CCDA
200-310
Official Cert Guide

ANTHONY BRUNO, CCIE No. 2738

STEVE JORDAN, CCIE No. 11293

Cisco Press
800 East 96th Street
Indianapolis, IN 46240

CCDA 200-310 Official Cert Guide

Anthony Bruno, CCIE No. 2738
Steve Jordan, CCIE No. 11293

Copyright © 2017 Pearson Education, Inc.

Published by:
Cisco Press
800 East 96th Street
Indianapolis, IN 46240 USA

Library of Congress Control Number: 2016940168

ISBN-10: 1-58714-454-9

ISBN-13: 978-1-58714-454-7

Warning and Disclaimer

Feedback Information

At Cisco Press, our goal is to create in-depth technical books of the highest quality and value. Each book is crafted with care and precision, undergoing rigorous development that involves the unique expertise of members of the professional technical community.

Reader feedback is a natural continuation of this process. If you have any comments on how we could improve the quality of this book, or otherwise alter it to better suit your needs, you can contact us through email at feedback@ciscopress.com. Please be sure to include the book title and ISBN in your message.

We greatly appreciate your assistance.

Corporate and Government Sales

Cisco Press offers excellent discounts on this book when ordered in quantity for bulk purchases or special sales. For more information, please contact:

U.S. Corporate and Government Sales
1-800-382-3419
corpsales@pearsontechgroup.com

For sales outside of the U.S., please contact:
International Sales
intlcs@pearson.com.

Trademark Acknowledgments

All terms mentioned in this book that are known to be trademarks or service marks have been appropriately capitalized. Cisco Press or Cisco Systems, Inc. cannot attest to the accuracy of this information. Use of a term in this book should not be regarded as affecting the validity of any trademark or service mark.

Editor-in-Chief: Mark Taub

Product Line Manager: Brett Bartow

Acquisitions Editor: Michelle Newcomb, Denise Lincoln

Managing Editor: Sandra Schroeder

Development Editor: Christopher Cleveland

Project Editor: Mandie Frank

Indexer: Ken Johnson

Cover Designer: Chuti Praesersith

Business Operation Manager, Cisco Press: Jan Cornelssen

Technical Editors: Jay McMickle, Kevin Yudong Wu

Copy Editor: Bart Reed

Editorial Assistant: Vanessa Evans

Composition: Studio Galou

Americas Headquarters
Cisco Systems, Inc.
San Jose, CA

Asia Pacific Headquarters
Cisco Systems (USA) Pte. Ltd.
Singapore

Europe Headquarters
Cisco Systems International BV
Amsterdam, The Netherlands

Cisco has more than 200 offices worldwide. Addresses, phone numbers, and fax numbers are listed on the Cisco Website at **www.cisco.com/go/offices.**

CCDE, CCENT, Cisco Eos, Cisco HealthPresence, the Cisco logo, Cisco Lumin, Cisco Nexus, Cisco StadiumVision, Cisco TelePresence, Cisco WebEx, DCE, and Welcome to the Human Network are trademarks; Changing the Way We Work, Live, Play, and Learn and Cisco Store are service marks; and Access Registrar, Aironet, AsyncOS, Bringing the Meeting To You, Catalyst, CCDA, CCDP, CCIE, CCIP, CCNA, CCNP, CCSP, CCVP, Cisco, the Cisco Certified Internetwork Expert logo, Cisco IOS, Cisco Press, Cisco Systems, Cisco Systems Capital, the Cisco Systems logo, Cisco Unity, Collaboration Without Limitation, EtherFast, EtherSwitch, Event Center, Fast Step, Follow Me Browsing, FormShare, GigaDrive, HomeLink, Internet Quotient, IOS, iPhone, iQuick Study, IronPort, the IronPort logo, LightStream, Linksys, MediaTone, MeetingPlace, MeetingPlace Chime Sound, MGX, Networkers, Networking Academy, Network Registrar, PCNow, PIX, PowerPanels, ProConnect, ScriptShare, SenderBase, SMARTnet, Spectrum Expert, StackWise, The Fastest Way to Increase Your Internet Quotient, TransPath, WebEx, and the WebEx logo are registered trademarks of Cisco Systems, Inc. and/or its affiliates in the United States and certain other countries.

All other trademarks mentioned in this document or website are the property of their respective owners. The use of the word partner does not imply a partnership relationship between Cisco and any other company. (0812R)

About the Authors

Anthony Bruno, CCIE No. 2738, is a Consulting Director with BT with more than 20 years of experience in the internetworking field. Previously, he worked for International Network Services, Lucent Technologies, and as a captain in the U.S. Air Force. His other industry certifications include CCDP, PMP, CCNP Security, Cisco Certified Business Value Practitioner, Cisco Data Center Network Infrastructure Specialist, Cisco Security Solutions & Design Specialist, and ITILv3 Foundation. He has consulted for many enterprise and service provider customers in the design, implementation, and optimization of large-scale networks. Anthony leads architecture and design teams in building next-generation networks for his customers. He completed his Master of Science in Electrical Engineering at the University of Missouri–Rolla in 1994 and his Bachelor of Science in Electrical Engineering at the University of Puerto Rico–Mayaguez in 1990. He is also a part-time instructor for the University of Phoenix–Online, teaching networking courses.

Outside of work Anthony enjoys running marathons, Spartan obstacle races, and Olympic and Ironman distance triathlons.

Steve Jordan, CCIE No. 11293, is a Senior Technology Manager with Accudata Systems and has 20 years experience in the field of internetworking. For the last 10 years, Steve has specialized in data center architectures involving compute, network, storage, virtualization, and SDN. Over the years, Steve has worked with many enterprise and service provider customers in both pre-sales and post-sales engineering and architecture roles, along with working at several Cisco Gold Partners. He has extensive experience in data center architecture and design and has implemented solutions in many financial, energy, retail, healthcare, education, and telecommunications industries. Steve is a 10-Year triple CCIE in the tracks of Routing & Switching, Storage Networking, and Data Center. His other certifications include VMware VCIX-NV, VCP-NV, VCP4-DCV, VCP5-DCV, CCDP, CCNP, ACI-SE, and ACI-FE.

Steve lives in Houston, Texas, with his wife and three sons. When he is not working on technology, Steve can be found traveling to new places, finding great food, and listening to live music.

Steve was also the coauthor for the previous editions of the *CCDA Official Cert Guide*.

About the Technical Reviewers

Kevin Yudong Wu, CCIE No. 10697 (Routing & Switching and Security), is a senior network consultant at British Telecom (BT). He has been engaged as a leading engineer in various network design projects, including LAN, WLAN, data center, and network security with BT's customers. Before joining BT, Kevin worked as customer support engineer at Cisco High Touch Technical Support (HTTS) to support both Cisco LAN switching and security products. He holds a master degree in both Computer Science (The University of Texas at Arlington, 2003) and Materials Engineering (Beijing University of Aeronautics and Astronautics, 1995).

Jay McMickle, CCIE No. 35355 (Routing & Switching and Security), is a double CCIE with 20 years of experience in the IT industry. He currently works as a Sr. Network and Security Consultant at Accudata Systems in Houston, Texas. Previously, he worked for Baker Hughes as a Technical Lead—first for the WAN team, followed by the Security team, and finally leading the Solution Architecture team. His other certifications include 3x CCNP (Routing & Switching, Design, and Security), Cisco Advanced Security Architect, Cisco Security Specializations, BCNE, CCSA, MCSE, and CCA. He specializes in routing designs and implementation as well as Security Architecture, implementation, and Security Operations. When he isn't working, you can find him teaching American Karate (ASK) or on the water wakeboarding or wakesurfing with friends and family. A big thank you to God. From the bottom to here, it is only through Him that I have the family, career, and friends that surround me. Thank you to Steve and Anthony. When we met (with you both as consultants) back in 2006, little did I know that we would remain in touch and become friends. Whether it's when I see Anthony at my neighborhood gym or Steve in the office, it goes to show how close our industry is and how you should nurture every relationship and not burn bridges. You might be working for them one day. Thank you to my wife for the patience she has with me in my work. Although I always "have one more thing to do," she understands my passion for IT and the dedication that comes along with it. Much love to both of my daughters, Avery (a.k.a. "The Goose") and Landyn (a.k.a. "The Bits"). I hope you both find a hobby that also serves as a career and funnels your passion for life as well. Much love to you both.

Dedications

This book is dedicated to my wife of 25 years, Yvonne Bruno, Ph.D., and to our daughters, Joanne and Dianne. Thanks for all of your support during the development of this book.

—Anthony Bruno

This book is dedicated to my wife of 22 years, Dorin Jordan, and my three sons, Blake, Lance, and Miles, for their support during the development of this book. I also want to dedicate this book to my mother Frances Brennan and my father-in law John Jordan for supporting me and being an inspiration to me throughout my life.

—Steve Jordan

Acknowledgments

This book would not have been possible without the efforts of many dedicated people. Thanks to Denise Lincoln and Michelle Newcomb for their guidance and support during the book development. Thanks to Chris Cleveland, development editor, for his guidance and special attention to detail. Thanks to Mandie Frank, project editor, for her accuracy. Thanks to Bart Reed, copy editor, for his attention to detail. Thanks to Brett Bartow, executive editor, for his vision. Thanks to all other Cisco Press team members who worked behind the scenes to make this a better book.

A special thanks my coauthor, Steve Jordan, for contributing five chapters. And a special thanks to the technical reviewers, Kevin Wu and Jay McMickle. Their technical advice and careful attention to detail made this book accurate.

—Anthony Bruno

This book would not be possible without all the great people who have assisted me. I would first like to thank Anthony Bruno for inviting me to assist him in this endeavor once more. Thanks to Denise Lincoln and Michelle Newcomb, project editors, for their guidance and support during the book development. Thanks again to Chris Cleveland, development editor, for supporting my schedule delays and keeping me on track.

Special thanks goes to the technical reviewers of this book, Kevin Wu and Jay McMickle, who provided wisdom and helped with keeping the book accurate.

Finally, thanks to all the managers and marketing people at Cisco Press who make all these books possible.

—Steve Jordan

Contents at a Glance

Elements Available on the Book Website

Contents

Elements Available on the Book Website

Appendix D   Memory Tables

Appendix E   Memory Tables Answer Key

Appendix F   Study Planner

Command Syntax Conventions

The conventions used to present command syntax in this book are the same conventions used in the IOS Command Reference. The Command Reference describes these conventions as follows:

- **Bold** indicates commands and keywords that are entered literally as shown. In actual configuration examples and output (not general command syntax), bold indicates commands that are manually input by the user (such as a **show** command).
- *Italic* indicates arguments for which you supply actual values.
- Vertical bars (|) separate alternative, mutually exclusive elements.
- Square brackets ([ ]) indicate an optional element.
- Braces ({ }) indicate a required choice.
- Braces within brackets ([{ }]) indicate a required choice within an optional element.

Introduction

So, you have worked on Cisco devices for a while, designing networks for your customers, and now you want to get certified? There are several good reasons to do so. The Cisco certification program allows network analysts, design engineers, and network architects to demonstrate their competence in different areas and levels of networking. The prestige and respect that come with a Cisco certification will definitely help you in your career. Your clients, peers, and superiors will recognize you as an expert in networking.

Cisco Certified Design Associate (CCDA) is the associate-level certification that represents knowledge of the design of Cisco internetwork infrastructure. The CCDA demonstrates skills required to design routed and switched networks, LANs, and WANs. The CCDA also has knowledge of campus designs, data centers, network security, voice, and wireless LANs.

Although it is not required, Cisco suggests taking the DESGN 3.0 course before you take the CCDA exam. For more information about the various levels of certification, career tracks, and Cisco exams, go to the Cisco Certifications page at http://www.cisco.com/c/en/us/training-events/training-certifications/certifications.html.

Our goal with this book is to help you pass the 200-310 CCDA exam. This is done by assessment on and coverage of all the exam topics published by Cisco. Reviewing tables and practicing test questions will help you practice your knowledge on all subject areas.

About the 200-310 CCDA Exam

The CCDA exam measures your ability to design networks that meet certain requirements for performance, security, capacity, and scalability. The exam focuses on small- to medium-sized networks. The candidate should have at least one year of experience in the design of small- to medium-sized networks using Cisco products. A CCDA candidate should understand internetworking technologies, including Cisco's enterprise network architecture, IPv4 subnets, IPv6 addressing and protocols, routing, switching, WAN technologies, LAN protocols, security, IP telephony, and network management. The new exam adds topics and updates to virtualization, data centers design, IPv6, voice and video design, wireless LANs, WAN technologies, and security.

The test to obtain CCDA certification is called Designing for Cisco Internetwork Solutions (DESGN) Exam #200-310. It is a computer-based test that has 55 to 65 questions and a 75-minute time limit. Because all exam information is managed by Cisco Systems and is therefore subject to change, candidates should continually monitor the Cisco Systems site for CCDA course and exam updates at http://www.cisco.com/c/en/us/training-events/training-certifications/certifications/associate/ccda.html.

You can take the exam at Pearson VUE testing centers. You can register with VUE at www.vue.com/cisco/. The CCDA certification is valid for three years. To recertify, you can pass a current CCDA test, pass a CCIE exam, or pass any 300 level, 642 level, or Cisco Specialist exam.

200-310 CCDA Exam Topics

Table I-1 lists the topics of the 200-310 CCDA exam and indicates the part in the book where they are covered.

Table I-1   200-310 CCDA Exam Topics

Exam Topic	Part
1.0 Design Methodologies	
1.1 Describe the Cisco Design lifecycle—PBM (plan, build, manage)	I
1.2 Describe the information required to characterize an existing network as part of the planning for a design change	I
1.3 Describe the use cases and benefits of network characterization tools (SNMP, NBAR, NetFlow)	I
1.4 Compare and contrast the top-down and bottom-up design approaches	I
2.0 Design Objectives	
2.1 Describe the importance and application of modularity in a network	I
2.2 Describe the importance and application of hierarchy in a network	I
2.3 Describe the importance and application of scalability in a network	I
2.4 Describe the importance and application of resiliency in a network	I
2.5 Describe the importance and application of concept of fault domains in a network	I
3.0 Addressing and Routing Protocols in an Existing Network	
3.1 Describe the concept of scalable addressing	
3.1.a Hierarchy	III
3.1.b Summarization	III
3.1.c Efficiency	III
3.2 Design an effective IP addressing scheme	
3.2.a Subnetting	III
3.2.b Summarization	III
3.2.c Scalability	III
3.2.d NAT	III
3.3 Identify routing protocol scalability considerations	
3.3.a Number of peers	III
3.3.b Convergence requirements	III
3.3.c Summarization boundaries and techniques	III

Exam Topic	Part
3.3.d Number of routing entries	III
3.3.e Impact of routing table of performance	III
3.3.f Size of the flooding domain	III
3.3.g Topology	III
3.4 Design a routing protocol expansion	
3.4.a IGP protocols (EIGRP, OSPF, IS-IS)	III
3.4.b BGP (eBGP peering, iBGP peering)	III
4.0 Enterprise Network Design	
4.1 Design a basic campus	
4.1.a Layer 2/Layer 3 demarcation	II
4.1.b Spanning tree	II
4.1.c Ether channels	II
4.1.d First Hop Redundancy Protocols (FHRP)	II
4.1.e Chassis virtualization	II
4.2 Design a basic enterprise network	
4.2.a Layer 3 protocols and redistribution	III
4.2.b WAN connectivity	II
4.2.b(i) Topologies (hub and spoke, spoke to spoke, point to point, full/partial mesh)	II
4.2.b(ii) Connectivity methods (DMVPN, get VPN, MPLS Layer 3 VPN, Layer 2 VPN, static IPsec, GRE, VTI)	II
4.2.b(iii) Resiliency (SLAs, backup links, QoS)	II
4.2.c Connections to the data center	II
4.2.d Edge connectivity	II
4.2.d(i) Internet connectivity	II
4.2.d(ii) ACLs and firewall placements	II
4.2.d(iii) NAT placement	II
4.3 Design a basic branch network	
4.3.a Redundancy	II
4.3.a(i) Connectivity	II
4.3.a(ii) Hardware	II
4.3.a(iii) Service provider	II
4.3.b Link capacity	II
4.3.b(i) Bandwidth	II

Exam Topic	Part
4.3.b(ii) Delay	II
5.0 Considerations for Expanding an Existing Network	
5.1 Describe design considerations for wireless network architectures	
5.1.a Physical and virtual controllers	II
5.1.b Centralized and decentralized designs	II
5.2 Identify integration considerations and requirements for controller-based wireless networks	
5.2.a Traffic flows	II
5.2.b Bandwidth consumption	II
5.2.c AP and controller connectivity	II
5.2.d QoS	II
5.3 Describe security controls integration considerations	
5.3.a Traffic filtering and inspection	IV
5.3.b Firewall and IPS placement and functionality	IV
5.4 Identify traffic flow implications as a result of security controls	
5.4.a Client access methods	IV
5.4.b Network access control	IV
5.5 Identify high-level considerations for collaboration (voice, streaming video, interactive video) applications	IV
5.5.a QoS (shaping vs. policing, trust boundaries, jitter, delay, loss)	IV
5.5.b Capacity	IV
5.5.c Convergence time	IV
5.5.d Service placement	IV
5.6 Describe the concepts of virtualization within a network design	II
5.7 Identify network elements that can be virtualized	
5.7.a Physical elements (chassis, VSS, VDC, contexts)	II
5.7.b Logical elements (routing elements, tunneling, VRFs, VLANs)	II
5.8 Describe the concepts of network programmability within a network design	
5.8.a APIs	II
5.8.b Controllers	II
5.8.c Application Centric Infrastructure (ACI)	II

Exam Topic	Part
5.9 Describe data center components	
5.9.a Server load balancing basics	II
5.9.b Blocking vs. non-blocking Layer 2	II
5.9.c Layer 2 extension	II

About the CCDA 200-310 Official Cert Guide

This book maps to the topic areas of the 200-310 CCDA exam and uses a number of features to help you understand the topics and prepare for the exam.

Objectives and Methods

This book uses several key methodologies to help you discover the exam topics for which you need more review, to help you fully understand and remember those details, and to help you prove to yourself that you have retained your knowledge of those topics. Therefore, this book does not try to help you pass the exams only by memorization, but by truly learning and understanding the topics. This book is designed to help you pass the CCDA exam by using the following methods:

- Helping you discover which exam topics you have not mastered
- Providing explanations and information to fill in your knowledge gaps
- Supplying exercises that enhance your ability to recall and deduce the answers to test questions
- Providing practice exercises on the topics and the testing process via test questions on the companion website

Book Features

To help you customize your study time using this book, the core chapters have several features that help you make the best use of your time:

- **"Do I Know This Already?" quiz:** Each chapter begins with a quiz that helps you determine how much time you need to spend studying that chapter.
- **Foundation Topics:** This is the core section of each chapter. It explains the concepts for the topics in that chapter.
- **Exam Preparation Tasks:** After the "Foundation Topics" section of each chapter, the "Exam Preparation Tasks" section lists a series of study activities that you should do at the end of the chapter. Each chapter includes the activities that make the most sense for studying the topics in that chapter:
  - **Review All the Key Topics:** The Key Topic icon appears next to the most important items in the "Foundation Topics" section of the chapter. The Review All the Key Topics activity lists the key topics from the chapter, along with their page numbers. Although the contents of the entire chapter could be on the exam, you should definitely know the information listed in each key topic, so you should review these.

- **Complete the Tables and Lists from Memory:** To help you memorize some lists of facts, many of the more important lists and tables from the chapter are included in a document on the CD. This document lists only partial information, allowing you to complete the table or list.

- **Define Key Terms:** Although the exam may be unlikely to ask a question such as "Define this term," the CCDA exams do require that you learn and know a lot of networking terminology. This section lists the most important terms from the chapter, asking you to write a short definition and compare your answer to the glossary at the end of the book.

- **Q&A:** Confirm that you understand the content you just covered.

How This Book Is Organized

This book contains 16 core chapters—Chapters 1 through 16. Chapter 17 includes some preparation tips and suggestions for how to approach the exam. Each core chapter covers a subset of the topics on the CCDA exam. The core chapters are organized into parts. They cover the following topics:

Part I: General Network Design

- **Chapter 1: Network Design Methodology** covers Cisco architectures for the enterprise network; the Plan, Design, Manage (PDM) network lifecycle; the Prepare, Plan, Design, Implement, Operate, and Optimize (PPDIOO) methodology; and the process of completing a network design.

- **Chapter 2: Network Design Models** covers hierarchical network models, the Cisco Enterprise Architecture model, and high-availability network services.

Part II: LAN and WAN Design

- **Chapter 3: Enterprise LAN Design** covers LAN media, campus LAN design and models, and best practices for campus networks.

- **Chapter 4: Data Center Design** covers enterprise data center design fundamentals, network programmability, data center challenges, virtualization technologies, data center interconnects, and load balancing in the DC.

- **Chapter 5: Wireless LAN Design** covers technologies and design options used for wireless LANs.

- **Chapter 6: WAN Technologies and the Enterprise Edge** examines technologies, design methodologies, DMZ connectivity, Internet connectivity, VPN network design, and requirements for the enterprise WANs.

- **Chapter 7: WAN Design** covers WAN design for the Enterprise WAN and enterprise branch, including remote access and virtual private network (VPN) architectures.

Part III: The Internet Protocol and Routing Protocols

- **Chapter 8: Internet Protocol Version 4 Design** covers the header, addressing, subnet design, and protocols used by IPv4.

- **Chapter 9: Internet Protocol Version 6 Design** covers the header, addressing, design best practices, and protocols used by IPv6.

- **Chapter 10: Routing Protocol Characteristics, RIP, EIGRP, and IS-IS** covers routing protocol characteristics, metrics, RIPv2, Enhanced Interior Gateway Routing Protocol (EIGRP), and Intermediate System to Intermediate System (IS-IS) characteristics and design.

- **Chapter 11: OSPF, BGP, Route Manipulation, and IP Multicast** covers Open Shortest Path First (OSPF) Protocol, Border Gateway Protocol (BGP), route summarization, route redistribution, route filtering, and IP multicast.

Part IV: Security, Convergence, Network Management

- **Chapter 12: Managing Security** examines security management, security policy, threats, risks, security compliance, and trust and identity management.

- **Chapter 13: Security Solutions** covers Cisco SAFE architecture, security technologies, and design options for securing the enterprise.

- **Chapter 14: Voice and Video Design** reviews traditional voice architectures, integrated multiservice networks, Cisco's IPT architecture and call processing deployment models, video deployment considerations, and IPT design.

- **Chapter 15: Network Management Protocols** covers Simple Network Management Protocol (SNMP), Remote Monitor (RMON), NetFlow, Cisco Discovery Protocol (CDP), Link Layer Discovery Protocol (LLDP), and syslog.

Part V: Comprehensive Scenarios and Final Prep

- **Chapter 16: Comprehensive Scenarios** provides network case studies for further comprehensive study.

- **Chapter 17: Final Preparation** identifies tools for final exam preparation and helps you develop an effective study plan. It contains tips on how to best use the web-based material to study.

Part VI: Appendixes

- **Appendix A: Answers to the "Do I Know This Already?" Quizzes and Q&A Questions** includes the answers to all the questions from Chapters 1 through 15.

- **Appendix B: CCDA Exam Updates: Version 1.0** provides instructions for finding updates to the exam and this book when and if they occur.

- **Appendix C: OSI Model, TCP/IP Architecture, and Numeric Conversion** reviews the Open Systems Interconnection (OSI) reference model to give you a better understanding of internetworking. It reviews the TCP/IP architecture and also reviews the techniques to convert between decimal, binary, and hexadecimal numbers. Although there might not be a specific question on the exam about converting a binary number to decimal, you need to know how to do so to do problems on the test.

- **Appendix D: Memory Tables** (a website-only appendix) contains the key tables and lists from each chapter, with some of the contents removed. You can print this appendix and, as a memory exercise, complete the tables and lists. The goal is to help you memorize facts that can be useful on the exam. This appendix is available in PDF format on the companion website; it is not in the printed book.

- **Appendix E: Memory Tables Answer Key** (a website-only appendix) contains the answer key for the memory tables in Appendix D. This appendix is available in PDF format on the companion website; it is not in the printed book.

- **Appendix F: Study Planner** is a spreadsheet, available from the book website, with major study milestones, where you can track your progress through your study.

Companion Website

Register this book to get access to the Pearson IT Certification test engine and other study materials plus additional bonus content. Check this site regularly for new and updated postings written by the authors that provide further insight into the more troublesome topics on the exam. Be sure to check the box that you would like to hear from us to receive updates and exclusive discounts on future editions of this product or related products.

To access this companion website, follow these steps:

1. Go to www.pearsonITcertification.com/register and log in or create a new account.
2. Enter the ISBN: 9781587144547.
3. Answer the challenge question as proof of purchase.
4. Click the Access Bonus Content link in the Registered Products section of your account page to be taken to the page where your downloadable content is available.

Please note that many of our companion content files can be very large, especially image and video files.

If you are unable to locate the files for this title by following the steps, please visit www.pearsonITcertification.com/contact and select the "Site Problems / Comments" option. Our customer service representatives will assist you.

Pearson IT Certification Practice Test Engine and Questions

The companion website includes the Pearson IT Certification Practice Test engine—software that displays and grades a set of exam-realistic multiple-choice questions. Using the Pearson IT Certification Practice Test engine, you can either study by going through the questions in Study Mode, or take a simulated exam that mimics real exam conditions. You can also serve up questions in Flash Card Mode, which will display just the question and no answers, challenging you to state the answer in your own words before checking the actual answers to verify your work.

The installation process requires two major steps: installing the software and then activating the exam. The website has a recent copy of the Pearson IT Certification Practice Test engine. The practice exam (the database of exam questions) is not on this site.

Note   The cardboard sleeve in the back of this book includes a piece of paper. The paper lists the activation code for the practice exam associated with this book. Do not lose the activation code. On the opposite side of the paper from the activation code is a unique, one-time-use coupon code for the purchase of the Premium Edition eBook and Practice Test.

Install the Software

The Pearson IT Certification Practice Test is a Windows-only desktop application. You can run it on a Mac using a Windows virtual machine, but it was built specifically for the PC platform. The minimum system requirements are as follows:

- Windows 10, Windows 8.1, or Windows 7
- Microsoft .NET Framework 4.0 Client
- Pentium-class 1GHz processor (or equivalent)
- 512 MB of RAM
- 650 MB of disk space plus 50 MB for each downloaded practice exam
- Access to the Internet to register and download exam databases

The software installation process is routine as compared with other software installation processes. If you have already installed the Pearson IT Certification Practice Test software from another Pearson product, there is no need for you to reinstall the software. Simply launch the software on your desktop and proceed to activate the practice exam from this book by using the activation code included in the access code card sleeve in the back of the book.

The following steps outline the installation process:

1. Download the exam practice test engine from the companion site.
2. Respond to Windows prompts as with any typical software installation process.

The installation process will give you the option to activate your exam with the activation code supplied on the paper in the cardboard sleeve. This process requires that you establish a Pearson website login. You need this login to activate the exam, so please do register when prompted. If you already have a Pearson website login, there is no need to register again. Just use your existing login.

Activate and Download the Practice Exam

Once the exam engine is installed, you should then activate the exam associated with this book (if you did not do so during the installation process) as follows:

1. Start the Pearson IT Certification Practice Test software from the Windows Start menu or from your desktop shortcut icon.

2. To activate and download the exam associated with this book, from the My Products or Tools tab, click the **Activate Exam** button.

3. At the next screen, enter the activation key from the paper inside the cardboard sleeve in the back of the book. Once this is entered, click the **Activate** button.

4. The activation process will download the practice exam. Click **Next**, and then click **Finish**.

When the activation process completes, the **My Products** tab should list your new exam. If you do not see the exam, make sure you have selected the My Products tab on the menu. At this point, the software and practice exam are ready to use. Simply select the exam and click the **Open Exam** button.

To update a particular exam you have already activated and downloaded, display the **Tools** tab and click the **Update Products** button. Updating your exams will ensure that you have the latest changes and updates to the exam data.

If you want to check for updates to the Pearson Cert Practice Test exam engine software, display the Tools tab and click the **Update Application** button. You can then ensure that you are running the latest version of the software engine.

Activating Other Exams

The exam software installation process, and the registration process, only has to happen once. Then, for each new exam, only a few steps are required. For instance, if you buy another Pearson IT Certification Cert Guide, extract the activation code from the cardboard sleeve in the back of that book; you do not even need the exam engine at this point. From there, all you have to do is start the exam engine (if not still up and running) and perform Steps 2 through 4 from the previous list.

Assessing Exam Readiness

Exam candidates never really know whether they are adequately prepared for the exam until they have completed about 30 percent of the questions. At that point, if you are not prepared, it is too late. The best way to determine your readiness is to work through the "Do I Know This Already?" quizzes at the beginning of each chapter and review the foundation and key topics presented in each chapter. It is best to work your way through the entire book unless you can complete each subject without having to do any research or look up any answers.

Premium Edition eBook and Practice Tests

This book also includes an exclusive offer for 70 percent off the Premium Edition eBook and Practice Tests edition of this title. Please see the coupon code included with the cardboard sleeve for information on how to purchase the Premium Edition.

This chapter covers the following subjects:

Cisco Architectures for the Enterprise

Plan, Build, and Manage Lifecycle

Prepare, Plan, Design, Implement, Operate, and Optimize Phases

Identifying Customer Requirements

Characterizing the Existing Network

Designing the Network Topology and Solutions

Networks can become complex and difficult to manage. Network architectures and design methodologies help you manage the complexities of networks. This chapter provides an overview of Cisco's architectures for the enterprise and the Plan, Build, Manage (PBM) network lifecycle. This chapter also describes steps in design methodology and contents of design documents.

CHAPTER 1

Network Design Methodology

"Do I Know This Already?" Quiz

The "Do I Know This Already?" quiz helps you identify your strengths and deficiencies in this chapter's topics.

The ten-question quiz, derived from the major sections in the "Foundation Topics" portion of the chapter, helps you determine how to spend your limited study time.

Table 1-1 outlines the major topics discussed in this chapter and the "Do I Know This Already?" quiz questions that correspond to those topics.

Table 1-1 "Do I Know This Already?" Foundation Topics Section-to-Question Mapping

Foundation Topics Section	Questions Covered in This Section
Cisco Architectures for the Enterprise	1, 2, 3, 4
Cisco Design Lifecycle: Plan, Design, Manage	5, 6
Identifying Customer Requirements	9, 10
Characterizing the Existing Network	7
Designing the Network Topology and Solutions	8

1. Which are the three Cisco network architectures for the enterprise?
   a. Hierarchical
   b. Borderless
   c. Integrated
   d. Data center/virtualization
   e. OSI model
   f. Collaboration

2. Which technology forces affect decisions for the enterprise network?
   a. Removal of borders
   b. Virtualization
   c. Growth of applications
   d. 10GigEthernet
   e. Regulation
   f. ROI
   g. Competitiveness

3. Network resiliency and control occur in which layer of the borderless network architecture?

   a. Policy and Control

   b. Borderless Network Services

   c. Borderless User Services

   d. Connection Management

4. Presence occurs in which collaboration architecture layer?

   a. Communication and Collaboration

   b. Collaboration Services

   c. Infrastructure

   d. Media Services

5. Which PBM process provides dedicated resources to troubleshoot issues within the network?

   a. Operations Management

   b. Solution Support

   c. Validation

   d. Product Support

6. In which PBM phase is the network designed?

   a. Plan phase

   b. Design phase

   c. Build phase

   d. Manage phase

7. What are the three primary sources of information in a network audit?

   a. CIO, network manager, network engineer

   b. Network manager, management software, CDP

   c. Network discovery, CDP, SNMP

   d. Existing documentation, existing management software, new management tools

8. Which design solution states that a design must start from the application layer and finish in the physical layer?

   a. OSI model

   b. PPDIOO

   c. Hierarchical architecture

   d. Top-down

9. Budget and personnel limitations are examples of what?

   a. Organization requirements

   b. Organization constraints

   c. Technical goals

   d. Technical constraints

10. Improving network response time and reliability are examples of what?

   a. Organization requirements

   b. Organization constraints

   c. Technical goals

   d. Technical constraints

Foundation Topics

With the complexities of networks, it is necessary to use architectures and methodologies in network design to support business goals. The Cisco Prepare, Plan, Design, Implement, Operate, and Optimize (PPDIOO) network lifecycle defines a continuous cycle of phases in a network's life. Each phase includes key steps in successful network planning, design, implementation, and operation. Cisco also introduces a simplified Plan, Build, Manage (PBM) network lifecycle that the CCDA should be familiar with. The top-down design approach to network design adapts the network infrastructure to the network applications' needs.

Cisco Architectures for the Enterprise

With the constant evolution of networks, Cisco keeps updating its enterprise architectures and frameworks. Business drivers can affect network architecture and technology forces that affect business.

Business forces affecting decisions for the enterprise network include the following:

- **Return on investment:** Companies expect a return (be it cost savings or increased productivity) on its investments in network infrastructure. The solutions need to use technology to work within a business solution.

- **Regulation:** Companies need to meet industry regulations; for example, the Health Insurance Portability and Accountability Act (HIPAA) for the health insurance industry and Payment Card Industry Data Security Standard (PCI DSS) for the credit card industry.

- **Competitiveness:** To maintain a competitive edge, companies need to use technology to make them more competitive than other businesses.

The technology forces affecting decisions for the enterprise network are

- **Removal of borders:** Traditional network boundaries have been removed. Access to network resources need to be enabled from branch offices, teleworkers, home offices, mobile devices, customers, and partner networks.

- **Virtualization:** Allows for the maximization of efficiencies through the reduction of hardware, power consumption, heating and cooling costs, facilities space, and management effort. Virtualization and its benefits are a key goal for almost all organizations. It has gained popularity by industry leaders such as VMware.

- **Growth of applications:** Customers continue to ask for new products, service offerings, improved customer service, greater security, and customization flexibility—all at a lower cost.

IT optimization areas are divided into three groups:

- Data center
- Network
- Applications

Each group has its own experts, budget, and challenges.

Cisco has created an interwoven framework to create three architectures for each group that provides for optimization at an individual level and the integration with other areas:

- Borderless networks architecture
- Collaboration architecture
- Data center and virtualization architecture

Figure 1-1 shows these three architectures, which are covered in more detail in the following sections.

Enterprise Architectures

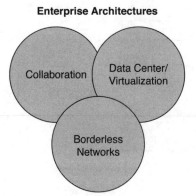

Figure 1-1   *Cisco enterprise architectures*

Borderless Networks Architecture

Cisco borderless networks architecture is a next-generation solution that enables connectivity to anyone and anything, anywhere, and at any time. The connectivity needs to be secure, reliable, and seamless. This architecture optimizes both business and network performance.

As shown in Figure 1-2, the Cisco borderless networks architecture blueprint consists of four major blocks:

- **Policy and Control:** Policies are applied to all users and devices across the architecture.
- **Network Services:** These services include resiliency and control. Cisco EnergyWise and MediaNet provide capabilities to borderless networks.
- **User Services:** These services include mobility, performance, and security.
- **Connection Management:** This block delivers secure access anytime and anywhere, regardless of how the network is accessed.

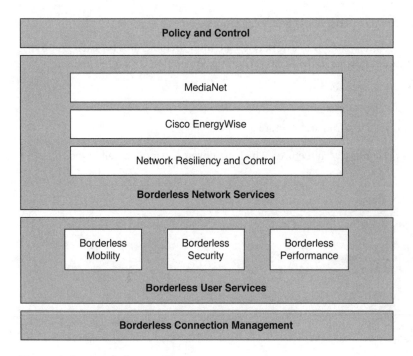

Figure 1-2 *Borderless architecture*

Collaboration and Video Architecture

The Cisco collaboration and video architecture is composed of three layers:

- **Communication and Collaboration Applications:** This layer contains conferencing, customer care, enterprise social software, IP communications, messaging, mobile applications, and TelePresence.

- **Collaboration Services:** This layer contains services that support the collaboration applications: presence, location, session management, contact management, client frameworks, tagging, and policy and security management.

- **Infrastructure:** This layer is responsible for allowing collaboration anytime, from anywhere, on any device. It includes virtual machines, the network, and storage.

Data Center and Virtualization Architecture

The Cisco data center and virtualization architecture comprises a comprehensive set of virtualization technologies and services that bring the network, computing, storage, and virtualization platforms together. This architecture consists of three components:

- **Unified Management:** Features automation, orchestration, and lifecycle management to simplify deployment and operation of physical/bare metal, virtual, and cloud infrastructures.

- **Unified Fabric:** This component delivers high-performance data and storage networking to simplify deployment, help ensure quality of experience, and reduce operating costs. Cisco integrated network services provide high-speed connectivity and high-availability, increase application performance, and reduce security risk in multitenant environments.

- **Unified Computing:** This component provides a highly scalable, system-level computing solution that integrates computing, access networking, and storage networking. Embedded management capabilities simplify operations across physical, virtual, and cloud infrastructures.

Figure 1-3 shows the architecture framework for data centers.

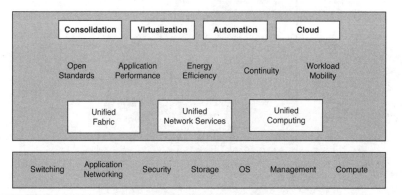

Figure 1-3 *Data center architecture framework*

Data center architecture and design is covered in Chapter 4, "Data Center Design."

Table 1-2 lists the benefits of the Cisco network architectures.

Table 1-2   Benefits of the Cisco Network Architectures

Benefit	Description
Functionality	Supports organizational requirements
Scalability	Supports growth and expansion of organizational tasks
Availability	Provides services reliability, anywhere and anytime
Performance	Provides responsiveness, throughput, and utilization on a per-application basis
Manageability	Provides control, performance monitoring, and fault detection
Efficiency	Provides network services and infrastructure with reasonable operational costs and appropriate capital investment

Cisco Design Lifecycle: Plan, Build, Manage

Cisco is introducing an updated network lifecycle with three phases: Plan, Build, and Manage (PBM), each with processes. Each phase is important in meeting customers' needs, organizational goals, and constraints. As shown in Figure 1-4, these phases are as follows:

- **Plan:** This phase includes processes for the assessment and network strategy, building the network design, and defining a plan.
- **Build:** This phase includes processes for the validation of the solution, the deployment of new IT and network solutions, and the migration to new infrastructures.

■ **Manage:** This phase includes processes for product support, solution support, optimization, and operations management of the network.

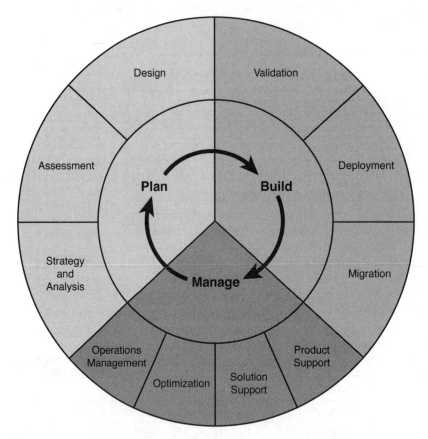

Figure 1-4   *The Cisco Plan, Build, Manage network lifecycle*

The sections that follow cover the processes under each phase.

Plan Phase

The Plan phase is divided into three processes:

■ Strategy and Analysis process

■ Assessment process

■ Design process

During the Strategy and Analysis process, network architecture strategies are created and roadmaps to transform the network architecture are developed. A cost-effective strategy is developed with a measurable return of investment (ROI). The network assessment helps determine the network infrastructure's compliance against industry and Cisco's best practices and corporate policies. The assessment also determines gaps in the network operation team's ability to support the new technologies being introduced. The Design process creates a resilient and scalable network design that can support the business requirements.

Build Phase

The Build phase is divided into three processes:

- Validation process
- Deployment process
- Migration process

The Validation process confirms that the proposed solution meets your requirements for availability, security, reliability, and performance through assessment and lab environments. This will mitigate the risks associated with upgrading the network.

The Deployment process installs and configures new IT and network solutions with minimal disruption to your production network. It accomplishes the business and technical goals of the new solution.

The Migration process upgrades the network infrastructure by a systematic and efficient approach, which could control costs, improve operational excellence, reduce network operation costs and system outages, and mitigate risk during device, network, and software refreshes.

Manage Phase

The Manage phase is divided into four processes:

- Product Support process
- Solution Support process
- Optimization process
- Operations Management process

The Product Support process provides automated network equipment inventory management, allowing better planning of equipment upgrades. It efficiently manages risk, lowers support costs, and increases operational efficiencies.

The Solution Support process provides dedicated and focused resources to manage and troubleshoot issues that might arise in new complex solutions. It increases solution uptime and employee productivity.

The Optimization process identifies gaps, delivers recommendations, and provides expert technical support to improve on the deployed solution. It increases the performance, availability, resiliency, and visibility of the network.

The Operation Management process ensures that the network staff has enough competence in the network technology to accelerate adoption of advanced technologies. It lowers the total cost of network ownership. Proactive monitoring and network management also occur in this process.

Table 1-3 summarizes the processes under each PBM phase.

Table 1-3   PBM Network Lifecycle Phases

PBM Phase	Processes Under Each Phase
Plan phase	Strategy and Analysis, Assessment, and Design
Build phase	Validation, Deployment, and Migration
Manage phase	Product Support, Solution Support, Optimization, and Operations Management

Prepare, Plan, Design, Implement, Operate, and Optimize Phases

The historical Cisco network lifecycle has six phases: Prepare, Plan, Design, Implement, Operate, and Optimize. These phases are collectively known as PPDIOO. The PPDIOO lifecycle provides four main benefits:

- It lowers the total cost of ownership by validating technology requirements and planning for infrastructure changes and resource requirements.
- It increases network availability by producing a sound network design and validating the network operation.
- It improves business agility by establishing business requirements and technology strategies.
- It speeds access to applications and services by improving availability, reliability, security, scalability, and performance.

These benefits are realized by the actions listed in Tables 1-4 through 1-7.

Table 1-4   Actions That Lower the Cost of Ownership

Actions That Lower the Cost of Ownership
Identifying and validating technology requirements
Planning for infrastructure changes and resource requirements
Developing a sound network design aligned with technical requirements and business goals
Accelerating successful implementation
Improving the efficiency of the network and the staff that supports it
Reducing operating expenses by improving the efficiency of operation processes and tools

Table 1-5   Actions That Increase Network Availability

Actions That Increase Network Availability
Assessing the state of the network and its ability to support the proposed design
Specifying the correct set of hardware and software releases and keeping them current
Producing a sound operations design and validating network operation
Staging and testing the proposed system before deployment
Improving staff skills
Proactively monitoring the system and assessing availability trends and alerts
Proactively identifying security breaches and defining remediation plans

Table 1-6   Actions That Improve Business Agility

Actions That Improve Business Agility
Establishing business requirements and technology strategies
Readying sites to support the system that will be implemented
Integrating technical requirements and business goals into a detailed design and demonstrating that the network is functioning as specified
Expertly installing, configuring, and integrating system components
Continually enhancing performance

Table 1-7   Actions That Accelerate Access to Applications and Services

Actions That Accelerate Access to Applications and Services
Accessing and improving operational preparedness to support current and planned network technologies and services
Improving service delivery efficiency and effectiveness by increasing availability, resource capacity, and performance
Improving the availability, reliability, and stability of the network and the applications that run on it
Managing and resolving problems that affect the system and keeping software applications current

Figure 1-5 shows the PPDIOO network lifecycle.

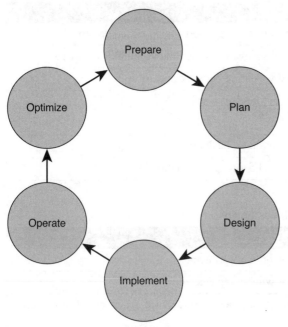

Figure 1-5   *Cisco PPDIOO network lifecycle*

The following sections discuss the PPDIOO phases in detail.

Prepare Phase

The Prepare phase establishes organization and business requirements, develops a network strategy, and proposes a high-level conceptual architecture to support the strategy. Technologies that support the architecture are identified. This phase creates a business case to establish a financial justification for a network strategy.

Plan Phase

The Plan phase identifies the network requirements based on goals, facilities, and user needs. This phase characterizes sites and assesses the network, performs a gap analysis against best-practice architectures, and looks at the operational environment. A project plan is developed to manage the tasks, responsible parties, milestones, and resources to do the design and implementation. The project plan aligns with the scope, cost, and resource parameters established with the original business requirements. This project plan is followed (and updated) during all phases of the cycle.

Design Phase

The network design is developed based on the technical and business requirements obtained from the previous phases. The network design specification is a comprehensive detailed design that meets current business and technical requirements. It provides high availability, reliability, security, scalability, and performance. The design includes network diagrams and an equipment list. The project plan is updated with more granular information for implementation. After the Design phase is approved, the Implement phase begins.

Implement Phase

New equipment is installed and configured, according to design specifications, in the Implement phase. New devices replace or augment the existing infrastructure. The project plan is followed during this phase. Planned network changes should be communicated in change control meetings, with necessary approvals to proceed. Each step in the implementation should include a description, detailed implementation guidelines, estimated time to implement, rollback steps in case of a failure, and any additional reference information. As changes are implemented, they are also tested before moving to the Operate phase.

Operate Phase

The Operate phase maintains the network's day-to-day operational health. Operations include managing and monitoring network components, routing maintenance, managing upgrades, managing performance, and identifying and correcting network faults. This phase is the design's final test. During operation, network management stations should monitor the network's general health and generate traps when certain thresholds are reached. Fault detection, correction, and performance monitoring events provide initial data for the Optimize phase.

Optimize Phase

The Optimize phase involves proactive network management by identifying and resolving issues before they affect the network. The Optimize phase may create a modified network design if too many network problems arise, or to improve performance issues or resolve application issues. The requirement for a modified network design leads to the network lifecycle beginning.

Summary of PPDIOO Phases

Table 1-8 summarizes the PPDIOO phases.

Table 1-8   PPDIOO Network Lifecycle Phases

PPDIOO Phase	Description
Prepare	Establishes organization and business requirements, develops a network strategy, and proposes a high-level architecture
Plan	Identifies the network requirements by characterizing and assessing the network as well as performing a gap analysis
Design	Provides high availability, reliability, security, scalability, and performance
Implement	Installation and configuration of new equipment
Operate	Day-to-day network operations
Optimize	Proactive network management and modifications to the design

Project Deliverables

During the lifecycle of the network, several documents are created. The first documents are high level in scope, and as the project works through the lifecycle phases, more details and generated. The following are the most common deliverables generated in a network project:

- **High-level design (HLD) document:** The HLD document includes business and technical requirements as well as proposed network architectures. No specific detailed design information such as proposed IP subnets and VLANs are created at this point.

- **Low-level design (LLD) document:** The LLD document takes the HLD document as its basis. The LLD document includes detailed design information such as network topology, specific hardware models, software versions, IP addressing, VLANs, routing protocols, redundancy and scalability details, and security considerations.

  - **Bill of materials (BOM):** Contains the part numbers, description, and quantities of the network equipment to be acquired for the network project.

  - **Network migration plan (NMP):** Explains the plan for migrating the network from the current state to the new design. The NMP is part of the LLD document.

- **Network implementation plan (NIP):** Contains the steps required to install and configure the network equipment and the steps that verify basic network operation. Information for each step should include step description, estimated implementation time, and design document references.

- **Network ready for use test plan (NRFU):** Contains the actions required to test the customer network to certify it's ready for use. The NRFU plan includes tests for devices, circuit throughput, routing, failover, QoS, management, security, and applications.

Design Methodology

The following sections focus on a design methodology for the PBM methodology. This design methodology has three steps:

Step 1.   Identifying customer network requirements

Step 2.   Characterizing the existing network

Step 3.   Designing the network topology and solutions

In Step 1, decision makers identify requirements, and a conceptual architecture is proposed. This step occurs in the Strategy and Analysis process of the PBM Plan phase.

In Step 2, the network is assessed, and a gap analysis is performed to determine the infrastructure necessary to meet the requirements. The network is assessed on function, performance, and quality. This step occurs in the Assessment process of the PBM Plan phase.

In Step 3, the network topology is designed to meet the requirements and close the network gaps identified in the previous steps. A detailed design document is prepared during this phase. Design solutions include network infrastructure, Voice over IP (VoIP), content networking, and intelligent network services. This set occurs in the Design process of the PBM Design phase.

Identifying Customer Design Requirements

To obtain customer requirements, you need to not only talk to network engineers, but also talk to business unit personnel and company managers. Networks are designed to support applications; you want to determine the network services you need to support.

As shown in Figure 1-6, the steps to identify customer requirements are as follows:

Step 1.   Identify network applications and services.

Step 2.   Define the organizational goals.

Step 3.   Define the possible organizational constraints.

Step 4.   Define the technical goals.

Step 5.   Define the possible technical constraints.

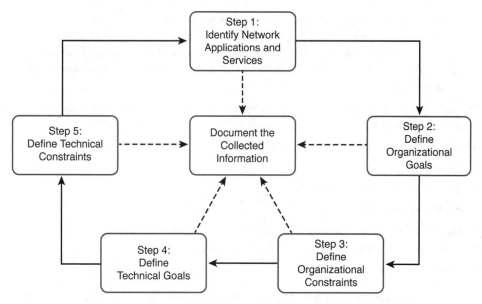

Figure 1-6   *Steps in identifying customer requirements*

After you complete these steps, you then analyze the data and develop a network design.

You need to identify current and planned applications and determine the importance of each application. Is email as important as customer support? Is IP telephony being deployed? High-availability and high-bandwidth applications need to be identified for the design to accommodate their network requirements. A table identifying applications should list the following:

- **Planned application types:** Such as email, collaboration, voice, web browsing, file sharing, and database

- **Concrete applications:** Such as Outlook and MeetingPlace

- **Business importance:** Labeled as critical, important, or unimportant

- **Comment:** Any additional information critical to the design of the network

Planned infrastructure services should also be gathered. Network services include security, quality of service (QoS), network management, high availability, unified communications, mobility, and virtualization.

For organizational goals, you should identify whether the company's goal is to improve customer support, add new customer services, increase competitiveness, or reduce costs. It might be a combination of these goals, with some of them being more important than others. Some organizational goals are as follows:

- Increase competitiveness
- Reduce costs
- Improve customer support
- Add new customer services

Organizational constraints include budget, personnel, policy, and schedule. The company might limit you to a certain budget or timeframe. The organization might require the project to be completed in an unreasonable timeframe. It might have limited personnel to support the assessment and design efforts, or it might have policy limitations to use certain protocols.

Technical goals support the organization's objectives and the supported applications. Technical goals include the following:

- Improve the network's response-time throughput
- Decrease network failures and downtime (high availability)
- Simplify network management
- Improve network security
- Improve reliability of mission-critical applications
- Modernize outdated technologies (technology refresh)
- Improve the network's scalability

Network design might be constrained by parameters that limit the solution. Legacy applications might still exist that must be supported going forward, and these applications might require a legacy protocol that may limit a design. Technical constraints include the following:

- Existing wiring does not support new technology.
- Bandwidth might not support new applications.
- The network must support existing legacy equipment.
- Legacy applications must be supported (application compatibility).

Characterizing the Existing Network

Characterizing the network is Step 2 of the design methodology. In this section, you learn to identify a network's major features, tools to analyze existing network traffic, and tools for auditing and monitoring network traffic.

Steps in Gathering Information

When arriving at a site that has an existing network, you need to obtain all the existing documentation. Sometimes no documented information exists. You should be prepared to use tools to obtain information and get access to log in to the network devices to obtain information. Here are the steps for gathering information:

Step 1.   Identify properties of the existing network: network topology, technologies, and applications. Use existing documentation and organizational input.

Step 2.   Perform a network audit that adds detail to the description of the network.

Step 3.   Analyze the gathered information.

When gathering existing documentation, you look for site information such as site names, site addresses, site contacts, site hours of operation, and building and room access. Network infrastructure information includes locations and types of servers and network devices, size of each site, data center and closet locations, LAN wiring, WAN technologies and circuit speeds, and power used. Logical network information includes IP addressing, routing protocols, network management, and security access lists used. You need to find out whether voice or video is being used on the network.

Network Audit Tools

When performing a network audit, you have three primary sources of information:

- Existing documentation
- Existing network management software tools
- New network auditing tools

After gathering the existing documentation, you must obtain access to the existing management software. The client may already have CiscoWorks tools, from which you can obtain hardware models and components and software versions. You can also obtain the existing router and switch configurations.

The network audit should provide the following information:

- Network device list
- Hardware specifications
- Software versions
- Configuration of network devices
- Auditing tools' output information
- Interface speeds
- Link, CPU, and memory utilization
- WAN technology types and carrier information

In a small network, you might be able to obtain the required information via a manual assessment. For a larger network, a manual assessment might be too time-consuming. Network assessment tools include the following:

- **Manual assessment**
    - **Manual commands:** Review of device configuration and operation though the use of **show** commands of network device configurations, interface loads, and router and switch logs
    - Scripting tools
- **Existing network management and auditing tools**
    - **Simple Network Management Protocol (SNMP):** Used to monitor performance of network devices and link utilization
    - **NetFlow:** Used for collecting and measuring data of every flow in a network segment.
    - **Cisco Discovery Protocol (CDP):** Used to discover how network devices are interconnected to each other. Link Layer Discovery Protocol (LLDP) is used in multivendor environments.
    - **Syslog:** Generates time-stamped log information of device and system events that are captured and exported to a syslog server.
    - **Network-Based Application Recognition (NBAR):** Intelligent classification engine.
    - **Cisco Prime Infrastructure and Solarwinds:** Collects SNMP and NetFLow information.
    - **Wireshark:** Utilizes SPAN port technology to capture real-time packets for analysis.
- **Additional tools with emphasis on VoIP, wireless, and security**
    - AirMagnet Analyzer Pro
    - Ekahau Site Survey for wireless site survey
    - LanGuard network security scanner for security

When performing manual auditing on network devices, you can use the following commands to obtain information:

- **show environment:** Displays temperature, voltage, and fan information
- **show processes cpu:** Displays the average CPU utilization information for the last 5 seconds, 1 minute, and 5 minutes
- **show version:** Displays software version and features, names and sources of configuration files, the boot image, device uptime, and reason for the last reboot
- **show memory:** Displays statistics on system memory, including total bytes as well as used and free bytes
- **show logging:** The state of the syslog error and event logging, including host addresses, and the logging destinations (console, monitor, buffer, or host) for which logging is enabled
- **show interfaces:** Displays interfaces' statistics, including input and output rate of packets and dropped packets
- **show policy-map interface:** Displays the statistics and the configurations of the input and output policies that are attached to an interface

- **show running-config:** Provides the full router or switch configuration currently in use
- **show startup-config:** Displays the configuration the router or switch will use at the next reboot

Example 1-1 shows the output of a **show version** command. This command shows the operating system version, the router type, the amount of flash and RAM memory, the router uptime, and the interface types.

Example 1-1   *Output of a* **show version** *Command*

```
R2>show version
Cisco IOS Software, 7200 Software (C7200-K91P-M), Version 12.2(25)S9, RELEASE SO
FTWARE (f)
Technical Support: http://www.cisco.com/techsupport
Copyright 1986-2006 by Cisco Systems, Inc.
Compiled Tue 28-Mar-06 23:12 by alnguyen


ROM: ROMMON Emulation Microcode
BOOTLDR: 7200 Software (C7200-K91P-M), Version 12.2(25)S9, RELEASE SOFTWARE (f
)


 R2 uptime is 5 minutes
System returned to ROM by unknown reload cause - suspect boot_data[BOOT_COUNT] 0
, BOOT_COUNT 0, BOOTDATA 19
System image file is "tftp://255.255.255.255/unknown"



This product contains cryptographic features and is subject to United
States and local country laws governing import, export, transfer and
use. Delivery of Cisco cryptographic products does not imply
third-party authority to import, export, distribute or use encryption.
Importers, exporters, distributors and users are responsible for
compliance with U.S. and local country laws. By using this product you
agree to comply with applicable laws and regulations. If you are unable
to comply with U.S. and local laws, return this product immediately.


A summary of U.S. laws governing Cisco cryptographic products may be found at:
http://www.cisco.com/wwl/export/crypto/tool/stqrg.html


If you require further assistance please contact us by sending email to
export@cisco.com.


Cisco 7206VXR (NPE400) processor (revision A) with 147456K/16384K bytes of memory.
Processor board ID 4294967295
R7000 CPU at 150Mhz, Implementation 39, Rev 2.1, 256KB L2 Cache
6 slot VXR midplane, Version 2.1
```

```
Last reset from power-on

PCI bus m_m (Slots 0, 1, 3 and 5) has a capacity of 600 bandwidth points.
Current configuration on bus m_m has a total of 200 bandwidth points.
This configuration is within the PCI bus capacity and is supported.

PCI bus m (Slots 2, 4, 6) has a capacity of 600 bandwidth points.
Current configuration on bus m has a total of 0 bandwidth points
This configuration is within the PCI bus capacity and is supported.

Please refer to the following document "Cisco 7200 Series Port
Adaptor Hardware Configuration Guidelines" on CCO <www.cisco.com>,
for 200 bandwidth points oversubscription/usage guidelines.


1 FastEthernet interface
8 Serial interfaces
125K bytes of NVRAM.

65536K bytes of ATA PCMCIA card at slot 0 (Sector size 512 bytes).
8192K bytes of Flash internal SIMM (Sector size 256K).
Configuration register is 0102
```

NetFlow provides extremely granular and accurate traffic measurements and a high-level collection of aggregated traffic. The output of NetFlow information is displayed via the **show ip cache flow** command on routers. Table 1-9 shows a description of the fields for NetFlow output.

Table 1-9   NetFlow Output Description

Field	Description
Bytes	Number of bytes of memory that are used by the NetFlow cache
Active	Number of active flows
Inactive	Number of flow buffers that are allocated in the NetFlow cache
Added	Number of flows that have been created since the start of the summary
Exporting flows	IP address and User Datagram Protocol (UDP) port number of the workstation to which flows are exported
Flows exported	Total number of flows exported and the total number of UDP datagrams
Protocol	IP protocol and well-known port number
Total flows	Number of flows for this protocol since the last time statistics were cleared
Flows/sec	Average number of flows for this protocol per second

Field	Description
Packets/flow	Average number of packets per flow per second
Bytes/pkt	Average number of bytes for this protocol
Packets/sec	Average number of packets for this protocol per second

Network Checklist

The following network checklist can be used to determine a network's health status:

- New segments should use switches and not use dated hub/shared technology.

- No WAN links are saturated (no more than 70 percent sustained network utilization).

- The response time is generally less than 100ms (one-tenth of a second); more commonly, less than 2ms in a LAN.

- No segments have more than 20 percent broadcasts or multicast traffic. Broadcasts are sent to all hosts in a network and should be limited. Multicast traffic is sent to a group of hosts but should also be controlled and limited to only those hosts registered to receive it.

- No segments have more than one cyclic redundancy check (CRC) error per million bytes of data.

- On the Ethernet segments, less than 0.1 percent of the packets result in collisions.

- A CPU utilization at or more than 75 percent for a 5-minute interval likely suggests network problems. Normal CPU utilization should be much lower during normal periods.

- The number of output queue drops has not exceeded 100 in an hour on any Cisco router.

- The number of input queue drops has not exceeded 50 in an hour on any Cisco router.

- The number of buffer misses has not exceeded 25 in an hour on any Cisco router.

- The number of ignored packets has not exceeded 10 in an hour on any interface on a Cisco router.

- QoS should be enabled on network devices to allow for prioritization of time-sensitive or bandwidth-sensitive applications.

Table 1-10 summarizes areas in characterizing the network.

Table 1-10   Characterizing the Network

Characteristic	Description
Steps in gathering information	1. Identify properties of the existing network via existing information and documentation.
	2. Perform a network audit.
	3. Analyze the gathered information.

Characteristic	Description
Primary sources of network audit information	Existing documentation
	Existing network management software
	New network management tools

Designing the Network Topology and Solutions

This section describes the top-down approach for network design, reviews pilot and prototype test networks, and describes the components of the design document. As part of the Design process of the PBM lifecycle, a top-down approach is used that begins with the organization's requirements before looking at technologies. Network designs are tested using a pilot or prototype network before moving into the Implement phase.

Top-Down Approach

Top-down design just means starting your design from the top layer of the OSI model and working your way down. Top-down design adapts the network and physical infrastructure to the network application's requirements. With a top-down approach, network devices and technologies are not selected until the applications' requirements are analyzed. To complete a top-down design, the following is accomplished:

- Analysis of application and organization requirements.
- Design from the top of the OSI reference model:
  - Define requirements for upper layers (application, presentation, session).
  - Specify infrastructure for lower OSI layers (transport, network, data link, physical).
- Gather additional data on the network.

Figure 1-7 shows a top-down structure design process. The design process begins with the applications and moves down to the network. Logical subdivisions are then incorporated with specifics.

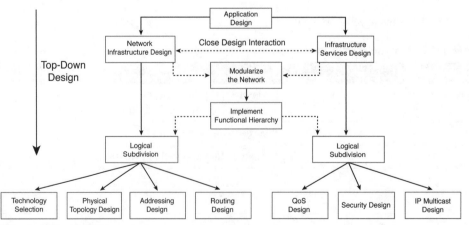

Figure 1-7 *Top-down design process*

Table 1-11 compares the top-down approach to the bottom-up approach to network design.

Table 1-11   Top-Down Design Compared to Bottom-Up Design

Design Approach	Benefits	Disadvantages
Top-down	Incorporates the organization's requirements. Provides the big picture. The design meets current and future requirements.	More time-consuming.
Bottom-up	The design is based on previous experience and allows for a quick solution.	May result in inappropriate design. Organizational requirements are not included.

Pilot and Prototype Tests

As soon as the design is complete and before the full implementation, it is a best practice to test the new solution. This testing can be done in one of two ways: prototype or pilot.

A prototype network is a subset of the full design, tested in an isolated environment. The prototype does not connect to the existing network. It is a non-production network. The benefit of using a prototype is that it allows testing of the network design before it is deployed prior to affecting a production network. When implementing a new technology such as IPsec, you might want to implement a prototype test before deploying it to the operational network.

A pilot site is an actual production network location that serves as a test site before the solution is deployed to all locations in an enterprise. A pilot allows real-world problems to be discovered before deploying a network design solution to the rest of the internetwork.

With both a prototype and a pilot, successful testing leads to proving the design and moving forward with implementation. A failure leads to correcting the design and repeating the tests to correct any deficiencies.

Design Document

The design document describes the business requirements; old network architecture; network requirements; and design, plan, and configuration information for the new network. The network architects and analysts use it to document the new network changes, and it serves as documentation for the enterprise. The design document should include the following sections:

- **Introduction:** This section describes the project's purpose and the reasons for the network design.

- **Design Requirements:** This section lists the organization's requirements, constraints, and goals.

- **Existing Network Infrastructure:** This section includes logical (Layer 3) topology diagrams; physical topology diagrams; audit results; network health analysis; routing protocols; a summary of applications; a list of network routers, switches, and other devices; configurations; and a description of issues.

- **Design:** This section contains the specific design information, such as logical and physical topology, IP addressing, routing protocols, and security configurations.
- **Proof of Concept:** This section results from live pilot or prototype testing.
- **Implementation Plan:** This section includes the detailed steps for the network staff to implement the new installation and changes. It also includes configuration templates for LAN switches and WAN routers.
- **Appendixes:** This section contains a list of existing network devices, configurations, and additional information used in the design of the network.

Table 1-12 summarizes the contents of the design document.

Table 1-12   Sections of the Design Document

Section	Description
Introduction	Purpose and goals of the network design
Design Requirements	Organization requirements and constraints
Existing Network Infrastructure	Contains diagrams, hardware and software versions, and existing configurations
Design	New logical topology, design, and IP addressing
Proof of Concept	Results from pilot or prototype
Implementation Plan	Detailed steps for implementation
Appendixes	Supporting information

The implementation of a network consists of several phases. Each step should contain the following information:

- Description of the step
- Reference to the design document
- Detailed implementation guidelines
- Network-verification checks
- Detailed rollback guidelines
- Estimated time to implement

References and Recommended Reading

Cisco Design Zone, www.cisco.com/en/US/netsol/n42/networking_solutions_program_category_home.html.

Design Zone for Borderless Networks, www.cisco.com/en/US/netsol/n063/networking_solutions_program_home.html.

Design Zone for Collaboration, www.cisco.com/en/US/netsol/n062/networking_solutions_program_home.html.

Design One for Data Center, www.cisco.com/en/US/netsol/n43/networking_solutions_program_home.html

Cisco Data Center and Virtualization, http://www.cisco.com/c/en/us/solutions/data-center-virtualization/architecture.html

Cisco Data Center, www.cisco.com/en/US/netsol/n40/n94/n24/architecture.html.

Smart Solutions for Mission Success, http://www.cisco.com/web/services/downloads/smart-solutions-maximize-federal-capabilities-for-mission-success.pdf

Exam Preparation Tasks

Review All Key Topics

Review the most important topics in the chapter, noted with the Key Topics icon in the outer margin of the page. Table 1-13 provides a reference of these key topics and the page number(s) on which each is found.

Table 1-13   Key Topics

Key Topic Element	Description	Page
List	Forces affecting decisions for the enterprise network	6
Section	Cisco Plan, Build, and Manage (PBM) design lifecycle	9
Table	PBM Network Lifecycle Phases	12
List	PPDIOO lifecycle's four main benefits	12
Table	PPDIOO Network Lifecycle Phases	15
List	Steps in gathering information	19
Summary	Describes the top-down approach to network design	24
Table	Top-Down Design Compared to Bottom-Up Design	25

Complete Tables and Lists from Memory

Print a copy of Appendix D, "Memory Tables," (found on the book website), or at least the section for this chapter, and complete the tables and lists from memory. Appendix E, "Memory Tables Answer Key," (also on the website) includes completed tables and lists to check your work.

Define Key Terms

Define the following key terms from this chapter, and check your answers in the glossary:

PBM, NBAR, NetFlow, policy control, virtualization

Q&A

The answers to these questions appear in Appendix A, "Answers to the 'Do I Know This Already?' Quizzes and Q&A Questions." For more practice with exam format questions, use the exam engine on the CD-ROM.

1. List the PPDIOO phases in order.

2. Which business forces affect decisions for the enterprise network?

   a. Removal of borders

   b. Virtualization

   c. Growth of applications

   d. 10GigEthernet

   e. Regulation

   f. ROI

   g. Competitiveness

3. Which design methodology step is important for identifying organizational goals?

   a. Identify customer requirements.

   b. Characterize the existing network.

   c. Design the network topology and solution.

   d. Examine the architecture.

   e. Validate the design.

   f. Obtain the ROI.

4. What needs to be obtained prior to designing the network?

   a. Expected ROI

   b. Organizational and technical goals

   c. Technical constraints

   d. Bill of materials

   e. Existing and new network applications

5. Match each PPDIOO phase with its description.

   i.   Implement

   ii. Optimize

   iii. Design

   iv. Prepare

   v.   Operate

   vi. Plan

   a. Establish requirements

   b. Gap analysis

   c. Provides high-availability design

   d. Installation and configuration

   e. Day to day

   f. Proactive management

6. Which borderless architecture provides mobility?

   a. Policy

   b. Network services

   c. User services

   d. Connection management

   e. Control services

7. Which are the three steps in the design methodology?

   a. Reviewing the project cost

   b. Designing the network topology and solution

   c. Characterizing the network

   d. Identifying customer requirements

   e. Validating the design

8. Match each infrastructure service with its description.

     i.   Identity

     ii. Mobility

     iii. Storage

     iv. Compute

     v.   Security

     vi. Voice/collaboration

   a. Access from a remote location

   b. Improved computational resources

   c. Unified messaging

   d. AAA, NAC

   e. Storage of critical data

   f. Secure communications

9. A company location is used to test a new VoIP solution. What is this type of test called?

   a. Prototype

   b. Pilot

   c. Implementation

   d. New

10. An isolated network is created to test a new design. What is this type of test called?

   a. Prototype

   b. Pilot

   c. Implementation

   d. New

11. NBAR, NetFlow, and EtherPeek are examples of what?

    a. Network audit tools

    b. Network analysis tools

    c. SNMP tools

    d. Trending tools

12. Monitoring commands, CiscoWorks, and WhatsUP are examples of what?

    a. Network audit tools

    b. Network analysis tools

    c. SNMP tools

    d. Trending tools

13. Which of the following are technical constraints? (Select all that apply.)

    a. Existing wiring

    b. Existing network circuit bandwidth

    c. Improving the LAN's scalability

    d. Adding redundancy

14. Which of the following are technical goals? (Select all that apply.)

    a. Existing wiring

    b. Existing network circuit bandwidth

    c. Improving the LAN's scalability

    d. Adding redundancy

15. Which of the following are organizational goals? (Select all that apply.)

    a. Improving customer support.

    b. Budget has been established.

    c. Increasing competitiveness.

    d. Completion in three months.

    e. Reducing operational costs.

    f. Network personnel are busy.

16. Which of the following are organizational constraints? (Select all that apply.)

    a. Improving customer support.

    b. Budget has been established.

    c. Increasing competitiveness.

    d. Completion in three months.

    e. Reducing operational costs.

    f. Network personnel are busy.

17. What components are included in the design document? (Select four.)

    a. IP addressing scheme

    b. Implementation plan

    c. List of Layer 2 devices

    d. Design requirements

    e. Selected routing protocols

    f. List of Layer 1 devices

18. Match each design document section with its description.

    i.   Introduction

    ii. Design Requirements

    iii. Existing Network Infrastructure

    iv. Design

    v.   Proof of Concept

    vi. Implementation Plan

    vii. Appendix

    a. Detailed steps

    b. Current diagram and configuration

    c. Organizational requirements

    d. Goals

    e. Pilot

    f. New logical topology

    g. Supporting information

19. The network health analysis is based on what information?

    a. The number of users accessing the Internet

    b. The statements made by the CIO

    c. Statistics from the existing network

    d. The IP addressing scheme

20. While performing a network audit, you encounter a Frame Relay WAN segment running at a sustained rate of 75 percent from 9 a.m. to 5 p.m. What do you recommend?

    a. Nothing. The daily 24-hour average rate is still 45 percent.

    b. Change from Frame Relay to MPLS.

    c. Increase the provisioned WAN bandwidth.

    d. Deny VoIP calls from 9 a.m. to 5 a.m.

21. What information is included in the network audit report? (Select all that apply.)

    a. Network device list

    b. IOS versions

c. Router models

d. Interface speeds

e. WAN utilization

22. Which three tasks are part of characterizing the existing network?

a. Speaking with the CIO

b. Using traffic analysis

c. Automated auditing of the network using tools

d. Collecting information

e. Obtaining organizational chart

f. Defining organizational goals

23. Which command provides the average CPU of a Cisco router?

a. show cpu

b. show processes cpu

c. show processes memory

d. show cpu utilization

e. show cpu average

24. Which parameters can be obtained by the use of a traffic analyzer?

a. Application importance

b. QoS requirements

c. Devices using a specific protocol

d. IP addresses of devices and TCP/UDP port number

e. Average bit rate and packet rate

25. Which commands provide information about individual applications, protocols, or flows? (Choose three.)

a. show process cpu

b. show ip interface

c. show ip cache flow

d. show ip nbar protocol-discovery

e. show process memory

f. show interface application

26. What is used to create the documentation of the existing network?

a. Router **show** commands

b. Network audit, documentation, and traffic analysis tools

c. Audit tools

d. Existing documentation and input from the organization

27. What is the sequence for the stages of top-down design?

28. Which are potential scopes for a network design project? (Choose three.)

    a. Network layer redundancy

    b. Campus upgrade

    c. Data link layer redundancy

    d. Network redesign

    e. WAN upgrade

    f. Application upgrade

29. A credit card company network is being designed. Secure transactions are emphasized throughout the initial requirements. Redundant links are required to reduce network outages. What is the order of importance of the following design issues?

    a. IP addressing design

    b. Physical topology design

    c. Network modules

    d. Security design

30. Which types of tools are used during the network design process?

    a. Network management tools

    b. Network trending tools

    c. Network modeling tools

    d. Network simulation and testing tools

    e. Network implementation tools

31. Which four items should be present in the implementation plan?

    a. Implementation description

    b. Estimated time to implement

    c. Reference to design document

    d. Rollback procedure

    e. Estimated cost of implementation

    f. Application profiles

32. A new design uses IPsec for the WAN. Which approach should be used to verify the design?

    a. Live network

    b. Pilot network

    c. Prototype network

    d. Cable network

    e. Internet network

33. Which three components are included in the design document?

   a. Design details

   b. Design requirements

   c. Current cable runs

   d. List of Layer 2 devices

   e. Implementation plan

34. Which sources are used to characterize a network?

   a. Sniffer, CIO meeting, **ip config/all**

   b. Network audit, input from staff, traffic analysis

   c. **show cdp, show lldp**

   d. Network assessment, server statistics, SNMP discovery

35. Which information should be included in the design implementation plan?

   a. Step description, time to implement, implementation guideline

   b. Step description, implementation explanation, rollback time

   c. Design document references, step description, estimated time to implement

   d. Implementation time, rollback time, implementation explanation

36. What layer of the OSI model is used to start a top-down design approach effort?

   a. Network Layer

   b. Presentation Layer

   c. Application Layer

   d. Political Layer

37. What are the benefits of the bottom-up design approach?

   a. Based on previous experience, allows for quick solution

   b. Uses the organization's requirements, allows for a quick solution

   c. Based on previous experience, meets future requirements

   d. Uses organization's requirements, meets future requirements

38. What are the benefits of the top-down design approach?

   a. Based on previous experience, allows for quick solution

   b. Uses the organization's requirements, allows for a quick solution

   c. Based on previous experience, meets future requirements

   d. Uses the organization's requirements, meets future requirements

39. Which PPDIOO phase is the design's final test?

  a. Prepare

  b. Plan

  c. Design

  d. Implement

  e. Operate

  d. Optimize

40. Which PPDIOO phase identifies and resolves issues before they affect the network?

  a. Prepare

  b. Plan

  c. Design

  d. Implement

  e. Operate

  f. Optimize

41. Which PPDIOO phase produces network diagrams and an equipment list?

  a. Prepare

  b. Plan

  c. Design

  d. Implement

  e. Operate

  f. Optimize

42. Which PPDIOO phase assesses the network and produces a gap list?

  a. Prepare

  b. Plan

  c. Design

  d. Implement

  e. Operate

  f. Optimize

43. Which PPDIOO phase develops a network strategy?

  a. Prepare

  b. Plan

  c. Design

  d. Implement

  e. Operate

  f. Optimize

44. Which PBM phase includes validation, deployment, and migration processes?

   a. Plan

   b. Design

   c. Build

   d. Manage

45. Which PBM phase includes product and solution support processes?

   a. Plan

   b. Design

   c. Build

   d. Manage

46. Which PBM phase includes strategy, assessment, and design processes?

   a. Plan

   b. Design

   c. Build

   d. Manage

This chapter covers the following subjects:

Hierarchical Network Models

Cisco Enterprise Architecture Model

High Availability Network Services

This chapter reviews the hierarchical network model and introduces Cisco's Enterprise Architecture model. This architecture model separates network design into more manageable modules. This chapter also addresses the use of device, media, and route redundancy to improve network availability.

CHAPTER 2

Network Design Models

"Do I Know This Already?" Quiz

The "Do I Know This Already?" quiz helps you identify your strengths and deficiencies in this chapter's topics.

The eight-question quiz, derived from the major sections in the "Foundation Topics" portion of the chapter, helps you determine how to spend your limited study time.

Table 2-1 outlines the major topics discussed in this chapter and the "Do I Know This Already?" quiz questions that correspond to those topics.

Table 2-1 "Do I Know This Already?" Foundation Topics Section-to-Question Mapping

Foundation Topics Section	Questions Covered in This Section
Hierarchical Network Models	1, 3
Cisco Enterprise Architecture Model	2, 5, 6, 7
High Availability Network Services	4, 8

1. In the hierarchical network model, which layer is responsible for fast transport?

    a. Network layer

    b. Core layer

    c. Distribution layer

    d. Access layer

2. Which Enterprise Architecture model component interfaces with the service provider (SP)?

    a. Campus infrastructure

    b. Access layer

    c. Enterprise edge

    d. Edge distribution

3. In the hierarchical network model, at which layer do security filtering, address aggregation, and media translation occur?

    a. Network layer

    b. Core layer

    c. Distribution layer

    d. Access layer

4. Which of the following is (are) a method (methods) of workstation-to-router redundancy in the access layer?

 a. AppleTalk Address Resolution Protocol (AARP)

 b. Hot Standby Router Protocol (HSRP)

 c. Virtual Router Redundancy Protocol (VRRP)

 d. Answers b and c

 e. Answers a, b, and c

5. The network-management module has tie-ins to which component(s)?

 a. Campus infrastructure

 b. Server farm

 c. Enterprise edge

 d. SP edge

 e. Answers a and b

 f. Answers a, b, and c

 g. Answers a, b, c, and d

6. Which of the following is an SP edge module in the Cisco Enterprise Architecture model?

 a. Public switched telephone network (PSTN) service

 b. Edge distribution

 c. Server farm

 d. Core layer

7. In which module would you place Cisco Unified Communications Manager (CUCM)?

 a. Campus core

 b. E-commerce

 c. Server farm

 d. Edge distribution farm

8. High availability, port security, and rate limiting are functions of which hierarchical layer?

 a. Network layer

 b. Core layer

 c. Distribution layer

 d. Access layer

Foundation Topics

With the complexities of network design, the CCDA needs to understand network models used to simplify the design process. The hierarchical network model was one of the first Cisco models that divided the network into core, distribution, and access layers.

The Cisco Enterprise Architecture model provides a functional modular approach to network design. In addition to a hierarchy, modules are used to organize server farms, network management, campus networks, WANs, and the Internet. A modular approach to network design allows for higher scalability, better resiliency, and easier fault isolation of the network.

Hierarchical Network Models

Hierarchical models enable you to design internetworks that use specialization of function combined with a hierarchical organization. Such a design simplifies the tasks required to build a network that meets current requirements and can grow to meet future requirements. Hierarchical models use layers to simplify the tasks for internetworking. Each layer can focus on specific functions, allowing you to choose the right systems and features for each layer. Hierarchical models apply to both LAN and WAN design.

Benefits of the Hierarchical Model

The benefits of using hierarchical models for your network design include the following:

- Cost savings
- Ease of understanding
- Modular network growth
- Improved fault isolation

After adopting hierarchical design models, many organizations report cost savings because they are no longer trying to do everything in one routing or switching platform. The model's modular nature enables appropriate use of bandwidth within each layer of the hierarchy, reducing the provisioning of bandwidth in advance of actual need.

Keeping each design element simple and functionally focused facilitates ease of understanding, which helps control training and staff costs. You can distribute network monitoring and management reporting systems to the different layers of modular network architectures, which also helps control management costs.

Hierarchical design facilitates changes and growth. In a network design, modularity lets you create design elements that you can replicate as the network grows—allowing maximum scalability. As each element in the network design requires change, the cost and complexity of making the upgrade are contained to a small subset of the overall network. In large, flat network architectures, changes tend to impact a large number of systems. Limited mesh topologies within a layer or component, such as the campus core or backbone connecting central sites, retain value even in the hierarchical design models.

Structuring the network into small, easy-to-understand elements improves fault isolation. Network managers can easily understand the transition points in the network, which helps identify failure points. It is more difficult to troubleshoot if hierarchical design is not used because the network is not divided into segments.

Today's fast-converging protocols were designed for hierarchical topologies. To control the impact of routing-protocol processing and bandwidth consumption, you must use modular hierarchical topologies with protocols designed with these controls in mind, such as the Open Shortest Path First (OSPF) routing protocol.

Hierarchical network design facilitates route summarization. Enhanced Interior Gateway Routing Protocol (EIGRP) and all other routing protocols benefit greatly from route summarization. Route summarization reduces routing-protocol overhead on links in the network and reduces routing-protocol processing within the routers. It is less possible to provide route summarization if the network is not hierarchical.

Hierarchical Network Design

As shown in Figure 2-1, a traditional hierarchical LAN design has three layers:

- The core layer provides fast transport between distribution switches within the enterprise campus.
- The distribution layer provides policy-based connectivity.
- The access layer provides workgroup and user access to the network.

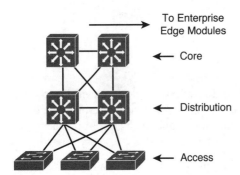

Figure 2-1 *Hierarchical network design has three layers: core, distribution, and access*

Each layer provides necessary functionality to the enterprise campus network. You do not need to implement the layers as distinct physical entities. You can implement each layer in one or more devices or as cooperating interface components sharing a common chassis. Smaller networks can "collapse" multiple layers to a single device with only an implied hierarchy. Maintaining an explicit awareness of hierarchy is useful as the network grows.

Core Layer

The core layer is the network's high-speed switching backbone that is crucial to corporate communications. It is also referred as the backbone. The core layer should have the following characteristics:

- Fast transport
- High reliability
- Redundancy
- Fault tolerance
- Low latency and good manageability
- Avoidance of CPU-intensive packet manipulation caused by security, inspection, quality of service (QoS) classification, or other processes
- Limited and consistent diameter
- QoS

When a network uses routers, the number of router hops from edge to edge is called the diameter. As noted, it is considered good practice to design for a consistent diameter within a hierarchical network. The trip from any end station to another end station across the backbone should have the same number of hops. The distance from any end station to a server on the backbone should also be consistent.

Limiting the internetwork's diameter provides predictable performance and ease of troubleshooting. You can add distribution layer routers and client LANs to the hierarchical model without increasing the core layer's diameter. Use of a block implementation isolates existing end stations from most effects of network growth.

Distribution Layer

The network's distribution layer is the isolation point between the network's access and core layers. The distribution layer can have many roles, including implementing the following functions:

- Policy-based connectivity (for example, ensuring that traffic sent from a particular network is forwarded out one interface while all other traffic is forwarded out another interface)
- Redundancy and load balancing
- Aggregation of LAN wiring closets
- Aggregation of WAN connections
- QoS
- Security filtering
- Address or area aggregation or summarization
- Departmental or workgroup access
- Broadcast or multicast domain definition
- Routing between virtual LANs (VLANs)
- Media translations (for example, between Ethernet and Token Ring)
- Redistribution between routing domains (for example, between two different routing protocols)
- Demarcation between static and dynamic routing protocols

You can use several Cisco IOS Software features to implement policy at the distribution layer:

- Filtering by source or destination address
- Filtering on input or output ports
- Hiding internal network numbers by route filtering
- Static routing
- QoS mechanisms, such as priority-based queuing

The distribution layer provides aggregation of routes providing route summarization to the core. In the campus LANs, the distribution layer provides routing between VLANs that also apply security and QoS policies.

Access Layer

The access layer provides user access to local segments on the network. The access layer is characterized by switched LAN segments in a campus environment. Microsegmentation using LAN switches provides high bandwidth to workgroups by reducing the number of devices on Ethernet segments. Functions of the access layer include the following:

- Layer 2 switching
- High availability
- Port security
- Broadcast suppression
- QoS classification and marking and trust boundaries
- Rate limiting/policing
- Address Resolution Protocol (ARP) inspection
- Virtual access control lists (VACLs)
- Spanning tree
- Trust classification
- Power over Ethernet (PoE) and auxiliary VLANs for VoIP
- Network Access Control (NAC)
- Auxiliary VLANs

You implement high availability models at the access layer. The section "High Availability Network Services" covers availability models. The LAN switch in the access layer can control access to the port and limit the rate at which traffic is sent to and from the port. You can implement access by identifying the MAC address using ARP, trusting the host, and using access lists.

Other chapters of this book cover the other functions in the list.

For small office/home office (SOHO) environments, the entire hierarchy collapses to interfaces on a single device. Remote access to the central corporate network is through traditional WAN technologies such as ISDN, Frame Relay, and leased lines. You can implement features such as dial-on-demand routing (DDR) and static routing to control costs. Remote access can include virtual private network (VPN) technology.

Table 2-2 summarizes the hierarchical layers.

Table 2-2   Cisco Enterprise Architecture Model

Hierarchical Layer	Description
Core	Fast transport
	High reliability
	Redundancy
	Fault tolerance
	Low latency and good manageability
	Avoidance of slow packet manipulation caused by filters or other processes
	Limited and consistent diameter
	QoS
Distribution	Policy-based connectivity
	Redundancy and load balancing
	Aggregation of LAN wiring closets
	Aggregation of WAN connections
	QoS
	Security filtering
	Address or area aggregation or summarization
	Departmental or workgroup access
	Broadcast or multicast domain definition
	Routing between VLANs
	Media translations (for example, between Ethernet and Token Ring)
	Redistribution between routing domains (for example, between two different routing protocols)
	Demarcation between static and dynamic routing protocols
Access	Layer 2 switching
	High availability
	Port security
	Broadcast suppression
	QoS

Hierarchical Layer	Description
Access *(continued)*	Rate limiting
	ARP inspection
	VACLs
	Spanning tree
	Trust classification
	Network Access Control (NAC)
	PoE and auxiliary VLANs for VoIP

Hierarchical Model Examples

You can implement the hierarchical model by using a traditional switched campus design or routed campus network. Figure 2-2 is an example of a switched hierarchical design in the enterprise campus. In this design, the core provides high-speed transport between the distribution layers. The building distribution layer provides redundancy and allows policies to be applied to the building access layer. Layer 3 links between the core and distribution switches are recommended to allow the routing protocol to take care of load balancing and fast route redundancy in the event of a link failure. The distribution layer is the boundary between the Layer 2 domains and the Layer 3 routed network. Inter-VLAN communications are routed in the distribution layer. Route summarization is configured under the routing protocol on interfaces towards the core layer. The drawback with this design is that Spanning Tree Protocol (STP) allows only one of the redundant links between the access switch and the distribution switch to be active. In the event of a failure, the second link becomes active, but at no point does load balancing occur.

Figure 2-3 shows examples of a routed hierarchical design. In this design, the Layer 3 boundary is pushed toward the access layer. Layer 3 switching occurs in access, distribution, and core layers. Route filtering is configured on interfaces toward the access layer. Route summarization is configured on interfaces toward the core layer. The benefit of this design is that load balancing occurs from the access layer since the links to the distribution switches are routed.

Another solution for providing redundancy between the access and distribution switching is the Virtual Switching System (VSS). VSS solves the STP looping problem by converting the distribution switching pair into a logical single switch. It removes STP and negates the need for Hot Standby Router Protocol (HSRP), Virtual Router Redundancy Protocol (VRRP), or Gateway Load Balancing Protocol (GLBP).

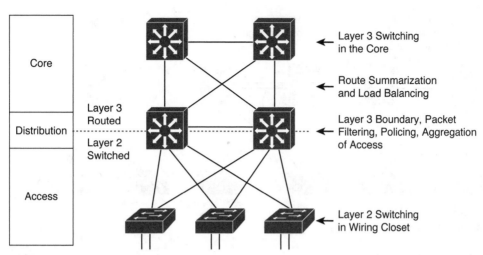

Figure 2-2 *Switched Hierarchical Design*

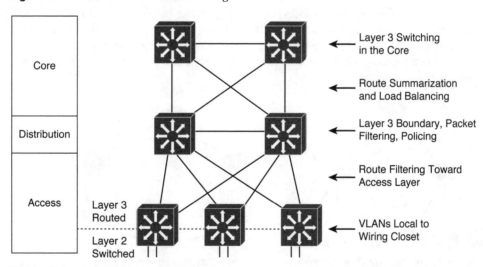

Figure 2-3 *Routed hierarchical design*

With VSS, the physical topology changes as each access switch has a single upstream distribution switch versus having two upstream distribution switches. VSS is configured only on Cisco 6500 switches using the VSS Supervisor 720-10G. As shown in Figure 2-4, the two switches are connected via 10GE links called virtual switch links (VSLs), which makes them seem as a single switch. The key benefits of VSS include the following:

- Layer 3 switching can be used toward the access layer, enhancing nonstop communication.
- Scales system bandwidth up to 1.44 Tbps.
- Simplified management of a single configuration of the VSS distribution switch.
- Better return on investment (ROI) via increased bandwidth between the access layer and the distribution layer.
- Supported on Catalyst 4500, 6500, and 6800 switches.

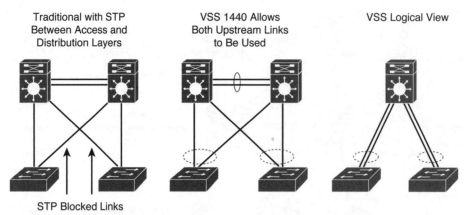

Figure 2-4   *VSS*

Hub-and-Spoke Design

For designing networks, the hub-and-spoke design provides better convergence times than ring topology. The hub-and-spoke design, illustrated in Figure 2-5, also scales better and is easier to manage than ring or mesh topologies. For example, implementing security policies in a full mesh topology would become unmanageable because you would have to configure policies at each point location.

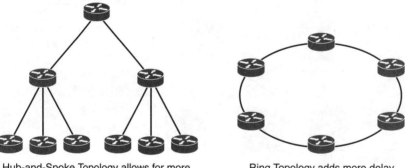

Hub-and-Spoke Topology allows for more
scalability and easier management.

Ring Topology adds more delay
as you add more nodes.

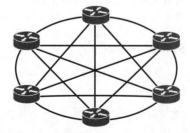

Mesh Topology requires a network
connection to all other devices.

Figure 2-5   *Hub-and-spoke design*

Collapsed Core Design

One alternative to the three-layer hierarchy is the collapsed core design. It is a two-layer hierarchy used with smaller networks. It is commonly used on sites with a single building with just multiple floors. As shown in Figure 2-6, the core and distribution layers are merged, providing all the services needed for those layers. Design parameters to decide if you need to migrate to the three-layer hierarchy include not enough capacity and throughput at the distribution layer, network resiliency, and geographic dispersion.

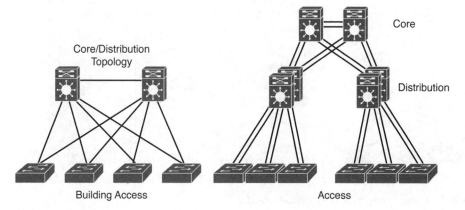

Figure 2-6 *Collapsed core design*

Cisco Enterprise Architecture Model

The Cisco Enterprise Architecture model facilitates the design of larger, more scalable networks.

As networks become more sophisticated, it is necessary to use a more modular approach to design than just WAN and LAN core, distribution, and access layers. The architecture divides the network into functional network areas and modules. These areas and modules of the Cisco Enterprise Architecture are

- Enterprise campus area
- Enterprise data center module
- Enterprise branch module
- Enterprise teleworker module

The Cisco Enterprise Architecture model maintains the concept of distribution and access components connecting users, WAN services, and server farms through a high-speed campus backbone. The modular approach in design should be a guide to the network architect. In smaller networks, the layers can collapse into a single layer, even a single device, but the functions remain.

Figure 2-7 shows the Cisco Enterprise Architecture model. The enterprise campus area contains a campus infrastructure that consists of core, building distribution, and building access layers, with a data center module. The enterprise edge area consists of the Internet, e-commerce, VPN, and WAN modules that connect the enterprise to the service provider's facilities. The SP edge area provides Internet, public switched telephone network (PSTN), and WAN services to the enterprise.

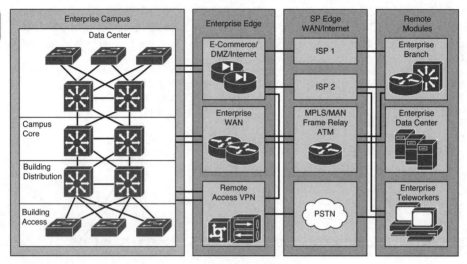

Figure 2-7 *Cisco Enterprise Architecture model*

The network management servers reside in the campus infrastructure but have tie-ins to all the components in the enterprise network for monitoring and management.

The enterprise edge connects to the edge-distribution module of the enterprise campus. In small and medium sites, the edge distribution can collapse into the campus backbone component. It provides connectivity to outbound services that are further described in later sections.

Enterprise Campus Module

The enterprise campus consists of the following submodules:

- Campus core
- Building distribution and aggregation switches
- Building access
- Server farm/data center

Figure 2-8 shows the Enterprise Campus model. The campus infrastructure consists of the campus core, building distribution, and building access layers. The campus core provides a high-speed switched backbone between buildings, to the server farm, and towards the enterprise edge. This segment consists of redundant and fast-convergence connectivity. The building distribution layer aggregates all the closet access switches and performs access control, QoS, route redundancy, and load balancing. The building access switches provide VLAN access, PoE for IP phones and wireless access points, broadcast suppression, and spanning tree.

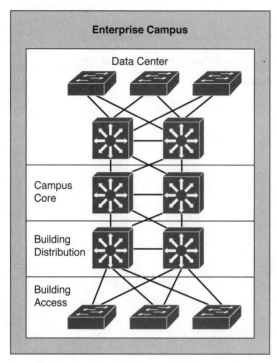

Figure 2-8   *Enterprise Campus model*

The server farm or data center provides high-speed access and high availability (redundancy) to the servers. Enterprise servers such as file and print servers, application servers, email servers, Dynamic Host Configuration Protocol (DHCP) servers, and Domain Name System (DNS) servers are placed in the server farm. Cisco Unified CallManager servers are placed in the server farm for IP telephony networks. Network management servers are located in the server farm, but these servers link to each module in the campus to provide network monitoring, logging, trending, and configuration management.

An enterprise campus infrastructure can apply to small, medium, and large locations. In most instances, large campus locations have a three-tier design with a wiring-closet component (building access layer), a building distribution layer, and a campus core layer. Small campus locations likely have a two-tier design with a wiring-closet component (Ethernet access layer) and a backbone core (collapsed core and distribution layers). It is also possible to configure distribution functions in a multilayer building access device to maintain the focus of the campus backbone on fast transport. Medium-sized campus network designs sometimes use a three-tier implementation or a two-tier implementation, depending on the number of ports, service requirements, manageability, performance, and availability required.

Enterprise Edge Area

As shown in Figure 2-9, the enterprise edge consists of the following submodules:

- Business web applications and databases, e-commerce networks and servers
- Internet connectivity and demilitarized zone (DMZ)
- VPN and remote access
- Enterprise WAN connectivity

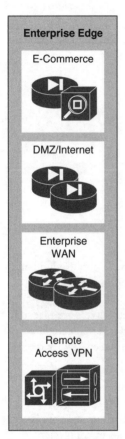

Figure 2-9   *Enterprise Edge module*

E-Commerce Module

The e-commerce submodule of the enterprise edge provides highly available networks for business services. It uses the high availability designs of the server farm module with the Internet connectivity of the Internet module. Design techniques are the same as those described for these modules. Devices located in the e-commerce submodule include the following:

- **Web and application servers:** Primary user interface for e-commerce navigation
- **Database servers:** Contain the application and transaction information

- **Firewall and firewall routers:** Govern the communication between users of the system

- **Network intrusion prevention systems (IPS):** Provide monitoring of key network segments in the module to detect and respond to attacks against the network

- **Multilayer switch with IPS modules:** Provide traffic transport and integrated security monitoring

Internet Connectivity Module

The Internet submodule of the enterprise edge provides services such as public servers, email, and DNS. Connectivity to one or several Internet service providers (ISPs) is also provided. Components of this submodule include the following:

- **Firewall and firewall routers:** Provide protection of resources, stateful filtering of traffic, and VPN termination for remote sites and users

- **Internet edge routers:** Provide basic filtering and multilayer connectivity

- **FTP and HTTP servers:** Provide for web applications that interface the enterprise with the world via the public Internet

- **SMTP relay servers:** Act as relays between the Internet and the intranet mail servers

- **DNS servers:** Serve as authoritative external DNS servers for the enterprise and relay internal requests to the Internet

Several models connect the enterprise to the Internet. The simplest form is to have a single circuit between the enterprise and the SP, as shown in Figure 2-10. The drawback is that you have no redundancy or failover if the circuit fails.

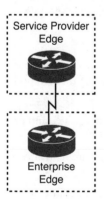

Figure 2-10   *Simple Internet connection*

You can use multihoming solutions to provide redundancy or failover for Internet service. Figure 2-11 shows four Internet multihoming options:

- **Option 1:** Single router, dual links to one ISP
- **Option 2:** Single router, dual links to two ISPs
- **Option 3:** Dual routers, dual links to one ISP
- **Option 4:** Dual routers, dual links to two ISPs

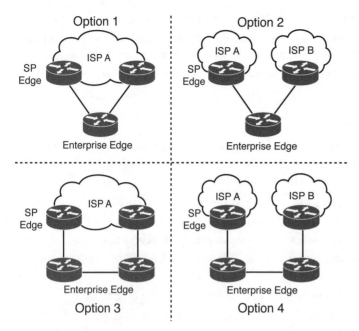

Figure 2-11   *Internet multihoming options*

Option 1 provides link redundancy but does not provide ISP and local router redundancy. Option 2 provides link and ISP redundancy but does not provide redundancy for a local router failure. Option 3 provides link and local router redundancy but does not provide for an ISP failure. Option 4 provides for full redundancy of the local router, links, and ISPs.

VPN/Remote Access

The VPN/remote access module of the enterprise edge provides remote-access termination services, including authentication for remote users and sites. Components of this submodule include the following:

- **Firewalls:** Provide stateful filtering of traffic, authenticate trusted remote sites, and provide connectivity using IPsec tunnels

- **Dial-in access concentrators:** Terminate legacy dial-in connections and authenticate individual users

- **Cisco Adaptive Security Appliances (ASAs):** Terminate IPsec tunnels, authenticate individual remote users, and provide firewall and intrusion prevention services

- Network intrusion prevention system (IPS) appliances

If you use a remote-access terminal server, this module connects to the PSTN. Today's networks often prefer VPNs over remote-access terminal servers and dedicated WAN links. VPNs reduce communication expenses by leveraging the infrastructure of SPs. For critical applications, the cost savings might be offset by a reduction in enterprise control and the loss of deterministic service. Remote offices, mobile users, and home offices access the Internet using the local SP with secured IPsec tunnels to the VPN/remote access submodule via the Internet submodule.

Figure 2-12 shows a VPN design. Branch offices obtain local Internet access from an ISP. Teleworkers also obtain local Internet access. VPN software creates secured VPN tunnels to the VPN server that is located in the VPN submodule of the enterprise edge.

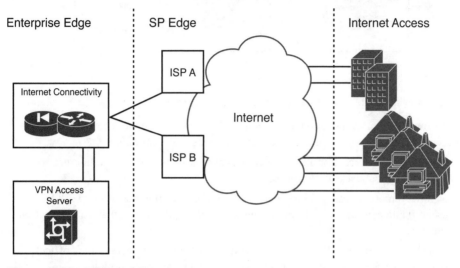

Figure 2-12   *VPN architecture*

Enterprise WAN

The enterprise edge of the enterprise WAN includes access to WANs. WAN technologies include the following:

- Multiprotocol Label Switching (MPLS)
- Metro Ethernet
- Leased lines
- Synchronous Optical Network (SONET) and Synchronous Digital Hierarchy (SDH)
- PPP
- Frame Relay
- ATM
- Cable
- Digital subscriber line (DSL)
- Wireless

Chapter 6, "WAN Technologies and the Enterprise Edge," and Chapter 7, "WAN Design," cover these WAN technologies. Routers in the enterprise WAN provide WAN access, QoS, routing, redundancy, and access control to the WAN. Of these WAN technologies, MPLS is the most popular WAN technology used today. For MPLS networks, the WAN routers prioritize IP packets based on configured differentiated services code point (DSCP) values to use one of several MPLS QoS levels. Figure 2-13 shows the WAN module connecting to the Frame Relay SP edge. The enterprise edge routers in the WAN module connect to the SP's Frame Relay switches.

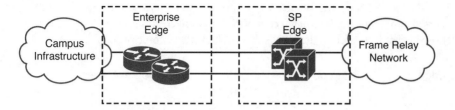

Figure 2-13   *WAN module*

Use the following guidelines when designing the enterprise edge:

- Determine the connection needed to connect the corporate network to the Internet. These connections are assigned to the Internet connectivity module.

- Create the e-commerce module for customers and partners that require Internet access to business and database applications.

- Design the remote access/VPN module for VPN access to the internal network from the Internet. Implement the security policy and configure authentication and authorization parameters.

- Assign the edge sections that have permanent connections to remote branch offices. Assign these to the WAN, metro area network (MAN), and VPN module.

Service Provider Edge Module

The SP edge module, shown in Figure 2-14, consists of SP edge services such as the following:

- Internet services
- PSTN services
- WAN services

Enterprises use SPs to acquire network services. ISPs offer enterprises access to the Internet. ISPs can route the enterprise's networks to their network and to upstream and peer Internet providers. ISPs can provide Internet services via Ethernet, DSL, or T1/DS3 access. It is common now for the SP to have their ISP router at the customer site and provide Ethernet access to the customer. Connectivity with multiple ISPs was described in the section "Internet Connectivity Module."

For voice services, PSTN providers offer access to the global public voice network. For the enterprise network, the PSTN lets dialup users access the enterprise via analog or cellular wireless technologies. It is also used for WAN backup using ISDN services.

WAN SPs offer MPLS, Frame Relay, ATM, and other WAN services for enterprise site-to-site connectivity with permanent connections. These and other WAN technologies are described in Chapter 6.

Figure 2-14 *WAN/Internet SP edge module*

Remote Modules

The remote modules of the Cisco Enterprise Architecture model are the enterprise branch, enterprise data center, and enterprise teleworker modules.

Enterprise Branch Module

The enterprise branch normally consists of remote offices or sales offices. These branch offices rely on the WAN to use the services and applications provided in the main campus. Infrastructure at the remote site usually consists of a WAN router and a small LAN switch, as shown in Figure 2-15. As an alternative to MPLS, it is common to use site-to-site IPsec VPN technologies to connect to the main campus.

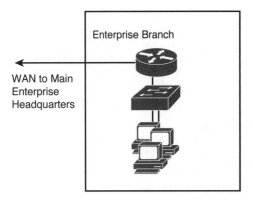

Figure 2-15 *Enterprise branch module*

Enterprise Data Center Module

The enterprise data center uses the network to enhance the server, storage, and application servers. The offsite data center provides disaster recovery and business continuance services for the enterprise. Highly available WAN services are used to connect the enterprise campus to the remote enterprise data center. The data center components include the following:

- **Network infrastructure:** Gigabit and 10 Gigabit Ethernet, InfiniBand, optical transport, and storage switching
- **Interactive services:** Computer infrastructure services, storage services, security, and application optimization
- **DC management:** Cisco Fabric Manager and Cisco VFrame for server and service management

The enterprise data center is covered in detail in Chapter 4, "Data Center Design."

Enterprise Teleworker Module

The enterprise teleworker module consists of a small office or a mobile user who needs to access services of the enterprise campus. As shown in Figure 2-16, mobile users connect from their homes, hotels, or other locations using dialup or Internet access lines. VPN clients are used to allow mobile users to securely access enterprise applications. The Cisco Virtual Office solution provides a solution for teleworkers that is centrally managed using small integrated service routers (ISRs) in the VPN solution. IP phone capabilities are also provided in the Cisco Virtual Office solution, providing corporate voice services for mobile users.

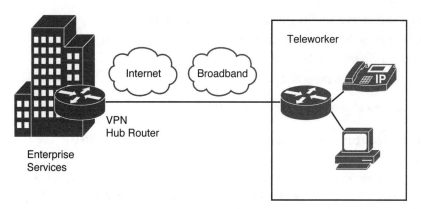

Figure 2-16 *Enterprise teleworker solution*

Table 2-3 summarizes the Cisco Enterprise Architecture.

Table 2-3 Cisco Enterprise Architecture Model

Enterprise Area or Module	Description
Enterprise campus area	The enterprise campus module includes the building access and building distribution components and the shared campus backbone component or campus core. Edge distribution provides connectivity to the enterprise edge. High availability is implemented in the server farm, and network management monitors the enterprise campus and enterprise edge.
Enterprise edge area	Consists of e-commerce, Internet, VPN/remote access, and WAN modules.
Enterprise WAN module	This module provides MPLS or other WAN technologies.
Enterprise remote branch module	The enterprise branch normally consists of remote offices, small offices, or sales offices. These branch offices rely on the WAN to use the services and applications provided in the main campus.
Enterprise data center module	The enterprise data center consists of using the network to enhance the server, storage, and application servers. The offsite data center provides disaster recovery and business continuance services for the enterprise.
Enterprise teleworker	The enterprise teleworker module supports a small office, mobile users, or home users providing access to corporate systems via VPN tunnels.

High Availability Network Services

This section covers designs for high availability network services in the access layer.

When designing a network topology for a customer who has critical systems, services, or network paths, you should determine the likelihood that these components will fail and then design redundancy where necessary. Consider incorporating one of the following types of redundancy into your design:

- Workstation-to-router redundancy in the building access layer
- Server redundancy in the server farm module
- Route redundancy within and between network components
- Link media redundancy in the access layer

The following sections discuss each type of redundancy.

Workstation-to-Router Redundancy and LAN High Availability Protocols

When a workstation has traffic to send to a station that is not local, the workstation has many possible ways to discover the address of a router on its network segment, including the following:

- ARP
- Explicit configuration
- ICMP Router Discovery Protocol (RDP)
- RIP
- HSRP
- VRRP
- GLBP
- VSS

The following sections cover each of these methods. VSS is covered earlier in the chapter.

ARP

Some IP workstations send an ARP frame to find a remote station. A router running proxy ARP can respond with its data link layer address. Cisco routers run proxy ARP by default.

Explicit Configuration

Most IP workstations must be configured with the IP address of a default router, which is sometimes called the default gateway.

In an IP environment, the most common method for a workstation to find a server is via explicit configuration (a default router). If the workstation's default router becomes unavailable, you must reconfigure the workstation with the address of a different router. Some IP stacks enable you to configure multiple default routers, but many other IP implementations support only one default router.

RDP

RFC 1256 specifies an extension to the Internet Control Message Protocol (ICMP) that allows an IP workstation and router to run RDP to let the workstation learn a router's address.

RIP

An IP workstation can run RIP to learn about routers, although this is not a common practice anymore and is not recommended. You should use RIP in passive mode rather than active mode. (Active mode means that the station sends RIP frames every 30 seconds.) Usually in these implementations, the workstation is a UNIX system running the routed or gated UNIX process.

HSRP

The Cisco HSRP provides a way for IP workstations that support only one default router to keep communicating on the internetwork even if their default router becomes unavailable. HSRP works by creating a virtual router that has its own IP and MAC addresses. The workstations use this virtual IP address as their default router.

HSRP routers on a LAN communicate among themselves to designate two routers as active and standby. The active router sends periodic hello messages. The other HSRP routers listen for the hello messages. If the active router fails and the other HSRP routers stop receiving hello messages, the standby router takes over and becomes the active router. Because the new active router assumes both the phantom's IP and MAC addresses, end nodes see no change. They continue to send packets to the phantom router's MAC address, and the new active router delivers those packets.

HSRP also works for proxy ARP. When an active HSRP router receives an ARP request for a node that is not on the local LAN, the router replies with the phantom router's MAC address instead of its own. If the router that originally sent the ARP reply later loses its connection, the new active router can still deliver the traffic.

Figure 2-17 shows a sample implementation of HSRP.

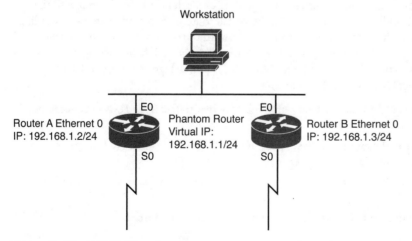

Figure 2-17   *HSRP: The phantom router represents the real routers*

In Figure 2-17, the following sequence occurs:

   1. The workstation is configured to use the phantom router (192.168.1.1) as its default router.

2. Upon booting, the routers elect Router A as the HSRP active router. The active router does the work for the HSRP phantom. Router B is the HSRP standby router.

3. When the workstation sends an ARP frame to find its default router, Router A responds with the phantom router's MAC address.

4. If Router A goes offline, Router B takes over as the active router, continuing the delivery of the workstation's packets. The change is transparent to the workstation.

VRRP

VRRP is a router redundancy protocol defined in RFC 3768. RFC 5768 defined VRRPv3 for both IPv4 and IPv6 networks. VRRP is based on Cisco's HSRP, but is not compatible. VRRP specifies an election protocol that dynamically assigns responsibility for a virtual router to one of the VRRP routers on a LAN. The VRRP router controlling the IP addresses associated with a virtual router is called the master, and it forwards packets sent to these IP addresses. The election process provides dynamic failover in the forwarding responsibility should the master become unavailable. This allows any of the virtual router IP addresses on the LAN to be used as the default first-hop router by end hosts. The virtual router backup assumes the forwarding responsibility for the virtual router should the master fail.

GLBP

GLBP protects data traffic from a failed router or circuit, such as HSRP, while allowing packet load sharing between a group of redundant routers. Methods for load balancing with HSRP and VRRP work with small networks, but GLBP allows for first-hop load balancing on larger networks.

The difference in GLBP from HSRP is that it provides for load balancing between multiple redundant routers—up to four gateways in a GLBP group. It load-balances by using a single virtual IP address and multiple virtual MAC addresses. Each host is configured with the same virtual IP address, and all routers in the virtual router group participate in forwarding packets. By default, all routers within a group forward traffic and load-balance automatically. GLBP members communicate between each other through hello messages sent every three seconds to the multicast address 224.0.0.102, User Datagram Protocol (UDP) port 3222. GLBP benefits include the following:

- **Load sharing:** GLBP can be configured in a way that traffic from LAN clients can be shared by multiple routers.

- **Multiple virtual routers:** GLBP supports up to 1024 virtual routers (GLBP groups) on each physical interface of a router.

- **Preemption:** GLBP enables you to preempt an active virtual gateway with a higher-priority backup.

- **Authentication:** Simple text password authentication is supported.

Server Redundancy

Some environments need fully redundant (mirrored) file and application servers. For example, in a brokerage firm where traders must access data to buy and sell stocks, two or more redundant servers can replicate the data. Also, you can deploy Cisco Unified Communications Manager (CUCM) servers in clusters for redundancy. The servers should be on different networks and use redundant power supplies. To provide high availability in the server farm module, you have the following options:

- **Single attachment:** This is not recommended because it requires alternate mechanisms (HSRP, GLBP) to dynamically find an alternate router.

- **Dual attachment:** This solution increases availability by using redundant network interface cards (NIC).

- Fast EtherChannel (FEC) and Gigabit EtherChannel (GEC) port bundles: This solution bundles 2 or 4 Fast or Gigabit Ethernet links to increase bandwidth.

Route Redundancy

Designing redundant routes has two purposes: balancing loads and increasing availability.

Load Balancing

Most IP routing protocols can balance loads across parallel links that have equal cost. Use the maximum-paths command to change the number of links that the router will balance over for IP; the default is four, and the maximum is six. To support load balancing, keep the bandwidth consistent within a layer of the hierarchical model so that all paths have the same cost. (Cisco Enhanced Interior Gateway Routing Protocol [EIGRP] is an exception because it can load-balance traffic across multiple routes that have different metrics by using a feature called variance.)

A hop-based routing protocol does load balancing over unequal-bandwidth paths as long as the hop count is equal. After the slower link becomes saturated, packet loss at the saturated link prevents full utilization of the higher-capacity links; this scenario is called pinhole congestion. You can avoid pinhole congestion by designing and provisioning equal-bandwidth links within one layer of the hierarchy or by using a routing protocol that takes bandwidth into account.

IP load balancing in a Cisco router depends on which switching mode the router uses. Process switching load balances on a packet-by-packet basis. Fast, autonomous, silicon, optimum, distributed, and NetFlow switching load balances on a destination-by-destination basis because the processor caches information used to encapsulate the packets based on the destination for these types of switching modes.

Increasing Availability

In addition to facilitating load balancing, redundant routes increase network availability.

You should keep bandwidth consistent within a given design component to facilitate load balancing. Another reason to keep bandwidth consistent within a layer of a hierarchy is that routing protocols converge much faster on multiple equal-cost paths to a destination network.

By using redundant, meshed network designs, you can minimize the effect of link failures. Depending on the convergence time of the routing protocols, a single link failure cannot have a catastrophic effect.

You can design redundant network links to provide a full mesh or a well-connected partial mesh. In a full-mesh network, every router has a link to every other router, as shown in

Figure 2-18. A full-mesh network provides complete redundancy and also provides good performance because there is just a single-hop delay between any two sites. The number of links in a full mesh is n(n–1)/2, where n is the number of routers. Each router is connected to every other router. A well-connected partial-mesh network provides every router with links to at least two other routing devices in the network.

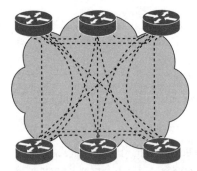

Figure 2-18 *Full-mesh network: Every router has a link to every other router in the network.*

A full-mesh network can be expensive to implement in WANs because of the required number of links. In addition, groups of routers that broadcast routing updates or service advertisements have practical limits to scaling. As the number of routing peers increases, the amount of bandwidth and CPU resources devoted to processing broadcasts increases.

A suggested guideline is to keep broadcast traffic at less than 20 percent of the bandwidth of each link; this amount limits the number of peer routers that can exchange routing tables or service advertisements. When designing for link bandwidth, reserve 80 percent of it for data, voice, and video traffic so that the rest can be used for routing and other link traffic. When planning redundancy, follow guidelines for simple, hierarchical design. Figure 2-19 illustrates a classic hierarchical and redundant enterprise design that uses a partial-mesh rather than a full-mesh topology. For LAN designs, links between the access and distribution layers can be Fast Ethernet, with links to the core at Gigabit Ethernet speeds.

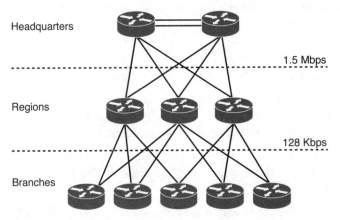

Figure 2-19 *Partial-mesh design with redundancy*

Link Media Redundancy

In mission-critical applications, it is often necessary to provide redundant media.

In switched networks, switches can have redundant links to each other. This redundancy is good because it minimizes downtime, but it can result in broadcasts continuously circling the network, which is called a broadcast storm. Because Cisco switches implement the IEEE 802.1d spanning-tree algorithm, you can avoid this looping in Spanning Tree Protocol (STP). The spanning-tree algorithm guarantees that only one path is active between two network stations. The algorithm permits redundant paths that are automatically activated when the active path experiences problems.

STP has a design limitation of only allowing one of the redundant paths to be active. VSS can be used with Catalyst 6500 switches to overcome this limitation.

You can use EtherChannel to bundle links for load balancing. Links are bundled in powers of 2 (2, 4, 8) groups. It aggregates the bandwidth of the links. Hence, two 10GE ports become 20 Gbps of bandwidth when they are bundled. For more granular load balancing, use a combination of source and destination per-port load balancing if available on the switch. In current networks, EtherChannel uses LACP, which is a standard-based negotiation protocol that is defined in IEEE 802.3ad (an older solution included the Cisco proprietary PAgP protocol). LACP helps protect against Layer 2 loops that are caused by misconfiguration. One downside is that it introduces overhead and delay when setting up the bundle.

Because WAN links are often critical pieces of the internetwork, WAN environments often deploy redundant media. As shown in Figure 2-20, you can provision backup links so that they become active when a primary link goes down or becomes congested.

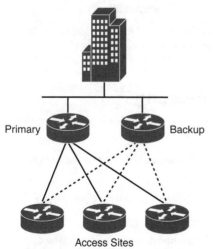

Primary   Backup

Access Sites

Figure 2-20 *Backup links can provide redundancy.*

Often, backup links use a different technology. For example, it is common to use Internet VPNs to back up primary MPLS links in today's networks. By using floating static routes, you can specify that the backup route must have a higher administrative distance (used by Cisco routers to select routing information) so that it is not normally used unless the primary route goes down.

> **Note** When provisioning backup links, learn as much as possible about the physical circuit routing. Different carriers sometimes use the same facilities, meaning that your backup path might be susceptible to the same failures as your primary path. Do some investigative work to ensure that your backup really is acting as a backup.

Cisco supports Multilink Point-to-Point Protocol (MPPP), which is an Internet Engineering Task Force (IETF) standard for ISDN B-channel (or asynchronous serial interface) aggregation. It bonds multiple WAN links into a single logical channel. MPPP is defined in RFC 1990. MPPP does not specify how a router should accomplish the decision-making process to bring up extra channels. Instead, it seeks to ensure that packets arrive in sequence at the receiving router. Then, the data is encapsulated within PPP and the datagram is given a sequence number. At the receiving router, PPP uses this sequence number to re-create the original data stream. Multiple channels appear as one logical link to upper-layer protocols. For Frame Relay networks, FRF.16.1 Multilink Frame Relay is used to perform a similar function.

Table 2-4 summarizes the four main redundancy models.

Table 2-4   Redundancy Models

Redundancy Type	Description
Workstation-to-router redundancy	Use of HSRP, VRRP, GLBP, and VSS
Server redundancy	Uses dual-attached NICs, FEC, or GEC port bundles
Route redundancy	Provides load balancing and high availability
Link redundancy	Uses multiple WAN links that provide primary and secondary failover for higher availability. On LANs, use EtherChannel.

References and Recommended Reading

Cisco Enterprise Teleworker Solution, http://www.cisco.com/c/en/us/solutions/enterprise-networks/teleworker/index.html.

Enterprise Architectures, http://www.cisco.com/c/en/us/solutions/enterprise-networks/index.html.

Cisco Enterprise Solutions Portal, http://www.cisco.com/c/en/us/solutions/enterprise/index.html.

Cisco TrustSec, http://www.cisco.com/c/en/us/solutions/enterprise-networks/trustsec/index.html.

Medianet at a Glance, www.cisco.com/web/solutions/medianet/docs/C45-511997-00medialnet_aag120308.pdf.

Application Performance white paper, www.cisco.com/en/US/solutions/ns1015/lippis_white_paper_application_velocity.pdf.

RFC 3758: Virtual Router Redundancy Protocol (VRRP).

RFC 1990: The PPP Multilink Protocol (MP).

Virtual Switching System, www.cisco.com/en/US/prod/collateral/switches/ps5718/ps9336/prod_qas0900aecd806ed74b.html.

2

Exam Preparation Tasks

Review All Key Topics

Review the most important topics in the chapter, noted with the Key Topics icon in the outer margin of the page. Table 2-5 lists a reference of these key topics and the page numbers on which each is found.

Table 2-5   Key Topic

Key Topic Element	Description	Page
Summary	Hierarchical Network models	41
List	Hierarchical Network Design	42
Figure 2-7	Cisco Enterprise Architecture model	50
Summary	High availability network services	59

Complete Tables and Lists from Memory

Print a copy of Appendix D, "Memory Tables" (found on the book website), or at least the section for this chapter, and complete the tables and lists from memory. Appendix E, "Memory Tables Answer Key," also on the website, includes completed tables and lists to check your work.

Define Key Terms

Define the following key terms from this chapter, and check your answers in the glossary:

core layer, distribution layer, access layer, VLAN, PoE, ARP, VSS, enterprise campus module, enterprise edge, enterprise WAN module, enterprise remote branch module, enterprise data center module, enterprise teleworker module, HSRP, VRRP, GLBP

Q&A

The answers to these questions appear in Appendix A, "Answers to the 'Do I Know This Already?' Quizzes and Q&A Questions." For more practice with exam format questions, use the exam engine from the website.

1. True or false: The core layer of the hierarchical model does security filtering and media translation.

2. True or false: The access layer provides high availability and port security.

3. You add Communications Manager to the network as part of a Voice over IP (VoIP) solution. In which submodule of the Enterprise Architecture model should you place Communications Manager?

4. True or false: HSRP provides router redundancy.

5. Which enterprise edge submodule connects to an ISP?

6. List the six modules of the Cisco Enterprise Architecture model for network design.

7. True or false: In the Cisco Enterprise Architecture model, the network management submodule does not manage the SP edge.

8. True or false: You can implement a full-mesh network to increase redundancy and reduce a WAN's costs.

9. How many links are required for a full mesh of six sites?

10. List and describe four options for multihoming to the SP between the enterprise edge and the SP edge. Which option provides the most redundancy?

11. To what enterprise edge submodule does the SP edge Internet submodule connect?

12. What are four benefits of hierarchical network design?

13. In an IP telephony network, in which submodule or layer are the IP phones and CUCM servers located?

14. Match the redundant model with its description:
  i. Workstation-router redundancy
  ii. Server redundancy
  iii. Route redundancy
  iv. Media redundancy
  a. Cheap when implemented in the LAN and critical for the WAN.
  b. Provides load balancing.
  c. Host has multiple gateways.
  d. Data is replicated.

15. True or false: Small-to-medium campus networks must always implement three layers of hierarchical design.

16. How many full-mesh links do you need for a network with ten routers?

17. Which layer provides routing between VLANs and security filtering?
  a. Access layer
  b. Distribution layer
  c. Enterprise edge
  d. WAN module

18. List the four modules of the enterprise edge area.

19. List the three submodules of the SP edge.

20. List the components of the Internet edge.

21. Which submodule contains firewalls, VPN concentrators, and ASAs?

    a. WAN

    b. VPN/remote access

    c. Internet

    d. Server farm

22. Which of the following describe the access layer? (Select two.)

    a. High-speed data transport

    b. Applies network policies

    c. Performs network aggregation

    d. Concentrates user access

    e. Provides PoE

    f. Avoids data manipulation

23. Which of the following describe the distribution layer? (Select two.)

    a. High-speed data transport

    b. Applies network policies

    c. Performs network aggregation

    d. Concentrates user access

    e. Provides PoE

    f. Avoids data manipulation

24. Which of the following describe the core layer? (Select two.)

    a. High-speed data transport

    b. Applies network policies

    c. Performs network aggregation

    d. Concentrates user access

    e. Provides PoE

    f. Avoids data manipulation

25. Which campus submodule connects to the enterprise edge module?

    a. SP edge

    b. WAN submodule

    c. Building distribution

    d. Campus core

    e. Enterprise branch

    f. Enterprise data center

26. Which remote module connects to the enterprise via the Internet or WAN submodules and contains a small LAN switch for users?

    a. SP edge

   b. WAN submodule

   c. Building distribution

   d. Campus core

   e. Enterprise branch

   f. Enterprise data center

27. Which three types of servers are placed in the e-commerce submodule?

   a. Web

   b. Application

   c. Database

   d. Intranet

   e. Internet

   f. Public share

Use Figure 2-21 to answer questions 28–33.

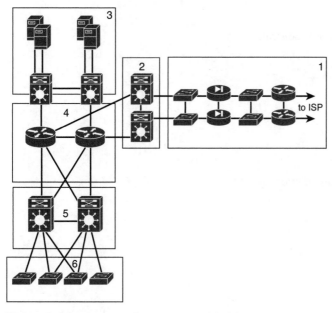

Figure 2-21   *Scenario for questions 28–33*

28. Which is the campus core layer?

   a. Block 1

   b. Block 2

   c. Block 3

   d. Block 4

   e. Block 5

   f. Block 6

29. Which is the enterprise edge?

    a. Block 1

    b. Block 2

    c. Block 3

    d. Block 4

    e. Block 5

    f. Block 6

30. Which is the campus access layer?

    a. Block 1

    b. Block 2

    c. Block 3

    d. Block 4

    e. Block 5

    f. Block 6

31. Which is the enterprise edge distribution?

    a. Block 1

    b. Block 2

    c. Block 3

    d. Block 4

    e. Block 5

    f. Block 6

32. Which is the campus distribution layer?

    a. Block 1

    b. Block 2

    c. Block 3

    d. Block 4

    e. Block 5

    f. Block 6

33. Which is the campus data center?

    a. Block 1

    b. Block 2

    c. Block 3

    d. Block 4

    e. Block 5

    f. Block 6

34. Which solution supports the enterprise teleworker?

    a. IP telephony

    b. Enterprise campus

    c. Cisco Virtual Office

    d. SP edge

    e. Hierarchical design

    f. Data Center 3.0

35. Which are two benefits of using a modular approach?

    a. Simplifies the network design

    b. Reduces the amount of network traffic on the network

    c. Often reduces the cost and complexity of the network

    d. Makes the network simple by using full mesh topologies

36. Which three modules provide infrastructure for remote users? (Select three.)

    a. Teleworker module

    b. WAN module

    c. Enterprise branch module

    d. Campus module

    e. Enterprise data center

    f. Core, distribution, access layers

37. Which are borderless networks infrastructure services? (Select three.)

    a. IP telephony

    b. Security

    c. QoS

    d. SP edge

    e. High availability

    f. Routing

38. Which module contains devices that supports AAA and stores passwords?

    a. WAN module

    b. VPN module

    c. Server farm module

    d. Internet connectivity module

    e. SP edge

    f. TACACS

39. Which topology is best used for connectivity in the building distribution layer?

   a. Full mesh

   b. Partial mesh

   c. Hub and spoke

   d. Dual ring

   e. EtherChannel

40. What are two ways that wireless access points are used? (Choose two.)

   a. Function as a hub for wireless end devices

   b. Connect to the enterprise network

   c. Function as a Layer 3 switch for wireless end devices

   d. Provide physical connectivity for wireless end devices

   e. Filter out interference from microwave devices

41. In which ways does application network services help resolve application issues? (Choose two.)

   a. It can compress, cache, and optimize content.

   b. Optimizes web streams, which can reduce latency and offload the web server.

   c. Having multiple data centers increases productivity.

   d. Improves application response times by using faster servers.

42. Which are key features of the distribution layer? (Select three.)

   a. Aggregates access layer switches

   b. Provides a routing boundary between access and core layers

   c. Provides connectivity to end devices

   d. Provides fast switching

   e. Provides transport to the enterprise edge

   f. Provides VPN termination

43. Which Cisco solution allows a pair of switches to act as a single logical switch?

   a. HSRP

   b. VSS

   c. STP

   d. GLB

44. Which module or layer connects the server layer to the enterprise edge?

   a. Campus distribution layer

   b. Campus data center access layer

   c. Campus core layer

   d. Campus MAN module

   e. WAN module

   f. Internet connectivity module

45. Which server type is used in the Internet connectivity module?

   a. Corporate

   b. Private

   c. Public

   d. Internal

   e. Database

   f. Application

46. Which server types are used in the e-commerce module for users running applications and storing data? (Select three.)

   a. Corporate

   b. Private

   c. Public

   d. Internet

   e. Database

   f. Application

   g. Web

47. Which are submodules of the enterprise campus module? (Select two.)

   a. WAN

   b. LAN

   c. Server farm/data center

   d. Enterprise branch

   e. VPN

   f. Building distribution

48. Which are the three layers of the hierarchical model? (Select three.)

   a. WAN layer

   b. LAN layer

   c. Core layer

   d. Aggregation layer

   e. Access layer

   f. Distribution layer

   g. Edge layer

49. You need to design for a packet load-sharing between a group of redundant routers. Which protocol allows you to do this?

   a. HSRP

   b. GLBP

   c. VRRP

   d. AARP

50. Which is a benefit of using network modules for network design?

   a. Network availability increases.

   b. Network becomes more secure.

   c. Network becomes more scalable.

   d. Network redundancy is higher.

51. The Cisco Enterprise Architecture takes which approach to network design?

   a. It takes a functional modular approach.

   b. It takes a sectional modular approach.

   c. It takes a hierarchical modular approach.

   d. It takes a regional modular approach.

52. Which is the recommended design geometry for routed networks?

   a. Design linear point-to-point networks

   b. Design in rectangular networks

   c. Design in triangular networks

   d. Design in circular networks

53. Which layer performs rate limiting, network access control, and broadcast suppression?

   a. Core layer

   b. Distribution layer

   c. Access layer

   d. Data link layer

54. Which layer performs routing between VLANs, filtering, and load balancing?

   a. Core layer

   b. Distribution layer

   c. Access layer

   d. Application layer

55. Which topology allows for maximum growth?

    a. Triangles

    b. Collapsed core-distribution

    c. Full mesh

    d. Core-distribution-access

56. Which layer performs port security and DHCP snooping?

    a. Core layer

    b. Distribution layer

    c. Access layer

    d. Application layer

57. Which layer performs Active Directory and messaging?

    a. Core layer

    b. Distribution layer

    c. Access layer

    d. Application layer

58. Which layers perform redundancy? (Select two.)

    a. Core layer

    b. Distribution layer

    c. Access layer

    d. Data Link Layer

59. Which statement is true regarding hierarchical network design?

    a. Makes the network harder since there are many submodules to use

    b. Provides better performance and network scalability

    c. Prepares the network for IPv6 migration from IPv4

    d. Secures the network with access filters in all layers

60. Based on Figure 2-22, and assuming that devices may be in more than one layer, list which devices are in each layer.

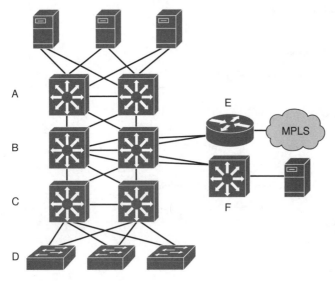

Figure 2-22   *Question 60*

Access layer:

Distribution layer:

Core:

Use Figure 2-23 to answer questions 61–63.

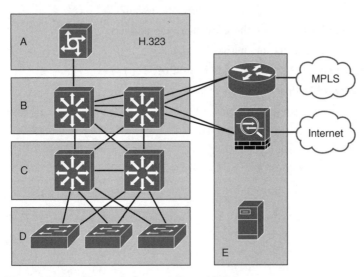

Figure 2-23   *Scenario for questions 61–63*

61. Which section(s) belong(s) to the core layer?

62. Which section(s) belong(s) to the distribution layer?

63. Which section(s) belong(s) to the access layer?

2

This chapter covers the following subjects:

LAN Media

LAN Hardware

Campus LAN Design and Best Practices

This chapter covers the design of campus local area networks (LANs). It reviews LAN media, components, and design models. The section "LAN Media" reviews the design characteristics of different Ethernet media technologies.

This chapter covers how you apply Layer 2 switches, Layer 3 switches, and routers in the design of LANs. It reviews several design models for large building, campus, and remote LANs.

CHAPTER 3

Enterprise LAN Design

"Do I Know This Already?" Quiz

The "Do I Know This Already?" quiz helps you identify your strengths and deficiencies in this chapter's topics.

The eight-question quiz, derived from the major sections in the "Foundation Topics" portion of the chapter, helps you determine how to spend your limited study time.

Table 3-1 outlines the major topics discussed in this chapter and the "Do I Know This Already?" quiz questions that correspond to those topics.

Table 3-1 "Do I Know This Already?" Foundation Topics Section-to-Question Mapping

Foundation Topics Section	Questions Covered in This Section
LAN Media	2
LAN Hardware	1, 3, 5, 8
Campus LAN Design and Best Practices	4, 6, 7

1. What device filters broadcasts?
   a. Layer 2 switch
   b. Hub
   c. Layer 3 switch
   d. Router
   e. a and c
   f. a and d
   g. a, c, and d

2. What is the maximum segment distance for Fast Ethernet over unshielded twisted-pair (UTP)?
   a. 100 feet
   b. 500 feet
   c. 100 meters
   d. 285 feet

3. What device limits the collision domain?

  a. Layer 2 switch

  b. Hub

  c. Layer 3 switch

  d. Router

  e. a and c

  f. c and d

  g. a, c, and d

4. The summarization of routes is a best practice at which layer?

  a. Access layer

  b. Distribution layer

  c. Core layer

  d. WAN layer

5. What type of LAN switches are preferred in the campus backbone of an enterprise network?

  a. Layer 2 switches

  b. Layer 3 switches

  c. Layer 3 hubs

  d. Hubs

6. Two workstations are located on separate VLANs. They exchange data directly. What type of application is this?

  a. Client/server

  b. Client-peer

  c. Peer-peer

  d. Client-enterprise

7. Which type of cable is the best solution in terms of cost for connecting an access switch to the distribution layer requiring 140 meters?

  a. UTP

  b. Copper

  c. Multimode fiber

  d. Single-mode fiber

8. Which mechanism transitions an access port directly to forwarding state?

  a. UplinkFast

  b. RootGuard

  c. PortFast

  d. AccessPortFast

Foundation Topics

This chapter covers the design of LANs. It reviews LAN media, components, and design models. Figure 3-1 shows the Enterprise Campus section of the Enterprise Composite Network model. Enterprise LANs have a campus backbone and one or more instances of building-distribution and building-access layers, with server farms and an enterprise edge to the WAN or Internet.

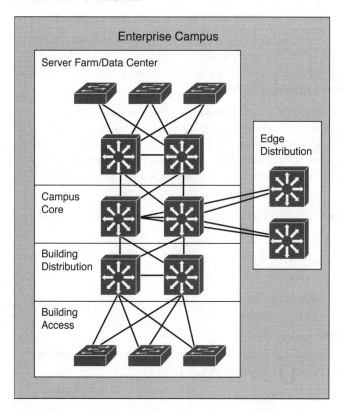

Figure 3-1   *Enterprise campus*

LAN Media

This section identifies some of the constraints you should consider when provisioning various LAN media types. It covers the physical specifications of Ethernet, Fast Ethernet, and Gigabit Ethernet.

You must also understand the design constraints of wireless LANs in the campus network. Specifications for wireless LANs are covered in Chapter 5, "Wireless LAN Design."

Ethernet Design Rules

Ethernet is the underlying basis for the technologies most widely used in LANs. In the 1980s and early 1990s, most networks used 10Mbps Ethernet, defined initially by Digital, Intel, and Xerox (DIX Ethernet Version II) and later by the IEEE 802.3 working group.

The IEEE 802.3-2002 standard contains physical specifications for Ethernet technologies through 10 Gbps.

100Mbps Fast Ethernet Design Rules

IEEE introduced the IEEE 802.3u-1995 standard to provide Ethernet speeds of 100 Mbps over UTP and fiber cabling. The 100BASE-T standard is similar to 10Mbps Ethernet in that it uses Carrier Sense Multiple Access Collision Detect (CSMA/CD); runs on Category (CAT) 3, 4, 5, and 6 UTP cable; and preserves the frame formats.

100Mbps Ethernet (or Fast Ethernet) topologies present some distinct constraints on the network design because of their speed. The combined latency due to cable lengths and repeaters must conform to the specifications for the network to work properly. This section discusses these issues and provides sample calculations.

The overriding design rule for 100Mbps Ethernet networks is that the round-trip collision delay must not exceed 512-bit times. However, the bit time on a 100Mbps Ethernet network is 0.01 microseconds, as opposed to 0.1 microseconds on a 10Mbps Ethernet network. Therefore, the maximum round-trip delay for a 100Mbps Ethernet network is 5.12 microseconds, as opposed to the more lenient 51.2 microseconds in a 10Mbps Ethernet network.

The following are specifications for Fast Ethernet, each of which is described in the following sections:

- 100BASE-TX
- 100BASE-T4
- 100BASE-FX

100BASE-TX Fast Ethernet

The 100BASE-TX specification uses CAT 5 or 6 UTP wiring. Fast Ethernet uses only two pairs of the four-pair UTP wiring. The specifications are as follows:

- Transmission over CAT 5 or 6 UTP wire.
- RJ-45 connector (the same as in 10BASE-T).
- Punchdown blocks in the wiring closet must be CAT 5 certified.
- 4B5B coding.

100BASE-T4 Fast Ethernet

The 100BASE-T4 specification was developed to support UTP wiring at the CAT 3 level. This specification takes advantage of higher-speed Ethernet without recabling to CAT 5 UTP. This implementation is not widely deployed. The specifications are as follows:

- Transmission over CAT 3, 4, 5, or 6 UTP wiring.
- Three pairs are used for transmission, and the fourth pair is used for collision detection.
- No separate transmit and receive pairs are present, so full-duplex operation is not possible.
- 8B6T coding.

100BASE-FX Fast Ethernet

The 100BASE-FX specification for fiber is as follows:

- It operates over two strands of multimode or single-mode fiber cabling.
- It can transmit over greater distances than copper media.
- It uses media interface connector (MIC), Stab and Twist (ST), or Stab and Click (SC) fiber connectors defined for FDDI and 10BASE-FX networks.
- 4B5B coding.

Gigabit Ethernet Design Rules

Gigabit Ethernet was first specified by two standards: IEEE 802.3z-1998 and 802.3ab-1999. The IEEE 802.3z standard specifies the operation of Gigabit Ethernet over fiber and coaxial cable and introduces the Gigabit Media-Independent Interface (GMII). These standards are superseded by the latest revision of all the 802.3 standards included in IEEE 802.3-2002.

The IEEE 802.3ab standard specified the operation of Gigabit Ethernet over CAT 5 UTP. Gigabit Ethernet still retains the frame formats and frame sizes, and it still uses CSMA/CD. As with Ethernet and Fast Ethernet, full-duplex operation is possible. Differences appear in the encoding; Gigabit Ethernet uses 8B10B coding with simple nonreturn to zero (NRZ). Because of the 20 percent overhead, pulses run at 1250 MHz to achieve 1000Mbps throughput.

Table 3-2 gives an overview of Gigabit Ethernet scalability constraints.

Table 3-2   Gigabit Ethernet Scalability Constraints

Type	Speed	Maximum Segment Length	Encoding	Media
1000BASE-T	1000 Mbps	100 m	Five-level	Cat 5 UTP
1000BASE-LX (long wavelength)	1000 Mbps	550 m	8B10B	Single-mode/ multimode fiber
1000BASE-SX (short wavelength)	1000 Mbps	62.5 micrometers: 220 m 50 micrometers: 500 m	8B10B	Multimode fiber
1000BASE-CX	1000 Mbps	25 m	8B10B	Shielded balanced copper

The following are the physical specifications for Gigabit Ethernet, each of which is described in the following sections:

- 1000BASE-LX
- 1000BASE-SX
- 1000BASE-CX
- 1000BASE-T

1000BASE-LX Long-Wavelength Gigabit Ethernet

IEEE 1000BASE-LX uses long-wavelength optics over a pair of fiber strands. The specifications are as follows:

- Uses long wave (1300 nm [nanometers]).
- For use on multimode or single-mode fiber.
- Maximum lengths for multimode fiber are
  - 62.5-micrometer fiber: 440 m
  - 50-micrometer fiber: 550 m
- Maximum length for single-mode fiber (9 micrometers) is 5 km.
- Uses 8B10B encoding with simple NRZ.

1000BASE-SX Short-Wavelength Gigabit Ethernet

IEEE 1000BASE-SX uses short-wavelength optics over a pair of multimode fiber strands. The specifications are as follows:

- Uses short wave (850 nm)
- For use on multimode fiber
- Maximum lengths:
  - 62.5-micrometer fiber: 260 m
  - 50-micrometer fiber: 550 m
- Uses 8B10B encoding with simple NRZ

1000BASE-CX Gigabit Ethernet over Coaxial Cable

IEEE 1000BASE-CX standard is for short copper runs between servers. The specifications are as follows:

- Used on short-run copper
- Runs over a pair of 150-ohm balanced coaxial cables (twinax)
- Maximum length of 25 m
- Mainly for server connections
- Uses 8B10B encoding with simple NRZ

1000BASE-T Gigabit Ethernet over UTP

The IEEE standard for 1000Mbps Ethernet over CAT 5 UTP was IEEE 802.3ab; it was approved in June 1999. It is now included in IEEE 802.3-2002. This standard uses the four pairs in the cable. (100BASE-TX and 10BASE-T Ethernet use only two pairs.) The specifications are as follows:

- CAT 5, four-pair UTP.
- Maximum length of 100 m.
- Encoding defined is a five-level coding scheme.
- One byte is sent over the four pairs at 1250 MHz.

10 Gigabit Ethernet Design Rules

The IEEE 802.3ae supplement to the 802.3 standard, published in August 2002, specifies the standard for 10 Gigabit Ethernet (10GE). It is defined for full-duplex operation over optical media, UTP, and copper. The IEEE 802.3an standard provides the specifications for running 10GE over UTP cabling. Hubs or repeaters cannot be used because they operate in half-duplex mode. It allows the use of Ethernet frames over distances typically encountered in metropolitan area networks (MANs) and wide area networks (WANs). Other uses include data centers, corporate backbones, and server farms.

10GE Media Types

10GE has seven physical media specifications based on different fiber types and encoding. Multimode fiber (MMF) and single-mode fiber (SMF) are used. Table 3-3 describes the different 10GE media types.

Table 3-3   10GE Media Types

10GE Media Type	Wavelength/Fiber (Short or Long)/UTP/Copper	Distance	Other Description
10GBASE-SR	Short-wavelength MMF	To 300 m	Uses 66B encoding
10GBASE-SW	Short-wavelength MMF	To 300 m	Uses the WAN interface sublayer (WIS)
10GBASE-LR	Long-wavelength SMF	To 10 km	Uses 66B encoding for dark fiber use
10GBASE-LW	Long-wavelength SMF	To 10 km	Uses WIS
10GBASE-ER	Extra-long-wavelength SMF	To 40 km	Uses 66B encoding for dark fiber use
10GBASE-EW	Extra-long-wavelength SNMP	To 40 km	Uses WIS
10GBASE-LX4	Uses division multiplexing for both MMF and SMF	To 10 km	Uses 8B/10B encoding
10GBASE-CX4	Four pairs of twinax copper	15 m	IEEE 802.3ak
10GBASE-T	CAT6a UTP	100 m	IEEE 802.3an
10GBASE-ZR	Long-wave SMF	80 km	Not in 802.3ae
10GBASE-PR	Passive optical Network	20 km	10G EPON 802.3av

Short-wavelength multimode fiber is 850 nm. Long-wavelength is 1310 nm, and extra-long-wavelength is 1550 nm. The WIS is used to interoperate with Synchronous Optical Network (SONET) STS-192c transmission format.

Looking ahead, both 40GE and 100GE have emerged and will become future backbone technologies for networks. IEEE 802.3ba is the designation given for the 802.3 standard, and speeds higher than 10 Gbps are paving the way for 40Gbps and 100Gbps Ethernet. Table 3-4 describes some of the physical standards.

Table 3-4   40GE and 100GE Physical Standards

Physical Layer	40 Gigabit Ethernet	100 Gigabit Ethernet
Backplane	—	100GBASE-KP4
Improved backplane	40GBASE-KR4	100GBASE-KR4
7 m over twinax copper cable	40GBASE-CR4	100GBASE-CR10
		100GBASE-CR4
30 m over Cat.8 UTP	40GBASE-T	—
100 m over OM3 MMF	40GBASE-SR4	100GBASE-SR10
125 m over OM4 MMF		100GBASE-SR4
2 km over SMF	40GBASE-FR	100GBASE-CWDM4
10 km over SMF	40GBASE-LR4	100GBASE-LR4
40 km over SMP	40GBASE-ER4	100GBASE-ER4

EtherChannel

The Cisco EtherChannel implementations provide a method to increase the bandwidth between two systems by bundling Fast Ethernet, Gigabit Ethernet, or 10GE links. When bundling Fast Ethernet links, use Fast EtherChannel. Gigabit EtherChannel bundles Gigabit Ethernet links. EtherChannel port bundles enable you to group multiple ports into a single logical transmission path between the switch and a router, host, or another switch. EtherChannels provide increased bandwidth, load sharing, and redundancy. If a link fails in the bundle, the other links take on the traffic load. You can configure EtherChannel bundles as trunk links.

Depending on your hardware, you can form an EtherChannel with up to eight compatibly configured ports on the switch. The participating ports in an EtherChannel trunk must have the same speed and duplex mode and belong to the same VLAN.

Comparison of Campus Media

As noted previously, several media types are used for campus networks. Table 3-5 provides a summary comparison of them. Wireless LAN (WLAN) is included here for completeness. WLAN technologies are covered in Chapter 5.

Table 3-5   Campus Transmission Media Comparison

Specification	Copper/UTP	Multimode Fiber	Single-Mode Fiber	Wireless LAN
Bandwidth	Up to 10 Gbps	Up to 10 Gbps	Up to 10 Gbps	Up to 300 Mbps
Distance	Up to 100 m	Up to 2 km (FE)	Up to 100 km (FE)	Up to 500 m at 1 Mbps
		Up to 550 m (GE)	Up to 5 km (GE)	

Specification	Copper/UTP	Multimode Fiber	Single-Mode Fiber	Wireless LAN
		Up to 300 m (10GE)	Up to 40 km (10GE)	
Price	Inexpensive	Moderate	Moderate to expensive	Moderate

LAN Hardware

This section covers the hardware devices and how to apply them to LAN design. Do note that repeaters and hubs are included here for historical reasons. You place devices in the LAN depending on their roles and capabilities. LAN devices are categorized based on how they operate in the Open Systems Interconnection (OSI) model. This section covers the following devices:

- Repeaters
- Hubs
- Bridges
- Switches
- Routers
- Layer 3 switches

Repeaters

Repeaters are the basic unit in networks that connect separate segments. Repeaters take incoming frames, regenerate the preamble, amplify the signals, and send the frame out all other interfaces. Repeaters operate at the physical layer of the OSI model. Because repeaters are unaware of packets or frame formats, they do not control broadcasts or collision domains. Repeaters are said to be "protocol transparent" because they are unaware of upper-layer protocols such as IP, Internetwork Packet Exchange (IPX), and so on. Repeaters were common in the 1980s and early 1990s in networks but were replaced by switches.

Hubs

With the increasing density of LANs in the late 1980s and early 1990s, hubs were introduced to concentrate thinnet and 10BASE-T networks in the wiring closet. Traditional hubs operate on the physical layer of the OSI model and perform the same functions as basic repeaters. The difference is that hubs have more ports than basic repeaters. Hubs were eventually replaced by switches.

Bridges

Bridges connect separate segments of a network. They differ from repeaters in that bridges are intelligent devices that operate in the data link layer of the OSI model. Bridges control the collision domains on the network. Bridges also learn the MAC layer addresses of each node on each segment and on which interface they are located. For any incoming frame, bridges forward the frame only if the destination MAC address is on another port or if the bridge is unaware of its location. The latter is called flooding. Bridges filter any incoming frames with destination MAC addresses that are on the same segment from where the frame arrives; they do not forward these frames.

Bridges are store-and-forward devices. They store the entire frame and verify the cyclic redundancy check (CRC) before forwarding. If the bridges detect a CRC error, they discard the frame. Bridges are protocol transparent; they are unaware of the upper-layer protocols such as IP, IPX, and AppleTalk. Bridges are designed to flood all unknown and broadcast traffic.

Bridges implement Spanning Tree Protocol (STP) to build a loop-free network topology. Bridges communicate with each other, exchanging information such as priority and bridge interface MAC addresses. They select a root bridge and then implement STP. Some interfaces are in a blocking state, whereas other bridges have interfaces in forwarding mode. Figure 3-2 shows a network with bridges. STP has no load sharing or dual paths, as there is in routing. STP provides recovery of bridge failure by changing blocked interfaces to a forwarding state if a primary link fails. Although DEC and IBM versions are available, the IEEE 802.1d standard is the STP most commonly used.

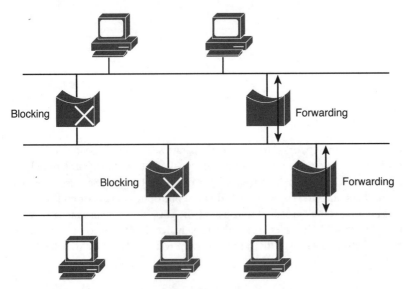

Figure 3-2   *Spanning Tree Protocol*

STP elects a root bridge as the tree's root. It places all ports that are not needed to reach the root bridge in blocking mode. The selection of the root bridge is based on the lowest numerical bridge priority. The bridge priority ranges from 0 to 65,535. If all bridges have the same bridge priority, the bridge with the lowest MAC address becomes the root. The concatenation of the bridge priority and the MAC address is the bridge identification (BID). Physical changes to the network force spanning-tree recalculation. Bridges have been replaced with the use of switches that perform the "bridging" functions.

Switches

Switches use specialized integrated circuits to reduce the latency common to regular bridges. Switches are the evolution of bridges. Some switches can run in cut-through mode, where the switch does not wait for the entire frame to enter its buffer; instead, it begins to forward the frame as soon as it finishes reading the destination MAC address. Cut-through operation increases the probability that frames with errors are propagated on the network, because it forwards the frame before the entire frame is buffered and checked for errors. Because of these problems, most switches today perform store-and-forward operation as bridges do. As shown in Figure 3-3, switches are exactly the same as bridges with respect to collision-domain and broadcast-domain characteristics. Each port on a switch is a separate collision domain. By default, all ports in a switch are in the same broadcast domain. Assignment to different VLANs changes that behavior.

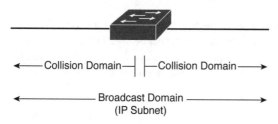

Figure 3-3 *Switches control collision domains.*

Switches have characteristics similar to bridges; however, they have more ports and run faster. Switches keep a table of MAC addresses per port, and they implement STP. Switches are data link layer devices. They are transparent to protocols operating at the network layer and above. Each port on a switch is a separate collision domain but is part of the same broadcast domain. Switches do not control broadcasts on the network.

The use of LAN switches instead of bridges or hubs is nearly universal. Switches are preferred over shared technology because they provide full bandwidth in each direction when configured in duplex mode. All the devices on a hub share the bandwidth in a single collision domain. Switches can also use VLANs to provide more segmentation.

Routers

Routers make forwarding decisions based on network layer addresses. When an Ethernet frame enters the router, the Layer 2 header is removed; the router forwards based on the Layer 3 IP address and adds a new Layer 2 address at the egress interface. In addition to controlling collision domains, routers bound data link layer broadcast domains. Each interface of a router is a separate broadcast domain. Routers do not forward data link layer broadcasts. IP defines network layer broadcast domains with a subnet and mask. Routers are aware of the network protocol, which means they can forward packets based on IP layer information. Figure 3-4 shows a router; each interface is a broadcast and a collision domain.

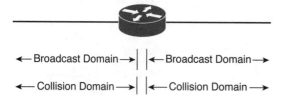

Figure 3-4 *Routers control broadcast and collision domains*

Routers exchange information about destination networks using one of several routing protocols. Routers use routing protocols to build a list of destination networks and to identify the best routes to reach those destinations. The following are examples of routing protocols:

- Enhanced Interior Gateway Routing Protocol (EIGRP)
- Open Shortest Path First (OSPF)
- Border Gateway Protocol (BGP)
- Routing Information Protocol (RIP)
- Intermediate System-to-Intermediate System (IS-IS)

Chapters 10 through 12 cover routing protocols in further detail. Routers translate data link protocols. They are the preferred method of forwarding packets between networks of differing media, such as Ethernet to serial. They also provide methods to filter traffic based on the network layer address, route redundancy, load balancing, hierarchical addressing, and multicast routing.

Layer 3 Switches

LAN switches that can run routing protocols are Layer 3 switches. These switches can run routing protocols and communicate with neighboring routers. They are also referred to as multilayer switches. Layer 3 switches have LAN technology interfaces that perform network layer packet forwarding. The use of switching technologies at the network layer greatly accelerates packet forwarding between connected LANs, including VLANs. You can use the router capacity you save to implement other features, such as security filtering and intrusion detection.

Layer 3 switches perform the functions of both data link layer switches and network layer routers. Each port is a collision domain. You can group ports into network layer broadcast domains (subnets). As with routers, a routing protocol provides network information to other network layer devices (subnets), and a routing protocol provides network information to other Layer 3 switches and routers.

Table 3-6 summarizes LAN devices for review.

Table 3-6   LAN Device Comparison

Device	OSI Layer	Is Domain Protocol Transparent or Protocol Aware?	Boundary	What It Understands
Bridge	Layer 2: data link	Transparent	Collision domain	Frames
Switch	Layer 2: data link	Transparent	Collision domain	Frames
Router	Layer 3: network	Aware	Broadcast domain	Packets
Layer 3 switch	Layer 3: network	Aware	Broadcast domain	Packets

Campus LAN Design and Best Practices

LANs can be classified as large-building LANs, campus LANs, or small and remote LANs. The large-building LAN typically contains a major data center with high-speed access and floor communications closets; the large-building LAN is usually the headquarters in larger companies. Campus LANs provide connectivity between buildings on a campus. Redundancy is usually a requirement in large-building and campus LAN deployments. Small and remote LANs provide connectivity to remote offices with a relatively small number of nodes.

Campus design factors include the following categories:

- **Network application characteristics:** Different application types
- **Infrastructure device characteristics:** Layer 2 and Layer 3 switching, hierarchy
- **Environmental characteristics:** Geography, wiring, distance, space, power, number of nodes

Applications are defined by the business, and the network must be able to support them. Applications may require high bandwidth or be time sensitive. The infrastructure devices influence the design. Decisions on switched or routed architectures and port limitations influence the design. The actual physical distances affect the design. The selection of copper or fiber media may be influenced by the environmental or distance requirements. The following sections show some sample LAN types. Table 3-7 summarizes the different application types.

Table 3-7 Application Types

Application Type	Description
Peer-to-peer	Includes instant messaging, file sharing, IP phone calls, and videoconferencing.
Client-local servers	Servers are located in the same segment as the clients or close by, normally on the same LAN. With 80/20 workgroup rule, 80 percent of traffic is local and 20 percent is not local.
Client/server farms	Mail, server, file, and database servers. Access is fast, reliable, and controlled.
Client-enterprise edge servers	External servers such as Simple Mail Transfer Protocol (SMTP), web, public servers, and e-commerce.

There is a wide range of network requirements for applications depending on the application types. Networks today are switched and not shared. Server farms require high-capacity links to the servers and redundant connections on the network to provide high availability. Costs are lower for peer-to-peer applications and become higher for applications that traverse the network with high redundancy. Table 3-8 summarizes network requirements for applications.

Table 3-8 Network Requirements for Application Types

Requirement	Peer-to-Peer	Client-Local Servers	Client/Server Farm	Client-Enterprise Edge Services
Connectivity type	Switched	Switched	Switched	Switched
Throughput required	Medium to high	Medium	High	Medium
Availability	Low to high	Medium	High	High
Network costs	Low to medium	Medium	High	Medium

Best Practices for Hierarchical Layers

Each layer of the hierarchical architecture contains special considerations. The following sections describe best practices for each of the three layers of the hierarchical architecture: access, distribution, and core.

Access Layer Best Practices

When designing the building access layer, you must consider the number of users or ports required to size up the LAN switch. Connectivity speed for each host should also be considered. Hosts might be connected using various technologies such as Fast Ethernet, Gigabit Ethernet, and port channels. The planned VLANs enter into the design.

Performance in the access layer is also important. Redundancy and QoS features should be considered.

There are several options for the access layer architectures:

- Traditional Layer 2 access layer design
- Updated Layer 2 access layer design
- Layer 3 access layer design
- Hybrid access layer design

Figure 3-5 shows the traditional Layer 2 access layer. This is the de facto model used where VLANs are defined in the distribution switches, HSRP gateways are configured for the VLANs with active and standby, and the STP root bridge is configured. There is no load balancing because STP is used, so only one uplink is active for each VLAN.

Layer 3 links are used between the core and distribution switches with a routing protocol.

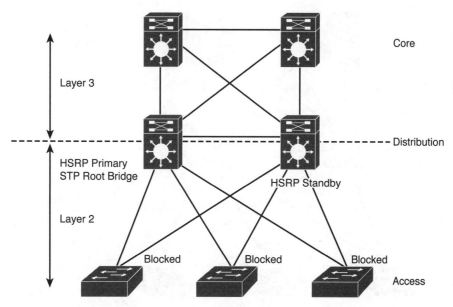

Figure 3-5   *Traditional Layer 2 access layer design*

Figure 3-6 shows the updated Layer 2 access layer. In this model, the distribution switches are still the demarcation between the Layer 2 and Layer 3 boundaries. The difference now is that VSS is configured in the distribution layer. VSS is supported on 4500, 6500, and 6800 series switches. With VSS, both access switch uplinks are used, doubling the bandwidth from access switches to the distribution pair. The bundled pair is called a *Multichassis EtherChannel (MEC)*, which creates a loop-free topology. With 1GE uplinks, you will now have 2 Gbps of uplink bandwidth. With 10GE uplinks, you will have 20 Gbps of uplink bandwidth!

Because VSS is used, there is no need for a first-hop routing protocol such as HSRP. This solution provides faster convergence than the traditional Layer 2 access design.

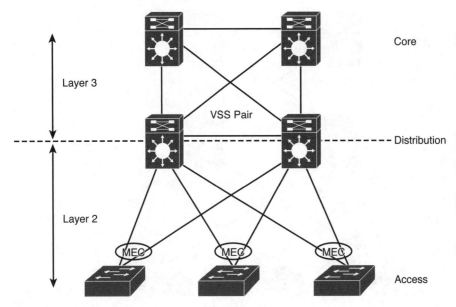

Figure 3-6   *Updated Layer 2 access layer design*

Figure 3-7 shows the Layer 3 access layer. With this design model, the Layer 3 demarc is pushed to the access layer. The access layer switches have VLANs defined and act as the default gateways. Notice that VLANs will not be able to span across access switches.

Layer 3 links are now used from the access layer to the distribution switches to the core. The use of HSRP is not necessary.

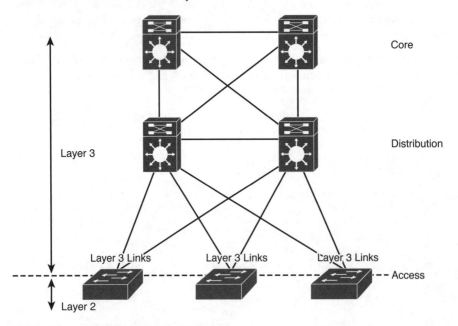

Figure 3-7   *Layer 3 access layer design*

The hybrid access layer combines the use of Layer 2 switching with Layer 3 at the access layer. In this design, some VLANs are defined in the access layer and others in the switch layer. There are Layer 3 and Layer 2 links between the distribution switches and the access switches. With the Layer 2 links, STP is still in the network. This design is not recommended because it has the added complexity of mixed Layer 2 and Layer 3 access layers per VLAN.

The following are the recommended best practices for the building access layer:

- Limit VLANs to a single closet when possible to provide the most deterministic and highly available topology.

- Use Rapid Per-VLAN Spanning Tree Plus (RPVST+) if STP is required. It provides for faster convergence than traditional 802.1d default timers.

- Set trunks to ON and ON with no-negotiate.

- Prune unused VLANs to avoid broadcast propagation (commonly done on the distribution switch). VTP v2 and v3 automatically prune unused VLANs.

- Use VLAN Trunking Protocol (VTP) Transparent mode, because there is little need for a common VLAN database in hierarchical networks.

- Disable trunking on host ports, because it is not necessary. Doing so provides more security and speeds up PortFast.

- Consider implementing routing in the access layer to provide fast convergence and Layer 3 load balancing.

- Use the **switchport host** commands on server and end-user ports to enable PortFast and disable channeling on these ports. Alternatively, you can use the **spanning-tree portfast default** global commands.

Use the Cisco STP Toolkit, which provides the following tools:

- **PortFast:** Bypasses the listening-learning phase for access ports

- **Loop Guard:** Prevents an alternate or root port from becoming designated in the absence of bridge protocol data units (BPDUs)

- **Root Guard:** Prevents external switches from becoming the root

- **Design Strategy:** Used to design an STP priority strategy with the highest priorities hardcoded at the top layers of the STP tree

- **BPDU Guard:** Disables a PortFast-enabled port if a BPDU is received

Distribution Layer Best Practices

As shown in Figure 3-8, the distribution layer aggregates all closet switches and connects to the core layer. Design considerations for the distribution layer include providing wire-speed performance on all ports, link redundancy, and infrastructure services.

The distribution layer should not be limited on performance. Links to the core must be able to support the bandwidth used by the aggregate access layer switches. Redundant links from the access switches to the distribution layer and from the distribution layer to the core layer allow for high availability in the event of a link failure. Infrastructure services include quality of service (QoS) configuration, security, and policy enforcement. Access lists are configured in the distribution layer.

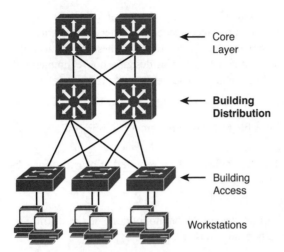

Figure 3-8   *Distribution layer*

The following are recommended best practices at the distribution layer:

- Use first-hop redundancy protocols. Hot Standby Router Protocol (HSRP) or Gateway Load Balancing Protocol (GLBP) should be used if you implement Layer 2 links between the Layer 2 access switches and the distribution layer.

- Use Layer 3 routing protocols between the distribution and core switches to allow for fast convergence and load balancing.

- Only peer on links that you intend to use as transit.

- Build Layer 3 triangles, not squares, as shown in Figure 3-9.

- Use the distribution switches to connect Layer 2 VLANs that span multiple access layer switches.

- Summarize routes from the distribution to the core of the network to reduce routing overhead.

- Use Virtual Switching System (VSS) as an option described in the following paragraph to eliminate the use of STP and the need for HSRP.

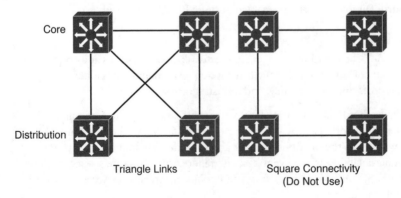

Figure 3-9   *Layer 3 triangles*

VSS solves the STP unused blocked links problem by converting the distribution switching pair into a logical single switch. With VSS, the physical topology changes as each access switch has a single upstream distribution switch versus having two upstream distribution switches. The bundled access switch pair is called a Multichassis EtherChannel (MEC), which creates a loop-free topology eliminated STP. VSS is configured only on Cisco 4500, 6500, and 6800 series switches. As shown in Figure 3-10, the two switches are connected via 10GE links called virtual switch links (VSLs), which makes them seem as a single switch. The key benefits of VSS include the following:

- Layer 3 switching can be used toward the access layer.

- Simplified management of a single configuration of the VSS distribution switch.

- Better return on investment (ROI) via increased bandwidth between the access layer and the distribution layer.

- No need to configure an FHRP such as HSRP or VRRP.

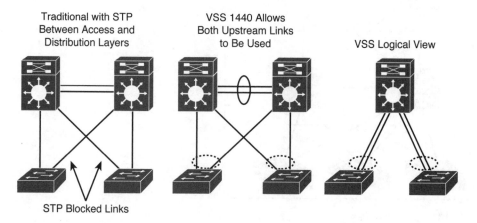

Figure 3-10 *Virtual switching system*

Core Layer Best Practices

Depending on the network's size, a core layer might or might not be needed. For larger networks, building distribution switches are aggregated to the core. This is called a collapsed core. This provides high-speed connectivity to the server farm or data center and to the enterprise edge (to the WAN and the Internet).

Figure 3-11 shows the criticality of the core switches. The core must provide high-speed switching with redundant paths for high availability to all the distribution points. The core must support gigabit speeds and data and voice integration.

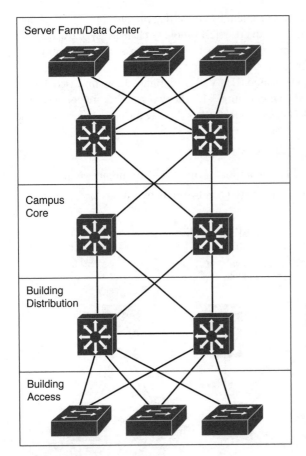

Figure 3-11   *Core switches*

The following are best practices for the campus core:

■ Reduce the switch peering by using redundant triangle connections between switches.

■ Use routing that provides a topology with no Layer 2 loops, which are seen in Layer 2 links using STP.

■ Use Layer 3 switches on the core that provide intelligent services that Layer 2 switches do not support.

■ Use two equal-cost paths to every destination network.

Table 3-9 summarizes campus layer best practices.

Table 3-9 Campus Layer Design Best Practices

Campus Layer	Best Practices
Access layer	Limit VLANs to a single closet when possible to provide the most deterministic and highly available topology.
	Use RPVST+ if STP is required. It provides the best convergence.
	Set trunks to ON and ON with no-negotiate.
	Manually prune unused VLANs to avoid broadcast propagation.
	Use VTP Transparent mode, because there is little need for a common VLAN database in hierarchical networks.
	Disable trunking on host ports, because it is not necessary. Doing so provides more security and speeds up PortFast.
	Consider implementing routing in the access layer to provide fast convergence and Layer 3 load balancing.
	Use Cisco STP Toolkit, which provides PortFast, Loop Guard, Root Guard, and BPDU Guard.
Distribution layer	Use first-hop redundancy protocols. Hot Standby Router Protocol (HSRP) or Gateway Load Balancing Protocol (GLBP) should be used if you implement Layer 2 links between the access and distribution.
	Use Layer 3 links between the distribution and core switches to allow for fast convergence and load balancing.
	Build Layer 3 triangles, not squares.
	Use the distribution switches to connect Layer 2 VLANs that span multiple access layer switches.
	Summarize routes from the distribution to the core of the network to reduce routing overhead.
	Use VSS as an option to eliminate the use of STP.
Core layer	Reduce the switch peering by using redundant triangle connections between switches.
	Use routing that provides a topology with no spanning-tree loops.
	Use Layer 3 switches on the core that provide intelligent services that Layer 2 switches do not support.
	Use two equal-cost paths to every destination network.

STP Design Considerations

Spanning Tree Protocol (STP) is defined by IEEE 802.1D. It prevents loops from being formed when switches or bridges are interconnected via multiple paths. STP is implemented by switches exchanging BPDU messages with other switches to detect loops, which are removed by shutting down selected bridge interfaces. This algorithm guarantees that there is one and only one active path between two network devices.

By default, the root bridge priority is 32768. If all switches have the same root bridge priority, the switch with the lowest MAC address will be elected as the root of the STP. Therefore, you should lower the root bridge priority on the switch that you want to be the STP root: the distribution legacy switch. You should also align the FHRP gateway to be the same switch.

STP switch ports enter the following states:

- **Blocking:** A port that would cause a switching loop if it were active. No user data is sent or received over a blocking port, but it may go into forwarding mode if the other links in use fail and the spanning tree algorithm determines the port may transition to the forwarding state. BPDU data is still received in the blocking state. It prevents the use of looped paths.

- **Listening:** The switch processes BPDUs and awaits possible new information that would cause it to return to the blocking state. It does not populate the MAC address table and it does not forward frames.

- **Learning:** While the port does not yet forward frames, it does learn source addresses from frames received and adds them to the filtering database (switching database). It populates the MAC address table, but does not forward frames.

- **Forwarding:** A port receiving and sending data, in normal operation. STP still monitors incoming BPDUs that would indicate it should return to the blocking state to prevent a loop.

- **Disabled:** Not strictly part of STP. A network administrator can manually disable a port.

Cisco Switches support three types of STPs:

- Per VLAN Spanning Tree Plus (PVST+)
- Rapid-PVST+
- Multiple Spanning Tree (MST)

PVST+ Per VLAN Spanning Tree Plus (PVST+) provides the same functionality as PVST using 802.1Q trunking technology rather than ISL. PVST+ is an enhancement to the 802.1Q specification and is not supported on non-Cisco devices. PVST+ is based on the IEEE 802.1D and adds Cisco proprietary features such as BackboneFast, UplinkFast, and PortFast.

Rapid_PVST+ is based on the Rapid STP (RSTP) IEEE 802.1W standard. RSTP (IEEE 802.1w) natively includes most of the Cisco proprietary enhancements to the 802.1D spanning tree, such as BackboneFast and UplinkFast. Rapid-PVST+ has these unique features:

- Uses Bridge Protocol Data Unit (BPDU) version 2, which is backward compatible with the 802.1D STP, which in turn uses BPDU version 0.

- All the switches generate BPDUs and send out on all the ports every 2 seconds, whereas in 802.1D STP only the root bridge sends the configuration BPDUs.

- **Port roles:** Root port, designated port, alternate port, and backup port.

- **Port states:** Discarding, Learning, and Forwarding.
- **Port types:** Edge Port (PortFast), Point-to-Point, and Shared port.

Rapid-PVST uses RSTP to provide faster convergence. When any RSTP port receives legacy 802.1D BPDU, it falls back to legacy STP and the inherent fast convergence benefits of 802.1W are lost when it interacts with legacy bridges. Cisco recommends that Rapid-PVST+ be configured for best convergence.

MST is defined by IEEE 802.1S. It is based on the Cisco Multiple Instance Spanning Tree Protocol (MISTP). MISTP (802.1S) is an IEEE standard that allows several VLANs to be mapped to a reduced number of spanning tree instances. This is possible because most networks do not need more than a few logical topologies. Each instance handles multiple VLANs that have the same Layer 2 topology.

Cisco STP Toolkit

STP has been the friend and enemy of network designers and network troubleshooters throughout the years. STP is required for a Layer 2 Ethernet network to function properly for path redundancy and prevention of Layer 2 loops. Cisco recommends that you design for the use of the Cisco STP Toolkit to enhance the performance of IEEE 802.1D STP on your network. Figure 3-12 shows where each mechanism is applied on the network.

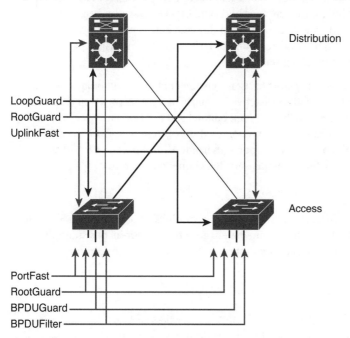

Figure 3-12 *Cisco STP Toolkit mechanisms*

PortFast

PortFast causes a Layer 2 LAN access port to enter the forwarding state immediately, bypassing the listening and learning states. When configured for PortFast, a port is still running STP and can immediately transition to the blocking state if necessary. PortFast should be used only when connecting a single end-station to the port. It can be enabled on trunk ports.

UplinkFast

UplinkFast provides fast convergence after a direct link failure and can achieve load balancing between redundant Layer 2 links using uplink groups. UplinkFast cannot be configured on *individual* VLANs; it is configured on *all* VLANs of the LAN switch. It is most useful when configured on the uplink ports of closet switches connecting to distribution switches. This mechanism is enabled when Rapid STP (RSTP) is enabled on the switch.

BackboneFast

BackboneFast provides fast failover when an indirect link failure occurs. It is initiated when a root port or blocked port on a network device receives inferior BPDUs from its designated bridge. It is configured on distribution and core switches. As with UplinkFast, this mechanism does not need to be enabled when RSTP is configured.

Loop Guard

Loop Guard helps prevent bridging loops that could occur because of a unidirectional link failure on a point-to-point link. It detects root ports and blocked ports and ensures they keep receiving BPDUs from the designated port on the segment. When Loop Guard is enabled, if a root or blocked port stops receiving BPDUs from its designated port, it transitions to the loop-inconsistent blocking state.

Loop Guard can be enabled on a per-port basis. It must be configured on point-to-point links only. It is automatically applied to all active instances or VLANs to which that port belongs. When enabled on an EtherChannel (link bundle) and the first link becomes unidirectional, it blocks the entire channel until the affected port is removed from the channel. Loop Guard cannot be enabled on PortFast ports, dynamic VLAN ports, or RootGuard-enabled switches. It does not affect UplinkFast or BackboneFast operation.

Root Guard

Root Guard prevents a port from becoming a root port or blocked port. When a RootGuard port receives a superior BPDU, the port immediately goes to the root-inconsistent (blocked) state. Root Guard is configured on access switches so that they do not become a root of the spanning tree.

BPDU Guard

BPDU Guard shuts down a port that receives a BPDU, regardless of PortFast configuration. In a valid configuration, PortFast-enabled ports do not receive BPDUs. Reception of a BPDU by a PortFast-enabled port signals an invalid configuration.

BPDU Filter

BPDU Filter prevents a port from sending or receiving BPDUs. It can be configured on a per-port basis. When configured globally, it applies to all operational PortFast ports.

Explicitly configuring PortFast BPDU filtering on a port that is not connected to a host can result in bridging loops. If a port configuration is not set to the default configuration, the PortFast setting will not affect PortFast BPDU filtering. When a PortFast port receives a BPDU, it immediately loses its operational PortFast status, BPDU filtering is automatically disabled on the port, and STP resumes sending BPDUs on the port.

Table 3-10 summarizes the mechanisms available within the STP Toolkit.

Table 3-10   Mechanisms Within the Cisco STP Toolkit

Mechanism	Improves STP Performance or Stability	Description
PortFast	STP performance	Bypasses listening-learning phases to transition directly to the forwarding state
UplinkFast	STP performance	Enables fast uplink failover on an access switch
BackboneFast	STP performance	Enables fast convergence in distribution and core layers when STP changes occur
Loop Guard	STP stability	Prevents an alternate or root port from being the designated port in the absence of bridge protocol data units (BPDUs)
Root Guard	STP stability	Prevents external switches from becoming the root of the STP tree
BPDU Guard	STP stability	Disables a PortFast-enable port if a BPDU is received
BPDU Filter	STP stability	Suppresses BPDU on ports

VLAN and Trunk Considerations

The following are some quick recommendations for VLANs and trunks:

- Cisco recommends the use of IEEE 802.1Q as the trunk protocol. Cisco ISL is obsolete.
- Do not use VLAN 1 as the management VLAN. Move it to a different VLAN number.
- Avoid automatic pruning of VLANs on trunk interfaces. Prune VLANs with manual configuration.
- Do not rely on the Dynamic Trunking Protocol (DTP). DTP provides the ability to negotiate the trunking method with the other device. Manual configuration is recommended by configuring the trunking protocol to 802.1Q.

Unidirectional Link Detection (UDLD) Protocol

STP relies on its operation of reception and transmission of the bridge protocol data units (BPDUs). If the STP process that runs on the switch with a blocking port stops receiving BPDUs from its upstream (designated) switch on the port, STP eventually ages out the STP information for the port and moves it to the forwarding state. This creates a forwarding loop or STP loop. Packets start to cycle indefinitely along the looped path, and they consume more and more bandwidth. This leads to a possible network outage.

An STP loop can occur on fiber networks if an SFP module fails. UDLD can be configured on a per-port basis on all redundant links. Because Loop Guard does not work on shared links, UDLD should be also configured to prevent loops. Loop Guard and Unidirectional Link Detection (UDLD) functionality overlap, partly in the sense that both protect against STP failures caused by unidirectional links. Cisco recommends that UDLD aggressive mode be configured on any fiber-optic interconnection and that UDLD be enabled in global mode. Table 3-11 compares describes Loop Guard and UDLD functionality.

Table 3-11   Loop Guard and UDLD Comparison

Functionality	Loop Guard	UDLD
Configuration	Per port	Per port
Action Granularity	Per VLAN	Per port
	STP performance	Enables fast convergence in the distribution and core layers when STP changes occur
Protection against STP failures caused by unidirectional links	Yes, when enabled on all root and alternate ports in a redundant topology	Yes, when enabled on all links in a redundant topology
Protection against STP failures caused by problems in the software (designated switch does not send BPDU)	Yes	No
Protection against mis-wiring.	No	Yes

Large-Building LANs

Large-building LANs are segmented by floors or departments. The building-access component serves one or more departments or floors. The building-distribution component serves one or more building-access components. Campus and building backbone devices connect the data center, building-distribution components, and the enterprise edge-distribution component. The access layer typically uses Layer 2 switches to contain costs, with more expensive Layer 3 switches in the distribution layer to provide policy enforcement. Current best practice is to also deploy multilayer switches in the campus and building backbone. Figure 3-13 shows a typical large-building design.

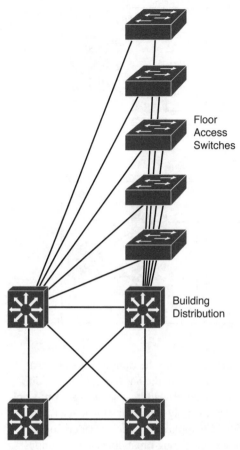

Figure 3-13 *Large-building LAN design*

Each floor can have more than 200 users. Following a hierarchical model of building access, building distribution, and core, Fast Ethernet nodes can connect to the Layer 2 switches in the communications closet. Fast Ethernet or Gigabit Ethernet uplink ports from closet switches connect back to one or two (for redundancy) distribution switches. Distribution switches can provide connectivity to server farms that provide business applications, Dynamic Host Configuration Protocol (DHCP), Domain Name System (DNS), intranet, and other services.

Enterprise Campus LANs

A campus LAN connects two or more buildings within a local geographic area using a high-bandwidth LAN media backbone. Usually the enterprise owns the medium (copper or fiber). High-speed switching devices minimize latency. In today's networks, Gigabit Ethernet campus backbones are the standard for new installations. In Figure 3-14, Layer 3 switches with Gigabit Ethernet media connect campus buildings.

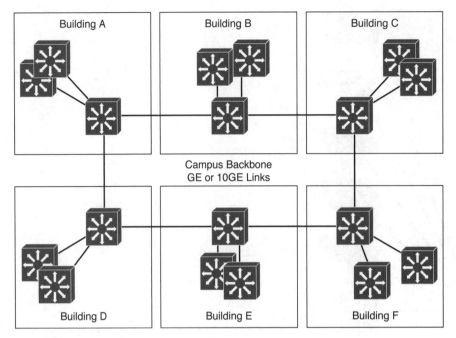

Figure 3-14 *Campus LAN*

Ensure that you implement a hierarchical composite design on the campus LAN and that you assign network layer addressing to control broadcasts on the networks. Each building should have addressing assigned in such a way as to maximize address summarization. Apply contiguous subnets to buildings at the bit boundary to apply summarization and ease the design. Campus networks can support high-bandwidth applications such as video conferencing. Remember to use Layer 3 switches with high-switching capabilities in the campus-backbone design. In smaller installations, it might be desirable to collapse the building-distribution component into the campus backbone. An increasingly viable alternative is to provide building access and distribution on a single device selected from among the smaller Layer 3 switches now available.

As shown in the previous sections, each individual module has different requirements. The building access layer is the only layer that uses Layer 2 switching. Both the campus core and the server farm have requirements for high availability, high performance, and a higher cost per port.

Table 3-12 shows network requirements for application types.

Table 3-12 Network Requirements for Application Types

Specification	Building Access	Distribution Layer	Campus Core	Server Farm
Technology	Layer 2 and Layer 3 switches	Layer 3 switches	Layer 3 switches	Layer 3 switches
Scalability	High	Medium	Low	Medium

Specification	Building Access	Distribution Layer	Campus Core	Server Farm
Availability	Medium	Medium	High	High
Performance	Medium	Medium	High	High
Cost per port	Low	Medium	High	High

Edge Distribution

For large campus LANs, the edge distribution module provides additional security between the campus LAN and the enterprise edge (WAN, Internet, and virtual private networks [VPNs]). The edge distribution protects the campus from the following threats:

- **IP spoofing:** The edge distribution switches protect the core from the spoofing of IP addresses.
- **Unauthorized access:** Controls access to the network core.
- **Network reconnaissance:** Filtering of network discovery packets to prevent discovery from external networks.
- **Packet sniffers:** The edge distribution separates the edge's broadcast domains from the campus, preventing possible network packet captures.

Medium-Size LANs

Medium-size LANs contain 200 to 1000 devices. Usually, the distribution and core layers are collapsed in the medium-size network. Access switches are still connected to both distribution/core switches to provide redundancy. Figure 3-15 shows the medium-size campus LAN.

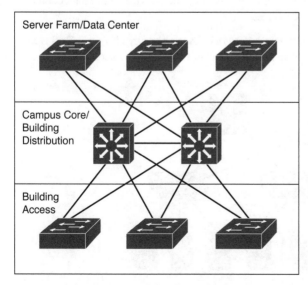

Figure 3-15   *Medium-size campus LAN*

Small and Remote Site LANs

Small and remote sites usually connect to the corporate network via a small router. The LAN service is provided by a small LAN switch. The router filters broadcast to the WAN circuit and forward packets that require services from the corporate network. You can place a server at the small or remote site to provide DHCP and other local applications such as a backup domain controller and DNS; if not, you must configure the router to forward DHCP broadcasts and other types of services. As the site grows, you need the structure provided by the Enterprise Composite Network model. Figure 3-16 shows a typical architecture of a remote LAN.

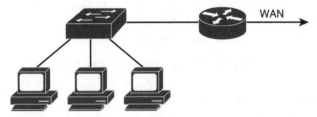

Figure 3-16 *Remote office LAN*

Server Farm Module

The server farm or data center module provides high-speed access to servers for the campus networks. You can attach servers to switches via Gigabit Ethernet or 10GE. Some campus deployments might need EtherChannel technology to meet traffic requirements. Figure 3-17 shows an example of a server farm module for a small network. Servers are connected via Fast Ethernet or Fast EtherChannel.

The server farm switches connect via redundant uplink ports to the core switches. The largest deployments might find it useful to hierarchically construct service to the data center using access and distribution network devices.

Server distribution switches are used in larger networks. Access control lists and QoS features are implemented on the server distribution switches to protect the servers and services and to enforce network policies.

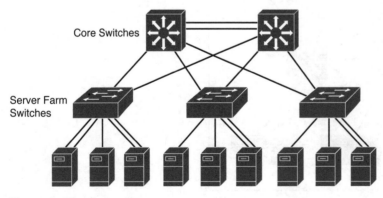

Figure 3-17 *Server farm*

Server Connectivity Options

Servers can be connected in three primary ways:

- Single network interface card (NIC)
- Dual NIC EtherChannel
- Dual NIC to separate access switches
- Content switching

Single NIC–connected servers contain Fast or Gigabit Ethernet full-duplex speeds with no redundancy. Servers requiring redundancy can be connected with dual NICs using switch EtherChannel or each link connected to separate access switches.

Advanced redundancy solutions use content switches that front-end multiple servers. This provides redundancy and load balancing per user request.

Enterprise Data Center Infrastructure

Data centers (DCs) contain different types of server technologies, including standalone servers, blade servers, mainframes, clustered servers, and virtual servers.

DC architecture is covered in detail in Chapter 4, "Data Center Design."

Campus LAN QoS Considerations

For the access layer of the campus LAN, you can classify and mark frames or packets to apply quality of service (QoS) policies in the distribution or at the enterprise edge. Classification is a fundamental building block of QoS and involves recognizing and distinguishing between different traffic streams. For example, you distinguish between HTTP/HTTPS, FTP, and VoIP traffic. Without classification, all traffic is treated the same.

Marking sets certain bits in a packet or frame that has been classified. Marking is also called coloring or tagging. Layer 2 has two methods to mark frames for CoS:

- **Inter-Switch Link (ISL):** This method is obsolete.
- **IEEE 802.1p/802.1Q:** This is the recommended method.

The IEEE 802.1D-1998 standard describes IEEE 802.1p traffic class expediting.

Both methods provide 3 bits for marking frames. The Cisco ISL is a proprietary trunk-encapsulation method for carrying VLANs over Fast Ethernet or Gigabit Ethernet interfaces. It is now an obsolete solution.

ISL appends tags to each frame to identify the VLAN it belongs to. As shown in Figure 3-18, the tag is a 30-byte header and CRC trailer that are added around the Fast Ethernet frame. This includes a 26-byte header and 4-byte CRC. The header includes a 15-bit VLAN ID that identifies each VLAN. The user field in the header also includes 3 bits for the class of service (CoS).

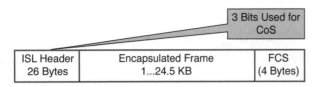

Figure 3-18 *ISL frame*

The IEEE 802.1Q standard trunks VLANs over Fast Ethernet and Gigabit Ethernet interfaces, and you can use it in a multivendor environment. IEEE 802.1Q uses one instance of STP for each VLAN allowed in the trunk. Like ISL, IEEE 802.1Q uses a tag on each frame with a VLAN identifier. Figure 3-19 shows the IEEE 802.1Q frame. Unlike ISL, 802.1Q uses an internal tag. IEEE 802.1Q also supports the IEEE 802.1p priority standard, which is included in the 802.1D-1998 specification. A 3-bit Priority field is included in the 802.1Q frame for CoS.

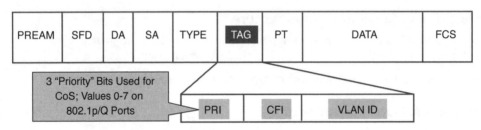

Figure 3-19 *IEEE 802.1Q frame*

The preferred location to mark traffic is as close as possible to the source. Figure 3-20 shows a segment of a network with IP phones. Most workstations send packets with CoS or IP precedence bits (ToS) set to 0. If the workstation supports IEEE 802.1Q/p, it can mark packets. VoIP traffic from the phone is sent with a Layer 2 CoS set to 5. The phone also reclassifies data from the PC to a CoS/ToS of 0. With differentiated services codepoint (DSCP) at Layer 3, VoIP bearer traffic is set to Expedited Forwarding (EF) (which implies a ToS set to 5), binary value 101110 (hexadecimal 2E). Signaling traffic is set to DSCP AF31.

As shown in Figure 3-20, switch capabilities vary in the access layer. If the switches in this layer are capable, configure them to accept the markings or remap them. The advanced switches in the distribution layer can mark traffic, accept the CoS/DSCP markings, or remap the CoS/DSCP values to different markings.

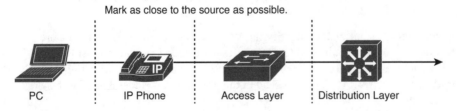

Figure 3-20 *Marking of frames or packets*

Multicast Traffic Considerations

Internet Group Management Protocol (IGMP) is the protocol between end workstations and the local Layer 3 switch. IGMP is the protocol used in multicast implementations between the end hosts and the local router. RFC 2236 describes IGMP Version 2 (IGMPv2). RFC 1112 describes the first version of IGMP. IP hosts use IGMP to report their multicast group memberships to routers. IGMP messages use IP protocol number 2. IGMP messages are limited to the local interface and are not routed.

RFC 3376 describes IGMP Version 3 (IGMPv3) IGMPv3 provides the extensions required to support source-specific multicast (SSM). It is designed to be backward compatible with both prior versions of IGMP. All versions of IGMP are covered in Chapter 11, "OSPF, BGP, Route Manipulation, and IP Multicast."

When campus LANs use multicast media, end hosts that do not participate in multicast groups might get flooded with unwanted traffic. Two solutions are

- Cisco Group Management Protocol (CGMP)
- IGMP snooping

CGMP

Cisco Group Management Protocol is a Cisco proprietary protocol implemented to control multicast traffic at Layer 2. Because a Layer 2 switch is unaware of Layer 3 IGMP messages, it cannot keep multicast packets from being sent to all ports.

As shown in Figure 3-21, with CGMP, the LAN switch can speak with the IGMP router to find out the MAC addresses of the hosts that want to receive the multicast packets. You must also enable the router to speak CGMP with the LAN switches. With CGMP, switches distribute multicast sessions to the switch ports that have group members.

When a CGMP-enabled router receives an IGMP report, it processes the report and then sends a CGMP message to the switch. The switch can then forward the multicast messages to the port with the host receiving multicast traffic. CGMP Fast-Leave processing allows the switch to detect IGMP Version 2 leave messages sent by hosts on any of the supervisor engine module ports. When the IGMPv2 leave message is sent, the switch can then disable multicast for the port.

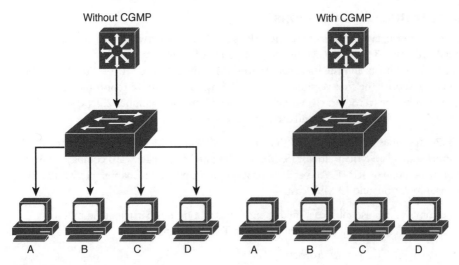

Figure 3-21   *CGMP*

IGMP Snooping

IGMP snooping is another way for switches to control multicast traffic at Layer 2. IGMP snooping has become the preferred solution over CGMP. With IGMP snooping, switches listen to IGMP messages between the hosts and routers. If a host sends an IGMP query message to the router, the switch adds the host to the multicast group and permits that port to receive multicast traffic. The port is removed from multicast traffic if an IGMP leave message is sent from the host to the router. The disadvantage of IGMP snooping is that it must listen to every IGMP control message, which can impact the switch's CPU utilization.

References and Recommended Readings

10Gigabit Alliance, www.10gea.org.

Cisco Data Center Network Architecture and Solutions Overview, www.cisco.com/en/US/solutions/collateral/ns340/ns517/ns224/ns377/net_brochure0900aecd802c9a4f.pdf.

"CSMA/CD Access Method, IEEE 802.3-2005." New York, NY: Institute of Electrical and Electronics Engineers, 2005.

IEEE P802.3ae 10Gb/s Ethernet Task Force, http://grouper.ieee.org/groups/802/3/ae/index.html.

"Token-Ring Access Method, IEEE 802.5-1998." Piscataway, NJ: Institute of Electrical and Electronics Engineers, 1998.

Cisco Spanning Tree Toolkit, http://www.cisco.com/c/dam/en_us/solutions/industries/docs/gov/turniton_stpt.pdf.

Spanning Tree From PVST+ to Rapid_PVST Migration, http://www.cisco.com/c/en/us/support/docs/switches/catalyst-6500-series-switches/72836-rapidpvst-mig-config.html.

Spanning Tree Protocol Enhancements Using Loop Guard and BPDU Skew Detection Features, http://www.cisco.com/c/en/us/support/docs/lan-switching/spanning-tree-protocol/10596-84.html.

Exam Preparation Tasks

Review All Key Topics

Review the most important topics in the chapter, noted with the Key Topic icon in the outer margin of the page. Table 3-13 lists a reference of these key topics and the page numbers on which each is found.

Table 3-13   Key Topics

Key Topic Element	Description	Page
List	Covers LAN devices, such as hubs, switches, and routers	89
Summary	Covers best practices for the access, distribution, and core layers	94
Table 3-9	Campus layer design best practices	101
Table 3-10	Mechanisms with the Cisco STP Toolkit	105

Complete Tables and Lists from Memory

Print a copy of Appendix D, "Memory Tables," (found on the CD), or at least the section for this chapter, and complete the tables and lists from memory. Appendix E, "Memory Tables Answer Key," also on the CD, includes completed tables and lists to check your work.

Define Key Terms

Define the following key terms from this chapter, and check your answers in the glossary:

CSMA/CD, 100BASE-TX, IEEE 802.3ab, EtherChannel, Layer 3 switches, access layer, distribution layer, core layer, VSS, Rapid-PVST+

Q&A

The answers to these questions appear in Appendix A, "Answers to the 'Do I Know This Already?'" Quizzes and Q&A Question." For more practice with exam format questions, use the exam engine on the CD.

1. True or false: Layer 2 switches control network broadcasts.
2. What technology can you use to limit multicasts at Layer 2?
3. True or false: Packet marking is also called coloring.
4. True or false: Usually, the distribution and core layers are collapsed in medium-size networks.
5. What are two methods to mark frames to provide CoS?

6. Which of the following is an example of a peer-to-peer application?

    a. IP phone call

    b. Client accessing file server

    c. Web access

    d. Using a local server on the same segment

7. What primary design factors affect the design of a campus network? (Select three.)

    a. Environmental characteristics

    b. Number of file servers

    c. Infrastructure devices

    d. Fiber and UTP characteristics

    e. Network applications

    f. Windows, Linux, and mainframe operating systems

8. You need to connect a building access switch to the distribution switch. The cable distance is 135 m. What type of cable do you recommend?

    a. UTP

    b. Coaxial cable

    c. Multimode fiber

    d. Single-mode fiber

9. Which layer of the campus network corresponds to the data center aggregation layer?

    a. Core layer

    b. Distribution layer

    c. Access layer

    d. Server farm

10. Which of the following is an access layer best practice?

    a. Reduce switch peering and routing.

    b. Use HSRP and summarize routes.

    c. Disable trunking and use RPVST+.

    d. Offload SSL sessions and use load balancers.

11. Which of the following is a distribution layer best practice?

    a. Reduce switch peering and routing.

    b. Use HSRP and summarize routes.

    c. Disable trunking and use RPVST+.

    d. Offload SSL sessions and use load balancers.

12. Which of the following is a core layer best practice?

    a. Reduce switch peering and routing.

    b. Use HSRP and summarize routes.

    c. Disable trunking and use RPVST+.

    d. Offload SSL sessions and use load balancers.

13. Which of the following is a DC aggregation layer best practice?

    a. Reduce switch peering and routing.

    b. Use HSRP and summarize routes.

    c. Disable trunking and use RPVST+.

    d. Offload SSL sessions and use load balancers.

14. Which of the following are threats to the edge distribution?

    a. IP spoofing

    b. Network discovery

    c. Packet-capture devices

    d. All of the above

15. An enterprise network has grown to multiple buildings supporting multiple departments. Clients access servers that are in local and other buildings. The company security assessment has identified policies that need to be applied. What do you recommend?

    a. Move all departments to a single building to prevent unauthorized access.

    b. Move all servers to one of the LAN client segments.

    c. Move all servers to a server farm segment that is separate from client LANs.

    d. Move all servers to the building distribution switches.

16. Link redundancy and infrastructure services are design considerations for which layers?

    a. Core layer

    b. Distribution layer

    c. Access layer

    d. All of the above

17. Which of the following are server connectivity methods in the server farm?

    a. Single NIC

    b. EtherChannel

    c. Content switch

    d. All of the above

18. What is the recommended method to connect the distribution switches to the core?

    a. Redundant triangle links

    b. Redundant cross-connect links

    c. Redundant Layer 3 squares

    d. Redundant Layer 2 links

19. A campus network of four buildings is experiencing performance problems. Each building contains 400 to 600 devices, all in one IP subnet. The buildings are connected in a hub-and-spoke configuration back to building 1 using Gigabit Ethernet with multimode fiber. All servers are located in building 1. What do you recommend to improve performance?

   a. Connect all buildings in a ring topology.

   b. Implement multiple VLANs in each building.

   c. Move servers to the buildings.

   d. Use single-mode fiber to make the Gigabit Ethernet links faster.

20. Which of the following is true about data link layer broadcasts?

   a. Not controlled by routers

   b. Not forwarded by routers

   c. Not forwarded by switches

   d. Not controlled by VLANs

21. Match each LAN medium with its original physical specification.

   i.   Fast Ethernet

   ii. Gigabit Ethernet

   iii. WLAN

   iv. Token Ring

   v.   10 Gigabit Ethernet

   a. IEEE 802.3ab

   b. IEEE 802.11b

   c. IEEE 802.3u

   d. IEEE 802.3ae

   e. IEEE 802.5

22. True or false: Layer 3 switches bound Layer 2 collision and broadcast domains.

23. Match each enterprise campus component with its description.

   i.   Campus infrastructure

   ii. Server farm

   iii. Edge distribution

   a. Consists of backbone, building-distribution, and building-access modules

   b. Connects the campus backbone to the enterprise edge

   c. Provides redundancy access to the servers

24. Match each LAN device type with its description.

      i.   Hub

      ii.   Bridge

      iii. Switch

      iv. Layer 3 switch

      v.   Router

    a. Legacy device that connects two data link layer segments

    b. Network layer device that forwards packets to serial interfaces connected to the WAN

    c. High-speed device that forwards frames between two or more data link layer segments

    d. High-speed device that bounds data link layer broadcast domains

    e. Device that amplifies the signal between connected segments

25. Match each application type with its description.

      i.   Peer to peer

      ii.   Client-local server

      iii. Client/server farm

      iv. Client-enterprise edge

    a. Server on the same segment

    b. IM

    c. Web access

    d. Client accesses database server

26. Match each transmission medium with its upper-limit distance.

      i.   UTP

      ii.   Wireless

      iii. Single-mode fiber

      iv. Multimode fiber

    a. 2 km

    b. 100 m

    c. 90 km

    d. 500 m

27. True or false: IP phones and LAN switches can reassign a frame's CoS bits.

28. Name two ways to reduce multicast traffic in the access layer.

29. What are two VLAN methods you can use to carry marking CoS on frames?

30. True or false: You can configure both CGMP and IGMP snooping in mixed Cisco switch and non-Cisco router environments.

Use Figure 3-22 to answer questions 31–36.

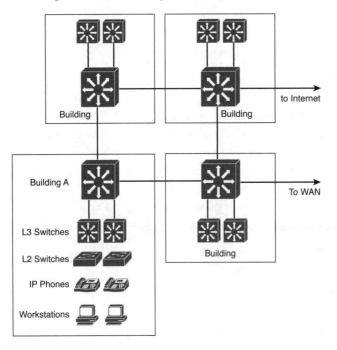

Figure 3-22   *Enterprise campus diagram*

31. The distance between buildings is around 950 meters. What medium do you recommend for the campus LAN backbone?

32. The workstations send frames with the DSCP set to EF. What should the IP phones do so that the network gives preference to VoIP traffic over data traffic?

33. If the Layer 2 switches in Building A cannot look at CoS and ToS fields, where should these fields be inspected for acceptance or reclassification: in the building Layer 3 switches or in the backbone Layer 3 switches?

34. Does the network have redundant access to the WAN?

35. Does the network have redundant access to the Internet?

36. Does Figure 3-22 use recommended devices for networks designed using the Enterprise Architecture model?

37. Which are environmental characteristics? (Select three.)

    a. Transmission media characteristics

    b. Application characteristics

    c. Distribution of network nodes

    d. Operating system used

    e. Remote-site connectivity requirements

38. Which network application type is most stringent on the network resources?

    a. Peer-to-peer

    b. Client to local server

    c. Client to server farm

    d. Client to enterprise edge

39. Why is LAN switching used more than shared LAN technology? (Select two.)

    a. Shared LANs do not consume all available bandwidth.

    b. Switched LANs offer increased throughput.

    c. Switched LANs allow two or more ports to communicate simultaneously.

    d. Switched LANs forward frames to all ports simultaneously.

40. An application used by some users in a department generates significant amounts of bandwidth. Which is a best design choice?

    a. Rewrite the application to reduce bandwidth.

    b. Use Gigabit Ethernet connections for those users.

    c. Put the application users into a separate broadcast domain.

    d. Add several switches and divide the users into these switches.

41. Users access servers located on a server VLAN and servers located in departmental VLANs. Users are located in the departmental VLAN. What is the expected traffic flow from users to servers?

    a. Most traffic is local.

    b. All traffic requires multilayer switching.

    c. There is no need for multilayer switching.

    d. Most of the traffic will have to be multilayer switched.

42. Company departments are located across several buildings. These departments use several common servers. Network policy and security are important. Where should servers be placed?

    a. Within all department buildings, and they should duplicate the common servers in each building.

    b. Connect the common servers to the campus core.

    c. Use a server farm.

    d. Connect the servers to the distribution layer.

43. A large company has a campus core. What is the best practice for the core campus network?

    a. Use triangles.

    b. Use squares.

    c. Use rectangles.

    d. Use point-to-point mesh.

44. A company has five floors. It has Layer 2 switches in each floor with servers. It plans to move servers to a new computer room and create a server farm. What should it use?

    a. Replace all Layer 2 switches with Layer 3 switches.

    b. Connect the Layer 2 switches to a Layer 3 switch in the computer room.

    c. Connect the Layer 2 switches to a new Layer 2 switch in the computer room.

    d. Connect the Layer 2 switches to each other.

45. A Fast Ethernet uplink is running at 80 percent utilization. Business-critical applications are used. What can be used to minimize packet delay and loss?

    a. Implement QoS with classification and policing in the distribution layer.

    b. Add additional VLANs so that the business applications are used on PCs on that VLAN.

    c. Perform packet bit rewrite in the distribution switches.

    d. Classify users in the access with different priority bits.

46. Which are four best practices used in the access layer?

    a. Disable trunking in host ports.

    b. Limit VLANS to one closet.

    c. Use PVST+ as the STP with multilayer switches.

    d. Enable trunking on host ports.

    e. Use VLAN spanning to speed convergence of STP.

    f. Use VTP Server mode in hierarchical networks.

    g. Use VTP Transparent mode in hierarchical networks.

    h. Use RPVST+ as the STP with multilayer switches.

47. Which are three best practices used in the distribution layer?

    a. Use HSRP or GLBP.

    b. Provide fast transport.

    c. Use Layer 3 routing protocols to the core.

    d. Use Layer 2 routing protocols to the core.

    e. Summarize routes to the core layer.

    f. Summarize routes to the access layer.

48. Which are four best practices used in the distribution layer?

    a. Disable trunking in host ports.

    b. Limit VLANs to one closet.

    c. Use HSRP.

    d. Use GLBP.

    e. Use VLAN spanning to speed convergence of STP.

    f. Use Layer 3 routing to the core.

    g. Summarize routes.

    h. Use RPVST+ as the STP with multilayer switches.

49. Which are three best practices used in the core layer?

    a. Use routing with no Layer 2 loops.

    b. Limit VLANs to one closet.

    c. Use HSRP.

    d. Use GLBP.

    e. Use Layer 3 switches with fast forwarding.

    f. Use Layer 3 routing to the core.

    g. Use two equal-cost paths to every destination network.

    h. Use RPVST+ as the STP with multilayer switches.

50. Which requirements drive the use of VLANs in a network?

    a. Use of non-Cisco equipment

    b. Separation of broadcast domains and prevention of traffic between departments

    c. Use of CCTV multicast traffic

    d. The company budget

51. What is a major requirement if you use a Layer 3 access layer design?

    a. The distribution switches are configured as a VSS pair.

    b. The core switches need to support EIGRP.

    c. The access layer switch needs to be able to route.

    d. HSRP is configured on the distribution switches.

52. What is an advantage of using the updated Layer 2 access layer design over the traditional model?

    a. There is an increase of uplink bandwidth.

    b. The updated model adds routing between distribution and access.

    c. The access layer switch needs to be able to route.

    d. Layer 3 load balancing is enabled.

53. Which Cisco IOS feature simplifies spanning tree topology?

    a. Rapid PVST+

    b. MST

    c. MISTP 802.1W

    d. VSS

54. Which Cisco STP Toolkit mechanisms are recommend on user access ports?

    a. PortFast

    b. RootGuard

    c. UplinkFast

    d. Loop Guard

    e. BPDU Guard

55. You want to enable physical device virtualization. Which feature provides that?

    a. VLAN

    b. VFR

    c. VSS

    d. VPN

56. A network has two distribution switches, A and B, connected via a Layer 2 trunk. Distribution A switch is the HSRP active gateway and STP root. Layer 2 links are used to connect access layer switches to both distribution switches. Which version of spanning tree is recommended?

    a. PVST+

    b. Rapid PVST+

    c. MST

    d. VSS

57. A network has two distribution switches, A and B, connected via a Layer 2 trunk. Distribution A switch is the STP root and distribution B is the active HSRP gateway. Layer 2 links are used to connect access layer switches to both distribution switches. Which statement is true?

    a. Traffic will transit from the access switches through distribution switch A through the Layer 2 trunk to distribution switch B.

    b. An STP loop will be created.

    c. The access switches will not be able to communicate.

    d. Loop Guard will prevent the loop from being created.

This chapter covers the following subjects:

Enterprise DC Architecture

Challenges in the DC

Enterprise DC Infrastructure

Virtualization Overview

Virtualization Technologies

Data Center Interconnects

Load Balancing in the DC

This chapter covers enterprise data center design fundamentals and challenges facing today's data center environments. General data center architecture, DC components, including security and storage integration, and design considerations are examined.

This chapter also provides an overview of virtualization, discusses the various virtualization technologies and network virtualization design considerations. The chapter finishes up with techniques for connecting DCs and load balancing in the DC.

The CCDA candidate can expect plenty of questions related to data center fundamentals, challenges, architecture, and virtualization.

CHAPTER 4

Data Center Design

"Do I Know This Already?" Quiz

The "Do I Know This Already?" quiz helps you identify your strengths and deficiencies in this chapter's topics.

The ten-question quiz, derived from the major sections in the "Foundation Topics" portion of the chapter, helps you determine how to spend your limited study time.

Table 4-1 outlines the major topics discussed in this chapter and the "Do I Know This Already?" quiz questions that correspond to those topics.

Table 4-1 "Do I Know This Already?" Foundation Topics Section-to-Question Mapping

Foundation Topics Section	Questions Covered in This Section
Enterprise DC Architecture	1, 2
Challenges in the DC	3, 4
Enterprise DC Infrastructure	5, 6
Virtualization Overview	7
Virtualization Technologies	8
Data Center Interconnects	9
Load Balancing in the DC	10

1. What are two methods for implementing unified fabric in the data center over 10 Gigabit Ethernet?

    a. VSS

    b. FCoE

    c. iSCSI

    d. vPC

2. What best describes the characteristics of the Cisco data center architecture foundation?

    a. Bare-metal servers

    b. Network, compute, storage

    c. Security, IPS, load balancing

    d. Email and file sharing

3. Which of the following data center facility aspects best corresponds with architectural and mechanical specifications?

  a. Space, load, and power capacity

  b. PCI, SOX, and HIPPA

  c. Operating temperature and humidity

  d. Site access, fire suppression, and security alarms

4. Which of the following uses the highest percentage of power within the overall data center power budget?

  a. Lighting

  b. Servers and storage

  c. Network devices

  d. Data center cooling

5. Which data center architecture layer provides Layer 2/Layer 3 physical port density for servers in the data center?

  a. Data center core

  b. Data center aggregation

  c. Data center access

  d. Data center distribution

6. Layer 4 security and application services, including server load balancing, Secure Sockets Layer (SSL) offloading, firewalling, and intrusion prevention system (IPS) services are provided by the data center _____ layer.

  a. Access

  b. Routed

  c. Core

  d. Aggregation

7. Virtualization technologies allow a _____ device to share its resources by creating multiple logical copies of itself.

  a. Software

  b. Virtual

  c. Logical

  d. Physical

8. Which of the following are examples of logical isolation techniques in which network segments share the same physical infrastructure? (Select all that apply.)

  a. VRF

  b. VLAN

  c. VSAN

  d. VSS

9. Which of the following DCI options does not require a service provider to implement?

   a. VPLS

   b. MPLS

   c. Dark Fiber

   d. VPWS

10. Which network load balancing option maintains TCP state information locally in its state tables?

    a. DNS based

    b. Anycast based

    c. Dedicated L4-7 load balancer

    d. ECMP

Foundation Topics

This chapter covers general enterprise data center considerations that you need to master for the CCDA exam. It starts with a discussion of the Cisco data center architecture to review the DC foundation, DC services, and user services layers. The next section, "Data Center Foundation Components," covers the virtualization technologies and services that unify network, storage, compute, and virtualization platforms. The section "Data Center Topology Components" shows how the virtualization technologies integrate with unified computing and the unified fabric.

The "Challenges in the DC" section describes the common server deployment challenges present in the data center. Major facility aspect issues involving rack space, power, cooling, and management are covered. Data center cabling is examined along with the data center cable considerations critical to the proper cable plant management.

Following that, the "Enterprise DC Infrastructure" section explores the Cisco multilayer architecture that is used for building out enterprise data centers to support blade servers and 1RU (rack unit) servers. Design aspects of the multilayer architecture involving data center access layer, aggregation layer, and core layer design considerations are also covered.

Next, an overview of virtualization is covered along with key drivers that are pushing the adoption of virtualization in the data center. The section "Virtualization Overview" compares the two main types of virtualization and provides several examples. Then the section "Network Virtualization Design Considerations" covers access control, path isolation, and services edge.

The chapter wraps up with Data Center Interconnects use cases, DCI options, and L2 considerations for connecting DCs. Lastly, we explore load balancing with application- and network-based options for the DC.

Enterprise DC Architecture

Enterprise DC architecture has three primary layers, called data center foundation, data center services, and user services. At the lower layer, we have the data center foundation supporting the data services, which ultimately support the user services or applications at the top of the stack.

The data center foundation layer provides the infrastructure for upper-layer services and applications that users rely on. The data center foundation must also be highly available, secure, scalable, and flexible to support the applications that run the business. The compute power in this layer processes the information between the servers, storage, and the users who access the applications in the data center. The data center foundation transparently provides end users application access through the intelligent use of the network, compute, and storage resources.

The data center services layer resides above the data center foundation and provides the necessary security firewall and IPS services that protect the applications and critical data in the data center. Data center services also include L4-7 load balancing to increase performance and provide better user experiences through improved user-response times.

The top of the architecture for the data center is the user services. These user services or applications are the driving force for enabling the employees to achieve the goals of the business. Examples of user services in the data center include email, file sharing, and order-processing applications.

Figure 4-1 illustrates the three primary layers of the enterprise Cisco data center architecture.

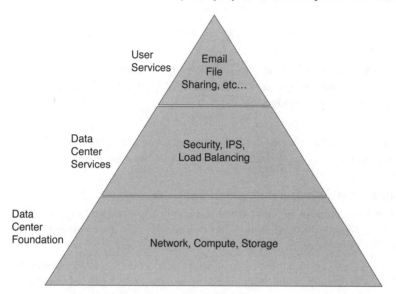

Figure 4-1   *Cisco data center architecture*

Data Center Foundation Components

Figure 4-2 highlights the Cisco data center foundation components.

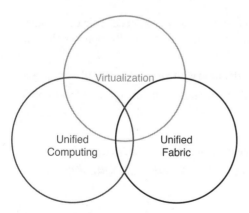

Figure 4-2   *Cisco data center foundation components*

The data center architectural components include virtualization technologies and services that unify network, storage, compute, and virtualization platforms. These technologies and network services enable incredible flexibility, visibility, and policy enforcement, which are critical for virtualized data centers. Here are the three main architecture components of the Cisco data center foundation:

- **Virtualization**

    - Virtual local area networks (VLANs), virtual storage area networks (VSANs), and virtual device contexts (VDCs) help to segment the LAN, SAN, and network devices instances.

    - Cisco Nexus 1000V virtual switches for VMware ESXi help to deliver visibility and policy control for virtual machines (VMs).

    - Flexible networking options with support for all server form factors and vendors, including support for blade servers from Cisco, Dell, IBM, and HP with integrated Ethernet and Fibre Channel switches.

- **Unified fabric**

    - Fibre Channel over Ethernet (FCoE) and Internet Small Computer Systems Interface (iSCSI) are two methods for implementing unified fabric in the data center over 10 Gigabit Ethernet networks.

    - FCoE is supported on VMware ESXi vSphere 5.0 and later.

    - The Cisco Catalyst, Cisco Nexus, and Cisco MDS family of switches all support iSCSI. The Cisco Nexus 5000 switches support unified fabric lossless operation, which improves the performance of iSCSI traffic using 10 Gigabit Ethernet.

    - The Cisco Nexus family of switches was designed to support unified fabric. Currently, the Cisco Nexus 7x00, 6000, 5x00, 4000, and 2000 and the MDS family of switches support data center bridging (DCB) and FCoE.

    - Converged network adapters (CNAs) run at 10GE and support FCoE. CNAs are available from both Emulex and QLogic. Additionally, a software stack is available for certain 10GE network interfaces from Intel.

- **Unified computing**

    - Cisco Unified Computing System (UCS) is an innovative next-generation data center platform that converges computing, network, storage, and virtualization together into one system.

    - It integrates lossless 10GE unified network fabric with x86 architecture-based servers.

    - It allows for Cisco Virtual Interface Card to virtualize your network interfaces on your server.

    - It offers Cisco VN-Link virtualization.

    - It increases productivity with just-in-time provisioning using service profiles.

    - There's a single point of management with the UCS Manager and XML API.

Data Center Topology Components

Figure 4-3 shows the Cisco data center topology.

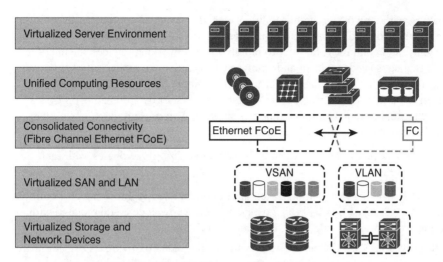

Figure 4-3 *Cisco data center topology*

At the top layer, we have virtual machines, which are software entities that have hardware-level abstraction capable of running a guest OS on top of a resource scheduler also known as a hypervisor.

Within the unified computing resources, the service profile defines the identity of the server. The identity contains many items such as memory, CPU, network cards, storage information, and boot image.

The 10 Gigabit Ethernet, FCoE, and Fibre Channel technologies provide the unified fabric and are supported on the Cisco Nexus 5000. FCoE is one of the key technologies that allow native Fibre Channel frames to be used on 10G Ethernet networks.

Virtualization technologies such as VLANs and VSANs provide for virtualized LAN and SAN connectivity by logically segmenting multiple LANs and SANs on the same physical equipment. Each VLAN and VSAN operates independently from one another.

At the lowest layer, we have virtualized hardware where storage devices can be virtualized into storage pools and network devices are virtualized using virtual device contexts (VDCs).

Data Center Network Programmability

Network programmability in the data center is constantly evolving, but it is definitely a skill that is highly desired for network engineers who want to stay relevant in the industry. Because a reliable and stable network infrastructure is essential for business continuity, network engineers have a lot of pressures put upon them to keep the network up and running at all times. When deploying new applications in the data center, network engineers usually consider the end-to-end path between the users and the applications. The end-to-end path might go through multiple network devices, which leads to a box-by-box configuration that is required to bring up the new applications. This box-by-box approach does not scale well and is more prone to human configuration errors.

As we progress with network programmability, we need to examine approaches that allow changes to the network via automation techniques that enable alignment with business velocity, agility, and continuity. In order to rapidly scale networking services, the mindset of network engineers needs to adapt and embrace automation, in a similar way that virtualization has improved the deployment timeframes of compute infrastructures. Automating doesn't need to be done all at once; network engineers can start by automating processes that are easy to do, but require a lot of time to complete. As more and more networking processes are automated, the fear of changes is reduced.

The path to network programmability can be broken down into three phases, with each building on the other:

Phase I: Configure: Implementation details are translated directly into syntax for configuration changes made box by box. Existing network knowledge is still required with underlying protocols such as IP, TCP, BGP, and OSPF.

Phase II: Provision: View the network as a whole rather than box by box. First, automate easy-to-do network processes before moving on to more advanced automation.

Phase III: Program: The network is programmed based on application requirements for network resources. This phase enables the network to rapidly provision new services and applications with speed, flexibility, and HA principles in mind.

SDN

Software-defined networking (SDN) architecture references points in the network that have open interfaces that enable software development. Centralized SDN software can control the flow of network traffic through a collection of network devices. Additionally, other services that include compute, storage, or network security functions can exist as well such as software inspection and modification applications. SDN is also commonly referred to as the separation of control planes and data planes. SDN is not OpenFlow or Network Functional Virtualization (NFV).

SDN architecture consists of three layers:

- **Application layer:** Business applications with direct API access to the control layer
- **Control layer:** Control plane services with direct APIs for connections to application and infrastructure layers
- **Infrastructure layer:** Data plane network devices that connect to endpoints and to the control layer for programming instructions

Controllers

SDN controllers provide centralized control of network devices in the data plane, including decisions regarding packet forwarding, routing, applying QoS, and/or security policy. SDN controllers communicate to the network devices using southbound interfaces, and some can integrate into orchestration systems via northbound interfaces. Many SDN controllers exist, including some from commercial vendors such as Cisco and VMware and others that are open source based.

Here is a list of some SDN controllers that are currently available:

- **Cisco APIC:** Policy-based controller and part of Cisco ACI. Policy-based controllers define a set of policies using a declarative model that tells the network device the intent of the policy but not how to implement it. Devices are trusted to implement the policy based on the intent provided, which implies a distributed control plane.

- **VMware NSX Controller:** Overlay controller that exposes network abstractions.

- **OpenDaylight:** Open-source controller from the Linux Foundation.

- **Pure OpenFlow:** Controller that can control switching and routing decisions for OpenFlow-enabled network devices.

APIs

Application programming interfaces (APIs) are used for communication between SDN controllers and network devices. Northbound APIs communicate with SDN applications, and southbound APIs communicate with network elements. For example, OpenFlow is an industry-standard API that works with white label–based switches, and NETCONF is a protocol used for the configuration of devices with XML-formatted messages that also uses APIs.

ACI

Application Centric Infrastructure (ACI) is the flagship Cisco data center architecture that takes a different approach to solving data center challenges. ACI enables the network to be programmed using an application-centric approach based on the requirements of the application and can support both bare-metal and virtualized compute infrastructures. In addition, ACI also provides feedback on the underlying physical network, which can be used for tuning or troubleshooting of the application. ACI is a stateless network infrastructure based on a white list model using a spine-leaf physical network fabric and is controlled via the APIC controller cluster.

The Cisco ACI solution consists of the following components:

- **APIC:** The Application Centric Infrastructure Controller is used for centralized management of the ACI fabric. APIC clusters are sets of three or more controllers for high availability.

- **Nexus 9000 series switches:** Physical network hardware based on a spine-leaf architecture to run Cisco ACI. There are chassis-based Nexus 9500 and fixed-based Nexus 9300 network devices to choose from, with specific models for spine and/or leaf functionality.

Cisco ACI defines the application requirements using what is called an application profile. The application profile is a logical mapping of how the application will be used on the network. For example, if you have a three-tier application consisting of Web, Application, and DB, the application will have policies defined for security, quality of service, and/or load balancing as the traffic moves between the tiers of the application.

Challenges in the DC

In the data center, server deployments are of great concern, along with facilities and network equipment. Here are some of the challenges that must be dealt with when deploying servers:

- Power required
- Physical rack space usage
- Limits to scale
- Management (resources, firmware)
- Server security
- Virtualization support
- Management effort required

Server growth is consistently rising, thus requiring more power, which is driving the need for energy efficiency for most data center server deployments. Although rack servers are low cost and provide high performance, unfortunately they take up space and consume a lot of energy to operate. Because both rack space and power increase costs, efficiency gains need to be considered in these areas.

Blade servers provide similar computing power when compared to rack mount servers, but they require less space, power, and cabling. The chassis in most blade servers allows for shared power, Ethernet LAN, and Fibre Channel SAN connections, which reduces the number of cables needed.

With both rack-mounted servers and blade servers, server virtualization software provides for better utilization of hardware resources, which requires less physical hardware to deploy servers, which in turn increases efficiency. Server virtualization also enables server scalability because more rack and cabinet space is available to deploy new virtualized hosts running additional virtual machines.

Server management is a key element for deploying servers, and there are solutions available from OEMs such as Integrated Lights Out (ILO), UCS Manager, and VMware vSphere Web-based Client. These products ease the management of larger server deployments and provide for secure remote management capabilities.

Data Center Facility Aspects

Multiple facility considerations go into the design and planning for a new data center build out.

During the planning sessions, data center architectural and mechanical specifications help define the following:

- How much space will be available
- How much load the floor can support
- The power and cooling capacity that will be available
- The cabling plant that will be needed and how to manage it

The facility also needs to meet certain environmental conditions, and the data center equipment selections process dictates the operating temperatures and humidity levels that need to be maintained in the data center.

Another important consideration is physical security. Because the data center usually stores data that needs to be secured from third parties, access to the site needs to be well controlled. In addition, fire suppression and alarm systems should be in place to protect equipment and data from natural disasters and theft.

Because the data center facilities are limited in capacity, they need to be designed properly to allow for the best use of employee space for today and into the future.

Most companies must now adhere to regulatory compliance, including environmental requirements, and provide disaster recovery in some form to enable business continuity. Data centers need to provide an infrastructure that can recover network communications, data, and applications and provide high availability.

To build a reliable data center that maximizes the investment, the design needs to be considered early in the building development process. It is important to include team members in several areas of expertise, including telecommunications, power, architectural, and heating, ventilating, and air conditioning (HVAC). Each team member needs to work together to ensure that the designed systems interoperate most effectively. The design of the data center needs to incorporate current requirements and support future growth.

Key Topic

Careful planning and close attention to design guidelines are crucial for the data center build out to be successful. Missing critical aspects of the design can cause the data center to be vulnerable to early obsolescence, which can impact data center availability and lead to a loss of revenue or increased cost to remediate.

Table 4-2 describes a number of data center facility considerations.

Table 4-2 Summary of Data Center Facility Considerations

Data Center Facility Considerations	Description
Architectural and mechanical specifications	Space available
	Load capacity
	Power and cooling capacity
	Cabling infrastructure
Environmental conditions	Operating temperature
	Humidity level
Physical security	Access to the site
	Fire suppression
	Security alarms
Capacity limits	Space for employees

Data Center Facility Considerations	Description
Compliance and regulation	Payment Card Industry (PCI), Sarbanes-Oxley (SOX), and Health Insurance Portability and Accountability Act (HIPAA)

Data Center Space

The space that the data center occupies makes up the physical footprint and helps answer many questions, including how to size the overall data center, where to position servers, how to make the DC flexible for future growth, and how to protect the valuable equipment inside.

The data center space element defines the number of racks for servers and telecommunications equipment that can be installed. The floor loading is affected by the rack weight after the racks are populated with equipment. Careful planning is needed to ensure that the floor loading is sufficient for current and future needs of the data center.

Selecting the proper size of the data center has a great influence on the cost, longevity, and flexibility of the data center. Although estimating the size of the data center is challenging, it is also critically importance that it be done correctly.

Several factors need to be considered, including the following:

- The number of employees who will be supporting the data center
- The number of servers and the amount of storage gear and networking equipment that will be needed
- The space needed for non-infrastructure areas:
    - Shipping and receiving
    - Server and network staging
    - Storage rooms, break rooms, and bath rooms
    - Employee office space

Keep in mind that if the data center is undersized, it will not sufficiently satisfy compute, storage, and network requirements and will negatively impact productivity and cause additional costs for expansion. On the flip side, a data center that is too spacious is a waste of capital and recurring operational expenses.

Right-size data center facilities consider the placement of infrastructure and equipment; if properly planned, the data center can grow and support the organization into the future without costly upgrades or relocations.

Here are some other rack and cabinet space considerations to keep in mind:

- Weight of the rack and equipment
- Heat expelled from the equipment

- The amount and type of power needed
    - Automatic transfer switch for equipment that has single power supplies
    - Uninterruptible power supplies (UPSs)
    - Redundant power distribution units (PDUs)
- Loading, which determines what and how many devices can be installed

Data Center Power

The power in the data center facility is used to power cooling devices, servers, storage equipment, the network, and some lighting equipment. Cooling down the data center requires the most power, next to servers and storage.

Because many variables make up actual power usage, determining power requirements for equipment in the data center can prove difficult. In server environments, the power usage depends on the computing load placed on the server. For example, if the server needs to work harder by processing more data, it has to draw more AC power from the power supply, which in turn creates more heat that needs to be cooled down.

The desired reliability drives the power requirements, which may include multiple power feeds from the power utility, UPS, redundant power circuits, and diesel generators. Depending on the options chosen, various levels of power redundancy can affect both capital and recurring operating expenses. Determining the right amount of power redundancy to meet the requirements takes careful planning to ensure success.

Estimating the power capacity needed involves collecting the requirements for all the current equipment, including the future requirements of the equipment for the data center. The complete power requirements must encompass the UPS, generators, HVAC, lighting, and all the network, server, and storage equipment.

Figure 4-4 shows an example of data center power usage.

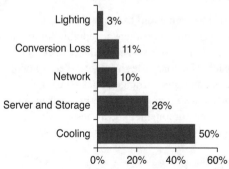

Figure 4-4 *Data center power usage example*

The designed power system should include electrical components such as PDUs, circuit breaker panels, electrical conduits, and wiring necessary to support the desired amount of physical redundancy. The power system also needs to provide protection for utility power failures, power surges, and other electrical problems by addressing the power redundancy requirements in the design.

Here are some key points related to data center power:

■ Defines the overall power capacity.

■ Provides physical electrical infrastructure and addresses redundancy.

■ Power is consumed by the following:

    ■ Cooling

    ■ Servers

    ■ Storage

    ■ Network

    ■ Conversion and lighting

Data Center Cooling

Devices in the data center produce variable amounts of heat, depending on the device load. Heat over time decreases the reliability of the data center devices. Cooling is used to control the temperature and humidity of the devices, and it is applied to zones, racks, or individual devices.

Environmental conditions need to be considered and measured by using probes to gauge temperature changes, hot spots, and relative humidity.

A major issue with high-density computing is overheating. There are more hot spots, and therefore more heat overall is produced. The increase in heat and humidity threatens equipment life spans. Computing power and memory requirements demand more power and thus generate more heat output. Space-saving servers increase the server density possible in a rack, but keep in mind that density equals heat. It might not be a big deal for one chassis at 3 kilowatts (kW), but with five or six servers per rack, the heat output increases to 20 kW. In addition, humidity levels can affect static electricity in the data center. Therefore, it is recommended that the relative humidity level be in the range of 40 percent to 55 percent. High levels of static electricity can cause damage to data center equipment.

Proper airflow is required to reduce the amount of heat generated by the high-density equipment. Sufficient cooling equipment must be available to produce acceptable temperatures within the data center. The cabinets and racks should be arranged in the data center with an alternating pattern of "cold" and "hot" aisles. The cold aisle should have equipment arranged face to face, and the hot aisle should have equipment arranged back to back. In the cold aisle, there should be perforated floor tiles drawing cold air from the floor into the face of the equipment. This cold air passes through the equipment and flushes out the back into the hot aisle. The hot aisle does not have any perforated tiles, and this design prevents the hot air from mixing with the cold air.

Figure 4-5 illustrates the alternating pattern of cold and hot aisles along with airflow.

For equipment that does not exhaust heat to the rear, here are some other cooling techniques:

■ Block unnecessary air escapes to increase airflow.

■ Increase the height of the raised floor.

- Spread out equipment into unused racks.
- Use open racks rather than cabinets where security is not a concern.
- Use cabinets with mesh fronts and backs.
- Use custom perforated tiles with larger openings.

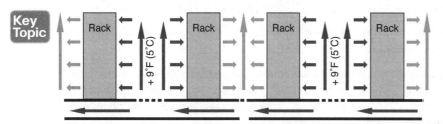

Figure 4-5 *Data center cold and hot aisles*

> **Note**   1 watt = 3.41214 British thermal units (BTU). Many manufacturers publish kW, kilo-volt ampere (kWA), and BTU in their equipment specifications. Sometimes dividing the BTU value by 3.413 does not equal the published wattage. Use the manufacturer information, if available; otherwise, this can be a helpful conversion formula to use.

Data Center Heat

Blade server deployments allow for more efficient use of space for servers, which is good, but there is also an increased amount of heat per server, which requires more cooling to maintain consistent temperatures.

The data center design must address the increased use of high-density servers and the heat that they produce. During the data center design, considerations for cooling need to be taken into account for the proper sizing of the servers and the anticipated growth of the servers, along with their corresponding heat output.

Here are some cooling solutions to address the increasing heat production:

- Increase the number of HVAC units.
- Increase the airflow through the devices.
- Increase the space between the racks and rows.
- Use alternative cooling technologies, such as water-cooled racks.

Data Center Cabling

The cabling in the data center is known as the passive infrastructure. Data center teams rely on a structured and well-organized cabling plant. Although the active electronics are crucial for keeping server, storage, and network devices up and running, the physical cabling infra-structure is what ties everything together. The cabling in the data center terminates connec-tions between devices and governs how each device communicates with one another.

Cabling has several key characteristics, such as the physical connector, media type, and cable length. Copper and fiber-optic cables are commonly used today. Fiber-optic cabling allows for longer distances and is less prone to interference than copper cabling. The two main types of optical fiber are single-mode and multimode. Copper cabling is widely available, costs less, and generally covers shorter distances (up to 100 meters, about 328 feet). Typical copper cabling found in the data center is CAT 6A with RJ-45 connectors.

Keep in mind that the 10GBASE-T standard requires CAT 6A twisted-pair cabling to support distances up to 100 meters.

It is important for cabling to be easy to maintain, abundant, and capable of supporting various media types and requirements for proper data center operations. Top-of-rack switches will help to keep most of the copper in the rack with short cable jumpers, with fiber used between top-of-rack switches and end-of-row switches.

Cable management and simplicity are affected by the following:

- Media selection
- Number of connections
- Type of cable termination organizers
- Space for cables on horizontal and vertical cable trays

These considerations must to be addressed during the data center facility design (for the server, storage, network, and all the associated technologies that are going to be implemented).

Figure 4-6 shows an example of cabling that is out of control.

Figure 4-6   *Data center cabling the wrong way*

Figure 4-7 shows the proper way to manage copper cabling.

The cabling infrastructure needs to avoid the following pitfalls:

- Inadequate cooling due to restricted airflow
- Outages due to accidental disconnect
- Unplanned dependencies resulting in more downtime
- Difficult troubleshooting options

Figure 4-7   *Proper data center cabling*

For example, using under-floor cabling techniques, especially with a high number of power and data cables, can restrict proper airflow. Another disadvantage with this approach is that cable changes require you to lift floor tiles, which changes the airflow and creates cooling inefficiencies.

One solution is a cable management system above the rack for server connectivity. Cables should be located in the front or rear of the rack to simplify cable connections. In most service provider environments, cabling is located in the front of the rack.

Enterprise DC Infrastructure

Today's enterprise data center infrastructure follows the Cisco multilayer architecture, which includes a DC core connecting to the local area network (LAN) core at the center. The LAN core provides access to the WAN, LAN, and the Internet/demilitarized zone (DMZ) via additional network connections. The DC core and the LAN core have high-speed L3 resilient interconnections between them. The LAN core and DC core networks maintain separate logical domains with respect to change-control processes and procedures. This model also allows for the DC core infrastructure to be moved offsite without a major redesign.

Figure 4-8 provides a high-level overview of an enterprise data center infrastructure.

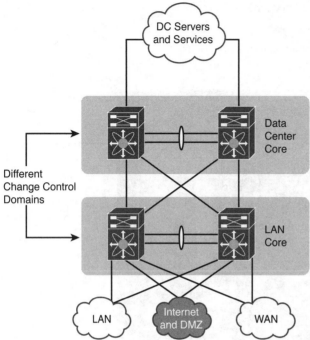

Figure 4-8   *Enterprise data center infrastructure overview*

Data Center Storage

For many companies, the nonstop demand for storage in the data center is a reality. Servers can use locally attached storage or they can access storage over the storage area network (SAN). Direct attached storage (DAS) is composed of local disks that are physically installed in the server. DAS is not very flexible because only the local host can use the storage in most cases. SANs, on the other hand, allow multiple servers to share a common pool of storage using either Fibre Channel (FC) or some form of IP storage such as iSCSI. Pools of storage can be easily expanded with more capacity using storage arrays. Fibre Channel SANs are dedicated storage networks that link servers using HBAs with storage arrays using SAN switches.

Figure 4-9 illustrates the legacy LAN and SAN separation approach to storage in the data center.

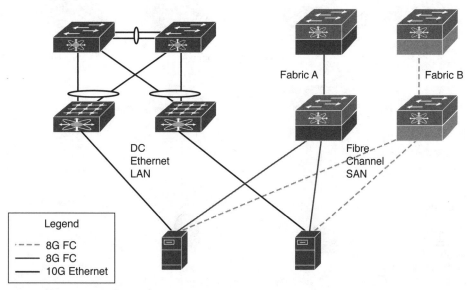

Figure 4-9   *Traditional LAN and SAN separation*

The legacy approach to storage in the data center is to use a separate infrastructure for LAN and FC SAN services. The use of two networks for LAN and FC SAN services not only takes up more space but is also more costly to operate and maintain. There is increased complexity with more equipment to manage and additional points of failure possible within the network.

The solution is to consolidate both LAN and FC SAN services within a single unified network. The consolidation allows for reduced management points within the network and better utilization of the space, cabling, and power resources. Nexus switches, for example, can provide a unified fabric that supports both Ethernet LAN and Fibre Channel SAN traffic on the same physical network.

Nexus 5500 switches support unified ports that can be configured and operated to run either 1G/10G Ethernet or 2G/4G/8G Fibre Channel. The Ethernet ports can also support Fibre Channel over Ethernet (FCoE). FCoE is a storage protocol that allows Fibre Channel frames to be encapsulated for transport over an Ethernet network. The 10G Ethernet network views the FC payloads as just another upper-layer protocol similar to IP protocol traffic.

Figure 4-10 shows the unified approach to Ethernet LAN and FC SAN in the data center.

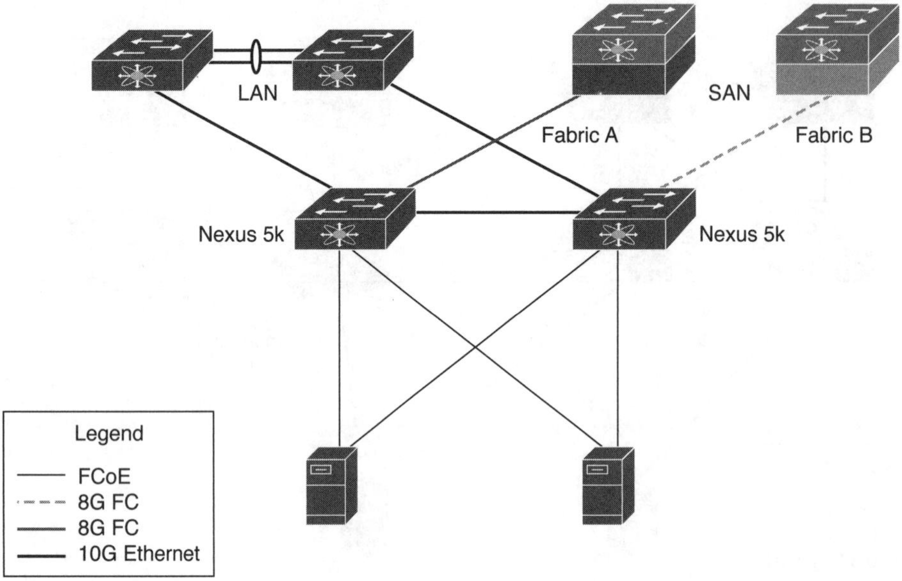

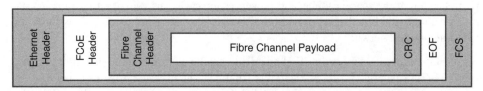

Figure 4-10   *Unified fabric for both the LAN and SAN*

The goal of the Fibre Channel over Ethernet (FcoE) protocol is to consolidate both the LAN and SAN on a single wire to reduce switch and cable complexity. From a server perspective, the local area network (LAN) and storage area network (SAN) I/O traffic leaving a server uses a 10G Ethernet adapter called a converged network adapter (CNA) instead of a separate Ethernet and host bus adapter (HBA). This further reduces the network interface requirements on the servers themselves.

Figure 4-11 illustrates the FC headers and payload in an Ethernet packet.

Ethernet Header	FCoE Header	Fibre Channel Header	Fibre Channel Payload	CRC	EOF	FCS

Figure 4-11   *Encapsulation of FC frame in an Ethernet packet*

Data Center Reference Architecture

The DC reference architecture is a three-tier hierarchy consisting of the DC core, DC aggregation, and DC access layers. This three-tier layered model is the most common model used in the enterprise, and it supports both blade servers and rack mount servers.

At the bottom edge of the data center infrastructure is the access layer. The data center access layer needs to provide physical port density and both Layer 2 and Layer 3 services for flexible server connectivity options.

The data center aggregation layer ties the DC core and DC access layers together, which provides a hierarchy for security and server farm services. Security services such as access control lists (ACLs), firewalls, and intrusion prevention systems (IPSs) should be implemented in the data center aggregation layer. In addition, server farm services such as content switching, caching, and Secure Sockets Layer (SSL) offloading should be deployed in the data center aggregation. Both the data center aggregation and core layers are commonly implemented in pairs for redundancy and to avoid single points of failure.

Defining the DC Access Layer

The data center access layer's main purpose is to provide Layer 2 and Layer 3 physical port density for various servers in the data center. In addition, data center access layer switches provide high-performance, low-latency switching and can support a mix of oversubscription requirements. Both Layer 2 and Layer 3 access (also called routed access) designs are available, but most data center access layers are built using Layer 2 connectivity. The Layer 2 access design uses VLAN trunks upstream, which allows data center aggregation services to be shared across the same VLAN and across multiple switches. Other advantages of Layer 2 access include support for NIC teaming and server clustering that requires network connections to be Layer 2 adjacent or on the same VLAN with one another.

Figure 4-12 highlights the data center access layer in the overall enterprise architecture.

The Spanning Tree Protocol (STP) manages physical loops by detecting and blocking loops that are present in the Layer 2 design. With DC designs, STP blocks loops in the network, thereby reducing the number of links by 50 percent that can be used to forward traffic. Currently, the recommended STP mode is Rapid per-VLAN Spanning Tree Plus (RPVST+), which ensures a logical loop-free topology and fast convergence.

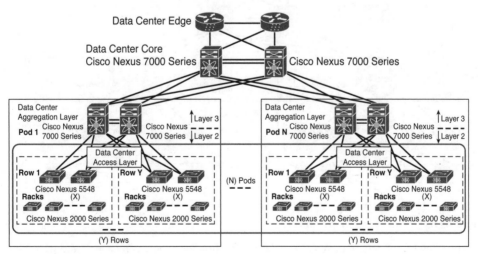

Figure 4-12 *Data center access layer*

New routed access designs aim to contain Layer 2 locally to avoid the use of the STP. With routed access designs, the default gateway function needs to be provided because the access switch becomes the first-hop router in the network.

Designs with both Layer 2 and Layer 3 access provide flexibility for multiple server solutions to be supported, including 1RU servers and modular blade server chassis.

Here are some of the data center access layer benefits:

■ Provides port density for server farms

■ Supports single-homed and dual-homed servers

■ Provides high-performance, low-latency Layer 2 switching

■ Supports a mix of oversubscription requirements

Defining the DC Aggregation Layer

The data center aggregation (distribution) layer aggregates Layer 2/Layer 3 links from the access layer and connects using upstream links to the data center core. Layer 3 connectivity is typically implemented between the data center aggregation and the data center core layers. The aggregation layer is a critical point for security and application services. The Layer 4-7 security and application services in the data center aggregation layer include server load balancing, SSL offloading, firewalling, and IPS services. These services maintain connection and session state for redundancy purposes and are commonly deployed in pairs using service modules or appliances. This design reduces the total cost of ownership (TCO) and eases the management overhead by simplifying the number of devices that must be managed. To support the scaling of the access layer, multiple aggregation layer switches can be used.

The highlighted section in Figure 4-13 illustrates the data center aggregation layer.

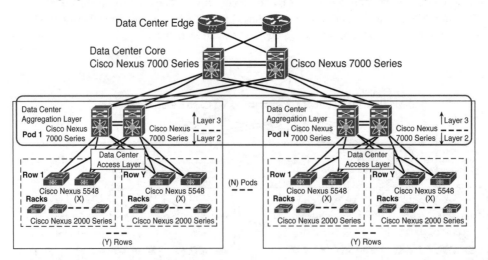

Figure 4-13 *Data center aggregation layer*

Depending on the requirements of the design, the boundary between Layer 2 and Layer 3 can be in the multilayer switches, firewalls, or content-switching devices in the aggregation layer. Multiple aggregation layers can be built out to support separate network environments, such as production, test, and PCI infrastructure, each with its own security zone and application services. First-hop redundancy protocols such as Hot Standby Router Protocol (HRSP) and Gateway Load Balancing Protocol (GLBP) are commonly used in the aggregation layer. Many aggregation designs include positioning STP primary and secondary root bridges to help control the loop-free topology and support a larger STP processing load.

Here are some of the data center aggregation layer benefits:

- Aggregates traffic from DC access and connects to DC core.
- Supports advanced application and security services.
- Layer 4-7 services include firewall, server load balancing, SSL offload, and IPS.
- Large STP processing load.
- Highly flexible and scalable.

Defining the DC Core Layer

The data center core connects the campus core to the data center aggregation layer using high-speed Layer 3 links. The core is a centralized Layer 3 routing layer in which one or more data center aggregation layers connect. The data center networks are summarized, and the core injects the default route into data center aggregation. The data center core also needs to support IP multicast to provide connectivity to the growing use of IP multicast applications.

The data center core layer is a best-practice component of larger data center networks. Smaller data centers may use a collapsed core design combining the aggregation layer and core layers together. However, if you are building a new or greenfield data center, it is recommended that you implement a data center core in the beginning to avoid network downtime later. Table 4-3 shows some drivers to help you decide whether a data center core is appropriate for your design.

Table 4-3 Data Center Core Drivers

Data Center Core Drivers	Description
10 and 40 Gigabit Ethernet density	Are there enough 10GE/40GE ports to connect the campus core to multiple data center aggregation layers?
Administrative domains and policies	Separate cores help to isolate campus distribution from DC aggregation for troubleshooting and quality of service/ access control list (QoS/ACL) policies.
Future growth	The impact and downtime from implementing a core at a later date makes it worthwhile to install sufficient core layers in the beginning.

The highlighted section in Figure 4-14 illustrates the data center core layer.

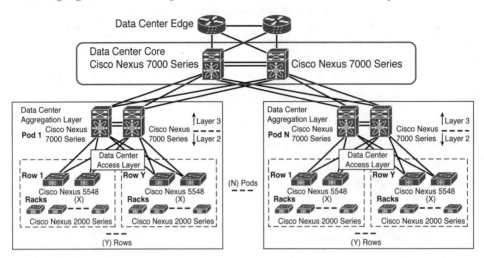

Figure 4-14 *Data center core layer*

Here are some of the data center core characteristics:

- Low-latency switching
- Distributed forwarding architecture
- 10 and 40 Gigabit Ethernet
- Scalable IP multicast support

Security in the DC

The data center hosts some of the most critical and valuable data assets for an organization. In order to protect and prevent unwanted network intrusions, firewalls and IPS sensors should be used between the critical data and the clients that need access to it. Data center firewalls should be deployed inline after the data center core to secure the critical-data VLANs. The IPS sensors can run on the hardware modules in the DC firewalls in either IDS (promiscuous) mode or IPS (blocking) mode. When the sensor is configured for IDS mode, there is only monitoring and alerting of abnormal traffic as it flows through the sensor. IPS mode, on the other hand, can actually detect and block malicious traffic before it reaches the critical-data VLANs.

Data center security designs should support the creation of multiple secure network segments to host applications and services with critical data that needs to be protected from outside threats. Security requirements and compliance reasons will drive the need for secure VLANs in the DC. For example, different levels of secure VLANs can be implemented to host applications and services that require separation, such as firewalled VLANs, firewalled-with-IPS VLANs, and open VLANs with ACLs. For example, secure VLANs can be used to segment a three-tier application such as Web, Application, or Database.

Fabric Extenders

A Fabric Extender (FEX) is a physical grouping of copper or fiber switch ports that uplinks to a parent switch such as the Nexus 5K or 7K. FEXs act as remote line cards to the upstream Nexus switch. There is no local management on the FEXs because they are completely managed by the parent Nexus switch. The same VLANs that are configured on the Nexus switch can be assigned to the ports on the FEX. The fabric uplinks on the FEXs can be port-channeled to a single or multiple upstream parent switches. However, the fabric extender non-fabric interfaces are designed to connect to host ports only, not to other downstream ethernet switches.

Virtualization Overview

As the demand for IT to do more with less while increasing efficiency has risen, virtualization has become a critical component in most enterprise networks. Virtualization technologies allow a physical device to share its resources by creating multiple logical copies of itself. Other forms of virtualization can enable multiple physical devices to logically appear as one.

Virtualization is a critical component of the Cisco network architectures for the enterprise data center and is changing the way data centers are architected. The use of virtualization improves network efficiency, provides enhanced flexibility, and reduces operational expenses.

Challenges

Network designers face many challenges that are driving the need to deploy virtualization technologies in the network. Data centers are growing rapidly, and these challenges directly impact the profitability of the business.

Take a look at some of the key driving forces for virtualization adoption in Table 4-4.

Table 4-4   Virtualization Key Drivers

Virtualization Driving Forces	Description
Operational cost	Need to reduce the rising cost of powering and cooling devices in the DC while getting more productivity.
Reducing the number of physical devices	DC consolidation of assets performing individual tasks.
Traffic isolation	Logical, separate user groups secured from other groups on the same network.
Increased performance/price ratio	Eliminate underutilized hardware that exhibits poor performance/price ratio.

Defining Virtualization and Benefits

Virtualization is an umbrella term used to represent several different technologies. Virtualization technologies share a common theme in their ability to abstract logical elements from hardware (applications or operating systems) or networks (LANs and SANs) and run them in a virtual state. Virtualization brings many benefits, from consolidation to increased efficiency.

Here are some of the common benefits achieved through virtualization techniques:

- Better use of computing resources, higher server densities, and simplified server migrations
- Flexibility for ease of management for adds, reassignments, or repurposing resources
- Separation of users group on the same physical network, enabling traffic isolation
- Ability to provide per-department security policies
- Reduction in power and space required
- Increased uptime and reduced operational costs

Virtualization Risks

Although virtualization has many benefits, it also introduces complexity and risks that need to be managed appropriately. For example, some solutions that are built to be redundant actually fail due to fate sharing. Fate sharing involves a dependency that is overlooked, such as two VPN tunnels over the same service provider network. If the service provider network fails, both VPN tunnels will be lost even though it was considered to be a redundant solution.

Another example is routing policy that redirects traffic over a longer path that has more latency instead of a much shorter direct path within the network. Maybe the routing policy is redirecting the traffic to a firewall instead of directly routing the traffic via the shortest path. The dynamic routing paths may also be altered due to a link failure that is causing traffic to take a suboptimal path to route around the failure.

In addition, virtualization network topologies and virtual machine sprawl are other aftereffects from virtualization. Many times, a new VM is created instead of finding an existing VM that can be reused. However, this uses up more of the available virtualization resources and creates more management complexity. These practices can also lead to creating new virtual network topologies, including creating unnecessary VLANs, which tends to make troubleshooting more difficult.

Types of Virtualization

Enterprise networks consist of two main types of virtualization technology groupings, called network virtualization and device virtualization:

- Network virtualization encompasses logical isolated network segments that share the same physical infrastructure. Each segment operates independently and is logically separate from the other segments. Each network segment appears with its own privacy, security, independent set of policies, QoS levels, and independent routing paths.

  Here are some examples of network virtualization technologies:

  - **VLAN:** Virtual local area network
  - **VSAN:** Virtual storage area network
  - **VRF:** Virtual routing and forwarding

- **VPN:** Virtual private network

- **vPC:** Virtual Port Channel

- Device virtualization allows for a single physical device to act like multiple copies of itself. Device virtualization enables many logical devices to run independently of each other on the same physical piece of hardware. The software creates virtual hardware that can function just like the physical network device. Another form of device virtualization entails using multiple physical devices to act as one logical unit.

Here are some examples of device virtualization technologies:

- Server virtualization: Virtual machines (VM)

- Virtual Switching System (VSS)

- Cisco Adaptive Security Appliance (ASA) firewall context

- Virtual device contexts (VDCs)

Virtualization Technologies

Virtualization is built from abstracting logical entities from pooled physical resources. The Cisco network architectures for the enterprise data center contain many forms of network and device virtualization technologies.

Figure 4-15 illustrates the many virtualization technologies in use today.

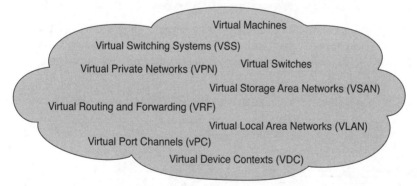

Figure 4-15 *Data center virtualization technologies*

VSS

Virtual Switching System (VSS) is a network virtualization technology used in the LAN that allows two physical Cisco Catalyst 4500, 6500, or 6800 series switches to act as a single logical virtual switch. VSS allows for the creation of Layer 2 port channels from the third downstream device to the pair of VSS switches, which eliminates STP blocking and allows for active/active forwarding. This technology is very similar to Multichassis EtherChannel (MEC) used with the Cisco Catalyst 3850 series product line, which enables switches stacked together to operate with a single control plane and use a single command-line interface (CLI) for management. However, VSS is limited to two physical chassis connected together. Furthermore, with VSS there is no longer a need for first-hop redundancy protocols (FHRPs) such as HSRP and GLBP because both switches share a single IP address for switched virtual interfaces (SVIs).

VRF

Virtual routing and forwarding (VRF) is a routing virtualization technology that creates multiple logical Layer 3 routing and forwarding instances (route tables) that can function on the same physical router. In Multiprotocol Label Switching (MPLS) VPN environments, the use of VRF technology plays a major role by allowing multiple networks to coexist on the same MPLS network. The routing information is contained inside the VRF and is visible only to routers participating in the same VRF. Because the routing information with VRF is separated, duplicate IP addressing schemes can be used.

vPC

Virtual Port Channel (vPC) technology works by combining two Cisco Nexus series switches with 10GE links, which are then represented to other switches as a single logical switch for port channeling purposes to the third downstream device. With vPC, the spanning-tree topology appears loop free, allowing for multiple active/active forwarding paths and creating redundancy while also increasing bandwidth in the physical topology. The downstream device can be a server, switch, firewall, or any other device that supports IEEE 802.3ad port channels. Cisco vPC is used heavily in data center design but also can be used in campus environments to aggregate port channels used with IDF switches.

VPC consists of two vPC peer switches connected by a peer link, which is a pair of 10GE links. The pair of vPC switches is referred to a vPC domain, and they use primary and secondary roles. The vPC peer switches are managed independently with separate control and forwarding planes.

Figure 4-16 depicts an example of a vPC design with Nexus 7700 and Nexus 5600.

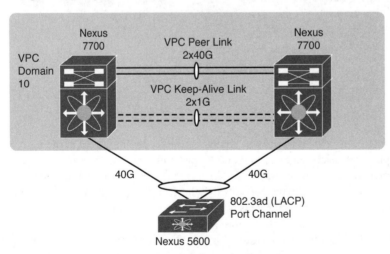

Figure 4-16 *Virtual Port Channel (vPC) example*

Device Contexts

Device contexts enable a single physical network device to host multiple virtual network devices. Each device context is an independent configuration with its own policy, network interfaces, and management accounts. The virtualized contexts that run on a single network device operate similarly to standalone network devices. Most of the same features present on the physical device are also supported on the individual device contexts.

The following Cisco network devices support the use of device contexts:

- Cisco Nexus 7000 series switches (VDC)
- Cisco Adaptive Security Appliance (ASA) firewall
- Cisco Catalyst 6500 ASA Services Module (ASA SM)
- Cisco intrusion prevention system (IPS)

Server Virtualization

The use of server virtualization has exploded onto the market over the past several years and can be found in most data center environments. Server virtualization is a software technique that abstracts server resources from the hardware to provide flexibility and to optimize the usage of the underlying hardware. As a result, many data center applications are no longer bound to bare-metal hardware resources.

The server-virtualized hypervisor provides the foundation for the virtualized environment on the host. The hypervisor controls the hardware and physical resources that can be allocated to virtual machines running on the host. This makes the VMs unaware of the physical hardware, but they can use CPUs, memory, and network infrastructure as shared pools available through the virtualization process.

The following represents several server virtualization vendors and their associated products:

- VMware ESX Server
- Citrix XenServer
- Microsoft Hyper-V

Server Scaling

Server farms in the data center need to be able to support the growth and the scaling to meet the needs of the business. As the demand on workloads increases, two main approaches are used to accommodate the growth:

- **Scale-up:** Buy larger servers with more memory and CPU cores. This is costly and easy to implement, but changing out physical servers can be disruptive to production. Virtualization can ease the burden here, where adding memory or CPU is not necessarily disruptive.
- **Scale-out:** Add additional servers with the application load distributed across the server farm pool. This approach is more cost-effective and flexible, but you need to add load balancing into the application design. Database locks can limit scaling if one server ties up database resources while other servers have to wait for access.

Virtual Switching

A virtual switch is software inside the hypervisor that provides connectivity between virtual machines. Virtual switches are similar to physical Ethernet switches in that they process and forward traffic based on L2 information. Virtual switches have uplinks that are tied to the physical NIC that resides in the hypervisor to allow reachability to the physical Ethernet network. Each VM has a virtual NIC attached to the virtual switch, along with a MAC and IP address that enables the VM to communicate with other VMs attached to the same virtual switch or outside to the physical network. The Nexus 1000v is an example of a virtual switch from Cisco.

Virtual workload mobility is a major benefit in virtualization environments. This functionality allows for running VMs to be moved between virtualized hosts running on separate physical hardware through the physical Ethernet network. During the migration, the host retains the same MAC and IP addressing information, which requires L2 connectivity between the hypervisor hosts. One of the challenges is the ability to move the VMs between the virtualized hosts along with the configured network and security policies without having to reconfigure each of the virtualized hosts.

Network Virtualization Design Considerations

Network solutions are needed to solve the challenges of sharing network resources but keeping users totally separate from one another. Although the users are separate, we still need to ensure that the network is highly available, secure, and can scale along with the business growth. Network virtualization offers solutions to these challenges and provides design considerations around access control, path isolation, and services edge.

Access Control

Access needs to be controlled to ensure that users and devices are identified and authorized for entry to their assigned network segment. Security at the access layer is critical for protecting the network from threats, both internal and external.

Path Isolation

Path isolation involves the creation of independent logical network paths over a shared network infrastructure. MPLS VPN is an example of a path-isolation technique whereby devices are mapped to a VRF to access the correct set of network resources. Other segmentation options include VLANs and VSANs, which logically separate LANs and SANs. The main goal when segmenting the network is to improve the scalability, resiliency, and security services as with non-segmented networks.

Services Edge

The services edge refers to making network services available to the intended users, groups, and devices with an enforced centralized managed policy. Separate groups or devices occasionally need to share information that may be on different VLANs, each with corresponding group policies. For example, traffic from the sales VLAN might need to talk to the engineering VLAN, but it needs to go through the firewall to permit the traffic and might even be tied to certain hours of the day. In such cases, the network should have a central way to manage the policy and control access to the resources. An effective way to address policy enforcement is to use an ASA SM in a Cisco Catalyst 6500 series switch to provide firewall services for the data center.

Table 4-5 describes network virtualization considerations.

Table 4-5 Network Virtualization Design Considerations

Network Virtualization Consideration	Description
Access control	Ensures users and devices are recognized, classified, and authorized for entry to their assigned network segments
Path isolation	Provides independent logical traffic paths over a shared network
Services edge	Ensures the right services are accessible to the intended users, groups, or devices

Data Center Interconnect

A Data Center Interconnect (DCI) is a network that connects two or more DCs together to transport traffic between them. Today's business is driving the need to be more mobile and flexible than ever before. As new DCs are built, it is expected that critical business workloads have high levels of resiliency and can move between DCs without restrictions to specific geographic locations. Users also expect secure network and application access with high performance from anywhere they are located.

DCI Use Cases

One of the most popular use cases for DCI is disaster recovery (DR). With the DR use case, the DR data center serves as a facility to run production workloads should a failure of the primary data center occur. The secondary DR data center is usually a smaller subset of the primary data center, but can allow the business to continue operations during and after a disaster. The DCI can also be used to move workloads and systems over to the DR data center if there is advanced warning of an impending DR event such as extreme flooding or a hurricane.

Figure 4-17 illustrates DCI connectivity between Houston and Dallas DCs.

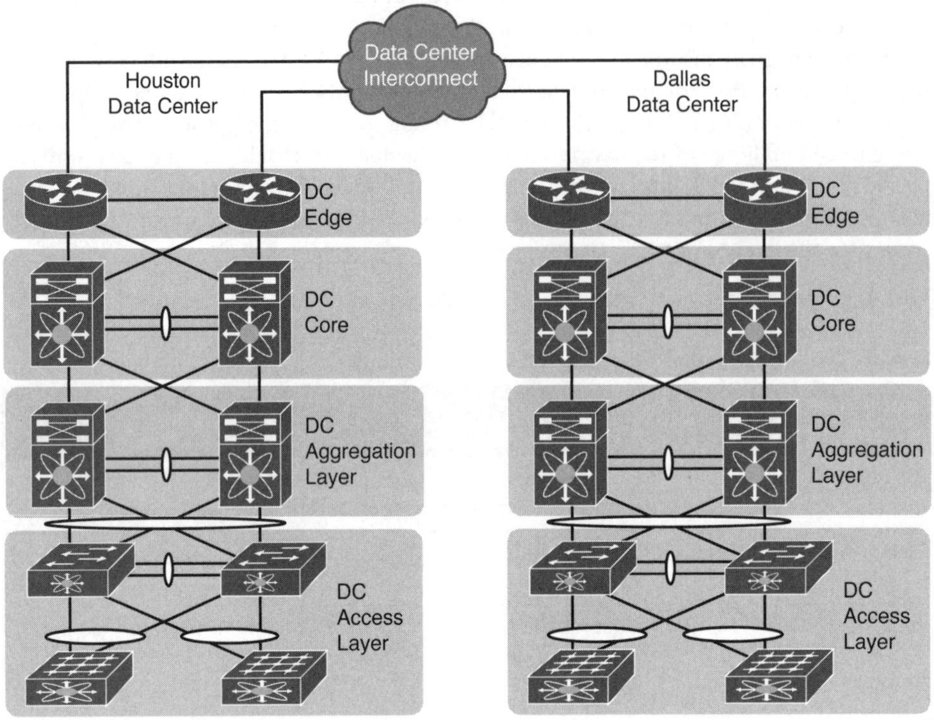

Figure 4-17 *Data Center Interconnect between Houston and Dallas DCs*

Another common use case for DCI is the Active/Active data center. This is where you actually use two data centers at the same time to run production workloads. For example, you may have one DC on the East Coast and another DC on the West Coast of the U.S. and need a way to move workloads between them. When Active/Active DCs are used, this can enable the organization to run the same applications in both DCs and improve the use of the available resources. Because the same applications exist at both DCs, this can optimize the performance and access to workloads based on proximity to the nearest DC.

DCI Transport Options

The transport options for DCI fall into three groupings based on Layer 1 through 3 of the OSI model. Table 4-6 shows the DCI transport options, descriptions, and encapsulations available.

Table 4-6   DCI Transport Options

Network Transport	Description	L2 and L3 Encapsulation Options
Layer 1—Dark Fiber and Service Provider offering	Privately owned or leased from SP, Private OTV for L2	Ethernet, IP, and MPLS
Layer 2—Service Provider offering	L2—VPLS or VPWS	Ethernet, IP, and MPLS
Layer 3—Service Provider offering	MPLS L3 VPN, Private OTV for L2	IP and MPLS

4

Note   Overlay Transport Virtualization (OTV) is a Nexus/ASR software feature that provides for L2 extension functionality between data centers over any IP network.

DCI L2 Considerations

You have several considerations to keep in mind when you extend Layer 2 between DCs. Within each DC, it is advisable to minimize the scope of L2 networks for better manageability. When providing connectivity between DCs, it is recommended that you do not extend L2, if at all possible. However, L2 connectivity is needed for scenarios that require HA clustering, server migrations, and VM mobility. Virtualization features such as VM mobility are the biggest drivers for L2 extensions between DCs. The VM mobility feature requires synchronization of software modules during the VM move over the L2 extension. With server migrations, IP renumbering can be complex, and some applications may be difficult to readdress, making it easier to just extend L2 to the other DC. With high-availability clusters, heartbeats are used to communicate over L2 between the servers that are part of the cluster.

Load Balancing in the DC

Load balancing in the DC is used for better application availability, performance, and scalability, as well as to give the users a more robust application experience. There are two main ways that we deploy load balancing in the DC: application load balancing and network load balancing.

Application Load Balancing

Application load balancing is when the application actually performs the load balancing between the tiers of the application stack. For example, with a standard three-tier application that uses Web, Application, and Database tiers, multiple web servers can redirect traffic to the different application servers without the need for network-based load balancing. The web servers themselves would control the load-balancing algorithms that can be used. This application load balancing functionality is not available with all applications; therefore, some applications may still need to use network-based load balancing.

Network Load Balancing

There are three general categories for network load balancing.

- **Dedicated L4-7 load balancers:** Can be hardware appliances, virtual appliances, or even software based. The load balancers use virtual IP addresses, which then map to a group of server IP addresses that make up server pools. Algorithms are used to make intelligent load-balancing decisions on which server to send the traffic to, and health checks are used to constantly verify the state of the servers. L4-7 load balancers also maintain TCP state information locally in their state tables.

- **DNS based:** Load balancing is where the DNS server keeps track of which server is available for use. The DNS server maintains a random list of servers' IPs for the specific DNS queries that it uses to respond to client requests. The DNS TTL periods are used to verify whether or not the server IPs are available. If the server IPs are not available, the server IPs are removed from the DNS server list. Applications that use hard-coded IP addresses or are not "DNS aware" prevent the use of DNS-based load balancing.

- **Anycast based:** Load balancing works between servers and a router that run a common dynamic routing protocol that supports ECMP. Each server in the pool shares the same virtual address and uses a different IP address on its physical Ethernet interface. The same virtual address is also used on the loopback of the router. The virtual address is then advertised from each server to the router via the routing protocol. This load-balancing approach only works reliably for UDP traffic because TCP uses sessions that cannot be maintained while the servers change.

References and Recommended Readings

Data Center Design Guide (CVD), http://www.cisco.com/c/dam/en/us/td/docs/solutions/CVD/Aug2014/CVD-DataCenterDesignGuide-AUG14.pdf.

Fibre Channel over Ethernet Storage Networking Evolution, http://www.cisco.com/c/en/us/products/collateral/data-center-virtualization/storage-area-network-solutions/white_paper_c11-472771.html.

Module 1 (Design Methodologies): Designing for Cisco Internetwork Solution Course (DESGN) 3.0.

Module 4 (Enterprise Network Design): Designing for Cisco Internetwork Solution Course (DESGN) 3.0.

Classic Network Design Using Cisco Nexus 9000 Series Switches, http://www.cisco.com/c/en/us/products/collateral/switches/nexus-9000-series-switches/guide-c07-730115.pdf.

Cisco Design Zone for Data Centers, www.cisco.com/en/US/netsol/ns743/networking_solutions_program_home.html.

Exam Preparation Tasks

Review All Key Topics

Review the most important topics in the chapter, indicated with the Key Topic icon in the outer margin of the page. Table 4-7 provides a reference of these key topics and the page numbers on which each is found.

Table 4-7   Key Topics

Key Topic Element	Description	Page
List	Virtualization, unified fabric, and unified computing.	132
Paragraphs	Virtualized servers, consolidated connectivity, and network devices.	133
List	Application-Centric Infrastructure (ACI) is the flagship Cisco data center architecture.	135
List	Power, space, security, and management.	136
Paragraph/table	Architectural and mechanical specifications, environmental conditions, physical security, capacities, and compliance.	137
Figure 4-4	Cooling, server, storage, and network.	139
Figure 4-5	Controls the temperature and humidity of the devices.	141
Figure 4-9	Traditional LAN and SAN separation approach to storage in the data center.	145
Section	Provides Layer 2 and Layer 3 physical port density for devices.	147
Section	Aggregates L2/L3 links from the access layer and connects using upstream links to the data center core.	148
Section	Centralized Layer 3 routing layer in which one or more data center aggregation layers connect.	149
Paragraph	Data center firewalls should be deployed inline after the data center core to secure the critical data VLANs.	150
Section	Operational cost, traffic isolation, and increased performance/price ratio.	151
List	Network and device virtualization.	152
Section	VRF, vPC, and VSS.	153
Section	VDC, ASA, and ACE.	155
Section	Secure network services available to users and groups with centralized managed policy.	157
Table 4-6	Layer 1 Dark Fiber through Layer 3 service provider	159
List	Dedicated L4-7 LBs, DNS based, anycast based	160

4

Complete Tables and Lists from Memory

Print a copy of Appendix D, "Memory Tables," (found on the book website), or at least the section for this chapter, and complete the tables and lists from memory. Appendix E, "Memory Tables Answer Key," also on the website, includes completed tables and lists to check your work.

Define Key Terms

Define the following key terms from this chapter, and check your answers in the glossary:

Cisco Nexus 1000V, Cisco Unified Computing System (UCS), Fibre Channel over Ethernet (FCoE), Internet Small Computer Systems Interface (iSCSI), data center space element, power, cabling, data center access, data center aggregation, data center core, scale-up, scale-out, Virtual Switching System (VSS), Virtual Port Channel (vPC), Fabric Extender (FEX), virtualization technologies, network virtualization, device virtualization, access control, path isolation, services edge, Data Center Interconnect (DCI), and network load balancing

Q&A

The answers to these questions appear in Appendix A, "Answers to the 'Do I Know This Already?' Quizzes and Q&A Questions." For more practice with exam format questions, use the exam engine on the website.

1. Which data center architecture layer involves security, IPS, and load balancing?

   a. User services

   b. Data center services

   c. Data center foundation

   d. Data Center Interconnect

2. What Cisco Nexus switch helps deliver visibility and policy control for virtual machines (VM)?

   a. Nexus 7000

   b. Nexus 4000

   c. Nexus 2000

   d. Nexus 1000V

3. Which of the following is a network adapter that can run at 10GE and support Fibre Channel over Ethernet (FCoE)?

   a. CNA

   b. VN-Link

   c. MDS

   d. NAS

4. What is an innovative next-generation data center platform that converges computing, network, storage, and virtualization all together into one system? (Select the best answer.)

   a. Cisco MDS

   b. Cisco Nexus 7000

   c. Cisco Nexus 5000

   d. Cisco UCS

5. Which of the following Cisco Nexus switches support virtual device contexts (VDCs)?

   a. Cisco Nexus 7000

   b. Cisco Nexus 2000

   c. Cisco Nexus 5000

   d. Cisco Nexus 4000

6. What services option provides an effective way to address firewall policy enforcement in a Cisco Catalyst 6500 series switch?

   a. IPS

   b. ASA SM

   c. Nexus 1000V

   d. VDCs

7. What has enabled applications to no longer be bound to bare-metal hardware resources?

   a. Unified fabric

   b. Device virtualization

   c. Network virtualization

   d. Server virtualization

8. Which of the following supports network virtualization technology that allows two physical Cisco Catalyst 6500 series switches to act as a single logical virtual switch?

   a. VN-Link technology

   b. Unified fabric

   c. Virtual Switching System (VSS)

   d. Virtual routing and forwarding (VRF)

9. What enables the spanning-tree topology to appear loop-free although multiple redundant paths that are present in the physical topology?

   a. vPC

   b. VRF

   c. Rapid PVST+

   d. VDC

10. Which of the following are data center core layer characteristics? (Select all that apply.)

   a. 10 and 40GE

   b. High-latency switching

   c. Distributed forwarding architecture

   d. Service modules

11. Which data center layer provides advanced application and security services and has a large STP processing load?

   a. Data center access layer

   b. Data center aggregation layer

   c. Data center services layer

   d. Data center core layer

12. Which of the following are drivers for the data center core layer? (Select all that apply.)

   a. Future growth

   b. 10 and 40 Gigabit Ethernet density

   c. Services edge

   d. Administrative domains and policies

13. Benefits such as port density for server farms, high-performance low-latency Layer 2 switching, and a mix of oversubscription requirements belong to which data center layer?

   a. Core

   b. Distribution

   c. Access

   d. Aggregation

14. Cable management is affected by which of the following? (Select all that apply.)

   a. Alternative cooling technologies

   b. Number of connections

   c. Media selection

   d. Increase in the number of HVAC units

15. Which of the following best describes how "cold" and "hot" aisles should be arranged in the data center?

   a. Hot and cold aisles facing each other

   b. Alternating pattern of cold and hot aisles

   c. Nonalternating pattern of hot and cold aisles

   d. None of the above

16. Within the unified computing resources, what defines the identity of the server?

   a. Virtualization

   b. Unified fabric

   c. Services profile

   d. Virtual machines

17. What DCI technology allows one to extend L2 over any IP network?

   a. VPLS

   b. MPLS VPN

   c. OTV

   d. VPWS

18. What network load-balancing option does not work with TCP?

   a. DNS based

   b. Anycast based

   c. Dedicated L4-7 load balancer

   d. ECMP

19. What involves the creation of independent logical paths over a shared network infrastructure?

   a. Access control

   b. Services edge

   c. Path isolation

   d. Device context

20. What Nexus technology allows for a physical grouping of copper or fiber switch ports that uplinks to a parent switch such as Nexus 5K or 7K?

   a. ASA SM

   b. Nexus 1000v

   c. VSS

   d. FEX

This chapter covers the following subjects:

Wireless LAN Technologies

Cisco Unified Wireless Network

Wireless LAN Design

Wireless LANs (WLANs) allow users to connect to network resources and services without using cables. With WLANs, users connect to the network in common areas, away from their desk, and in areas that do not easily accommodate the installation of wired cabling, such as outdoors and in designated historical sites. This chapter describes WLAN technologies, design, and Cisco solutions.

CHAPTER 5

Wireless LAN Design

"Do I Know This Already?" Quiz

The "Do I Know This Already?" quiz helps you identify your strengths and deficiencies in this chapter's topics.

The eight-question quiz, derived from the major sections in the "Foundation Topics" portion of the chapter, helps you determine how to spend your limited study time.

Table 5-1 outlines the major topics discussed in this chapter and the "Do I Know This Already?" quiz questions that correspond to those topics.

Table 5-1 "Do I Know This Already?" Foundation Topics Section-to-Question Mapping

Foundation Topics Section	Questions Covered in This Section
Wireless LAN Technologies	1, 2
Cisco Unified Wireless Network	3, 4, 5
Wireless LAN Design	6, 7, 8

1. What technology provides 1.3 Gbps of bandwidth using 5GHz frequencies?

   a. IEEE 802.11b

   b. IEEE 802.11g

   c. IEEE 802.11n

   d. IEEE 802.11ac

2. What frequency allotment provides 11 channels for unlicensed use for WLANs in North America?

   a. UNII

   b. ISM

   c. Bluetooth

   d. FM

3. What standard is used for control messaging between access points and controllers?

   a. IEEE 802.11

   b. CSMA/CA

   c. IEEE 802.1X

   d. CAPWAP

4. Which WLAN controller interface is used for out-of-band management?

   a. Management interface

   b. Service-port interface

   c. AP manager interface

   d. Virtual interface

5. How many access points are supported by a Cisco WiSM WLC module?

   a. 6

   b. 50

   c. 100

   d. 1000

6. Which WLAN controller redundancy scheme uses a backup WLC configured as the tertiary WLC in the APs?

   a. N+1

   b. N+N

   c. N+N+1

   d. N+N+B

7. What is the recommended maximum number of data devices associated to a WLAN?

   a. 8

   b. 20

   c. 50

   d. 100

8. Which device of Cisco's Wireless Mesh Networking communicates with the rooftop AP (RAP)?

   a. WLC

   b. WCS

   c. RAP

   d. MAP

Foundation Topics

Cisco has developed a strategy to address the increasing wireless demands placed on today's networks. The Cisco Unified Wireless Network (UWN) architecture combines elements of wireless and wired networks to deliver scalable, manageable, and secure WLANs. Control and Provisioning for Wireless Access Point (CAPWAP) allows the placement of lightweight access points (LAPs) that are remotely configured and easily deployable versus them being manually configured on autonomous APs. Cisco provides solutions for client roaming, radio frequency management, and controller designs that make wireless networks scalable. This chapter covers the Cisco UWN architecture and general WLAN technologies and design.

Wireless LAN Technologies

This section reviews the Institute of Electronics and Electrical Engineers (IEEE) 802.11 WLAN standards, WLAN frequencies, access methods, security, and authentication.

WLAN Standards

WLAN applications include inside-building access, LAN extension, outside building-to-building communications, public access, and small office/home office (SOHO) communications. The first standard for WLANs was IEEE 802.11, approved by the IEEE in 1997. The current specification is IEEE 802.11-1999, with many amendments thereafter.

IEEE 802.11 implemented WLANs at speeds of 1 Mbps and 2 Mbps using direct sequence spread spectrum (DSSS) and frequency-hopping spread spectrum (FHSS) at the physical layer of the Open Systems Interconnection (OSI) model. DSSS divides data into separate sections; each section travels over different frequencies at the same time. FHSS uses a frequency-hopping sequence to send data in bursts. With FHSS, some data transmits at Frequency 1, and then the system hops to Frequency 2 to send more data, and so on, returning to transmit more data at Frequency 1. The interoperability certification for IEEE 802.11 WLANs is wireless fidelity (Wi-Fi). The Wireless Ethernet Compatibility Alliance (WECA) governs the Wi-Fi certification.

In 1999, the 802.11b amendment was introduced, providing an 11Mbps data rate. It provides speeds of 11, 5.5, 2, and 1 Mbps and uses 11 channels of the Industrial, Scientific, and Medical (ISM) frequencies. IEEE 802.11b uses DSSS and is backward compatible with 802.11 systems that use DSSS.

The IEEE approved a second standard in 1999. IEEE 802.11a provides a maximum 54Mbps data rate but is incompatible with 802.11b. It provides speeds of 54, 48, 36, 24, 18, 12, 9, and 6 Mbps. IEEE 802.11a uses 13 channels of the Unlicensed National Information Infrastructure (UNII) frequencies and is incompatible with 802.11b and 802.11g. IEEE 802.11a is also known as WiFi5.

In 2003, the IEEE 802.11g standard was approved, providing a 54Mbps data rate using the ISM frequencies. The advantage of 802.11g over 802.11a is that it is backward compatible with 802.11b.

The IEEE 802.11n standard was ratified in 2009. It added multiple-input multiple-output (MIMO) antennas and expected maximum data rates up to 600 Mbps using four spatial streams, each with a 40MHz width. In addition to DSSS, it uses orthogonal frequency-division multiplexing (OFDM) as a digital carrier modulation method. IEEE 802.11n uses both the 2.4GHz and 5GHz bands.

The latest wireless standard is IEEE 802.11ac, ratified in 2013. It comes in two waves. The first, 802.11ac Wave 1, provides improvements over 802.11n, with greater channel bonding at 80 MHz, up to eight MIMO single-user spatial streams, and denser modulation using 256 quadrature amplitude modulation (QAM; up from 64 QAM). The PHY rate for 802.11ac Wave 1 is 1.3 Gbps.

The second wave for 802.11ac includes the following features:

- Support for multiuser multiple-input, multiple-output (MU-MIMO)
- Support for speeds up to 2.34 Gbps
- 160MHz channel width
- 256 QAM modulation
- Four spatial streams
- PHY rate of 2.34 to 3.47 Gbps

ISM and UNII Frequencies

ISM frequencies are set aside by ITU-R radio regulations 5.138 and 5.150. In the United States, the Federal Communications Commission (15.247) specifies the ISM bands for unlicensed use. ISM bands are specified in the following ranges:

- 900 MHz to 928 MHz
- 2.4 GHz to 2.5 GHz
- 5.75 GHz to 5.875 GHz

Of these, channels located in the 2.4GHz range are used for 802.11b and 802.11g. As shown in Figure 5-1, 11 overlapping channels are available for use. Each channel is 22 MHz wide. It is common to use channels 1, 6, and 11 in the same areas because these three channels do not overlap.

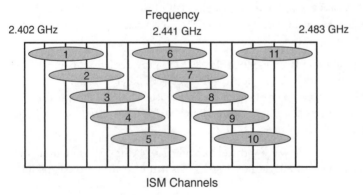

Figure 5-1   *ISM 2.4 channels*

The UNII radio bands were initially specified for use with 802.11a wireless, but are also used by 802.11n and 802.11ac. UNII operates over three ranges:

- **UNII 1:** 5.150 GHz to 5.250 GHz.
- **UNII 2:** 5.230 GHz to 5.350 GHz and 5.470 GHz to 5.725 GHz.
- **UNII 3:** 5.725 GHz to 5.875 GHz. This range overlaps with ISM.

UNII provides 12 nonoverlapping channels.

Summary of WLAN Standards

Table 5-2 summarizes the WLAN standards, frequencies, and data rates.

Table 5-2 WLAN Standards Summary

IEEE Protocol	Standard Release Date	Frequency	Typical Data Rate	Maximum Data Rate
Legacy	1997	ISM	1 Mbps	2 Mbps
802.11a	1999	UNII	25 Mbps	54 Mbps
802.11b	1999	ISM	6.5 Mbps	11 Mbps
802.11g	2003	ISM	25 Mbps	54 Mbps
802.11n	2009	ISM or UNII	200 Mbps	600 Mbps
802.11ac Wave 1	2013	ISM and UNII 5GHz bands	870 Mbps	1.3 Gbps
802.11ac Wave 2	2015 deployments	ISM and UNII 5GHz bands	2.4 Gbps	3.5 Gbps

Service Set Identifier

WLANs use a service set identifier (SSID) to identify the WLAN's "network name." The SSID can be 2 to 32 characters long. The network engineer will then map the wireless SSID to a VLAN. All devices in the WLAN must have the same configured SSID to communicate. It is similar to a VLAN identifier in a wired network. The difficulty in large networks is in configuring the SSID, frequency, and power settings for hundreds of remotely located access points. Cisco addresses this problem with the Cisco Wireless Control System (WCS), which allows the network engineer to manage thousands of APs from a single controller. WCS is covered in more detail in the "Cisco UWN Architecture" section.

A single AP can broadcast multiple SSIDs simultaneously. Each of the SSIDs should get mapped to its own VLAN and IP subnets. Based on the purpose of the wireless network, different SSIDs will get different security and access to different parts of the network. Many companies implement "guest" SSIDs to allow visitors basic access to the Internet. Internal corporate SSIDs will have stronger security and authentication before allowing the user access to corporate internal resources. Table 5-3 provides a basic example of SSIDs and mappings.

Table 5-3 Example SIDs, VLANs, and IP Subnets

SSID	VLAN	IP Subnet
Guests	999	192.168.100.0/24
Employees	100	10.10.10.0/24
Contractors	200	10.100.10.0/24

WLAN Layer 2 Access Method

The IEEE 802.11 Media Access Control (MAC) layer implements carrier sense multiple access with collision avoidance (CSMA/CA) as an access method. With CSMA/CA, each WLAN station listens to see whether a station is transmitting. If no activity is occurring, the station transmits. If activity is occurring, the station uses a random countdown timer. When the timer expires, the station transmits. The difference from wired networks is that in wired networks, collisions are detected on the physical wire; hence, CSMA/CD (collision detection) is used.

WLAN Security

WLANs provide an effective solution for hard-to-reach locations and enable mobility to a level that was previously unattainable. However, the reach of wireless beyond physical connections and boundaries presents additional security concerns. Several standards have been developed to address these security concerns. The Wired Equivalent Privacy (WEP) security protocol, used in the IEEE 802.11b standard, is considered faulty and vulnerable to numerous attacks.

In June 2004, the IEEE 802.11i standard was ratified to provide additional security in WLAN networks. It supersedes WEP security, and introduces the 4-way Handshake and the Group Key Handshake. IEEE 802.11i is also known as Wi-Fi Protected Access 2 (WPA2) and Robust Security Network (RSN). The 802.11i architecture contains the following components:

- **4-way Handshake and Group Key Handshake:** Both use 802.1X for authentication, thus entailing the use of Extensible Authentication Protocol (EAP) and an authentication server.

- **Robust Security Network (RSN):** Used for the establishment and tracking of robust security network associations.

- **Advanced Encryption Standard (AES):** Used for confidentiality, integrity, and origin authentication.

Unauthorized Access

A problem that confronts WLANs comes from the fact that wireless signals are not easily controlled or contained. WEP works at the data link layer, sharing the same key for all nodes that communicate. The 802.11 standard was deployed because it allows bandwidth speed up to 11 Mbps and it is based on DSSS technology. DSSS also enables APs to identify WLAN cards via their MAC addresses. Because traditional physical boundaries do not apply to wireless networks, attackers can gain access using wireless from outside the physical security perimeter. Attackers achieve unauthorized access if the wireless network does not have a mechanism to compare a MAC address on a wireless card to a database that contains a directory with access rights. An individual can roam within an area, and each AP that comes into contact with that card must also rely on a directory. Statically allowing access via a MAC address is also unsecure because MAC addresses can be spoofed.

Some APs can implement MAC address and protocol filtering to enhance security or limit the protocols used over the WLAN. With hundreds of WLAN clients, MAC address filtering is not a scalable solution. Again, attackers can hack MAC address filtering. A user can listen for transmissions, gather a list of MAC addresses, and then use one of those MAC addresses to connect to the AP. This is why additional security protocols such as WEP, WPA, and WPA2 have to be implemented so that the attacker has to attempt to crack the security keys to gain access.

WLAN Security Design Approach

The WLAN security design approach makes two assumptions, which this chapter describes. The assumptions are that all WLAN devices are connected to a unique IP subnet and that most services available to the wired network are also available to the wireless nodes. Using these two assumptions, the WLAN security designs offer two basic security approaches:

- Use of EAP-Flexible Authentication via Secure Tunneling (EAP-FAST) to secure authentication
- Use of virtual private networks (VPNs) with IP Security (IPsec) to secure traffic from the WLAN to the wired network

Considering WLAN as an alternative access methodology, remember that the services these WLAN users access are often the same as those accessed by the wired users. WLANs potentially open many new attack vectors for hackers, and you should consider the risks before deployment.

To enhance security, you can implement WLANs with IPsec VPN software, use the IEEE 802.1X-2001 port-based access control protocol, and use WPA.

IEEE 802.1X-2001 Port-Based Authentication

IEEE 802.1X-2001 is a port-based authentication standard for LANs. It authenticates a user before allowing access to the network. You can use it on Ethernet, Fast Ethernet, and WLAN networks.

With IEEE 802.1X-2001, client workstations run client software to request access to services. Clients use EAP to communicate with the LAN switch. The LAN switch verifies client information with the authentication server and relays the response to the client. LAN switches use a Remote Authentication Dial-In User Service (RADIUS) client to communicate with the server. The RADIUS authentication server validates the client's identity and authorizes the client. But note that it does not provide encryption privacy. The server uses RADIUS with EAP extensions to make the authorization.

Dynamic WEP Keys and LEAP

Cisco also offers dynamic per-user, per-session WEP keys to provide additional security over statically configured WEP keys, which are not unique per user. For centralized user-based authentication, Cisco developed LEAP. LEAP uses mutual authentication between the client and the network server and uses IEEE 802.1X for 802.11 authentication messaging. LEAP can be used with the Temporal Key Integrity Protocol (TKIP) rather than WEP to overcome the weaknesses of WEP. LEAP uses a RADIUS server to manage user information.

LEAP is a combination of 802.1X and EAP. It combines the capability to authenticate to various servers such as RADIUS with forcing the WLAN user to log on to an access point that compares the logon information to RADIUS. This solution is more scalable than MAC address filtering.

Because the WLAN access depends on receiving an address, using Dynamic Host Configuration Protocol (DHCP), and the authentication of the user using RADIUS, the WLAN needs constant access to these back-end servers. In addition, LEAP does not support one-time passwords (OTPs), so you must use good password-security practices. The password issue and maintenance practice are a basic component of corporate security policy.

Controlling WLAN Access to Servers

In the same way you place Domain Name System (DNS) servers accessible via the Internet on a demilitarized zone (DMZ) segment, you should apply a similar strategy to the RADIUS and DHCP servers accessible to the WLAN. These servers should be secondary servers that are on a different segment (separate VLAN) from their primary counterparts. Access to this VLAN is filtered. Such placement ensures that any attacks launched on these servers are contained within that segment.

You should control network access to the servers. Consider the WLAN an unsecured segment and apply appropriate segmentation and access lists. Such a step ensures that WLAN access is controlled and directed to only those areas that need it. For example, you might not want to permit WLAN access to management servers and HR servers.

You must also protect these servers against network attack. The criticality of these servers makes them an ideal target for denial-of-service (DoS) attacks. Consider using network-based intrusion detection systems (IDSs) to detect network attacks against these devices.

Cisco Unified Wireless Network

This section covers the Cisco Unified Wireless Network (UWN) architecture, Control and Provisioning for Wireless Access Point (CAPWAP), WLAN controller components, roaming, and mobility groups. Cisco UWN components provide scalable WLAN solutions using WLAN controllers to manage lightweight access points (LAPs). The CCDA must understand how these components work with each other, how they scale, and how roaming and mobility groups work.

Cisco UWN Architecture

With the explosion of wireless solutions in and out of the enterprise, designers must create solutions that provide mobility and business services while maintaining network security. The Cisco UWN architecture combines elements of wireless and wired networks to deliver scalable, manageable, and secure WLANs. As shown in Figure 5-2, the Cisco UWN architecture is composed of five network elements:

- **Client devices:** These include laptops, workstations, IP phones, PDAs, and manufacturing devices to access the WLAN.

- **Access points:** These devices provide access to the wireless network. APs are placed in strategic locations to minimize interference.

- **Network unification:** The WLAN system should be able to support wireless applications by providing security policies, QoS, intrusion prevention, and radio frequency (RF) management. Cisco WLAN controllers provide this functionality and integration into all major switching and routing platforms.

- **Network management:** The Cisco Wireless Control System (WCS) provides a central management tool that lets you design, control, and monitor wireless networks.

- **Mobility services:** These include guest access, location services, voice services, and threat detection and mitigation.

Cisco UWN provides the following benefits:

- Reduced total cost of ownership (TCO)
- Enhanced visibility and control
- Dynamic RF management
- WLAN security
- Unified wired and wireless network
- Enterprise mobility
- Enhanced productivity and collaboration

5

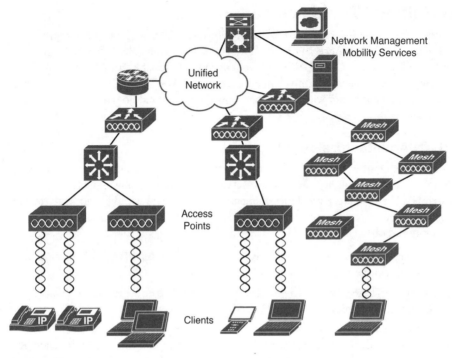

Figure 5-2   *Cisco UWN architecture*

Table 5-4 covers the Cisco UWN architecture.

Table 5-4   Cisco UWN Architecture

Cisco UWN Element	Description
Client devices	These include laptops, workstations, IP phones, PDAs, and manufacturing devices to access the WLAN.
Access points	Provide access to the network.
Network unification	The WLAN system should be able to support wireless applications by providing security policies, QoS, intrusion prevention, RF management, and wireless controllers.
Network management	Cisco Wireless Control System (WCS) provides a central management tool that lets you design, control, and monitor wireless networks.
Mobility services	Include guest access, location services, voice services, and threat detection and mitigation.

Autonomous Access Points

Access points (APs) provide wireless access to client devices to the network. In older networks, APs were configured autonomously. Autonomous APs operate independently of each other and have to be individually configured. This method of configuration might be okay for small networks but would be very difficult to manage for hundreds and thousands of APs.

Centralized WLAN Architecture

In the centralized WLAN architecture, autonomous APs are replaced by lightweight access points (LAPs). These LAPs are then configured and managed by a wireless LAN controller (WLC). Furthermore, user traffic is placed on the wired network at the controller and not at the LAP. As shown in Figure 5-3, wireless 802.11 traffic is placed in CAPWAP tunnels over the 802.3 wired network. Traffic then goes from the WLC to its IP destination.

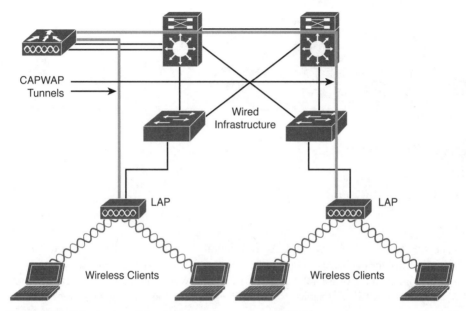

Figure 5-3 *Centralized WLAN architecture using WLC*

LWAPP

Lightweight Access Point Protocol (LWAPP) is a Cisco standard for control messaging for setup, authentication, and operations between APs and WLAN controllers (WLCs). LWAPP has been deprecated in favor of CAPWAP.

LWAPP control messages can be transported at Layer 2 tunnels or Layer 3 tunnels. Layer 2 LWAPP tunnels were the first method developed in which the APs did not require an IP address. The disadvantage of Layer 2 LWAPP was that the WLC needed to be on every subnet on which the AP resides. Layer 2 LWAPP is a deprecated solution for Cisco. Layer 3 LWAPP was the preferred solution before CAPWAP. In the configuration, Layer 2 or Layer 3 transport modes can be selected. When set to Layer 3, the LWAPP uses IP addresses to communicate with the access points; these IP addresses are collected from a mandatory DHCP server. When set to Layer 2, the LWAPP uses proprietary code to communicate with the access points.

Note   Layer 2 LWAPP tunnels use EtherType code 0xBBBB. Layer 3 LWAPP uses UDP ports 12222 and 12223.

As shown in Figure 5-4, Layer 3 LWAPP tunnels are used between the LAP and the WLC. Messages from the WLC use User Datagram Port (UDP) port 12223 for control and UDP port 12222 for data messages. In this solution, APs require an IP address, but the WLC does not need to reside on the same segment.

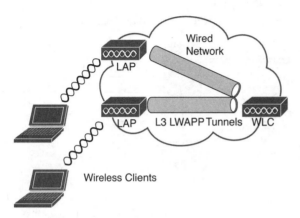

Figure 5-4   *Layer 3 LWAPP*

CAPWAP

Control and Provisioning for Wireless Access Point (CAPWAP) is an IETF standard (RFC 5415) for control messaging for setup, authentication, and operations between APs and WLCs. In Controller Software 5.2, Cisco LAPs use CAPWAP communication between the WLC and LAPs. CAPWAP is similar to LWAPP, except for the following differences:

- CAPWAP uses Datagram Transport Layer Security (DTLS) for authentication and encryption to protect traffic between APs and controllers. LWAPP uses AES.
- CAPWAP has a dynamic maximum transmission unit (MTU) discovery mechanism.
- CAPWAP control messages run over UDP 5246.
- CAPWAP data messages use UDP 5247.

CAPWAP uses a Layer 3 tunnel between the LAP and the WLC. Figure 5-5 shows the architecture. The APs obtain an IP address via DHCP. On the AP side, the control and data messages use an ephemeral UDP port that is derived from a hash between the AP MAC addresses. CAPWAP uses UDP port 5247 for data messages and UDP port 5246 for control messages.

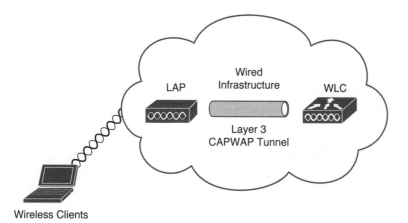

Figure 5-5 *CAPWAP tunnel*

Cisco Unified Wireless Network Split-MAC Architecture

With the Cisco UWN split-MAC operation, the control and data messages are split. LAPs communicate with the WLCs using control messages over the wired network. LWAPP or CAPWAP data messages are encapsulated and forwarded to and from wireless clients. The WLC manages multiple APs, providing configuration information and firmware updates as needed.

LAP MAC functions are

- **802.11:** Beacons, probe response
- **802.11 Control:** Packet acknowledgment and transmission
- **802.11e:** Frame queuing and packet prioritization
- **802.11i:** MAC layer data encryption/decryption

Controller MAC functions are

- **802.11 MAC Management:** Association requests and actions
- **802.11e Resource Reservation:** To reserve resources for specific applications
- **802.11i:** Authentication and key management

Local MAC

CAPWAP supports local MAC. Local MAC moves the MAC management from the WLC to the local AP. This allows for termination of client traffic at the wired port of the AP. The functionality is useful for small and remote branch offices, which would not require a WLC.

LAP MAC functions are

- **802.11:** Beacons, probe response
- **802.11 Control:** Packet acknowledgment and transmission
- **802.11e:** Frame queuing and packet prioritization

- **802.11i:** MAC layer data encryption/decryption
- **802.11 MAC Management:** Association requests and actions

Controller MAC functions are

- **802.11:** Proxy association requests and actions
- **802.11e Resource Reservation:** To reserve resources for specific applications
- **802.11i:** Authentication and key management

Figure 5-6 shows the difference between an autonomous AP and a CAPWAP using WLC. Autonomous APs act as a 802.1Q translational bridge with a trunk to the LAN switch. In CAPWAP with WLC, the AP uses a CAPWAP tunnel, and the WLC establishes the 802.1Q trunk to the LAN switch.

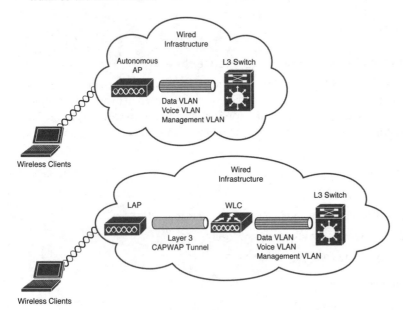

Figure 5-6   *Autonomous AP versus CAPWAP AP with WLC*

AP Modes

For the CCDA test, make sure you understand the different AP modes. APs operate in one of six different modes:

- **Local mode:** This is the default mode of operation. In this mode, every 180 seconds the AP measures noise floor and interference, and scans for IDS events. This scanning activity occurs on unused channels and lasts for 60 milliseconds.
- **Hybrid Remote Edge AP (H-REAP) mode:** This mode enables a LAP to reside across a WAN link and still be able to communicate with the WLC and provide the functionality of a regular LAP. It allows local MAC.

- **Monitor mode:** Monitor mode is a feature designed to allow specified CAPWAP-enabled APs to exclude themselves from handling data traffic between clients and the infrastructure. They instead act as dedicated sensors for location-based services (LBS), rogue AP detection, and intrusion detection (IDS). When APs are in Monitor mode, they cannot serve clients and continuously cycle through all configured channels, listening to each channel for approximately 60 ms.

- **Rogue detector mode:** LAPs that operate in Rogue Detector mode monitor for rogue APs. They do not transmit or contain rogue APs. The idea is that the rogue detector (RD) should be able to see all the VLANs in the network, because rogue APs can be connected to any of the VLANs in the network. (Therefore, we connect it to a trunk port.) The LAN switch sends all the rogue AP/client MAC address lists to the RD. The RD then forwards those to the WLC to compare with the MAC addresses of clients that the WLC APs have heard over the air. If the MAC addresses match, the WLC knows that the rogue AP to which those clients are connected is on the wired network.

- **Sniffer mode:** A CAPWAP that operates in Sniffer mode functions as a sniffer and captures and forwards all the packets on a particular channel to a remote machine that runs AiroPeek. These packets contain information on the timestamp, signal strength, packet size, and so on. The Sniffer feature can be enabled only if you run AiroPeek, a third-party network analyzer software that supports decoding of data packets.

- **Bridge mode:** Applications supported are point-to-point bridging, point-to-multipoint bridging, point-to-point wireless access with integrated wireless backhaul, and point-to-multipoint wireless access with integrated wireless backhaul.

Table 5-5 summarizes the AP modes.

Table 5-5   Access Point Modes

AP Mode	Description
Local mode	The default mode of operation.
H-REAP mode	For remote LAP management across WAN links.
Monitor mode	The APs exclude themselves from handling data traffic and dedicate themselves to location-based services (LBS).
Rogue Detector mode	Monitors for rouge APs.
Sniffer mode	Captures and forwards all packets of a remote sniffer.
Bridge mode	For point-to-point and point-to-multipoint solutions.

LAP Discovery of WLC Using CAPWAP

When LAPs are placed on the network, they first perform DHCP discovery to obtain an IP address.

For controllers that have a CAPWAP image, the AP follows the following process:

1. The CAPWAP AP starts the discovery process to find the controller by using a CAPWAP request. The WLC responds with a CAPWAP response.

    2. If a CAPWAP response is not received after 60 seconds, the AP starts the discovery process using LWAPP discovery.

    3. If the AP cannot find a controller using LWAPP within 60 seconds, it returns to step 1.

WLC selection by a CAPWAP is a design decision. This is configurable in the WLC. The AP selects the WLC to create a CAPWAP tunnel based on the information configured in the WLC. The WLC responses contain controller sysName, controller type, controller AP capacity and load, the master controller status, and the AP manager IP addresses. The AP selects one or several WLCs to send a CAPWAP tunnel request based on Table 5-6. The WLC validates the AP and sends a CAPWAP tunnel response, an encryption key is derived, and future messages are encrypted. The AP then selects one WLC and sends a join request.

Table 5-6   WLAN Controller Platforms

Order	WLC
First	Primary sysName (preconfigured)
Second	Second sysName (preconfigured)
Third	Tertiary sysName (preconfigured)
Fourth	Master controller
Fifth	WLC with greatest capacity for AP associations

WLAN Authentication

Wireless clients first associate to an AP. Then wireless clients need to authenticate with an authentication server before the AP allows access to services. As shown in Figure 5-7, the authentication server resides in the wired infrastructure. An EAP/RADIUS tunnel occurs between the WLC and the authentication server. Cisco's Secure Access Control Server (ACS) using EAP is an example of an authentication server.

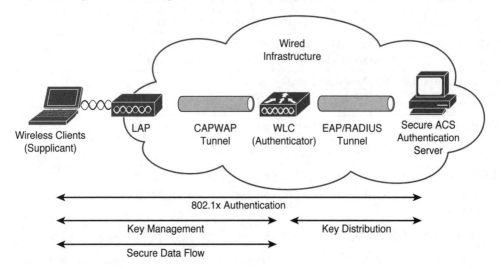

Figure 5-7   *WLAN authentication*

Authentication Options

Wireless clients communicate with the authentication server using EAP. Each EAP type has advantages and disadvantages. Trade-offs exist between the security provided, EAP type manageability, the operating systems supported, the client devices supported, the client software and authentication messaging overhead, certificate requirements, user ease of use, and WLAN infrastructure device support. The following summarizes the authentication options:

- **EAP-Transport Layer Security (EAP-TLS)** is an IETF open standard that is well sup-ported among wireless vendors but rarely deployed. It uses Public Key Infrastructure (PKI) to secure communications to the RADIUS authentication server using TLS and digital certificates.

- **Protected Extensible Authentication Protocol (PEAP)** is a joint proposal by Cisco Systems, Microsoft, and RSA Security as an open standard. PEAP/MSCHAPv2 is the most common version, and it is widely available in products and widely deployed. It is similar in design to EAP-TTLS, requiring only a server-side PKI certificate to create a secure TLS tunnel to protect user authentication. PEAP-GTC allows more generic authentication to a number of databases such as Novell Directory Services (NDS).

- **EAP-Tunneled TLS (EAP-TTLS)** was co-developed by Funk Software and Certicom. It is widely supported across platforms and offers good security, using PKI certificates only on the authentication server.

- **Cisco Lightweight Extensible Authentication Protocol (LEAP)** is an early proprietary EAP method supported in the Cisco Certified Extensions (CCX) program. It is vulner-able to dictionary attacks.

- **EAP-Flexible Authentication via Secure Tunneling (EAP-FAST)** is a proposal by Cisco Systems to fix the weaknesses of LEAP. EAP-FAST uses a Protected Access Credential (PAC), and use of server certificates is optional. EAP-FAST has three phases. Phase 0 is an optional phase in which the PAC can be provisioned manually or dynamically. In Phase 1, the client and the AAA server use the PAC to establish the TLS tunnel. In Phase 2, the client sends user information across the tunnel.

WLAN Controller Components

The CCDA candidate must understand the three major components of WLCs:

- WLANs
- Interfaces
- Ports

WLANs are identified by unique SSID network names. The LAN is a logical entity. Each WLAN is assigned to an interface in the WLC. Each WLAN is configured with radio poli-cies, quality of service (QoS), and other WLAN parameters.

A WLC interface is a logical connection that maps to a VLAN on the wired network. Each interface is configured with a unique IP address, default gateways, physical ports, VLAN tag, and DHCP server.

Table 5-7 covers the WLC components.

Table 5-7   WLC Components

WLC Component	Description
WLAN	Identified by a unique SSID and assigned to an interface
Interface	A logical connection that maps to a VLAN in the wired network
Port	A physical connection to the wired LAN

The port is a physical connection to the neighboring switch or router. By default, each port is an IEEE 802.1Q trunk port. There may be multiple ports on a WLC into a single port-channel interface. These ports can be aggregated using link aggregation (LAG). Some WLCs have a service port that is used for out-of-band management. Figure 5-8 shows the WLC components.

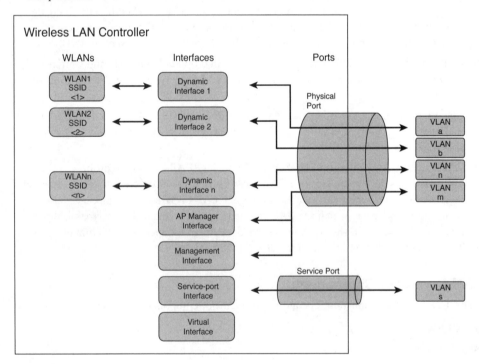

Figure 5-8   *WLAN controller components*

WLC Interface Types

A WLC has five interface types:

- **Management interface** (static, configured at setup, mandatory) is used for in-band management, connectivity to AAA, and Layer 2 discovery and association.

- **Service-port interface** (static, configured at setup, optional) is used for out-of-band management. It is an optional interface that is statically configured.

- **AP manager interface** (static, configured at setup, mandatory except for 5508 WLC) is used for Layer 3 discovery and association. It has the source IP address of the AP that is statically configured.

- **Dynamic interface** (dynamic) is analogous to VLANs and is designated for WLAN client data.

- **Virtual interface** (static, configured at setup, mandatory) is used for Layer 3 security authentication, DHCP relay support, and mobility management.

Table 5-8 summarizes WLC interface types.

Table 5-8   WLC Interface Types

WLC Interface Type	Description
Management interface	For in-band management
Service-port interface	For out-of-band management
AP manager interface	For Layer 3 discovery and association
Dynamic interface	Dedicated to WLAN client data; analogous to VLANs
Virtual interface	For Layer 3 authentication and mobility management

AP Controller Equipment Scaling

Cisco provides different solutions to support the differing numbers of APs present in enterprise customers. Standalone devices, modules for Integrated Services Routers (ISRs), and modules for 6500 switches support numerous APs. Table 5-9 lists the platforms and the number of APs supported.

Table 5-9   WLAN Controller Platforms

Platform	Number of Supported Access Points
CTVM virtual controller	200
Cisco 2500 series WLC	75
Cisco WLC for ISR G2	200
Catalyst 3850 Integrated WLC	50
WiSM2 WLC module	1000
Cisco 5508 WLC	500
Cisco 5520 WLC	1500
Cisco 8540 WLC	6000

To scale beyond the default number of APs on a Cisco WLC, use *link aggregation (LAG)*. This option is supported by 5500 series controllers and is the default for 3850G Integrated WLC and Catalyst 6500 series WiSM.

Figure 5-9 shows the use of LAG. With LAG, the system dynamically manages port redundancy and load-balances APs across an EtherChannel interface transparently. The default limit of APs per port does not apply when LAG is enabled.

One limitation of LAG is that the WLC platforms only support one LAG group per controller. When LAG is enabled, all the physical ports, excluding the services port, are included in the bundle. Therefore, the WLC using LAG cannot be connected to more than one neighbor device.

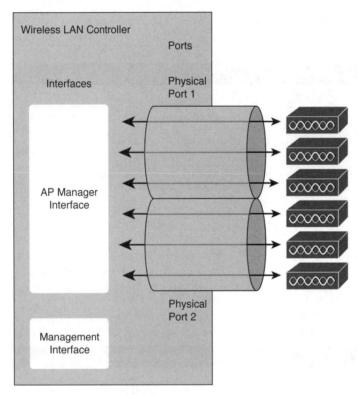

Figure 5-9 *WLC LAG*

Roaming and Mobility Groups

The primary reason to have wireless networks is roaming: the ability to access network resources from common areas and in areas where it is difficult to run cabling. End clients might want to move from one location to another. Mobility allows users to access the network from several locations. Roaming occurs when the wireless client changes association from one AP to another. The challenge is to scale the wireless network to allow client roaming that is seamless and secure. Roaming can be intracontroller or intercontroller.

Intracontroller Roaming

Intracontroller roaming, shown in Figure 5-10, occurs when a client moves association from one AP to another AP that is joined to the same WLC. The WLC updates the client database with the new associated AP and does not change the client's IP address. If required, clients are reauthenticated, and a new security association is established. The client database remains on the same WLC.

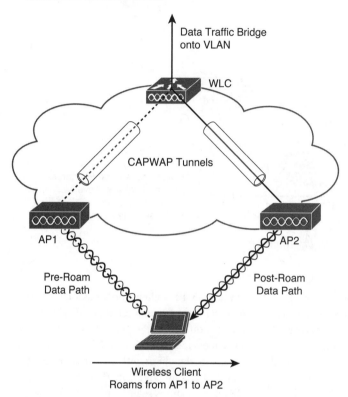

Figure 5-10 *Intracontroller roaming*

Layer 2 Intercontroller Roaming

Intercontroller roaming occurs when a client moves association from one AP to another AP that is joined to a different WLC that is on the same subnet. The Layer 2 roam occurs when the client traffic is bridged to the same IP subnet. Figure 5-11 shows Layer 2 intercontroller roaming. Traffic remains of the same IP subnet, and no IP address changes to the client occur. The client database is moved from WLC1 to WLC2. The client is reauthenticated transparently, and a new security session is established.

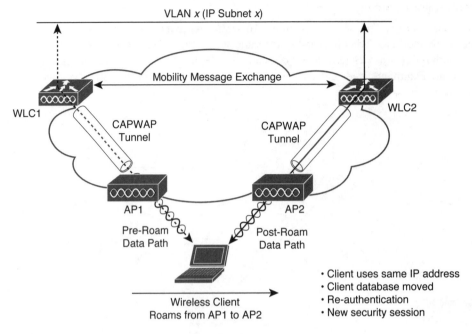

Figure 5-11   *Layer 2 intercontroller roaming*

Layer 3 Intercontroller Roaming

With Layer 3 intercontroller roaming, shown in Figure 5-12, a client moves association from one AP to another AP that is joined to a different WLC that is on a different IP subnet than the first WLC. Then the traffic is bridged onto a different IP subnet. When the client associates to AP2, WLC2 then exchanges mobility messages with WLC1. The original client database is not moved to WLC2. Instead, WLC1 marks the client with an "Anchor" entry in its database. The database entry is copied to WLC2's database and is marked as a "Foreign" entry. The wireless client maintains its original IP address and is reauthenticated. A new security session is then established.

Client traffic then routes in an asymmetric manner. Traffic from the client is forwarded by the Foreign WLC, but traffic to the client arrives at the Anchor WLC, which forwards it through an Ethernet-in-IP (EtherIP) tunnel to the Foreign WLC. The Foreign WLC forwards the data traffic to the client.

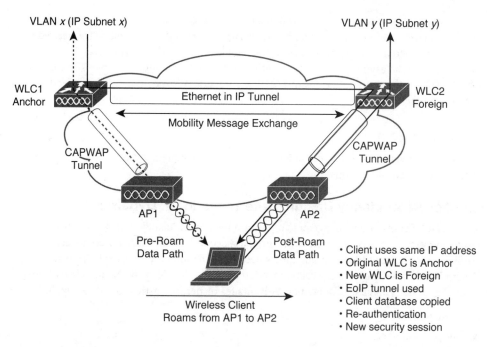

Figure 5-12 *Layer 3 intercontroller roaming*

Mobility Groups

Mobility groups allow controllers to peer with each other to support roaming across controller boundaries. This also allows for AP load balancing and controller redundancy.

When you assign WLCs to mobility groups, the WLCs dynamically exchange mobility messages and data is tunneled via EtherIP between the Anchor and Foreign AP. WLCs should be placed in mobility groups when intercontroller roaming is possible and for controller redundancy.

Mobility groups support up to 24 controllers. The upper limit of APs supported in a mobility group is determined by the number of APs that the controllers support, which varies by controller type. A mobility list is a group of controllers configured on a single controller that specifies members in different mobility groups. Controllers can communicate across mobility groups, and clients can roam between APs in different mobility groups if the controllers are included in each other's mobility lists. Each WLC is configured with a list of the members in the mobility group. Mobility lists can support up to 72 controllers with Release 5.1 or later, or up to 48 controllers with Release 5.0.

The WLCs exchange messages using UDP port 16666 for unencrypted messages or UDP port 16667 for encrypted messages. APs learn the IP addresses of other members of the mobility group after the CAPWAP join process.

As an example of the scalability, if 24 Cisco 2504 WLCs (75 APs supported per 2504 WLC) are used, then 1800 APs (24 * 75 = 1800) are supported.

As a best practice, Cisco recommends minimizing intercontroller roaming in the network. It is also recommended that there be less than 10 ms of round-trip time latency between controllers. Cisco also states that Layer 2 roaming is more efficient than Layer 3 roaming because of the asymmetric communication of Layer 3 roaming. Proactive key caching (PKC) or Cisco Compatible Extensions (CCKM) Version 4 is recommended to speed up and secure roaming.

WLAN Design

This section covers controller redundancy design, radio frequency groups, site survey, and WLAN design considerations.

Controller Redundancy Design: Deterministic vs. Dynamic

WLCs can be configured for dynamic or deterministic redundancy. For deterministic redundancy, the AP is configured with a primary, secondary, and tertiary controller. This requires more upfront planning but allows better predictability and faster failover times. Deterministic redundancy is the recommended best practice. N+1, N+N, and N+N+1 are examples of deterministic redundancy. Advantages of deterministic redundancy include

- Predictability
- Network stability
- Flexible and powerful redundancy design options
- Faster failover times
- A fallback option in case of failover

The disadvantage of deterministic controller redundancy is that it requires more upfront planning and configuration.

Dynamic controller redundancy uses CAPWAP to load-balance APs across WLCs. CAPWAP populates APs with a backup WLC. This solution works better when WLCs are in a centralized cluster. The disadvantages are longer failover times and unpredictable operation. An example is adjacent APs registering with differing WLCs.

Advantages of dynamic controller redundancy include

- Easy to deploy and configure
- Access points dynamically load-balance

Disadvantages include longer failover times, unpredictable operation, more intercontroller roaming, and no fallback option in the event of controller failure.

N+1 WLC Redundancy

With N+1 redundancy, shown in Figure 5-13, a single WLC acts as the backup of multiple WLCs. The backup WLC is configured as the secondary WLC on each AP. One design constraint is that the backup WLC might become oversubscribed if there are too many failures of the primary controllers. The secondary WLC is the backup controller for all APs and it is normally placed in the data center.

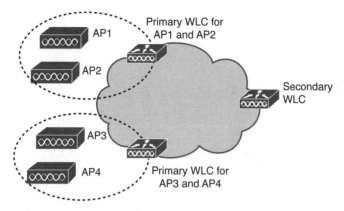

Figure 5-13 *N+1 controller redundancy*

N+N WLC Redundancy

With N+N redundancy, shown in Figure 5-14, an equal number of controllers back up each other. For example, a pair of WLCs on one floor serves as a backup to a second pair on another floor. The top WLC is primary for AP1 and AP2 and secondary for AP3 and AP4. The bottom WLC is primary for AP3 and AP4 and secondary for AP1 and AP2. The provisioned controllers should be sized with enough capacity to manage a failover situation.

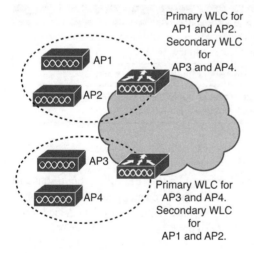

Figure 5-14 *N+N controller redundancy*

N+N+1 WLC Redundancy

With N+N+1 redundancy, shown in Figure 5-15, an equal number of controllers back up each other (as with N+N), plus a backup WLC is configured as the tertiary WLC for the APs. N+N+1 redundancy functions the same as N+N redundancy, plus there's a tertiary controller that backs up the secondary controllers. The tertiary WLC is placed in the data center or network operations center.

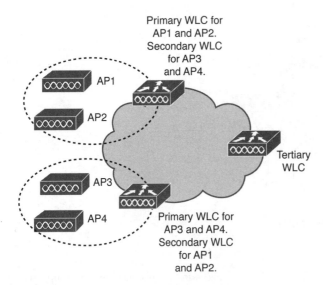

Figure 5-15 *N+N+1 controller redundancy*

Table 5-10 summarizes WLC redundancy.

Table 5-10   WLC Redundancy

WLC Redundancy	Description
N+1	A single WLC acts as the backup for multiple WLCs. The backup WLC is configured as the secondary on APs.
N+N	An equal number of controllers back up each other.
N+N+1	An equal number of controllers back up each other. The backup WLC is configured as the tertiary on APs.

Radio Management and Radio Groups

The limit of available channels in the ISM frequencies used by the IEEE 802.11b/g/n standard presents challenges to the network designer. There are three nonoverlapping channels (channels 1, 6, and 11). The recommended best practice is to limit the number of data devices connected to each AP to 20, or no more than seven concurrent voice over WLAN (VoWLAN) calls using G.711 or eight concurrent VoWLAN calls using G.729. Additional APs should be added as user population grows to maintain this ratio of data and voice per AP.

Cisco Radio Resource Management (RRM) is a method to manage AP RF channel and power configuration. Cisco WLCs use the RRM algorithm to automatically configure, optimize, and self-heal. Cisco RRM functions are as follows:

- **Radio resource monitoring:** Cisco LAPs monitor all channels. Collected packets are sent to the WLC, which can detect rogue APs, clients, and interfering APs.

- **Dynamic channel assignment:** WLCs automatically assign channels to avoid interference.

- **Interference detection and avoidance:** As Cisco LAPs monitor all channels, interference is detected by a predefined threshold (10 percent by default). Interference can be generated by rogue APs, microwaves, cordless telephones, Bluetooth devices, neighboring WLANs, or other electronic devices.

- **Dynamic transmit power control:** The WLCs automatically adjust power levels.

- **Coverage hole detection and correction:** WLCs may adjust the power output of APs if clients report that a low received signal strength indication (RSSI) level is detected.

- **Client and network load balancing:** Clients can be influenced to associate with certain APs to maintain network balance.

With AP self-healing, WLCs use RRM to raise the power levels and adjust the channel selection of neighbor APs to compensate for loss of coverage of a failed AP. APs report a lost neighbor when they no longer receive neighbor messages at –70 dBm.

RF Groups

An RF group is a cluster of WLC devices that coordinate their RRM calculations. When the WLCs are placed in an RF group, the RRM calculation can scale from a single WLC to multiple floors, buildings, or even the campus. As shown in Figure 5-16, APs send neighbor messages to other APs. If the neighbor message is above –80 dBm, the controllers form an RF group. The WLCs elect an RF group leader to analyze the RF data. The RF group leader exchanges messages with the RF group members using UDP port 12114 for 802.11b/g/n and UDP port 12115 for 802.11a.

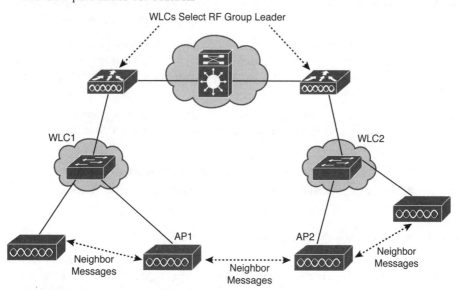

Figure 5-16   *RF groups*

RF groups are formed with the following process:

1. APs send out neighbor messages over the air. The message includes an encrypted shared secret that is configured in the WLC and pushed to each AP.

2. APs sharing the same secret are able to validate messages from each other. Neighbor messages need to be over –80 dBm to form an RF group.

3. The members in the RF group elect an RF group leader to maintain a "master" power and channel scheme for the RF group. The RF group leader analyzes real-time radio data collected by the system and calculates the master power and channel plan.

RF Site Survey

Similar to performing an assessment for a wired network design, RF site surveys are done to determine design parameters for WLANs and customer requirements. RF site surveys help determine the coverage areas and check for RF interference. This helps determine the appropriate placement of wireless APs.

The RF site survey has the following steps:

Step 1. Define customer requirements, such as service levels and support for VoIP. Determine devices to support as well as sites where wireless devices will be located.

Step 2. Obtain a facility diagram to identify the potential RF obstacles.

Step 3. Visually inspect the facility to look for potential barriers to the propagation of RF signals, such as metal racks, elevator shafts, and stairwells.

Step 4. Identify user areas that may be intensively used, such as conference rooms, and areas that are not heavily used, such as stairwells.

Step 5. Determine preliminary AP locations, which need power, wired network access, cell coverage and overlap, channel selection, mounting locations, and antennas.

Step 6. Perform the actual survey by using an AP to survey the location and received RF strength based on the targeted AP placement. Consider the effects of electrical machinery. Microwave ovens and elevators might distort the radio signal from the APs.

Step 7. Document the findings by recording the target AP locations, log signal readings, and data rates at outer boundaries. Information included in the report includes the following:

- Detail customer requirements; describe and diagram AP coverage.
- Parts list, including APs, antennas, accessories, and network components.
- Describe tools used and methods used for the survey.

Using EoIP Tunnels for Guest Services

Basic solutions use separate VLANs for guest and corporate users to segregate guest traffic from corporate traffic. The guest SSID is broadcast, but the corporate SSID is not. All other security parameters are configured. Another solution is to use Ethernet over IP (EoIP) to tunnel the guest traffic from the CAPWAP to an anchor WLC.

As shown in Figure 5-17, EoIP is used to logically segment and transport guest traffic from the edge AP to the Anchor WLC. There is no need to define guest VLANs in the internal network, and corporate traffic is still locally bridged. The Ethernet frames from the guest clients are maintained across the CAPWAP and EoIP tunnels.

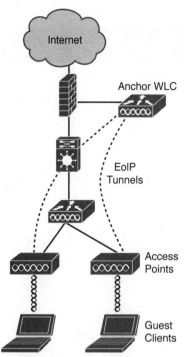

Figure 5-17 *EoIP tunnels*

Wireless Mesh for Outdoor Wireless

Traditionally, outdoor wireless solutions have been limited to point-to-point and point-to-multipoint bridging between buildings. With these solutions, each AP is wired to the network. The Cisco wireless mesh networking solution, shown in Figure 5-18, eliminates the need to wire each AP and allows users to roam from one area to another without having to reconnect.

The wireless mesh components are shown in Table 5-11.

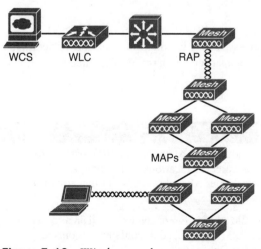

Figure 5-18 *Wireless mesh components*

Table 5-11   Wireless Mesh Components

Wireless Mesh Component	Description
Wireless Control System (WCS)	The wireless mesh SNMP management system allows networkwide configuration and management.
WLAN controller (WLC)	Links the mesh APs to the wired network and performs all the tasks previously described for a WLC, such as managing multiple APs, mitigating radio interference, managing security, and providing Layer 3 mobility.
Rooftop AP (RAP)	Connects the mesh to the wired network and serves as the root. It also communicates with the MAPs. RAPs are typically located on rooftops or towers.
Mesh access point (MAP)	Remote APs that provide access to wireless clients. They communicate with the RAP to connect to the wired network. MAPs are typically located on top of a pole, such as a lamp post.

Mesh Design Recommendations

The following are Cisco recommendations (and considerations) for mesh design:

- There is a < 10ms latency per hop. Typically 2 ms to 3 ms.
- For outdoor deployment, four or fewer hops are recommended for best performance. A maximum of eight hops is supported.
- For indoor deployment, one hop is supported.
- For best performance, 20 MAP nodes per RAP is recommended. Up to 32 MAPs is supported per RAP.
- Throughput: one hop =14 Mbps, two hops = 7 Mbps, three hops = 3 Mbps, four hops = 1 Mbps.

Campus Design Considerations

When designing for the Cisco Unified Wireless Network, you need to be able to determine how many LAPs to place and how they will be managed with the WLCs. Table 5-12 summarizes campus design considerations.

Table 5-12   WLAN Design Considerations

Design Item	Description
Number of APs	The design should have enough APs to provide full RF coverage for wireless clients for all the expected locations in the enterprise. Cisco recommends 20 data devices per AP and seven G.711 concurrent or eight G.729 concurrent VoWLAN calls.
Placement of APs	APs are placed in a centralized location of the expected area for which they are to provide access. APs are placed in conference rooms to accommodate peak requirements.

Design Item	Description
Power for APs	Traditional wall power can be used, but the preferred solution is to use Power over Ethernet (PoE) to power APs and provide wired access. Monitor the power budget of the LAN switch.
Number of WLCs	The number of WLCs depends on the selected redundancy model based on the client's requirements. The number of controllers is also dependent on the number of required APs and the number of APs supported by the differing WLC models.
Placement of WLCs	WLCs are placed in secured wiring closets or in the data center. Deterministic redundancy is recommended, and intercontroller roaming should be minimized. WLCs can be placed in a central location or distributed in the campus distribution layer. WLCs can also be placed in the cloud, where only management traffic is routed to the cloud (user traffic remains on the local network).*

* Cloud controllers are via the Cisco Meraki solution, where Cisco Meraki APs establish SSL connections to the cloud controllers to register.

Power over Ethernet (PoE)

The use of PoE is an important aspect to the design of a campus network. PoE plays a role in powering IP phones and wireless APs. There are two PoE standards:

- **IEEE 802.3af:** Standard that provides 15.4 watts per port.
- **IEEE 802.3at:** Newer standard for higher power requirements. Provides 30 watts.

Newer wireless standards, such as 802.11ac, provide high bandwidth but with the requirement of higher power requirements. The 802.3at standard provides 30 watts of power using two pairs of Category 5e (or better) UTP cable.

Ensure that the switch can provide enough power for all its ports. For example, if a 48-port switch needs to provide 15.4 watts for each port, it will need to provide a total 740 watts of power.

Wireless and Quality of Service (QoS)

Wireless networks operate differently from wired networks because they are multiple access broadcast networks. Whereas IEEE 802.1p is used for Layer 2 QoS in wired networks, IEEE 802.1e defines mechanisms for implementing Layer 2 QoS in wireless LANs. A translation between IP DSCP, 802.3e, and 802.3p values needs to occur. Table 5-13 describes Cisco's recommendations where four Wi-Fi Multimedia (WMM) categories are used:

- **AC_VO:** Access category for voice
- **AC_VI:** Access category for video
- **AC_BE:** Access category for best effort
- **AC_BK:** Access category for background traffic

Table 5-13   Wireless 802.1e QoS Markings

Traffic Type	IP DSCP	802.1p	802.1e	Controller Profile
Network control	—	7	—	Reserved for network control
Inter-network control	48	6	7 (AC_VO)	CAPWAP control
Voice	46 (EF)	5	6 (AC_VO)	Platinum profile
Video	34 (AF41)	4	5 (AC_VI)	Gold profile
Voice control	26 (AF31)	3	4 (AC_VI)	—
Best effort	0 (BE)	0	3 (AC_BE) 0 (AC_BE)	Silver profile (normal)
Background Gold	18 (AF21)	2	2 (AC_BK)	—
Background Silver	10 AF11)	1	1 (AC_BK)	Bronze profile

For traffic traveling from the client to the WLC and the wired network, CoS/QoS works as follows:

1. The 802.11e CoS marking on the frame arriving at the AP is translated to a DSCP value on the outside of the CAPWAP tunnel.

2. The CAPWAP packet is decapsulated at the WLC, and the original DSCP value of the IP packet is used for translation to the wired CoS value.

3. The DSCP marking on the packet leaving the WLC on its way to the wired network will, by default, have the DSCP setting equal to the packet that left the WLAN client.

For traffic from the wired network to the wireless client, CoS/QoS works as follows:

1. The 802.1p markings are read at the WLC's wired interface.

2. The WLC reads the DSCP value and copies it to the DSCP value of the CAPWAP header.

3. The AP translates the DSCP value of the CAPWAP packet into the 802.11e value of the outgoing wireless Ethernet frame.

Table 5-14 compares the indoor AP features for Cisco APs.

Table 5-14   Supported Features and Specifications for Cisco APs

Feature	1700 Series	1830 Series	1850 Series	2700 Series	3700 Series
Ideal for	Small and midsize enterprises	Small and midsize enterprises	Small and midsize enterprises	Midsize or large enterprises that require advanced features	Midsize or large enterprises that require advanced features
Power requirement	802.3af, 802.3at PoE+, Enhanced PoE	802.3af, 802.3at PoE+, Enhanced PoE	802.3at PoE+, Enhanced PoE	802.3at PoE+, Enhanced PoE	4 × 4:3 operation: 802.3at PoE+, Enhanced PoE, Universal PoE (UPOE) 3 × 3:3 operation: 802.3af PoE
Installation	For carpeted offices	For carpeted offices	For carpeted offices	Rugged	Rugged
Antennas	1700i: Internal	Internal	1850i: Internal 1850e: External	2700i: Internal 2700e: External	3700i: Internal 3700e: External
Wi-Fi standards	a/b/g/n/ac	a/b/g/n/ac (Wave 2)	a/b/g/n/ac (Wave 2)	a/b/g/n/ac	a/b/g/n/ac
Number of radios	Dual (2.4 GHz and 5.0 GHz)	Dual (2.4 GHz and 5.0 GHz)	Dual (2.4 GHz and 5.0 GHz)	Dual (2.4 GHz and 5.0 GHz)	Dual (2.4 GHz and 5.0 GHz)
Max data rate 5 GHz	867 Mbps	867 Mbps	1.7 Gbps	1.3 Gbps	1.3 Gbps

Branch Design Considerations

For branch networks, you need to consider the number and placement of APs, which depends on the location and expected number of wireless clients at the branch office. It may not be cost-justifiable to place a WLC at each branch office of an enterprise. One requirement is that the round-trip time (RTT) between the AP and the WLC should not exceed 300 ms. For centralized controllers, it is recommended that you use REAP or Hybrid REAP (H-REAP).

Local MAC

CAPWAP supports local media access control (local MAC), which can be used in branch deployments. Unlike with split-MAC, the AP provides MAC management support for association requests and actions. Local MAC terminates client traffic at the wired port of the AP versus at the WLC. This allows direct local access to branch resources without requiring the data to travel to the WLC at the main office. Local MAC also allows the wireless client to function even if a WAN link failure occurs.

REAP

REAP is designed to support remote offices by extending LWAPP control timers. With REAP control, traffic is still encapsulated over an LWAPP tunnel and is sent to the WLC. Management control and RF management are done over the WAN. Client data is locally bridged. With REAP, local clients still have local connectivity if the WAN fails.

WLCs support the same number of REAP devices as APs. REAP devices support only Layer 2 security policies, do not support Network Address Translation (NAT), and require a routable IP address.

Hybrid REAP

H-REAP is an enhancement to REAP that provides additional capabilities such as NAT, more security options, and the ability to control up to three APs remotely. It is the preferred solution for remote or small office APs to connect to the wireless controllers over the WAN.

H-REAP operates in two security modes:

- **Standalone mode:** H-REAP does the client authentication itself when the WLC cannot be reached. In standalone mode, H-REAP supports WPA-PSK and WPA2-PSK for client authentication.
- **Connected mode:** The device uses the WLC for client authentication. In connected mode, H-REAP supports WPA-PSK, WPA2-PSK, VPNs, L2TP, EAP, and web authentication for client authentication.

H-REAP is delay sensitive. The RTT must not exceed 300 ms between the AP and the WLC. And, CAPWAP must be prioritized over other traffic.

Branch Office Controller Options

For branch offices, Cisco recommends one of four options:

- **CTVM virtual controller:** Supports up to 200 LAPs.
- **WLC module in Integrated Services Router (ISR):** The ISR-G2-UCS-E supports up to 200 LAPs.
- **3650 WLAN controller:** Supports 50 LAPs.
- **Cisco 2500 series controllers:** Supports up to 75 LAPs

The following points summarize WLAN design:

■ An RF site survey is used to determine a wireless network's RF characteristics and AP placement.

■ Guest services are easily supported using EoIP tunnels in the Cisco Unified Wireless Network.

■ Outdoor wireless networks are supported using outdoor APs and Cisco wireless mesh networking APs.

■ Campus wireless network design provides RF coverage for wireless clients in the campus using LAPs. The LAPs are managed by WLCs.

■ Branch wireless network design provides RF coverage for wireless clients in the branch. Central management of REAP or H-REAP APs can be supported.

■ Each AP should be limited to 30 data devices per WLAN SSID.

■ For voice over wireless design, it is recommended that a separate SSID be used for voice and that each AP support roughly seven (G.711) to eight (G.729) voice calls over VoWLAN. This is because all devices share bandwidth.

Table 5-15 provides a quick summary of the UDP ports used by wireless protocols.

Table 5-15   UDP Ports Used by WLAN Protocols

WLAN Protocol	UDP Port
LWAPP control	UDP 12223
LWAPP data	UDP 12222
WLC exchange messages (unencrypted)	UDP 16666
WLC exchange messages (encrypted)	UDP 16667
RF group IEEE 802.11b/g/n	UDP 12114
RF group IEEE 802.11a	UDP 12115
CAPWAP control	UDP 5246
CAPWAP data	UDP 5247

References and Recommended Readings

Cisco Outdoor Wireless Network Solution, http://www.cisco.com/c/en/us/products/wireless/outdoor-wireless/index.html.

Cisco Unified Wireless Network, http://www.cisco.com/c/en/us/products/wireless/index.html.

Cisco Wireless Control System, http://www.cisco.com/c/en/us/products/wireless/wireless-control-system/index.html.

Cisco Compare Wireless LAN Controllers, http://www.cisco.com/c/en/us/products/wireless/buyers-guide.html#~controllers.

802.11ac: The Fifth Generation of Wi-Fi Technical White Paper, http://www.cisco.com/c/en/us/products/collateral/wireless/aironet-3600-series/white_paper_c11-713103.html?cachemode=refresh.

QoS on Wireless LAN Controllers and Lightweight APs Configuration Example, http://www.cisco.com/c/en/us/support/docs/wireless-mobility/wireless-lan-wlan/81831-qos-wlc-lap.html.

Cisco 802.11ac Wave 2 FAQ, http://www.cisco.com/c/en/us/solutions/collateral/enterprise-networks/802-11ac-solution/q-and-a-c67-734152.html.

802.11 WLAN Roaming and Fast-Secure Roaming on CUWN, http://www.cisco.com/c/en/us/support/docs/wireless-mobility/wireless-lan-wlan/116493-technote-technology-00.html#anc8.

Enterprise Mobility 8.1 Design Guide, http://www.cisco.com/c/en/us/td/docs/wireless/controller/8-1/Enterprise-Mobility-8-1-Design-Guide/Enterprise_Mobility_8-1_Deployment_Guide.html.

IEEE Std 802.11g-2003. Amendment to IEEE Std 802.11, 1999 Edition.

Lightweight Access Point FAQ, http://www.cisco.com/c/en/us/support/docs/wireless/aironet-1200-series/70278-lap-faq.html.

Light Weight Access Point Protocol (LWAPP), draft-ohara-capwap-lwapp-02, http://tools.ietf.org/html/draft-ohara-capwap-lwapp-02.

RFC 5415: Control and Provisioning of Wireless Access Points (CAPWAP) Protocol Specification, http://tools.ietf.org/search/rfc5415.

RFC 5416: Control and Provisioning of Wireless Access Points (CAPWAP) Protocol Binding for IEEE 802.11, http://tools.ietf.org/search/rfc54156.

Cisco Wireless LAN Controller FAQ, http://www.cisco.com/c/en/us/support/docs/wireless/4400-series-wireless-lan-controllers/69561-wlc-faq.html.

Cisco Wireless LAN Controller Best Practices, http://www.cisco.com/c/en/us/support/docs/wireless-mobility/wireless-lan-wlan/82463-wlc-config-best-practice.html.

"Wireless LAN MAC and Physical Layer (PHY) Specifications," IEEE 802.11-1999. Piscataway, New Jersey: Institute of Electrical and Electronics Engineers, 1999.

Exam Preparation Tasks

Review All Key Topics

Review the most important topics in the chapter, noted with the Key Topic icon in the outer margin of the page. Table 5-16 lists a reference of these key topics and the page numbers on which each is found.

Table 5-16   Key Topics

Key Topic Element	Description	Page
Summary	WLAN standards campus media	169
Table	WLAN Standards Summary	171
Summary	Cisco Unified Wireless Network Architecture	175
Table	Cisco UWN Architecture	176
Summary	CAPWAP	178
List	Access point modes	180
Table	Access Point Modes	181
List	WLAN controller components	183
List	WLC interface types	184
Summary	Roaming and mobility groups	186
Summary	Controller redundancy design	190
Summary	Radio frequency groups	193
Summary	Wireless mesh for outdoor wireless	195

Complete Tables and Lists from Memory

Print a copy of Appendix D, "Memory Tables" (found on the book website), or at least the section for this chapter, and complete the tables and lists from memory. Appendix E, "Memory Tables Answer Key," also on the website, includes completed tables and lists to check your work.

Define Key Terms

Define the following key terms from this chapter, and check your answers in the glossary:

AP, CAPWAP, CSMA/CA, DSSS, FHSS, H-REAP, IEEE 802.1x, LAG, , MIMO, MAP, N+1 redundancy, N+N redundancy, N+N+1 redundancy, RF groups, RRM, RAP, SSID, split-MAC, WLAN, WLC

Q&A

The answers to these questions appear in Appendix A. For more practice with exam format questions, use the exam engine on the book website.

1. What is the maximum data rate of IEEE 802.11ac Wave 1?

2. What is the typical data rate of IEEE 802.11n?

3. What are some difficulties with having to manage hundreds of standalone APs?

4. What standard does IEEE 802.11i use for confidentiality, integrity, and authentication?

5. List at least four benefits of Cisco UWN.

6. True or false: With split-MAC, the control and data frames are load-balanced between the LAP and the WLC.

7. True or false: With split-MAC, the WLC, not the LAP, is responsible for authentication and key management.

8. What CAPWAP transport mode is the preferred and most scalable?

    a. Intra

    b. Layer 2

    c. Layer 3

    d. EoIP

9. What is the preferred intercontroller roaming option?

    a. Intra

    b. Layer 2

    c. Layer 3

    d. EoIP

10. What device places user traffic on the appropriate VLAN?

    a. LAP

    b. WLAN controller

    c. MAP

    d. RAP

11. How many access points are supported in a mobility group using Cisco series WLCs?

    a. 144

    b. 1200

    c. 2400

    d. 7200

12. What is the recommended number of data devices an AP can support for best performance?

   a. About 6

   b. 7 to 8

   c. 10 to 15

   d. About 20

13. What is the recommended number of VoWLAN devices an AP can support for best performance?

   a. 2 to 3

   b. 7 to 8

   c. 10 to 15

   d. About 20

14. What method is used to manage radio frequency channels and power configuration?

   a. WLC

   b. WCS

   c. RRM

   d. MAP

15. What is the typical latency per wireless mesh hop in milliseconds?

   a. 1 to 3

   b. 7 to 8

   c. 10 to 15

   d. About 20

16. What is the recommended maximum RTT between an AP and the WLC?

   a. 20 ms

   b. 50 ms

   c. 100 ms

   d. 300 ms

17. What is the recommended controller redundancy technique?

   a. N+1+N

   b. Static

   c. Dynamic

   d. Deterministic

18. What is the recommended best practice for guest services?

   a. Use separate VLANs.

   b. Use separate routers and access lists.

   c. Obtain a DSL connection and bridge to the local LAN.

   d. Use EoIP to isolate traffic to the DMZ.

5

19. What is the recommended best practice for branch WLANs?

   a. Use H-REAP with centralized controllers.

   b. Use local-MAP.

   c. Use wireless mesh design.

   d. Use EoIP.

20. What are two recommended best practices for WLC design?

   a. Maximize intercontroller roaming.

   b. Minimize intercontroller roaming.

   c. Use distributed controller placement.

   d. Use centralized controller placement.

21. How many APs does the Cisco 6500 WLC module support?

   a. 6

   b. 50

   c. 100

   d. 300

22. Match each access point mode with its description:

      i.   Local

      ii.   REAP

      iii.   Monitor

      iv.   Rogue detector

      v.   Sniffer

      vi.   Bridge

   a. For location-based services

   b. Captures packets

   c. For point-to-point connections

   d. Default mode

   e. Management across the WAN

   f. Monitors rogue APs

23. Match each WLC interface type with its description.

      i.   Management

      ii.   Service port

      iii.   AP manager

      iv.   Dynamic

      v.   Virtual

   a. Authentication and mobility

   b. Analogous to user VLANs

    c. Discovery and association

    d. Out-of-band management

    e. In-band management

24. Match each roaming technique with its client database entry change.

    i.   Intracluster roaming

    ii.   Layer 2 intercluster roaming

    iii. Layer 3 intercluster roaming

    a. The client entry is moved to a new WLC.

    b. The client entry is updated on the same WLC.

    c. The client entry is copied to a new WLC.

25. Match each UDP port with its protocol.

    i.   LWAPP data

    ii.   RF group 802.11b/g

    iii. WLC encrypted exchange

    iv. LWAPP control

    v.   WLC unencrypted exchange

    vi. CAPWAP control

    vii. CAPWAP data

    a. UDP 12114

    b. UDP 12222

    c. UDP 5246

    d. UDP 5247

    e. UDP 12223

    f. UDP 16666

    g. UDP 16667

26. Match each wireless mesh component with its description.

    i.   WCS

    ii.   WLC

    iii. RAP

    iv. MAP

    a. Root of the mesh network

    b. Remote APs

    c. Networkwide configuration and management

    d. Links APs to the wired network

27. How many MAP nodes are recommended per rooftop AP?

    a. 6

    b. 20

    c. 500

    d. 100

28. Which of the following shows the correct order of the steps in an RF site survey?

    a. Define requirements, document findings, perform the survey, determine preliminary AP locations, identify coverage areas.

    b. Define requirements, perform the survey, determine preliminary AP locations, identify coverage areas, document findings.

    c. Identify coverage areas, define requirements, determine preliminary AP locations, perform the survey, document findings.

    d. Define requirements, identify coverage areas, determine preliminary AP locations, perform the survey, document findings.

29. What technique performs dynamic channel assignment, power control, and interference detection and avoidance?

    a. CAPWAP

    b. RRM

    c. Mobility

    d. LEAP

30. What are the three nonoverlapping channels of IEEE 802.11b/g/n?

    a. Channels A, D, and G

    b. Channels 1, 6, and 11

    c. Channels 3, 8, and 11

    d. Channels A, E, and G

31. Which of the following statements is true?

    a. IEEE 802.11g is backward compatible with 802.11b; 802.11a is not compatible with 802.11b.

    b. IEEE 802.11a is backward compatible with 802.11b; 802.11g is not compatible with 802.11b.

    c. IEEE 802.11b is backward compatible with 802.11a; 802.11g is not compatible with 802.11b.

    d. IEEE 802.11n is backward compatible with 802.11a and 802.11g.

32. What is necessary when you use H-LEAP for authentication?

    a. WLC

    b. WCS

    c. RADIUS server

    d. LAP

33. A LAP is added to a network. What sequence accurately reflects the process it will use to associate with the WLAN controller?

   a. First master, secondary, tertiary, greatest AP capacity

   b. Primary, secondary, tertiary, greatest AP capacity, master

   c. Primary, secondary, tertiary, master, greatest AP capacity

   d. Greatest AP capacity, primary, secondary, master

34. A LAP is added to a network that is in a separate IP subnet from the WLAN controller. OTAP has not been enabled. Which two methods can be used by the LAP to find the WLAN controller?

   a. DHCP

   b. Primary, secondary, tertiary, greatest AP capacity, master

   c. Primary, secondary, tertiary, master, greatest AP capacity

   d. Greatest AP capacity, primary, secondary, master

   e. DNS

   f. Local subnet broadcast

35. Which statement is true regarding wireless QoS?

   a. When the WLC receives a packet from the wired network, it copies the 802.1e value to the DSCP value of the CAPWAP header.

   b. When the WLC receives a packet from the wired network, it copies the DSCP value to the DSCP value of the CAPWAP header.

   c. When the WLC receives a packet from the wired network, it copies the 802.1e value to the 802.1p value of the CAPWAP header.

   d. When the WLC receives a packet from the wireless network, it copies the 802.1e value to the DSCP value of the CAPWAP header.

36. Which two of the following statements represent a preferred split-MAC LWAPP implementation? (Select two.)

   a. IEEE 802.1Q trunking extends from the wired infrastructure to a WLAN controller. Then the 802.1Q packet is encapsulated in CAPWAP or LWAPP and sent to the access point for transmission over the SSID.

   b. Each wireless client authentication type maps to a unique SSID, which in turn maps to a common shared VLAN.

   c. 802.1Q trunking extends from the wired infrastructure to the access point for translation into SSIDs.

   d. Each wireless client authentication type maps to a unique SSID, which in turn maps to a unique VLAN.

   e. 802.1Q trunking extends from the wired infrastructure to a WLAN controller for translation into SSIDs.

5

37. Which two of the following are required for Cisco wireless client mobility deployment?

   a. Matching security

   b. Matching mobility group name

   c. Matching RF channel

   d. Matching RF group name

   e. Matching RF power

   f. Assigned master controller

38. Which of the following describe best practices for Cisco outdoor wireless mesh networks? (Select three.)

   a. RAP implemented with 20 or fewer MAP nodes

   b. RAP implemented with 20 to 32 MAP nodes

   c. Mesh hop counts of four or fewer

   d. Mesh hop counts of eight to four

   e. Client access via 802.11b/g and backhaul with 802.11a

   f. Client access via 802.11a and backhaul with 802.11b/g

39. Which of the following describe best practices for Cisco WLAN guest access? (Select two.)

   a. Guest tunnels have limitations on which wireless controllers can originate the tunnel.

   b. Guest tunnels have limitations on which wireless controllers can terminate the tunnel.

   c. Dedicated guest VLANs are only extended to the wireless controllers in the network to ensure path isolation.

   d. Dedicated guest VLANs are extended throughout the network to the access points for path isolation.

   e. Dedicated guest access in the DMZ extends from the origination to the termination controllers without dedicated guest VLANs.

   f. Guest tunnels can originate and terminate on any wireless controller platform.

40. How are WLANs identified?

   a. MAC addresses

   b. IP subnet

   c. SSID

   d. WEP key

   e. LAN ports

   f. Secure encryption key

41. Which description is correct regarding wireless solutions that provide higher bandwidth than point-to-multipoint (p2mp) wireless?

   a. P2p links tend to be slower than p2mp.

   b. P2mp wireless connections can provide up to 1.544 Mbps of raw bandwidth.

   c. P2p wireless connections can provide up to 44 Mbps of raw bandwidth.

   d. P2mp links tend to be faster than p2mp.

42. Which WLAN attributes should be considered during a site survey? (Select two.)

   a. Channels

   b. Power

   c. SSID

   d. Network name

   e. Authentication

   f. Encryption

43. Which WLC interfaces are mandatory? (Select all that apply.)

   a. Management

   b. AP manager

   c. Dynamic

   d. Virtual

   e. Service port

   f. Extended

44. Which are differences between CAPWAP and LWAPP? (Select three.)

   a. CAPWAP uses the newer AES. LWAPP uses DTLS.

   b. CAPWAP uses DTLS. LWAPP uses AES.

   c. CAPWAP control uses UDP 5246. LWAPP control uses UDP 12223.

   d. CAPWAP control uses UDP 12223. LWAPP control uses UDP 5246.

   e. CAPWAP is preferred.

   f. LWAPP is preferred.

45. Which two of the following are functions of an access point in a split MAC architecture? (Choose two.)

   a. 802.1Q encapsulation

   b. EAP authentication

   c. MAC layer encryption/decryption

   d. Process probe response

46. Which WLC redundancy design allows for grouping of APs to minimize intercontroller roaming events?

   a. N

   b. N+1

   c. N+N

   d. N+N+1

47. Which AP mode excludes the AP from handling data traffic between clients and the infrastructure, allowing it to perform LBS functions?

   a. Local mode

   b. Monitor mode

   c. Rogue Detector mode

   d. Sniffer mode

48. Which AP mode allows the AP to receive a list MAC addresses from the LAN switch and then forwards that list and a list of MAC addresses listened over the air to the WLC?

   a. Local mode

   b. Monitor mode

   c. Rogue Detector mode

   d. Sniffer mode

49. Which AP mode is the default mode of operation?

   a. Local mode

   b. Monitor mode

   c. Rogue Detector mode

   d. Sniffer mode

50. A switch needs to provide 802.3af power to each of its 48 ports. How much power needs to be supplied?

   a. 100 watts

   b. 320 watts

   c. 740 watts

   d. 1440 watts

This chapter covers the following subjects:

WAN and Enterprise Edge Overview

WAN Transport Technologies

WAN and Edge Design Methodologies

DMZ Connectivity

Internet Connectivity

VPN Network Design

This chapter reviews wide area network technologies. Expect plenty of questions about the selection and use of WAN technologies and the enterprise edge. The CCDA must understand the various WAN technology options and what makes them different from each other. This chapter also covers WAN design methodologies and how quality of service (QoS) techniques can make better use of the available bandwidth. Finally, this chapter looks at the DMZ, Internet, and VPN network design in the enterprise edge.

CHAPTER 6

WAN Technologies and the Enterprise Edge

"Do I Know This Already?" Quiz

The "Do I Know This Already?" quiz helps you identify your strengths and deficiencies in this chapter's topics.

The ten-question quiz, derived from the major sections in the "Foundation Topics" portion of the chapter, helps you determine how to spend your limited study time.

Table 6-1 outlines the major topics discussed in this chapter and the "Do I Know This Already?" quiz questions that correspond to those topics.

Table 6-1 "Do I Know This Already?" Foundation Topics Section-to-Question Mapping

Foundation Topics Section	Questions Covered in This Section
WAN and Enterprise Edge Overview	1
WAN Transport Technologies	2–4
WAN and Edge Design Methodologies	5–6
DMZ Connectivity	7
Internet Connectivity	8
VPN Network Design	9–10

1. What are two modules or blocks used in the enterprise edge?

    a. Internet and campus core

    b. Core and building access

    c. Internet and DMZ

    d. WAN and building distribution

2. What MAN/WAN technology has bandwidth available from 100 Mbps to 10 Gbps?

    a. DSL

    b. Metro Ethernet

    c. TDM

    d. Frame Relay

3. How much bandwidth does a T1 circuit provide?

    a. 155 Mbps

    b. 64 kbps

    c. 15 Mbps

    d. 1.544 Mbps

4. What methodology is used when designing the enterprise edge?

    a. Cisco-powered network

    b. ISL

    c. PBM

    d. IEEE

5. What technology delivers IP services using labels to forward packets from the source to the destination?

    a. ADSL

    b. Cable

    c. Frame Relay

    d. MPLS

6. Which of the following adds strict PQ to modular class-based QoS?

    a. LLQ

    b. FIFO

    c. CBWFQ

    d. WFQ

7. Which of the following VPNs provides an alternative to MPLS WAN services?

    a. GRE VPN

    b. Extranet VPN

    c. Remote access VPN

    d. Site-to-site VPN

8. What Internet connectivity option provides the highest level of resiliency for services?

    a. Single-router dual-homed

    b. Single-router single-homed

    c. Shared DMZ

    d. Dual-router dual-homed

9. What VPN application gives mobile users connectivity to corporate services over the Internet?

    a. Remote access VPN

    b. Site-to-site VPN

    c. MPLS VPN

    d. Extranet VPN

10. What VPNs are better suited for routing protocols such as OSPF and EIGRP?

    a. Site-to-site VPN with IPsec over GRE

    b. Remote access VPN

    c. Site-to-site VPN

    d. IPsec VPN

6

Foundation Topics

This chapter describes the WAN topics you need to master for the CCDA exam. These topics include the WAN modules included in the enterprise edge, WAN technologies, WAN technology selection considerations, and WAN design methodologies. In addition, this chapter describes quality of service (QoS) and how it can be used to prioritize network traffic and better utilize the available WAN bandwidth.

WAN and Enterprise Edge Overview

WANs provide network connectivity for the enterprise core and the remote branch locations. The enterprise edge, on the other hand, securely connects the enterprise core to the Internet in order to provide DMZ-type services such as VPN connectivity and other cloud-related services. Many WAN and Internet transport options are available, and new ones are continually emerging. When you are selecting WAN transport technologies, it is important to consider factors such as cost, bandwidth, reliability, and manageability, in addition to the hardware and software capabilities of the equipment. Moreover, enterprise branch offices can take advantage of a shared network such as MPLS WAN or use the Internet as a transport for secure VPN connectivity back to the headquarters or main office, which many are using today as a backup to their high-cost WAN circuits.

WAN Defined

Wide area networks (WAN) are communications networks used to connect geographically disperse network locations. Generally, WAN services are offered by service providers or telecommunication carriers. WANs can transport data, voice, and video traffic. Service providers charge fees, called tariffs, for providing WAN services or communications to their customers. Sometimes the term service is referred to as the WAN communications provided by the carrier.

When designing a WAN, you should become familiar with the design's requirements, which typically derive from these two important goals:

- **Service level agreement (SLA):** Defines the availability of the network. Networked applications rely on the underlying network between the client and server to provide its functions. There are multiple levels of application availability that can be part of a negotiated SLA with a service provider. Organizations have to work with the carrier to define what level of service, such as bandwidth, allowed latency, and loss, is acceptable to the organization.

- **Cost and usage:** To select the correct reliable WAN service, you must consider the budget and usage requirements of the WAN service.

There are three key objectives of an effective WAN design:

- The WAN needs to support the goals and policies of the organization.

- The WAN technologies selected need to meet the current application requirements and provide for growth of the organization in the future.

- The proposed design should incorporate security throughout and ensure high availability where applicable while staying within budget.

Figure 6-1 shows a typical enterprise with Multiprotocol Label Switching (MPLS) WAN and Internet connections.

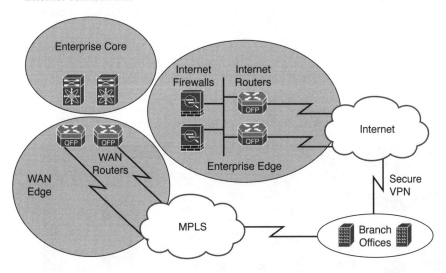

Figure 6-1 *WAN and enterprise edge*

WAN Edge Module

Enterprises can have multiple WAN interconnections. WAN connectivity between an organization's headquarters and the remote sites is generally across a service provider network, such as with an MPLS WAN. Alternative options for connecting branch offices involve using broadband technologies, coupled with IPsec VPNs over the Internet, such as DMVPN.

WAN technologies can be point-to-point (P2P) or multipoint, such as Frame Relay or MPLS WAN services. Most WAN service providers offer MPLS WAN solutions where the enterprise edge router interacts with service providers at Layer 3. Public WAN connections over the Internet are available, ranging from broadband technologies all the way up to multigigabit connectivity options. Typically, these services do not provide any guarantee of network availability, so they are considered a "best effort" service. Frame Relay and MPLS network solutions usually have a much higher degree of reliability and availability.

Note   When you are seeking a WAN service, the options can vary depending on the service provider's offerings, so it is recommended to review options from multiple WAN service providers.

Enterprise Edge Modules

The enterprise edge modules include the demilitarized zone (DMZ) and SP edge. Internet service providers (ISPs) offer many connectivity options for the SP edge and DMZ modules in the Enterprise Edge:

- **Demilitarized zone (DMZ):** DMZ zones are used to further divide network applications and are deployed with firewall policy protections. Common DMZs include Internet DMZs for e-commerce applications, remote access VPNs for corporate users, and site-to-site VPNs for connections to remote sites.

- **Service provider edge (SP):** The SP edge is used to connect to Internet service providers and provide reliable Internet connectivity. Internet service typically needs high availability and is frequently deployed with multiple ISP connections as well as redundant routers and switches for aggregating the multiple network connections.

Figure 6-2 illustrates the use of modules, or blocks, in the enterprise.

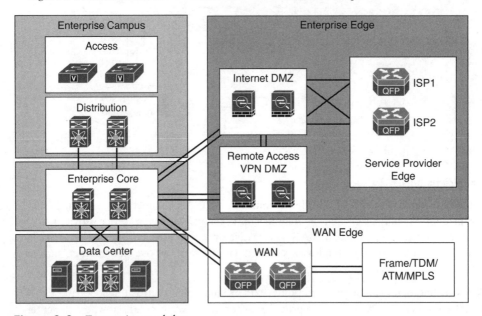

Figure 6-2 *Enterprise modules*

WAN Transport Technologies

Several factors should be considered when selecting a WAN transport technology. Some WAN options are public Internet based, and some are private WAN based. Geography also plays a key role in what WAN technologies are available in a given area. Major cities have the most WAN transport options, and rural areas are more limited as to the availability of WAN service options.

Table 6-2 examines some WAN technologies and highlights some common factors used to make WAN technology selections. This information also reflects the different characteristics of each WAN technology. However, keep in mind that your service provider offerings limit the WAN technology choices available to you during your selection.

Table 6-2   WAN Comparison

WAN Technology	Bandwidth	Reliability	Latency	Cost
ISDN	Low	Medium	Medium	Low
DSL	Low/Medium	Low	Medium	Low
Cable	Low/Medium	Low	Medium	Low
Wireless	Low/Medium	Low	Medium	Medium
Frame Relay	Low/Medium	Medium	Low	Medium
TDM	Medium	High	Low	Medium
Metro Ethernet	Medium/High	High	Low	Medium
SONET/SDH	High	High	Low	High
MPLS	High	High	Low	High
Dark fiber	High	High	Low	High
DWDM	High	High	Low	High

The following sections offer more details about each WAN technology covered in Table 6-2.

ISDN

Integrated Services Digital Network (ISDN) is an all-digital phone line connection that was standardized in the early 1980s. ISDN allows both voice and data to be transmitted over the digital phone line instead of the analog signals used in dialup connections. ISDN provides greater bandwidth and lower latency compared to dialup analog technology. ISDN comes in two service types: Basic Rate Interface (BRI) and Primary Rate Interface (PRI).

ISDN BRI Service

ISDN BRI consists of two B channels and one D channel (2B+D). Both of the BRI B channels operate at 64 Kbps and carry user data. The D channel handles the signaling and control information and operates at 16 Kbps. Another 48 Kbps is used for framing and synchronization, for a total bit rate of 192 Kbps.

ISDN PRI Service

ISDN PRI service offers 23 B channels and 1 D channel (23B+D) in both North America and Japan. Each channel (including the D channel) operates at 64 Kbps, for a total bit rate of 1.544 Mbps, including overhead. In other parts of the world, such as Europe and Australia, the ISDN PRI service provides 30 B channels and 1 64Kbps D channel.

Note   Although ISDN has been around for many years, the industry has moved toward using broadband technologies such as cable, DSL, and public wireless with IPsec VPNs for WAN services. However, ISDN PRI still remains as an effective UC solution used for terminating voice circuits on voice gateway routers.

Digital Subscriber Line

Digital subscriber line (DSL) is a technology that provides high-speed Internet data services over ordinary copper telephone lines. It achieves this by using frequencies that are not used in normal voice telephone calls.

The term *xDSL* describes the various competing forms of DSL available today.

ADSL is the most popular DSL technology and is widely available. The key to ADSL is that the downstream bandwidth is asymmetric or higher than the upstream bandwidth. Some limitations include that ADSL can be used only in close proximity to the local DSLAM, typically less than 2 km. The local DSLAM, or digital subscriber line access multiplexer, allows telephone lines to make DSL connections to the Internet. Download speeds usually range from 768 Kbps to 9 Mbps, and upload speeds range from 64 Kbps to 1.5 Mbps. The customer premises equipment (CPE) refers to a PC along with a DSL modem or DSL router that connects back to the network access provider (NAP) DSLAMs.

The ADSL circuit consists of a twisted-pair telephone line that contains three information channels:

- Medium-speed downstream channel
- Low-speed upstream channel
- Basic telephone service channel

DSL splitters are used to separate basic telephone service from the ADSL modem/router to provide service even if the ADSL signaling fails.

Although DSL is primarily used in the residential community, this technology can also be used as a WAN technology for an organization. However, keep in mind that because this is a public network connection over the Internet, it is recommended that this technology be used in conjunction with a firewall/VPN solution back into your corporate enterprise network. The high speeds and relatively low cost make this a popular Internet access WAN technology.

Cable

Broadband cable is a technology used to transport data using a coaxial cable medium over cable distribution systems. The equipment used on the remote-access side or customer premises is the cable modem, and it connects to the Cable Modem Termination System (CMTS) on the ISP side. The Universal Broadband Router (uBR) or CMTS provides the CMTS services, which forward traffic upstream through the provider's Internet connections.

Cable modems support data, voice, and video TCP/IP traffic. Generally, cable modems are installed at the customer premises to provide service to small businesses, branch offices, and corporate teleworkers.

The Data Over Cable Service Interface Specifications (DOCSIS) protocol defines the cable procedures that the equipment needs to support.

Figure 6-3 illustrates how a cable modem connects to the CMTS. The PC connects to the TCP/IP network using PPP over Ethernet (PPPoE) or Dynamic Host Configuration Protocol (DHCP).

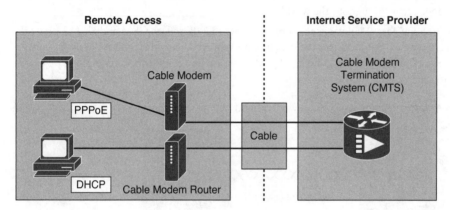

Figure 6-3   *Data over cable*

Wireless

Wireless as a technology uses electromagnetic waves to carry the signal between endpoints. Everyday examples of wireless technology include cell phones, wireless LANs, cordless computer equipment, and global positioning systems (GPS).

Here are some examples of wireless implementations:

- **Bridge wireless:** Wireless bridges connect two separate networks, typically located in two separate buildings. This technology enables high data rates for use with line-of-sight applications. When interconnecting hard-to-wire sites, temporary networks, or warehouses, a series of wireless bridges can be connected to provide connectivity.

- **Wireless LAN:** WLANs have increased, too, in both residential and business environments to meet the demands of LAN connections over the air. Wi-Fi networks are based on IEEE 802.11a/b/g/n standards or the newest 802.11ac Wave 1 standard, providing data rates up to 1.3 Gbps. The growing range of applications includes guest access, voice over wireless, advanced security, and location-based services. A key advantage of WLANs is the ability to save time and money by avoiding costly physical layer wiring installations.

- **Mobile wireless:** Consists of cellular applications and mobile phones. Most wireless technologies, such as the second and third generations, are migrating to more digital services to take advantage of the higher speeds. Mobile wireless technologies include GSM, GPRS, and UMTS:

- **GSM:** Global System for Mobile Communications. A digital mobile radio standard that uses time-division multiplex access (TDMA) technology in three bands (900, 1800, and 1900 MHz). The data transfer rate is 9600 bps and includes the ability to roam internationally.

- **GPRS:** General Packet Radio Service. Extends the capability of GSM speeds from 64 Kbps to 128 Kbps.

- **UMTS:** Universal Mobile Telecommunications Service. Also known as 3G broadband. Provides packet-based transmission of digitized voice, video, and data at rates up to 2.0 Mbps. UMTS also provides a set of services available to mobile users, location-independent throughout the world.

- **LTE:** Long Term Evolution, also known as 4G LTE. Based on GSM and UMTS network technologies, but increases the capacity and speed using a different radio along with network improvements. Download peak rates are up to 300 Mbps and upload peak rates are up to 75 Mbps.

Figure 6-4 shows examples of bridge wireless and wireless LANs.

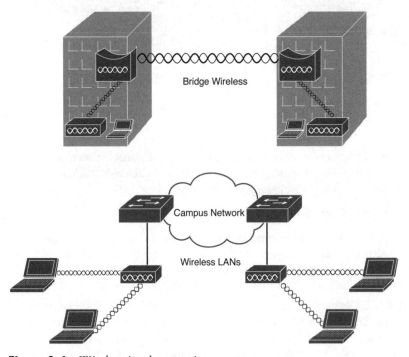

Figure 6-4   *Wireless implementations*

Frame Relay

Frame Relay is a packet-switched connection-oriented Layer 2 WAN protocol. Frame Relay is an industry standard networking protocol that uses virtual circuits between connected devices. The data link layer in Frame Relay establishes connections using a DTE device such as a router and a DCE device such as a frame switch.

Frame Relay circuits between sites can be either permanent virtual circuits (PVCs) or switched virtual circuits (SVCs). PVCs are used more predominantly because of the connections' permanent nature. SVCs, on the other hand, are temporary connections created for each data transfer session.

A point-to-point PVC between two routers or endpoints uses a data-link connection identifier (DLCI) to identify the local end of the PVC. The DLCI is a locally significant numeric value that can be reused throughout the Frame Relay WAN if necessary.

Frame Relay has been deployed since the late 1980s, but the use of Frame Relay is on the decline because of the popularity of MPLS.

Time-Division Multiplexing

Time-division multiplexing (TDM) is a type of digital multiplexing in which multiple channels such as data, voice, and video are combined over one communication medium by interleaving pulses representing bits from different channels. Basic DS0 channel bandwidth is defined at 64 Kbps. In North America, a DS1 or T1 circuit provides 1.544 Mbps of bandwidth consisting of 24 time slots of 64 Kbps each and an 8Kbps channel for control information. In addition, a DS3 or T3 circuit provides 44.736 Mbps of bandwidth. Other parts of the world, such as Europe, follow E1 standards, which allow for 30 channels at 2.048 Mbps of bandwidth. Service providers can guarantee or reserve the bandwidth used on TDM networks. The customers' TDM transmissions are charged for their exclusive access to these circuits. On the other hand, packet-switched networks typically are shared, thereby allowing the service providers more flexibility in managing their networks and the services they offer.

Metro Ethernet

Metro Ethernet uses well-known "Ethernet" to deliver low-cost and high-speed MAN/WAN connectivity for organizations. Many service providers now offer Metro Ethernet solutions to deliver a wide range of converged network services such as data, voice, and video on the same wire. Metro Ethernet provides enterprise LAN type functionality out in the MAN and WAN, increasing the throughput available for applications. Metro Ethernet bandwidths can range from 100 Mbps to 10 Gbps, and even higher in some cases, allowing for support for higher performance and increased QoS requirements. In contrast to the rigid nature of traditional TDM provisioning, metro Ethernet services are much easier to deploy and scale due to the flexible bandwidth increments. Metro Ethernet technology is appealing to many customers because they are already comfortable using Ethernet throughout their LAN environments.

SONET/SDH

The architecture of SONET/SDH is circuit based and delivers high-speed services over an optical network. SONET is defined by the American National Standards Institute (ANSI) specification, and the International Telecommunications Union (ITU) defines SDH. SONET/SDH guarantees bandwidth and has line rates of 155 Mbps to more than 10 Gbps. Common circuit sizes are OC-3, or 155 Mbps, and OC-12, or 622 Mbps.

SONET/SDH uses a ring topology by connecting sites and providing automatic recovery capabilities and has self-healing mechanisms. SONET/SDH rings support ATM or Packet over SONET (POS) IP encapsulations. The Optical Carrier (OC) rates are the digital band-width hierarchies that are part of the SONET/SDH standards. The optical carrier speeds supported are as follows:

- OC-1 = 51.85 Mbps
- OC-3 = 155.52 Mbps
- OC-12 = 622.08 Mbps
- OC-24 = 1.244 Gbps
- OC-48 = 2.488 Gbps
- OC-192 = 9.952 Gbps
- OC-255 = 13.21 Gbps

Figure 6-5 shows an OC-48 SONET ring with connections to three sites that share the ring.

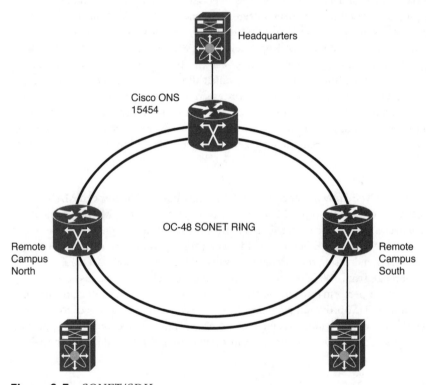

Figure 6-5   *SONET/SDH*

Multiprotocol Label Switching (MPLS)

MPLS is technology for the delivery of IP services using labels (numbers) to forward pack-ets. In normal routed environments, packets are forwarded hop by hop from the sources to the destination. Each router in the path performs a Layer 3 destination address lookup, rewrites the Layer 2 address, and forwards the packet to the destination. However, MPLS functions by marking packet headers that include label information. As soon as packets are marked with a label, specific paths through the network can be designed to correspond to that distinct label. MPLS labels can be set on parameters such as source addresses, Layer 2 circuit ID, or QoS value. Packets that are destined to the same endpoint with the same requirements can be forwarded based on the labels, without a routing decision at every hop. Typically, the labels correspond to the Layer 3 destination address, which makes MPLS the same as destination-based routing.

MPLS labels can also be used to implement traffic engineering by overriding the routing tables. MPLS packets can run over most Layer 2 technologies, such as ATM, Frame Relay, POS, and Ethernet. The goal of MPLS is to maximize switching using labels and minimize Layer 3 routing.

In MPLS implementations, there are customer edge (CE) routers, provider edge (PE) routers, and provider (P) routers. The CE router resides at the customer premises, and that is typically where internal and external routing information is exchanged. The CE router then connects to the PE router, which is the ingress to the MPLS service provider network. After that, the PE routers connect to P routers in the core of the service provider network. To exit the MPLS network, the process is reversed, with the last router being the CE router at the other customer premises.

Figure 6-6 shows the end-to-end MPLS WAN connectivity with CE, PE, and P routers.

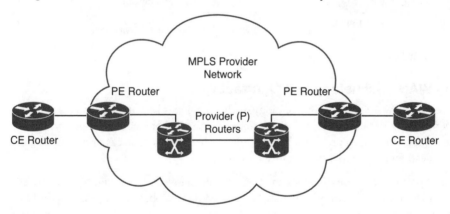

Figure 6-6   *MPLS*

Dark Fiber

Dark fiber is fiber-optic cable that has been installed in the ground or where right-of-way issues are evident. To maintain signal integrity and jitter control over long distances, signal regenerators are used in some implementations. The framing for dark fiber is determined by the enterprise, not the provider. The edge devices can use the fiber just like within the enterprise, which allows for greater control of the services provided by the link. Dark fiber is owned by service providers in most cases and can be purchased similarly to leased-line circuits for use in both the MAN and WAN. The reliability of these types of links also needs to be designed by the enterprise and is not provided by the service provider. High availability using dark fiber needs to be designed with multiple links, which differs from SONET/SDH technology that has redundancy built into the architecture.

Dense Wavelength-Division Multiplexing

Dense wavelength-division multiplexing (DWDM) increases fiber optic's bandwidth capabilities by using different wavelengths of light called *channels* over the same fiber strand. Each fiber channel is the equivalent to several (Nx) 10 Gigabit Ethernet links. It maximizes the use of the installed base of fiber used by service providers and is a critical component of optical networks. DWDM allows for service providers to increase the services offered to customers by adding new bandwidth to existing channels on the same fiber. DWDM lets a variety of devices access the network, including IP routers, ATM switches, and SONET terminals.

Figure 6-7 illustrates the use of DWDM using Cisco Nexus and Cisco ONS devices with a SONET/SDH ring.

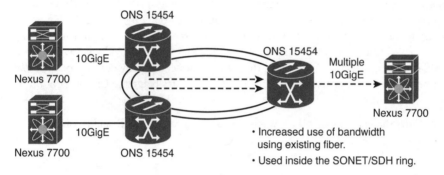

Figure 6-7   *DWDM*

Ordering WAN Technology and Contracts

When you order WAN transport technology, early planning is key. It usually takes at least 60 days for the carrier to provision circuits. Generally, the higher a circuit's capacity, the more lead time required to provision. When ordering bandwidth overseas or between hemispheres, a lead time of 60 to 120 days is fairly common.

WAN transport in most cases includes an access circuit charge and, at times, distance-based charges. However, some carriers have eliminated TDM distance-based charges because T1s are readily available from most carriers. Metro Ethernet availability is spotty at best, and the lead times are long. In rare cases, construction is necessary to provide fiber access, which requires more cost and time delays. You should compare pricing and available WAN technology options from competing carriers.

When ordering Frame Relay and ATM, a combination of access circuit charges, per-PVC charges, and per-bandwidth committed information rate (CIR) charges are customary. CIR is the rate the provider guarantees it will provide. Some carriers set the CIR to half the circuit's speed, thereby allowing customers to burst two times above the CIR. Frame Relay speeds can be provisioned up to T3 speeds, but typically they are less than 10 Mbps.

MPLS VPNs have been competitive with ATM and Frame Relay rates. Service providers are offering MPLS VPNs with higher bandwidth at lower rates to persuade their customers away from traditional ATM and Frame Relay services. However, other service providers see more value in MPLS VPNs and price them higher than ATM and Frame Relay because of the added benefits of traffic engineering. Some carriers will also charge more additional CoS queues, so it is important to design the proper amount of CoS queues, factoring in room for growth.

When you are selecting a standard carrier package, it takes about a month to contract a WAN circuit. If you want to negotiate a detailed SLA, expect to take another five months or more, including discussions with the service provider's legal department. The bigger the customer, the more influence it has over the SLAs and the contract negotiations.

Contract periods for most WAN services are one to five years. Contracts are usually not written for longer durations because of the new emerging technologies and better offerings from providers. An exception is dark fiber, which is usually contracted for a 20-year term. In this case, you also want to have the right of non-reversion written in the SLA. This means that no matter what happens to the service provider, the fiber is yours for the 20-year period. The process to repair fiber cuts needs to be defined in the SLA.

Tariffed commercial WAN services are available at published rates but are subject to restrictions. However, carriers are moving toward unpublished rates to be more competitive and to offer more options.

WAN and Edge Design Methodologies

The Plan, Build, and Manage methodology should be used when designing enterprise edge networks. Some keys to PBM are the processes of identifying business and technology strategies, assessing the existing network, and creating a design that is scalable, flexible, and resilient:

- **Identifying the network requirements** includes reviewing the types of applications, the traffic volume, and the traffic patterns in the network.
- **Assessing the existing network** reviews the technologies used and the locations of hosts, servers, network equipment, and other end nodes.
- **Designing the topology** is based on the availability of technology as well as the projected traffic patterns, technology performance, constraints, and reliability.

When designing the WAN topology, remember that the design should describe the functions that the enterprise modules should perform. The expected service levels provided by each WAN technology should be explained. WAN connections can be characterized by the cost of renting the transmission media from the service provider to connect two or more sites together.

New network designs should be flexible and adaptable to future technologies and should not limit the customer's options going forward. Voice over IP and video are examples of technologies that network designs should be able to support if the customer decides to move to a converged network. The customer should not have to undergo major hardware upgrades to implement these types of technologies. In addition, the ongoing support and management of the network is another important factor, along with the design's cost-effectiveness.

Table 6-3 lists key design principles that can help serve as the basis for developing network designs.

Table 6-3 Key Design Principles

Design Principle	Description
High availability	Redundancy through hardware, software, and connectivity
Scalability	Modularity with additional devices, services, and technologies
Security	Integrating security throughout to protect business data
Performance	Providing enough capacity and bandwidth for applications
Manageability	Ease of managing and maintaining the infrastructure
Standards and regulations	Compliance with applicable laws, regulations, and standards
Cost	Balancing the amount of security and technologies with the budget

High availability is often what most businesses and organizations strive for in sound network designs. The key components of application availability are response time, throughput, and reliability. Real-time applications such as voice and video are not very tolerant to jitter and delay.

Table 6-4 identifies various application requirements for data, voice, and video traffic.

Table 6-4 Application Requirements

	Data File Transfer	Interactive Data Application	Real-time Voice	Real-time Video
Response time	Reasonable	Within a second	Round trip less than 400 ms with the delay and low jitter	Minimum delay and jitter
Throughput and packet loss tolerance	High/medium	Low/low	Low/low	High/medium
Downtime (high reliability has low downtime)	Reasonable	Low	Low	Minimum

Response Time

Response time measures the time between the client user request and the response from the server host. The end user will accept a certain level of delay in response time and still be satisfied. However, there is a limit to how long the user will wait. This amount of time can be measured and serves as a basis for future application response times. Users perceive the network communication in terms of how quickly the server returns the requested information and how fast the screen updates. Some applications, such as a request for an HTML web page, require short response times. On the other hand, a large FTP transfer might take a while, but this is generally acceptable.

Throughput

In network communications, throughput is the measure of data transferred from one host to another in a given amount of time. Bandwidth-intensive applications have more of an impact on a network's throughput than interactive traffic such as a Telnet session. Most high-throughput applications usually involve some type of file-transfer activity. Because throughput-intensive applications have longer response times, you can usually schedule them when time-sensitive traffic volumes are lower, such as after hours.

Reliability

Reliability is the measure of a given application's availability to its users. Some organizations require rock-solid application reliability, such as five-nines (99.999 percent); this has a higher price than most other applications. For example, financial and security exchange commissions require nearly 100 percent uptime for their applications. These types of networks are built with a high amount of physical and logical redundancy. It is important to ascertain the level of reliability needed for a network that is being designed. Reliability goes further than availability by measuring not only whether the service is there but whether it is performing as it should.

Bandwidth Considerations

Table 6-5 compares a number of different WAN technologies, along with the speeds and media types associated with them.

Table 6-5   Physical Bandwidth Comparison

WAN Connectivity	Bandwidth: Less Than 2 Mbps	Bandwidth: 2 Mbps to 45 Mbps	Bandwidth: 45 Mbps to 100 Mbps	Bandwidth: 100 Mbps to 10 Gbps
Copper	Serial, ISDN, Frame Relay, TDM, ADSL	Frame Relay, Ethernet, ADSL, cable, T3	Fast Ethernet	Gigabit Ethernet, 10 Gigabit Ethernet (10GBASE-CX4)
Fiber	N/A	Ethernet	Fast Ethernet, ATM	Gigabit Ethernet, 10 Gigabit Ethernet, ATM, SONET/SDH, POS, dark fiber
Wireless	802.11b	802.11b, wireless WAN (varies)	802.11a/g	802.11n/ac Wave1

The WAN designer must engineer the network with enough bandwidth to support the needs of the users and applications that will use the network. How much bandwidth a network needs depends on the services and applications that will require network bandwidth. For example, VoIP requires more bandwidth than interactive Secure Shell (SSH) traffic. A large number of graphics or CAD drawings require an extensive amount of bandwidth compared to file or print sharing information being transferred on the network. A big driver in increasing demands for more bandwidth is the expanded use of collaboration applications that use video interactively.

When designing bandwidth for the WAN, remember that implementation and recurring costs are always important factors. It is best to begin planning for WAN capacity early. When the link utilization reaches around 50 percent to 60 percent, you should consider increases and closely monitor the capacity at that point. When the link utilization reaches around 75 percent, immediate attention is required to avoid congestion problems and packet loss that will occur when the utilization nears full capacity.

QoS techniques become increasingly important when delay-sensitive traffic such as VoIP is using the limited bandwidth available on the WAN. LAN bandwidth, on the other hand, is generally inexpensive and plentiful; in the age of robust real-time applications, however, QoS can be necessary. To provide connectivity on the LAN, you typically need to be concerned only with hardware and implementation costs.

WAN Link Categories

When you start to evaluate WAN link characteristics, they generally fall into three broad categories: private, leased, and shared. There are many factors to consider, such as how the WAN is used, the cost, advantages, and what technologies are available in a given area.

Table 6-6 identifies various WAN link characteristics.

Table 6-6   WAN Link Characteristics

	Use	Cost	Advantages	Examples
Private	WAN to connect distant LANs	Owner must buy and configure network. Expensive to maintain.	High security. Transmission quality.	Metro Ethernet using dark fiber
Leased	WAN to connect distant LANs	High cost. Equipment is leased or private.	Provider is responsible for maintenance. Dedicated bandwidth.	TDM, SONET
Shared	Shared-circuit or packet-switched WAN	Cost is fair. Bandwidth is leased. Equipment is leased or private.	Provider is responsible for maintenance. Shared network for multiple sites.	MPLS or Frame Relay

There are fixed and recurring costs in most WAN environments. Fixed costs include the network equipment, circuit provisioning, and network management tools. The recurring costs include the service provider monthly WAN service fees, maintenance costs of the WAN, and the network operations personnel.

Optimizing Bandwidth Using QoS

QoS is an effective tool for managing a WAN's available bandwidth. Keep in mind that QoS does not add bandwidth; it only helps you make better use of it. For chronic congestion problems, QoS is not the answer; you need to add more bandwidth. However, by prioritizing traffic, you can make sure that your most critical traffic gets the best treatment and available bandwidth in times of congestion. One popular QoS technique is to classify your traffic based on a protocol type or a matching access control list (ACL) and then give policy treatment to the class. You can define many classes to match or identify your most important traffic classes. The remaining unmatched traffic then uses a default class in which the traffic can be treated as best effort.

Queuing, Traffic Shaping, and Policing

Cisco has developed many different QoS mechanisms, such as queuing, policing, and traffic shaping, to enable network operators to manage and prioritize the traffic flowing on the network. Applications that are delay sensitive, such as VoIP, require special treatment to ensure proper application functionality. Queuing refers to the buffering process used by routers and switches when they receive traffic faster than can be transmitted. Different queuing mechanisms can be implemented to influence the order in which the different queues are serviced (that is, how different types of traffic are emptied from the queues).

Table 6-7 identifies QoS considerations to optimize bandwidth.

Table 6-7 QoS Considerations

QoS Category	Description
Classification	Identifies and marks flow
Congestion management	Mechanism to handle traffic overflow using a queuing algorithm
Link-efficiency mechanisms	Reduces latency and jitter for network traffic on low-speed links
Traffic shaping and policing	Avoids congestion by policing ingress and egress flows

Classification

For a flow to have priority, it first must be identified and marked. Both of these tasks are referred to as classification. The following technologies have features that support classification:

- **Network-based application recognition (NBAR)** is a technology that uses deep packet content inspection to identify network applications. An advantage of NBAR is that it can recognize applications even when they do not use standard network ports. Furthermore, it matches fields at the application layer. Before NBAR, classification was limited to Layer 4 TCP and User Datagram Protocol (UDP) port numbers.

- **Committed access rate (CAR)** uses an ACL to set precedence and allows customization of the precedence assignment by user, source or destination IP address, and application type.

Congestion Management

Two types of output queues are available on routers: the hardware queue and the software queue. The hardware queue uses the strategy of first in, first out (FIFO). The software queue schedules packets first and then places them in the hardware queue. Keep in mind that the software queue is used only during periods of congestion. The software queue uses QoS techniques such as priority queuing, custom queuing, weighted fair queuing, class-based weighted fair queuing, low-latency queuing, and traffic shaping and policing.

Priority Queuing

Priority queuing (PQ) is a queuing method that establishes four interface output queues that serve different priority levels: high, medium, default, and low. Unfortunately, PQ can starve other queues if too much data is in one queue because higher-priority queues must be emptied before lower-priority queues.

Custom Queuing

Custom queuing (CQ) uses up to 16 individual output queues. Byte size limits are assigned to each queue so that when the limit is reached, it proceeds to the next queue. The network operator can customize these byte size limits. CQ is fairer than PQ because it allows some level of service to all traffic. This queuing method is considered legacy due to the improvements in the queuing methods.

Weighted Fair Queuing

Weighted fair queuing (WFQ) ensures that traffic is separated into individual flows or sessions without requiring that you define ACLs. WFQ uses two categories to group sessions: high bandwidth and low bandwidth. Low-bandwidth traffic has priority over high-bandwidth traffic. High-bandwidth traffic shares the service according to assigned weight values. WFQ is the default QoS mechanism on interfaces below 2.0 Mbps.

Class-Based Weighted Fair Queuing

Class-based weighted fair queuing (CBWFQ) extends WFQ capabilities by providing support for modular user-defined traffic classes. CBWFQ lets you define traffic classes that correspond to match criteria, including ACLs, protocols, and input interfaces. Traffic that matches the class criteria belongs to that specific class. Each class has a defined queue that corresponds to an output interface.

After traffic has been matched and belongs to a specific class, you can modify its characteristics, such as assigning bandwidth, maximum queue limit, and weight. During periods of congestion, the bandwidth assigned to the class is the guaranteed bandwidth that is delivered to the class.

One of CBWFQ's key advantages is its modular nature, which makes it extremely flex-ible for most situations. It is often referred to as MQC, or Modular QoS CLI, which is the framework for building QoS policies. Many classes can be defined to separate your net-work traffic as needed in the MQC.

Low-Latency Queuing

Low-latency queuing (LLQ) adds a strict priority queue (PQ) to CBWFQ. The strict PQ allows delay-sensitive traffic such as voice to be sent first, before other queues are serviced. That gives voice preferential treatment over the other traffic types. Unlike priority queuing, LLQ provides for a maximum threshold on the PQ to prevent lower priority traffic from being starved by the PQ.

Without LLQ, CBWFQ would not have a priority queue for real-time traffic. The additional classification of other traffic classes is done using the same CBWFQ techniques. LLQ is the standard QoS method for many VoIP networks.

Traffic Shaping and Policing

Traffic shaping and policing are mechanisms that inspect traffic and take an action based on the traffic's characteristics, such as DSCP or IP precedence bits set in the IP header.

Traffic shaping slows down the rate at which packets are sent out an interface (egress) by matching certain criteria. Traffic shaping uses a token bucket technique to release the pack-ets into the output queue at a preconfigured rate. Traffic shaping helps eliminate potential bottlenecks by throttling back the traffic rate at the source. In enterprise environments, traf-fic shaping is used to smooth the flow of traffic going out to the provider. This is desirable for several reasons. In provider networks, it prevents the provider from dropping traffic that exceeds the contracted rate.

Policing tags or drops traffic depending on the match criteria. Generally, policing is used to set the limit of incoming traffic coming into an interface (ingress) and uses a "leaky bucket mechanism." Policing is also referred to as committed access rate, or CAR. One example of using policing is to give preferential treatment to critical application traffic by elevating to a higher class and reducing best-effort traffic to a lower-priority class.

When you contrast traffic shaping with policing, remember that traffic shaping buffers packets while policing can be configured to drop packets. In addition, policing propagates bursts, but traffic shaping does not.

Link Efficiency

Within Cisco IOS, several link-efficiency mechanisms are available. Link fragmentation and interleaving (LFI), Multilink PPP (MLP), and Real-Time Transport Protocol (RTP) header compression provide for more efficient use of available bandwidth.

Table 6-8 describes Cisco IOS link-efficiency mechanisms.

Table 6-8   Link-Efficiency Mechanisms

Mechanisms	Description
Link fragmentation and interleaving (LFI)	Reduces delay and jitter on slower-speed links by breaking up large packet flows and inserting smaller data packets (Telnet, VoIP) in between them.
Multilink PPP (MLP)	Bonds multiple links together between two nodes, which increases the available bandwidth. MLP can be used on analog or digital links and is based on RFC 1990.
Real-Time Transport (RTP) header compression	Provides increased efficiency for applications that take advantage of RTP on slow links. Compresses RTP/UDP/IP headers from 40 bytes down to 2 bytes to 5 bytes.

Window Size

The window size defines the upper limit of frames that can be transmitted without getting a return acknowledgment. Transport protocols, such as TCP, rely on acknowledgments to provide connection-oriented reliable transport of data segments. For example, if the TCP window size is set to 8192, the source stops sending data after 8192 bytes if no acknowledgment has been received from the destination host. In some cases, the window size might need to be modified because of unacceptable delay for larger WAN links. If the window size is not adjusted to coincide with the delay factor, retransmissions can occur, which affects throughput significantly. It is recommended that you adjust the window size to achieve better connectivity conditions.

DMZ Connectivity

Inside the enterprise edge module, the main purpose of DMZs is to provide access to services through control and isolation techniques. Firewalls are used to segment the DMZs by function (Internet DMZ or remote access VPN DMZ, for example). DMZs are typically segmented and controlled by ACLs on stateful firewalls such as Cisco ASA. In addition, security controls such as virtual devices contexts, NAT, proxying, and split routing/DNS can also be used to enforce enhanced levels of security. Services within the DMZs can be hosted on physical or virtual appliances located in the data center.

DMZ types include the following:

- **Internet DMZ:** These types of DMZs provide Internet-facing services such as web, email, DNS, and e-commerce services for corporate users and/or customers.

- **Remote access VPN DMZ:** DMZ for network access by corporate users via SSL or IPsec VPN sessions.

- **Site-to-site VPN DMZ:** DMZ for remote site or branch office connectivity via IPsec VPN tunnels as an alternative to private network WAN service.

- **Cloud services DMZ:** DMZ to connect to public cloud services such as Amazon Web Services (AWS) or Microsoft Azure via encrypted tunnels.

- **Unified communications DMZ:** DMZ to host UC services such as voice and video over the Internet.

- **Security services DMZ:** Security-based DMZ for services such as web application firewalls (WAPs), intrusion prevention services (IPSs), email, and URL filtering services.

Figure 6-8 depicts the use of FW DMZs with access control entries (ACEs) in the enterprise edge.

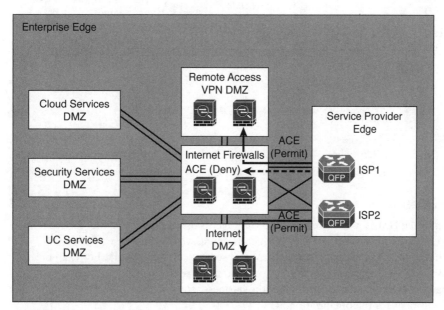

Figure 6-8   *DMZ types with ACEs*

Segmenting DMZs

The primary method of segmenting DMZs takes advantage of using separate physical or logical interfaces on a firewall. In addition, it is important to consider dedicating DMZs per service and even dividing up critical services into multiple DMZs, thereby increasing security. These levels of classification reduce the risk of compromise by splitting up the services. There is also an increased use of virtual machines and virtual appliances that need to be leveraged that reside in the data center infrastructure. From the enterprise edge, additional segmentation techniques such as VLANs, VRFs, IPsec VPNs, and virtual device contexts can be used to extend the traffic and provide path isolation.

Figure 6-9 illustrates the use of a virtual appliance in the data center being used in the public-facing DMZ.

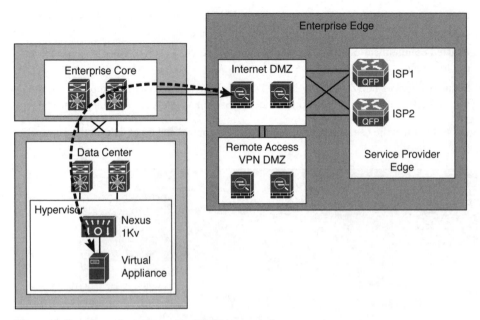

Figure 6-9   *Virtual appliances—DMZ extended*

DMZ Services

When designing DMZs, you have two main options for distributing the DMZ services—
per-service DMZs and shared DMZs. When considering which one to use, think about
how each option will impact the management and security of the network. For example,
too many DMZs will increase security but will also increase the management overhead.
Balancing cost versus risk in order to meet the business requirements will help you determine what is right for the organization.

- **Per-service DMZ:** Good for traffic isolation and security because all traffic will have to
  go through the firewall, but there is an impact on management and performance.

- **Shared DMZs:** More services in a DMZ will ease the management overhead and perfor-
  mance, but also will decrease the security because all of the traffic is locally switched.
  However, you can use enhanced Layer 2 features such as port security and private
  VLANs to further increase security.

Internet Connectivity

Most enterprises have multiple sites with a varying number of users at each site, but are
usually grouped into two site types: larger central sites and smaller branch sites. The larger
site types will typically host more of the users and services. The smaller branch offices will
have a low user count and a smaller number of hosted services. Both central and branch sites
typically need Internet access, but there are high availability considerations to think about
when selecting the Internet access design for a given site type. When choosing an Internet
connectivity option, remember to take into account the business requirements and the budget allocated for the design.

Internet connectivity options include the following:

Dual-router dual-homed: Provides the highest level of resiliency for Internet connectivity with full redundancy in hardware, links, and Internet service providers.

Single-router dual-homed: Provides a good level of redundancy for the Internet connectivity through the use of multiple links and multiple Internet service providers.

Single-router single-homed: Provides the bare minimum for Internet connectivity, providing no levels of redundancy for the hardware, links, or Internet service providers.

Figure 6-10 shows Internet connectivity options with different levels of redundancy.

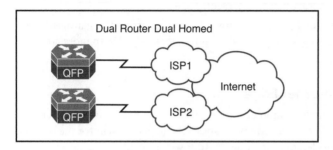

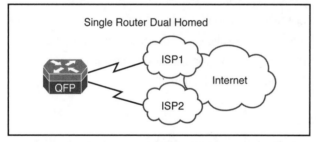

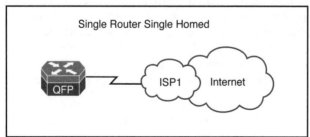

Figure 6-10 *Internet connectivity options*

Because central sites have higher user populations, they will normally have higher Internet bandwidth connectivity and centralized access control for the Internet traffic flows. Although most branch offices will have an Internet connection, many of them will still have their Internet traffic backhauled over the WAN to the central site where centralized access control can occur. Another Internet connectivity option for branches sites is to have their own direct Internet access, but there are security challenges with adhering to the same set of security policies in place at the centralized site. Even though the performance for the traffic flows is better with direct Internet access, there is a greater security risk for the enterprise due to more Internet connection points for attackers to target.

Centralized Internet (Branch) vs. Direct Internet (Branch)

Whether or not to backhaul Internet traffic from branches offices versus branches having direct Internet is a common decision that many companies now need to face. Here are some pros and cons of each:

- **Centralized Internet for each branch:** Higher bandwidth available and centralized security policies, but suboptimal traffic flows. This might require additional redundancy at the Internet edge, which may or may not be present.
- **Direct Internet for branches:** Optimal traffic flows, but more difficult to manage distributed security policies. This also has a higher risk of Internet attacks due to more attachment points.

High Availability for the Internet Edge

Once you have decided on having two Internet routers, each with a link to two different Internet service providers, it is time to start thinking about the logical design for the routers. Logical Internet HA design considerations include the following:

- Use a public BGP AS number for EBGP connections to the ISPs.
- Use provider-independent IP address space to allow for advertisement to both ISPs.
- Receive full or partial Internet routing tables to optimize forwarding outbound.
- Use HSRP/GLBP or an IGP such as EIGRP or OSPF internally.

VPN Network Design

VPNs are typically deployed over some kind of shared or public infrastructure. VPNs are similar to tunnels in that they carry traffic over an existing IP infrastructure. VPN technologies use the Internet, ATM/Frame Relay WANs, and point-to-point connected IP infrastructures to transport data from end to end. A disadvantage of using VPNs over public networks is that the connectivity is best effort in nature, and troubleshooting is also difficult because you do not have visibility into the service provider's infrastructure.

One of the goals of remote-access network design is to provide a unified solution that allows for seamless connectivity as if the users are on the HQ LAN. The primary function of remote access is to provide your users access to internal resources and applications. Because connection requirements drive the technology selection process, it is important that you analyze the application and network requirements in addition to reviewing the available service provider options.

The following summarizes typical remote-access requirements:

- Best-effort interactive and low-volume traffic patterns
- Connections to the enterprise edge using Layer 2 WAN technologies (consider capital and recurring costs)
- Voice and IPsec VPN support

Remote-access network connections are enabled over permanent always-on connections or on-demand connections. Technologies include any Internet connection technology such as cable, wireless 802.11 a/b/g/n LAN, and 3G/4G wireless WAN (WWAN). However, these remote-access technologies might or might not be available, so it is best to check the availability for the location in your network design.

VPN types divided by application, include the following:

- **Remote access VPN:** These types of VPN connections give mobile users, home users, and partners connectivity to corporate intranets over the Internet. Users typically connect remotely using cable, wireless LAN, or 3G/4G WWAN. Remote access VPNs usually terminate on Cisco ASA appliances and can be grouped together to form a load-balancing cluster in a dedicated DMZ, or existing Cisco ASA firewalls can be used in smaller organizations. Both SSL and IPsec protocols are supported with remote access VPNs, but SSL is recommended. With an SSL VPN, client design options include full tunnel or split tunnel, local LAN access, a web or Anyconnect client, an authentication mechanism, and endpoint assessments, all enforced by the ASA appliance.

- **Site-to-site VPN:** Site-to-site VPNs over the Internet offer an alternative WAN transport for interconnecting sites. Generally, the remote sites use their Internet connection to establish the VPN connection back to the corporate head-end office. Site-to-site VPNs can also use an IP backbone provided by the service provider. The main use cases for site-to-site VPNs are for primary WAN transport, lower-cost MPLS WAN backup, and connecting to secure cloud services. ASAs, Cisco ISR, and Cisco ASR series routers are commonly used for site-to-site VPNs with IPsec over GRE to support the deployment of IGPs.

- **Extranet VPNs:** This is another form of site-to-site VPN infrastructure for business partner connectivity that also uses the Internet or a private infrastructure for network access. Keep in mind that it is important to have secure extranet network policies to restrict the business partners' access. Typically, these types of VPNs terminate in a partner-designated firewalled demilitarized zone (DMZ).

Figure 6-11 shows VPN examples for home users, mobile users, and site-to-site VPNs.

6

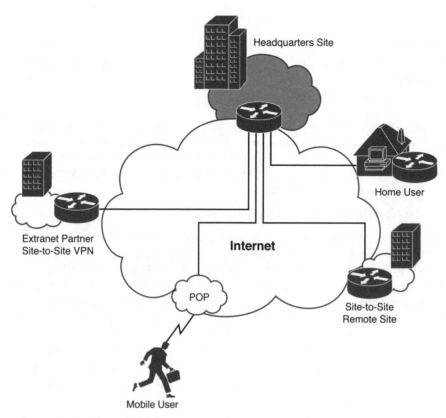

Figure 6-11   *VPN examples*

References and Recommended Readings

Cisco IOS Quality of Service Solutions Configuration Guide Library, Cisco IOS Release 15M&T, http://www.cisco.com/c/en/us/td/docs/ios-xml/ios/qos/config_library/15-mt/qos-15-mt-library.html.

Frame Relay, www.cisco.com/univercd/cc/td/doc/cisintwk/ito_doc/frame.htm.

Integrated Services Digital Network, www.cisco.com/univercd/cc/td/doc/cisintwk/ito_doc/isdn.htm.

Module 4, "Enterprise Network Design," Designing for Cisco Internetwork Solution Course (DESGN) v3.0.

RFC 1990, www.ietf.org/rfc/rfc1990.txt.

TDM: Time Division Multiplex and Multiplexer, www.networkdictionary.com/telecom/tdm.php.

LTE: LTE (telecommunications), en.wikipedia.org/wiki/LTE_(telecommunication).

10GE DWDM Interconnections in Enterprise Campus Networks, www.cisco.com/c/en/us/products/collateral/interfaces-modules/transceiver-modules/prod_white_paper0900aecd8054d53d.html.

Exam Preparation Tasks

Review All Key Topics

Review the most important topics in the chapter, noted with the Key Topic icon in the outer margin of the page. Table 6-9 lists a reference of these key topics and the page numbers on which each is found.

Table 6-9   Key Topics

Key Topic Element	Description	Page
List	WAN design goals	218
Table 6-2	WAN comparison	221
Summary	Metro Ethernet	225
Summary	MPLS	226
List	Keys to PBM	229
Table 6-4	Application requirements	230
Table 6-5	Physical bandwidth comparison	231
Table 6-6	WAN link characteristics	232
Table 6-7	QoS considerations	233
Table 6-8	Link-efficiency mechanisms	236
List	DMZ types	236
List	Internet connectivity options	239
List	High availability for the Internet edge	240
List	VPN types	241

Complete Tables and Lists from Memory

Print a copy of Appendix D, "Memory Tables," (found on the book website), or at least the section for this chapter, and complete the tables and lists from memory. Appendix E, "Memory Tables Answer Key," also on the website, includes completed tables and lists to check your work.

Define Key Terms

Define the following key terms from this chapter, and check your answers in the glossary:

service level agreement, digital subscriber line, broadband cable, wireless, time-division multiplexing, Frame Relay, MPLS, SONET/SDH, DWDM, DMZ, remote access VPN, site-to-site VPN

Q&A

The answers to these questions appear in Appendix A, "Answers to the 'Do I Know This Already?' Quizzes and Q&A Questions." For more practice with exam format questions, use the exam engine on the CD.

1. When using PBM design methodology, what should a network designer do after identifying the customer requirements?

    a. Design the network topology.

    b. Design a test network.

    c. Plan the implementation.

    d. Characterize the existing network.

2. Which module is within the enterprise edge module?

    a. Data center module

    b. Campus core

    c. Building distribution

    d. Remote access VPN module

3. What WAN technology is most cost effective and suitable for the telecommuter?

    a. MPLS

    b. Dark fiber

    c. ISDN

    d. DSL

4. What two modules are found in the enterprise edge?

    a. Campus core

    b. Building access

    c. Internet

    d. DMZ

5. Which of the following statements best describes window size for good throughput?

    a. A large window size reduces the number of acknowledgments.

    b. A small window size reduces the number of acknowledgments.

    c. A small window size provides better performance.

    d. None of the above.

6. What is the default queuing mechanism for router interfaces below 2.0 Mbps?

    a. Traffic shaping

    b. WFQ

    c. CBWFQ

    d. LLQ

7. Which of the following best describe the PBM design methodology? (Select three.)

   a. Analyze the network requirements.

   b. Characterize the existing network.

   c. Implement the network management.

   d. Design the network topology.

8. Which of the following modules belongs in the enterprise edge?

   a. Building distribution

   b. Campus core

   c. Network management

   d. DMZ/e-commerce

9. Which network module connects to ISPs in the enterprise edge?

   a. Building distribution

   b. Campus core

   c. WAN edge

   d. Service provider edge

10. Which network module connects using the MPLS connectivity?

   a. Remote access VPN

   b. Campus core

   c. Building access

   d. WAN edge

11. Which network module connects using Frame Relay or ATM?

   a. Remote access VPN

   b. WAN edge

   c. Building distribution

   d. Server farm

12. During which part of the PBM design methodology does implementation planning occur?

   a. Analyze the network requirements.

   b. Design the topology.

   c. Characterize the existing network.

   d. None of the above.

13. What functional area provides connectivity between the central site and remote sites?

   a. Access

   b. Campus core

   c. Building distribution

   d. WAN edge

6

14. What WAN technology allows the enterprise to control framing?

    a. Cable

    b. Wireless

    c. DWDM

    d. Dark fiber

15. Which QoS method uses a strict PQ in addition to modular traffic classes?

    a. CBWFQ

    b. Policing

    c. WFQ

    d. LLQ

16. A T1 TDM circuit uses how many timeslots?

17. Which wireless implementation is designed to connect two wireless networks in different buildings?

    a. Mobile wireless

    b. GPRS

    c. Bridge wireless

    d. UMTS

18. What improves the utilization of optical-fiber strands?

19. On the ISP side of a cable provider, cable modems connect to what system?

20. If Frame Relay, ATM, and SONET technologies are used, what enterprise network module would they connect to?

    a. WAN/MAN

    b. VPN/remote access

    c. Internet

    d. DMZ/e-commerce

21. What protocol describes data-over-cable procedures that the equipment must support?

22. Into what WAN technology category does ISDN fit?

    a. Cell switched

    b. UTMS switched

    c. Circuit switched

    d. Packet switched

23. What do service providers use to define their service offerings at different levels?

    a. SWAN

    b. WAN tiers

    c. WWAN

    d. SLA

24. When is it appropriate to use various queuing solutions?

    a. The WAN has frequent congestion problems.

    b. The WAN occasionally becomes congested.

    c. The WAN is consistently at 50 percent utilized.

    d. The WAN is consistently at 40 percent utilized.

6

This chapter covers the following subjects:

Traditional WAN Technologies

Remote Site Connectivity

Enterprise VPN vs. Service Provider VPN

WAN Backup Design

Enterprise WAN Architecture

Enterprise WAN Components

Enterprise Branch Architecture

Enterprise Teleworker Design

This chapter covers wide area network (WAN) designs for the enterprise WAN and enterprise branch architecture. The chapter starts out by reviewing traditional WAN technologies and network topologies. Remote site connectivity is examined with an emphasis on virtual private networks (VPNs). Next, enterprise VPNs are compared and contrasted with service provider VPNs. Then, the chapter explores WAN architecture, WAN components, and WAN backup design. Finally, the chapter wraps up with enterprise branch architecture and enterprise teleworker design.

CHAPTER 7

WAN Design

"Do I Know This Already?" Quiz

The "Do I Know This Already?" quiz helps you identify your strengths and deficiencies in this chapter's topics.

The ten-question quiz, derived from the major sections in the "Foundation Topics" portion of the chapter, helps you determine how to spend your limited study time.

Table 7-1 outlines the major topics discussed in this chapter and the "Do I Know This Already?" quiz questions that correspond to those topics.

Table 7-1 "Do I Know This Already?" Foundation Topics Section-to-Question Mapping

Foundation Topics Section	Questions Covered in This Section
Traditional WAN Technologies	1
Remote Site Connectivity	2
Enterprise VPN vs. Service Provider VPN	3-4
WAN Backup Design	5
Enterprise WAN Architecture	6, 7
Enterprise WAN Components	8
Enterprise Branch Architecture	9, 10
Enterprise Teleworker Design	N/A

1. Which of the following are examples of packet- and cell-switched technologies used in the enterprise edge?

    a. Frame Relay and ATM

    b. ISDN and T1

    c. Cable and DSL

    d. Analog voice and T1

2. Which remote site network connectivity option has the highest cost?

    a. Enterprise Managed VPN over Internet

    b. IPsec over the Internet

    c. SP Managed VPN over Private Network

    d. Leased lines

3. What Enterprise VPN option does not support routing protocols?

   a. GRE over IPsec

   b. IPsec VPN

   c. DMVPN

   d. GETVPN

4. What IPsec technology in the enterprise uses routers along with NHRP and mGRE?

   a. IPsec direct encapsulation

   b. Easy VPN

   c. GET VPN

   d. DMVPN

5. What backup option allows for both a backup link and load-sharing capabilities using the available bandwidth?

   a. Dial backup

   b. Secondary WAN link

   c. Shadow PVC

   d. IPsec tunnel

6. Which common factor is used for WAN architecture selection that involves eliminating single points of failure to increase uptime and growth?

   a. Network segmentation

   b. Ease of management

   c. Redundancy

   d. Support for growth

7. What WAN/MAN architecture is provided by the service provider and has excellent growth support and high availability?

   a. Private WAN

   b. ISP service

   c. SP MPLS/IP VPN

   d. Private MPLS

8. Which Cisco IOS Software family has been designed for low-end to mid-range LAN switching?

   a. IOS15.1

   b. IOS S Releases 12.2SE and IOS XE 3.7

   c. IOS XR

   d. IOS 12.2SX

9. For designing enterprise branch architecture, which of the following are common network components? (Select all that apply.)

   a. Routers supporting WAN edge connectivity

   b. Switches providing the Ethernet LAN infrastructure

   c. Network management servers

   d. IP phones

10. Which branch design supports 50 to 100 users and provides Layer 3 redundancy features?

   a. Small branch

   b. Medium branch

   c. Large branch

   d. Enterprise teleworker

7

Foundation Topics

This chapter covers WAN design topics that you need to master for the CCDA exam. It begins by discussing physical WAN technology and WAN topologies used in the enterprise. Next is a review of remote site network connectivity options that are used to design remote sites. The chapter goes on to cover the different connectivity options available for enterprise VPNs and service provider (SP) VPNs.

Next, several backup strategies are explored that are used when designing WANs. Then the chapter reviews the considerations used in developing WAN architectures, including the hardware and software options used when selecting components for network designs. In addition, the design of branch offices is discussed, with a review of several options for designing different sizes of branch offices.

Traditional WAN Technologies

When selecting a particular WAN technology, you should be familiar with the three major categories that represent traditional WANs:

- **Circuit switched:** Data connections that can be brought up when needed and terminated when finished. Examples include ordinary public switched telephone network (PSTN) phone service, analog modems, and ISDN. Carriers reserve that call path through the network for the duration of the call.

- **Leased lines:** A dedicated connection provided by the SP. These types of connections are point to point and generally more expensive. Time-division multiplexing (TDM) based leased lines usually use synchronous data transmission.

- **Packet and cell switched:** Connections that use virtual circuits (PVC/SVC) established by the SP. Packet-switched technologies include Frame Relay and cell-switched technologies such as ATM. ATM uses cells and provides support for multiple quality of service (QoS) classes. The virtual circuits are part of the shared ATM/Frame Relay SP backbone network. This gives the SP greater flexibility with its service offerings.

When planning and designing a packet-switched WAN, you should become familiar with some basic WAN topologies. These WAN topologies include hub-and-spoke, partial-mesh, and full-mesh topologies, as shown in Figure 7-1.

Hub-and-Spoke Topology

A star or hub-and-spoke topology provides a hub router with connections to the spoke routers through the WAN cloud. Network communication between the sites flows through the hub router. Significant WAN cost savings, lower circuit counts, and simplified management are benefits of the hub-and-spoke topology. In addition, hub-and-spoke topologies provide WAN hierarchy and can provide high availability through the use of dual routers at the hub site.

A major disadvantage of this approach is that if you use a single hub router, it can represent a single point of failure. The hub-and-spoke topology can also limit the overall performance when resources are accessed through the central hub router from the spoke routers, such as with spoke-to-spoke network traffic.

Figure 7-1 illustrates the full mesh, partial mesh, and hub-and-spoke topologies.

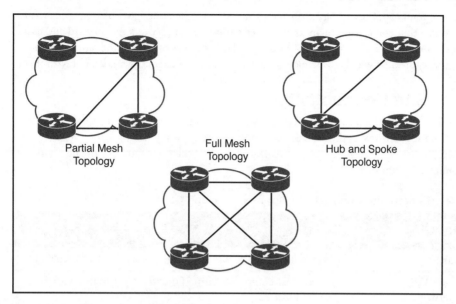

Figure 7-1 *WAN topologies*

Full-Mesh Topology

With full-mesh topologies, each site has a connection to all other sites in the WAN cloud (any-to-any). As the number of sites grows, so does the number of spoke connections that are ultimately required. Consequently, the full-mesh topology is not viable in very large networks. However, a key advantage of this topology is that it has plenty of redundancy in the event of network failures. But redundancy implemented with this approach does have a high price associated with it.

Here are some issues inherent with full-mesh topologies:

- Many virtual circuits (VCs) are required to maintain the full mesh.
- Issues occur with the amount of broadcast and multicast replication packets for each site.
- Complex configurations are needed.
- High cost.

The number of VCs required for a full mesh can be calculated using the formula $((N - 1) \times N / 2)$. For example, if you have four sites, the six VCs are required: $((4 - 1) \times 4 / 2) = 6$.

Partial-Mesh Topology

A partial-mesh topology has fewer VC connections than a full-mesh topology. Therefore, not all sites in the cloud are required to be connected to each other. However, some sites on the WAN cloud have full-mesh characteristics. Partial-mesh topologies can give you more options and flexibly for where to place the high-redundancy VCs based on your specific requirements, such as with core hub sites, but not at other noncritical branch offices.

Point-to-Point Topology

A point-to-point topology or back-to-back connection is when you have just two sites with a single connection connecting them together. This topology is very straightforward and easy to work with, but it lacks scalability if you consider hundreds of sites, for example. Point-to-point links are also widely available but generally have a higher cost associated with them.

Remote Site Connectivity

Several WAN technologies can be used for connecting remote sites back to the headquarters or main site. However, these three main options are typically used for remote site connectivity, each with its own pros and cons. Table 7-2 lists the pros and cons of the remote site connectivity options.

Table 7-2   Remote Site Connectivity Options: Pros and Cons

Remote Site Connectivity Option	Pros	Cons
Leased Lines	Very reliable and secure	Higher cost and lacks scalability
SP Managed VPN over Private Network	Lower cost compared with leased lines	Potential trust issues with SP
Enterprise Managed VPN over the Internet	Low cost and scalable	Lower reliability and best effort

Figure 7-2 illustrates the three main options for connecting remote offices and HQ locations.

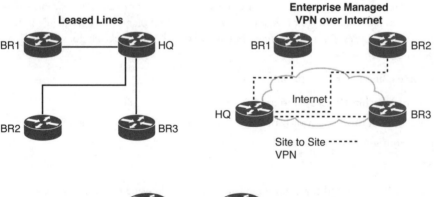

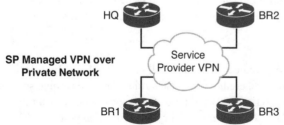

Figure 7-2 *Remote site connectivity*

Leased lines are private point-to-point network connections between a pair of sites. With leased lines, you get the same upload and download bandwidths, and the speeds are usually between 10 Mbps to 1 Gbps or more. Leased lines provide consistent and reliable bandwidth along with security; however, leased lines are more expensive when compared to SP Managed VPN or Enterprise Managed VPN over the Internet. Given that VPNs over private or public networks generally have lower costs than leased lines, they have become the most popular method for remote site connectivity.

A Service Provider Managed VPN is where the SP builds and manages the VPN. The SP VPN is thereby acting as a transport network between HQ locations and remote branch offices for multiple customers. MPLS L3 VPN is the most common service offering, but other L2 services are usually available as well. With SP Managed VPNs, the provider will typically offer to manage voice and Internet services along with the WAN services.

Enterprise Managed VPN is a method of building secure tunnels between your sites using the Internet as the transport network. There are many VPN technologies available, but as long as the tunnels are protected with IPsec, they can be safe to use over the Internet. Using these types of site-to-site tunnels is the lowest cost option but lacks SLAs and traffic reliability for availability, delay, and jitter.

Enterprise VPN vs. Service Provider VPN

When you need to provide secure remote access using VPNs, you must consider several things. One key consideration is the use of enterprise VPNs or service provider–based VPNs. Enterprise VPNs typically require in-house VPN design, implementation, and support. An SP VPN, on the other hand, is a managed VPN service from the service provider. Table 7-3 provides an overview of some technology options that are available when selecting VPNs.

Table 7-3   VPNs Found in Enterprise and Service Provider Environments

Enterprise VPNs	Service Provider VPNs
IP Security (IPsec)	Multiprotocol Label Switching (MPLS)
Generic routing encapsulation (GRE)	Metro Ethernet
Dynamic Multipoint Virtual Private Network (DMVPN)	Virtual Private Wire Services (VPWS)
IPsec Virtual tunnel interface (VTI)	Virtual Private LAN Services (VPLS)
GETVPN	

Enterprise Managed VPN: IPsec

What is IPsec? IPsec is a network layer protocol suite for encrypting IP packets between two hosts and thereby creating a secure "tunnel." The IETF defined IPsec in RFC 4301. IPsec uses open standards and provides secure communication between peers to ensure data confidentiality, integrity, and authenticity through network layer encryption. IPsec connections are commonly configured between firewalls, VPN appliances, or routers that have IPsec features enabled. IPsec can scale from small to very large networks.

The IPsec protocols include Internet Security Association and Key Management Protocol (ISAKMP) and two other IPsec IP protocols: Encapsulating Security Payload (ESP) and Authentication Header (AH). IPsec uses symmetrical encryption algorithms to provide data protection. These algorithms need a secure method to exchange keys to ensure that the data is protected. Internet Key Exchange (IKE) ISAKMP protocols provide these functions. ESP is used to provide confidentiality, data origin authentication, connectionless integrity, and anti-replay services. AH is used to provide integrity and data origin authentication, usually referred to as just authentication.

In addition, IPsec can secure data from eavesdropping and modification using transform sets, which give you varying levels of strength for the data protection. IPsec also has several Hash Message Authentication Codes (HMAC) available to provide protection from attacks such as man-in-the-middle, packet-replay, and data-integrity attacks.

IPsec Direct Encapsulation

IPsec provides a tunnel mode of operation that enables it to be used as a standalone connection method and is the most fundamental VPN design model. When you are using IPsec direct encapsulation, dynamic routing protocols and IP multicast are not supported. The headend IPsec terminating device needs to use static IP addressing, but the remote IPsec endpoints can use static or dynamic IP addressing. Redundancy can be provided at the headend by using multiple IPsec terminating devices, and each remote IPsec endpoint can be populated with a list of headend endpoints to make connections with.

IPsec packet payloads can be encrypted, and IPsec receivers can authenticate packet origins. Internet Key Exchange (IKE) and Public Key Infrastructure (PKI) can also be used with IPsec. IKE is the protocol used to set up a security association (SA) with IPsec. PKI is an arrangement that provides for third-party verification of identities.

Figure 7-3 shows the topology for IPsec direction encapsulation with multiple headend sites to provide resiliency for the branch offices.

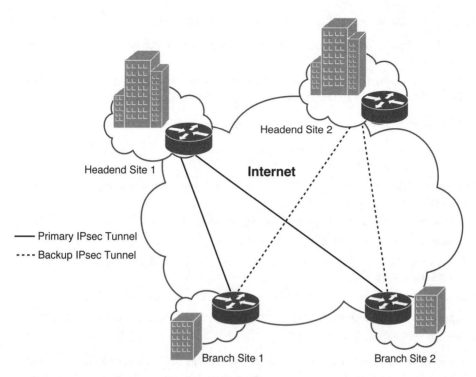

Figure 7-3 *IPsec direct encapsulation example*

Generic Routing Encapsulation

GRE was developed by Cisco to encapsulate a variety of protocols inside IP tunnels. This approach consists of minimal configuration for basic IP VPNs but lacks in both security and scalability. In fact, GRE tunnels do not use any encryption to secure the packets during transport.

Using IPsec with GRE tunnels provides for secure VPN tunnels by encrypting the GRE tunnels. There are many advantages with this approach, such as the support for dynamic IGP routing protocols, non-IP protocols, and IP multicast. Other advantages include support for QoS policies and deterministic routing metrics for headend IPsec termination points. Because all the primary and backup GRE over IPsec tunnels are pre-established, there is built-in redundancy to support failure scenarios. The IP addressing for the remote sites can have dynamic or static addressing, but the headend site requires static IP addressing. Primary tunnels can be differentiated from backup tunnels by modifying the routing metrics slightly to prefer the one or the other.

IPsec DMVPN

Dynamic Multipoint VPN (DMVPN) is a Cisco IOS solution for building IPsec + GRE VPNs in a dynamic and scalable manner.

DMVPN relies on two key technologies called NHRP and mGRE:

- Next Hop Resolution Protocol (NHRP) creates a mapping database for all spoke tunnels to real public addresses.

- Multipoint GRE (mGRE) is a single GRE interface, which provides support for multiple GRE and IPsec tunnels to reduce the complexity and the size of the configuration.

DMVPN supports a reduced configuration framework and supports the following features:

- Hub router configuration reduction, with a single mGRE interface and a single IPsec profile to manage all spoke routers

- Automatic IPsec initiation and auto-creation of GRE tunnels without any IPsec peering configuration

- IP unicast, IP multicast, and dynamic routing protocol support

- Remote spoke routers with dynamic IP addressing

- Spoke routers behind dynamic Network Address Translation (NAT) and hub routers behind static NAT

- Dynamic spoke-to-spoke tunnels for partial scaling or fully meshed VPNs

- Support for all the GRE tunnel benefits such as QoS, deterministic routing, and redundancy scenarios

Each remote site is connected using a point-to-point (P2P) GRE tunnel interface to a single mGRE headend interface. The headend mGRE interface dynamically accepts new tunnel connections.

Redundancy can be achieved by configuring spokes to terminate to multiple headends at one or more hub locations. IPsec tunnel protection is typically used to map the cryptographic attributes to the tunnel that is originated by the remote peer.

Dead peer detection (DPD) can be used to detect the loss of a peer IPsec connection. NHRP is configured on both the headend and spoke routers and is a requirement for using mGRE interfaces.

IPsec Virtual Tunnel Interface Design

Virtual tunnel interface (VTI) is an IPsec VPN design option available in Cisco IOS Software. VTI has some interesting advantages over previous IPsec design options, including support for dynamic routing protocols and IP multicast without using GRE- or mGRE-type interfaces. Also, because VTI tunnels are assigned a unique interface, specific tunnel-level features such as QoS can be configured for each tunnel separate from other VTI tunnels. The physical topology for VTI designs can be designed the same way as IPsec direct encapsulation using multiple headends and two tunnels from the remote sites, one to each headend.

GETVPN

Group Encrypted Transport VPN (GETVPN) is similar to IPsec VPNs; however, it differs by preserving the original IP addresses in the outer IP header of the packets. Because the original IP source and destination addresses are preserved, no overlay routing control plane is needed, thereby allowing routing and multicast to route natively within the underlying network. GETVPN is not typically used on the Internet because NAT does not work due to the original IP addressing preservation. However, GETVPN is a good solution for private MPLS networks or where you have end-to-end control of the private IP address space.

Table 7-4 shows a comparison of enterprise VPN options.

Table 7-4 Enterprise VPN Comparison

Characteristic	IPsec VPN	GRE over IPsec	DMVPN	VTI	GETVPN
Network Topology	Hub-and-spoke & partial mesh	Hub-and-spoke & partial mesh	Hub-and-spoke & any-to-any	Hub-and-spoke	Any-to-any
Routing Protocols	No	Yes	Yes	Yes	Yes
Multicast	No	Yes	Yes	Yes	Yes
NAT	Yes	Yes	Yes	Yes	No
Scalability	No	No	Yes	Yes, dynamic	Yes
Network Type	Public or private	Public or private	Public or private	Public or private	Mostly private
Standard	Yes	Yes	Cisco proprietary	Cisco proprietary	Cisco proprietary

Service Provider–Managed Offerings

Next, we will explore service provider managed offerings that include Metro Ethernet and Service Provider VPNs for L2 and L3 services. Metro Ethernet is available in most cities and can provide a flexible WAN solution for connectivity between sites that are local to a city. However, you might need a more scalable WAN solution for connectivity between multiple cities. Service provider VPNs for L2 and L3 enable increased scalability and flexibility along with SLAs, which make it an excellent choice for critical applications.

Metro Ethernet

Demand for bandwidth in the metro area network (MAN) is increasing due to the result of the high throughput requirements of data-intensive applications. Today, many SPs are offering Metro Ethernet services to fulfill the demand; these are based on Ethernet, IP, and optical technologies such as dense wavelength-division multiplexing (DWDM) or coarse wavelength-division multiplexing.

Metro Ethernet services can provide more bandwidth, the ability to upgrade the bandwidth as needed, and higher levels of redundancy through multiple route processors. Because Metro Ethernet can support the higher bandwidth requirements, it is often better suited to support converged network services (for example, voice, video, and data services combined on the same link).

7

Most service providers are using Ethernet as a method to access their backbone network. Ethernet handoff is becoming common even if the transport is based on SONET/SDH, MPLS, Frame Relay, or the Internet.

Table 7-5 shows the benefits Ethernet handoffs at the customer edge provide.

Table 7-5 Benefits of Ethernet Handoffs at the Customer Edge

Benefit	Description
Service-enabling solution	Layering value-added services in addition to the network
Flexible architecture	No need for a truck roll for increasing port speeds
	No need for new customer premises equipment (CPE)
	Evolving existing Frame/ATM services to an IP-based solution
Seamless enterprise integration	Ease of integration with existing LAN network equipment

Service Provider VPNs: L2 vs. L3

Service Provider VPN offerings typically include Layer 2 or Layer 3 connectivity options. Layer 2 VPNs are more expensive than Layer 3, but serve a couple of important use cases. Layer 2 VPNs are useful for application requirements that need Layer 2 adjacencies between sites or to support customer edge routers that need to exchange routes directly. Layer 3 options, on the other hand, are lower cost and more scalable than Layer 2; however, the customer routers will need to exchange routes with provider edge routers at each site.

Layer 2 VPN service connects your HQ with one or more of your branches at Layer 2 across the SP backbone network. Layer 2 VPN services allow for attached routers at each site to connect using the same IP subnet. IGP routing protocols such as OSPF and EIGRP can then establish neighbor adjacencies and exchange routes directly. This is useful if the customer wants to manage their own routing information instead of the provider doing so. Layer 2 VPN provider options include either Virtual Private LAN Service (VPLS) or Virtual Private Wire Service (VPWS).

Layer 3 VPN service provides routed L3 connections between your sites. With L3 VPNs, you are exchanging routes with the provider. Customer routes are exchanged from the customer edge (CE) routers to the provider edge (PE) router before entering the L3 VPN. The SP uses BGP for routing inside the L3 VPN, and then routes are exchanged at each remote site from the PE router back to the CE router. Routing protocols such as OSPF and EIGRP are normally used at the exchange point between the CE and PE routers, but static or BGP routing can also be used. Multiprotocol Label Switching (MPLS) is an example of a Layer 3 VPN service.

Virtual Private Wire Services

VPWS is a Layer 2 VPN technology commonly referred to as *pseudowires*. VPWS provides a point-to-point WAN link between two sites over an MPLS provider backbone. It's similar in concept to a leased line service, except that the provider transports multiple customer VPNs on the MPLS equipment connecting your sites. Two popular VPWS use cases include connecting a pair of data centers together and point-to-point WAN transport for legacy services.

VPWS L2 VPN Considerations

There are several traffic considerations to think about with the VPWS L2 VPN service. It is important to understand whether the service will transparently pass all traffic, such as Spanning Tree Protocol (STP) frames as well as broadcast, unknown unicast, and multicast (BUM) type traffic. Also, does the provider offer quality of service (QoS) mechanisms to prioritize voice, video, and critical traffic over best-effort traffic? Another consideration to think about is the maximum transmission unit (MTU) size throughout the provider network for the L2 VPN. If you are using VPWS for Data Center Interconnect (DCI), you might need to support jumbo frames within the provider network. Additionally, you will want to make sure the provider is passing link loss signaling from end to end. This way, you can detect when the far side link is down.

Virtual Private LAN Services

Virtual Private LAN Services (VPLS) expands on VPWS and defines an architecture that enables Ethernet Multipoint Service (EMS) over an MPLS network. The operation of VPLS allows for connecting L2 domains over an IP/MPLS network, which emulates an IEEE Ethernet bridge.

Figure 7-4 depicts a VPLS topology in an MPLS network.

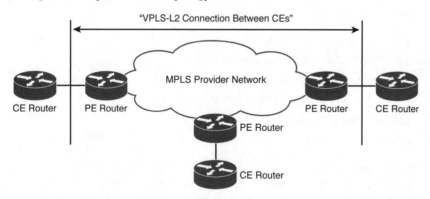

Figure 7-4   *VPLS topology example*

VPLS is a type of VPN that allows for the connection of multiple sites into a single L2 domain over a managed IP/MPLS network. VPLS presents an Ethernet interface, which simplifies the LAN/WAN demarc for service providers. This enables rapid and flexible service provisioning because the service bandwidth is not tied to the physical interface. All the VPLS services appear to be on the same VLAN regardless of physical locations in the WAN.

VPLS uses edge routers that learn L2 domains, bridges them, and replicates them through the VPN. Within the IP/MPLS cloud is a collection of full-mesh connections providing any-to-any connectivity between sites. VPLS supports many of the new applications and services that need to be on the same L2 network to function properly. Some services lack network layer addressing or are transparent to the upper-layer protocols.

VPLS L2 VPN Considerations

Because VPLS provides an L2 switched segment between your sites, you can choose and control the L3 routing between the sites, not the provider. That means you can use routing protocols such as EIGRP, OSPF, and BGP. However, you can run into scalability problems with IGP routing protocols if you try to connect hundreds of routers to the same L2 segment. With VPLS providing the connectivity, BGP is the only routing protocol that you should use in larger L2 domains.

MPLS

MPLS is a technology for the delivery of IP services using an efficient encapsulation mechanism. MPLS uses labels appended to IP packets or L2 frames for the transport of data. The labels can be used as designators to identify IP prefixes, ATM VCs, and can be used to guarantee bandwidth. MPLS can run on many L2 technologies, including ATM, Frame Relay, PPP, Packet over SONET (POS), and Ethernet.

MPLS is an economical solution that can be easily integrated over any existing infrastructure offering flexibility, because MPLS is independent of access technologies. SPs can offer intelligent network services to their customers over a single infrastructure. Each of the SP's customers can have one or more VPNs within the overall MPLS network, called virtual routing and forwarding (VRF) instances.

MPLS Layer 3 Design Overview

MPLS Layer 3 VPNs have the following characteristics:

- The MPLS network distributes labels to each VPN.
- Only labels for other VPN members are distributed.
- Each VPN is automatically provisioned by IP routing.
- Each MPLS network is as secure as the Frame Relay connections.
- Encryption can be added to the VPN to provide privacy.
- Only one label is needed for both QoS and VPN.

MPLS Layer 3 VPNs represent the most popular deployed MPLS technology. MPLS Layer 3 VPNs leverage Border Gateway Protocol (BGP) to distribute VPN-related information. The SP typically manages the BGP routing domain within the MPLS cloud. This can significantly reduce the operational costs and complexities for enterprise environments.

Inside the MPLS cloud, network routes are learned with a dynamic Interior Gateway Protocol (IGP) routing protocol such as Open Shortest Path First (OSPF), Enhanced Interior Gateway Routing Protocol (EIGRP), or Border Gateway Protocol (BGP), or with static routes that are manually configured.

MPLS L3 VPN Considerations

MPLS VPNs use labels to specify the VRF and the corresponding VPN destination networks, which prevent the overlapping of addresses between VPNs. With MPLS Layer 3 VPNs, other valued-added services can be layered on, such as QoS and traffic engineering.

These services might offer enhanced network services such as voice, video, and data, for example. In addition, MPLS TE and Fast Reroute (FRR) features can be used to provide tight service level agreements (SLAs), including up to five levels of QoS SLAs.

VPN Benefits

The major benefits of using VPNs are flexibility, cost, and scalability. VPNs are easy to set up and deploy over an existing infrastructure in most cases. VPNs enable network access to remote users, remote sites, and extranet business partners. VPNs lower the cost of ownership by reducing the WAN recurring monthly charges and standardizing VPN security policies. The geographic coverage of VPNs is nearly everywhere Internet access is available, which makes VPNs highly scalable. In addition, VPNs simplify WAN operations because they can be deployed in a secure and consistent manner.

WAN Backup Design

Redundancy is a critical component of WAN design for the remote site because of the unreliable nature of WAN links, when compared to LANs that they connect. Most enterprise edge solutions require high availability between the primary and remote site. Because WAN links have lower reliability and lack bandwidth, they are good candidates for most WAN backup designs.

Branch offices should have some type of backup strategy in the event of a primary link failure. Backup links can be either permanent WAN or Internet-based connections.

WAN backup options are as follows:

- **Secondary WAN link:** Adding a secondary WAN link makes the network more fault tolerant. This solution offers two key advantages:
    - **Backup link:** Provides for network connectivity if the primary link fails. Dynamic or static routing techniques can be used to provide routing consistency during backup events. Application availability can also be increased because of the additional backup link.
    - **Additional bandwidth:** Load sharing allows both links to be used at the same time, increasing the available bandwidth. Load balancing can be achieved over the parallel links using automatic routing protocol techniques.
- **IPsec tunnel across the Internet:** An IPsec VPN backup link can redirect traffic to the corporate headquarters when a network failure has been detected.

WAN Backup over the Internet

Another alternative for WAN backup is to use the Internet as the connectivity transport between sites. However, keep in mind that this type of connection does not support bandwidth guarantees. The enterprise also needs to set up the tunnels and advertise the company's networks internally so that remote offices have reachable IP destinations.

Security is of great importance when you rely on the Internet for network connectivity, so a secure tunnel using IPsec needs to be deployed to protect the data during transport.

Figure 7-5 illustrates connectivity between the headend or central site and a remote site using traditional MPLS L3 VPN IP connections for the primary WAN link. The IPsec tunnel is a backup tunnel that provides redundancy for the site if the primary WAN link fails.

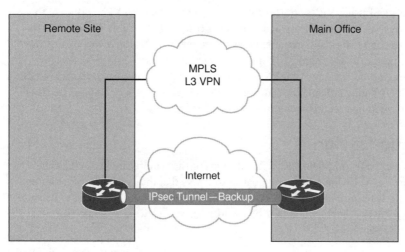

Figure 7-5 *WAN backup over the Internet*

IPsec tunnels are configured between the source and destination routers using tunnel interfaces. Packets that are destined for the tunnel have the standard formatted IP header. IP packets that are forwarded across the tunnel need an additional GRE/IPsec header placed on them, as well. As soon as the packets have the required headers, they are placed in the tunnel with a destination address of the tunnel endpoint. After the packets cross the tunnel and arrive on the far end, the GRE/IPsec headers are removed. The packets are then forwarded normally using the original IP packet headers. An important design consideration to keep in mind is that you might need to modify the MTU sizes between the source and destination of the tunnel endpoints to account for the larger header sizes of the additional GRE/IPsec headers.

Enterprise WAN Architecture

When selecting an enterprise WAN architecture, you should identify and understand the business and technical requirements. It is important to review sample network designs that could help identify requirements. Here are some common factors that influence decisions for WAN architecture selection:

- **High availability:** Most businesses need a high level of availability, especially for their critical applications. The goal of high availability is to remove the single points of failure in the design, either by software features or hardware-based resiliency. Redundancy is critical in providing high levels of availability for the enterprise. Some technologies have built-in techniques that enable them to be highly available. For technologies that do not, other techniques can be used, such as using additional WAN circuits or backup power supplies.

- **Support for growth:** Often, enterprises want to provide for growth in their WAN architectures, considering the amount of effort and time required to connect additional sites. High-growth WAN technologies can reduce the amount of effort and cost involved in network expansions. WAN technologies that do not provide growth require significantly more effort, time, and cost to add new branches or remote offices.

- **Operational expenses:** Private line and traditional ATM/Frame Relay tend to have higher recurring expenses than Internet-based IP VPNs. Public networks such as the Internet can be used for WAN services to reduce cost, but there are some tradeoffs with reliability and security compared to private or ATM/Frame Relay–type transports. Moreover, public networks make it more difficult to provide advanced technologies such as real-time voice and video.

- **Operational complexity:** The expertise of the technical staff who are required to maintain and support MAN and WAN technologies varies. Most enterprises have the internal IT knowledge to handle most traditional MAN and WAN upgrades without the need for much training. However, some of the advanced technologies usually reserved for SPs may require additional training for the IT staff if the support is brought in-house. Depending on the technology and the design, you have opportunities to reduce the complexity through network management.

- **Cost to implement:** In most cases, the implementation cost is a major concern. During the design process, it is important to evaluate the initial and recurring costs along with the design's benefits. Sometimes an organization can migrate from legacy connectivity to new technology with minimal investment in terms of equipment, time, and resources. In other cases, a network migration can require a low initial cost in terms of equipment and resources but can provide recurring operational savings and greater flexibility over the long term.

- **Network segmentation support:** Segmentation provides for Layer 2/3 logical separations between networks instead of physically separate networks. Advantages include reduced costs associated with equipment, maintenance, and carrier charges. In addition, separate security polices can be implemented per department or by functional area of the network to restrict access as needed.

- **Support for voice and video:** There is an increasing demand for the support of voice over MAN and WAN technologies. Some WAN providers offer Cisco QoS-Certified IP VPNs, which can provide the appropriate levels of QoS needed for voice and video deployments. In cases where Internet or public network connections are used, QoS cannot always be ensured. When voice and video are required for small offices, teleworkers, or remote agents, 768Kbps upstream bandwidth or greater is recommended.

Cisco Enterprise MAN/WAN

The Cisco Enterprise MAN/WAN architecture uses several technologies that work together in a cohesive relationship.

Here is the list of Cisco enterprise MAN/WAN technologies:

- Private WAN (optional encryption)
- Private WAN with self-deployed MPLS

- ISP service (Internet with site-to-site and remote-access VPN)
- SP-managed IP/MPLS VPN

These architectures provide integrated QoS, security, reliability, and ease of management that is required to support enterprise business applications and services. As you can see, these architectures provide a number of alternative technologies to the traditional private WAN and can allow for network growth and reduced monthly carrier charges.

Enterprise WAN/MAN Architecture Comparison

Enterprise WAN/MAN architectures have common characteristics that allow the network designer to compare the advantages and disadvantages of each approach. Table 7-6 compares the characteristics of private WAN, ISP service, SP MPLS/IP VPN, and private MPLS architectures.

Table 7-6   WAN/MAN Architecture Comparison

Characteristic	Private WAN	ISP Service	SP MPLS/IP VPN	Private MPLS
High availability	Excellent	Good	Excellent	Excellent
Growth support	Moderate	Good	Excellent	Excellent
Security	IPsec (optional)	IPsec (mandatory)	IPsec (optional)	IPsec (optional)
Ongoing expenses	High	Low	Moderate to high	Moderate to high
Ease of management	High	Medium	Medium	High
Voice/video support	Excellent	Low	Excellent	Excellent
Effort to migrate from private WAN	Low	Moderate	Moderate	High
Multicast	Good	Good	Good	Excellent

The Cisco enterprise MAN/WAN architectures include private WAN, ISP service, SP MPLS/IP VPN, and private MPLS:

- **Private WAN** generally consists of Frame Relay, ATM, private lines, and other traditional WAN connections. If security is needed, private WAN connections can be used in conjunction with encryption protocols such as Digital Encryption Standard (DES), Triple DES (3DES), and Advanced Encryption Standard (AES). This technology is best suited for an enterprise with moderate growth outlook where some remote or branch offices will need to be connected in the future. Businesses that require secure and reliable connectivity to comply with IT privacy standards can benefit from IPsec-encrypted connectivity over the private WAN. Disadvantages of private WANs are that they have high recurring costs from the carriers and they are not the preferred technology for teleworkers and remote call center agents. Some enterprises may use encryption on the network, connecting larger sites and omitting encryption on the smaller remote offices with IP VPNs.

- **ISP service (Internet with site-to-site and remote-access VPN)** uses strong encryption standards such as 3DES and AES, which make this WAN option more secure than the private WAN. ISP service also provides compliance with many new information security regulations imposed on some industries, such as healthcare and finance. This technology is best suited for basic connectivity over the Internet. However, if you need to support voice and video, consider IPsec VPN solutions that have the desired QoS support needed to meet your network requirements. The cost of this technology is relatively low. It is useful for connecting large numbers of teleworkers, remote contact agents, and small remote offices.

- **SP MPLS/IP VPN** is similar to private WAN technology, but with added scalability and flexibility. MPLS-enabled IP VPNs enable mesh-like behavior or any-to-any branch-type connectivity. SP MPLS networks can support enterprise QoS requirements for voice and video, especially those with high growth potential. SP MPLS features secure and reliable technology with generally lower carrier fees. This makes it a good option for connecting branch offices, teleworkers, and remote call center agents.

- **Private WAN with self-deployed MPLS** enables the network to be segmented into multiple logical segments allowing for multiple VPNs internally. Self-deployed MPLS is usually reserved for large enterprises that are willing to make substantial investments in equipment and training to build out the MPLS network. The IT staff needs to be well trained and comfortable with supporting complex networks.

Figure 7-6 illustrates the SP MPLS, private WAN with encryption, and IPsec VPNs WAN architectures.

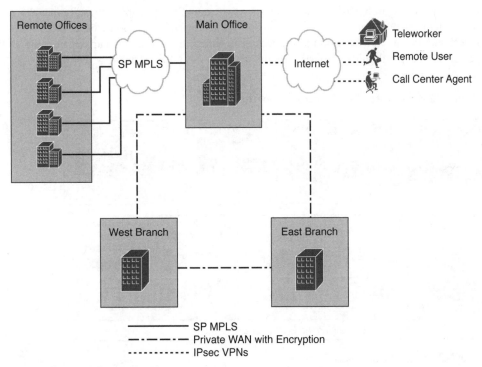

Figure 7-6 *WAN Architectures*

Enterprise WAN Components

When selecting enterprise edge components, you want to keep several considerations in mind. Here are some factors to examine during the selection process:

- Hardware selection involves the data-link functions and features offered by the device. Considerations include the following:
  - Port density
  - Types of ports supported
  - Modularity (add-on hardware)
  - Backplane and packet throughput
  - Redundancy (CPU and/or power)
  - Expandability for future use
- Software selection focuses on the network performance and the feature sets included in the software. Here are some factors to consider:
  - Forwarding decisions
  - Technology feature support
  - Bandwidth optimization
  - Security vulnerabilities
  - Software issues

When evaluating hardware, it is recommended that you use the latest Cisco product datasheets to research hardware and determine the equipment's capabilities. Remember to consider the port densities and types of ports the device offers. Some other areas to investigate include device modularity, packet throughput, redundancy capabilities, and the device's expandability options. Finally, remember to factor in what power options the hardware supports.

Figure 7-7 shows Cisco ISR G2 hardware options.

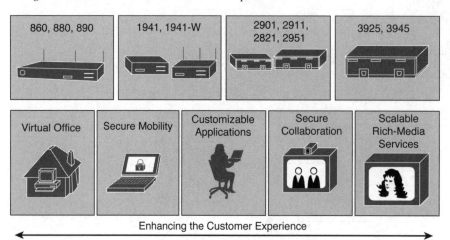

Figure 7-7 *Cisco ISR G2 hardware*

Cisco's second generation of Integrated Services Routers (ISR G2) is part of the Borderless Networks with the Cisco Network Architectures for the Enterprise. These ISR G2 routers provide the platform for business innovation by meeting the performance requirements for the next generation of WAN and network services. This architecture allows cost-effective delivery of high-definition (HD) collaboration solutions at the branch office and supports the secure transition to the private cloud. Cisco ISR G2 routers enable the business to deploy on-demand services, which reduces the overall cost of ownership.

Here are some key advantages of the ISR G2 routers:

- Deliver next-gen WAN and network service capabilities
- Provide video-based collaboration and rich-media services
- Enable secure transition to cloud and virtualized network services
- Reduced energy consumption and costs to support corporate responsibility

In addition, the new Cisco 4000 series Integrated Services Router offers four to ten times performance increase for the same price as the ISR G2. Cisco 4000s support many of the same features as the ISR G2, but with added capabilities such as Integrated Service Container, multicore hardware VPN acceleration, and the IOS XE operating system.

Comparing Hardware and Software

Table 7-7 compares the Cisco router and switch hardware platforms and their associated software families, releases, and functional descriptions.

Table 7-7   Cisco Router/Switch Platform and Software Comparison

Router/Switch Hardware	Software	Description
800, 1900, 2900, 3900	Cisco IOS 15.1	Delivers security, voice, and IP services with support for rich-media applications such as HD video and on-demand services.
4000	Cisco IOS XE 3.16	Delivers converged routing platforms with network, compute, and WAN services for branch networks.
ASR 1000	Cisco IOS XE 3S	Delivers high-performance routing for the network edge and data center. Also supports Metro Ethernet for the SP edge.
ASR 9000, CRS-1	Cisco IOS XR 5.3	High availability, providing large scalability and flexibility for the SP core and edge (takes advantage of highly distributed processing capabilities of the Cisco CRS-1 routing systems and the Cisco ASR 9000).
3560, 3850	Cisco IOS S Release 12.2SE and Cisco IOS XE 3.7	Provides low-end to mid-range LAN switching for enterprise access and distribution deployments.

Router/Switch Hardware	Software	Description
4500, 4900	Cisco IOS S Release 15.2	Provides mid-range LAN switching for enterprise access and distribution in the campus. Also supports Metro Ethernet.
6500, 6800	Cisco IOS S Release 12.2SX and 15.1SY	Delivers high-end LAN switching for enterprise access, distribution, core, and data center. Also supports Metro Ethernet for the SP edge.

Enterprise Branch Architecture

Enterprise branch architectures encompass a wide range of services that customers want to deploy at the edge of the enterprise. These architectures allow for a variety of connection options, and distance typically is not an issue. The services in this architecture give customers new opportunities to increase security, converge their voice and data traffic, improve productivity, and reduce costs.

Common branch network components found within the enterprise framework include

- Routers supporting the WAN edge connectivity
- Switches providing the Ethernet LAN infrastructure
- Security appliances securing the branch devices
- Wireless access points (APs) allowing for roaming mobility
- Call processing providing Unified Communications and video support
- IP phones and PCs for the end-user devices

In the past, we had applications local to the branch along with WAN connectivity to the headquarters for some of our critical applications. Currently, IT trends are moving most of the applications to the data center or the public cloud, such as VDI and Office 365. The move of these applications offsite is increasing the demands for bandwidth on the WAN links connecting the branches. If the WAN is not designed with sufficient bandwidth, users can have bad experiences, such as slow response times accessing their applications due to the congested WAN links.

Branch Design

It is important to characterize the existing network by gathering requirements to develop a suitable design for the branch.

Here are some questions you should ask:

- How much scalability is expected (for network devices, servers, users)?
- What level of high availability or redundancy is required?
- Is support for a specific server or network protocol needed?
- Will network management or support be centralized or distributed?

- Are there any network segmentation restrictions, such as DMZ segments or internal networks versus external networks?

- Will wireless services be needed, and to what extent?

- What is the estimated budget for the branch design?

Branch Connectivity

There are three common deployment models for branch connectivity, each with its own pros and cons:

- **MPLS WAN:** Single- or dual-router MPLS VPN

- **Hybrid WAN:** MPLS VPN and Internet VPN

- **Internet WAN:** Single- or dual-router Internet VPN

MPLS WAN involves single or dual routers for the MPLS VPN connections. MPLS WAN provides for the highest in SLA guarantees for both QoS capabilities and network availability. However, this option is the most expensive, and you need to be tied to the provider in this case.

Hybrid WAN combines MPLS VPN and Internet VPN on a single router split between a pair of routers. This deployment model offers a balanced cost option between the higher-cost MPLS VPN connection and the lower-cost Internet VPN for backup. With Hybrid WAN, traffic can be split between the MPLS VPN for higher-priority-based traffic and Internet VPN for lower-priority-based traffic.

Internet WAN includes a single router or dual routers using Internet-based VPN only. This deployment model is the lowest cost option, but lacks service level agreements (SLAs) and QoS capabilities offered by carriers. In this case, the enterprise would be responsible for providing any SLAs to the end users.

Redundancy for Branches

Depending on the cost of downtime for an organization, different levels of redundancy can be implemented for a branch site. The more critical branch sites will use higher levels or redundancy options. With any of the deployment options—MPLS WAN, Hybrid WAN, or Internet WAN—you can design redundant links with redundant routers, a single router with redundant links, or a single router with a single link.

For the most critical branch sites, you will typically want to eliminate single points of failure by designing with dual routers and dual WAN links along with dual power supplies. However, this highly available option comes with a higher price tag and is more complex to manage. Another option available to reduce cost is to use a single router with dual power supplies and multiple WAN links providing power and link redundancy. Non-redundant, single-homed sites are the lowest cost but they have multiple single points of failure inherent with the design, such as the WAN carrier or WAN link.

Single WAN Carrier vs. Dual WAN Carriers

The advantages of working with a single WAN carrier are that you only have one vendor to manage and you can work out a common QoS model that can be used throughout your

WAN. The major drawback with a single carrier is that if the carrier has an outage, it can be catastrophic to your overall WAN connectivity. This also makes it difficult to transition to a new carrier because all your WAN connectivity is with a single carrier.

On the other hand, if you have dual WAN carriers, the fault domains are increased and you have more WAN offerings to choose from because you are working with two different carriers for WAN services. The disadvantages with dual WAN carriers are that the overall design is more complex to manage and there will be higher recurring WAN costs.

Single MPLS Carrier Site

In a single MPLS carrier design, each site is connected to a single MPLS VPN from one provider. For example, you might have some sites that are single homed and some sites that are dual homed to the MPLS VPN. Each site will consist of CE routers peering with the provider using EBGP, and IBGP will be used for any CE-to-CE peering. Each CE will advertise any local prefixes to the provider with BGP and redistribute any learned BGP routes from the provider into the IGP or use default routing. Common IGPs are standard-based OSPF and EIGRP.

Figure 7-8 illustrates a single MPLS carrier design with single- and dual-homed sites.

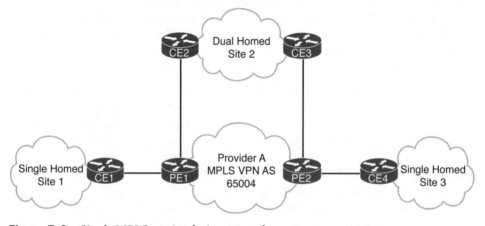

Figure 7-8   *Single MPLS carrier design example*

Dual MPLS Carriers

In a dual MPLS carrier design, each site is connected to both provider A and provider B. Some sites might have two routers for high availability, and others will only have a single router but with two links for link and provider redundancy. For example, each CE router will redistribute local routes from EIGRP into BGP. Routes from other sites will be redistributed from BGP into EIGRP as external routes. For sites that have two routers, filtering or tagging of the routes in and out of BGP will be needed to prevent routing loops.

Figure 7-9 illustrates a dual MPLS carrier design with single and dual routers.

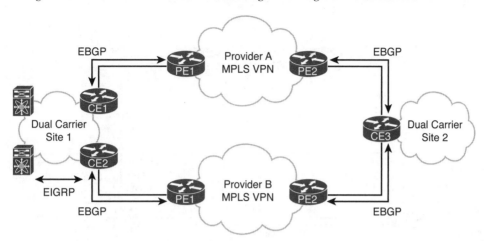

Figure 7-9   *Dual MPLS carrier design example*

Hybrid WAN: L3 VPN with IPsec VPN

Hybrid WAN designs involve using MPLS VPN for the primary connection and an Internet VPN for the backup connection. In this example design, EBGP would be used to peer with the MPLS VPN provider, and EIGRP would be used for routing for the IGP internally. At each site, the CE router would learn routes from the MPLS VPN via BGP and redistribute the routes from BGP into EIGRP. Then, each site would redistribute EIGRP routes into BGP and use EIGRP to peer with other local routers at each site. The Internet VPN routers would use EIGRP to exchange routes inside the IPsec VPN tunnels, and they would not need to redistribute routing information because they would only run EIGRP. On the MPLS VPN router, BGP-learned routes will be preferred, because the BGP routes that would be redistributed into EIGRP routes would have a higher administrative distance. In this case, if you want the MPLS VPN router to be the primary path, you need to run HSRP between the dual-homed routers, with the active router being the MPLS VPN connected router. That way, it would choose the MPLS VPN path as the primary and use the Internet VPN path as the backup.

Figure 7-10 illustrates a hybrid WAN design with MPLS VPN and Internet VPN.

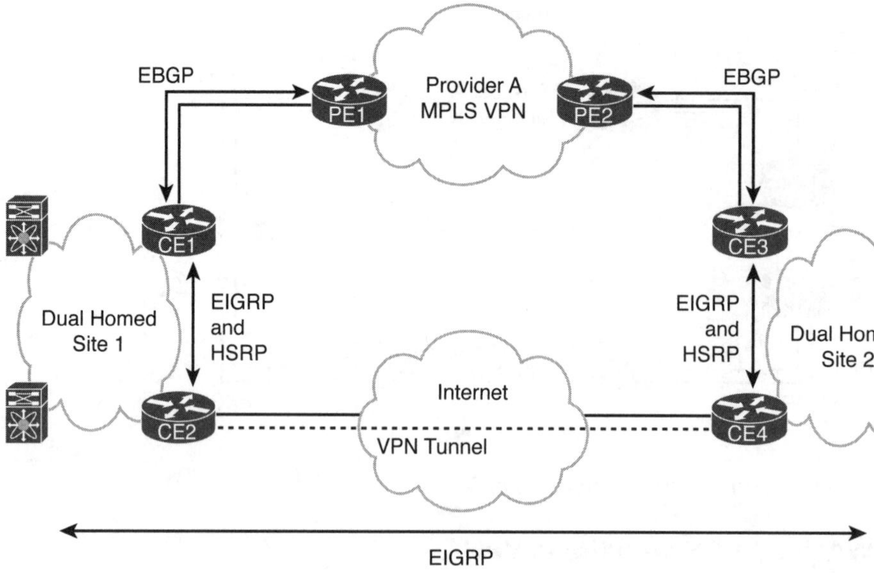

Figure 7-10   *Hybrid WAN design example*

Internet for Branches

When designing the Internet traffic flows for your branch locations, you have two main options to consider. One option is to tunnel all the Internet traffic back to the DC or main site, referred to as centralized Internet access. With this option, you have more control over the Internet traffic with centralized security services such as URL filtering, firewalling, and intrusion prevention. However, there are some drawbacks with this approach, because the bandwidth requirements and cost will be higher for your WAN links to the branch locations, and this will also increase the delay for any Internet-based traffic. Another option is to allow Internet-destined traffic at each branch to use the dedicated local Internet connection or VPN split tunneling. There are some advantages with this approach because your bandwidth requirements and the cost for your MPLS VPN links will be lower for your branch locations because you do not need to transport Internet traffic on them. This approach does have some drawbacks, however, because the local Internet access may violate your security policy by exposing more Internet points within your organization that need protection with security services.

Flat Layer 2 vs. Collapsed Core

Flat Layer 2 designs are commonly used to design branch small locations. Flat Layer 2 is where you use a Layer 2 switch to separate your network services with VLANs and then use an 802.1Q trunk to a router for the L3 gateway function for the network segments. With this design, you can also add a secondary router and run a First Hop Redundancy Protocol (FHRP) such as Hot Standby Routing Protocol (HSRP)/Gateway Load Balancing Protocol (GLBP) on a transit to provide redundancy for the default gateways. If an IGP is used, such as EIGRP, another transit link or VLAN will be needed to provide redundancy for dynamic L3 IP routing.

Collapsed core design is another approach for designing branch locations that are typically for larger branch locations. This design uses an L3 distribution layer switch to aggregate the 802.1Q trunk links from L2 access switches. Then, the L3 distribution layer switch connects with a single link or multiple links with EtherChannel to the L3 edge router. This design can also support high availability by using a pair of L3 edge routers and a pair of L3 distribution layer switches. Transit links are used between the routers and the L3 switches for EIGRP to support dynamic routing failover. FHRP, such as HSRP/GLBP, is then used to provide redundancy for a pair of L3 distribution switches; however, if a switch stack is used, then FHRPs are not needed.

Enterprise Branch Profiles

The enterprise branch has three profiles categorized by size and the number of users. The profiles are not intended to be the only architectures for branch offices but rather a common set of services that each branch should include. These profiles serve as a basis on which integrated services and application networking are built. The three profiles for the enterprise branch are as follows:

- **Small office:** Up to 50 users (single-tier design)
- **Medium office:** Between 50 and 100 users (dual-tier design)
- **Large office:** Between 100 and 1000 users (three-tier design)

Requirements such as high availability, scalability, and redundancy influence the branch profile selected for a branch office.

To integrate the WAN edge and the LAN infrastructure, an ISR can be used to provide voice, security, and data services. The ISR supports triple-speed interfaces (10/100/1000), high-speed WAN interface cards (HWICs), network modules, and embedded security capabilities.

Small Branch Design

The small branch design is recommended for branch offices that do not require hardware redundancy and that have a small user base supporting up to 50 users. This profile consists of an access router providing WAN and Internet services and connections for the LAN services. The access router can connect the Layer 2 switch ports in one of three ways:

- Integrated Layer 2 switching using an optional EtherSwitch module that provides 16 to 48 Ethernet ports for client connections. Some modules support PoE.
- External Layer 2 switching using a trunk connection to an access switch that aggregates the Ethernet connections. The access switch can also include PoE to support IP phones and wireless APs.
- Logical EtherChannel interface between the ISR and the access switches using the EtherSwitch module. The access switches can also provide PoE as needed.

The Layer 3 WAN services are based on the WAN and Internet deployment model. A T1 is used for the primary link, and an Internet-based secondary link with VPN is used for backup. Other network fundamentals are supported, such as EIGRP, floating static routes, and QoS for bandwidth protection.

The ISR can support the default gateway function and other Layer 3 services such as DHCP, NAT, IPsec VPN, and IOS Firewall.

Layer 2 services can be provided by the Cisco ISR using switch modules or the Cisco Catalyst 2960-X/XR, 3560, 3750, or 3850 series-based access switches. It is recommended that you use Rapid Per VLAN Spanning Tree Plus (PVST+) for all Layer 2 branch offices where loops are present. Rapid PVST+ ensures a loop-free topology when multiple Layer 2 connections are used for redundancy purposes.

Both the Cisco 2921 and the 2951 ISRs support three integrated 10/100/1000 Ethernet interfaces, which support Layer 3 routing, and service modules. There are also 16-, 24-, and 48-port Cisco Enhanced EtherSwitch service modules available.

Figure 7-11 illustrates the small branch design connecting back to the corporate office where the corporate resources are located.

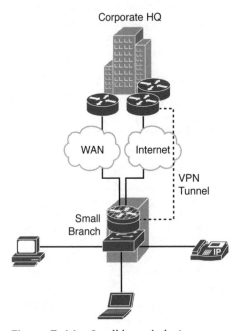

Figure 7-11 *Small branch design*

Medium Branch Design

The medium branch design is recommended for branch offices of 50 to 100 users, which is similar to the small branch but with an additional access router in the WAN edge (slightly larger) allowing for redundancy services. Typically, two 2921 or 2951 routers are used to support the WAN and Internet, and separate access switches are used to provide LAN connectivity.

The infrastructure components are dual-access routers, external Layer 2/3 switches, laptops, desktops, printers, and IP phones. Dual Ethernet WAN links provide the private WAN services, which are used to connect back to the corporate offices via both of the access routers.

Layer 3 protocols such as EIGRP are typically deployed. Because there are two routers, Hot Standby Router Protocol (HSRP) or Gateway Load Balancing Protocol (GLBP) can be used to provide redundant gateway services. QoS can also be used to provide guaranteed bandwidth for VoIP, and policing can be used to restrict certain traffic classes from overwhelming the available bandwidth. Cisco IOS features such as QoS, access control lists (ACLs), and RIP/EIGRP stub routing capabilities are available in the LAN base feature set, but advanced IP unicast routing (OSPF/EIGRP/BGP) and multicast routing protocols (PIM-SM/SSM) require an upgraded IP Services feature set.

The medium branch design supports using a higher-density external switch or using the Enhanced EtherSwitch module with the ISR to create trunks to the external access switches. The Cisco Catalyst 3850 series switches have StackWise technology, allowing multiple switches to be connected and managed as one. This also increases the port density available for end-user connections. With Cisco StackWise technology, customers can create a single, 480Gbps switching unit that can connect up to nine 3850 series switches using a variety of fiber and copper ports, allowing greater flexibility with the connection options.

Figure 7-12 illustrates the medium branch design using dual routers back to the corporate office where the corporate resources are located.

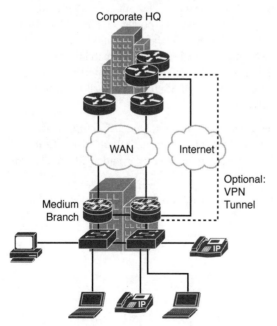

Figure 7-12 *Medium branch design*

Large Branch Design

The large branch design is the largest of the branch profiles, supporting between 100 and 1000 users. This design profile is similar to the medium branch design in that it also provides dual access routers in the WAN edge. In addition, dual Adaptive Security Appliances (ASAs) are used for stateful firewall filtering, and dual distribution switches provide the multilayer switching component. The WAN services use an MPLS deployment model with dual WAN links into the WAN cloud.

Because there are dual routers, redundant network routing can be achieved through EIGRP load balancing. On the distribution layer switches, first-hop redundancy protocols such as HSRP/GLBP can be used to provide gateway redundancy. The dual ASA configuration allows for redundancy and stateful failover. QoS services such as shaping and policing can be applied to all the routers and switches, as required.

To meet the requirements of the larger user base, a distribution layer of multilayer switches is added to aggregate the connected access switches. A multilayer switch provides the additional LAN switching capabilities to meet the port density requirements and allows flexibility to support additional network devices.

A couple of hardware options for this design are the Cisco Catalyst 3850 with StackWise technology and using a modular approach with a Cisco Catalyst 4500. The Cisco 3850 series of switches provide great port density options and can even provide the redundant power. The Cisco 4500 switch platform is a modular chassis-based switch that not only allows for flexibility by increasing port densities through additional modules but can also provide redundant power internally for the entire chassis by using dual power supplies. All of these switch models have PoE options available for both IEEE 802.3af (PoE) and IEEE 802.3at (PoE+). The Cisco Catalyst 4507 switch also supports dual supervisor capabilities for high-availability types of environments. The Cisco 4500 switches also support the Virtual Switching System (VSS) feature, which virtualizes a pair of 4500 switches, allowing them to act as a single switch to downstream devices.

If Cisco Catalyst 3560 and 3850 switches are used, additional Layer 2 security features such as dynamic Address Resolution Protocol (ARP) inspection, Dynamic Host Control Protocol (DHCP) snooping, and IP Source Guard can be used to provide additional security enhancements.

Figure 7-13 illustrates the large branch design using dual routers, ASAs, and distribution switches.

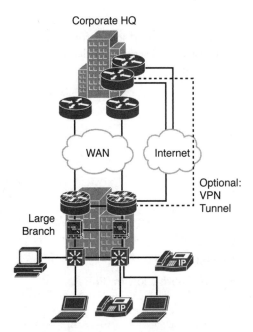

Figure 7-13 *Large branch design*

Enterprise Teleworker Design

At the remote edges of the network is another branch office known as enterprise teleworkers. Cisco developed a solution called Cisco Virtual Office Solution, which was designed with the enterprise teleworker in mind. As organizations continually try to reduce costs and improve employee productivity, working from home is becoming an increasingly popular option for businesses and organizations. This approach allows employees to manage their work schedules more effectively and increase their productivity. This also results in greater job satisfaction and flexibility in the work schedules. The work-from-home teleworker is an extension of the enterprise and serves as the basis for the enterprise teleworker solution.

Enterprise teleworkers need to be differentiated from the occasional remote worker. The full-time enterprise teleworker has more extensive application access and requirements than the occasional remote worker. Occasionally, remote users connect to the corporate network at a hotspot, but generally they do not have the same application demands of an enterprise teleworker. Generally, enterprise teleworkers connect to a local ISP through a cable or DSL connection in their residence.

The Cisco Virtual Office Solution for the Enterprise Teleworker is implemented using the Cisco 800 series ISRs. Each ISR has integrated switch ports that then connect to the user's broadband connection. The solution uses a permanent always-on IPsec VPN tunnel back to the corporate network. This architecture provides for centralized IT security management, corporate-pushed security policies, and integrated identity services. In addition, this solution supports the enterprise teleworker needs through advanced applications such as voice and video. For example, the enterprise teleworker can take advantage of toll bypass, voicemail, and advanced IP phone features not available in the PSTN.

ISRs for Teleworkers

The Cisco 860 and 880 series offer integrated services at broadband speeds for small offices and enterprise teleworkers. Depending on the Cisco 800 series ISR selected, features include support for data, security, and wireless technologies.

Cisco 860 ISRs provide the following:

- Broadband services for small office and teleworkers
- Four-port 10/100/1000 switching with VLAN support
- Security: SPI firewall, IPsec VPN (3DES/AES)
- Wireless 802.11n access point support
- CON/AUX port or web-based management tools

Cisco 880 ISRs provide the following:

- Broadband services for small office and teleworkers
- WAN diversity, FE, DSL, 3G wireless WAN, and ISDN
- Four-port 10/100 FE switch with VLAN support; two ports allow for PoE
- Security
    - SPI firewall with control for email, IM, and HTTP
    - IPsec VPN (3DES/AES), DMVPN, GET VPN, and Secure Sockets Layer (SSL) VPN
    - IPS (intrusion prevention system; inline deep-packet inspection)
    - Content filtering (category-based reputation rating, keyword/URL blocking)
- Wireless 802.11n access point support (unified or autonomous)
- Integrated WAN optimization (1.5 Mbps; 30–75 TCP connections with license)
- CON/AUX port or web-based management tools

References and Recommended Readings

Services Ready Large Branch Network System Assurance Guide, www.cisco.com/en/US/docs/voice_ip_comm/cvd/G2srlgbrnt/G2srlgbrnt_Book.html.

Module 4, "Enterprise Network Design," Designing for Cisco Internetwork Solutions Course (DESGN) v3.0.

RFC 4301: Security Architecture for the Internet Protocol, www.ietf.org/rfc/rfc4301.

RFC 2406: IP Encapsulating Security Payload, www.ietf.org/rfc/rfc2406.txt.

RFC 2402: IP Authentication Header, www.ietf.org/rfc/rfc2402.txt.

What's New on Cisco ISR G2? www.cisco.com/assets/prod/rt/isr/whats-new-isrg2.html.

Benefits of Migrating to Cisco 4000 Series Integrated Services Routers, http://www.cisco.com/c/dam/en/us/products/collateral/routers/4000-series-integrated-services-routers-isr/aag_c83-731053.pdf.

Cisco Enhanced Power over Ethernet (PoE), http://www.cisco.com/c/en/us/products/switches/epoe.html.

Exam Preparation Tasks

Review All Key Topics

Review the most important topics in the chapter, noted with the Key Topic icon in the outer margin of the page. Table 7-8 lists a reference of these key topics and the page numbers on which each is found.

Table 7-8   Key Topics

Key Topic Element	Description	Page
List	The three major categories that represent traditional WANs	252
Table 7-2	Remote site connectivity options	254
Table 7-3	Enterprise VPN vs. Service Provider VPN	255
Table 7-4	Enterprise VPN comparison	259
List	WAN backup options	263
List	Common factors that influence decisions for WAN architecture selection	264
Table 7-6	WAN/MAN architecture comparison	266
List	Enterprise edge component considerations	268
Table 7-7	Cisco Router/Switch Platform and Software Comparison	269
List	Branch connectivity deployment options	271
List	Three ways access routers can connect the Layer 2 switch ports	275
Summary	Medium branch design	276
Summary	Large branch design	278
Summary	Enterprise teleworker design	279

Complete Tables and Lists from Memory

Print a copy of Appendix D, "Memory Tables" (found on the book website), or at least the section for this chapter, and complete the tables and lists from memory. Appendix E, "Memory Tables Answer Key," also on the website, includes completed tables and lists to check your work.

Define Key Terms

Define the following key terms from this chapter, and check your answers in the glossary:

circuit switched, leased lines, packet and cell switched, hub-and-spoke (or star) topology, partial-mesh topology, full-mesh topology, leased lines, IPsec, MPLS, Virtual Private LAN Services (VPLS), DMVPN, GETVPN, Metro Ethernet, dial backup, secondary WAN link, small branch design, medium branch design, large branch design

Q&A

The answers to these questions appear in Appendix A, "Answers to the 'Do I Know This Already?' Quizzes and Q&A Questions." For more practice with exam format questions, use the exam engine on the website.

1. What type of WAN technology provides a dedicated connection from the service provider?

   a. Circuit-switched data connection

   b. Leased lines

   c. Packet switched

   d. Cell switched

2. What type of topology suffers from a single point of failure?

   a. Hub-and-spoke topology

   b. Full-mesh topology

   c. Partial-mesh topology

   d. None of the above

3. What kind of topology requires that each site be connected to every other site in the cloud?

   a. Hub-and-spoke topology

   b. Full-mesh topology

   c. Partial-mesh topology

   d. All of the above

4. Which two of the following best describe WAN backup over the Internet deployments?

   a. Private WAN

   b. Redundancy for primary WAN connection

   c. VPLS

   d. Best-effort performance

5. Which of the following provides an L2 connection over an MPLS network?

   a. MPLS VPN

   b. VPLS

   c. GETVPN

   d. None of the above

6. What are three types of WAN topologies that can be used with Cisco enterprise architectures in the WAN?

   a. Ring

   b. Full mesh

   c. Partial mesh

   d. Hub and spoke

7. The service provider plays an active role in enterprise routing with what kind of VPNs?

   a. Leased lines

   b. MPLS L3 VPN

   c. VPLS

   d. Enterprise VPN over the Internet

8. Which WAN backup option uses load sharing in addition to providing backup services?

   a. Secondary WAN link

   b. IPsec tunnel – Backup link

   c. VRF stitching

   d. VLANs

9. Which of the following best describes the difference between a small branch and a medium branch?

   a. Small branches use dual external switches.

   b. Medium branches use a single ASA firewall.

   c. Small branches use a single ASA firewall.

   d. Medium branches use dual routers and dual external L2 switches.

10. How many users are supported in a large branch design?

    a. Up to 50

    b. Between 50 to 100

    c. Between 100 to 1000

    d. Between 200 to 5000

11. What two methods are used to enable private networks over public networks?

    a. IPsec

    b. PKI

    c. DMVPN

    d. PSTN

12. What is not a factor for WAN architecture selection?

    a. Ease of management

    b. Ongoing expenses

    c. Spanning-tree inconsistencies

    d. High availability

7

13. Which Layer 3 tunneling technique enables basic IP VPNs without encryption?

    a. GRE

    b. IPsec

    c. HMAC

    d. IKE

14. Which of the following is not recommended for designing WANs?

    a. Analyze customer requirements.

    b. Characterize the existing network.

    c. Design the new WAN.

    d. Implement the new WAN.

15. What WAN architecture uses the Internet with site-to-site VPNs?

    a. Private WAN

    b. ISP service

    c. SP MPLS/IP VPN

    d. Private WAN with self-deployed MPLS

16. Which WAN backup method does not typically use the Internet as a transport?

    a. IPsec tunnel

    b. GRE tunnel

    c. DMVPN

    d. GETVPN

17. What branch design uses ASA firewalls?

    a. Small branch

    b. Medium branch

    c. Large branch

    d. Secure branch

18. What WAN/MAN architecture is usually reserved for large enterprises that are willing to make substantial investments in equipment and training?

    a. Private WAN

    b. Private WAN with self-deployed MPLS

    c. ISP service

    d. SP MPLS/IP VPN

19. Match each branch profile design with its description.

      i.   Single access router

      ii. Cable modem/router

      iii. Pair of access routers

      iv. Pair of firewalls

a. Small branch

b. Medium branch

c. Large branch

d. Enterprise teleworker

This chapter covers the following subjects:

IPv4 Header

IPv4 Addressing

IP Address Subnets

Address Assignment and Name Resolution

IP Addressing Design

This chapter covers the concepts and terminology for Internet Protocol Version 4 (IPv4) address design. It reviews IPv4 address structures and IPv4 address types. IPv4 is the version of the protocol that the Internet has used since the initial allocation of IPv4 addresses in 1981. The size of the enterprise indicated the address class that was allocated. This chapter covers the IPv4 header to give you an understanding of IPv4 characteristics. The mid-1990s saw the implementation of classless interdomain routing (CIDR), network address translation (NAT), and private address space to prevent the apparent exhaustion of the IPv4 address space. Companies implement variable-length subnet masks (VLSMs) in their networks to provide intelligent address assignment and summarization. Separate IP subnets are used for IP phones and wireless LANs to segregate this traffic from data traffic. As of February 2011, the Internet Assigned Numbers Authority (IANA) allocated the last remaining address blocks of the IPv4 address space, making the free pool of IPv4 address space depleted. Furthermore, on September 24, 2015, the American Registry for Internet Numbers (ARIN) issued the final IPv4 addresses in its free pool. Careful allocation of available IPv4 address space must be part of the network design. The CCDA candidate needs to understand all these concepts to design IPv4 addressing for a network.

CHAPTER 8

Internet Protocol Version 4 Design

"Do I Know This Already?" Quiz

The "Do I Know This Already?" quiz helps you identify your strengths and deficiencies in this chapter's topics.

The ten-question quiz, derived from the major sections in the "Foundation Topics" portion of the chapter, helps you determine how to spend your limited study time.

Table 8-1 outlines the major topics discussed in this chapter and the "Do I Know This Already?" quiz questions that correspond to those topics.

Table 8-1 "Do I Know This Already?" Foundation Topics Section-to-Question Mapping

Foundation Topics Section	Questions Covered in This Section
IPv4 Header	4, 10
IPv4 Addressing	1, 5, 9
IPv4 Address Subnets	2, 3, 6, 7
Address Assignment and Name Resolution	8

1. Which of the following addresses is an IPv4 private address?
   a. 198.176.1.1
   b. 172.31.16.1
   c. 191.168.1.1
   d. 224.130.1.1

2. How many IP addresses are available for hosts in the subnet 198.10.100.64/27?
   a. 14
   b. 30
   c. 62
   d. 126

3. What subnet mask should you use in loopback addresses?
   a. 255.255.255.252
   b. 255.255.255.254
   c. 255.255.255.0
   d. 255.255.255.255

4. In what IPv4 field are the precedence bits located?

   a. Priority field

   b. IP Protocol field

   c. Type of Service field

   d. IP Options field

5. What type of address is 225.10.1.1?

   a. Unicast

   b. Multicast

   c. Broadcast

   d. Anycast

6. Which subnetworks are summarized by the following summary route: 150.10.192.0/21?

   a. 150.10.192.0/24, 150.10.193.0/24

   b. 150.10.192.0/22, 150.10.196.0/23, 150.10.197.0/24

   c. 150.10.192.0/22, 150.10.199.0/22

   d. 150.10.192.0/23, 150.10.194.0/23, 150.10.196.0/23, 150.10.199.0/24, 150.10.198.0/24

7. What type of network and subnet mask would you use to save address space in a point-to-point WAN link?

   a. 100.100.10.16/26

   b. 100.100.10.16/28

   c. 100.100.10.16/29

   d. 100.100.10.16/30

8. What protocol is used to automatically assign IP addresses?

   a. Dynamic Host Control Protocol

   b. Dedicated Host Configuration Protocol

   c. Dynamic Host Configuration Protocol

   d. Automatic Host Configuration Protocol

9. A company needs to use public IP addresses so that four network servers are accessible from the Internet. What technology is used to meet this requirement?

   a. DNS

   b. IPsec

   c. Static NAT

   d. Dynamic NAT

10. The DS field of DSCP is capable of how many codepoints?

   a. 8

   b. 32

   c. 64

   d. 128

Foundation Topics

This chapter reviews IPv4 headers, address classes, and assignment methods.

IP is the network layer protocol in TCP/IP. It contains logical addressing and information for routing packets throughout the internetwork. IP is described in RFC 791, which was prepared for the Defense Advanced Research Projects Agency (DARPA) in September 1981.

IP provides for the transmission of blocks of data, called datagrams or packets, from a source to a destination. The sources and destinations are identified by 32-bit IP addresses. The source and destination devices are workstations, servers, printers, and routers. The CCDA candidate must understand IPv4 logical address classes and assignment. The IPv4 protocol also provides for the fragmentation and reassembly of large packets for transport over networks with small maximum transmission units (MTUs). The CCDA candidate must have a good understanding of this packet fragmentation and reassembly.

Appendix C, "OSI Model, TCP/IP Architecture, and Numeric Conversion," provides an overview of the TCP/IP architecture and how it compares with the OSI model. It also reviews binary numbers and numeric conversion (to decimal), which is a skill needed to understand IP addresses and subnetting.

IPv4 Header

The best way to understand IPv4 is to know the IPv4 header and all its fields. Segments from TCP or the User Datagram Protocol (UDP) are passed on to IP for processing. The IP header is appended to the TCP or UDP segment. The TCP or UDP segment then becomes the IP data. The IPv4 header is 20 bytes in length when it uses no optional fields. The IP header includes the addresses of the sending host and destination host. It also includes the upper-layer protocol, a field for prioritization, and a field for fragmentation. Figure 8-1 shows the IP header format.

```
0                   1                   2                   3
0 1 2 3 4 5 6 7 8 9 0 1 2 3 4 5 6 7 8 9 0 1 2 3 4 5 6 7 8 9 0 1
```

Version	IHL	Type of Service		Total Length	
Identification			flags	Fragment Offset	
Time to Live		Protocol		Header Checksum	
Source Address					
Destination Address					
IP Options Field				Padding	

Figure 8-1 *IP header*

The following is a description of each field in the IP header:

- **Version:** This field is 4 bits in length. It indicates the IP header's format, based on the version number. Version 4 is the current version; therefore, this field is set to 0100 (4 in binary) for IPv4 packets. This field is set to 0110 (6 in binary) in IPv6 networks.

- **IHL (Internet Header Length):** This field is 4 bits in length. It indicates the length of the header in 32-bit words (4 bytes) so that the beginning of the data can be found in the IP header. The minimum value for a valid header (five 32-bit words) is 5 (0101).

- **ToS (Type of Service):** This field is 8 bits in length. Quality of service (QoS) parameters such as IP precedence or DSCP are found in this field. These are explained further in this chapter.

- **Total Length:** This field is 16 bits in length. It represents the length of the datagram or packet in bytes, including the header and data. The maximum length of an IP packet can be $2^{16} - 1 = 65,535$ bytes. Routers use this field to determine whether fragmentation is necessary by comparing the total length with the outgoing MTU.

- **Identification:** This field is 16 bits in length. It identifies fragments for reassembly.

- **Flags:** This field is 3 bits in length. It indicates whether the packet can be fragmented and whether more fragments follow. Bit 0 is reserved and set to 0. Bit 1 indicates May Fragment (0) or Do Not Fragment (1). Bit 2 indicates Last Fragment (0) or More Fragments to Follow (1).

- **Fragment Offset:** This field is 13 bits in length. It indicates (in bytes) where in the packet this fragment belongs. The first fragment has an offset of 0.

- **Time to Live:** This field is 8 bits in length. It indicates the maximum time the packet is to remain on the network. Each router decrements this field by 1 for loop avoidance. If this field is 0, the packet must be discarded. This scheme permits routers to discard undeliverable packets.

- **Protocol:** This field is 8 bits in length. It indicates the upper-layer protocol. The Internet Assigned Numbers Authority (IANA) is responsible for assigning IP protocol values. Table 8-2 shows some key protocol numbers. You can find a full list at www.iana.org/assignments/protocol-numbers.

Table 8-2 IP Protocol Numbers

Protocol Number	IP Protocol
1	Internet Control Message Protocol (ICMP)
2	Internet Group Management Protocol (IGMP)
6	Transmission Control Protocol (TCP)
17	User Datagram Protocol (UDP)
41	IPv6 encapsulation
50	Encapsulating Security Payload (ESP)
51	Authentication Header (AH)
58	ICMPv6
88	Enhanced Interior Gateway Routing Protocol (EIGRP)
89	Open Shortest Path First (OSPF)
103	Protocol-Independent Multicast (PIM)
112	Virtual Router Redundancy Protocol (VRRP)

- **Header Checksum:** This field is 16 bits in length. The checksum does not include the data portion of the packet in the calculation. The checksum is recomputed and verified at each point the IP header is processed.

- **Source Address:** This field is 32 bits in length. It is the sender's IP address.

- **Destination Address:** This field is 32 bits in length. It is the receiver's IP address.

- **IP Options:** This field is variable in length. The options provide for control functions that are useful in some situations but unnecessary for the most common communications. Specific options are security, loose source routing, strict source routing, record route, and timestamp.

- **Padding:** This field is variable in length. It ensures that the IP header ends on a 32-bit boundary.

Table 8-3 summarizes the fields of the IP header.

Table 8-3   IPv4 Header Fields

Field	Length	Description
Version	4 bits	Indicates the IP header's format, based on the version number. Set to 0100 for IPv4.
IHL	4 bits	Length of the header in 32-bit words.
ToS	8 bits	QoS parameters.
Total Length	16 bits	Length of the packet in bytes, including header and data.
Identification	16 bits	Identifies a fragment.
Flags	3 bits	Indicates whether a packet is fragmented and whether more fragments follow.
Fragment Offset	13 bits	Location of the fragment in the total packet.
Time to Live	8 bits	Decremented by 1 by each router. When this is 0, the router discards the packet.
Protocol	8 bits	Indicates the upper-layer protocol.
Header Checksum	16 bits	Checksum of the IP header; does not include the data portion.
Source Address	32 bits	IP address of the sending host.
Destination Address	32 bits	IP address of the destination host.
IP Options	Variable	Options for security, loose source routing, record route, and timestamp.
Padding	Variable	Added to ensure that the header ends in a 32-bit boundary.

ToS

The ToS field of the IP header is used to specify QoS parameters. Routers and Layer 3 switches look at the ToS field to apply policies, such as priority, to IP packets based on the markings. An example is a router prioritizing time-sensitive IP packets over regular data traffic such as web or email, which is not time sensitive.

The ToS field has undergone several definitions since RFC 791. Figure 8-2 shows the several formats of the ToS service field based on the evolution of RFCs 791 (1981), 1349 (1992), 2474 (1998), and 3168 (2001). The following paragraphs describe this evolution.

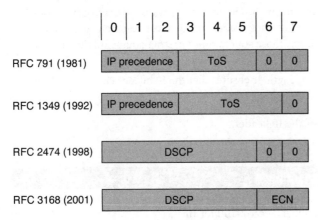

Figure 8-2   *Evolution of the IPv4 ToS field*

The first 3 (leftmost) bits are the IP precedence bits. These bits define values that are used by QoS methods. The precedence bits especially help in marking packets to give them differentiated treatment with different priorities. For example, Voice over IP (VoIP) packets can get preferential treatment over regular data packets. RFC 791 describes the precedence bits as shown in Table 8-4.

Table 8-4   IP Precedence Bit Values

Decimal	Binary	IP Precedence Description
0	000	Routine
1	001	Priority
2	010	Immediate
3	011	Flash
4	100	Flash override
5	101	Critical
6	110	Internetwork control
7	111	Network control

All default traffic is set with 000 in the precedence bits. Voice traffic is usually set to 101 (critical) to give it priority over normal traffic. An application such as FTP is assigned a normal priority because it tolerates network latency and packet loss. Packet retransmissions are typically acceptable for normal traffic.

Note   It is common to see voice traffic classified as IP precedence 5, video traffic classified as IP precedence 4, and voice and video signaling classified as IP precedence 3. Default traffic remains as IP precedence 0.

RFC 1349 redefined bits 3 and 6 (expanding for ToS bits) to reflect a desired type of service optimization. Table 8-5 shows the ToS field values that indicate service parameters to use for IP packets.

Table 8-5   ToS Field Values

ToS Bits 3 to 6	Description
0000	Normal service
1000	Minimize delay
0100	Maximize throughput
0010	Maximize reliability
0001	Minimize monetary cost

In 1998, RFC 2474 redefined the ToS octet as the Differentiated Services (DS) field and further specified bits 0 through 5 as the Differentiated Services Codepoint (DSCP) bits to support differentiated services. RFC 3168 (2001) updates RFC 2474, with the specification of an Explicit Congestion Notification (ECN) field.

The DS field takes the form shown in Figure 8-2. The DS field provides more granular levels of packet classification by using 6 bits for packet marking. DS has $2^6 = 6^4$ levels of classification, which is significantly higher than the eight levels of the IP precedence bits. These 64 levels are called codepoints, and they have been defined to be backward compatible with IP precedence values. RFC 2474 defines three sets of PHBs: Class Selector (CS), Assured Forwarding (AF), and Expedited Forwarding (EF). The CS PHB set is for DSCP values that are compatible with IP precedence bits. The AF PHB set is used for queuing and congestion avoidance. The EF PHB set is used for premium service. The CS per-hop behaviors (PHB), in the form of xxx000, make it backward compatible with IP precedence.

The network designer uses DSCP to give priority to IP packets using Cisco routers. Routers should be configured to map these codepoints to PHBs with queuing or other bandwidth-management techniques. Table 8-6 compares DSCP and IP precedence values used to assign priority and apply policies to IP packets.

8

Table 8-6 DSCP and IP Precedence Values

IP Precedence	Limitation		DSCP		
Service Type	Decimal	Binary	Class	Decimal	Codepoint
Routine	0	000	Best effort	0	000xxx
Priority	1	001	Assured Forwarding (AF) Class 1	8 to 14	001xxx
Immediate	2	010	AF Class 2	16 to 22	010xxx
Flash	3	011	AF Class 3	24 to 30	011xxx
Flash override	4	100	AF Class 4	32 to 38	100xxx
Critical	5	101	Expedited Forwarding (EF)	40 to 46	101xxx
Internetwork control	6	110	Control	48	110xxx
Network control	7	111	Control	56	111xxx

RFC 2597 defines recommended values for AF codepoints with low, medium, and high packet-drop precedence. Table 8-7 shows the recommended AF codepoint values.

Table 8-7 DSCP AF Packet-Drop Precedence Values

Precedence	AF Class 1	AF Class 2	AF Class 3	AF Class 4
Low drop precedence	001010	010010	011010	100010
Medium drop precedence	001100	010100	011100	100100
High drop precedence	001110	010110	011110	100110

RFC 2598 defines the EF PHB for low loss, loss latency, and assured bandwidth types of traffic. This is considered a premium service. Traffic such as VoIP is classified as EF. The codepoint for EF is 101110, which corresponds to a DSCP value of 46.

When you are configuring Cisco routers, the following options are preconfigured and summarize the defined values for DSCP. Table 8-8 shows the IP DSCP values predefined in Cisco values.

Table 8-8 IP DSCP Values

DSCP Class	DSCP Codepoint Value	DSCP Decimal
Default	000000	0
CS1	001000	8
AF11	001010	10
AF12	001100	12

DSCP Class	DSCP Codepoint Value	DSCP Decimal
AF13	001110	14
CS2	010000	16
AF21	010010	18
AF22	010100	20
AF23	010110	22
CS3	011000	24
AF31	011010	26
AF32	011100	28
AF33	011110	30
CS4	100000	32
AF41	100010	34
AF42	100100	36
AF43	100110	38
CS5	101000	40
EF	101110	46
CS6	110000	48
CS7	111000	56

8

IPv4 Fragmentation

One key characteristic of IPv4 is fragmentation and reassembly. Although the maximum length of an IP packet is 65,535 bytes, most of the common lower-layer protocols do not support such large MTUs. For example, the MTU for Ethernet is approximately 1518 bytes. When the IP layer receives a packet to send, it first queries the outgoing interface to get its MTU. If the packet's size is greater than the interface's MTU, the layer fragments the packet.

When a packet is fragmented, it is not reassembled until it reaches the destination IP layer. The destination IP layer performs the reassembly. Any router in the path can fragment a packet, and any router in the path can fragment a fragmented packet again. Each fragmented packet receives its own IP header and is routed independently from other packets. Routers and Layer 3 switches in the path do not reassemble the fragments. The destination host performs the reassembly and places the fragments in the correct order by looking at the identification and fragment offset fields.

If one or more fragments are lost, the entire packet must be retransmitted. Retransmission is the responsibility of the higher-layer protocol (such as TCP). Also, you can set the Flags field in the IP header to "Do Not Fragment" the packet. If the field indicates Do Not Fragment, the packet is discarded if the outgoing MTU is smaller than the packet.

IPv4 Addressing

This section covers the IPv4 address classes, private addressing, and NAT. The IPv4 address space was initially divided into five classes. Each IP address class is identified by the initial bits of the address. Classes A, B, and C are unicast IP addresses, meaning that the destination is a single host. IP Class D addresses are multicast addresses, which are sent to multiple hosts. IP Class E addresses are reserved. This section introduces IPv4 private addresses, which are selected address ranges that are reserved for use by companies in their private networks. These private addresses are not routed in the Internet. NAT translates between private and public addresses.

An IP address is a unique logical number to a network device or interface. An IP address is 32 bits in length. To make the number easier to read, the dotted-decimal format is used. The bits are combined into four 8-bit groups, each converted into decimal numbers (for example, 10.1.1.1). If you are not familiar with binary numbers, Appendix C, "OSI Model, TCP/IP Architecture, and Numeric Conversion," contains a review of binary and hexadecimal number manipulation.

The following example shows an IP address in binary and decimal formats:

Binary IP address: 01101110 00110010 11110010 00001010

Convert each byte into decimal.

For the first octet:

0	1	1	0	1	1	1	0
0	+64	+32	+0	+8	+4	+2	+0 = 110

01101110 = 110

For the second octet:

0	0	1	1	0	0	1	0
0	+0	+32	+16	+0	+0	+2	+0 = 50

00110010 = 50

For the third octet:

1	1	1	1	0	0	1	0
128	+64	+32	+16	+0	+0	+2	+0 = 242

11110010 = 242

For the fourth octet:

0	0	0	0	1	0	1	0
0	+0	+0	+0	+8	+0	+2	+0 = 10

00001010 = 10

The IP address is 110.50.242.10.

IPv4 Address Classes

IPv4 addresses have five classes: A, B, C, D, and E. In classful addressing, the most significant bits of the first byte determine the address class of the IP address. Table 8-9 shows the high-order bits of each IP address class.

Table 8-9 High-Order Bits of IPv4 Address Classes

Address Class	High-Order Bits
A	0xxxxxxx
B	10xxxxxx
C	110xxxxx
D	1110xxxx
E	1111xxxx

Again, the IPv4 Class A, B, and C addresses are unicast addresses. Unicast addresses represent a single destination. Class D is for multicast addresses. Packets sent to a multicast address are sent to a group of hosts. Class E addresses are reserved for experimental use. IANA allocates the IPv4 address space. IANA delegates regional assignments to Regional Internet Registries (RIR). The five RIRs are

- ARIN (American Registry for Internet Numbers)
- RIPE NCC (Reseaux IP Europeens Network Control Center)
- APNIC (Asia Pacific Network Information Center)
- LACNIC (Latin America and Caribbean Network Information Center)
- AfriNIC (African Network Information Centre)

Updates to the IPv4 address space can be found at www.iana.org/assignments/ipv4-address-space.

The following sections discuss each of these classes in detail.

Class A Addresses

Class A addresses range from 0 (00000000) to 127 (01111111) in the first byte. Network numbers available for assignment to organizations are from 1.0.0.0 to 126.0.0.0. Networks 0 and 127 are reserved. For example, 127.0.0.1 is reserved for local host or host loopback. A packet sent to a local host address is sent to the local machine.

By default, for Class A addresses, the first byte is the network number, and the three remaining bytes are the host number. The format is $N.H.H.H$, where N is the network part and H is the host part. With 24 bits available, there are $2^{24} - 2 = 16,777,214$ IP addresses for host assignment per Class A network. We subtract two for the network number (all 0s) and broadcast address (all 1s). A network with this many hosts will surely not work with so many hosts attempting to broadcast on the network. This section discusses subnetting later as a method of defining smaller networks within a larger network address.

Class B Addresses

Class B addresses range from 128 (10000000) to 191 (10111111) in the first byte. Network numbers assigned to companies or other organizations are from 128.0.0.0 to 191.255.0.0. This section discusses the 16 networks reserved for private use later.

By default, for Class B addresses, the first two bytes are the network number, and the remaining two bytes are the host number. The format is *N.N.H.H*. With 16 bits available, there are $2^{16} - 2 = 65,534$ IP addresses for host assignment per Class B network. As with Class A addresses, having a segment with more than 65,000 hosts broadcasting will surely not work; you resolve this issue with subnetting.

Class C Addresses

Class C addresses range from 192 (11000000) to 223 (11011111) in the first byte. Network numbers assigned to companies are from 192.0.0.0 to 223.255.255.0. The format is N.N.N.H. With 8 bits available, there are $2^8 - 2 = 254$ IP addresses for host assignment per Class C network. H = 0, which is the network number; H = 255, which is the broadcast address.

Class D Addresses

Class D addresses range from 224 (11100000) to 239 (11101111) in the first byte. Network numbers assigned to multicast groups range from 224.0.0.1 to 239.255.255.255. These addresses do not have a host or network part. Some multicast addresses are already assigned; for example, 224.0.0.10 is used by routers running EIGRP. You can find a full list of assigned multicast addresses at www.iana.org/assignments/multicast-addresses.

Class E Addresses

Class E addresses range from 240 (11110000) to 254 (11111110) in the first byte. These addresses are reserved for experimental networks. Network 255 is reserved for the broadcast address, such as 255.255.255.255. Table 8-10 summarizes the IPv4 address classes. Again, each address class can be uniquely identified in binary by the high-order bits.

Table 8-10 IPv4 Address Classes

Address Class	High-Order Bits	Network Numbers
A	0xxxxxxx	1.0.0.0 to 126.0.0.0*
B	10xxxxxx	128.0.0.0 to 191.255.0.0
C	110xxxxx	192.0.0.0 to 223.255.255.0
D	1110xxxx	224.0.0.1 to 239.255.255.255
E	1111xxxx	240.0.0.0 to 254.255.255.255

*Networks 0.0.0.0 and 127.0.0.0 are reserved as special-use addresses.

IPv4 Address Types

IPv4 addresses can also be classified in one of three types:

- Unicast
- Broadcast
- Multicast

A unicast address represents a single interface of a host (PC, router, server). It can be a source or destination IP address. A broadcast address is a destination IP address that is set to all other devices in a given address range; normally it is sent to all devices in the IP subnet. A multicast address is a destination IP address sent to a specific set of hosts. Table 8-11 summarizes IPv4 address types.

Table 8-11   IPv4 Address Type

IPv4 Address Type	Description
Unicast	The IP address of an interface on a single host. It can be a source or destination address.
Broadcast	An IP address that reaches all hosts in an address range. It is only a destination address.
Multicast	An IP address that reaches a group of hosts. It is only a destination address.

IPv4 Private Addresses

Some network numbers within the IPv4 address space are reserved for private use. These numbers are not routed on the Internet, so there is no way to reach them over an Internet connection. Many organizations today use private addresses in their internal networks with NAT to access the Internet. (NAT is covered later in this chapter.) Private addresses are explained in RFC 1918: Address Allocation for Private Internets, published in 1996. Private addresses were one of the first steps dealing with the concern that the globally unique IPv4 address space would become exhausted. The availability of private addresses combined with NAT reduces the need for organizations to carefully define subnets to minimize the waste of assigned, public, global IP addresses.

The IP network address space reserved for private internets is 10/8, 172.16/12, and 192.168/16. It includes one Class A network, 16 Class B networks, and 256 Class C networks. Table 8-12 summarizes private address space. Large organizations can use network 10.0.0.0/8 to assign address space throughout the enterprise. Midsize organizations can use one of the Class B private networks 172.16.0.0/16 through 172.31.0.0/16 for IP addresses. The smaller Class C addresses, which begin with 192.168, can be used by corporations and are commonly used in home routers.

8

Table 8-12   IPv4 Private Address Space

Class Type	Start Address	End Address
Class A	10.0.0.0	10.255.255.255
Class B	172.16.0.0	172.31.255.255
Class C	192.168.0.0	192.168.255.255

NAT

NAT devices convert IP address space into globally unique IP addresses. NAT was originally specified by RFC 1631; the current specification is RFC 3022. It is common for companies to use NAT to translate internal private addresses to public addresses, and vice versa, although it can also translate public IP addresses to public IP addresses.

The translation can be from many private addresses to a single public address or from many private addresses to a range of public addresses. When NAT performs a many-to-one translation, the process is called port address translation (PAT) because different port numbers identify translations.

As shown in Figure 8-3, the source addresses for outgoing IP packets are converted to globally unique IP addresses. The conversion can be configured statically, or it can dynamically use a global pool of addresses.

NAT has several forms:

■ **Static NAT:** Maps an unregistered or private IP address to a registered IP address; it is configured manually. It is commonly used to assign a network device with an internal private IP address a unique public address so that it can be accessed from the Internet.

■ **Dynamic NAT:** Dynamically maps an unregistered or private IP address to a registered IP address from a pool (group) of registered addresses. The two subsets of dynamic NAT are overloading and overlapping:

  ■ **Overloading:** Maps multiple unregistered or private IP addresses to a single registered IP address by using different ports. This is also known as PAT, single-address NAT, or port-level multiplexed NAT.

  ■ **Overlapping:** Maps registered internal IP addresses to outside registered IP addresses. It can also map external addresses to internal registered addresses.

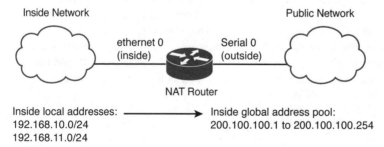

Figure 8-3   *Network address translation*

When designing for NAT, you should understand the following terminology:

- **Stub domain:** The internal network that might be using private IP addresses.

- **Public network:** Outside the stub domain, it resides in the Internet. Addresses in the public network can be reached from the Internet.

- **Inside local address:** The real IP address of the device that resides in the internal network. This address is used in the stub domain.

- **Inside global address:** The translated IP address of the device that resides in the internal network. This address is used in the public network.

- **Outside global address:** The real IP address of a device that resides in the Internet, outside the stub domain.

- **Outside local address:** The translated IP address of the device that resides in the Internet. This address is used inside the stub domain.

Figure 8-4 illustrates the terms described in the list. The real IP address of the host in the stub network is 192.168.10.100; it is the inside local address. The NAT router translates the inside local address into the inside global address (200.100.10.100). Hosts located in the Internet have their real IP address (outside global address) translated; in the example, 30.100.2.50 is translated into the outside local address of 192.168.100.50.

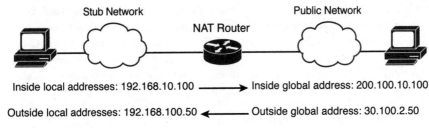

Inside local addresses: 192.168.10.100 ⟶ Inside global address: 200.100.10.100

Outside local addresses: 192.168.100.50 ⟵ Outside global address: 30.100.2.50

Figure 8-4 *Terminology example*

Table 8-13 summarizes the NAT concepts.

Table 8-13 NAT Concepts

NAT Address Type	Description
Static NAT	Commonly used to assign a network device with an internal private IP address a unique public address so that it can be accessed from the Internet.
Dynamic NAT	Dynamically maps an unregistered or private IP address to a registered IP address from a pool (group) of registered addresses.
PAT	Maps multiple unregistered or private IP addresses to a single registered IP address by using different ports.
Inside local address	The real IP address of the device that resides in the internal network. This address is used in the stub domain.
Inside global address	The translated IP address of the device that resides in the internal network. This address is used in the public network.

NAT Address Type	Description
Outside global address	The real IP address of a device that resides in the Internet, outside the stub domain.
Outside local address	The translated IP address of the device that resides in the Internet. This address is used inside the stub domain.

IPv4 Address Subnets

Subnetting plays an important part in IPv4 addressing. The subnet mask helps determine the network, subnetwork, and host part of an IP address. The network architect uses subnetting to manipulate the default mask to create subnetworks for LAN and WAN segments. These subnetworks provide enough addresses for LANs of different sizes. Point-to-point WAN links usually get a subnet mask that allows for only two hosts because only two routers are present in the point-to-point WAN link. You should become familiar with determining subnetwork numbers, broadcast addresses, and host address ranges given an IP address and mask.

Subnet masks are used for Class A, B, and C addresses only. Multicast addresses do not use subnet masks. A subnet mask is a 32-bit number in which bits are set to 1 to identify the network portion of the address, and a 0 is the host part of the address. The mask's bits set to 1 are contiguous on the left portion of the mask; the bits set to 0 are contiguous on the right portion of the mask. Table 8-14 shows the default masks for Class A, B, and C addresses. This section addresses various ways to represent IP subnet masks. Understanding these ways is significant because the representation of a network and its mask can appear differently in Cisco documentation or on the command-line interface.

Table 8-14   IPv4 Default Network Address Masks

Class	Binary Mask	Dotted-Decimal Mask
A	11111111 00000000 00000000 00000000	255.0.0.0
B	11111111 11111111 00000000 00000000	255.255.0.0
C	11111111 11111111 11111111 00000000	255.255.255.0

Mask Nomenclature

There are several ways to represent IP subnet masks. The mask can be binary, hexadecimal, dotted decimal, or a prefix "bit mask." Historically, the most common representation was the dotted-decimal format (255.255.255.0). The prefix bit mask format is now more popular. This format represents the mask by using a slash followed by the number of leading address bits that must be set to 1 for the mask. It is also referred to as classless interdomain routing (CIDR) prefix notation. For example, 255.255.0.0 is represented as /16. Table 8-15 shows most of the mask representations. The /24 mask is common on LAN segments. The /30 mask is common for WAN point-to-point links, and /32 is used for router loopback addresses.

Table 8-15 Subnet Masks

Dotted Decimal	Bit Mask	Hexadecimal
255.0.0.0	/8	FF000000
255.192.0.0	/10	FFC00000
255.255.0.0	/16	FFFF0000
255.255.224.0	/19	FFFFE000
255.255.240.0	/20	FFFFF000
255.255.255.0	/24	FFFFFF00
255.255.255.128	/25	FFFFFF80
255.255.255.192	/26	FFFFFFC0
255.255.255.224	/27	FFFFFFE0
255.255.255.240	/28	FFFFFFF0
255.255.255.248	/29	FFFFFFF8
255.255.255.252	/30	FFFFFFFC
255.255.255.255	/32	FFFFFFFF

IP Address Subnet Design Example

The development of an IP address plan or IP address subnet design is an important concept for the network designer. You should be capable of creating an IP address plan based on many factors:

- Number of locations
- Number of devices per location
- IP addressing requirements for each individual location or building
    - Number of devices to be supported in each communication closet
    - Site requirements: VoIP devices, wireless LAN, video
- Subnet size

The following example shows subnetting for a small company. Suppose the company has 200 hosts and is assigned the Class C network of 195.10.1.0/24. The 200 hosts need to be in six different LANs.

You can subnet the Class C network using a mask of 255.255.255.224. Looking at the mask in binary (11111111 11111111 11111111 11100000), the first 3 bytes are the network part, the first 3 bits of the fourth byte determine the subnets, and the five remaining 0 bits are for host addressing.

Table 8-16 shows the subnetworks created with a mask of 255.255.255.224. Using this mask, $2n$ subnets are created, where n is the number of bits taken from the host part for the subnet mask. This example uses 3 bits, so $2^3 = 8$ subnets. The first column of the table lists the LANs. The second column shows the binary of the fourth byte of the IP address. The third column shows the subnet number, and the fourth and fifth columns show the first host and broadcast address of the subnet.

Table 8-16   Subnets for Network 195.1.1.0

LAN	Fourth Byte	Subnet Number	First Host	Broadcast Address
LAN 0	00000000	195.10.1.0	195.10.1.1	195.10.1.31
LAN 1	00100000	195.10.1.32	195.10.1.33	195.10.1.63
LAN 2	01000000	195.10.1.64	195.10.1.65	195.10.1.95
LAN 3	01100000	195.10.1.96	195.10.1.97	195.10.1.127
LAN 4	10000000	195.10.1.128	195.10.1.129	195.10.1.159
LAN 5	10100000	195.10.1.160	195.10.1.161	195.10.1.191
LAN 6	11000000	195.10.1.192	195.10.1.193	195.10.1.223
LAN 7	11100000	195.10.1.224	195.10.1.225	195.10.1.255

Use the formula $2n - 2$ to calculate the number of hosts per subnet, where n is the number of bits for the host portion. The preceding example has 5 bits in the fourth byte for host addresses. With $n = 5$, $2^5 - 2 = 30$ hosts. For LAN 1, host addresses range from 195.10.1.33 to 195.10.1.62 (30 addresses). The broadcast address for the subnet is 195.10.1.63. Each LAN repeats this pattern with 30 hosts in each subnet.

Determining the Network Portion of an IP Address

Given an address and mask, you can determine the classful network, the subnetwork, and the subnetwork's broadcast number. You do so with a logical AND operation between the IP address and subnet mask. You obtain the broadcast address by taking the subnet number and making the host portion all 1s. Table 8-17 shows the logical AND operation. Notice that the AND operation is similar to multiplying bit 1 and bit 2; if any 0 is present, the result is 0.

Table 8-17   AND Logical Operation

Bit 1	Bit 2	AND
0	0	0
0	1	0
1	0	0
1	1	1

As an example, take the IP address 150.85.1.70 with a subnet mask of 255.255.255.224, as shown in Table 8-18. Notice the 3 bold bits in the subnet mask. These bits extend the default Class C prefix (/24) 3 bits to a mask of /27. As shown in Table 8-18, you perform an AND operation of the IP address with the subnet mask to obtain the subnetwork. You obtain the broadcast number by making all the host bits 1. As shown in bold, the subnet mask reaches 3 bits in the fourth octet. The subnetwork is identified by the five rightmost 0s in the fourth octet, and the broadcast is identified by all 1s in the 5 rightmost bits.

Table 8-18   Subnetwork of IP Address 150.85.1.70

	Binary First, Second, and Third Octets	Binary Fourth Octet		Dotted-Decimal IP
IP address	10010110 01010101 00000001	010	00110	150.85.1.70
Subnet mask	11111111 11111111 11111111	**111**	00000	255.255.255.224
Subnetwork	10010110 01010101 00000001	010	**00000**	150.85.1.64
	Major network portion	**Subnet**	**Host**	
Broadcast address	10010110 01010101 00000001	010	**11111**	150.85.1.95

Variable-Length Subnet Masks

Variable-length subnet masks (VLSMs) divide a network into subnets of various sizes to prevent wasting IP addresses. If a Class C network uses 255.255.255.240 as a subnet mask, 16 subnets are available, each with 14 IP addresses. If a point-to-point link needs only 2 IP addresses, 12 IP addresses are wasted. This problem scales further with Class B and Class A address spaces. With VLSMs, small LANs can use /28 subnets with 14 hosts, and larger LANs can use /23 and /22 masks with 510 and 1022 hosts, respectively. Point-to-point networks use a /30 mask, which supports two hosts.

There isn't one way to subdivide a network, so there is no single correct way to create subnets. The best practice is to divide large networks into smaller subnets that can be assigned to sites. Further divide each site subnet into smaller subnets for data, VoIP, wireless LAN, and other subnets to be used in site VLANs. Furthermore, WAN and point-to-point links, router, and switch loopback addresses are allocated IP subnets.

VLSM Address Assignment: Example 1

Let's look at a VLSM IP address assignment example. Take Class B network 130.20.0.0/16 as an example. Using a /20 mask produces 16 subnetworks. Table 8-19 shows the subnetworks. With the /20 subnet mask, the first 4 bits of the third byte determine the subnets.

Table 8-19   Subnets with the /20 Mask

Third Byte	Subnetwork
00000000	130.20.0.0/20
00010000	130.20.16.0/20
00100000	130.20.32.0/20
00110000	130.20.48.0/20
01000000	130.20.64.0/20

8

Third Byte	Subnetwork
01010000	130.20.80.0/20
01100000	130.20.96.0/20
01110000	130.20.112.0/20
10000000	130.20.128.0/20
10010000	130.20.144.0/20
10100000	130.20.160.0/20
10110000	130.20.176.0/20
11000000	130.20.192.0/20
11010000	130.20.208.0/20
11100000	130.20.224.0/20
11110000	130.20.240.0/20

With fixed-length subnet masks, the network supports only 16 networks. Any LAN or WAN link has to use a /20 subnet. In this scenario, if the sites involved vary in size, this "one network size fits all" solution might be a waste of address space and therefore is inefficient. With VLSMs, you can further subnet the /20 subnets.

For example, take 130.20.64.0/20 and subdivide it to support LANs with about 500 hosts. A /23 mask has 9 bits for hosts, producing $2^9 - 2 = 510$ IP addresses for hosts. Table 8-20 shows the subnetworks for LANs within a specified subnet.

Table 8-20   Subnetworks for 130.20.64.0/20

Third Byte	Subnetwork
01000000	130.20.64.0/23
01000010	130.20.66.0/23
01000100	130.20.68.0/23
01000110	130.20.70.0/23
01001000	130.20.72.0/23
01001010	130.20.74.0/23
01001100	130.20.76.0/23
01001110	130.20.78.0/23

With VLSMs, you can further subdivide these subnetworks of subnetworks. Take subnetwork 130.20.76.0/23 and use it for two LANs that have fewer than 250 hosts. It produces subnetworks 130.20.76.0/24 and 130.20.77.0/24. Also, subdivide 130.20.78.0/23 for serial links. Because each point-to-point serial link needs only two IP addresses, use a /30 mask. Table 8-21 shows the subnetworks produced.

Table 8-21   Serial-Link Subnetworks

Third Byte	Fourth Byte	Subnetwork
01001110	00000000	130.20.78.0/30
01001110	00000100	130.20.78.4/30
01001110	00001000	130.20.78.8/30
01001110	00001100	130.20.78.12/30
...	...	...
01001111	11110100	130.20.79.244/30
01001111	11111000	130.20.79.248/30
01001111	11111100	130.20.79.252/30

Each /30 subnetwork includes the subnetwork number, two IP addresses, and a broadcast address. Table 8-22 shows the bits for 130.20.78.8/30.

Table 8-22   Addresses Within Subnetwork 110.20.78.8/30

Binary Address	IP Address	Function
10000010 00010100 01001110 00001000	130.20.78.8	Subnetwork
10000010 00010100 01001110 00001001	130.20.78.9	IP address 1
10000010 00010100 01001110 00001010	130.20.78.10	IP address 2
10000010 00010100 01001110 00001011	130.20.78.11	Broadcast address

Loopback Addresses

You can also reserve a subnet for router loopback addresses. There are several reasons to use loopback addresses:

- Loopback addresses provide an always-up interface to use for router-management connectivity.
- Loopback addresses can also serve as the router ID for some routing protocols.
- They are reachable even if a single interface goes down on a device that has multiple interfaces.
- They are used for IP telephony (for example, in the configuration of dial peers).
- They are used as the source IP address for network management and monitoring.

The loopback address is a single IP address with a 32-bit mask. In the previous example, network 130.20.75.0/24 could provide 256 loopback addresses for network devices, starting with 130.20.75.0/32 and ending with 130.20.75.255/32.

IP Telephony Networks

You should reserve separate subnets for LANs using IP phones. IP phones are normally placed in a VLAN that is in a logical segment separate from that of the user workstations. Separating voice and data on different subnets or VLANs also aids in providing QoS for voice traffic with regard to classifying, queuing, and buffering. This design rule also facilitates troubleshooting.

Table 8-23 shows an example of allocating IP addresses for a small network for a company located within three buildings. Notice that separate VLANs are used for the VoIP devices.

Table 8-23   IP Address Allocation for VoIP Networks

Building Floor/Function	VLAN Number	IP Subnet
First-floor data	VLAN 11	172.16.11.0/24
Second-floor data	VLAN 12	172.16.12.0/24
Third-floor data	VLAN 13	172.16.13.0/24
First-floor VoIP	VLAN 111	172.16.111.0/24
Second-floor VoIP	VLAN 112	172.16.112.0/24
Third-floor VoIP	VLAN 113	172.16.113.0/24

Overlay subnets can be used where IP subnets have already been allocated and no spare subnets are available. A different class of private address can be used. This solves the scalability issues with the addressing plan. Table 8-24 shows an example similar to that in Table 8-23, but using overlay subnets.

Table 8-24   Overlay IP Address Allocation for VoIP Networks

Building Floor/Function	VLAN Number	IP Subnet
First-floor data	VLAN 11	172.16.11.0/24
Second-floor data	VLAN 12	172.16.12.0/24
Third-floor data	VLAN 13	172.16.13.0/24
First-floor VoIP	VLAN 111	10.16.11.0/24
Second-floor VoIP	VLAN 112	10.16.12.0/24
Third-floor VoIP	VLAN 113	10.16.13.0/24

VLSM Address Assignment: Example 2

Because this is an important topic, here is another example of a VLSM design. Take network 10.0.0.0/8, which is commonly used by companies in their internal networks because this is private IP address space.

Global companies divide this address space into continental regions for the Americas, Europe/Middle East, Africa, and Asia/Pacific. An example is shown in Table 8-25, where the address space has been divided into four major blocks:

- 10.0.0.0 to 10.63.0.0 is reserved.
- 10.64.0.0 to 10.127.0.0 for the Americas.
- 10.128.0.0 to 10.191.0.0 for Europe, Middle East, and Africa.
- 10.192.0.0 to 10.254.0.0 for Asia Pacific.

Table 8-25 Global IP Address Allocation

Region	Network
Reserved	10.0.0.0/10
North America	10.64.0.0/10
South America	10.96.0.0/11 *part of the above
Europe/Middle East	10.128.0.0/10
Africa	10.160.0.0/11 *part of the above
Asia Pacific	10.192.0.0/10

From each of these regions, address blocks can be allocated to company sites. Large sites may require 4, 8, or 16 Class C equivalent (/24) subnets to assign to data, voice, wireless, and management VLANs. Table 8-26 shows an example. The large site is allocated network 10.64.16.0/20. The first four /24 subnets are assigned for data VLANs, the second four /24 subnets are assigned for voice VLANs, and the third four /24 subnets are assigned for wireless VLANs. Other subnets are used for router and switch interfaces, point-to-point links, and network management devices.

Table 8-26 IP Address Allocation in a Large Site

Function	IP Subnet
Data VLAN 1	10.64.16.0/24
Data VLAN 2	10.64.17.0/24
Data VLAN 3	10.64.18.0/24
Data VLAN 4	10.64.19.0.24
Voice VLAN 1	10.64.20.0/24
Voice VLAN 2	10.64.21.0/24
Voice VLAN 3	10.64.22.0/24
Voice VLAN 4	10.64.23.0/24
Wireless VLAN 1	10.64.24.0/24
Wireless VLAN 2	10.64.25.0/24
Wireless VLAN 3	10.64.26.0/24
Wireless VLAN 4	10.64.27.0/24

Function	IP Subnet
Reserved	10.64.28.0/24
Reserved	10.64.29.0/24
Router/switch loopbacks	10.64.30.0/24
P2P links, misc.	10.64.31.0/24

IPv4 Addressing Design

This section covers IPv4 design topics that the CCDA candidate should be aware of. There is no perfect way to address a network, and each company will have a unique set of requirements that will drive the allocation and subnetting of the IPv4 address space.

Goal of IPv4 Address Design

What is the goal of IPv4 addressing? As a designer, you want to provide enough address capacity to address all nodes in the network and allow for future growth! You will want to allow enough IPv4 subnets for data networks, wireless LANs, IP Telephony (IPT) networks, video/CCTV networks, access control systems, network management, server farms, and router/switch loopback addresses. This allows communications via the network's applications and to and from the Internet.

With your addressing, you will want to assign specific subnets that allow you to easily segment communications between different traffic types—for example, assigning 192.168.x.x subnets for data and 172.16.x.x for IPT at a particular site. This makes it easier to configure filters that prevent nodes on 192.168.x.x from attempting to connect to 172.16.x.x devices, thus protecting your IP phones.

Plan for Future Use of IPv4 Addresses

When assigning subnets for a site or perhaps a floor of a building, do not assign subnets that are too small. You want to assign subnets that allow for growth! Many applications and services get added to your "data-only" network, such as VoIP, security cameras, access control systems, and video conference systems.

For example, if a floor has a requirement for 50 users, do you assign a /26 subnet (which allows 62 addressable nodes)? Or do you assign a /25 subnet, which allows up to 126 nodes? You need to balance between the scalability of the address space and the efficiency of its use. Assigning too large of a subnet will prevent you from having other subnets for IPT and video conferencing.

Sometimes new network additions do not allow you to adhere to a network design. The company might make an acquisition or new offices might be created. Although a new address design would be the cleanest solution, the recommendation is to avoid re-addressing of networks. Here are some other options:

- If you use 10.0.0.0/8 as your network, then use the other private IP addresses for the additions.

- Use NAT as a workaround.

Performing Route Summarization

As a designer you will want to allocate IPv4 address space to allow for route summarization. Large networks can grow quickly from 500 routes to 1000, and higher. Route summarization reduces the size of the routing table and as a result reduces the amount the route update traffic on the network. Route summarization allows the network address space to scale as the company grows.

As an example, suppose a company has assigned the following subnets to a site:

- 10.10.130.0/24 to 10.10.140.0/24 for data networks

- 10.10.146.0/24 to 10.10.156.0/24 for VoIP networks

- 10.10.160.0/24 to 10.10.166/24 for wireless networks

- 10.10.170.0/29 for access control systems

- 10.10.176.0/28 for server farm and other systems

Instead of announcing each and every subnet of this network to the WAN, the recommendation is to summarize the site with a 10.10.128.0/26 route. This subnet encompasses networks from 10.10.128.0/24 to 10.10.191.0/24, so this address block would be assigned to this site.

Plan for a Hierarchical IP Address Network

Looking at IPv4 addressing for a higher/company-wide network, recommended practice dictates that you allocate contiguous address blocks to regions of the network. Hierarchical IPv4 addressing enables summarization, which makes the network easier to manage and troubleshoot.

As an example, consider the IPv4 deployment shown in Figure 8-5. Network subnets cannot be aggregated because /24 subnets from many different networks are deployed in different areas of the network. For example, subnets under 10.10.0.0/16 are deployed in Asia (10.10.4.0/24), the Americas (10.10.6.0/24), and Europe (10.10.8.0/24). The same occurs with networks 10.70.0.0/16 and 10.128.0.0/16. This increases the size of the routing table, making it less efficient. It also makes it harder for network engineers to troubleshoot because it is not obvious in which part of the world a particular subnet is located.

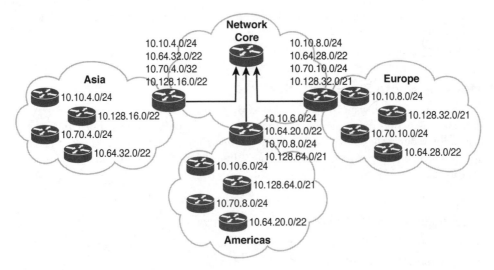

Figure 8-5 *Not summarized network*

By contrast, Figure 8-6 shows a network that allocates a high-level block to each region:

- 10.0.0.0/18 for Asia Pacific networks
- 10.64.0.0/18 for Americas networks
- 10.128.0.0/18 for European/Middle East networks

This solution provides for summarization of regional networks at area borders and improves control over growth of the routing table.

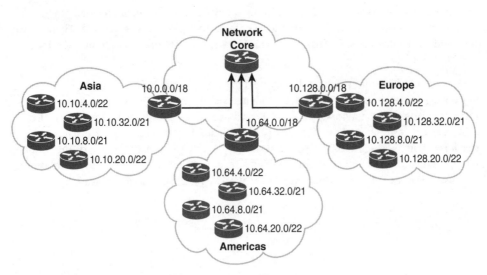

Figure 8-6 *Summarized network*

Private and Public IP Address and NAT Guidelines

Use public IPv4 addresses on external-facing devices that require connectivity to the Internet and external organizations. Examples include the following:

- Internet connectivity module, such as publicly accessible web and DNS servers
- E-commerce or cloud module
- Remote access and virtual private network (VPN) module, where public IP addresses are used for selected connections

The following are some public/private IP addressing best practices:

- Use private IP addresses throughout the internal enterprise network.
- Use NAT and PAT as needed to translate between private internal IP addresses to public external addresses.
- Use one private address to one public address NAT when servers on the internal network need to be visible from the public network. In firewalls, this is a "static" NAT configuration.
- Use PAT for many private address translations to one public address translation for end systems that need to access the public network.

Table 8-27 provides examples of where public or private IP addresses should be used in the Cisco network architecture.

Table 8-27   Public Versus Private IP Addresses

Network Location	Public or Private Address
E-commerce module	Public
Intranet website	Private
External DNS servers	Public
Remote-access/VPN module	Public
Inside global address	Public
Real IP address of a web server located in internal network	Private

Steps for Creating an IPv4 Address Plan

As a CCDA candidate, follow these three steps to create an IPv4 address plan:

Step 1.   Define addressing standards

Step 2.   Plan the IPv4 range and allocate it

Step 3.   Document the IPv4 addressing plan

Addressing standards vary per company and per the situation for which you are designing. Define the standards that you want to use for your network, use them, and document them. Using standards will make it easier for operations to troubleshoot any network issue. Here are some examples of standards:

- Use .1 or .254 (in the last octet) as the default gateway of the subnet.

- Match the VLAN ID number with the third octet of an IP address (for example, the IP subnet 10.10.150.0/25 is assigned to VLAN 150).

- Reserve .1 to .15 of a subnet for static assignments and .16 to .239 for the DHCP pool.

- Employ router and switch naming using international two-digit country codes, city airport codes, device codes, and numeric codes (for example, ushourtr01 for a router located in Houston).

For the allocation of IPv4 subnets, stick to the following best practices:

- Private addresses are used for internal networks.

- Allocate /24 subnets for user devices (laptops, PCs).

- Allocate a parallel /24 subset for VoIP devices (IP phones).

- Allocate subnets for access control systems and video conference systems.

- Reserve subnets for future use.

- Use /30 subnets for point-to-point links.

- Use /32 for loopback addresses.

- Allocate subnets for remote access and network management.

- Use public addresses for the public facing network.

Case Study: IP Address Subnet Allocation

Consider a company that has users in several buildings in a campus network. In building A there are four floors and in building B there are two floors, with the address requirements shown in Table 8-28.

Table 8-28   Building Address Requirements

Network Location	Addresses Required
Building A: Floor 1	40
Building A: Floor 2	70
Building A: Floor 3	30
Building A: Floor 4	90
Building B: Floor 1	80
Building B: Floor 2	120

As shown in Figure 8-7, the building's Layer 3 switches will be connected via a dual-fiber link between switch A and switch B. Both switches will connect to the WAN router R1. Assume that you have been allocated network 10.10.0.0/17 for this campus and that IP phones will be used.

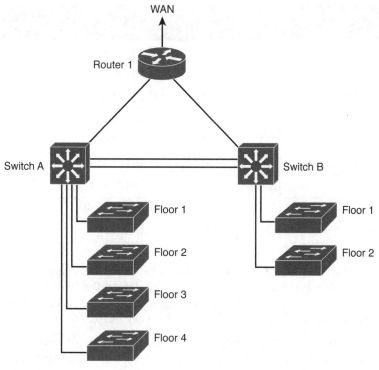

Figure 8-7 *Campus network connectivity*

Many different possible solutions meet the requirements for IPv4 address assignment. Table 8-29 shows one solution.

Table 8-29 Building IPv4 Address Allocation

Network Location	Addresses Required	Subnet Size	VLANs	Addresses Assigned
Building A: Floor 1	40	/24	11	10.10.11.0/24
Building A: Floor 2	70	/24	12	10.10.12.0/24
Building A: Floor 3	30	/24	13	10.10.13.0/24
Building A: Floor 4	90	/24	14	10.10.14.0/24
Building B: Floor 1	80	/24	21	10.10.21.0/24
Building B: Floor 2	120	/24	22	10.10.22.0/24
Switch A – Switch B links		/30	/	10.10.2.4/30 and 10.10.2.8/30
Switch A R1 link		/30	/	10.10.2.12/30
Switch B R1 link		/30	/318	10.10.2.16/30
R1 Loopback		/32	/	10.10.1.1/32

Network Location	Addresses Required	Subnet Size	VLANs	Addresses Assigned
Switch A Loopback		/32	/	10.10.1.2/32
Switch B Loopback		/32	/	10.10.1.4/32
Building A: Floor 1 IPT	40	/24	111	10.10.111.0/24
Building A: Floor 2 IPT	70	/24	112	10.10.112.0/24
Building A: Floor 3 IPT	30	/24	113	10.10.113.0/24
Building A: Floor 4 IPT	90	/24	114	10.10.114.0/24
Building B: Floor 1	80	/24	121	10.10.121.0/24
Building B: Floor 2	120	/24	122	10.10.122.0/24
Access Control System	40	/24	300	10.10.3.0/24

Data subnets are assigned starting with IP subnet 10.10.11.0/24 for floor 1 in building A. Notice that the VLAN number matches the third octet of the IP subnet. The second floor is assigned VLAN 12 and IP subnet 10.10.12.0/24. For building B, VLAN numbers in the 20s are used, with floor 1 having a VLAN of 21 assigned with IP subnet 10.10.21.0/24.

VLANs for IP Telephony (IPT) are similar to data VLANs, with the correlation of using numbers in the 100s. For example, floor 1 of building A uses VLAN 11 for data and VLAN 111 for voice, and the corresponding IP subnets are 10.10.11.0/24 (data) and 10.10.111.0.24 (voice). This is repeated for all floors.

This solution uses /30 subnets for point-to-point links from the 10.10.2.0/24 subnet. Loopback addresses are taken from the 10.10.1.0/24 network starting with 10.10.1.1/32 for the WAN router. Subnet 10.10.3.0/24 is reserved for the building access control system.

Address Assignment and Name Resolution

Device network configuration parameters such as IP addresses, subnet masks, default gateways, and DNS server IP addresses can be assigned statically by the administrator or dynamically by DHCP or BOOTP servers. You should statically assign most shared network systems such as routers and servers, but dynamically assign most client systems such as end-user PCs and laptops. This section covers the protocols you use to dynamically assign IP address parameters to a host, which are the Bootstrap Protocol (BOOTP) and the Dynamic Host Configuration Protocol (DHCP). This section also covers Domain Name System (DNS) and Address Resolution Protocol (ARP), which are two significant protocols in IP networks. DNS maps domain names to IP addresses, and ARP resolves IP addresses to MAC addresses. These protocols are important in TCP/IP networks because they simplify the methods of address assignment and resolution.

Recommended Practices of IP Address Assignment

IP addresses can be assigned statically (manual configuration) or dynamically:

- Use static IP address assignment for network infrastructure devices.
- Use dynamic IP address assignment for end-user devices.

Use static IP address assignment for routers, switches, printers, and servers. These static IP addresses are assigned in the network infrastructure, data center modules, and in modules of the enterprise edge and WAN. You need to manage and monitor these systems, so you must access them via a stable IP address.

You should dynamically assign end-client workstations to reduce the configuration tasks required to connect these systems to the network. Cisco IP phones and mobile devices are also assigned an IP address dynamically. Wireless access points also learn their IP address and the IP address of the wireless controller via DHCP. When you assign client workstation characteristics dynamically, the system automatically learns which network segment it is assigned to and how to reach its default gateway as the network is discovered. One of the first methods used to dynamically assign IP addresses was BOOTP. The current method to assign IP addresses is DHCP.

BOOTP

The basic BOOTP was first defined in RFC 951. It has been updated by RFC 1497 and RFC 1542. It is a protocol that allows a booting host to configure itself by dynamically obtaining its IP address, IP gateway, and other information from a remote server. You can use a single server to centrally manage numerous network hosts without having to configure each host independently.

BOOTP is an application layer protocol that uses UDP/IP for transport. The BOOTP server port is UDP port 67. The client port is UDP port 68. Clients send BOOTP requests to the BOOTP server, and the server responds to UDP port 68 to send messages to the client. The destination IP of the BOOTP requests uses the all-hosts address (255.255.255.255), which the router does not forward. If the BOOTP server is one or more router hops from the subnet, you must configure the local default gateway router to forward the BOOTP requests.

BOOTP requires that you build a "MAC address to IP address" table on the server. You must obtain every device's MAC address, which is a time-consuming effort. BOOTP has been replaced by the more sophisticated DHCP.

DHCP

DHCP provides a way to dynamically configure hosts on the network. Based on BOOTP, it is defined in RFC 2131 and adds the capability to reuse network addresses and additional configuration options. DHCP improves on BOOTP by using a "lease" for IP addresses and providing the client with all the IP configuration parameters needed to operate in the network.

DHCP servers allocate network addresses and deliver configuration parameters dynamically to hosts. With DHCP, the computer can obtain its configuration information—IP address, subnet mask, IP default gateway, DNS servers, WINS servers, and so on—when needed.

8

DHCP also includes other optional parameters that you can assign to clients. The configuration information is managed centrally on a DHCP server.

Routers act as relay agents by passing DHCP messages between DHCP clients and servers. Because DHCP is an extension of BOOTP, it uses the message format defined in RFC 951 for BOOTP. It uses the same ports as BOOTP: DHCP servers use UDP port 67, and DHCP clients use UDP port 68.

DHCP has three address allocation mechanisms:

- **Manual:** In manual allocation, DHCP is used to dispatch a preallocated IP address to a specific MAC address.

- **Automatic:** For automatic allocation, IP addresses are permanently assigned to a host. The IP address does not expire.

- **Dynamic:** For dynamic allocation, IP addresses are assigned for a limited time or until the host explicitly releases the address. This dynamic allocation mechanism can reuse the IP address after the lease expires.

An IP address is assigned as follows:

1. The client sends a DHCPDISCOVER message to the local network using a 255.255.255.255 broadcast.

2. DHCP relay agents (routers and switches) can forward the DHCPDISCOVER message to the DHCP server in another subnet.

3. The server sends a DHCPOFFER message to respond to the client, offering IP address, lease expiration, and other DHCP option information.

4. Using DHCPREQUEST, the client can request additional options or an extension on its lease of an IP address. This message also confirms that the client is accepting the DHCP offer.

5. The server then sends a DHCPACK (acknowledgment) message that confirms the lease and contains all the pertinent IP configuration parameters.

6. If the server is out of addresses or it determines that the client request is invalid, it sends a DHCPNAK message to the client.

One important note for the CCDA to remember is to place DHCP servers in the Enterprise Campus Data Center/Server Farm module and the enterprise branch of the enterprise campus architecture.

Table 8-30 summarizes DHCP allocation mechanisms.

Table 8-30   DHCP Allocation Mechanisms

Network Location	Address Allocation Mechanism
This mechanism can reuse the IP address after the lease expires.	Dynamic
Dispatches an IP address allocated to a specific MAC address.	Manual
Allocations of IP addresses are permanently assign to a host.	Automatic

DNS

The Domain Name System (DNS) is an Internet-based directory system that returns the destination IP addresses given a domain name (such as www.cisco.com). DNS is a distributed database. Separate, independent organizations administer their assigned domain name spaces and can break their domains into a number of subdomains. For example, given www. cisco.com, DNS returns the IP address 198.133.219.25. DNS was first specified by RFCs 882 and 883. The current specifications are specified in RFCs 1034 and 1035. DNS has also been updated by RFCs 1101, 1122, 1183, 1706, 1876, 1982, 1995, 1996, 2136, 2137, 2181, 2308, 2535, 2782, 2845, 3425, 3658, 3755, 4033, 4034, 4035, 6014, and 6840. As you can see, a lot of work has gone into making DNS efficient and more secure.

Figure 8-8 shows a simplified view of the DNS process for name resolution. The client device queries its configured DNS server (the resolver) for the IP address of a fully qualified domain name (FQDN; for example, www.cisco.com). The resolver in turn queries the DNS server of the foreign or remote DNS server, which responds with the IP address of www. cisco.com. This response is stored in cache on the resolver so that it can be used for future queries. The resolver provides the response to the client machine, which can then communicate via the IP address to the destination.

Figure 8-8   *DNS name resolution*

DNS was implemented to overcome the limitations of managing a single text host table. Imagine creating and maintaining text files with the names and IP addresses of all the hosts on the Internet! DNS scales hostname-to-IP-address translation by distributing responsibility for the domain name space. DNS follows a reversed tree structure for domain name space, as shown in Figure 8-9. IANA (www.iana.org) manages the tree's root.

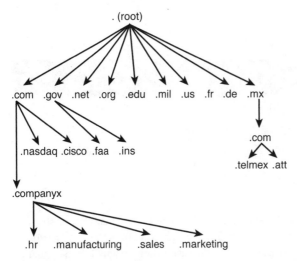

Figure 8-9 *DNS tree*

DNS data is called resource records (RR). Resource records are the data within a DNS zone. Table 8-31 lists some common resource records.

Table 8-31 DNS Resource Records

DNS RR	Description
A	Address. Provides the name-to-address mapping. It contains the IP address in dotted-decimal form.
AAAA	Secure IPv6 address.
CNAME	Canonical name. Used for aliases or nicknames.
MX	Mail Exchanger. Specifies the IP of the server where mail should be delivered.
NS	Name server. Specifies the name of the device that provides DNS for a particular domain.
PTR	Pointer. Used for reverse mapping from the translation of IP addresses to names.
SOA	Start of Authority. Designates the start of a zone. This is the device that is the master of DNS data for a zone.

DNS uses TCP and UDP port 53. UDP is the recommended transport protocol for DNS queries. TCP is the recommended protocol for zone transfers between DNS servers. A zone transfer occurs when you place a secondary server in the domain and transfer the DNS information from the primary DNS server to the secondary server. A DNS query searches for the IP address of an FQDN, such as www.cnn.com.

One important note for the CCDA to remember is to place DNS servers in the Enterprise Campus Server Farm module and enterprise branch of the enterprise campus architecture (see Figure 8-10).

Table 8-32 summarizes the placement of DHCP and DNS servers on the Cisco enterprise network.

Table 8-32   DHCP and DNS Servers

Network Location	Server Type
Campus data center	DHCP and Internal DNS
Enterprise branch	DHCP and Internal DNS
E-commerce	External DNS
Internet	External DNS
SP edge premises	Internal DNS
Remote enterprise data center	Internal and External DNS

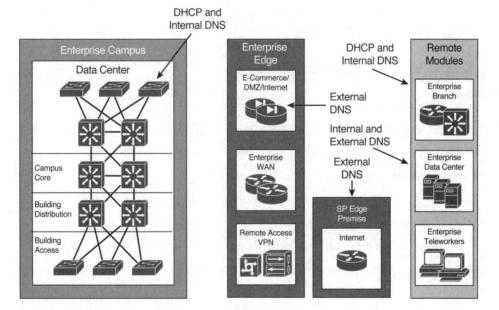

Figure 8-10   *DHCP and DNS servers in the network*

ARP

When an IP host needs to send an IP packet over an Ethernet network, it needs to find out what 48-bit MAC physical address to send the frame to. Given the destination IP, ARP obtains the destination MAC. The destination MAC can be a local host or the gateway router's MAC address if the destination IP is across the routed network. ARP is described in RFC 826. The local host maintains an ARP table with a list relating IP address to MAC address.

ARP operates by having the sender broadcast an ARP request. Figure 8-11 shows an example of an ARP request and reply. Suppose a router with the IP address 10.1.1.1 has a packet to send to 10.1.1.10 but does not have the destination MAC address in its ARP table. It broadcasts an ARP request to all hosts in a subnet. The ARP request contains the sender's IP and MAC address and the target IP address. All nodes in the broadcast domain receive the ARP request and process it. The device with the target IP address sends an ARP reply to the sender with its MAC address information; the ARP reply is a unicast message sent to 10.1.1.1. The sender now has the target MAC address in its ARP cache and sends the frame.

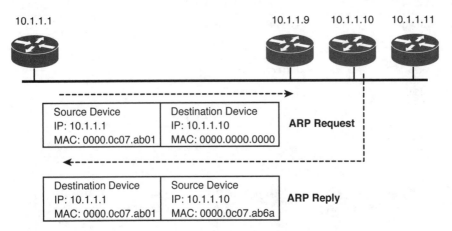

Figure 8-11   *ARP Request and Reply*

References and Recommended Readings

RFC 1349: Type of Service in the Internet Protocol Suite, www.ietf.org/rfc.

RFC 951: Bootstrap Protocol (BOOTP), www.ietf.org/rfc.

RFC 3246: An Expedited Forwarding PHB (Per-Hop Behavior), www.ietf.org/rfc.

RFC 2131: Dynamic Host Configuration Protocol, www.ietf.org/rfc.

RFC 1631: The IP Network Address Translator (NAT), www.ietf.org/rfc.

RFC 2597: Assured Forwarding PHB Group, www.ietf.org/rfc.

RFC 791: Internet Protocol, www.ietf.org/rfc.

RFC 1034: Domain Names—Concepts and Facilities, www.ietf.org/rfc.

RFC 1035: Domain Names—Implementation and Specification, www.ietf.org/rfc.

RFC 2474: Definition of the Differentiated Services Field (DS Field) in the IPv4 and IPv6 Headers, www.ietf.org/rfc.

RFC 826: Ethernet Address Resolution Protocol: Or Converting Network Protocol Addresses to 48-bit Ethernet Address for Transmission on Ethernet Hardware, www.ietf.org/rfc.

RFC 3168: The Addition of Explicit Congestion Notification (ECN) to IP, www.ietf.org/rfc.

RFC 1918: Address Allocation for Private Internets, www.ietf.org/rfc.

RFC 3022: Traditional IP Network Address Translator (Traditional NAT), www.ietf.org/rfc.

RFC 5798: Virtual Router Redundancy Protocol (VRRP), www.ietf.org/rfc.

RFC 2598: An Expedited Forwarding PHB, www.ietf.org/rfc.

RFC 2474: Differentiated Services Field, www.ietf.org/rfc.

RFC 4033: DNS Security Introduction and Requirements, www.ietf.org/rfc.

RFC 6014: Cryptographic Algorithm Identifier Allocation for DNSSEC, www.ietf.org/rfc.

RFC 6840: Clarification and Implementation Notes for DNS Security (DNSSEC) , www.ietf.org/rfc.

www.cisco.com/en/US/products/sw/netmgtsw/ps1982/products_user_guide_chapter09186a00800ade55.html.

https://www.arin.net/resources/request/ipv4_depletion.html.

8

Exam Preparation Tasks

Review All Key Topics

Review the most important topics in the chapter, noted with the Key Topic icon in the outer margin of the page. Table 8-33 lists a reference of these key topics and the page numbers on which each is found.

Table 8-33 Key Topics

Key Topic Element	Description	Page
Figure 8-1	IP header	289
Table 8-2	IP Protocol Numbers	290
Table 8-3	IPv4 Header Fields	291
Summary	The Type of Service field of the IP header is used to specify QoS parameters.	291
Table 8-4	IP Precedence Bit Values	292
Table 8-8	IP DSCP Values	294
List	IPv4 address types.	299
Table 8-11	IPv4 Address Type	299
Summary	IPv4 private addresses.	299
Table 8-12	IPv4 Private Address Space	300
Summary	NAT.	300
Table 8-13	NAT Concepts	301
Summary	IPv4 address subnets.	302
Table 8-15	Subnet Masks	303
Summary	VLSM.	305
Section	IPv6 addressing design.	310
Table 8-27	Public Versus Private IP Addresses	313
List	Three address-allocation mechanisms of DHCP.	318
Summary	DNS.	319
Table 8-31	DNS Resource Records	320

Complete Tables and Lists from Memory

Print a copy of Appendix D, "Memory Tables," (found on the CD), or at least the section for this chapter, and complete the tables and lists from memory. Appendix E, "Memory Tables Answer Key," also on the CD, includes completed tables and lists to check your work.

Define Key Terms

Define the following key terms from this chapter, and check your answers in the glossary:

IPv4, DHCP, DNS, DSCP, NAT, PAT, ToS, VLSM

Q&A

The answers to these questions appear in Appendix A, "Answers to the 'Do I Know This Already?' Quizzes and Q&A Questions." For more practice with exam format questions, use the exam engine on the CD.

1. List the RFC 1918 private address ranges.

2. True or false: You can use DHCP to specify the TFTP host's IP address to a client PC.

3. True or false: 255.255.255.248 and /28 are two representations of the same IP mask.

4. True or false: Upper-layer protocols are identified in the IP header's protocol field. TCP is protocol 6, and UDP is protocol 17.

5. Fill in the blank: Without any options, the IP header is _____ bytes in length.

6. The IP header's ToS field is redefined as the DS field. How many bits does DSCP use for packet classification, and how many levels of classification are possible?

7. True or false: NAT uses different IP addresses for translations. PAT uses different port numbers to identify translations.

8. True or false: The IP header's header checksum field performs the checksum of the IP header and data.

9. Calculate the subnet, the address range within the subnet, and the subnet broadcast of the address 172.56.5.245/22.

10. When packets are fragmented at the network layer, where are the fragments reassembled?

11. Which protocol can you use to configure a default gateway setting on a host?

   a. ARP

   b. DHCP

   c. DNS

   d. RARP

12. How many host addresses are available with a Class B network with the default mask?

   a. 63,998

   b. 64,000

   c. 65,534

   d. 65,536

13. Which of the following is a dotted-decimal representation of a /26 prefix mask?

   a. 255.255.255.128

   b. 255.255.255.192

   c. 255.255.255.224

   d. 255.255.255.252

8

14. Which network and mask summarize both the 192.170.20.16/30 and 192.170.20.20/30 networks?

    a. 192.170.20.0/24

    b. 192.170.20.20/28

    c. 192.170.20.16/29

    d. 192.170.20.0/30

15. Which AF class is backward compatible with IP precedence bits' flash traffic?

    a. AF2

    b. AF3

    c. AF4

    d. EF

16. Which of the following is true about fragmentation?

    a. Routers between source and destination hosts can fragment IPv4 packets.

    b. Only the first router in the network can fragment IPv4 packets.

    c. IPv4 packets cannot be fragmented.

    d. IPv4 packets are fragmented and reassembled at each link through the network.

17. A packet sent to a multicast address reaches what destinations?

    a. The nearest destination in a set of hosts.

    b. All destinations in a set of hosts.

    c. Broadcasts to all hosts.

    d. Reserved global destinations.

18. What are three types of IPv4 addresses?

    a. Anycast

    b. Multicast

    c. Dynamic

    d. Broadcast

    e. Unicast

    f. Global

    g. Static

19. Which devices should be assigned an IP address dynamically? (Select three.)

    a. Cisco IP phones

    b. LAN switches

    c. Workstations

    d. Mobile devices

    e. Routers

20. Which name resolution method reduces administrative overhead?

   a. Static name resolution

   b. Dynamic name resolution

   c. DHCP name resolution

   d. Host.txt name resolution

21. How many hosts can be addressed with the following IPv4 subnet: 172.30.192.240/28?

   a. 6

   b. 14

   c. 126

   d. 1024

22. What is the smallest subnet and mask that can be used in a DMZ network that needs to have only three hosts?

   a. 192.168.10.32/30

   b. 192.168.10.32/29

   c. 192.168.10.32/28

   d. 192.168.10.32/27

23. Which modules cannot use private IPv4 address space? (Select all that apply.)

   a. Access

   b. Distribution

   c. Core

   d. E-commerce

   e. LAN

   f. WAN

   g. Internet Connection

   h. Data Center

   i. Remote Access/VPN

24. Which technology allows a company to use a single public IP address when using private IPv4 addresses in the internal LAN?

   a. NAT

   b. Redistribution

   c. PAT

   d. access list

25. Which of the following is the European RIR?

   a. IANA

   b. ARIN

   c. RIPE

   d. ERIR

26. Which technology allows you to divide address blocks into subnets of different sizes?

   a. NAT

   b. VLSM

   c. PAT

   d. Variable division subnet masks

27. Which regional registry allocates address blocks in North America?

   a. IANA

   b. RIPE

   c. ARIN

   d. APNIC

   e. LACNIC

   d. AFRINIC

28. Which regional registry allocates address blocks in China?

   a. IANA

   b. RIPE

   c. ARIN

   d. APNIC

   e. LACNIC

   d. AFRINIC

Answer the following questions based on the given scenario and Figure 8-12.

Company VWX has the network shown in Figure 8-12. The main site has three LANs, with 100, 29, and 60 hosts. The remote site has two LANs, each with 100 hosts. The network uses private addresses. The Internet service provider assigned the company the network 210.200.200.8/26.

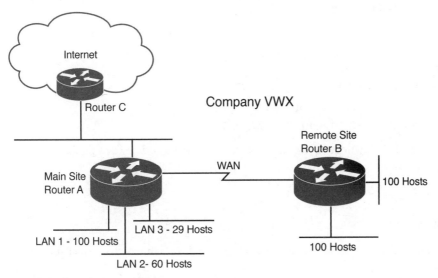

Figure 8-12 *Scenario diagram*

29. The remote site uses the network prefix 192.168.10.0/24. What subnets and masks can you use for the LANs at the remote site and conserve address space?

   a. 192.168.10.64/26 and 192.168.10.192/26

   b. 192.168.10.0/25 and 192.168.10.128/25

   c. 192.168.10.32/28 and 192.168.10.64/28

   d. 192.168.10.0/30 and 192.168.10.128/30

30. The main site uses the network prefix 192.168.15.0/24. What subnets and masks can you use to provide sufficient addresses for LANs at the main site and conserve address space?

   a. 192.168.15.0/25 for LAN 1, 192.168.15.128/26 for LAN 2, and 172.15.192.0/27 for LAN 3

   b. 192.168.15.0/27 for LAN 1, 192.168.15.128/26 for LAN 2, and 172.15.192.0/25 for LAN 3

   c. 192.168.15.0/100 for LAN 1, 192.168.15.128/60 for LAN 2, and 172.15.192.0/29 for LAN 3

   d. 192.168.15.0/26 for LAN 1, 192.168.15.128/26 for LAN 2, and 172.15.192.0/29 for LAN 3

31. Which network and mask would you use for the WAN link to save the most address space?

   a. 192.168.11.240/27

   b. 192.168.11.240/28

   c. 192.168.11.240/29

   d. 192.168.11.240/30

32. What networks does Router C announce to the Internet service provider's Internet router?

   a. 210.200.200.8/26

   b. 192.168.10.0/24 and 192.168.11.0/24

   c. 192.168.10.0/25 summary address

   d. 201.200.200.8/29 and 192.168.10.0/25

33. What technology does Router C use to convert private addresses to public addresses?

   a. DNS

   b. NAT

   c. ARP

   d. VLSM

34. What mechanism supports the ability to divide a given subnet into smaller subnets based on need?

   a. DNS

   b. NAT

   c. ARP

   d. VLSM

This chapter covers the following subjects:

Introduction to IPv6

IPv6 Header

IPv6 Address Representation

IPv6 Address Scope Types and Address Allocations

IPv6 Mechanisms

IPv6 Routing Protocols

IPv4-to-IPv6 Transition Strategies and Deployments

IPv6 Comparison with IPv4

This chapter reviews Internet Protocol Version 6 (IPv6) address structures, address assignments, representations, and mechanisms used to deploy IPv6. Expect plenty of questions about IPv6 on the exam. The CCDA candidate must understand how an IPv6 address is represented and the different types of IPv6 addresses. This chapter also covers the benefits of IPv6 over IPv4, compares the protocols, and examines migration to IPv6 options.

As IPv6 matures, different deployment models will be used to implement the new protocol with existing IPv4 networks. This chapter covers these models at a high level. This chapter does not discuss the configuration of IPv6 because it is not a requirement for CCDA certification.

CHAPTER 9

Internet Protocol Version 6 Design

"Do I Know This Already?" Quiz

The "Do I Know This Already?" quiz helps you identify your strengths and deficiencies in this chapter's topics.

The 13-question quiz, derived from the major sections in the "Foundation Topics" portion of the chapter, helps you determine how to spend your limited study time.

Table 9-1 outlines the major topics discussed in this chapter and the "Do I Know This Already?" quiz questions that correspond to those topics.

Table 9-1 "Do I Know This Already?" Foundation Topics Section-to-Question Mapping

Foundation Topics Section	Questions Covered in This Section
Introduction to IPv6	11
IPv6 Header	1, 2
IPv6 Address Representation	5, 8, 9
IPv6 Address Types and Address Allocations	3, 4, 7
IPv6 Mechanisms	10
IPv4-to-IPv6 Transition Strategies and Deployments	6
IPv6 Routing Protocols	12
IPv6 comparison with IPv4	13

1. IPv6 uses how many more bits for addresses than IPv4?
   a. 32
   b. 64
   c. 96
   d. 128

2. What is the length of the IPv6 header?
   a. 20 bytes
   b. 30 bytes
   c. 40 bytes
   d. 128 bytes

3. What address type is the IPv6 address FE80::300:34BC:123F:1010?

   a. Aggregatable global

   b. Unique-local

   c. Link-local

   d. Multicast

4. What are three scope types of IPv6 addresses?

   a. Unicast, multicast, broadcast

   b. Unicast, anycast, broadcast

   c. Unicast, multicast, endcast

   d. Unicast, anycast, multicast

5. What is a compact representation of the address 3f00:0000:0000:a7fb:0000:0000:b100:0023?

   a. 3f::a7fb::b100:0023

   b. 3f00::a7fb:0000:0000:b100:23

   c. 3f::a7fb::b1:23

   d. 3f00:0000:0000:a7fb::b1:23

6. What is NAT-PT?

   a. Network Address Translation–Port Translation. Translates RFC 1918 addresses to public IPv4 addresses.

   b. Network Addressable Transparent–Port Translation. Translates network addresses to ports.

   c. Network Address Translation–Protocol Translation. Translates between IPv4 and IPv6 addresses.

   d. Next Address Translation–Port Translation.

7. What IPv6 address scope type replaces the IPv4 broadcast address?

   a. Unicast

   b. Multicast

   c. Broadcast

   d. Anycast

8. What is the IPv6 equivalent to 127.0.0.1?

   a. 0:0:0:0:0:0:0:0

   b. 0:0:0:0:0:0:0:1

   c. 127:0:0:0:0:0:0:1

   d. FF::1

9. Which of the following is an "IPv4-compatible" IPv6 address?

   a. ::180.10.1.1

   b. f000:0:0:0:0:0:180.10.1.1

   c. 180.10.1.1::

   d. 2010::180.10.1.1

10. Which protocol maps names to IPv6 addresses?

   a. Address Resolution Protocol (ARP)

   b. Network Discovery (ND)

   c. Domain Name System (DNS)

   d. DNSv2

11. Which of the following are IPv6 enhancements over IPv4?

   a. Larger address space, globally private IP address, multicast

   b. Larger address space, globally unique IP addresses, no broadcasts

   c. Larger address space, globally private IP address, multicast

   d. Larger address space, address auto-configuration, enhanced broadcasts

12. Which of the following supports routing on IPv6 networks?

   a. RIPv3, OSPFv3, EIGRP for IPv6

   b. RIPng, OSPFv3, EIGRPv6

   c. RIPng, OSPFv3, EIGRP for IPv6

   d. RIPv2, OSPFv2, EIGRP

13. What changed from IPv4 header to the IPv6?

   a. Protocol Type became the Next Header field.

   b. ND is used rather than ARP.

   c. AAAA records are used rather than A records.

   d. All of these answers are correct.

9

Foundation Topics

The following sections cover topics that you need to master for the CCDA exam. The section "IPv6 Header" covers each field of the IPv6 header, which helps you understand the protocol. The section "IPv6 Address Representation" covers the hexadecimal representation of IPv6 addresses and the compressed representation. The section "IPv6 Address Scope Types and Address Allocations" covers unicast, multicast, and anycast IPv6 addresses, special address types, and the current allocations of IPv6 addresses.

The section "IPv6 Mechanisms" covers Internet Control Message Protocol Version 6 (ICMPv6), ND, and address assignment and resolution, and it introduces IPv6 routing protocols. The section "IPv4-to-IPv6 Transition Mechanisms and Deployment Models" covers dual-stack backbones, IPv6 over IPv4 tunnels, dual-stack hosts, and Network Address Translation–Protocol Translation (NAT-PT).

Introduction to IPv6

You should become familiar at a high level with IPv6 specifications, addressing, and design. The driving motivation for the adoption of a new version of IP is the limitation imposed by the 32-bit address field in IPv4. In the 1990s, there was concern that the IP address space would be depleted soon. Although classless interdomain routing (CIDR) and NAT have slowed down the deployment of IPv6, its standards and deployments are becoming mature. IPv6 is playing a significant role in the deployment of IP services for wireless phones. Some countries such as Japan directed IPv6 compatibility back in 2005. Other countries, such as China, France, and Korea, have been implementing IPv6. The 2008 Summer Olympics was accessible from the IPv6 Internet. The U.S. federal government had mandated all agencies to support IPv6 by mid 2008. Operating systems such as Windows 10, Windows 7, Linux, Mac OS, and others all support IPv6. Google and Facebook are also accessible in the IPv6 Internet.

The IPv6 specification provides 128 bits for addressing, a significant increase from 32 bits. The overall specification of IPv6 is in RFC 2460. Other RFCs describing IPv6 specifications are 4921, 3513, 3587, 3879, 2373, 2374, 2461, 1886, and 1981.

IPv6 includes the following enhancements over IPv4:

- **Larger address space:** IPv6 uses 128-bit addresses rather than the 32-bit addresses in IPv4. This supports more address hierarchy levels and uses simpler address autoconfiguration.

- **Globally unique IP addresses:** The additional address space allows each node to have a unique address and eliminates the need for NAT.

- **Header format efficiency:** The IPv6 header length is fixed, lowering header processing time and thus allowing vendors to improve packet switching efficiency.

- **Improved option mechanism:** IPv6 options are placed in separate optional headers that are located between the IPv6 header and the transport layer header. The option headers are not required.

- **Address autoconfiguration:** This capability provides for dynamic assignment of IPv6 addresses. IPv6 hosts can automatically configure themselves, with or without a Dynamic Host Configuration Protocol (DHCP) server. Stateful and stateless autoconfiguration is supported.

- **Flow labeling capability:** Instead of the Type of Service field in IPv4, IPv6 enables the labeling of packets belonging to a particular traffic class for which the sender requests special handling, such as quality of service (QoS) and real-time service. This support aids specialized traffic, such as real-time voice or video.

- **Security capabilities:** IPv6 includes features that support authentication and privacy. IP Security (IPsec) is a requirement.

- **Maximum transmission unit (MTU) path discovery:** IPv6 eliminates the need to fragment packets by implementing MTU path discovery before sending packets to a destination.

- **Site multihoming:** IPv6 allows multihoming by allowing hosts to have multiple IPv6 addresses and networks to have multiple IPv6 prefixes, which facilitates connection to multiple ISPs.

- **Support for mobility and multicast:** Mobile IPv6 allows for IPv6 nodes to change its location on a network and maintain its existing connection. The Mobile node is always reachable via one permanent address.

- **Eliminate the use of broadcasts:** IPv6 reduces unnecessary bandwidth by eliminating the use of broadcasts, replacing them with multicasts.

IPv6 Header

This section covers each field of the IPv6 header. The IPv6 header is simpler than the IPv4 header. Some IPv4 fields have been eliminated or changed to optional fields. The IPv6 header size is 40 bytes. The fragment offset fields and flags in IPv4 have been eliminated from the header. IPv6 adds a flow label field for QoS mechanisms to use.

The use of 128 bits for source and destination addresses provides a significant improvement over IPv4. With 128 bits, there are $3.4 * 10^{38}$ or 340 billion billion billion billion IPv6 addresses, compared to only 4.3 billion IPv4 addresses.

IPv6 improves over IPv4 by using a fixed-length header. The IPv6 header appears in Figure 9-1.

The following is a description of each field in the IP header:

- **Version:** This field is 4 bits long. It indicates the format, based on the version number, of the IP header. These bits are set to 0110 for IPv6 packets.

- **Traffic Class:** This field is 8 bits in length. It describes the class or priority of the IPv6 packet and provides functionality similar to the IPv4 Type of Service field.

- **Flow Label:** This field is 20 bits in length. It indicates a specific sequence of packets between a source and destination that requires special handling, such as real-time data (voice and video).

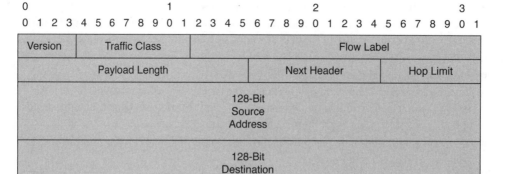

Figure 9-1   *IPv6 header format*

- **Payload Length:** This field is 16 bits in length. It indicates the payload's size in bytes. Its length includes any extension headers.

- **Next Header:** This field is 8 bits in length. It indicates the type of header that follows this IPv6 header. In other words, it identifies the upper-layer protocol. It uses values defined by the Internet Assigned Numbers Authority (IANA). Table 9-2 shows some key protocol numbers. You can find a full list at www.iana.org/assignments/protocol-numbers.

Table 9-2   IP Protocol Numbers

Protocol Number	Protocol
6	Transmission Control Protocol (TCP)
17	User Datagram Protocol (UDP)
50	Encapsulating Security Payload (ESP)
51	Authentication Header (AH)
85	ICMP for IPv6
59	No Next Header for IPv6
60	Destination Options for IPv6
88	Enhanced IGRP (EIGRP)
89	Open Shortest Path First (OSPF)

- **Hop Limit:** This field is 8 bits in length. It is decremented by 1 by each router that forwards the packets. If this field is 0, the packet is discarded.

- **Source Address:** This field is 128 bits in length. It indicates the sender's IPv6 address.

- **Destination Address:** This field is 128 bits in length. It indicates the destination host's IPv6 address.

Notice that although the IPv6 address is four times the length of an IPv4 address, the IPv6 header is only twice the length (40 bytes). Optional network layer information is not included in the IPv6 header; instead, it is included in separate extended headers. Some extended headers are the routing header, fragment header, and hop-by-hop options header. The routing header is used for source routing. The fragment header is included in fragmented datagrams to provide information to allow the fragments to be reassembled. The hop-by-hop extension header is used to support jumbo-grams.

Two important extended headers are the Authentication Header (AH) and the Encapsulating Security Payload (ESP) header. These headers are covered later in the chapter.

IPv6 Address Representation

RFC 4291 (which obsoletes RFC 3513 and RFC 2373) specifies the IPv6 addressing architecture. IPv6 addresses are 128 bits in length. For display, the IPv6 addresses have eight 16-bit groups. Each 16-bit group is represented using hexadecimal numbers. (See Appendix C, "OSI Model, TCP/IP Architecture, and Numeric Conversion," for a quick review on hexadecimal numbers.) The hexadecimal value is $x:x:x:x:x:x:x:x$, where each x represents four hexadecimal digits (16 bits).

An example of a full IPv6 address is 1111111000011010 0100001010111001 0000000000011011 0000000000000000 0000000000000000 0001001011010000 0000000001011011 0000011010110000.

The hexadecimal representation of the preceding IPv6 binary number is

FE1A:42B9:001B:0000:0000:12D0:005B:06B0

Groups with a value of 0 can be represented with a single 0. For example, you can also represent the preceding number as

FE1A:42B9:01B:0:0:12D0:05B:06B0

You can represent multiple groups of 16-bit 0s with ::, which is allowed to appear only once in the number. Also, you do not need to represent leading 0s in a 16-bit group. The preceding IPv6 address can be further shortened to

FE1A:42B9:1B::12D0:5B:6B0

> **Tip** Remember that the fully expanded address has eight blocks and that the double colon represents only 0s. You can use the double colon only once.

You expand a compressed address by reversing the process described earlier: add leading 0s in groups where they have been omitted, then add 0s represented by ::. For example, the IPv6 address 2001:4C::50:0:0:741 expands as follows:

2001:004C::0050:0000:0000:0741

Because there should be eight blocks of addresses and you have six, you can expand the double colon to two blocks as follows:

2001:004C:0000:0000:0050:0000:0000:0741

IPv4-Compatible IPv6 Addresses

IPv6 allows for IPv4-compatible IPv6 addresses. In a mixed IPv6/IPv4 environment, the IPv4 portion of the address requires the last two 16-bit blocks, or 32 bits of the address, which is represented in IPv4 dotted-decimal notation. The portion of the IPv6 address preceding the IPv4 information is all 0s. Six hexadecimal 16-bit blocks are concatenated with the dotted-decimal format. The first 96 bits are 0, and the last 32 bits are used for the IPv4 address. This form is *x:x:x:x:x:x:d.d.d.d*, where each *x* represents the hexadecimal digits and *d.d.d.d* is the dotted-decimal representation.

An example of a mixed full address is 0000:0000:0000:0000:0000:0000:100.1.1.1; this example can be shortened to 0:0:0:0:0:0:100.1.1.1 or ::100.1.1.1.

RFC 4921 mentions that IPv4-compatible IPv6 addresses have been deprecated since updated IPv6 transition mechanisms no longer use these addresses.

IPv6 Prefix Representation

IPv6 prefixes are represented similar to IPv4, with the following format:

   IPv6-address/prefix

The *IPv6-address* portion is a valid IPv6 address. The *prefix* portion is the number of leftmost contiguous bits that represent the *prefix*. You use the double colon only once in the representation. An example of an IPv6 prefix is 200C:001b:1100:0:0:0:0:0/40 or 200C:1b:1100::/40.

For another example, look at the representations of the 60-bit prefix 2001000000000ab0:

   2001:0000:0000:0ab0:0000:0000:0000:0000/60

   2001:0000:0000:0ab0:0:0:0:0/60

   2001:0000:0000:ab0::/60

   2001:0:0:ab0::/60

The rules for address representation are still valid when using a prefix. The following is not a valid representation of the preceding prefix:

   2001:0:0:ab0/60

The preceding representation is missing the trailing double colon:

   2001::ab0/60

The preceding representation expands to 2001:0:0:0:0:0:0:0ab0, which is not the prefix 2001:0000:0000:0ab0::/60.

When representing an IPv6 host address with its subnet prefix, you combine the two. For example, the IPv6 address 2001:0000:0000:0ab0:001c:1bc0:08ba:1c9a in subnet prefix 2001:0000:0000:0ab0::/60 is represented as the following:

   2001:0000:0000:0ab0:001c:1bc0:08ba:1c9a/60

IPv6 Address Scope Types and Address Allocations

This section covers the major types of IPv6 addresses. IPv4 addresses are unicast, multicast, or broadcast. IPv6 maintains each of these address functions, except that the IPv6 address types are defined a little differently. A special "all-nodes" IPv6 multicast address handles the broadcast function. IPv6 also introduces the anycast address type.

Also important to understand are the IPv6 address allocations. Sections of the IPv6 address space are reserved for particular functions, each of which is covered in this section. To provide you with a full understanding of address types, the following sections describe each one.

IPv6 Address Allocations

The leading bits of an IPv6 address can define the IPv6 address type or other reservations. These leading bits are of variable length and are called the format prefix (FP). Table 9-3 shows the allocation of address prefixes. The IPv6 address space was delegated to IANA. You can find current IPv6 allocations at www.iana.org/assignments/ipv6-address-space. Many prefixes are still unassigned.

Table 9-3   IPv6 Prefix Allocation

Binary Prefix	Hexadecimal/Prefix	Allocation
0000 0000	0000::/8	Unspecified, loopback, IPv4-compatible
0000 0001	0100::/8	Unassigned
0000 001	0200:/7	Unassigned
0000 010	0400::/7	Reserved for Internetwork Packet Exchange (IPX) allocation
0000 1	0800::/5	Unassigned
0001	1000::/4	Unassigned
001	2000::/3	Global unicast address
010	4000::/3	Unassigned
011	6000::/3	Unassigned
100	8000::/3	Reserved for geographic-based unicast addresses
101	A000::/3	Unassigned
110	C000::/3	Unassigned
1110	E000::/3	Unassigned
1111 0	F000::/5	Unassigned
1111 10	F800::/6	Unassigned
1111 110	FC00::/7	Unique local unicast
1111 1110 0	FE00::/9	Unassigned
1111 1110 10	FE80:/10	Link-local unicast addresses
1111 1110 11	FEC0::/10	Unassigned; was site-local unicast addresses (deprecated)
1111 1111	FF00::/8	Multicast addresses

9

An unspecified address is all 0s: 0:0:0:0:0:0:0:0. It signifies that an IPv6 address is not specified for the interface. Unspecified addresses are not forwarded by an IPv6 router.

The IPv6 loopback address is 0:0:0:0:0:0:0:1. This address is similar to the IPv4 loopback address of 127.0.0.1.

IPv6 Unicast Address

The IPv6 *unicast* (one-to-one) address is the logical identifier of a single-host interface. With a unicast address, a single source sends to a single destination. It is similar to IPv4 unicast addresses. Unicast addresses are divided into:

- Global unicast address
- Link-local address
- Unique local address

Global Unicast Addresses

IPv6 global addresses connect to the public network. These unicast addresses are globally unique and routable. This address format is initially defined in RFC 2374. RFC 3587 provides updates to the format.

The original specification defined the address format with a three-layer hierarchy: public topology, site topology, and interface identifier. The *public topology* consisted of service providers that provided transit services and exchanges of routing information. It used a top-level aggregator (TLA) identifier and a next-level identifier (NLA). A site-level aggregator (SLA) was used for site topology. The *site topology* is local to the company or site and does not provide transit services. The TLA, NLA, and SLA identifiers are deprecated by RFC 3587. RFC 3587 simplifies these identifiers with a global routing prefix and subnet identifier for the network portion of the address.

Figure 9-2 shows the format of the standard IPv6 global unicast address. The global routing prefix is generally 48 bits in length, and the subnet ID is 16 bits. The interface ID is 64 bits in length and uniquely identifies the interface on the link.

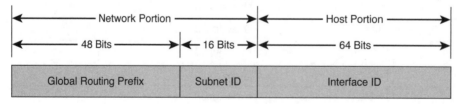

Figure 9-2   *IPv6 global unicast address format*

The interface ID is obtained from the 48-bit MAC address of the host. The MAC is converted to the EUI-64 identifier format by inserting the FFFE hexadecimal value in between the 24-bit leftmost and rightmost values.

For example, with the following MAC address 01:00:0C:A4:BC:D0, the leftmost 24 bits are 01:00:0C and the rightmost bits are A4:BC:D0. By inserting FFFE, the IPv6 64-bit identifier becomes

01:00:0C:FF:FE:A4:BC:D0.

Link-Local Addresses

IPv6 link-local addresses are significant only to nodes on a single link. Routers do not forward packets with a link-local source or destination address beyond the local link. Link-local addresses are identified by leading FE8 hexadecimal numbers. Link-local addresses are configured automatically or manually.

As shown in Figure 9-3, the format of the link-local address is an FP of 1111111010, followed by 54 0s and a 64-bit interface identifier (ID). The interface ID is obtained from the device MAC address and verified automatically through communication with other nodes in the link. The interface ID is then concatenated with the link-local address prefix of FE80::/64 to obtain the interface link-local address.

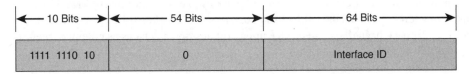

Figure 9-3   *IPv6 link-local address format*

Unique Local IPv6 Address

RFC 4193 defines the unique local address. Unique local addresses designed for use in local networks and are not routable in the Internet. It substitutes the deprecated site-local addresses. As shown in Figure 9-4, the format of the unique local address is an FP of 1111 110 (FC00::/7) followed by global ID, followed by the subnet ID and then the 64-bit interface identifier (ID). The bit labeled L is set to 1 if the prefix is locally assigned and setting it to 0 has not been defined.

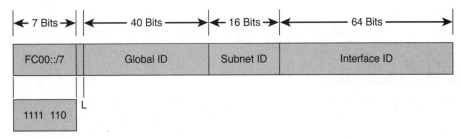

Figure 9-4   *IPv6 unique local address*

Global Aggregatable IPv6 Address

Global aggregatable unicast addresses are a type of global unicast address that allows the aggregation of routing prefixes. This enables a reduction in the number of routes in the global routing table. These addresses are used in links to aggregate (summarize) routes upward to the core in large organizations or to ISPs. Global aggregatable addresses are identified by a fixed prefix of 2000:/3. As shown in Figure 9-5, the format of the global aggregatable IPv6 address is a global routing prefix starting with binary 001, followed by the subnet ID and then the 64-bit interface identifier (ID). The device MAC address is normally used as the interface ID.

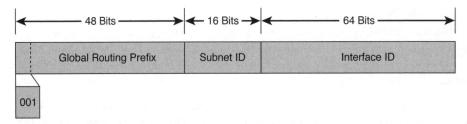

Figure 9-5 *IPv6 link-local address format*

IPv4-Compatible IPv6 Address

IPv4-compatible IPv6 addresses begin with 96 binary 0s (six 16-bit groups) followed by the 32-bit IPv4 address, as in 0:0:0:0:0:0:130.100.50.1, or just ::130.100.50.1. IPv4-compatible IPv6 addresses have been deprecated since updated transition mechanisms no longer require this format.

IPv6 Anycast Addresses

The IPv6 *anycast* (one-to-nearest) address identifies a set of devices. An anycast address is allocated from a set of unicast addresses. These destination devices should share common characteristics and are explicitly configured for anycast.

You can use the anycast address to identify a set of routers or servers within an area. When a packet is sent to the anycast address, it is delivered to the nearest device as determined by the routing protocol. An example of the use of anycast addresses is to assign an anycast address to a set of servers—one in North America and the other in Europe. Users in North America would be routed to the North American server, and those in Europe to the European server.

You cannot use an anycast address as a source address. Also, you must explicitly configure nodes to which the anycast address is assigned to recognize the anycast address.

IPv6 Multicast Addresses

The IPv6 *multicast* (one-to-many) address identifies a set of hosts. The packet is delivered to all the hosts identified by that address. This type is similar to IPv4 multicast (Class D) addresses. IPv6 multicast addresses also supersede the broadcast function of IPv4 broadcasts. You use an "all-nodes" multicast address instead. One additional function of IPv6 multicast is to provide the IPv4 broadcast equivalent with the all-nodes multicast group.

Some IPv6 multicast addresses are

FF01:0:0:0:0:0:0:1—Indicates all-nodes address for interface-local scope

FF02:0:0:0:0:0:0:2—All-routers address for link-local

RFC 4291 specifies the format of IPv6 multicast addresses. As shown in Figure 9-6, the fields of the IPv6 multicast address are the FP, a value of 0xFF, followed by a 4-bit flags field, a 4-bit scope field, and 112 bits for the group identifier (ID). Again, a quick way to recognize an IPv6 multicast address is that it begins with FF::/8.

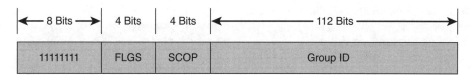

Figure 9-6 *Multicast address format*

The FLGS (flags) field consists of three leading 0s followed by a T bit: 000T. If T = 0, the address is a well-known multicast address assigned by the global IANA. If T = 1, the address is not a permanently assigned address.

The SCOP (scope) field limits the scope of the multicast group. Table 9-4 shows the assigned scope values.

Table 9-4 Multicast Scope Assignments

SCOP (Binary)	SCOP (Hexadecimal)	Assignment
0000	0	Reserved
0001	1	Node-local scope
0010	2	Link-local scope
0011	3	Unassigned
0100	4	Admin-local scope
0101	5	Site-local scope
0110	6	Unassigned
0111	7	Unassigned
1000	8	Organization-local scope
1001	9	Unassigned
1010	A	Unassigned
1011	B	Unassigned
1100	C	Unassigned
1101	D	Unassigned
1110	E	Global scope
1111	F	Reserved

The group ID identifies the multicast group within the given scope. The group ID is independent of the scope. A group ID of 0:0:0:0:0:0:1 identifies nodes, whereas a group ID of 0:0:0:0:0:0:2 identifies routers. Some well-known multicast addresses appear in Table 9-5 associated with a variety of scope values.

Table 9-5 Well-Known IPv6 Multicast Addresses

Multicast Address	Multicast Group
FF01::1	All nodes (node-local)
FF02::1	All nodes (link-local)
FF01::2	All routers (node-local)
FF02::2	All routers (link-local)
FF02::5	Open Shortest Path First Version 3 (OSPFv3)
FF02::6	OSPFv3 designated routers
FF02::9	Routing Information Protocol (RIPng)
FF02::A	EIGRP routers
FF02::B	Mobile agents
FF02::C	DHCP servers/relay agents
FF02::D	All Protocol Independent Multicast (PIM) routers
FF05::1	All nodes in the local network site
FF0x::FB	Multicast DNS
FF02::1:2	All DHCP and relay agents on the local network site (RFC 3313)
FF05::1:3	All DHCP servers on the local network site (RFC 3313)

Table 9-6 summarizes the IPv6 address types.

Table 9-6 IPv6 Address Types

IPv6 Address Type	Description
Unicast	The IP address of an interface on a single host. It can be a source or destination address.
Anycast	An IP address that identifies a set of devices within an area. It is only a destination address.
Multicast	An IP address that reaches a group of hosts identified by the address. It is only a destination address

The CCDA should know how to identify address types based from the prefix. Table 9-7 summarizes the prefixes their respective address type.

Table 9-7 IPv6 Addresses Prefix

IPv6 Address Type	Description
Loopback	0000::0001
Unspecified address	0000::0000

IPv6 Address Type	Description
Global unicast address	2000::/3
Unique local unicast	FC00::/7
Link-local unicast address	FE80:/10
Multicast address	FF00::/8
OSPFv3	FF02::5
EIGRP routers	FF02::A
DHCP	FF02::C

IPv6 Mechanisms

The changes to the 128-bit address length and IPv6 header format modified the underlying protocols that support IP. This section covers ICMPv6, IPv6 ND, address resolution, address assignment, and IPv6 routing protocols. These protocols must now support 128-bit addresses. For example, DNS adds a new record locator for resolving fully qualified domain names (FQDNs) to IPv6 addresses. IPv6 also replaces ARP with the IPv6 ND protocol. IPv6 ND uses ICMPv6.

ICMPv6

ICMP needed some modifications to support IPv6. RFC 2463 describes the use of ICMPv6 for IPv6 networks. All IPv6 nodes must implement ICMPv6 to perform network layer functions. ICMPv6 performs diagnostics (ping), reports errors, and provides reachability information. Although IPv4 ICMP uses IP protocol 1, IPv6 uses a next header number of 58.

Informational messages are

- Echo request
- Echo reply

Some error messages are

- Destination unreachable
- Packet too big
- Time exceeded
- Parameter problem

The destination-unreachable messages also provide further details:

- No route to destination
- Destination administratively prohibited
- Address unreachable
- Port unreachable

9

Other IPv6 mechanisms use ICMPv6 to determine neighbor availability, path MTU, destination address, or port reachability.

IPv6 Neighbor Discovery Protocol

IPv6 does not implement the ARP that is used in IPv4. Instead, IPv6 implements the Neighbor Discovery (ND) protocol described in RFC 2461. Hosts use ND to implement plug-and-play functions that discover all other nodes in the same link, check for duplicate addresses, and find routers in the link. The protocol also searches for alternative routers if the primary fails.

The IPv6 ND protocol performs the following functions:

- **Stateless address autoconfiguration:** The host can determine its full IPv6 address without the use of DHCP.
- **Duplicate address detection:** The host can determine whether the address it will use is already in use on the network.
- **Prefix discovery:** The host finds out the link's IPv6 prefix.
- **Parameter discovery:** The host finds out the link's MTU and hop count.
- **Address resolution:** The host can determine the MAC address of other nodes without the use of ARP.
- **Router discovery:** The host finds local routers without the use of DHCP.
- **Next-hop determination:** The host can determine a destination's next hop.
- **Neighbor unreachability detection:** The host can determine whether a neighbor is no longer reachable.
- **Redirect:** The host can tell another host if a preferred next hop exists to reach a particular destination.

IPv6 ND uses ICMPv6 to implement some of its functions. These ICMPv6 messages are

- **Router Advertisement (RA):** Sent by routers to advertise their presence and link-specific parameters
- **Router Solicitation (RS):** Sent by hosts to request RA from local routers
- **Neighbor Solicitation (NS):** Sent by hosts to request link layer addresses of other hosts (also used for duplicate address detection)
- **Neighbor Advertisement (NA):** Sent by hosts in response to an NS
- **Redirect:** Sent to a host to notify it of a better next hop to a destination

The link address resolution process uses NS messages to obtain a neighbor's link layer address. Nodes respond with an NA message that contains the link layer address.

IPv6 Name Resolution

Name resolution for IPv6 addresses can be static or dynamic. Just as with IPv4, static names to IPv6 addresses can be manually configured in the host configuration file. Dynamic name resolution relies on the Domain Name System (DNS).

IPv4 uses A records to provide FQDN-name-to-IPv4-address resolution. DNS adds a resource record (RR) to support name-to-IPv6-address resolution. RFC 3596 describes the addition of a new DNS resource record type to support transition to IPv6 name resolution. The new record type is AAAA, commonly known as "quad-A." Given a domain name, the AAAA record returns an IPv6 address to the requesting host.

RFC 2874 specifies another DNS record for IPv6; it defines the A6 resource record. The A6 record provides additional features and was intended as a replacement for the AAAA RR. But RFC 3363 has changed the status of the A6 RR to deprecated.

Current DNS implementations need to be able to support A (for IPv4) and AAAA resource records, with type A having the highest priority and AAAA the lowest.

For hosts that support dual-stack (IPv4 and IPv6), the application decides which stack to use and accordingly requests an AAAA or A record. As shown in Figure 9-7, the client device requests the AAAA record of the destination IPv6 server. The DNS server returns the IPv6 address. Note that this is the same DNS server that supports IPv4 addresses; no separate DNS servers are needed for IPv6 networks.

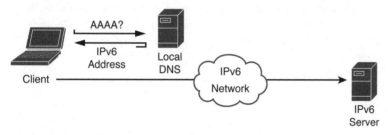

Figure 9-7   *IPv6 DNS AAAA request*

Path MTU Discovery

IPv6 does not allow packet fragmentation throughout the internetwork. Only sending hosts are allowed to fragment. Routers are not allowed to fragment packets. RFC 2460 specifies that the MTU of every link in an IPv6 must be 1280 bytes or greater. RFC 1981 recommends that nodes should implement IPv6 path MTU discovery to determine whether any paths are greater than 1280 bytes. ICMPv6 packet-too-big error messages determine the path MTU. Nodes along the path send the ICMPv6 packet-too-big message to the sending host if the packet is larger than the outgoing interface MTU.

Figure 9-8 shows a host sending a 2000-byte packet. Because the outgoing interface MTU is 1500 bytes, Router A sends an ICMPv6 packet-too-big error message back to Host A. The sending host then sends a 1500-byte packet. The outgoing interface MTU at Router B is 1300 bytes. Router B sends an ICMPv6 packet-too-big error message to Host A. Host A then sends the packet with 1300 bytes.

9

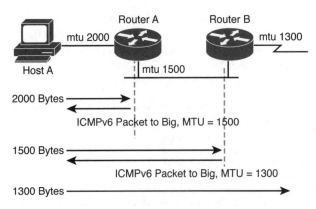

Figure 9-8 *ICMPv6 packet-too big message*

IPv6 Address-Assignment Strategies

Assignment of IPv6 addresses to a host can be statically or dynamically configured. Static IPv6 address assignment just involves manual configuration on the host's configuration files. Dynamic IPv6 address assignment can be done via stateless or stateful methods. The stateless method may result in a link-local or globally unique address. The three methods to assign IPv6 addresses are:

- Manual configuration
- Stateless address autoconfiguration (SLAAC)
- Stateful configuration with DHCPv6

Manual Configuration

As with IPv4, devices such as routers, switches, servers, and firewalls should be configured with their IPv6 addresses manually.

SLAAC of Link-Local Address

The dynamic configuration of link-local IPv6 addresses is a stateless autoconfiguration method, without DHCP. Hosts obtain their link-local addresses automatically as an interface is initialized. First, the host performs a duplicate address-detection process. The host joins the all-nodes multicast group to receive neighbor advertisements from other nodes. The neighbor advertisements include the subnet or prefix associated with the link. The host then sends a neighbor-solicitation message with the tentative IP address (interface identifier) as the target. If a host is already using the tentative IP address, that host replies with a neighbor advertisement. If the host receives no neighbor advertisement, the target IP address becomes the link-local address of the originating host. It uses the link-local prefix FE80::/10 (binary: 1111 1110 10). An alternate is to manually configure the link-local address.

SLAAC of Globally Unique IPv6 Address

RFC 4862 describes IPv6 stateless address autoconfiguration. With autoconfiguration of globally unique IP addresses, IPv6 hosts can use SLAAC, without DHCP, to acquire their own IP address information. This is done on a per-interface basis. As shown in Figure 9-9, after a host has autoconfigured a link-local address, it listens for router advertisement (RA) messages. These router messages contain the prefix address to be used for the network. The IPv6 address is then formed from the prefix plus the interface ID (derives from the MAC address).

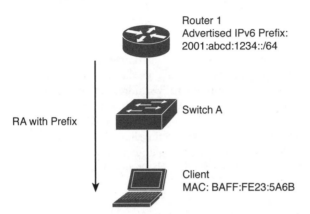

Figure 9-9   *Stateless autoconfiguration*

The process takes the following steps to create the globally unique IPv6 address:

1. Router advertisements (RA) are sent by Router 1.

2. The client learns the prefix from the RA. In the case of Figure 9-9, the prefix is 2001:abcd:1234/64.

3. The client identifier is created by splitting the local MAC address and adding FF:FE in the middle. Hence, in our example, the MAC 0200:FE23:5A6B becomes 0200:FEFF:FE23:5A6B.

4. The seventh bit is flipped (binary 00000010 becomes binary 0000000); thus, the identifier becomes 0000:FEFF:FE23:5A6B.

5. The merging of the prefix and identifier becomes 2001:abcd:1234:0000:0000: FEFF:FE23:5A6B.

6. The address is shortened to 2001:abcd:1234:: FEFF:FE23:5A6B.

Table 9-8 summarizes IPv6 address schemes.

Table 9-8   IPv6 Address Autoconfiguration Scheme

IPv6 Address Configuration Scheme	Description
Manual configuration	Routers, switches, servers, and firewalls.
SLAAC link-local	Host sends a neighbor-solicitation message that includes the target IPv6 address that begins with FE80::.
SLAAC global unique	Combines the router prefix with the local MAC address.
DHCPv6	Provides stateful address allocation.

DHCPv6

DHCPv6 is the updated version of DHCP that provides dynamic IP address assignment for IPv6 hosts. DHCPv6 is described in RFC 3315. It provides the same functions as DHCP, with more control than stateless autoconfiguration, and it supports renumbering without routers. DHCPv6 assignment is stateful, whereas IPv6 link-local and global unique autoconfiguration is not.

DHCPv6 Lite

SLAAC is simpler than DHCPv6, although it offers less control and fewer capabilities. For example, SLAAC is not able to send DNS parameters. To overcome this limitation, there is another (special case) option for clients to receive both their IPv6 address and other information via stateless method. This is accomplished using SLAAC initially and then using stateless DHCPv6 service, also known as DHCPv6 Lite. With DHCPv6 Lite DNS server, domain name, SIP server, and other information can be sent to the client. With DHCPv6 Lite, the client performs the SLAAC to obtain its IPv6 address and then sends a DHCP information request to the router. The router then responds with a reply message in the requested information.

IPv6 Security

IPv6 has two integrated mechanisms to provide security for communications. It natively supports IP Security (IPsec). IPsec is mandated at the operating system level for all IPsec hosts. RFC 2401 describes IPsec. Extension headers carry the IPsec AH and ESP headers. The AH provides authentication and integrity. The ESP header provides confidentiality by encrypting the payload. For IPv6, the AH defaults to message digest algorithm 5 (MD5), and the ESP encryption defaults to Data Encryption Standard–cipher block chaining (DES-CBC).

A description of the IPsec mechanisms appears in Chapter 13, "Security Solutions." More information also appears in RFC 2402: IP Authentication Header, and in RFC 2406: IP Encapsulating Security Payload (ESP).

Table 9-9 summarizes IPv6 mechanisms.

Table 9-9   IPv6 Mechanisms

IPv6 Mechanism	Description
ICMPv6	Performs diagnostics and reachability information. Next header number of 58.
IPv6 neighbor discovery	Discovers all nodes in the same link and checks for duplicate addresses.
AAAA	DNS resource record for IPv6.
SLAAC	Performs stateless IPv6 address assignment.
DHCPv6	Provides stateful IPv6 address assignment.
RIPng	Routing protocol that uses UDP port 521.
EIGRP for IPv6	Cisco routing protocol for IPv6.
OSPFv3	Link-state routing protocol for IPv6.

IPv6 Routing Protocols

New routing protocols have been developed to support IPv6, such as RIPng, Intermediate System-to-Intermediate System (IS-IS), Enhanced Interior Gateway Routing Protocol (EIGRP) for IPv6, and Open Shortest Path First Version 3 (OSPFv3) Protocol. Border Gateway Protocol (BGP) also includes changes that support IPv6. These routing protocols are only briefly mentioned here because they are covered in detail in Chapter 10, "Routing Protocol Characteristics, RIP, EIGRP, and IS-IS," and Chapter 11, "OSPF, BGP, Route Manipulation, and IP Multicast."

RIPng

RFC 2080 describes changes to RIP to support IPv6 networks, called RIP next generation (RIPng). RIP mechanisms remain the same. RIPng still has a 15-hop limit, counting to infinity, and split horizon with poison reverse. Instead of User Datagram Protocol (UDP) port 520 for RIPv2, RIPng uses UDP port 521. RIPng supports IPv6 addresses and prefixes. Cisco IOS software currently supports RIPng. RIPng uses multicast group FF02::9 for RIP updates to all RIP routers.

EIGRP for IPv6

Cisco has developed EIGRP support for IPv6 networks to route IPv6 prefixes. EIGRP for IPv6 is configured and managed separately from EIGRP for IPv4; no network statements are used. EIGRP for IPv6 retains all the characteristics (network discovery, DUAL, modules) and functions of EIGRP for IPv4. EIGRP uses multicast group FF02::A for EIGRP updates.

OSPFv3

RFC 5340 describes OSPFv3 to support IPv6 networks. OSPF algorithms and mechanisms (flooding, designated router [DR] election, areas, and shortest path first [SPF] calculations) remain the same. Changes are made for OSPF to support IPv6 addresses, address hierarchy, and IPv6 for transport. Cisco IOS software currently supports OSPFv3.

OSPFv3 uses multicast group FF02::5 for all OSPF routers and FF02::6 for all DRs.

IS-IS for IPv6

Specifications for routing IPv6 with integrated IS-IS is described in RFC 5308: Routing IPv6 with IS-IS. The draft specifies new type, length, and value (TLV) objects, reachability TLVs, and an interface address TLV to forward IPv6 information in the network. IOS supports IS-IS for IPv6 as currently described in the draft standard.

BGP4 Multiprotocol Extensions (MP-BGP) for IPv6

RFC 2545 specifies the use of BGP attributes for passing on IPv6 route information. MP-BGP is also referred as BGP4+. The MP_REACH_NLRI (multiprotocol-reachable) attribute describes reachable destinations. It includes the next-hop address and a list of Network Layer Reachability Information (NLRI) prefixes of reachable networks. The MP_UNREACH_NLRI (multiprotocol-unreachable) attribute conveys unreachable networks. IOS currently supports these BGP4 multiprotocol attributes to communicate reachability information for IPv6 networks.

9

IPv6 Addressing Design

This section covers IPv6 design topics that the CCDA should be aware of: planning for IPv6 addressing, IPv6 route summarization, IPv6 address allocation, and IPv6 private addressing. Some IPv6 design concepts are similar to IPv6 (such as the goal to do summarization), and some concepts are unique to IPv6. As with IPv4, each company will have a unique set of requirements that will drive the allocation and subnetting of the IPv6 address space.

Planning for Addressing with IPv6

When designing LAN subnets with IPv6, it is recommended that you use a /64 subnet. This is similar to the /24 subnet in IPv4. It provides more than enough addresses for devices contained in the subnet, allows for future growth, and avoids having to do renumbering in the future. It also allows ease of aggregation of subnets.

If you are allocated IPv6 addresses from an Internet service provider (ISP), you most likely will have to renumber your IPv6 addresses if you move to a different ISP. The best way to avoid this is to obtain an IPv6 address block from a Regional Internet Registry (RIR). This way, your IPv6 addresses are independent of which ISP you use. The five RIRs are

- **AFRINIC:** Africa region
- **APNIC:** Asia Pacific region
- **ARIN:** Canada, U.S., and some Caribbean Islands region
- **LACNIC:** Latin America and some Caribbean Islands region
- **RIPE NCC:** Europe, Middle East, and Central Asia region

Route Summarization with IPv6

As a designer, you will want to allocate IPv6 address space to allow for route summarization. Large networks can grow quickly from 500 routes to 1000, and higher. Route summarization reduces the amount of route traffic on the network and unnecessary route computation, regardless of IPv4 or IPv6 addressing. Route summarization allows the network address space to scale as the company grows.

As an example, say a company has assigned the following IPv6 subnets to a site:

- 2001:db8:2a3e:8180::/64 for data networks
- 2001:db8:2a3e:8184::/64 for VoIP networks
- 2001:db8:2a3e:8188:/64 for wireless networks
- 2001:db8:2a3e:818F::/64 for small server farm and other systems

Instead of announcing each and every subnet of this network to the WAN, the recommendation is to summarize the site with a 2001:db8:2a3e:8180::/60 route. This summary encompasses 16 subnets from 2001:db8:2a3e:8180::/64 to 2001:db8:2a3e:818F::/64, so this address block would be assigned to this site.

IPv6 Private Addressing

IPv6 private addressing should be very limited as compared to its use in IPv4. IPv6 private IP addresses are referred to unique local addresses (ULAs) and use the prefix FC00::/7. Regardless of small or large companies, you should not expect to use ULAs in IPv6 networks. Furthermore, the Internet Engineering Task Force (IETF) does not recommend the use of NAT for IPv6. In the remote event that ULAs are needed, you will also use NAT66 for the IPv6-to-IPv6 private-to-public translation.

IPv6 for the Enterprise

IPv6 addresses are assigned in a hierarchical manner. The IANA allocates IPv6 addresses to the RIRs. The RIRs, in turn, allocate address blocks to local Internet registries (LIRs), and most LIRs are ISPs. In some regions (for example APNIC), RIRs allocate addresses to national Internet registries (NIRs), which in turn allocate addresses to ISPs. Normally, ISPs are allocated /32 blocks of addresses. Companies are allocated an address block from /40 to /64. Large companies are allocated a /40 block of IPv6 addresses. Small companies might receive a /56 block, but a normal allocation is a /48 block of IPv6 addresses. Private consumers, such as residential user, are allocated a /64 address block.

A /48 address block is equal to two to the power of sixteen (2^{16}) /64 subnets. As an example, if a company is allocated 2001:DB8:0ABC::/48, this allows it to assign subnets from 2001:DB8:0ABC:0000::/64, 2001:DB8:0ABC:0001::/64, 2001:DB8:0ABC:0002::/64, all the way to 2001:DB8:0ABC:FFFF::/64. That is 2^{16} = 65,536 subnets!

IPv6 Address Allocation

There are several schemas to allocate IPv6 addresses within an organization. Because IPv6 addresses are usually allocated to a network that already has IPv4 addresses, you can attempt to use the IPv4 address or subnet as part of the IPv6 address. You can also allocate IPv6 address space to show a location and type.

Partly Linked IPv4 Address into IPv6

IPv6 deployments are not expected to be greenfield; there will be IPv4 subnets on the network. One method to allocate IPv6 addresses is to match the IPv6 /64 bit subnet with the IPv4 /24 bit subnet. In addition, the IP subnet can match the VLAN number used. Table 9-10 shows an example. The third octet of the IPv4 subnet is used as the subnet for the IPv6 /64 subnet; furthermore, it matches the VLAN number. Do note that this works very well with IPv4 /24 subnets, but will not work optimally with /30 and other smaller links.

Table 9-10 IPv6 Address Allocation Partly Linked to IPv4

VLAN Number	IPv4 Subnet	IPv6 Subnet
VLAN 11	172.16.11.0/24	2001:DB8:0ABC:11::/64
VLAN 12	172.16.12.0/24	2001:DB8:0ABC:12::/64
VLAN 13	172.16.13.0/24	2001:DB8:0ABC:13::/64
VLAN 111	172.16.111.0/24	2001:DB8:0ABC:111::/64

VLAN Number	IPv4 Subnet	IPv6 Subnet
VLAN 112	172.16.112.0/24	2001:DB8:0ABC:112::/64
VLAN 113	172.16.113.0/24	2001:DB8:0ABC:113::64

Whole IPv4 Address Linked into IPv6

Another method is to link the whole IPv4 address into the lowest significant bits of the IPv6 address. Table 9-11 shows an example using the same subnets. Converting the numbers, 172 decimal is 0xAC and 16 is 0x10. The drawback with this schema is that it is not obvious that the IPv6 and IPv4 subnets are linked. At first sight, can you tell that 0xAC10 is 172.16?

Table 9-11   IPv6 Address Allocation Completely Linked to IPv4

VLAN Number	IPv4 Subnet	IPv6 Subnet
VLAN 11	172.16.11.0/24	2001:DB8:0ABC::AC10:0B:00/120
VLAN 12	172.16.12.0/24	2001:DB8:0ABC::AC10:0C00/120
VLAN 13	172.16.13.0/24	2001:DB8:0ABC::AC10:0D00/120
VLAN 111	172.16.111.0/24	2001:DB8:0ABC:AC10:6F00/120
VLAN 112	172.16.112.0/24	2001:DB8:0ABC:AC10:7000/120
VLAN 113	172.16.113.0/24	2001:DB8:0ABC:AC10:7100/120

IPv6 Addresses Allocated Per Location and/or Type

Another schema for allocating IPv6 addresses is to use assign bits to identify a location and/or other bits to identify a site type. *Location* refers to data center, core, edge, and branch. *Type* refers to the use of the subnet, such as server, end client, router, switch, and so on. As shown in Figure 9-10, 4 bits can be used for Location codes and 4 additional bits used for Type codes. The remaining bits of the /64 subnet can be used within the sites for specific VLANs.

2001:DB8:ABC:	L	L	L	L	T	T	T	T	0000	0000	::/64

L = Location
T = Type

Figure 9-10   *IPv6 address allocated per Location/Type*

IPv4-to-IPv6 Transition Mechanisms and Deployment Models

This section describes transition mechanisms and deployment models to migrate from IPv4 to IPv6. During a transition time, both protocols can coexist in the network. The three major transition mechanisms are

- **Dual-stack:** IPv4 and IPv6 coexist in hosts and networks.
- **Tunneling:** IPv6 packets are encapsulated into IPv4 packets.
- **Translation:** IPv6 packets are translated to IPv4 packets.

IPv6 deployment models are also divided into three major categories:

- **Dual-stack model:** IPv4 and IPv6 coexist on hosts and the network.
- **Hybrid model:** Combination of Intra-Site Automatic Tunneling Addressing Protocol (ISATAP) or manually configured tunnels and dual-stack mechanisms.
- **Service block model:** Combination of ISATAP and manually configured tunnels and dual-stack mechanisms.

Each model provides several advantages and disadvantages; familiarize yourself with those. Of all these models, the dual-stack model is recommended because it requires no tunneling and is easier to manage.

Dual-Stack Mechanism

Devices running dual-stack can communicate with both IPv4 and IPv6 devices. The IPv4 protocol stack is used between IPv4 hosts, and the IPv6 protocol stack is used between IPv6 hosts. The application decides which stack to use to communicate with destination hosts. As shown in Figure 9-11, when a frame is received, the Ethernet type code identifies whether the packet needs to be forwarded to IPv4 (0x0800) or IPv6 (ox86DD). When using dual stacks, a host also uses DNS to determine which stack to use to reach a destination. If DNS returns an IPv6 (AAAA record) address to the host, the host uses the IPv6 stack. If DNS returns an IPv4 (A record) address to the host, the host uses the IPv4 stack.

IPv6 over IPv4 Tunnels

In this deployment model, pockets of IPv6-only networks are connected using IPv4 tunnels. With tunneling, IPv6 traffic is encapsulated within IPv4 packets so that they are sent over the IPv4 WAN. The advantage of this method is that you do not need separate circuits to connect the IPv6 networks. A disadvantage of this method is the increased protocol over-head of the encapsulated IPv6 headers. Tunnels are created manually, semiautomatically, or automatically.

9

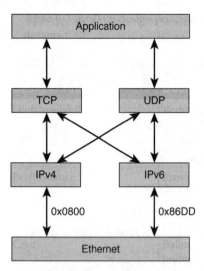

Figure 9-11   *Dual-stack mechanism*

Manually configured (static configuration) tunnels are configured with IPv4 and IPv6 addresses for tunnel source and destination. Tunnels can be built between border routers or between routers and hosts.

In semiautomatic configured tunnels, a tunnel broker is used. The tunnel broker is a server on the IPv4 network that receives requests from dual-stack clients and builds a tunnel on the tunnel router and associates it with the client.

Automatic tunnel mechanisms are

- IPv4 compatible
- 6to4
- 6over4
- ISATAP

IPv4-compatible tunnels use IPv4-compatible addresses. This mechanism does not scale, and IP-compatible addresses have been deprecated, so this mechanism is appropriate only for testing.

RFC 3056 specifies the 6to4 method for transition by assigning an interim unique IPv6 prefix. 2002::/16 is the assigned range for 6to4. Each 6to4 site uses a /48 prefix that is concatenated with 2002. The border router extracts the IPv4 address that is embedded in the IPv6 destination address and encapsulates the IPv6 packet in an IPv4 packet with the extracted destination IPv4 address. The destination router extracts the IPv6 packet and forwards it to the IPv6 destination.

Figure 9-12 shows a network using IPv4 tunnels. Site A and Site B both have IPv4 and IPv6 networks. The IPv6 networks are connected using an IPv4 tunnel in the WAN.

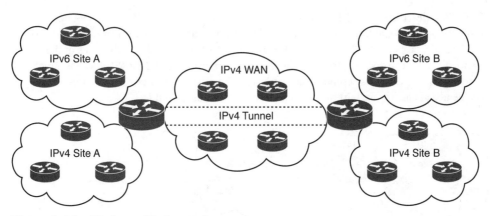

Figure 9-12 *IPv6 over IPv4 tunnels*

6over4 is another tunnel method that requires an IPv4 multicast-enabled network. IPv6 multicast packets get encapsulated into IPv4 multicast packets to communicate with other 6over4 hosts. 6over4 is of limited practical use.

Another method to tunnel IPv6 over IPv4 is the Intra-Site Automatic Tunnel Addressing Protocol (ISATAP). With ISATAP, a tunnel is created between dual-stack hosts or routers to transmit IPv6 packets over an IPv4 network. Unlike the 6over4 mechanism, ISATAP does not require IPv4 to be multicast enabled.

With ISATAP, the link-local address is generated by concatenating FE80:0000:0000:0000: 0000:5EFE: with the IPv4 address expressed in hexadecimal. For example, with IPv4 192.168.10.10, the link-local address is FE80:0000:0000:0000:0000:5EFE:C0A8:0A0A. ISATAP also requires the use of a routable address (for example, a global unicast IPv6 address that uses the same 0000:5EFE IANA reserved value for the interface ID along with the 32-bit IPv4 embedded address).

Protocol Translation Mechanisms

One of the mechanisms for an IPv6-only host to communicate with an IPv4-only host without using dual stacks is protocol translation. Translation is basically an extension to IPv4 NAT techniques. Some techniques are

- **Application layer gateways (ALG):** These use dual stacks and allow one host on the IPv4 domain to communicate with the host on the IPv6 domain.

- **Application programming interfaces (API):** An API module intercepts IP traffic through an API and converts it for the IPv6 counterpart.

- **Translation techniques:** Include NAT-PT and Dual-Stack Transition Mechanism (DSTM).

DSTM proposes the use of a dual stack that uses IPv4 addresses only when needed and the use of IPv4-over-IPv6 tunneling to reach a destination IPv4 address. It is used when there is an IPv6-only backbone but an application needs to reach an IPv4 address.

RFC 2766 describes NAT-PT, which provides translation between IPv6 and IPv4 hosts. NAT-PT operates similarly to the NAT mechanisms to translate IPv4 private addresses to public address space. NAT-PT binds addresses in the IPv6 network to addresses in the IPv4 network, and vice versa. Figure 9-13 shows a network using NAT-PT. RFC 4699 is a recent Informational RFC that recommends that NAT-PT be placed into historical status and recommends against its use (although the protocol is still supported in IOS).

Figure 9-13   *Network Address Translation–Protocol Translation*

Cisco also introduces the Cisco 6PE for Multiprotocol Label Switching (MPLS) service providers. Cisco 6PE allows IPv6 islands to communicate over an MPLS/IPv4 core network using MPLS label-switched paths (LSP). The Cisco 6PE routers are dual stack. The method relies on BGP extensions in the IPv4 6PE routers to exchange IPv6 reachability information, along with an MPLS label for each IPv6 address prefix announced.

IPv6 Deployment Models

Deployment of IPv6 can be done in one of the following models:

- **Dual-stack model:** IPv4 and IPv6 coexist on hosts and the network.
- **Hybrid model:** Combination of ISATAP or manually configured tunnels and dual-stack mechanisms.
- **Service block model:** Combination of ISATAP and manually configured tunnels and dual-stack mechanisms.

Dual-Stack Model

In the dual-stack model, both devices and the network routers and switches all run both IPv4 and IPv6 protocol stacks. The applications on the devices decide which stack to use to communicate with destination hosts. Alternatively, DNS is used to decide which stack to use. A DNS AAAA RR return uses IPv6, and a DNS A RR return uses IPv4. Because most mature operating systems now support IPv6, this is the preferred technique for transition to IPv6. Figure 9-14 shows a dual-stack network where both protocols reside. Older IPv4 sites that have not migrated to the dual-stack model can communicate throughout the network with other IPv4 devices.

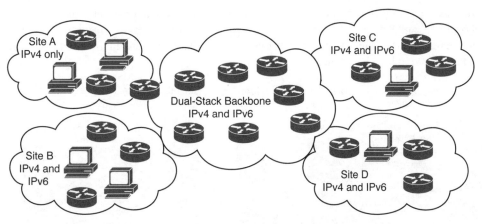

Figure 9-14   *Dual-stack Network Address Translation–Protocol Translation*

Hybrid Model

The hybrid model uses a combination of transition mechanisms. The transition mechanisms used are based on multiple network criteria such as number of hosts, IPv6-capable hardware, and location of IPv6 services. The hybrid model uses a combination of transition mechanisms:

- Dual-stack mechanism
- ISATAP
- Manually configured tunnels

The hybrid model can be used to tunnel a dual-stack host on an IPv4 access layer to an IPv6 core. As shown in Figure 9-15, the dual-stack computer establishes an ISATAP tunnel to the core layer to access services from the dual-stack server on the right.

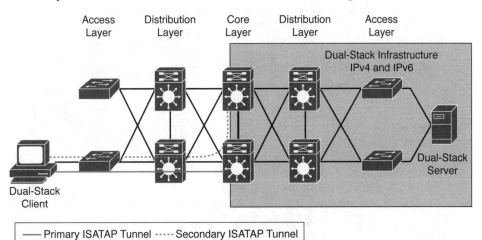

Figure 9-15   *IPv6 hybrid model with ISATAP tunnel*

Another scenario is to tunnel dual-stack distribution layers over an IPv4-only core. As shown in Figure 9-16, the dual-stack computer on the left can access the dual-stack server on the right via the manually configured tunnels. Multiple tunnels are configured to provide redundancy and load balancing.

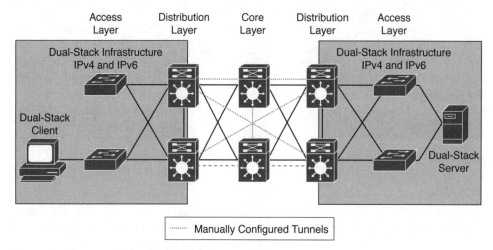

Figure 9-16 *IPv6 hybrid model with manually configured tunnels*

Service Block Model

In the service block model, a centralized layer that services dual-stack devices is created with tunnels manually configured between the distribution layer and the service block. Dual-stack hosts also connect via ISATAP tunnels. In Figure 9-17, the dual-stack client on the left connects to the service block to establish connectivity with the dual-stack server on the right.

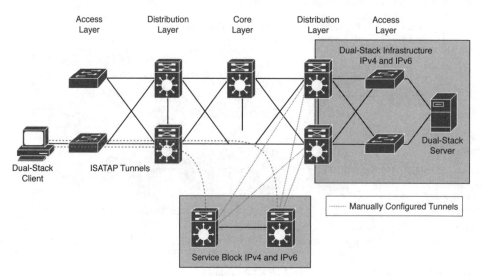

Figure 9-17 *Service block deployment model*

IPv6 Deployment Model Comparison

Table 9-12 summarizes the advantages and disadvantages of the IPv6 deployment models.

Table 9-12   IPv6 Deployment Model Comparison

IPv6 Deployment Model	Advantages	Disadvantages
Dual-stack model	Tunneling not required. Better processing performance. IPv4 and IPv6 independent routing, QoS, security, and multicast policies.	Network equipment upgrades.
Hybrid model 1	Existing network can be leveraged with no upgrades.	IPv6 multicast not supported within ISATAP tunnels. Terminating ISATAP tunnels in the core makes the core appear to be in IPv6 access layer.
Hybrid model 2	IPv4 and IPv6 have independent routing, QoS, security, and multicast policies.	Many static tunnels, which makes it difficult to manage.
Server block model	Lesser impact on existing network. Flexible when controlling access to IPv6-enabled applications.	Large amounts of tunneling. Cost of additional equipment.

Table 9-13 provides a simple description of the deployment model and matches it with its name. Study this table for the test.

Table 9-13   IPv6 Deployment Models

IPv6 Deployment Model	Description
Dual-stack model	All routers and hosts run IPv6 and IPv4.
Hybrid model	Uses ISATAP or manually configured tunnels to allow dual-stack clients to connect to dual-stack servers over an IPv4 core.
Service block model	Uses ISATAP and manually configured tunnels to a service module.

IPv6 Comparison with IPv4

This section provides a summary comparison of IPv6 to IPv4. Become knowledgeable about the characteristics summarized in Table 9-14. The use of 128 bits over 32 bits is an obvious change. The upper-layer protocol is identified with the Next Header field in IPv6, which was the Protocol Type field used in IPv4. ARP is replaced by IPv6 ND.

Table 9-14   IPv6 and IPv4 Characteristics

Characteristic	IPv6	IPv4
Address length	128 bits	32 bits
Address representation	Hexadecimal	Dotted decimal
Header length	Fixed (40 bytes)	Variable
Upper-layer protocols	Next header field	Protocol Type field
Link address resolution	ND	ARP
Address configuration	SLAAC or stateful DHCP	Stateful DHCP
DNS (name-to-address resolution)	AAAA records	A records
Interior routing protocols	EIGRPv6, OSPFv3, RIPng, IS-IS for IPv6	EIGRP, OSPFv2, RIPv2, IS-IS
Classification and marking	Traffic Class and Flow Label fields, differentiated services codepoint (DSCP)	IP Precedence bits, Type of Service field, DSCP
Private addresses	Unique local addresses	RFC 1918 private address space
Fragmentation	Sending host only	Sending host and intermediate routers
Loopback address	0:0:0:0:0:0:0:1	127.0.0.1
Address scope types	Unicast, anycast, multicast	Unicast, multicast, broadcast

References and Recommended Readings

RFC 3056: Connection of IPv6 Domains via IPv4 Clouds, www.ietf.org/rfc.

RFC 2740: OSPF for IPv6, www.ietf.org/rfc.

RFC 2463: Internet Control Message Protocol (ICMPv6) for the Internet Protocol Version 6 (IPv6) Specification, www.ietf.org/rfc.

RFC 2874: DNS Extensions to Support IPv6 Address Aggregation and Renumbering, www.ietf.org/rfc.

RFC 2460: Internet Protocol, Version 6 (IPv6) Specification, www.ietf.org/rfc.

Doyle, J. and J. Carroll. *Routing TCP/IP, Volume I, Second Edition*. Indianapolis: Cisco Press, 2005.

Doyle, J. and J. Carroll. *Routing TCP/IP, Volume II*. Indianapolis: Cisco Press, 2001.

RFC 3315: Dynamic Host Configuration Protocol for IPv6 (DHCPv6), www.ietf.org/rfc.

RFC 2373: IP Version 6 Addressing Architecture, www.ietf.org/rfc.

RFC 3513: Internet Protocol Version 6 (IPv6) Addressing Architecture, www.ietf.org/rfc.

RFC 3587: IPv6 Global Unicast Address Format, www.ietf.org/rfc.

RFC 2374: An IPv6 Aggregatable Global Unicast Address Format, www.ietf.org/rfc.

Hopps, C. Routing IPv6 for IS-IS (draft), www.simpleweb.org/ietf/internetdrafts/complete/draft-ietf-isis-ipv6-03.txt.

RFC 3879: Deprecating Site Local Addresses, www.ietf.org/rfc.

Implementing IPv6 Networks Training, www.cisco.com/application/pdf/en/us/guest/tech/tk373/c1482/ccmigration_09186a008019d70b.pdf.

RFC 2401: Security Architecture for the Internet Protocol, www.ietf.org/rfc.

RFC 2402:, IP Authentication Header, www.ietf.org/rfc.

RFC 2406: IP Encapsulating Security Payload (ESP), www.ietf.org/rfc.

RFC 2080: RIPng for IPv6, www.ietf.org/rfc.

RFC 2545: Use of BGP-4 Multiprotocol Extensions for IPv6 Inter-Domain Routing, www.ietf.org/rfc.

RFC 1981: Path MTU Discovery for IP version 6, www.ietf.org/rfc.

RFC 2461: Neighbor Discovery for IP Version 6 (IPv6), www.ietf.org/rfc.

RFC 1886: DNS Extensions to Support IP Version 6, www.ietf.org/rfc.

RFC 2766: Network Address Translation–Protocol Translation (NAT-PT), www.ietf.org/rfc.

RFC 4291: IP Version 6 Addressing Architecture, www.ietf.org/rfc.

www.cisco.com/web/strategy/docs/gov/IPv6FedGov_wp.pdf.

RFC 3587: IPv6 Global Unicast Address Format, www.ietf.org/rfc.

RFC 363: Representing Internet Protocol Version 6 (IPv6) Addresses in the Domain Name System (DNS), www.ietf.org/rfc.

Cisco IOS IPv6 Provider Edge Router (6PE) over MPLS, www.cisco.com/en/US/products/sw/iosswrel/ps1835/products_data_sheet09186a008052edd3.html.

www.isatap.org/.

RFC 5214: Intra-Site Automatic Tunnel Addressing Protocol (ISATAP), www.ietf.org/rfc.

IPv6 Extension Headers Review and Considerations, www.cisco.com/en/US/technologies/tk648/tk872/technologies_white_paper0900aecd8054d37d.html.

IPv6 Documentation Prefix – FAQs, https://www.apnic.net/services/services-apnic-provides/helpdesk/faqs/ipv6-documentation-prefix---faqs.

RFC 3849: IPv6 Address Prefix Reserved for Documentation, www.ietf.org/rfc.

RFC 4291: IP Version 6 Addressing Architecture, www.ietf.org/rfc.

9

RFC 5952: A Recommendation for IPv6 Address Text Representation, www.ietf.org/rfc.

RFC 6052: IPv6 Addressing of IPv4/IPv6 Translators, www.ietf.org/rfc.

RFC 7136: Significance of IPv6 Interface Identifiers, www.ietf.org/rfc.

RFC 7346: IPv6 Multicast Address Scopes, www.ietf.org/rfc.

RFC 7371: Updates to the IPv6 Multicast Addressing Architecture, www.ietf.org/rfc.

RFC 5340: OSFP for IPv6, www.ietf.org/rfc.

RFC 6845: OSFP Hybrid Broadcast and Point-to-Multipoint Interface Type, www.ietf.org/rfc.

RFC 6860: Hiding Transit-Only Networks in OSPF, www.ietf.org/rfc.

RFC 7503: OSPFv3 Autoconfiguration, www.ietf.org/rfc.

RFC 5308: Routing IPv6 with IS-IS, www.ietf.org/rfc.

Understanding IPv6 Link Local Address, http://www.cisco.com/c/en/us/support/docs/ip/ip-version-6-ipv6/113328-ipv6-lla.html.

RFC 4862: IPv6 Stateless Address Autoconfiguration, www.ietf.org/rfc.

RFC 7527: Enhanced Duplicate Address Detection, www.ietf.org/rfc.

RFC 3014: Privacy Extensions for Stateless Address Autoconfiguration in IPv6, www.ietf.org/rfc.

RFC 3736: Stateless Dynamic Host Configuration Protocol (DHCP) for IPv6, www.ietf.org/rfc.

ARIN Info Center, https://www.arin.net/knowledge/ipv6_info_center.html.

RFC 6296: IPv6-to-IPv6 Network Prefix Translation, www.ietf.org/rfc.

http://www.ipv6forum.com/dl/presentations/IPv6-addressing-plan-howto.pdf

Exam Preparation Tasks

Review All Key Topics

Review the most important topics in the chapter, noted with the Key Topic icon in the outer margin of the page. Table 9-15 lists a reference of these key topics and the page numbers on which each is found.

Table 9-15   Key Topics

Key Topic Element	Description	Page
List	Lists the enhancements of IPv6 over IPv4	336
Summary	Describes each field of the IPv6 header	337
Table 9-2	IP Protocol Numbers	338
Summary	Describes how IPv6 addresses are represented	339
Table 9-3	IPv6 Prefix Allocation	341
Summary	Describes unicast address types	342
Summary	Describes anycast address types	344
Summary	Describes multicast address types	344
Table 9-4	Multicast Scope Assignments	345
Table 9-5	Well-Known IPv6 Multicast Addresses	346
Table 9-7	IPv6 Addresses Prefix	346
Summary	Describes mechanisms such as ICMPv6, IPv6 ND, and address resolution	347
List	Describes stateless autoconfiguration or stateful DHCP address assignment	350
Table 9-8	IPv6 Address Autoconfiguration Scheme	351
Table 9-9	IPv6 Mechanisms	352
List	Describes dual-stack, tunneling, and translation-transition mechanisms	357
List	Describes dual-stack, hybrid, and service block deployment models	360
Table 9-12	IPv6 Deployment Model Comparison	363
Table 9-13	IPv6 Deployment Models	363
Table 9-14	Summarizes IPv6 characteristics as they compare with IPv4	364

9

Complete Tables and Lists from Memory

Print a copy of Appendix D, "Memory Tables," (found on the book website), or at least the section for this chapter, and complete the tables and lists from memory. Appendix E, "Memory Tables Answer Key," also on the website, includes completed tables and lists to check your work.

Define Key Terms

Define the following key terms from this chapter, and check your answers in the glossary:

ALG, AGI, ICMPv6, IANA, ID, ISATAP, FQDN, DHCPv6, IPsec, MTU, NAT-PT, ND, RIPng, OSPFv3, MP-BGP

Q&A

The answers to these questions appear in Appendix A, "Answers to the 'Do I Know This Already?' Quizzes and Q&A Questions." For more practice with exam format questions, use the exam engine on the CD.

1. True or false: OSPFv2 supports IPv6.

2. True or false: DNS AAAA records are used in IPv6 networks for name-to-IPv6-address resolution.

3. Fill in the blank: IPv6 ND is similar to what _____ does for IPv4 networks.

4. How many bits are there between the colons of IPv6 addresses?

5. The first field of the IPv6 header is 4 bits in length. What binary number is it always set to?

6. True or false: DHCP is required for dynamic allocation of IPv6 addresses.

7. IPv6 multicast addresses begin with what hexadecimal numbers?

8. IPv6 link-local addresses begin with what hexadecimal prefix?

9. True or false: ISATAP allows tunneling of IPv6 through IPv4 networks.

10. List the eight fields of the IPv6 header.

11. Which of the following is not an IPv6 address type?

    a. Unicast

    b. Broadcast

    c. Anycast

    d. Multicast

12. True or false: The IPv6 address 2001:0:0:1234:0:0:0:abcd can be represented as 2001::1234:0:0:0:abcd and 2001:0:0:1234::abcd.

13. What is the subnet prefix of 2001:1:0:ab0:34:ab1:0:1/64?

14. The IPv6 address has 128 bits. How many hexadecimal numbers does an IPv6 address have?

15. What type of IPv6 address is the following?

FF01:0:0:0:0:0:0:2

16. What is the compact format of the address 2102:0010:0000:0000:0000:fc23:0100:00ab?

    a. 2102:10::fc23:01:ab

    b. 2102:001::fc23:01:ab

    c. 2102:10::fc23:100:ab

    d. 2102:0010::fc23:01:ab

17. When using the dual-stack backbone, which of the following statements is correct?

    a. The backbone routers have IPv4/IPv6 dual stacks, and end hosts do not.

    b. The end hosts have IPv4/IPv6 dual stacks, and backbone routers do not.

    c. Both the backbone routers and end hosts have IPv4/IPv6 dual stacks.

    d. Neither the backbone routers nor end hosts have IPv4/IPv6 dual stacks.

18. How does a dual-stack host know which stack to use to reach a destination?

    a. It performs an ND, which returns the destination host type.

    b. It performs a DNS request that returns the IP address. If the returned address is IPv4, the host uses the IPv4 stack. If the returned address is IPv6, the host uses the IPv6 stack.

    c. The IPv6 stack makes a determination. If the destination is IPv4, the packet is sent to the IPv4 stack.

    d. The IPv4 stack makes a determination. If the destination is IPv6, the packet is sent to the IPv6 stack.

19. What protocol numbers are used by Ethernet to identify IPv4 versus IPv6?

    a. Protocol 6 for IPv4 and protocol 17 for IPv6.

    b. 0x86DD for IPv6 and 0x0800 for IPv4.

    c. 0x8000 for IPv4 and 0x86DD for IPv6.

    d. 0x0800 for both IPv4 and IPv6; they are identified in the packet layer.

20. Which of the following describe the IPv6 header? (Select two.)

    a. It is 40 bytes in length.

    b. It is of variable length.

    c. The Protocol Number field describes the upper-layer protocol.

    d. The Next Header field describes the upper-layer protocol.

9

21. Which of the following is true about fragmentation?

    a. Routers between source and destination hosts can fragment IPv4 and IPv6 packets.

    b. Routers between source and destination hosts cannot fragment IPv4 and IPv6 packets.

    c. Routers between source and destination hosts can fragment IPv6 packets only. IPv4 packets cannot be fragmented.

    d. Routers between source and destination hosts can fragment IPv4 packets only. IPv6 packets cannot be fragmented.

22. A packet sent to an anycast address reaches what?

    a. The nearest destination in a set of hosts

    b. All destinations in a set of hosts

    c. Broadcasts to all hosts

    d. Global unicast destinations

23. Which of the following is/are true about IPv6 and IPv4 headers?

    a. The IPv6 header is of fixed length, and the Next Header field describes the upper-layer protocol.

    b. The IPv4 header is of variable length, and the Protocol field describes the upper-layer protocol.

    c. The IPv6 header is of fixed length, and the Protocol field describes the upper-layer protocol.

    d. A and B

    e. B and C

24. An organization uses an IPv6 address range that it received from its ISP. The IPv6 addresses will be used internally, and employees will access the Internet using Port Address Translation. What is required for DNS?

    a. DNS servers need to support only IPv4 addresses.

    b. DNS servers need to support only IPv6 addresses.

    c. No changes are needed to the DNS servers.

    d. DNS servers need to support both IPv4 and IPv6 addresses.

    e. Additional DNS servers for IPv6 addresses are needed.

    f. DNS servers are not needed for PAT.

25. Which statements about IPv6 addresses are true? (Select two.)

    a. Leading 0s are required.

    b. Two colons (::) are used to separate fields.

    c. Two colons (::) are used to represent successive hexadecimal fields of 0s.

    d. A single interface will have multiple IPv6 addresses of different types.

26. You have duplicate file servers at multiple locations. Which IPv6 address type allows each end station to send a request to the nearest file server using the same destination address, regardless of the location of that end station?

   a. Anycast

   b. Broadcast

   c. Unicast

   d. Global unicast

   e. Multicast

27. Which strategy allows both IPv4 and IPv6 addressing/stacks to coexist on a host to facilitate a migration?

   a. Deploy NAT-PT between the networks.

   b. Hosts run IPv4 and routers run native IPv6.

   c. Enable anycast in the routing protocol.

   d. Run both IPv4 and IPv6 address stacks on devices.

   e. Redistribute between the IPv4 and IPv6 networks.

28. Which strategy would be most flexible for a corporation with the following characteristics?

2,400,000 hosts

11,000 routers

Internet connectivity

High volume of traffic with customers and business partners

   a. Deploy NAT-PT between business and Internet networks.

   b. Hosts run IPv4 and routers run native IPv6.

   c. Both hosts and routers run dual stack.

   d. Enable anycast in the routing protocol.

   e. Redistribute between the IPv4 and IPv6 networks.

29. What is the hierarchy for IPv6 aggregatable addresses?

   a. Global, site, loop

   b. Public, site, interface

   c. Internet, site, interface

   d. Multicast, anycast, unicast

30. NAT-PT translates between what address types?

   a. Translates RFC 1918 private addresses to public IPv4 addresses

   b. Translates between IPv4 and IPv6 addresses

   c. Translates between network addresses and IPv6 ports

   d. Translates between private IPv6 addresses to public IPv6 addresses

9

31. In a network where IPv6 exists within an IPv4 network, which two strategies allow both schemes to coexist? (Select two.)

  a. Translate between the protocols.

  b. Hosts run IPv4 and routers run native IPv6.

  c. Encapsulate IPv6 packets into IPv4 packets.

  d. Enable anycast in the routing protocol.

  e. Redistribute between the IPv4 and IPv6 networks.

32. Which IPv6 feature enables routing to distribute connection requests to the nearest content server?

  a. Anycast

  b. Link-local

  c. Aggregatable

  d. Multicast

  e. Site-local

33. Which statement best describes the efficiency of the IPv6 header?

  a. It is less efficient than the IPv4 header.

  b. It has the same efficiency as the IPv4 header; the larger IPv6 address makes it faster.

  c. It is more efficient than the IPv4 header.

  d. It is larger than the IPv4 header.

34. What does one-to-nearest communication mean for IPv6?

  a. Anycast

  b. Broadcast

  c. Multicast

  d. Unicast

35. Which tunneling protocol allows dual-stack hosts to tunnel over IPv4 network that is not multicast enabled?

  a. 6to4

  b. 6over4

  c. IPsec

  d. ISATAP

36. How would you summarize the networks listed below?

2001:0db8:2a3e:4490::/64

2001:0db8: 2a3e:4a1b::/64

2001:0db8: 2a3e:4ff2::/64

2001:0db8: 2a3e:4c5b::/64

   a. 2001:0db8:2a3e:4000::/52

   b. 2001:0db8: 2a3e:4000::/56

   c. 2001:0db8: 2a3e:4000::/60

   d. 2001:0db8: 2a3e:4000::/64

37. Select the statement that is true about IPv6 address assignment.

   a. Configure devices manually using IPv6 address assignment.

   b. Configure servers using SLAAC.

   c. Use SLAAC to assign IPv6 addresses and then DHCPv6 to assign additional information to hosts.

   d. You cannot use DHCPv6 after a host is assigned an IPv6 via SLAAC.

38. Which IPv6 feature allows a single node to send packets that are routed to the nearest receiver from a group of potential receivers?

   a. Link-local

   b. Site-local

   c. Anycast

   d. Multicast

39. Which statement is correct?

   a. IPv6 does not use multicast addresses.

   b. IPv6 routers do not forward packets if the packet has a link-local source address.

   c. DHCPv6 is the only method for dynamic address assignment.

   d. IPv6 routers forward packets if the packet has a link-destination address.

40. Which two link-state routing protocols support IPv6 routing?

   a. RIPng

   b. OSPF

   c. EIGRP

   d. IS-IS

   e. BGP4+

9

41. Which are transition models to IPv6 for an enterprise network?

   a. Dual-stack

   b. Top-down

   c. Tunneled

   d. Service block

   e. Translation

   f. Fork-lift

   g. Hybrid

42. Which are deployment models to IPv6 for an enterprise network?

   a. Dual-stack

   b. Top-down

   c. Tunneled

   d. Service block

   e. Translation

   f. Fork-lift

   g. Hybrid

43. If an application uses broadcast traffic for IPv4, how will it communicate using IPv6?

   a. Anycast

   b. Broadcast

   c. Multicast

   d. Unicast

44. What type of address begins with the following prefix?

   FC00::/7

   a. Local-link

   b. Broadcast

   c. Multicast

   d. Unique local unicast

45. Which regional registry allocates address blocks in the Middle East?

   a. IANA

   b. RIPE

   c. ARIN

   d. APNIC

   e. LACNIC

   f. AFRINIC

Questions 46 through 49 are based on the following scenario and Figure 9-18.

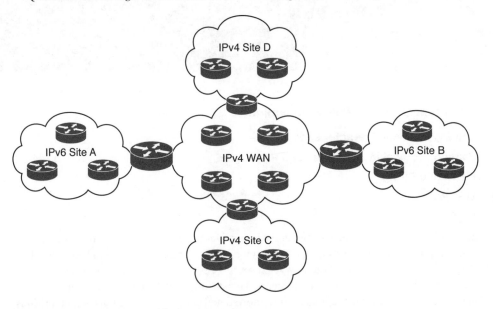

Figure 9-18   *Company adds Sites A and B.*

A company has an existing WAN that uses IPv4. Sites C and D use IPv4. As shown in Figure 9-18, the company plans to add two new locations (Sites A and B). The new sites will implement IPv6. The company does not want to lease more WAN circuits.

46. What options does the company have to connect Site A to Site B?

47. What mechanism needs to be implemented so that IPv6 hosts can communicate with IPv4 hosts, and vice versa?

48. If a dual-stack backbone is implemented, do all WAN routers and all hosts need an IPv6-IPv4 dual stack?

49. If an IPv4 tunnel is implemented between Sites A and B, do all WAN routers require an IPv6-IPv4 dual stack?

9

This chapter covers the following subjects:

Routing Protocol Characteristics

Routing Protocol Metrics and Loop Prevention

RIPv2 and RIPng

EIGRP

IS-IS

This chapter covers the metrics used and other characteristics of routing protocols. Routing protocols can be categorized as distance-vector or link-state and as hierarchical or flat. The CCDA must understand how each routing protocol is categorized to select the one that meets the customer's requirements. This chapter covers the routing protocols at a high level. The following chapters go into more detail about the operations and algorithms used in each routing protocol.

CHAPTER 10

Routing Protocol Characteristics, RIP, EIGRP, and IS-IS

"Do I Know This Already?" Quiz

The "Do I Know This Already?" quiz helps you identify your strengths and deficiencies in this chapter's topics.

The ten-question quiz, derived from the major sections in the "Foundation Topics" portion of the chapter, helps you determine how to spend your limited study time.

Table 10-1 outlines the major topics discussed in this chapter and the "Do I Know This Already?" quiz questions that correspond to those topics.

Table 10-1 "Do I Know This Already?" Foundation Topics Section-to-Question Mapping

Foundation Topics Section	Questions Covered in This Section
Routing Protocol Characteristics	2, 4, 7, 8
Routing Protocol Metrics and Loop Prevention	6, 9
RIPv2 and RIPng	5, 8
EIGRP	3, 7, 8, 9, 10
IS-IS	1

1. What is the default metric for any interface for the IS-IS routing protocol?
   a. 5
   b. 10
   c. 70
   d. 100

2. Which type of routing protocol would you use when connecting to an Internet service provider?
   a. Classless routing protocol
   b. Interior gateway protocol
   c. Exterior gateway protocol
   d. Classful routing protocol

3. Which routing protocol is distance-vector and classless?

    a. RIPv2

    b. EIGRP

    c. OSPF

    d. IS-IS

4. Which type of routing protocol sends periodic routing updates?

    a. Static

    b. Distance-vector

    c. Link state

    d. Hierarchical

5. Which distance-vector routing protocol is used for IPv6 networks?

    a. OSPFv2

    b. RIPng

    c. OSPFv3

    d. BGPv3

6. Which of the following is true regarding routing metrics?

    a. If the metric is bandwidth, the path with the lowest bandwidth is selected.

    b. If the metric is bandwidth, the path with the highest bandwidth is selected.

    c. If the metric is bandwidth, the highest sum of the bandwidth is used to calculate the highest cost.

    d. If the metric is cost, the path with the highest cost is selected.

7. Both OSPF and EIGRP are enabled on a router with default values. Both protocols have a route to a destination network in their databases. Which route is entered into the routing table?

    a. The OSPF route.

    b. The EIGRP route.

    c. Both routes are entered with load balancing.

    d. Neither route is entered; an error has occurred.

8. Which of the following are classless routing protocols?

    a. RIPv1 and RIPv2

    b. EIGRP and RIPv2

    c. IS-IS and OSPF

    d. Answers B and C

9. Which parameters are included in the computation of the EIGRP composite metric used by default?

    a. Bandwidth and load

    b. Bandwidth and delay

    c. Bandwidth and reliability

    d. Bandwidth and maximum transmission unit (MTU)

10. Which routing protocol implements the Diffusing Update Algorithm (DUAL)?

    a. IS-IS

    b. IGRP

    c. EIGRP

    d. OSPF

10

Foundation Topics

This chapter covers the high-level characteristics of routing protocols and their metrics. You should become familiar with the different categories of routing protocols and their characteristics for the exam. Understand how each metric is used and, based on the metric, which path is preferred. For example, you need to know that a path with the highest bandwidth is preferred over a path with a lower bandwidth. This chapter also covers distance-vector routing protocols: RIPv2, RIPng, and EIGRP.

Routing Protocol Characteristics

This section discusses the different types and characteristics of routing protocols.

Characteristics of routing-protocol design are

- **Distance-vector, link-state, or hybrid:** How routes are learned.
- **Interior or exterior:** For use in private networks or the public Internet.
- **Classless (classless interdomain routing [CIDR] support) or classful:** CIDR enables aggregation of network advertisements (supernetting) between routers.
- **Fixed-length or variable-length subnet masks (VLSMs):** Conserve addresses within a network.
- **Flat or hierarchical:** Addresses scalability in large internetworks.
- **IPv4 or IPv6:** Newer routing protocols are used for IPv6 networks.

This section also covers the default administrative distance assigned to routes learned from each routing protocol or from static assignment. Routes are categorized as statically (manually) configured or dynamically learned from a routing protocol. The following sections cover all these characteristics.

Static Versus Dynamic Route Assignment

Static routes are manually configured on a router. When configured manually and not learned from a neighbor, they do not react to network outages. The one exception is when the static route specifies the outbound interface or the next hop is not resolved in the routing table. In this situation, if the interface goes down, the static route is removed from the routing table. Because static routes are unidirectional, they must be configured for each outgoing interface the router will use. The size of today's networks makes it impossible to manually configure and maintain all the routes in all the routers in a timely manner. Human configuration can involve many mistakes. Dynamic routing protocols were created to address these shortcomings. They use algorithms to advertise, learn about, and react to changes in the network topology.

The main benefit of static routing is that a router generates no routing protocol overhead. Because no routing protocol is enabled, no bandwidth is consumed by route advertisements between network devices. Another benefit of static routing protocols is that they are easier to configure and troubleshoot than dynamic routing protocols. Static routing is recommended for hub-and-spoke topologies with low-speed remote connections and where only a single path to the network exists. A default static route is configured at each remote site because the hub is the only route used to reach all other sites. Static routes are also used at network boundaries (Internet or partners) where routing information is not exchanged. These static routes are then redistributed into the internal dynamic routing protocol used.

Figure 10-1 shows a hub-and-spoke WAN where static routes are defined in the remote WAN routers because no routing protocols are configured. This setup eliminates routing protocol traffic on the low-bandwidth WAN circuits.

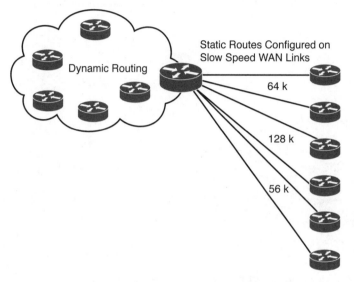

Figure 10-1 *Static routes in a hub-and-spoke network*

Routing protocols dynamically determine the best route to a destination. When the network topology changes, the routing protocol adjusts the routes without administrative intervention. Routing protocols use a metric to determine the best path toward a destination network. Some use a single measured value such as hop count. Others compute a metric value using one or more parameters. Routing metrics are discussed later in this chapter. The following is a list of dynamic routing protocols:

- RIPv1
- RIPv2
- EIGRP
- OSPF
- IS-IS
- RIPng
- OSPFv3
- EIGRP for IPv6
- Border Gateway Protocol (BGP)

10

Interior Versus Exterior Routing Protocols

Routing protocols can be categorized as interior gateway protocols (IGPs) or exterior gateway protocols (EGPs). IGPs are meant for routing within an organization's administrative domain (in other words, the organization's internal network). EGPs are routing protocols used to communicate with exterior domains, where routing information is exchanged between administrative domains. Figure 10-2 shows where an internetwork uses IGPs and EGPs with multiple autonomous administrative domains. BGP exchanges routing information between the internal network and an ISP. IGPs appear in the internal private network.

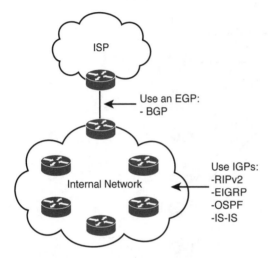

Figure 10-2 *Interior and exterior routing protocols*

One of the first EGPs was called exactly that: Exterior Gateway Protocol. Today, BGP is the de facto (and the only available) EGP.

Potential IGPs for an IPv4 network are

- RIPv2
- OSPFv2
- IS-IS
- EIGRP

Potential IGPs for an IPv6 network are

- RIPng
- OSPFv3
- EIGRP for IPv6

RIPv1 is no longer recommended because of its limitations. RIPv2 addresses many of the limitations of RIPv1 and is the most recent version of RIP. IGRP is an earlier version of EIGRP. RIPv1, RIPv2, and IGRP are no longer CCDA exam topics. Table 10-2 provides a quick high-level summary of which protocol should be selected.

Table 10-2 IGP and EGP Protocol Selection

Routing Protocol	Description
BGP	Used to connect to an ISP.
OSPF	IGP used in enterprise networks. Supports large networks and is multivendor.
EIGRP	IGP used in large enterprise networks with Cisco routers.

Distance-Vector Routing Protocols

The first IGP routing protocols introduced were distance-vector routing protocols. They used the Bellman-Ford algorithm to build the routing tables. With distance-vector routing protocols, routes are advertised as vectors of distance and direction. The distance metric is usually router hop count. The direction is the next-hop router (IP address) toward which to forward the packet. For RIP, the maximum number of hops is 15, which can be a serious limitation, especially in large nonhierarchical internetworks.

Distance-vector algorithms call for each router to send its entire routing table to only its immediate neighbors. The table is sent periodically (30 seconds for RIP). In the period between advertisements, each router builds a new table to send to its neighbors at the end of the period. Because each router relies on its neighbors for route information, it is commonly said that distance-vector protocols "route by rumor."

Having to wait half a minute for a new routing table with new routes is too long for today's networks. This is why distance-vector routing protocols have slow convergence.

RIPv2 and RIPng can send triggered updates—full routing table updates sent before the update timer has expired. A router can receive a routing table with 500 routes with only one route change, which creates serious overhead on the network (another drawback). Furthermore, RFC 2091 updates RIP with triggered extensions to allow triggered updates with only route changes. Cisco routers support this on fixed point-to-point interfaces.

The following is a list of IP distance-vector routing protocols:

- RIPv1 and RIPv2
- EIGRP (which could be considered a hybrid)
- RIPng

EIGRP

EIGRP is a hybrid routing protocol. It is a distance-vector protocol that implements some link-state routing protocol characteristics. Although EIGRP uses distance-vector metrics, it sends partial updates and maintains neighbor state information just as link-state protocols do. EIGRP does not send periodic updates as other distance-vector routing protocols do. The important thing to consider for the test is that EIGRP could be presented as a hybrid protocol. EIGRP metrics and mechanisms are discussed later in this chapter.

10

Link-State Routing Protocols

Link-state routing protocols address some of the limitations of distance-vector protocols. When running a link-state routing protocol, routers originate information about themselves (IP addresses), their connected links (the number and types of links), and the state of those links (up or down). The information is flooded to all routers in the network as changes in the link state occur. Each router makes a copy of the information received and forwards it without change. Each router independently calculates the best paths to each destination network by using the Dijkstra shortest path algorithm, creating a shortest path tree with itself as the root, and maintains a map of the network.

After the initial exchange of information, link-state updates are not sent unless a change in the topology occurs. Routers do send small hello messages between neighbors to maintain neighbor relationships. If no updates have been sent, the link-state route database is refreshed after 30 minutes.

The following is a list of link-state routing protocols:

■ OSPFv2

■ IS-IS

■ OSPFv3

OSPFv2 and OSPFv3 are covered in Chapter 11, "OSPF, BGP, Route Manipulation, and IP Multicast."

Distance-Vector Routing Protocols Versus Link-State Protocols

When choosing a routing protocol, consider that distance-vector routing protocols use more network bandwidth than link-state protocols. Distance-vector protocols generate more bandwidth overhead because of the large periodic routing updates. Link-state routing protocols do not generate significant routing update overhead but do use more router CPU and memory resources than distance-vector protocols. This occurs because with link-state routing protocols (generally speaking), WAN bandwidth is a more expensive resource than router CPU and memory in modern devices.

Table 10-3 compares distance-vector to link-state routing protocols.

 Table 10-3 Distance-Vector Versus Link-State Routing Protocols

Characteristic	Distance Vector	Link State
Scalability	Limited	Good
Convergence	Slow	Fast
Routing overhead	More traffic	Less traffic
Implementation	Easy	More complex
Protocols	RIPv1, RIPv2, EIGRP, RIPng	OSPF, IS-IS, OSPFv3

EIGRP is a distance-vector protocol with link-state characteristics (hybrid) that give it high scalability, fast convergence, less routing overhead, and relatively easy configuration. If "distance-vector" is not an answer to a question, then "hybrid" would be a valid option.

Hierarchical Versus Flat Routing Protocols

Some routing protocols require a network topology that must have a backbone network defined. This network contains some, or all, of the routers in the internetwork. When the internetwork is defined hierarchically, the backbone consists of only some devices. Backbone routers service and coordinate the routes and traffic to or from routers not in the local internetwork. The supported hierarchy is relatively shallow. Two levels of hierarchy are generally sufficient to provide scalability. Selected routers forward routes into the backbone. OSPF and IS-IS are hierarchical routing protocols. By default, EIGRP is a flat routing protocol, but it can be configured with manual summarization to support hierarchical designs.

Flat routing protocols do not allow a hierarchical network organization. They propagate all routing information throughout the network without dividing or summarizing large networks into smaller areas. Carefully designing network addressing to naturally support aggregation within routing-protocol advertisements can provide many of the benefits offered by hierarchical routing protocols. Every router is a peer of every other router in flat routing protocols; no router has a special role in the internetwork. EIGRP, RIPv1, and RIPv2 are flat routing protocols.

Classless Versus Classful Routing Protocols

Routing protocols can be classified based on their support of VLSM and CIDR. Classful routing protocols do not advertise subnet masks in their routing updates; therefore, the configured subnet mask for the IP network must be the same throughout the entire internetwork. Furthermore, the subnets must, for all practical purposes, be contiguous within the larger internetwork. For example, if you use a classful routing protocol for network 130.170.0.0, you must use the chosen mask (such as 255.255.255.0) on all router interfaces using the 130.170.0.0 network. You must configure serial links with only two hosts and LANs with tens or hundreds of devices with the same mask of 255.255.255.0. The big disadvantage of classful routing protocols is that the network designer cannot take advantage of address summarization across networks (CIDR) or allocation of smaller or larger subnets within an IP network (VLSM). For example, with a classful routing protocol that uses a default mask of /25 for the entire network, you cannot assign a /30 subnet to a serial point-to-point circuit. Classful routing protocols are

- RIPv1
- IGRP (this protocol is not a test topic)

Classless routing protocols advertise the subnet mask with each route. You can configure subnetworks of a given IP network number with different subnet masks (VLSM). You can configure large LANs with a smaller subnet mask and configure serial links with a larger subnet mask, thereby conserving IP address space. Classless routing protocols also allow flexible route summarization and supernetting (CIDR). You create supernets by aggregating

10

classful IP networks. For example, 200.100.100.0/23 is a supernet of 200.100.100.0/24 and 200.100.101.0/24. Classless routing protocols are

- RIPv2
- OSPF
- EIGRP
- IS-IS
- RIPng
- OSPFv3
- EIGRP for IPv6
- BGP

IPv4 Versus IPv6 Routing Protocols

With the increasing use of the IPv6 protocol, the CCDA must be prepared to design networks using IPv6 routing protocols. As IPv6 was defined, routing protocols needed to be updated to support the new IP address structure. None of the IPv4 routing protocols support IPv6 networks, and none of the IPv6 routing protocols are backward compatible with IPv4 networks. But both protocols can coexist on the same network, each with its own routing protocol. Devices with dual stacks recognize which protocol is being used by the IP Version field in the IP header.

RIPng is the IPv6-compatible RIP routing protocol. EIGRP for IPv6 is the new version of EIGRP that supports IPv6 networks. OSPFv3 was developed for IPv6 networks, and OSPFv2 remains for IPv4 networks. Internet drafts were written to provide IPv6 routing using IS-IS. Multiprotocol extensions for BGP provide IPv6 support for BGP. Table 10-4 summarizes IPv4 versus IPv6 routing protocols.

Table 10-4   IPv4 and IPv6 Routing Protocols

IPv4 Routing Protocols	IPv6 Routing Protocols
RIPv2	RIPng
EIGRP	EIGRP for IPv6
OSPFv2	OSPFv3
IS-IS	IS-IS for IPv6
BGP	Multiprotocol BGP

Administrative Distance

On Cisco routers running more than one routing protocol, it is possible for two different routing protocols to have a route to the same destination. Cisco routers assign each routing protocol an administrative distance. When multiple routes exist for a destination, the router selects the longest match. For example, if to reach a destination of 170.20.10.1 OSPF has a route prefix of 170.20.10.0/24 and EIGRP has a route prefix of 170.20.0.0/16, the OSPF route is preferred because the /24 prefix is longer than the /16 prefix. It is more specific.

If two or more routing protocols offer the same route (with same prefix length) for inclusion in the routing table, the Cisco IOS router selects the route with the lowest administrative distance.

The administrative distance is a rating of the trustworthiness of a routing information source. Table 10-5 shows the default administrative distance for configured (static) or learned routes. In the table, you can see that static routes are trusted over dynamically learned routes. Within IGP routing protocols, EIGRP internal routes are trusted over OSPF, IS-IS, and RIP routes.

Table 10-5   Default Administrative Distances for IP Routes

IP Route	Administrative Distance
Connected interface	0
Static route directed to a connected interface	1
Static route directed to an IP address	1
EIGRP summary route	5
External BGP route	20
Internal EIGRP route	90
IGRP route	100
OSPF route	110
IS-IS route	115
RIP route	120
EGP route	140
External EIGRP route	170
Internal BGP route	200
Route of unknown origin	255

The administrative distance establishes the precedence used among routing algorithms. Suppose a router has an EIGRP route to network 172.20.10.0/24 with the best path out Ethernet 0 and an OSPF route for the same network out Ethernet 1. Because EIGRP has an administrative distance of 90 and OSPF has an administrative distance of 110, the router enters the EIGRP route in the routing table and sends packets with destinations of 172.20.10.0/24 out Ethernet 0.

Static routes have a default administrative distance of 1. There is one exception. If the static route points to a connected interface, it inherits the administrative distance of connected interfaces, which is 0. You can configure static routes with a different distance by appending the distance value to the end of the command.

10

Table 10-6 provides a summary of routing protocol characteristics.

Table 10-6   Routing Protocol Characteristics

Routing Protocol	Distance Vector or Link State	Interior or Exterior	Classful or Classless	Administrative Distance
RIPv2	DV	Interior	Classless	120
EIGRP	DV (hybrid)	Interior	Classless	90
OSPF	LS	Interior	Classless	110
IS-IS	LS	Interior	Classless	115
BGP	Path vector	Both	Classless	20

Routing Protocol Metrics and Loop Prevention

Routing protocols use a metric to determine best routes to a destination. Some routing protocols use a combination of metrics to build a composite metric for best path selection. This section describes metrics and also covers routing loop-prevention techniques. You must understand each metric for the CCDA exam.

Some routing metric parameters are

- Hop count
- Bandwidth
- Cost
- Load
- Delay
- Reliability
- Maximum transmission unit (MTU)

Hop Count

The hop count parameter counts the number of links between routers the packet must traverse to reach a destination. The RIP routing protocol uses hop count as the metric for route selection. If all links were the same bandwidth, this metric would work well. The problem with routing protocols that use only this metric is that the shortest hop count is not always the most appropriate path. For example, between two paths to a destination network—one with two 56Kbps links and another with four T1 links—the router chooses the first path because of the lower number of hops (see Figure 10-3). However, this is not necessarily the best path. You would prefer to transfer a 20MB file via the T1 links rather than the 56Kbps links.

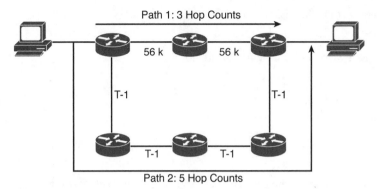

Figure 10-3 *Hop count metric*

Bandwidth

The bandwidth parameter uses the interface bandwidth to determine a best path to a destination network. When bandwidth is the metric, the router prefers the path with the highest bandwidth to a destination. For example, a Fast Ethernet (100 Mbps) is preferred over a DS-3 (45 Mbps). As shown in Figure 10-3, a router using bandwidth to determine a path would select Path 2 because of the larger bandwidth (1.5 Mbps over 56 Kbps).

If a routing protocol uses only bandwidth as the metric and the path has several different speeds, the protocol can use the lowest speed in the path to determine the bandwidth for the path. EIGRP and IGRP use the minimum path bandwidth, inverted and scaled, as one part of the metric calculation. In Figure 10-4, Path 1 has two segments, with 256 Kbps and 512 Kbps of bandwidth. Because the smaller speed is 256 Kbps, this speed is used as Path 1's bandwidth. The smallest bandwidth in Path 2 is 384 Kbps. When the router has to choose between Path 1 and Path 2, it selects Path 2 because 384 Kbps is larger than 256 Kbps.

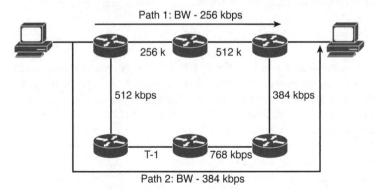

Figure 10-4 *Bandwidth metric example*

Cost

Cost is the name of the metric used by OSPF and IS-IS. In OSPF on a Cisco router, a link's default cost is derived from the interface's bandwidth. Cisco's implementation of IS-IS assigns a default cost of 10 to all interfaces.

The formula to calculate cost in OSPF is

$10^8/BW$

where BW is the interface's default or configured bandwidth.

For 10Mbps Ethernet, cost is calculated as follows:

BW = 10 Mbps = $10 * 10^6$ = 10,000,000 = 10^7

cost (Ethernet) = 10^8 / 10^7 = 10

The sum of all the costs to reach a destination is the metric for that route. The lowest cost is the preferred path.

Figure 10-5 shows an example of how the path costs are calculated. The path cost is the sum of all costs in the path. The cost for Path 1 is 350 + 180 = 530. The cost for Path 2 is 15 + 50 + 100 + 50 = 215.

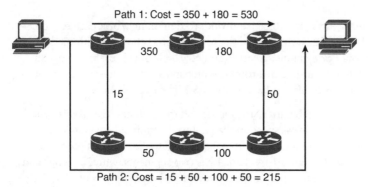

Figure 10-5   *Cost metric example*

Because the cost of Path 2 is less than that of Path 1, Path 2 is selected as the best route to the destination.

Load

The load parameter refers to the degree to which the interface link is busy. The router keeps track of interface utilization; routing protocols can use this metric when calculating the best route. Load is one of the five parameters included in the definition of the EIGRP metric. By default, it is not used to calculate the composite metric. If you have 512Kbps and 256Kbps links to reach a destination, but the 512Kbps circuit is 99 percent busy and the 256Kbps circuit is only 5 percent busy, the 256Kbps link is the preferred path. On Cisco routers, the percentage of load is shown as a fraction over 255. Utilization at 100 percent is shown as 255/255, and utilization at 0 percent is shown as 0/255. Example 10-1 shows the load of a serial interface at 5/255 (1.9 percent).

Example 10-1   *Interface Load*

```
router3>show interface serial 1
Serial1 is up, line protocol is up
  Hardware is PQUICC Serial
  Internet address is 10.100.1.1/24
  MTU 1500 bytes, BW 1544 Kbit, DLY 20000 usec, rely 255/255, load 5/255
```

Delay

The delay parameter refers to how long it takes to move a packet to the destination. Delay depends on many factors, such as link bandwidth, utilization, port queues, and physical distance traveled. Total delay is one of the five parameters included in the definition of the EIGRP composite metric. By default, it is used to calculate the composite metric. You can configure an interface's delay with the **delay** *tens-of-microseconds* command, where *tens-of-microseconds* specifies the delay in tens of microseconds for an interface or network segment. The interface delay can be checked with the **show interface** command. As shown in Example 10-2, the interface's delay is 20,000 microseconds.

Example 10-2   *Interface Delay*

```
router3>show interface serial 1
Serial1 is up, line protocol is up
 Hardware is PQUICC Serial
 Internet address is 10.100.1.1/24
 MTU 1500 bytes, BW 1544 Kbit, DLY 20000 usec, rely 255/255, load 1/255
```

Reliability

The reliability parameter is the dependability of a network link. Some WAN links tend to go up and down throughout the day. These links get a small reliability rating. Reliability is measured by factors such as a link's expected received keepalives and the number of packet drops and interface resets. If the ratio is high, the line is reliable. The best rating is 255/255, which is 100 percent reliability. Reliability is one of the five parameters included in the definition of the EIGRP metric. By default, it is not used to calculate the composite metric. As shown in Example 10-3, you can verify an interface's reliability using the **show interface** command.

Example 10-3   *Interface Reliability*

```
router4#show interface serial 0
Serial0 is up, line protocol is up
 Hardware is PQUICC Serial
 MTU 1500 bytes, BW 1544 Kbit, DLY 20000 usec, rely 255/255, load 1/255
```

Maximum Transmission Unit

The MTU parameter is simply the maximum size of bytes a unit can have on an interface. If the outgoing packet is larger than the MTU, the IP protocol might need to fragment it. If a packet larger than the MTU has the Do Not Fragment flag set, the packet is dropped. As shown in Example 10-4, you can verify an interface's MTU using the **show interface** command.

Example 10-4   *Interface MTU*

```
router4#show interface serial 0
Serial0 is up, line protocol is up
 Hardware is PQUICC Serial
 MTU 1500 bytes, BW 1544 Kbit, DLY 20000 usec, rely 255/255, load 1/255
```

10

Routing Loop-Prevention Schemes

Some routing protocols employ schemes to prevent the creation of routing loops in the network. These schemes are

- Split horizon
- Poison reverse
- Counting to infinity

Split Horizon

Split horizon is a technique used by distance-vector routing protocols to prevent routing loops. Routes that are learned from a neighboring router are not sent back to that neighboring router, thus suppressing the route. If the neighbor is already closer to the destination, it already has a better path.

In Figure 10-6, Routers 1, 2, and 3 learn about Networks A, B, C, and D. Router 2 learns about Network A from Router 1 and also has Networks B and C in its routing table. Router 3 advertises Network D to Router 2. Now, Router 2 knows about all networks. Router 2 sends its routing table to Router 3 without the route for Network D because it learned that route from Router 3.

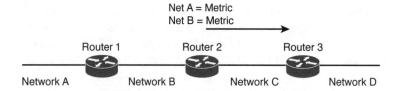

Figure 10-6 *Simple split-horizon example*

Poison Reverse

Poison reverse is a route update sent out an interface with an infinite metric for routes learned (received) from the same interface. Poison reverse simply indicates that the learned route is unreachable. It is more reliable than split horizon alone. Examine Figure 10-7. Instead of suppressing the route for Network D, Router 2 sends that route in the routing table marked as unreachable. In RIP, the poison-reverse route is marked with a metric of 16 (infinite) to prevent that path from being used.

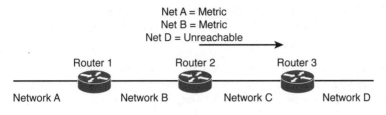

With Poison Reverse, Router 2 sends Net A
and Net B routes to Router 3; also, a
route for Net D with an infinite metric.

Figure 10-7 *Poison reverse*

Counting to Infinity

Some routing protocols keep track of router hops as the packet travels through the network. In large networks where a routing loop might be present because of a network outage, routers might forward a packet without it reaching its destination.

Counting to infinity is a loop-prevention technique in which the router discards a packet when it reaches a maximum limit. It assumes that the network diameter is smaller than the maximum allowed hops. RIP has a maximum of 16 hops, and EIGRP has a maximum of 100 hops by default. These values are considered infinity.

Triggered Updates

Another loop-prevention and fast-convergence technique used by routing protocols is triggered updates. When a router interface changes state (up or down), the router is required to send an update message, even if it is not time for the periodic update message. Immediate notification about a network outage is key to maintaining valid routing entries within all routers in the network by allowing faster convergence. Some distance-vector protocols, including RIP, specify a small time delay to avoid having triggered updates generate excessive network traffic. The time delay is variable for each router.

Summarization

Another characteristic of routing protocols is the ability to summarize routes. Protocols that support VLSMs can perform summarization outside of IP class boundaries. By summarizing, the routing protocol can reduce the size of the routing table, and fewer routing updates on the network occur.

RIPv2 and RIPng

This section covers RIPv2 and RIPng. Although Cisco has removed RIP from the exam topics for the test, this section is included for reference. It is possible that you will see questions on RIP or see RIPv2 and RIPng mentioned as possible answers to a test question.

RIPv2 is used for IPv4 networks, and RIPng was created to support IPv6 networks. RIPv2 was first described in RFC 1388 and RFC 1723 (1994); the current RFC is 2453, written in November 1998. Although current environments use advanced routing protocols such as

OSPF and EIGRP, some networks still use RIP. The need to use VLSMs and other requirements prompted the definition of RIPv2. RIPv1 was the first version of RIP, which did not support VLSMs. RIPv1 is not a CCDA topic.

RIPv2 improves on RIPv1 with the ability to use VLSM, support for route authentication, and multicasting of route updates. RIPv2 supports CIDR. It still sends updates every 30 seconds and retains the 15-hop limit; it also uses triggered updates. RIPv2 still uses UDP port 520; the RIP process is responsible for checking the version number. It retains the loop-prevention strategies of split-horizon, poison reverse, and counting to infinity. On Cisco routers, RIPv2 has the same administrative distance as RIPv1, which is 120. Finally, RIPv2 uses the IP address 224.0.0.9 when multicasting route updates to other RIP routers. As in RIPv1, RIPv2 by default summarizes IP networks at network boundaries. You can disable autosummarization if required.

You can use RIPv2 in small networks where VLSM is required. It also works at the edge of larger networks.

Authentication

Authentication can prevent communication with any RIP routers that are not intended to be part of the network, such as UNIX stations running **routed**. Only RIP updates with the authentication password are accepted. RFC 1723 defines simple plain-text authentication for RIPv2.

MD5 Authentication

In addition to plaintext passwords, the Cisco implementation provides the ability to use message digest 5 (MD5) authentication, which is defined in RFC 1321. MD5 is a hashing algorithm that takes a variable-length string of text and produces a fixed-length 128-bit output. One significant advantage to hashing plaintext is that the original message cannot be reconstituted even with knowledge of the hash algorithm. This provides greater security than using plaintext authentication.

RIPv2 Routing Database

RIPv2 maintains a routing table database, as in Version 1. The difference is that it also keeps the subnet mask information. The following list repeats the table information of RIPv1:

- **IP Address:** The IP address of the destination host or network, with subnet mask
- **Gateway:** The first gateway along the path to the destination
- **Interface:** The physical network that must be used to reach the destination
- **Metric:** A number indicating the number of hops to the destination
- **Timer:** The amount of time since the route entry was last updated

RIPv2 Message Format

The RIPv2 message format takes advantage of the unused fields in the RIPv1 message format by adding subnet masks and other information. Figure 10-8 shows the RIPv2 message format.

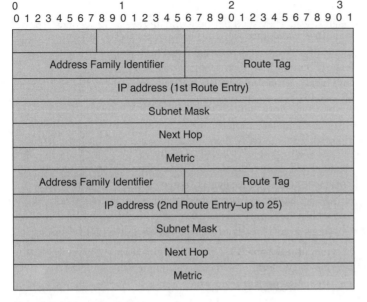

Figure 10-8 *RIPv2 message format*

The following list describes each field:

- **Command:** Indicates whether the packet is a request or response message. The request message asks that a router send all or a part of its routing table. Response messages contain route entries. The router sends the response periodically or as a reply to a request.

- **Version:** Specifies the RIP version used. It is set to 2 for RIPv2 and to 1 for RIPv1.

- **AFI:** Specifies the address family used. RIP is designed to carry routing information for several different protocols. Each entry has an AFI to indicate the type of address specified. The AFI for IP is 2. The AFI is set to 0xFFF for the first entry to indicate that the remainder of the entry contains authentication information.

- **Route tag:** Provides a method for distinguishing between internal routes (learned by RIP) and external routes (learned from other protocols). You can add this optional attribute during the redistribution of routing protocols.

- **IP Address:** Specifies the IP address (network) of the destination.

- **Subnet Mask:** Contains the subnet mask for the destination. If this field is 0, no subnet mask has been specified for the entry.

- **Next Hop:** Indicates the IP address of the next hop where packets are sent to reach the destination.

- **Metric:** Indicates how many router hops to reach the destination. The metric is between 1 and 15 for a valid route or 16 for an unreachable or infinite route.

Again, as in RIPv1, the router permits up to 25 occurrences of the last five 32-bit words (20 bytes), for up to 25 routes per RIP message. If the AFI specifies an authenticated message, the router can specify only 24 routing table entries. The updates are sent to the multicast address of 224.0.0.9.

10

RIPv2 Timers

RIPv2 timers are the same as in RIPv1. They send periodic updates every 30 seconds. The default invalid timer is 180 seconds, the hold-down timer is 180 seconds, and the flush timer is 240 seconds. You can write this list as 30/180/180/240, representing the U/I/H/F timers.

RIPv2 Design

Things to remember in designing a network with RIPv2 include that it supports VLSM within networks and allows for the summarization of routes in a hierarchical network. RIPv2 is still limited to 16 hops; therefore, the network diameter cannot exceed this limit. RIPv2 multicasts its routing table every 30 seconds to the multicast IP address 224.0.0.9. RIPv2 is usually limited to accessing networks where it can interoperate with servers running routed or with non-Cisco routers. RIPv2 also appears at the edge of larger internetworks. RIPv2 further provides for route authentication.

As shown in Figure 10-9, when you use RIPv2, all segments can have different subnet masks.

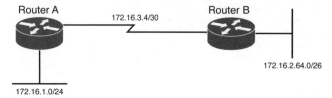

Figure 10-9 *RIPv2 design*

RIPv2 Summary

The characteristics of RIPv2 follow:

- Distance-vector protocol.
- Uses UDP port 520.
- Classless protocol (support for CIDR).
- Supports VLSMs.
- Metric is router hop count.
- Low scalability: maximum hop count is 15; infinite (unreachable) routes have a metric of 16.
- Periodic route updates are sent every 30 seconds to multicast address 224.0.0.9.
- There can be 25 routes per RIP message (24 if you use authentication).
- Supports authentication.
- Implements split horizon with poison reverse.
- Implements triggered updates.
- Subnet mask is included in the route entry.
- Administrative distance for RIPv2 is 120.
- Not scalable. Used in small, flat networks or at the edge of larger networks.

RIPng

RIPng (RIP next generation) is the version of RIP that can be used in IPv6 networks. It is described in RFC 2080. Most of the RIP mechanisms from RIPv2 remain the same. RIPng still has a 15-hop limit, counting to infinity, and split horizon with poison reverse. A hop count of 16 still indicates an unreachable route.

Instead of using UDP port 520, as in RIPv2, RIPng uses UDP port 521. RIPng supports IPv6 addresses and prefixes. RIPng uses multicast group FF02::9 for RIPng updates to all RIPng routers.

RIPng Timers

RIPng timers are similar to RIPv2. Periodic updates are sent every 30 seconds. The default invalid timeout for routes to expire is 180 seconds, the default hold-down timer is 180 seconds, and the default garbage-collection timer is 120 seconds.

Authentication

RIPng does not implement authentication methods in its protocol as RIPv2 does. RIPng relies on built-in IPv6 authentication functions.

RIPng Message Format

Figure 10-10 shows the RIPng routing message. Each route table entry (RTE) consists of the IPv6 prefix, route tag, prefix length, and metric.

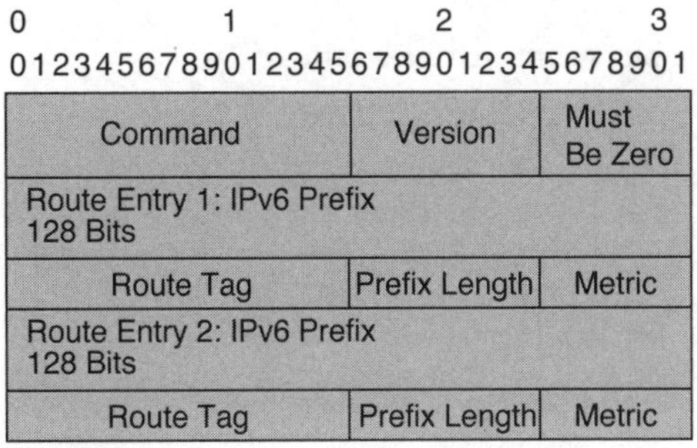

Figure 10-10   *RIPng update message format*

The following list describes each field:

- **Command:** Indicates whether the packet is a request or response message. This field is set to 1 for a request and to 2 for a response.
- **Version:** Set to 1, the first version of RIPng.
- **IPv6 prefix:** The destination 128-bit IPv6 prefix.
- **Route Tag:** As with RIPv2, this is a method that distinguishes internal routes (learned by RIP) from external routes (learned by external protocols). Tagged during redistribution.
- **Prefix Length:** Indicates the significant part of the prefix.
- **Metric:** This 8-bit field contains the router hop metric.

RIPv2 has a Next Hop field for each of its route entries. An RTE with a metric of 0xFF indicates the next-hop address to reduce the number of route entries in RIPng. It groups all RTEs after it to summarize all destinations to that particular next-hop address. Figure 10-11 shows the format of the special RTE indicating the next-hop entry.

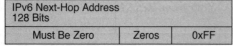

Figure 10-11 *RIPng next-hop route table entry*

RIPng Design

RIPng has low scalability. As with RIPv2, it is limited to 15 hops; therefore, the network diameter cannot exceed this limit. RIPng also broadcasts its routing table every 30 seconds, which causes network overhead. RIPng can be used only in small networks.

RIPng Summary

The characteristics of RIPng are as follows:

- Distance-vector protocol for IPv6 networks only.

- Uses UDP port 521.

- Metric is router hop count.

- Maximum hop count is 15; infinite (unreachable) routes have a metric of 16.

- Periodic route updates are sent every 30 seconds to multicast address FF02::9.

- Uses IPv6 functions for authentication.

- Implements split horizon with poison reverse.

- Implements triggered updates.

- Prefix length included in route entry.

- Administrative distance for RIPv2 is 120.

- Not scalable. Used in small networks.

EIGRP

Cisco Systems released EIGRP in the early 1990s as an evolution of IGRP toward a more scalable routing protocol for large internetworks. EIGRP is a classless protocol that permits the use of VLSMs and that supports CIDR for the scalable allocation of IP addresses. EIGRP does not send routing updates periodically, as does IGRP. EIGRP allows for authentication with MD5. EIGRP autosummarizes networks at network borders and can load-share over unequal-cost paths. Packets using EIGRP use IP 88. Only Cisco routers use EIGRP. However, Cisco has released EIGRP as an IETF draft, so it might be possible that other vendors implement EIGRP in their network devices.

EIGRP is an advanced distance-vector protocol that implements some characteristics similar to those of link-state protocols. Some Cisco documentation refers to EIGRP as a hybrid protocol. EIGRP advertises its routing table to its neighbors as distance-vector protocols do, but it uses hellos and forms neighbor relationships as link-state protocols do. EIGRP sends partial updates when a metric or the topology changes on the network. It does not send full routing-table updates in periodic fashion as do distance-vector protocols. EIGRP uses Diffusing Update Algorithm (DUAL) to determine loop-free paths to destinations. This section discusses DUAL.

By default, EIGRP load-balances traffic if several paths have an equal cost to the destination. EIGRP performs unequal-cost load sharing if you configure it with the **variance** *n* command. EIGRP includes routes that are equal to or less than *n* times the minimum metric route to a destination. As in RIP and IGRP, EIGRP also summarizes IP networks at network boundaries.

EIGRP internal routes have an administrative distance of 90. EIGRP summary routes have an administrative distance of 5, and EIGRP external routes (from redistribution) have an administrative distance of 170.

EIGRP Components

EIGRP has four components that characterize it:

- Protocol-dependent modules
- Neighbor discovery and recovery
- Reliable Transport Protocol (RTP)
- Diffusing Update Algorithm (DUAL)

You should know the role of the EIGRP components, which are described in the following sections.

Protocol-Dependent Modules

EIGRP uses different modules that independently support IP, Internetwork Packet Exchange (IPX), and AppleTalk routing protocols. These modules are the logical interface between DUAL and routing protocols such as IPX RIP, and AppleTalk Routing Table Maintenance Protocol (RTMP). The EIGRP module sends and receives packets but passes received information to DUAL, which makes routing decisions.

When configured to support IPX, EIGRP communicates with the IPX RIP and forwards the route information to DUAL to select the best paths. AppleTalk EIGRP automatically redistributes routes with AppleTalk RTMP to support AppleTalk networks. IPX and AppleTalk are not CCDA objectives and are therefore not covered in this book.

Neighbor Discovery and Recovery

EIGRP discovers and maintains information about its neighbors. It multicasts hello packets (224.0.0.10) every 5 seconds on most interfaces. The router builds a table with EIGRP neighbor information. The holdtime to maintain a neighbor is three times the hello time: 15 seconds. If the router does not receive a hello in 15 seconds, it removes the neighbor from

10

the table. EIGRP multicasts hellos every 60 seconds on multipoint WAN interfaces (X.25, Frame Relay, ATM) with speeds less than a T-1 (1.544 Mbps), inclusive. The neighbor hold-time is 180 seconds on these types of interfaces. To summarize, hello/holdtime timers are 5/15 seconds for high-speed links and 60/180 seconds for low-speed links.

Example 10-5 shows an EIGRP neighbor database. The table lists the neighbor's IP address, the interface to reach it, the neighbor holdtime timer, and the uptime.

Example 10-5 *EIGRP Neighbor Database*

```
Router#  show ip eigrp neighbor
IP-EIGRP neighbors for process 100
H  Address         Interface    Hold Uptime     SRTT      RTO       Q       Seq Type
                   c            (sec)           (ms)                Cnt     Num
1  172.17.1.1      Se0          11 00:11:27     16        200       0       2
0  172.17.2.1      Et0          12 00:16:11     22        200       0       3
```

RTP

EIGRP uses RTP to manage EIGRP packets. RTP ensures the reliable delivery of route updates and uses sequence numbers to ensure ordered delivery. It sends update packets using multicast address 224.0.0.10. It acknowledges updates using unicast hello packets with no data.

DUAL

EIGRP implements DUAL to select paths and guarantee freedom from routing loops. J.J. Garcia Luna-Aceves developed DUAL. It is mathematically proven to result in a loop-free topology, providing no need for periodic updates or route holddown mechanisms that make convergence slower.

DUAL selects a best path and a second-best path to reach a destination. The best path selected by DUAL is the successor, and the second-best path (if available) is the feasible successor. The feasible distance is the lowest calculated metric of a path to reach the destination. The topology table in Example 10-6 shows the feasible distance. The example also shows two paths (Ethernet 0 and Ethernet 1) to reach 172.16.4.0/30. Because the paths have different metrics, DUAL chooses only one successor.

Example 10-6 *Feasible Distance as Shown in the EIGRP Topology Table*

```
Router8#  show ip eigrp topology
IP-EIGRP Topology Table for AS(100)/ID(172.16.3.1)


Codes: P - Passive, A - Active, U - Update, Q - Query, R - Reply,
       r - reply Status, s - sia Status
```

```
P 172.16.4.0/30, 1 successors, FD is 2195456
          via 172.16.1.1 (2195456/2169856), Ethernet0
          via 172.16.5.1 (2376193/2348271), Ethernet1
P 172.16.1.0/24, 1 successors, FD is 281600
          via Connected, Ethernet0
```

The route entries in Example 10-6 are marked with a P for the passive state. A destination is in passive state when the router is not performing any recomputations for the entry. If the successor goes down and the route entry has feasible successors, the router does not need to perform any recomputations and does not go into active state.

DUAL places the route entry for a destination into active state if the successor goes down and there are no feasible successors. EIGRP routers send query packets to neighboring routers to find a feasible successor to the destination. A neighboring router can send a reply packet that indicates it has a feasible successor or a query packet. The query packet indicates that the neighboring router does not have a feasible successor and will participate in the recomputation. A route does not return to passive state until it has received a reply packet from each neighboring router. If the router does not receive all the replies before the "active-time" timer expires, DUAL declares the route as stuck in active (SIA). The default active timer is 3 minutes.

EIGRP Timers

EIGRP sets updates only when necessary and sends them only to neighboring routers. There is no periodic update timer.

EIGRP uses hello packets to learn of neighboring routers. On high-speed networks, the default hello packet interval is 5 seconds. On multipoint networks with link speeds of T1 and slower, hello packets are unicast every 60 seconds.

The holdtime to maintain a neighbor adjacency is three times the hello time: 15 seconds. If a router does not receive a hello within the holdtime, it removes the neighbor from the table. Hellos are multicast every 60 seconds on multipoint WAN interfaces (X.25, Frame Relay, ATM) with speeds less than 1.544 Mbps, inclusive. The neighbor holdtime is 180 seconds on these types of interfaces. To summarize, hello/holdtime timers are 5/15 seconds for high-speed links and 60/180 seconds for multipoint WAN links less than 1.544 Mbps, inclusive.

Note EIGRP does not send updates using a broadcast address; instead, it sends them to the multicast address 224.0.0.10 (all EIGRP routers). It also can send any updates using unicast packets if the **neighbor** command is used.

EIGRP Metrics

EIGRP uses the same composite metric as IGRP, but the bandwidth (BW) term is multiplied by 256 for finer granularity. The composite metric is based on bandwidth, delay, load, and reliability. MTU is not an attribute for calculating the composite metric.

EIGRP calculates the composite metric with the following formula:

$EIGRP_{metric} = \{k1 * BW + [(k2 * BW)/(256 - load)] + k3 * delay\} * \{k5/(reliability + k4)\}$

In this formula, BW is the lowest interface bandwidth in the path, and delay is the sum of all outbound interface delays in the path. The router dynamically measures reliability and load. It expresses 100 percent reliability as 255/255. It expresses load as a fraction of 255. An interface with no load is represented as 1/255.

Bandwidth is the inverse minimum bandwidth (in Kbps) of the path in bits per second scaled by a factor of $256 * 10^7$. The formula for bandwidth is

$(256 * 10^7)/BW_{min}$

The delay is the sum of the outgoing interface delays (in tens of microseconds) to the destination. A delay of all 1s (that is, a delay of hexadecimal FFFFFFFF) indicates that the network is unreachable. The formula for delay is

[sum of delays] * 256

Reliability is a value between 1 and 255. Cisco IOS routers display reliability as a fraction of 255. That is, 255/255 is 100 percent reliability, or a perfectly stable link; a value of 229/255 represents a 90 percent reliable link.

Load is a value between 1 and 255. A load of 255/255 indicates a completely saturated link. A load of 127/255 represents a 50 percent saturated link.

By default, k1 = k3 = 1 and k2 = k4 = k5 = 0. EIGRP's default composite metric, adjusted for scaling factors, is

$EIGRP_{metric} = 256 * \{ [10^7/BW_{min}] + [sum\_of\_delays] \}$

BW_{min} is in Kbps, and sum_of_delays is in 10s of microseconds. The bandwidth and delay for an Ethernet interface are 10 Mbps and 1 ms, respectively.

The calculated EIGRP BW metric is

$256 * 10^7/BW = 256 * 10^7/10,000$

$= 256 * 10,000$

$= 256,000$

The calculated EIGRP delay metric is

256 * sum of delay = 256 * 1 ms

= 256 * 100 * 10 microseconds

= 25,600 (in 10s of microseconds)

Table 10-7 shows some default values for bandwidth and delay.

Table 10-7   Default EIGRP Values for Bandwidth and Delay

Media Type	Delay	Bandwidth
Satellite	5120 (2 seconds)	5120 (500 Mbps)
Ethernet	25,600 (1 ms)	256,000 (10 Mbps)
T-1 (1.544 Mbps)	512,000 (20,000 ms)	1,657,856
64 Kbps	512,000	40,000,000
56 Kbps	512,000	45,714,176

The **metric weights** subcommand is used to change EIGRP metric computation. You can change the k values in the EIGRP composite metric formula to select which EIGRP metrics to use. The command to change the k values is the **metric weights tos** *k1 k2 k3 k4 k5* subcommand under **router eigrp** *n*. The **tos** value is always 0. You set the other arguments to 1 or 0 to alter the composite metric. For example, if you want the EIGRP composite metric to use all the parameters, the command is as follows:

```
router eigrp n
 metric weights 0 1 1 1 1 1
```

EIGRP Packet Types

EIGRP uses five packet types:

- **Hello:** EIGRP uses hello packets in the discovery of neighbors. They are multicast to 224.0.0.10. By default, EIGRP sends hello packets every 5 seconds (60 seconds on WAN links with 1.544 Mbps speeds or less).

- **Acknowledgment:** An acknowledgment packet acknowledges the receipt of an update packet. It is a hello packet with no data. EIGRP sends acknowledgment packets to the unicast address of the sender of the update packet.

- **Update:** Update packets contain routing information for destinations. EIGRP unicasts update packets to newly discovered neighbors; otherwise, it multicasts update packets to 224.0.0.10 when a link or metric changes. Update packets are acknowledged to ensure reliable transmission.

- **Query:** EIGRP sends query packets to find feasible successors to a destination. Query packets are always multicast unless they are sent as a response; then they are unicast back to the originator.

- **Reply:** EIGRP sends reply packets to respond to query packets. Reply packets provide a feasible successor to the sender of the query. Reply packets are unicast to the sender of the query packet.

10

EIGRP Design

When designing a network with EIGRP, remember that it supports VLSMs and network summarization. EIGRP allows for the summarization of routes in a hierarchical network. EIGRP is not limited to 16 hops as RIP is; therefore, the network diameter can exceed this limit. In fact, the EIGRP diameter can be 225 hops. The default diameter is 100. EIGRP can be used in the site-to-site WAN and IPsec virtual private networks (VPNs). In the enterprise campus, EIGRP can be used in data centers, server distribution, building distribution, and the network core.

EIGRP does not broadcast its routing table periodically, so there is no large network overhead. You can use EIGRP for large networks; it is a potential routing protocol for the core of a large network. EIGRP further provides for route authentication.

As shown in Figure 10-12, when you use EIGRP, all segments can have different subnet masks.

Figure 10-12 *EIGRP design*

EIGRP is suited for almost all enterprise environments, including LANs and WANs, and is simple to design. The only caveat is that it is a Cisco proprietary routing protocol that cannot be used with routers from other vendors. The use of EIGRP is preferred over RIP in all environments.

EIGRP Stub Routers

EIGRP allows for the configuration of stub routers for remote branches. It is used to reduce EIGRP query traffic between hub routers and remote branch routers that are connected over WAN links. Figure 10-13 shows an example of an EIGRP stub router operation. If the LAN network 10.10.10.0/24 goes down, the Hub1 router sends query packets everywhere; however, there is no need to send query packets to stub branches because there are no alternate routes there. Once you configure the branch routers as EIGRP stub routers, the query is sent only to the Hub2 router.

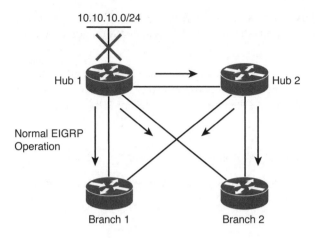

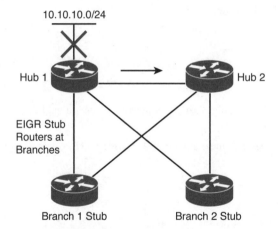

Figure 10-13 *EIGRP stub routers*

There are different options when configuring the EIGRP stub routers:

- **Receive-only:** The stub router will not advertise any network.
- **Connected:** Allows the stub router to advertise directly connected networks.
- **Static:** Allows the stub router to advertise static routes.
- **Summary:** Allows the stub router to advertise summary routes.
- **Redistribute:** Allows the stub router to advertise redistributed routes.

EIGRP Variance Command

EIGRP allows unequal-cost routing with the use of the **variance #** command. If you have an active route with a metric of 10 and have feasible successors of 15, 25, and 55, you can adjust the variance number to make those routes active. If you use **variance 2**, then the

10

active metric of 10 gets multiplied by 2, which equals 20. Any feasible successor less than 20 gets added as an active route. The route with a metric of 15 is added, thus you have two active routes.

If you use **variance 3**, the routes with a metric of 10, 15, 25 become active (3 × 10 =30). Note that for this example, using a variance of 4 or 5 does not add the route with a metric of 55. You will need to use a variance of 6 to add the route with a metric of 55 (6 × 10 = 60).

EIGRP for IPv4 Summary

The characteristics of EIGRP for IPv4 networks follow:

- Hybrid routing protocol (a distance-vector protocol that has link-state protocol characteristics).
- Uses IP protocol number 88.
- Classless protocol (supports VLSMs).
- Default composite metric uses bandwidth and delay.
- You can factor load and reliability into the metric.
- Sends partial route updates only when there are changes.
- Supports MD5 authentication.
- Uses DUAL for loop prevention.
- Fast convergence.
- By default, it uses equal-cost load balancing with equal metrics. Uses unequal-cost load sharing with the **variance** command.
- Administrative distance is 90 for EIGRP internal routes, 170 for EIGRP external routes, and 5 for EIGRP summary routes.
- High scalability; used in large networks.
- Multicasts updates to 224.0.0.10.
- Does not require a hierarchical physical topology.
- Provides routing for IPv4, plus legacy protocols such as AppleTalk and IPX.

EIGRP for IPv6 (EIGRPv6) Networks

EIGRP was originally an IPv4 routing protocol, although Cisco has developed IPv6 support into EIGRP to route IPv6 prefixes. EIGRP for IPv6 is configured and managed separately from EIGRP for IPv4; no network statements are used. EIGRP for IPv6 retains all the same characteristics (network discovery, DUAL, modules) and functions as EIGRP for IPv4. The major themes with EIGRP for IPv6 are as follows:

- Implements the protocol-independent modules.
- EIGRP neighbor discovery and recovery.
- Reliable transport.
- Implements the DUAL algorithm for a loop-free topology.
- Uses same metrics as EIGRP for IPv4 networks.

- Uses same timers as EIGRP for IPv4.

- Uses same concepts of feasible successors and feasible distance as EIGRP for IPv4.

- Uses the same packet types as EIGRP for IPv4.

- Managed and configured separately from EIGRP for IPv4.

- Requires a router ID before it can start running.

- Configured on interfaces. No network statements are used.

The difference is the use of IPv6 prefixes and the use of IPv6 multicast group FF02::A for EIGRP updates, which are sourced from the link-local IPv6 address. This means that neighbors do not need to share the same global prefix, except for those neighbors that are explicitly specified for unicast updates.

Another difference is that EIGRP for IPv6 defaults to a shutdown state for the routing protocols and must be manually or explicitly enabled on an interface to become operational. Because EIGRP for IPv6 uses the same characteristics and functions as EIGRP for IPv4, as covered in the previous section on EIGRP, they are not repeated here.

EIGRP for IPv6 Design

Use EIGRP for IPv6 in large geographic IPv6 networks. EIGRP's diameter can scale up to 255 hops, but this network diameter is not recommended. EIGRP authentication can be used instead of IPv6 authentication.

EIGRP for IPv6 can be used in the site-to-site WAN and IPsec VPNs. In the enterprise campus, EIGRP can be used in data centers, server distribution, building distribution, and the network core.

EIGRP's DUAL algorithm provides for fast convergence and routing loop prevention. EIGRP does not broadcast its routing table periodically, so there is no large network overhead. The only constraint is that EIGRP for IPv6 is restricted to Cisco routers.

EIGRP for IPv6 Summary

The characteristics of EIGRP for IPv6 are as follows:

10

- Uses the same characteristics and functions as EIGRP for IPv4.

- Hybrid routing protocol (a distance-vector protocol that has link-state protocol characteristics).

- Uses Next Header protocol 88.

- Routes IPv6 prefixes.

- Default composite metric uses bandwidth and delay.

- You can factor load and reliability into the metric.

- Sends partial route updates only when there are changes.

- Supports EIGRP MD5 authentication.

- Uses DUAL for loop prevention and fast convergence.

- By default, uses equal-cost load balancing. Uses unequal-cost load balancing with the **variance** command.

- Administrative distance is 90 for EIGRP internal routes, 170 for EIGRP external routes, and 5 for EIGRP summary routes.

- Uses IPv6 multicast FF02::A for EIGRP updates.

- High scalability; used in large networks.

The CCDA should understand EIGRP-specific characteristics and benefits. Table 10-8 provides a summary for reference.

Table 10-8   EIGRP Protocol Characteristics

Characteristic	EIGRP Support
Distance vector or link state	Hybrid: distance-vector routing protocol with link-state characteristics
Convergence	Fastest convergence with DUAL for a loop-free topology
Classless or classful	Classless routing protocol, supports VLSMs
Scalability	Highly scalable, supports large networks
Multiprotocol support	Supports IPv4, IPv6, plus legacy protocols such as IPX and AppleTalk
Multicast address for updates	224.0.0.10 for IPv4; FF02::A for IPv6

IS-IS

IS-IS is an International Organization for Standardization (ISO) dynamic routing specification. IS-IS is described in ISO/IEC 10589, reprinted by the Internet Engineering Task Force (IETF) as RFC 1195. IS-IS is a link-state routing protocol that floods link-state information throughout the network to build a picture of network topology. IS-IS was primarily intended for routing OSI Connectionless Network Protocol (CNLP) packets, but has the capability to route IP packets. IP packet routing uses Integrated IS-IS, which provides the capability to route protocols such as IP.

IS-IS is a common alternative to other powerful routing protocols such as OSPF and EIGRP in large networks. Although not seen much in enterprise networks, IS-IS is commonly used for internal routing in large ISP networks. IS-IS is also getting more use in data center technologies such as Overlay Transport Virtualization (OTV) and fabric path. As with OSPF, IS-IS uses the Dijkstra algorithm to calculate the shortest path tree (SPF) as well as uses link-state packets (LSPs) instead of OSPF link-state advertisements (LSAs). Also, both are not proprietary protocols.

IS-IS creates two levels of hierarchy, with Level 1 for intra-area routing and Level 2 for inter-area routing. IS-IS distinguishes between Level 1 and Level 2 intermediate systems (ISs). Level 1 ISs communicate with other Level 1 ISs in the same area. Level 2 ISs route between Level 1 areas and form an inter-area routing backbone. Hierarchical routing simplifies backbone design because Level 1 ISs only need to know how to get to the nearest Level 2 IS.

> **Note**   In IS-IS, a router is usually the IS, and personal computers, workstations, and servers are end systems (ESs). ES-to-IS links are Level 0.

IS-IS Metrics

IS-IS, as originally defined, uses a composite metric with a maximum path value of 1024. The required default metric is arbitrary and typically assigned by a network administrator. By convention, it is intended to measure the capacity of the circuit for handling traffic, such as its throughput in bits per second. Higher values indicate a lower capacity. Any single link can have a maximum value of 64. IS-IS calculates path values by summing link values. The standard set the maximum metric values to provide the granularity to support various link types, while at the same time ensuring that the shortest-path algorithm used for route computation is reasonably efficient.

In Cisco routers, all interfaces have a default metric of 10. The administrator must configure the interface metric to get a different value. This small metric value range has proved insufficient for large networks and provides too little granularity for new features such as traffic engineering and other applications, especially with high-bandwidth links. Cisco IOS software addresses this issue with the support of a 24-bit metric field, the so-called "wide metric." Wide metrics are also required for route leaking. Using the new metric style, link metrics now have a maximum value of 16,777,215 ($2^{24} - 1$) with a total path metric of 4,261,412,864 ($254 \times 2^{24} = 2^{32}$). Deploying IS-IS in the IP network with wide metrics is recommended for enabling finer granularity and supporting future applications such as traffic engineering.

IS-IS also defines three optional metrics (costs): delay, expense, and error. Cisco routers do not support the three optional metrics. The wide metric noted earlier uses the octets reserved for these metrics.

IS-IS Operation and Design

This subsection discusses IS-IS areas, designated routers, authentication, and the Network Entity Title (NET). IS-IS defines areas differently from OSPF; area boundaries are links and not routers. IS-IS has no BDRs. Because IS-IS is an OSI protocol, it uses a NET to identify each router.

IS-IS NET Addressing

Although you can configure IS-IS to route IP, the communication between routers uses OSI PDUs. The NET is the OSI address used for each router to communicate with OSI PDUs. A NET address ranges from 8 to 20 bytes in length and is hexadecimal. It consists of an Authority and Format Identifier (AFI), area ID, system ID, and selector (SEL), as shown in Figure 10-14. The system ID must be unique within the network. An example of an IS-IS NET is 49.0001.1290.6600.1001.00, which consists of the following parts:

- AFI: 49
- Area ID: 0001

10

- System ID: 1290.6600.1001
- SEL: 00

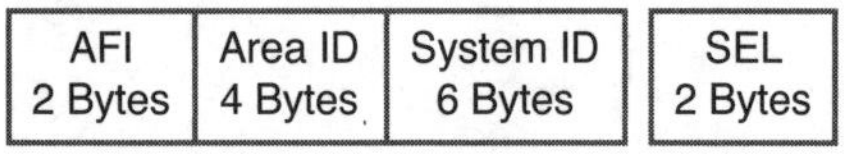

AFI 2 Bytes	Area ID 4 Bytes	System ID 6 Bytes	SEL 2 Bytes

Figure 10-14 *IS-IS NET*

Level 2 routers use the area ID. The system ID must be the same length for all routers in an area. For Cisco routers, it must be 6 bytes in length. Usually, a router MAC address identifies each unique router. The SEL is configured as 00. You configure the NET with the **router isis** command. In this example, the domain authority and format identifier (AFI) is 49, the area is 0001, the system ID is 00aa.0101.0001, and the SEL is 00:

```
router isis
net 49.0001.00aa.0101.0001.00
```

IS-IS DRs

As with OSPF, IS-IS selects DRs on multiaccess networks. It does not choose a backup DR as does OSPF. By default, the priority value is 64. You can change the priority value to a value from 0 to 127. If you set the priority to 0, the router is not eligible to become a DR for that network. IS-IS uses the highest system ID to select the DR if there is a tie with the priorities. On point-to-point networks, the priority is 0 because no DR is elected. In IS-IS, all routers in a multiaccess network establish adjacencies with all others in the subnetwork, and IS-IS neighbors become adjacent upon the discovery of one another. Both these characteristics are different from OSPF behavior.

IS-IS Areas

IS-IS uses a two-level hierarchy. Routers are configured to route Level 1 (L1), Level 2 (L2), or both Level 1 and Level 2 (L1/L2). Level 1 routers are like OSPF internal routers in a Cisco totally stubby area. An L2 router is similar to an OSPF backbone router. A router that has both Level 1 and 2 routes is similar to an OSPF area border router (ABR). IS-IS does not define a backbone area like OSPF's area 0, but you can consider the IS-IS backbone a continuous path of adjacencies among Level 2 ISs.

The L1/L2 routers maintain a separate link-state database for the L1 routes and L2 routes. Also, the L1/L2 routers do not advertise L2 routes to the L1 area. L1 routers do not have information about destinations outside the area and use L1 routes to the L1/L2 routers to reach outside destinations.

As shown in Figure 10-15, IS-IS areas are not bounded by the L1/L2 routers but by the links between L1/L2 routers and L2 backbone routers.

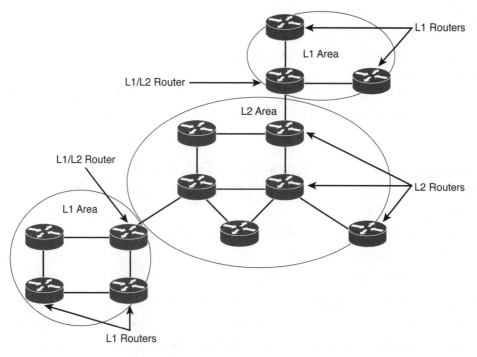

Figure 10-15 *IS-IS areas and router types*

IS-IS Authentication

IS-IS supports three types of clear-text authentication: link authentication, area authentication, and domain authentication. All these types support only cleartext password authentication. Recently, an RFC draft has added support for an IS-IS MD5. The design recommendation is to not use any plaintext authentication and to use MD5 hash for authentication. With MD5, a cryptographic hash is used instead of plaintext, and the password is never included in the PDU, thus making it more secure.

Routers in a common subnetwork (Ethernet, private line) use link authentication. The cleartext password must be common only between the routers in the link. Level 1 and Level 2 routes use separate passwords. With area authentication, all routers in the area must use authentication and must have the same password.

Only L2 and L1/L2 routers use domain authentication. All L2 and L1/L2 routers must be configured for authentication and must use the same password.

IS-IS Summary

The characteristics of IS-IS follow:

- Link-state protocol.
- Uses OSI CNLP to communicate with routers.
- Classless protocol (supports VLSMs and CIDR).

10

- Default metric is set to 10 for all interfaces.

- Single metric: single link max = 64, path max = 1024.

- Sends partial route updates only when there are changes.

- Authentication with cleartext passwords.

- Administrative distance is 115.

- Used in large networks. Sometimes attractive as compared to OSPF and EIGRP.

- Described in ISO/IEC 10589; reprinted by the IETF as RFC 1142.

References and Recommended Readings

Bruno, A. CCIE Routing and Switching Exam Certification Guide. Indianapolis: Cisco Press, 2002.

RFC 1058: Routing Information Protocol, www.ietf.org/rfc.

RFC 2453: RIP Version 2, www.ietf.org/rfc.

RFC 2328: OSPF Version 2, www.ietf.org/rfc.

RFC 1142: OSI IS-IS Intra-domain Routing Protocol, www.ietf.org/rfc.

Doyle, J. Routing TCP/IP, Volume I. Indianapolis: Cisco Press, 1998.

"Enhanced IGRP," www.cisco.com/univercd/cc/td/doc/cisintwk/ito_doc/en_igrp.htm.

"Enhanced Interior Gateway Routing Protocol," www.cisco.com/en/US/tech/tk365/tk207/technologies_white_paper09186a0080094cb7.shtml.

"Implementing EIGRP for IPv6," www.cisco.com/en/US/partner/products/sw/iosswrel/ps5187/products_configuration_guide_chapter09186a00805fc867.html#wp1049317.

RFC 1723: RIP Version 2 – Carrying Additional Information, www.ietf.org/rfc.

RFC 2080: RIPng for IPv6, www.ietf.org/rfc.

RFC 1321: The MD5 Message-Digest Algorithm, www.ietf.org/rfc.

"Routing Information Protocol," www.cisco.com/univercd/cc/td/doc/cisintwk/ito_doc/rip.htm.

"Tech Notes: How Does Unequal Cost Path Load Balancing (Variance) Work in IGRP and EIGRP?", http://www.cisco.com/c/en/us/support/docs/ip/enhanced-interior-gateway-routing-protocol-eigrp/13677-19.html.

RFC 7142: Reclassification of RFC 1142 to Historic, www.ietf.org/rfc

RFC 1195: Use of OSI IS-IS for Routing in TCP/IP and Dual Environments, www.ietf.org/rfc.

RFC 5302: Domain-Wide Prefix Distribution with Two-Level IS-IS, www.ietf.org/rfc.

EIGRP Stub Router Functionality, http://www.cisco.com/en/US/technologies/tk648/tk365/technologies_white_paper0900aecd8023df6f.html

"IPv6 Deployment Strategies," www.cisco.com/en/US/docs/ios/solutions_docs/ipv6/IPv6dswp.html#wp1028199.

Exam Preparation Tasks

Review All Key Topics

Review the most important topics in the chapter, noted with the Key Topic icon in the outer margin of the page. Table 10-9 provides a reference of these key topics and the page numbers on which each is found.

Table 10-9   Key Topics

Key Topic Element	Description	Page
List	Routing protocol characteristics	380
Table 10-2	IGP and EGP Protocol Selection	383
Table 10-3	Distance-vector routing protocols versus link-state protocols	384
Table 10-4	IPv4 and IPv6 Routing Protocols	386
Table 10-5	Default Administrative Distances for IP Routes	387
Table 10-6	Routing Protocol Characteristics	388
List	RIPv2 summary	396
List	RIPng summary	398
List	EIGRP components	399
List	EIGRP for IPv4 summary	406
List	EIGRP for IPv6 summary	407
List	IS-IS summary	411

Complete Tables and Lists from Memory

Print a copy of Appendix D, "Memory Tables," (found on the book website), or at least the section for this chapter, and complete the tables and lists from memory. Appendix E, "Memory Tables Answer Key," also on the website, includes completed tables and lists to check your work.

Define Key Terms

Define the following key terms from this chapter, and check your answers in the glossary:

administrative distance, BW, delay, distance vector, DUAL, EIGRP, EGP, hop count, IGP, link state, load, RIPng, RIPv2, VLSM

10

Q&A

The answers to these questions appear in Appendix A, "Answers to the 'Do I Know This Already?' Quizzes and Q&A Questions." For more practice with exam format questions, use the exam engine on the CD.

1. True or false: Link-state routing protocols send periodic routing updates.

2. True or false: RIPv2 was created to support IPv6.

3. True or false: The path with the lowest cost is preferred.

4. True or false: A link with a reliability of 200/255 is preferred over a link with a reliability of 10/255.

5. True or false: A link with a load of 200/255 is preferred over a link with a load of 10/255.

6. On a router, both EIGRP and OSPF have internal routes to 198.168.10.0/24. Which route is injected into the routing table?

7. On a router, both RIPv2 and IS-IS have a route to 198.168.10.0/24. Which route is injected into the routing table?

8. On a router, EIGRP has a route to the destination with a prefix of /28, and OSPF has a route to the destination with a prefix of /30. Which is used to reach the destination?

9. Which of the following is the best measurement of an interface's reliability and load?

    a. Reliability 255/255, load 1/255

    b. Reliability 255/255, load 255/255

    c. Reliability 1/255, load 1/255

    d. Reliability 1/255, load 255/255

10. Which routing protocols permit an explicit hierarchical topology?

    a. BGP

    b. EIGRP

    c. IS-IS

    d. RIP

    e. OSPF

    f. B and D

    g. C and E

11. What routing protocol parameter is concerned with how long a packet takes to travel from one end to another in the internetwork?

12. For what routing protocol metric is the value of a Fast Ethernet interface calculated as $10^8/10^8 = 1$?

13. Match the loop-prevention technique (numerals) with its description (letters).

    i.   Split horizon

    ii. Poison reverse

    iii. Triggered updates

    iv. Counting to infinity

    a. Sends an infinite metric from which the route was learned

    b. Drops a packet when the hop count limit is reached

    c. Suppresses a route announcement from which the route was learned

    d. Sends a route update when a route changes

14. True or false: Link-state routing protocols are more CPU and memory intensive than distance-vector routing protocols.

15. Which routing protocols would you select if you needed to take advantage of VLSMs? (Select all that apply.)

    a. RIPv1

    b. RIPv2

    c. IGRP

    d. EIGRP

    e. OSPF

    f. IS-IS

16. Which standards-based protocol would you select in a large IPv6 network?

    a. RIPng

    b. OSPFv3

    c. EIGRP for IPv6

    d. RIPv2

17. Which of the following routing protocols are fast in converging when a change in the network occurs? (Select three.)

    a. RIPv1

    b. RIPv2

    c. EIGRP

    d. OSPF

    e. IS-IS

    f. BGP

10

18. If you are designing a large corporate network that cannot be designed in a hierarchy, which routing protocol would you recommend?

    a. RIPv1

    b. RIPv2

    c. EIGRP

    d. OSPF

    e. IS-IS

    f. BGP

19. Which routing protocols support VLSMs? (Select all that apply.)

    a. RIPv1

    b. RIPv2

    c. EIGRP

    d. OSPF

    e. IS-IS

    f. All of the above

20. You are connecting your network to an ISP. Which routing protocol would you use to exchange routes?

    a. RIPv1

    b. RIPv2

    c. EIGRP

    d. OSPF

    e. IS-IS

    f. BGP

    g. All of the above

21. Which routing protocol requires only Cisco routers on the network?

    a. RIPv1

    b. RIPv2

    c. EIGRP

    d. OSPF

    e. IS-IS

    f. BGP

    g. All of the above

22. Which routing protocol would be supported on an IPv6 network with multiple vendor routers?

    a. RIPv2

    b. EIGRP for IPv6

    c. BGPv6

    d. OSPFv3

    e. RIPv3

    f. All of the above

    g. B and D

23. Which of the following characteristics are implemented differently between distance-vector and link-state routing protocols?

    a. IP route tables

    b. Route information distribution

    c. Routing tables

    d. Forwarding of traffic

    e. Verification of route information sources

    f. Administrative distance

24. Which two statements are true for IGPs and EGPs?

    a. IGPs can be substituted with static routing.

    b. IGPs are better at finding the fastest paths across the network.

    c. IGPs must converge quickly, but EGPs do not.

    d. IGPs are for inter-autonomous system connections, EGPs are used for intra-autonomous system connections.

25. How is convergence related to routing information?

    a. The speed of convergence affects the frequency of routing updates.

    b. The faster the convergence, less consistent routing information is produced.

    c. The faster the convergence, more consistent routing information is produced.

    d. There is no relation between convergence and routing information consistency.

26. What is a major advantage of a classless structured network over a classless network?

    a. There is less overhead in classless networks.

    b. There is more overhead in classless networks.

    c. Less IP addresses are used in classful networks.

    d. Classless networks do not have advantages over classful networks.

27. Which two EIGRP features make it appropriate for a company's network?

    a. Slow convergence

    b. VLSM support

    c. DUAL

    d. Automatic summarization

    e. Multivendor support

10

28. Match the protocol with the characteristic.

   i.   EIGRP for IPv6

   ii. RIPv2

   iii. RIPng

   iv. EIGRP

  a. Uses multicast FF02::9

  b. Uses multicast 224.0.0.9

  c. Uses multicast 224.0.0.10

  d. Uses multicast FF02::A

29. A small network is experiencing excessive broadcast traffic and slow response times. The current routing protocol is RIPv1. What design changes would you recommend?

  a. Migrate to RIPv2.

  b. Migrate to RIPng.

  c. Migrate to EIGRP for IPv4.

  d. Migrate to EIGRPv6.

30. Match the EIGRP component with its description.

   i.   RTP

   ii. DUAL

   iii. Protocol-dependent modules

   iv. Neighbor discovery

  a. An interface between DUAL and IPX RIP, IGRP, and AppleTalk

  b. Used to deliver EIGRP messages reliably

  c. Builds an adjacency table

  d. Guarantees a loop-free network

31. Match each EIGRP parameter with its description.

   i.   Feasible distance

   ii. Successor

   iii. Feasible successor

   iv. Active state

  a. The best path selected by DUAL.

  b. The successor is down.

  c. The lowest calculated metric of a path to reach the destination.

  d. The second-best path.

32. On an IPv6 network, you have RIPng and EIGRP running. Both protocols have a route to destination 10.1.1.0/24. Which route gets injected into the routing table?

  a. The RIPng route

  b. The EIGRP route

   c. Both routes

   d. Neither route because of a route conflict

33. Which routing protocol should be used if the network requirements include fastest convergence time and unequal load balancing?

   a. BGP

   b. OSPF

   c. EIGRP

   d. RIPv2

34. Which IGP protocol is a common alternative to EIGRP and OSPF as a routing protocol for large service provider networks?

   a. OSPFv3

   b. RIPv2

   c. BGP4

   d. IS-IS

35. What is the default IS-IS metric for a T1 interface?

   a. 5

   b. 10

   c. 64

   d. 200

36. In IS-IS networks, the backup designated router (BDR) forms adjacencies to what routers?

   a. Only to the DR.

   b. To all routers.

   c. The BDR only becomes adjacent when the DR is down.

   d. There is no BDR is IS-IS.

37. Which routing protocol converges most quickly?

   a. BGP

   b. OSPF

   c. EIGRP

   d. RIPv2

   e. IS-IS

38. Which routing protocol allows for unequal cost multipath routing?

   a. IS-IS

   b. OSPF

   c. EIGRP

   d. RIPv2

10

39. Which two link-state routing protocols support IPv6?

   a. BGP4

   b. EIGRP

   c. OSPF

   d. RIPng

   e. IS-IS

40. Select those answers that are characteristics of EIGRP? (Select four.)

   a. ASN and K values must match to form neighbors

   b. Can use multiple unequal paths

   c. Summary routes have an AD of 150.

   d. External routes have an AD of 170.

   e. Exchanges the full routing table every 60 seconds.

   f. Uses multicast address 224.0.0.10 for updates.

   g. Does not support MD5 authentication

41. A hierarchical design of EIGRP helps with which of the following? (Select two.)

   a. Redistribution

   b. Route summarization

   c. Faster convergence

   d. Load balancing

42. Which are design considerations with EIGRP?

   a. The **neighbor** command is used to enable unicast communication.

   b. The **neighbor** command can be used to establish adjacency with non-Cisco routers.

   c. The ASN and K values must match to establish neighbors.

   d. Virtual links can be used to establish neighbors over an area.

43. Which are the two fastest converging routing protocols?

   a. IS-IS

   b. OSPF

   c. EIGRP

   d. RIPv2

   e. BGP4

44. Which routing protocol uses multicast FF28::A and Next Header protocol 88?

   a. IS-IS for IPv6

   b. OSPFv3

   c. EIGRP for IPv6

   d. RIPng

45. What is the system ID of the following NET?

49.0001.1900.6500.0001.00

   a. 49.0001

   b. 0001.1900.6500

   c. 1900.6500.0001

   d. 0001.00

46. Loops can cause broadcast storms and congestion. How do distance-vector routing protocols handle this? (Select all that apply.)

   a. Counting to infinity

   b. Poison reverse

   c. Split horizon

   d. Vector routing

47. EIGRP has a route with a metric of 20. There are two feasible successors with metrics of 35 and 45. If the **variance 2** command is invoked, how many active routes are there for this route?

   a. 1.

   b. 2.

   c. 3.

   d. Variance has to be used for equal-cost routes.

48. Which routing protocol has the highest admin distance?

   a. RIP

   b. EIGRP

   c. OSPF

   d. IS-IS

   c. BGP

49. Which routing protocol has the lowest admin distance?

   a. RIP

   b. EIGRP

   c. OSPF

   d. IS-IS

   c. iBGP

10

50. Which routing protocol represents each column of Table 10-10?

Table 10-10 Routing Protocol Characteristics

Characteristic	A	B	C	D	E
Supports VLSM	Yes	Yes	Yes	Yes	Yes
Convergence	Fast	Fast	Slow	Fast	Fast
Scalability	High	High	Low	High	High
Supports IPv6	Yes	No	No	No	Yes
Proprietary	Yes	No	No	Yes	No

Answer questions 51–53 based on Figure 10-16.

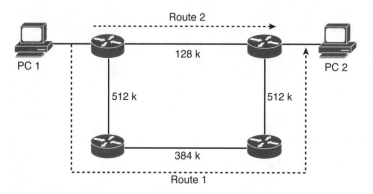

Figure 10-16 *Scenario diagram*

51. A user performs a Telnet from PC 1 to PC 2. If the metric used by the configured routing protocol is the bandwidth parameter, which route will the packets take?

   a. Route 1.

   b. Route 2.

   c. Neither, because the information is insufficient.

   d. One packet takes Route 1, the following packet takes Route 2, and so on.

52. A user performs a Telnet from PC 1 to PC 2. If the metric used by the configured routing protocol is hop count, which route will the packets take?

   a. Route 1.

   b. Route 2.

   c. Neither, because the information is insufficient.

   d. One packet takes Route 1, the following packet takes Route 2, and so on.

53. A user performs a Telnet from PC 1 to PC 2. If the metric used by the configured routing protocol is OSPF cost, which route will the packets take?

   a. Route 1.

   b. Route 2.

   c. Neither, because the information is insufficient.

   d. One packet takes Route 1, the following packet takes Route 2, and so on.

Use Figure 10-17 to answer the remaining questions.

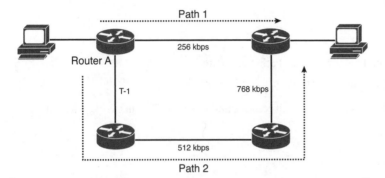

Figure 10-17 *Path selection*

54. By default, if RIPv2 is enabled on all routers, what path is taken?

   a. Path 1

   b. Path 2

   c. Unequal load balancing with Path 1 and Path 2

   d. Equal load balancing with Path 1 and Path 2

55. By default, if RIPng is enabled on all routers, what path is taken?

   a. Path 1

   b. Path 2

   c. Unequal load balancing with Path 1 and Path 2

   d. Equal load balancing with Path 1 and Path 2

56. By default, if EIGRP is enabled on all routers, what path is taken?

   a. Path 1

   b. Path 2

   c. Unequal load balancing with Path 1 and Path 2

   d. Equal load balancing with Path 1 and Path 2

10

57. EIGRP is configured on the routers. If it is configured with the variance command, what path is taken?

    a. Path 1

    b. Path 2

    c. Unequal load sharing Path 1 and Path 2

    d. Equal load balancing with Path 1 and Path 2

58. By default, if EIGRP for IPv6 is enabled on all routers, and this is an IPv6 network, what path is taken?

    a. Path 1

    b. Path 2

    c. Unequal load balancing with Path 1 and Path 2

    d. Equal load balancing with Path 1 and Path 2

59. By default, if IS-IS is enabled on all routers, and this is an IPv6 network, what path is taken?

    a. Path 1

    b. Path 2

    c. Unequal load balancing with Path 1 and Path 2

    d. Equal load balancing with Path 1 and Path 2

This chapter covers the following subjects:

OSPFv2

OSPFv3

BGP

Route Manipulation

IP Multicast Review

This chapter reviews the characteristics and design issues of the Open Shortest Path First Version 2 (OSPFv2) routing protocol. For IPv6 networks, OSPFv3 is also covered. OSPFv2 and OSPFv3 are link-state routing protocols. They do not broadcast their route tables as distance-vector routing protocols do. Routers using link-state routing protocols send information about the status of their interfaces to all other routers in the area. Then they perform database computations to determine the shortest paths to each destination. This chapter also covers the Border Gateway Protocol (BGP), which is used to exchange routes between autonomous systems. It is most frequently used between enterprises and service providers. The "Route Manipulation" section covers route summarization, route filtering, and redistribution of route information between routing protocols. The CCDA should know where redistribution occurs when required by the network design. This chapter concludes by covering IP multicast protocols.

CHAPTER 11

OSPF, BGP, Route Manipulation, and IP Multicast

"Do I Know This Already?" Quiz

The "Do I Know This Already?" quiz helps you identify your strengths and deficiencies in this chapter's topics.

The 12-question quiz, derived from the major sections in the "Foundation Topics" portion of the chapter, helps you determine how to spend your limited study time.

Table 11-1 outlines the major topics discussed in this chapter and the "Do I Know This Already?" quiz questions that correspond to those topics.

Table 11-1 "Do I Know This Already?" Foundation Topics Section-to-Question Mapping

Foundation Topics Section	Questions Covered in This Section
OSPFv2	1, 2, 3, 4, 6,
OSPFv3	7
BGP	8, 12
Route Manipulation	9
IP Multicast Review	5, 10, 11

1. Which protocol defines an Area Border Router (ABR)?

   a. Enhanced Interior Gateway Routing Protocol (EIGRP)

   b. Open Shortest Path First (OSPF)

   c. Intermediate System-to-Intermediate System (IS-IS)

   d. Routing Information Protocol (RIP)

2. Which routing protocols support variable-length subnet masks (VLSMs)?

   a. EIGRP

   b. OSPF

   c. IS-IS

   d. A and B

   e. A and C

   f. B and C

   g. A, B, and C

3. What is an ASBR?

   a. Area Border Router

   b. Autonomous System Boundary Router

   c. Auxiliary System Border Router

   d. Area System Border Router

4. What is the OSPFv2 link-state advertisement (LSA) type for autonomous system external LSAs?

   a. Type 1

   b. Type 2

   c. Type 3

   d. Type 4

   e. Type 5

5. What address do you use to multicast to the OSPFv2 designated router (DR)?

   a. 224.0.0.1

   b. 224.0.0.5

   c. 224.0.0.6

   d. 224.0.0.10

6. To where are OSPF Type 1 LSAs flooded?

   a. The OSPF area

   b. The OSPF domain

   c. From the area to the OSPF backbone

   d. Through the virtual link

7. What OSPFv3 LSA carries address prefixes?

   a. Network LSA

   b. Summary LSA

   c. Inter-area-router LSA

   d. Intra-area-prefix LSA

8. What protocol do you use to exchange IP routes between autonomous systems?

   a. IGMP

   b. eBGP

   c. EIGRP

   d. OSPF

9. Where should routes be summarized?

   a. On the core routers

   b. On the distribution routers

   c. On the access routers

   d. None of the above

10. What is IGMP?

    a. Interior Group Management Protocol

    b. Internet Group Management Protocol

    c. Interior Gateway Routing Protocol

    d. Interior Gateway Media Protocol

11. How many bits are mapped from the Layer 3 IPv4 multicast address to a Layer 2 MAC address?

    a. 16 bits

    b. 23 bits

    c. 24 bits

    d. 32 bits

12. What is the administrative distance of eBGP routes?

    a. 20

    b. 100

    c. 110

    d. 200

11

Foundation Topics

This chapter covers the link-state routing protocol OSPF. OSPF is an Interior Gateway Protocol (IGP) used within an autonomous system. Is it the most widely used IGP in enterprises, government networks, and service providers. OSPFv2 is used for IPv4 networks, and OSPFv3 is used for IPv6 networks. IS-IS is another link-state routing protocol covered in the previous chapter.

The "BGP" section covers the characteristics and design of BGP. eBGP exchanges routes between autonomous systems. eBGP is commonly used between enterprises and their service providers.

The section "Route Manipulation" covers how you use policy-based routing (PBR) to change packets' destination addresses based on policies. This section also covers route summarization, filtering, and redistribution of route information between routing protocols.

The section "IP Multicast Review" covers multicast protocols such as Internet Group Management Protocol (IGMP), Cisco Group Management Protocol (CGMP), and Protocol Independent Multicast (PIM).

OSPFv2

RFC 2328 defines OSPFv2, a link-state routing protocol that uses Dijkstra's shortest path first (SPF) algorithm to calculate paths to destinations. OSPFv2 is used in IPv4 networks. OSPF was created for its use in large networks where RIP failed. OSPF improved the speed of convergence, provided for the use of variable-length subnet masks (VLSMs), and improved the path calculation.

In OSPF, each router sends link-state advertisements (LSAs) about itself and its links to all other routers in the area. Note that it does not send routing tables but rather link-state information about its interfaces. Then, each router individually calculates the best routes to the destination by running the SPF algorithm. Each OSPF router in an area maintains an identical database describing the area's topology. The routing table at each router is individually constructed using the local copy of this database to construct a shortest-path tree.

OSPFv2 is a classless routing protocol that permits the use of VLSMs. With Cisco routers, OSPF also supports equal-cost multipath load balancing and neighbor authentication. OSPF uses multicast addresses to communicate between routers. OSPF uses IP protocol 89.

This section covers OSPF theory and design concepts. It discusses OSPF LSAs, area types, and router types. OSPF uses a two-layer hierarchy with a backbone area at the top and all other areas below. Routers send LSAs informing other routers of the status of their interfaces. The use of LSAs and the characteristics of OSPF areas are important concepts to understand for the exam.

OSPFv2 Metric

The metric that OSPFv2 uses is cost. It is an unsigned 16-bit integer in the range of 1 to 65,535. The default cost for interfaces is calculated based on the bandwidth in the formula 10^8 / BW, where BW is the bandwidth of the interface expressed as a full integer of bits per second (bps). If the result is smaller than 1, the cost is set to 1. A 10BASE-T (10 Mbps = 10^7 bps) interface has a cost of 10^8 / 10^7 = 10. OSPF performs a summation of the costs to reach a destination; the lowest cost is the preferred path. Table 11-2 shows some sample interface metrics.

Table 11-2 OSPF Default Interface Costs

Interface Type	OSPF Cost
10 Gigabit Ethernet	.01 → 1
Gigabit Ethernet	.1 → 1
OC-3 (155 Mbps)	.64516 → 1
Fast Ethernet	$10^8/10^8$ = 1
DS-3 (45 Mbps)	2
Ethernet	$10^8/10^7$ = 10
T1	64
512 kbps	195
256 kbps	390

The default reference bandwidth used to calculate OSPF costs is 10^8 (cost = 10^8 / BW). Notice that for technologies that support speeds greater than 100 Mbps, the default metric gets set to 1 without regard for the network's different capabilities (speed).

Because OSPF was developed prior to high-speed WAN and LAN technologies, the default metric for 100 Mbps was 1. Cisco provides a method to modify the default reference bandwidth. The cost metric can be modified on every interface. It is highly recommended that you change the default reference bandwidth to a higher number on all routers in the OSPF network if OSPF links have a speed higher than 100 Mbps.

OSPFv2 Adjacencies and Hello Timers

OSPF uses Hello packets for neighbor discovery. The default Hello interval is 10 seconds (30 seconds for nonbroadcast multiaccess [NBMA] networks). For point-to-point networks, the Hello interval is 10 seconds. Hellos are multicast to 224.0.0.5 (ALLSPFRouters). Hello packets include such information as the router ID, area ID, authentication, and router priority.

11

After two routers exchange Hello packets and set two-way communication, they establish adjacencies.

Figure 11-1 shows a point-to-point network and an NBMA network.

For point-to-point networks, valid neighbors always become adjacent and communicate using multicast address 224.0.0.5. For broadcast (Ethernet) and NBMA networks (Frame Relay), all routers become adjacent to the designated router (DR) and backup designated router (BDR), but not to each other. All routers reply to the DR and BDR using the multicast address 224.0.0.6. The section "OSPF DRs" covers the DR concept.

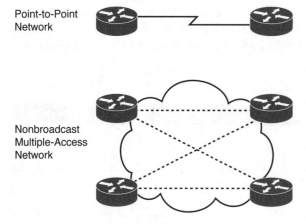

Figure 11-1 *OSPF networks*

On OSPF point-to-multipoint nonbroadcast networks, it is necessary to configure the set of neighbors that are directly reachable over the point-to-multipoint network. Each neighbor is identified by its IP address on the point-to-multipoint network. Nonbroadcast point-to-multipoint networks do not elect DRs, so the DR eligibility of configured neighbors is undefined. OSPF communication in point-to-point networks use unicast or multicast addresses for neighbor communication.

OSPF virtual links unicast OSPF packets. Later, the section "Virtual Links" discusses virtual links.

OSPFv2 Areas

As a network grows, the initial flooding and database maintenance of LSAs can burden a router's CPU. OSPF uses areas to reduce these effects. An area is a logical grouping of routers and links that divides the network. Routers share link-state information with only the routers in their areas. This setup reduces the size of the database and the cost of computing the SPF tree at each router.

Using a topology with multiple areas provides the following benefits:

■ The segmentation of the network reduces the number of SFP tree calculations.

■ The segmentation of the network reduces the amount of LSA flooding.

■ Multi-area design allows for summarization at the Area Border Routers (ABRs).

■ One OSPF area hides the topology from another area.

Each area is assigned a 32-bit integer number. Area 0 (or 0.0.0.0) is reserved for the backbone area. Every OSPF network should have a backbone area. The backbone area must exist in any internetwork using OSPF over multiple areas as a routing protocol. As you can see in Figure 11-2, communication between Area 1 and Area 2 must flow through Area 0. This communication can be internal to a single router that has interfaces directly connected to Areas 0, 1, and 2.

Intra-area traffic is packets passed between routers in a single area.

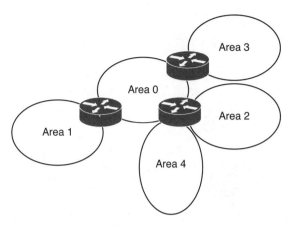

Figure 11-2 *OSPF areas*

OSPF Area Design Considerations

The CCDA should be aware of a few considerations in the design of OSPF areas. First, in a hub-and-spoke design, you have a remote branch keep the OSPF boundary at the hub side, as shown in Figure 11-3. This allows the branch router to only calculate SPFs within its own area and limits the LSA flooding. If the OSPF Area 0 boundary was extended to the branch, then the branch router would have to do OSPF calculations for Area 0 and its own area, and LSAs would flood over the WAN link.

The second design consideration is not to group remote branches into a single area. Having all remote branches in the same area is not scalable. Instead, place each remote branch in its own area to limit LSA flooding and SPF recalculations.

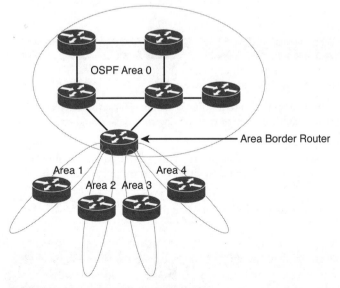

Figure 11-3 *OSPF area design*

OSPF Router Types

OSPF classifies participating routers based on their place and function in the area architecture. Figure 11-4 shows OSPF router types.

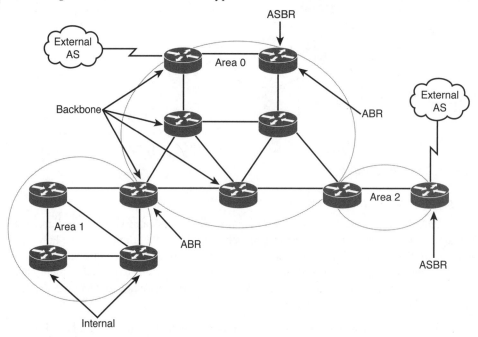

Figure 11-4 *OSPF router types*

Table 11-3 explains each router type in Figure 11-4.

Table 11-3 OSPF Router Types

Type	Description
Internal router	Any router whose interfaces all belong to the same OSPF area. These routers keep only one link-state database.
ABR	Routers that are connected to more than one area. These routers maintain a link-state database for each area they belong to. These routers generate summary LSAs.
ASBR	Routers that inject external LSAs into the OSPF database (redistribution). These external routes are learned via either other routing protocols or static routes.
Backbone router	Routers with at least one interface attached to Area 0.

Tip An OSPF router can be an ABR, an ASBR, and a backbone router at the same time. The router is an ABR if it has an interface on Area 0 and another interface in another area. The router is a backbone router if it has one or more interfaces in Area 0. The router is an ASBR if it redistributes external routes into the OSPF network.

OSPF DRs

On multiaccess networks (such as Ethernet), some routers get selected as DRs. The purpose of the DR is to collect LSAs for the multiaccess network and to forward the LSA to all non-DR routers; this arrangement reduces the amount of LSA traffic generated. A router can be the DR for one multiaccess network and not the DR in another attached multiaccess network.

The DR also floods the network LSAs to the rest of the area. OSPF also selects a BDR; it takes over the function of the DR if the DR fails. Both the DR and BDR become adjacent to all routers in the multiaccess network. All routers that are not DR and BDR are sometimes called DRothers. These routers are only adjacent to the DR and BDR. The DR generates a Type 2 (network) LSA, which advertises all other routers on the multiaccess segment. This allows the DRothers routers to get the Type 1 LSAs. OSPF routers multicast LSAs only to adjacent routers. DRothers multicast packets to the DR and BDR using the multicast address 224.0.0.6 (ALLDRouters). The DR floods updates using ALLSPFRouters (224.0.0.5).

DR and BDR selection is based on an OSPF DR interface priority. The default value is 1, and the highest priority determines the DR. In a tie, OSPF uses the numerically highest router ID. The router ID is the IP address of the configured loopback interface. The router ID is the highest configured loopback address, or if the loopback is not configured, it's the highest physical address. Routers with a priority of 0 are not considered for DR/BDR selection. The dotted lines in Figure 11-5 show the adjacencies in the network.

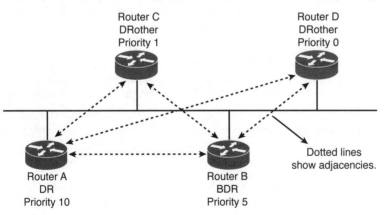

Figure 11-5 *DRs*

In Figure 11-5, Router A is configured with a priority of 10, and Router B is configured with a priority of 5. Assuming that these routers are turned on simultaneously, Router A becomes the DR for the Ethernet network. Router C has a lower priority, becoming adjacent to Router A and Router B but not to Router D. Router D has a priority of 0 and therefore is not a candidate to become a DR or BDR.

If you introduce a new router to the network with a higher priority than that of the current DR and BDR, it does not become the selected DR unless both the DR and BDR fail. If the DR fails, the current BDR becomes the DR.

LSA Types

OSPF routers generate LSAs that are flooded within an area, between areas, and throughout the entire autonomous system. OSPF defines different LSA types for participating routers, DRs, ABRs, and ASBRs. Understanding the LSA types can help you with other OSPF concepts. Table 11-4 describes the major LSA types. You will need to know OSPF LSAs by type code (number) and by type name. Note that there are other LSA types that are not covered in this book.

Table 11-4   Major LSA Types

Type Code	Type	Description
1	Router LSA	Produced by every router. Includes all the router's links, interfaces, state of links, and cost. This LSA type is flooded within a single area and does not travel into other areas.
2	Network LSA	Produced by every DR on every broadcast or NBMA network. It lists all the routers in the multiaccess network. This LSA type is contained within an area.
3	Summary LSA for ABRs	Produced by ABRs. It is sent into an area to advertise destinations outside the area.
4	Summary LSA for ASBRs	Originated by ABRs. Sent into an area by the ABR to advertise the IP address of the ASBRs. It does not advertise networks outside the OSPF network, just the ASBR.
5	Autonomous system external LSA	Originated by ASBRs. Advertises destinations external to the OSPF autonomous system, flooded throughout the whole OSPF autonomous system.
7	Not-so-stubby area (NSSA) external LSA	Originated by ASBRs in an NSSA. It is not flooded throughout the OSPF autonomous system, only to the NSSA. Similar to the Type 5 LSA.

Type 1 and Type 2 LSAs are intra-area LSAs that have an area-flooding scope. Type 3 LSAs are a summary of destinations outside the local area but within the OSPF domain. Type 4 LSAs provide reachability about the ASBR. Type 3 and Type 4 LSAs are inter-area LSAs that have an area-flooding scope. ABRs exchange Type 3 and Type 4 LSAs. Type 5 LSAs advertise external destinations. Type 5 LSAs have a domain-flooding scope, meaning they are flooded throughout all areas. Type 7 LSAs are originated by ASBRs in an NSSA and are similar to the Type 5 LSA and only flooded within the NSSA.

Autonomous System External Path Types

The two types of autonomous system external paths are Type 1 (E1) and Type 2 (E2), and they are associated with Type 5 LSAs. ASBRs advertise external destinations whose cost can be just a redistribution metric (E2) or a redistribution metric plus the costs of each segment (E1) used to reach the ASBR.

By default, external routes are of Type 2, which is the metric (cost) used in the redistribution. Type 1 external routes have a metric that is the sum of the redistribution cost plus the cost of the path to reach the ASBR.

OSPF Stub Area Types

OSPF provides support for stub areas. The concept is to reduce the number of inter-area or external LSAs that get flooded into a stub area. RFC 2328 defines OSPF stub areas. RFC 1587 defines support for NSSAs. Cisco routers use totally stubby areas, such as Area 2, as shown in Figure 11-6.

Stub Areas

Consider Area 1 in Figure 11-6. Its only path to the external networks is via the ABR through Area 0. All external routes are flooded to all areas in the OSPF autonomous system. You can configure an area as a stub area to prevent OSPF external LSAs (Type 5) from being flooded into that area. A single default route is injected into the stub area instead. If multiple ABRs exist in a stub area, all inject the default route. Traffic originating within the stub area routes to the closest ABR.

Note that network summary LSAs (Type 3) from other areas are still flooded into the stub Area 1.

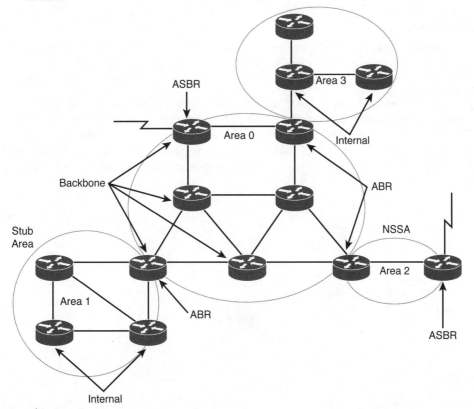

Figure 11-6   *OSPF stub networks*

Totally Stubby Areas

Let's take Area 1 in Figure 11-6 one step further. The only path for Area 1 to get to Area 0 and other areas is through the ABR. A totally stubby area does not flood network summary LSAs (Type 3). It stifles Type 4 LSAs, as well. Like regular stub areas, totally stubby areas do not flood Type 5 LSAs. They send just a single LSA for the default route. If multiple ABRs exist in a totally stubby area, all ABRs inject the default route. Traffic originating within the totally stubby area routes to the closest ABR.

NSSAs

Notice that Area 2 in Figure 11-6 has an ASBR. If this area is configured as an NSSA, it generates the external LSAs (Type 7) into the OSPF system while retaining the characteristics of a stub area to the rest of the autonomous system. There are two options for the ABR. First, the ABR for Area 2 can translate the NSSA external LSAs (Type 7) to autonomous system external LSAs (Type 5) and flood the rest of the internetwork. Second, the ABR is not configured to convert the NSSA external LSAs to Type 5 external LSAs, and therefore the NSSA external LSAs remain within the NSSA.

There is also an NSSA totally stub area. The difference is that the default NSSA has no default route unless the ABR is explicitly configured to advertise one. The NSSA totally stub area does receive a default route.

Virtual Links

OSPF requires that all areas be connected to a backbone router. Sometimes, WAN link provisioning or failures can prevent an OSPF area from being directly connected to a backbone router. You can use virtual links to temporarily connect (virtually) the area to the backbone.

As shown in Figure 11-7, Area 4 is not directly connected to the backbone. A virtual link is configured between Router A and Router B. The flow of the virtual link is unidirectional and must be configured in each router of the link. Area 2 becomes the transit area through which the virtual link is configured. Traffic between Areas 2 and 4 does not flow directly to Router B. Instead, the traffic must flow to Router A to reach Area 0 and then pass through the virtual link.

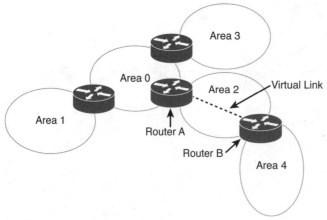

Figure 11-7 *OSPF virtual link*

OSPFv2 Router Authentication

OSPFv2 supports the authentication of routes using 64-bit clear text or cryptographic message digest 5 (MD5) authentication. Authentication can be performed on a per-area or per-interface basis. Plaintext authentication passwords do not need to be the same for the routers throughout the area, but they must be the same between neighbors.

MD5 authentication provides higher security than plaintext authentication. As with plaintext authentication, passwords do not have to be the same throughout an area, but they do need to be the same between neighbors.

OSPFv2 Summary

OSPFv2 is used in large enterprise IPv4 networks. The network topology must be hierarchical. OSPF is used in the enterprise campus building access, distribution, and core layers. OSPF is also used in the enterprise data center, WAN/MAN, and branch offices.

The characteristics of OSPFv2 follow:

- Link-state routing protocol.
- Uses IP protocol 89.
- Classless protocol (supports VLSMs and CIDR).
- Metric is cost (based on interface bandwidth by default).
- Fast convergence. Uses link-state updates and SPF calculation.
- Reduced bandwidth use. Sends partial route updates only when changes occur.
- Routes are labeled as intra-area, inter-area, external Type 1, or external Type 2.
- Support for authentication.
- Uses the Dijkstra algorithm to calculate the SPF tree.
- Default administrative distance is 110.
- Uses multicast address 224.0.0.5 (ALLSPFRouters).
- Uses multicast address 224.0.0.6 (ALLDRouters).
- Good scalability. Recommended for large networks.

OSPFv3

RFC 5340 describes OSPF Version 3 as a routing protocol for IPv6 networks. Note that OSPFv3 is for IPv6 networks only and that it is not backward compatible with OSPFv2 (used in IPv4). OSPF algorithms and mechanisms, such as flooding, router types, designated router election, areas, stub and NSSA, and SPF calculations, remain the same. Changes are made for OSPF to support IPv6 addresses, address hierarchy, and IPv6 for transport. OSPFv3 uses multicast group FF02::5 for all OSPF routers and FF02::6 for all designated routers.

11

OSPFv3 Changes from OSPFv2

The following are the major changes for OSPFv3:

- **Version number is 3:** Obviously, this is a newer version of OSPF, and it runs over IPv6 only.

- **Support for IPv6 addressing:** New LSAs created to carry IPv6 addresses and prefixes.

- **Per-link processing:** OSPFv2 uses per-subnet processing. With link processing, routers in the same link can belong to multiple subnets.

- **Address semantics removed:** Addresses are removed from the router and network LSAs. These LSAs now provide topology information.

- **No authentication in the OSPFv3 protocol:** OSPFv3 uses the authentication schemes inherited in IPv6.

- **New link LSA:** For local-link flooding scope.

- **New intra-area-prefix LSA:** Carries all the IPv6 prefix information. Similar to an OSPFv2 router and network LSAs.

- **Identifying neighbors by router ID:** Neighbors are always identified by the router ID. This does not occur in OSPFv2 point-to-point and broadcast networks.

- **Options field changes:** Two Options bits, the R-bit and the V6-bit, have been added to the Options field for processing router LSAs during the SPF calculation.

Note In OSPFv3, the router IDs, area IDs, and LSA link-state IDs remain at the size of 32 bits. Larger IPv6 addresses cannot be used.

OSPFv3 Areas and Router Types

OSPFv3 retains the same structure and concepts as OSPFv2. The area topology, interfaces, neighbors, link-state database, and routing table remain the same. RFC 2740 does not define new area types or router types.

The OSPF areas shown in Figure 11-2 and the router types shown in Figure 11-4 remain the same. The router types in relation to the OSPF areas are

- **Internal router:** Any router whose interfaces all belong to the same OSPF area. These routers keep only one link-state database.

- **ABR:** Routers that are connected to more than one area, where one area is Area 0. These routers maintain a link-state database for each area they belong to. These routers generate summary LSAs.

- **ASBR:** Routers that inject external LSAs into the OSPF database (redistribution). These external routes are learned via either other routing protocols or static routes.

- **Backbone router:** Routers with at least one interface attached to Area 0.

OSPFv3 LSAs

OSPFv3 retains the LSA types used by OSPFv2 with some modifications and introduces two new LSAs: link LSA and intra-area-prefix.

All LSAs use a common 20-byte header that indicates the LS type, the advertising router, and the sequence number. Figure 11-8 shows the format of the LSA header.

The LS Age indicates the time in seconds since the LSA was generated.

The LS Type indicates the function performed by this LSA. This field includes a U bit and S2 and S1 bits. When the U bit is set to 0, the LSA is flooded only locally. When the U bit is set to 1, the LSA is stored and flooded. The S1 and S2 bits have the functions indicated in Table 11-5.

```
0               1               2               3
```

LS Age	LS Type
Link State ID	
Advertising Router	
LS Sequence Number	
LS Checksum	Length

Figure 11-8 *LSA header*

Table 11-5 LSA Header S2 S1 Bits

S2 S1	Flooding Scope
00	Link-local scope
01	Flood to all routers within the area
10	Flood to all routers within the autonomous system
11	Reserved

The Link State ID is used with the LS type and advertising router to identify the link-state database. The Advertising Router field contains the 32-bit router ID of the router that generated the LSA. The LS Sequence Number is used to detect old or duplicate LSAs. The LS Checksum is for error checking. The Length field indicates the length of the LSA, including the header.

Table 11-6 summarizes the nine LSAs that can be used in OSPF. Most LSAs retain the same function used in OSPFv2 for IPv4. Each OSPFv3 LSA is described in more detail following the table.

11

Table 11-6   OSPFv3 LSA Types

LSA Name	LS Type	Description
Router LSA	0x2001	State of router interfaces
Network LSA	0x2002	Generated by DR routers in broadcast or NBMA networks
Inter-area-prefix LSA	0x2003	Routes to prefixes in other areas
Inter-area-router LSA	0x2004	Routes to routers in other areas
Autonomous system external LSA	0x4005	Routes to networks external to the autonomous system
Group-membership LSA	0x2006	Networks that contain multicast groups
NSSA Type 7 LSA	0x2007	Routers to networks external to the autonomous system, injected into the NSSA
Link LSA	0x0008	Tells neighbors about link-local addresses and list IPv6 prefixes associated with the link
Intra-area-prefix LSA	0x2009	IPv6 prefixes connected to a router, a stub network, or an associated transit network segment

Router LSAs describe the cost and state of all the originating router's interfaces. These LSAs are flooded within the area only. Router LSAs are LS type 0x2001. No IPv6 prefixes are contained in this LSA.

Network LSAs are originated by DRs in broadcast or NBMA networks. They describe all routers attached to the link that are adjacent to the DR. These LSAs are flooded within the area only. The LS type is 0x2002. No IPv6 prefixes are contained in this LSA.

Inter-area-prefix LSAs describe routes to IPv6 prefixes that belong to other areas. They are similar to OSPFv2 type 3 summary LSAs. The inter-area-prefix LSA is originated by the ABR and has an LS type of 0x2003. It is also used to send the default route in stub areas. These LSAs are flooded within the area only.

Each inter-area-router LSA describes a route to a router in another area. It is similar to OSPF Type 4 summary LSAs. It is originated by the ABR and has an LS type of 0x2004. These LSAs are flooded within the area only.

Autonomous system-external LSAs describe networks that are external to the autonomous system. These LSAs are originated by ASBRs, have an LS type of 0x4005, and therefore are flooded to all routers in the autonomous system.

The group-membership LSA describes the directly attached networks that contain members of a multicast group. This LSA is limited to the area and has an LS type of 0x2006. This LSA is described further in RFC 1584. This LSA is not supported in Cisco IOS Software.

Type 7 LSAs describe networks that are external to the autonomous system, but they are flooded to the NSSA area only. NSSAs are covered in RFC 1587. This LSA is generated by the NSSA ASBR and has a type of 0x2007.

Link LSAs describe the router's link-local address and a list of IPv6 prefixes associated with the link. This LSA is flooded to the local link only and has a type of 0x0008.

The intra-area-prefix LSA is a new LSA type that is used to advertise IPv6 prefixes associated with a router, a stub network, or an associated transit network segment. This LSA contains information that used to be part of the router LSAs and network LSAs.

OSPFv3 Summary

OSPFv3 is used in large enterprise IPv6 networks. The network topology must be hierarchical. OSPF is used in the enterprise campus building access, distribution, and core layers. OSPF is also used in the enterprise data center, WAN/MAN, and branch offices.

The characteristics of OSPFv3 follow:

- Link-state routing protocol for IPv6.
- Uses IPv6 Next Header 89.
- Metric is cost (based on interface bandwidth by default).
- Sends partial route updates only when changes occur.
- Routes are labeled as intra-area, inter-area, external Type 1, or external Type 2.
- Uses IPv6 for authentication.
- Uses the Dijkstra algorithm to calculate the SPF tree.
- Default administrative distance is 110.
- Uses multicast address FF02::5 (ALLSPFRouters).
- Uses multicast address FF02::6 (ALLDRouters).
- Fast convergence, scalable, and reduces bandwidth.
- Recommended for large IPv6 networks.

BGP

This section covers Border Gateway Protocol theory and design concepts. The current version of BGP, Version 4, is defined in RFC 4271 (January 2006). BGP is an interdomain routing protocol. What this means is that you use BGP to exchange routing information between autonomous systems. (It is used for inter-autonomous system routing.) The primary function of BGP is to provide and exchange network-reachability information between domains or autonomous systems. BGP is a path-vector protocol. BGP is best suited for setting routing policies between autonomous systems. In the enterprise campus architecture, BGP is used in the Internet connectivity module.

BGP is the de facto standard for routing between service providers on the Internet because of its rich features. You can also use it to exchange routes in large internal networks. The Internet Assigned Numbers Authority (IANA) reserved TCP port 179 to identify the BGP protocol. BGPv4 was created to provide CIDR, a feature that was not present in the earlier versions of BGP. BGP is a path-vector routing protocol; it is neither a distance-vector nor link-state routing protocol.

11

> **Note** RFC 1519 describes CIDR, which provides the capability to forward packets based on IP prefixes only, with no concern for IP address class boundaries. CIDR was created as a means to constrain the growth of the routing tables in the Internet core through the summarization of IP addresses across network class boundaries. The early 1990s saw an increase in the growth of Internet routing tables and a reduction in Class B address space. CIDR provides a way for service providers to assign address blocks smaller than a Class B network but larger than a Class C network.

BGP Neighbors

BGP is usually configured between two directly connected routers that belong to different autonomous systems. Each autonomous system is under different technical administration. BGP is frequently used to connect the enterprise to service providers and to interconnect service providers, as shown in Figure 11-9. The routing protocol within the enterprise could be any Interior Gateway Protocol (IGP). Common IGP choices include RIPv2, EIGRP, OSPF, and IS-IS. BGPv4 is the only deployed Exterior Gateway Protocol (EGP).

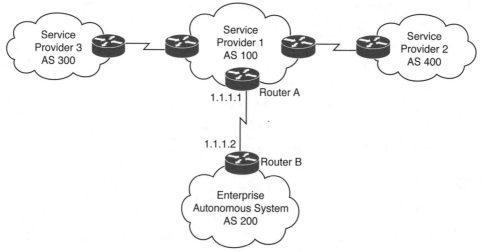

Figure 11-9 *BGP neighbors*

BGP is an interdomain routing protocol that allows BGP speakers residing in different autonomous systems to exchange routing (NLRI) information. An autonomous system is a collection of devices under common administration. BGP autonomous systems range from 1 through 65,535. Autonomous system numbers (ASN) 1 through 64,511 are considered public ASNs. These are allocated by IANA to Regional Internet Registries (RIR). Entities wanting to receive an ASN must complete the application process of their local RIR and be approved before being assigned an ASN. ASNs 65,512 through 65,535 are considered private ASNs. These ASNs can be used by any organization, but, like RFC 1918 addresses, cannot be used on the Internet.

Before two BGP routers can exchange routing updates, they must become established neighbors. After BGP routers establish a TCP connection, exchange information, and accept the information, they become established neighbors and start exchanging routing updates. If the neighbors do not reach an established state, they do not exchange BGP updates. The information exchanged before the neighbors are established includes the BGP version number, ASN, BGP router ID, and BGP capabilities.

eBGP

External Border Gateway Protocol is the term used to describe BGP peering between neighbors in different autonomous systems. As required by RFC 1771, the eBGP peers share a common subnet (although Cisco does allow some flexibility to avoid doing so). In Figure 11-10, all routers speak eBGP with routers in other autonomous systems. Within autonomous system 500, the routers communicate using iBGP, which is covered next.

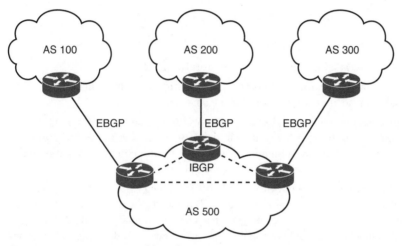

Figure 11-10   *eBGP used between autonomous systems*

iBGP

Internal Border Gateway Protocol is the term used to describe the peering between BGP neighbors in the same autonomous system. iBGP is used primarily in transit autonomous systems. Transit autonomous systems forward traffic from one external autonomous system to another external autonomous system. If transit autonomous systems did not use iBGP, the eBGP-learned routes would have to be redistributed into an IGP and then redistributed into the BGP process in another eBGP router. Normally, the number of eBGP routes is too large for an IGP to handle.

iBGP provides a better way to control the routes within the transit autonomous system. With iBGP, the external route information (attributes) is forwarded. The various IGPs that might be used do not understand or forward BGP attributes, including autonomous system paths, between eBGP routers.

Another use of iBGP is in large corporations where the IGP networks are in smaller independent routing domains along organizational or geographic boundaries. In Figure 11-11, a company has decided to use three independent IGPs: one for the Americas; another for Asia and Australia; and another for Europe, the Middle East, and Africa. Routes are redistributed into an iBGP core.

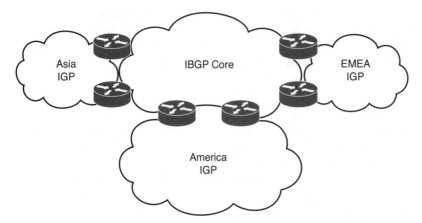

Figure 11-11 *iBGP in a large corporation*

The CCDA should know at a high level these other uses for iBGP:

■ **Applying policies in the internal autonomous system with the help of BGP path attributes:** BGP path attributes are covered in a later section.

■ **QoS policy propagation on BGP (QPPB):** QPPB uses iBGP to spread common QoS parameters from one router to other routers in the network. It classifies packets using IP precedence bits based on BGP community lists, BGP autonomous system paths, and access lists. After packets are classified, QoS features can enforce policies.

■ **Multiprotocol BGP peering of Multiprotocol Label Switching (MPLS) virtual private networks (VPNs):** The multiprotocol version of BGP is used to carry MPLS VPN information between all provider edge (PE) routers within a VPN community. MP-BGP is defined in RFC 2858. It introduces a new BGP capabilities advertisement to determine whether a BGP peer supports MP-BGP. It introduces optional nontransitive attributes used to advertise feasible routes to a peer, network layer reachability information, and other characteristics. It defines an address family identifier (AFI) of 2 to identify IPv6, which is used to convey an IPv4 address as the BGP next hop for the advertised IPv6 prefixes.

Route Reflectors

iBGP requires that all routers be configured to establish a logical connection with all other iBGP routers. The logical connection is a TCP link between all iBGP-speaking routers. The routers in each TCP link become BGP peers. In large networks, the number of iBGP-meshed peers can become very large. Network administrators can use route reflectors to reduce the number of required mesh links between iBGP peers. Some routers are selected to become the route reflectors to serve several other routers that act as route-reflector clients. Route reflectors allow a router to advertise or reflect routes to clients. The route reflector and its clients form a cluster. All client routers in the cluster peer with the route reflectors within the cluster. The route reflectors also peer with all other route reflectors in the internetwork. A cluster can have more than one route reflector.

In Figure 11-12, without route reflectors, all iBGP routers are configured in an iBGP mesh, as required by the protocol. When Routers A and G become route reflectors, they peer with Routers C and D; Router B becomes a route reflector for Routers E and F. Routers A, B, and G peer among each other.

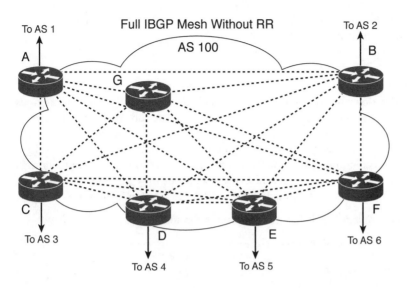

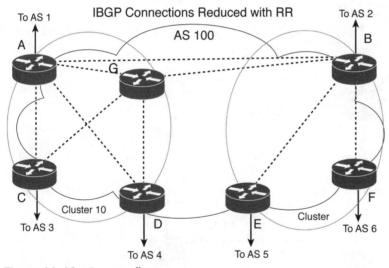

Figure 11-12 *Route reflectors*

11

> **Note** The combination of the route reflector and its clients is called a cluster. In Figure
> 11-12, Routers A, G, C, and D form a cluster. Routers B, E, and F form another cluster.

Routers A and G are configured to peer with each other and with Routers B, C, and D. The
configuration of Routers C and D is different from the rest; they are configured to peer
with Routers A and G only. All route reflectors in the same cluster must have the same cluster ID number.

Router B is the route reflector for the second cluster. Router B peers with Routers A and G
and with Routers E and F in its cluster. Routers E and F are route-reflector clients and peer

only with Router B. If Router B goes down, the cluster on the right goes down because no second route reflector is configured.

Confederations

Another method to reduce the iBGP mesh within an autonomous system is BGP confederations. With confederations, the autonomous system is divided into smaller, sub-autonomous systems, and the whole group is assigned a confederation ID. The sub-ASNs or identifiers are not advertised to the Internet but are contained within the iBGP networks. The routers within each private autonomous system are configured with the full iBGP mesh. Each sub-autonomous system is configured with eBGP to communicate with other sub-autonomous systems in the confederation. External autonomous systems see only the ASN of the confederation, and this number is configured with the BGP confederation identifier.

In Figure 11-13, a confederation divides the autonomous system into two.

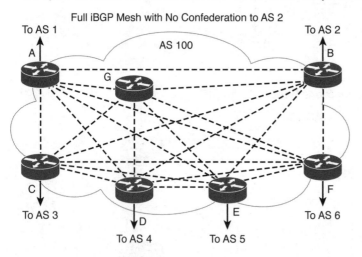

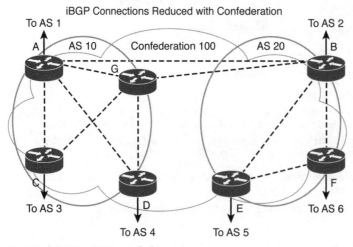

Figure 11-13 *BGP confederations*

Routers A, B, and G are configured for eBGP between the sub-autonomous systems. You configure the **bgp confederation identifier** command on all routers The confederation identifier number is the same for all routers in the network. You use the **bgp confederation peers** command to identify the ASN of other sub-autonomous systems in the confederation. Because Routers A and G are in autonomous system 10, the peer confederation to Router B is autonomous system 20. Router B is in autonomous system 20, and its peer confederation to Routers A and G is autonomous system 10. Routers C and D are part of autonomous system 10 and peer with each other and with Routers A and G. Routers E and F are part of autonomous system 20 and peer with each other and with Router B.

BGP Administrative Distance

The Cisco IOS software assigns an administrative distance to eBGP and iBGP routes, as it does with other routing protocols. For the same prefix, the route with the lowest administrative distance is selected for inclusion in the IP forwarding table. For BGP, the administrative distances are

- eBGP routes: 20
- iBGP routes: 200

BGP Attributes, Weight, and the BGP Decision Process

The BGP protocol uses path attributes to select the best path to a destination. This subsection describes BGP attributes, the use of weight to influence path selection, and the BGP decision process.

BGP Path Attributes

BGP uses several attributes for the path-selection process. BGP uses path attributes to communicate routing policies. BGP path attributes include next hop, local preference, autonomous system path, origin, multi-exit discriminator (MED), atomic aggregate, and aggregator. Of these, the autonomous system path is one of the most important attributes: It lists the number of autonomous system paths to reach a destination network.

BGP attributes can be categorized as *well known* or *optional*. Well-known attributes are recognized by all BGP implementations. Optional attributes do not have to be supported by the BGP process.

Well-known attributes can be further subcategorized as *mandatory* or *discretionary*. Mandatory attributes are always included in BGP update messages. Discretionary attributes might or might not be included in the BGP update message.

Optional attributes can be further subcategorized as *transitive* or *nontransitive*. Routers must advertise the route with transitive attributes to its peers even if it does not support the attribute locally. If the path attribute is nontransitive, the router does not have to advertise the route to its peers.

The following subsections cover each attribute category.

11

Next-Hop Attribute

The next-hop attribute is the IP address of the next IP hop that will be used to reach the destination. The next-hop attribute is a well-known mandatory attribute.

Local Preference Attribute

The local preference attribute indicates which path to use to exit the autonomous system. It is a well-known discretionary attribute used between iBGP peers and is not passed on to external BGP peers. In Cisco IOS Software, the default local preference is 100. The higher local preference is preferred.

The default local preference is configured on the BGP router with an external path; it then advertises its local preference to internal iBGP peers. Figure 11-14 shows an example of the local preference attribute where Routers B and C are configured with different local preference values. Router A and other iBGP routers then receive routes from both Router B and Router C. Between the two possible paths (shown with arrows), Router A prefers using Router C to route Internet packets because it has a higher local preference (400) than Router B (300).

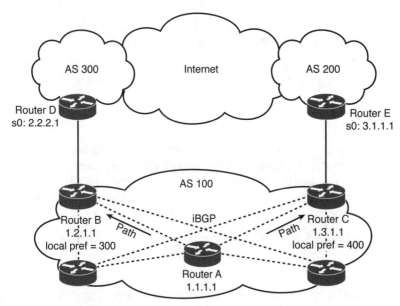

Figure 11-14   *BGP local preference*

Origin Attribute

Origin is a well-known mandatory attribute that defines the source of the path information. Do not confuse the origin with comparing whether the route is external (eBGP) or internal (iBGP). The origin attribute is received from the source BGP router. There are three types:

- **IGP:** Indicated by an *i* in the BGP table. Present when the route is learned by way of the network statement.

- **EGP:** Indicated by an *e* in the BGP table. Learned from EGP.

■ **Incomplete:** Indicated by a question mark (?) in the BGP table. Learned from redistribution of the route.

In terms of choosing a route based on origin, BGP prefers routes that have been verified by an IGP over routes that have been learned from EGP peers, and BGP prefers routes learned from eBGP peers over incomplete paths.

Autonomous System Path Attribute

The autonomous system path is a well-known mandatory attribute that contains a list of ASNs in the path to the destination. Each autonomous system prepends its own ASN to the autonomous system path. The autonomous system path describes all the autonomous systems a packet would have to travel to reach the destination IP network. It is used to ensure that the path is loop free. When the autonomous system path attribute is used to select a path, the route with the fewest autonomous system hops is preferred. In the case of a tie, other attributes, such as MED, break the tie. Example 11-1 shows the autonomous system path for network 200.50.32.0/19. To reach the destination, a packet must pass autonomous systems 3561, 7004, and 7418. The command **show ip bgp 200.50.32.0** displays the autonomous system path information.

Example 11-1   *Autonomous System Path Attribute*

```
Router# show ip bgp 200.50.32.0
BGP routing table entry for 200.50.32.0/19, version 93313535
Paths: (1 available, best #1)
 Not advertised to any peer
 3561 7004 7418
   206.24.241.181 (metric 490201) from 165.117.1.219 (165.117.1.219)
     Origin IGP, metric 4294967294, localpref 100, valid, internal, best
     Community: 2548:182 2548:337 2548:666 3706:153
```

MED Attribute

The MED attribute, also known as a metric, tells an external BGP peer the preferred path into the autonomous system when multiple paths into the same autonomous system exist. In other words, MED influences which one of many paths a neighboring autonomous system uses to reach destinations within the autonomous system. It is an optional nontransitive attribute carried in eBGP updates. The MED attribute is not used with iBGP peers. The lowest MED value is preferred, and the default value is 0. Paths received with no MED are assigned a MED of 0. The MED is carried into an autonomous system but does not leave the autonomous system.

Consider the diagram shown in Figure 11-15. With all attributes considered equal, consider that Router C selects Router A as its best path into autonomous system 100 based on Router A's lower router ID (RID). If Router A is configured with a MED of 200, that will make Router C select Router B as the best path to autonomous system 100. No additional configuration is required on Router B because the default MED is 0.

11

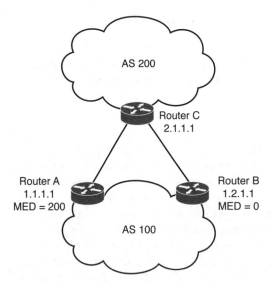

Figure 11-15   *MED attribute*

Community Attribute

Although it is not an attribute used in the routing-decision process, the community attribute groups routes and applies policies or decisions (accept, prefer) to those routes. It is a group of destinations that share some common property. The community attribute is an optional transitive attribute of variable length.

Atomic Aggregate and Aggregator Attributes

The atomic aggregate attribute informs BGP peers that the local router used a less specific (aggregated) route to a destination without using a more specific route.

The purpose of the attribute is to alert BGP speakers along the path that some information has been lost due to the route aggregation process and that the aggregate path might not be the best path to the destination. When some routes are aggregated by an aggregator, the aggregator does attach its Router-ID to the aggregated route in the AGGREGATOR _ ID attribute, and it sets the ATOMIC _ AGGREGATE attribute (or not) based on whether or not the AS _ PATH information of the aggregated routes was preserved. The atomic aggregate attribute lets the BGP peers know that the BGP router used an aggregated route. A more-specific route must be in the advertising router's BGP table before it propagates an aggregate route.

When the atomic aggregate attribute is used, the BGP speaker has the option to send the aggregator attribute. The aggregator attribute includes the ASN and the IP address of the router that originated the aggregated route. In Cisco routers, the IP address used is the RID of the router that performs the route aggregation. Atomic aggregate is a well-known discretionary attribute, and aggregator is an optional transitive attribute.

Weight

Weight is assigned locally on a router to specify a preferred path if multiple paths exist out of a router for a destination. Weights can be applied to individual routes or to all routes received from a peer. Weight is specific to Cisco routers and is not propagated to other routers. The weight value ranges from 0 to 65,535. Routes with a higher weight are preferred when multiple routes exist to a destination. Routes that are originated by the local router have a default weight of 32,768. The default weight for learned routes is 0.

You can use weight rather than local preference to influence the selected path to external BGP peers. The difference is that weight is configured locally and is not exchanged in BGP updates. On the other hand, the local preference attribute is exchanged between iBGP peers and is configured at the gateway router.

When the same destinations are advertised from both Router B and Router C, as shown in Figure 11-16, Router A prefers the routes from Router C over Router B because the routes received from Router C have a larger weight (600) locally assigned.

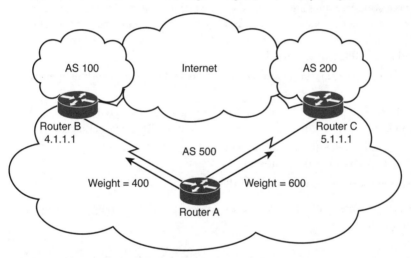

Figure 11-16 *BGP weight*

BGP Decision Process

By default, BGP selects only a single path to reach a specific destination (unless you specify maximum paths). The Cisco implementation of BGP uses a simple decision process. When the path is selected, BGP puts the selected path in its routing table and propagates the path to its neighbors.

To select the best path to a destination, Cisco routers running BGP use the following algorithm in the following order:

1. If the specified next hop is inaccessible, drop the path.

2. If the path is internal, and synchronization is enabled, and the path is not in the IGP, drop the path.

3. Prefer the path with the highest weight. (This step is Cisco specific, and weight is localized to the router.)

4. Prefer the path with the highest local preference. **iBGP** uses this path only to reach the preferred external BGP router.

5. Prefer the path that was locally originated via a **network** or **aggregate** BGP subcommand or through redistribution from an IGP. Local paths sourced by **network** or **redistribute** commands are preferred over local aggregates sourced by the **aggregate-address** command. (This step is Cisco specific.)

6. If no route was originated, prefer the route that has the shortest autonomous system path.

7. If all paths have the same autonomous system path length, prefer the path with the lowest origin type. Paths with an origin type of IGP (lower) are preferred over paths originated from an EGP such as BGP, and EGP origin is preferred over a route with an incomplete origin. (IGP < EGP < incomplete.)

8. If the origin codes are the same, prefer the path with the lowest MED attribute. An eBGP peer uses this attribute to select a best path to the autonomous system. This attribute is exchanged between autonomous systems. (This step is a tiebreaker, as described in the RFC that defines the BGP.)

9. If the paths have the same MED, prefer the external (eBGP) path over the internal (iBGP) path.

10. If the paths are still the same, prefer the path through the closest IGP neighbor (best IGP metric). (This step is a tiebreaker, as described in the RFC that defines the BGP.)

11. Prefer the path with the BGP neighbor with the lowest BGP router ID. (The RFC that defines the BGP describes the router ID.)

12. Prefer the path with the lowest neighbor IP address.

After BGP decides on a best path, it marks it with a > sign in the **show ip bgp** table and adds it to the IP routing table.

> **Note** Options for influencing outbound routing decisions include Weight, Local Preference, and AS Path Length. Options for influencing inbound routing decisions include AS Path Length, BGP Communities, and MED.

BGP Summary

The characteristics of BGP follow:

- BGP is an Exterior Gateway Protocol (EGP) used in routing in the Internet. It is an inter-domain routing protocol.

- BGP is a path-vector routing protocol suited for strategic routing policies.

- It uses TCP port 179 to establish connections with neighbors.

- BGPv4 implements CIDR.

- eBGP is used for external neighbors. It is used between different autonomous systems.

- iBGP is used for internal neighbors. It is used within an autonomous system.

- BGP uses several attributes in the routing-decision algorithm.

- It uses confederations and route reflectors to reduce BGP peering overhead.

- The MED (metric) attribute is used between autonomous systems to influence inbound traffic.

- Weight is used to influence the path of outbound traffic from a single router, configured locally.

Route Manipulation

This section covers policy-based routing (PBR), route summarization, route filtering, and route redistribution. You can use PBR to modify the next hop of packets from what is selected by the routing protocol. PBR is useful when the traffic engineering of paths is required. Routes are summarized to reduce the size of routing tables and at network boundaries. Redistribution between routing protocols is required to inject route information from one routing protocol to another. Route filtering is used to control network addresses that get redistributed or to control access to certain parts of the network. The CCDA must understand the issues with the redistribution of routes.

PBR

You can use PBR to modify the next-hop address of packets or to mark packets to receive differential service. Routing is based on destination addresses; routers look at the routing table to determine the next-hop IP address based on a destination lookup. PBR is commonly used to modify the next-hop IP address based on the source address. You can also use PBR to mark the IP precedence bits in outbound IP packets so that you can apply QoS policies. In Figure 11-17, Router A exchanges routing updates with routers in the WAN. The routing protocol might select Serial 0 as the preferred path for all traffic because of the higher bandwidth. The company might have business-critical systems that use the T1 but does not want systems on Ethernet 1 to affect WAN performance. You can configure PBR on Router A to force traffic from Ethernet 1 out on Serial 1.

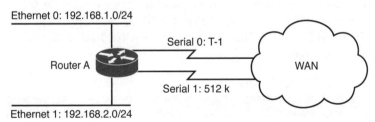

Figure 11-17 *Policy-based routing*

Route Summarization

Large networks can grow quickly, from 500 routes to 1000, to 2000, and higher. Network IP addresses should be allocated to allow for route summarization. Route summarization reduces the amount of route traffic on the network, unnecessary route computation, and the perceived complexity of the network. Route summarization also allows the network to scale as a company grows.

The recommended location for route summarization is to summarize at the distribution layer of the network topology. Figure 11-18 shows a hierarchical network. It has a network core, regional distribution routers, and access routes for sites.

All routes in Brazil are summarized with a single 10.1.0.0/16 route. The North American and European routes are also summarized with 10.2.0.0/16 and 10.3.0.0/16, respectively. Routers in Europe need to know only the summarized route to get to Brazil and North America, and vice versa. Again, a design best practice is to summarize at the distribution toward the core. The core needs to know only the summarized route of the regional areas.

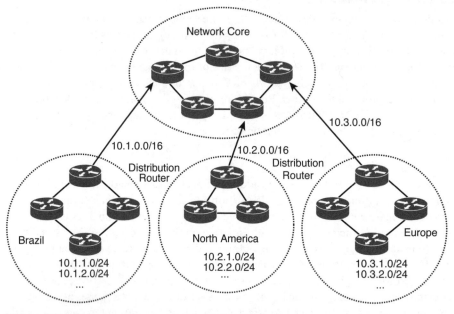

Figure 11-18   *Route summarization to the network core*

You can also use summarization to aggregate four contiguous Class C networks at the /22 bit level. For example, networks 200.1.100.0, 200.1.101.0, 200.1.102.0, and 200.1.103.0 share common bits, as shown in Table 11-7. The resulting network is 200.1.100.0/22, which you can use for a 1000-node network.

Table 11-7   Common Bits Within Class C Networks

Binary Address	IP Address
11001000 00000001 01100100 00000000	200.1.100.0
11001000 00000001 01100101 00000000	200.1.101.0
11001000 00000001 01100110 00000000	200.1.102.0
11001000 00000001 01100111 00000000	200.1.103.0

It is important for an Internet network designer to assign IP networks in a manner that permits summarization. It is preferred that a neighboring router receive one summarized route, rather than 8, 16, 32, or more routes, depending on the level of summarization. This setup reduces the size of the routing tables in the network.

For route summarization to work, the multiple IP addresses must share the same leftmost bits, and routers must base their routing decisions on the IP address and prefix length. Figure 11-19 shows another example of route summarization. All the edge routers send network information to their upstream routers. Router E summarizes its two LAN networks by sending 192.168.16.0/23 to Router A. Router F summarizes its two LAN networks by sending 192.168.18.0/23. Router B summarizes the networks it receives from Routers C and D. Routers B, E, and F send their routes to Router A. Router A sends a single route (192.168.16.0/21) to its upstream router, instead of sending eight routes. This process reduces the number of networks that upstream routers need to include in routing updates.

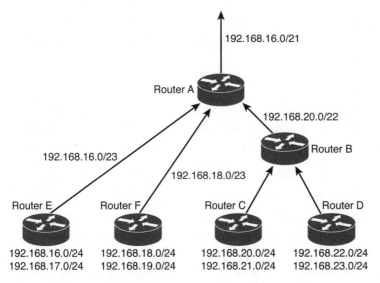

Figure 11-19 *Route summarization of networks*

Notice in Table 11-8 that all the Class C networks share a bit boundary with 21 common bits. The networks are different on the 22nd bit and thus cannot be summarized beyond the 21st bit. All these networks are summarized with 192.168.16.0/21.

Table 11-8   Summarization of Networks

Binary Address	IP Network
11000000 10101000 00010000 00000000	192.168.16.0
11000000 10101000 00010001 00000000	192.168.17.0
11000000 10101000 00010010 00000000	192.168.18.0
11000000 10101000 00010011 00000000	192.168.19.0

Binary Address	IP Network
11000000 10101000 00010100 00000000	192.168.20.0
11000000 10101000 00010101 00000000	192.168.21.0
11000000 10101000 00010110 00000000	192.168.22.0
11000000 10101000 00010111 00000000	192.168.23.0

To summarize, the recommended practices regarding summarization include the following:

- Implement summarization at WAN connectivity and remote-access points toward the network core, to reduce the routing table size.

- Summarize at the distribution layer for all network interfaces that point to the network core.

- Implement passive interfaces on access layer interfaces so that neighbor adjacencies are not established through the access layer. A more-specific route might be created, which would be taken over a summarized route.

Route Redistribution

Route redistribution is an exchange of routes between routing protocols (for example, between EIGRP and OSPF). You configure the redistribution of routing protocols on routers that reside at the service provider edge of the network or an autonomous system boundary within the internal network. These routers exchange routes with other autonomous systems. Redistribution is also done on routers that run more than one routing protocol. Here are some reasons to do redistribution:

- Migration from an older routing protocol to a new routing protocol.

- Mixed-vendor environment in which Cisco routers might be using EIGRP and other vendor routers might be using OSPF.

- Different administrative domain between company departments using different routing protocols.

- Mergers and acquisitions in which the networks initially need to communicate. In this scenario, two different EIGRP processes might exist.

Routes can be learned from different sources. The first is a static route that is configured when not peering with the AS-external router. Another source is a different routing protocol where you might be running EIGRP and the other network uses OSPF. Another common example is when peering with an ISP, the enterprise is commonly using OSPF and your Internet routers peer with the ISP router using BGP.

Figure 11-20 shows an example of the exchange of routes between two autonomous systems. Routes from autonomous system 100 are redistributed into BGP on Router A. Routes from autonomous system 200 are redistributed into BGP on Router B. Then, Routers A and B exchange BGP routes. Router A and Router B also implement filters to redistribute only the desired networks.

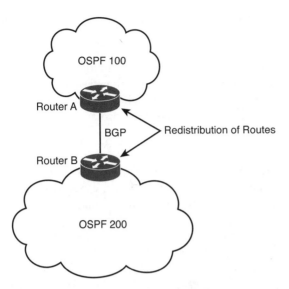

Figure 11-20 *IDS and IPS operational differences*

A company might also acquire another company that might be running another routing protocol. Figure 11-21 shows a network that has both OSPF and EIGRP routing protocols. Routers A and B perform redistribution between OSPF and EIGRP. Both routers must filter routes from OSPF before redistributing them into EIGRP and filter routes from EIGRP before redistributing them into OSPF. This setup prevents route feedback.

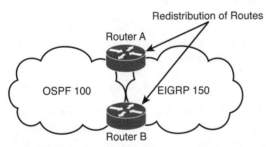

Figure 11-21 *Redistribution between IGPs*

Route feedback occurs when a routing protocol learns routes from another routing protocol and then announces the routes to the other routing protocol. In Figure 11-21, OSPF should not advertise the routes it learned from EIGRP on Router A back to EIGRP on Router B. And EIGRP should not announce the routes it learned from OSPF on Router B back to OSPF on Router A.

You can use access lists, distribution lists, and route maps when redistributing routes. You can use these methods to specify (select) routes for redistribution, to set metrics, or to set other policies for the routes. They are used to prevent loops in the redistribution. They are also used to control routes' redistribution direction. Redistribution can be accomplished by two methods:

11

- Two-way redistribution
- One-way redistribution

In two-way redistribution, routing information is exchanged between both routing protocols. No static routes are used in this exchange. Route filters are used to prevent routing loops. Routing loops can be caused by one route protocol redistributing routes that were learned from a second route protocol back to that second routing protocol.

One-way redistribution only allows redistribution from one routing protocol to another. Normally, it is used in conjunction with a default or static route at the edge of a network. Figure 11-22 shows an example of one-way redistribution. The routing information from the WAN routes is redistributed into the campus, but campus routes are not redistributed out to the WAN. The WAN routers use a default route to get back to the campus.

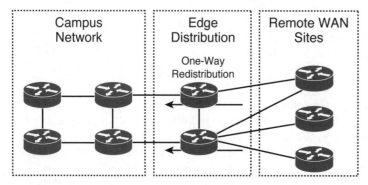

Figure 11-22   *One-way route redistribution*

Other locations for one-way redistribution are from building access networks, BGP routes or static routes into the IGP, and from VPN static routes into the IGP.

Default Metric

You should configure the metric of the redistributed routes to a metric other than 0. You can configure the metric in the **redistribution** command or configure a default seed metric. You can also use the command in OSPF. IS-IS does not use the **default-metric** command. The **default-metric** command is used to specify the seed metric that is used if one is not specified during redistribution The **default-metric** command has the following syntax for EIGRP:

```
default-metric bandwidth delay reliability load mtu
```

OSPF Redistribution

This subsection reviews a few things you need to remember when designing a network that will redistribute with OSPF.

When redistributing routes into OSPF, use the **subnets** keyword to permit subnetted routes to be received. If you do not use it, only the major network route is redistributed, without any subnetworks. In other words, OSPF performs automatic summarization to IP classful network values. Also, unlike EIGRP and RIPv2, OSPF does not need a metric to be specified during redistribution; neither does it need a seed metric to be specified because it uses a default metric for redistributed routes.

By default, redistributed routes are classified as external Type 2 (E2) in OSPF. You can use the **metric-type** keyword to change the external route to an external Type 1 (E1). The network design can take into account the after-redistribution cost (Type 2) or the after-redistribution cost plus the path's cost (Type 1).

In Figure 11-23, Router B is configured to perform mutual redistribution between EIGRP 100 and OSPF process ID 50. In this example, you can use route maps and access lists to prevent routing loops. The route maps permit or deny the networks that are listed in the access lists. The **subnets** keyword redistributes every subnet in EIGRP into OSPF. This book does not cover exact configurations.

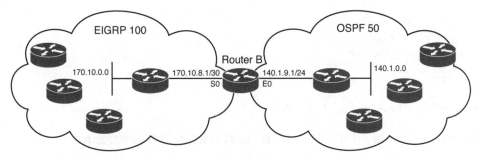

Figure 11-23   *OSPF and EIGRP redistribution*

Route Filtering

Filtering of routes can occur on either a redistribution point or in the routing domain to prevent some parts of the network from accessing other sections of the network. Route filtering is used to filter routes at the redistribution of BGP into IGPs such as OSPF, EIGRP, or IS-IS.

Filtering at a redistribution point provides the following benefits:

- Avoids routing loops
- Avoids suboptimal routing
- Prevents certain routes from entering the domain

Transit Traffic

With BGP, you should be attentive to not configure your network as a transit network between autonomous systems. This commonly occurs when you connect your enterprise network to two ISPs in a multihomed BGP configuration. When BGP routes get exchanged with multiple Internet service providers (ISPs), route filtering is used to prevent advertisement of private addresses and addresses that are out of scope of the domain. The recommendation is to filter routes so that only the enterprise prefixes are advertised to the ISPs, as illustrated in Figure 11-24.

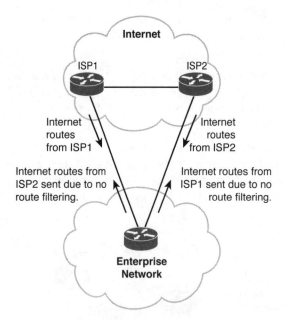

Figure 11-24   *Avoiding BGP transit traffic*

Routing Protocols on the Hierarchical Network Infrastructure

The selected routing protocol should be used based on the network design goals and the network module being used. As shown in Figure 11-25, high-speed routing is recommended for the network core and distribution layers. These routing protocols react fast to network changes. It is a best practice that the same routing protocol be used in the three layers (core, distribution, access) of the enterprise network.

The enterprise edge connects the campus network with external connectivity, including WAN, Internet, VPN, and remote-access modules. Routing protocols in the enterprise edge may be EIGRP, OSPF, BGP, and static routes. Specifically in the Internet module you will find BGP/static routes.

Table 11-9 shows a summary of the recommended routing protocols in the network infrastructure.

Table 11-9   Routing Protocols on the Hierarchical Network Infrastructure

Network Module	Routing Protocols
Campus core	EIGRP, OSPF
Campus distribution	EIGRP, OSPF
Enterprise edge	EIGRP, OSPF, BGP, Static
Internet and VPN modules	BGP, Static

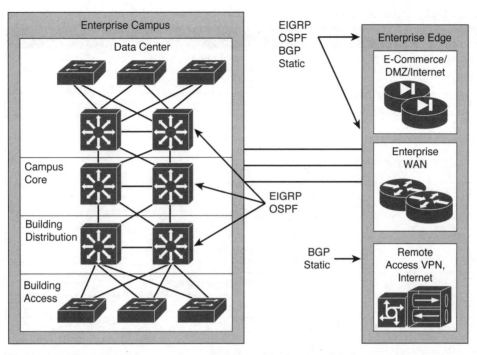

Figure 11-25 *Routing protocols on the hierarchical network infrastructure*

IP Multicast Review

With multicast, packets are sent to a multicast group, which is identified with an IP multicast address. Multicast supports the transmission of IP packets from one source to multiple hosts. Packets with unicast addresses are sent to one device, and broadcast addresses are sent to all hosts; packets with multicast addresses are sent to a group of hosts.

Multicast Addresses

Multicast addressing uses Class D addresses from the IPv4 protocol. Class D addresses range from 224.0.0.0 to 239.255.255.255. IANA manages multicast addresses.

Routing protocols (RIPv2, EIGRP, and OSPF) use multicast addresses to speak to their neighbors. For example, OSPF routers use 224.0.0.6 to speak to the designated router (DR) in a multiaccess network. Class D multicast addresses range from 224.0.0.0 to 239.255.255.255. Multicast addresses in the range of 224.0.0.1 to 224.255.255.255 are reserved for special addresses or network protocols on a multiaccess link. RFC 2365 reserves multicast addresses in the range of 239.192.000.000 to 239.251.255.255 for organization-local scope. Similarly, 239.252.000.000 to 239.252.255.255, 239.254.000.000 to 239.254.255.255, and 239.255.000.000 to 239.255.255.255 are reserved for site-local scope.

Table 11-10 lists some well-known and multicast address blocks.

11

Table 11-10   Multicast Addresses

Multicast Address	Description
224.0.0.0/24	Local network control block
224.0.0.1	All hosts or all systems on this subnet
224.0.0.2	All multicast routers
224.0.0.4	Distance-Vector Multicast Routing Protocol (DVMRP) routers
224.0.0.5	All OSPF routers
224.0.0.6	All OSPF DR routers
224.0.0.9	RIPv2 routers
224.0.0.10	EIGRP routers
224.0.0.13	All PIM routers
224.0.1.0/24	Internetwork control block
224.0.1.39	Rendezvous point (RP) announce
224.0.1.40	RP discovery
224.0.2.0 to 224.0.255.0	Ad hoc block
239.000.000.000 to 239.255.255.255	Administratively scoped
239.192.000.000 to 239.251.255.255	Organization-local scope
239.252.000.000 to 239.254.255.255	Site-local scope

Layer 3 to Layer 2 Mapping

Multicast-aware Ethernet, Token Ring, and Fiber Distributed Data Interface (FDDI) network interface cards use the reserved IEEE 802 address 0100.5e00 for multicast addresses at the MAC layer. This includes Fast Ethernet and Gigabit Ethernet. Notice that for the address, the high-order byte 0x01 has the low-order bit set to 1. This bit is the Individual/Group (I/G) bit. It signifies whether the address is an individual address (0) or a group address (1). Hence, for multicast addresses, this bit is set to 1.

Ethernet interfaces map the lower 23 bits of the IP multicast address to the lower 23 bits of the MAC address 0100.5e00.0000. As an example, the IP multicast address 224.0.0.2 is mapped to the MAC layer as 0100.5e00.0002. Figure 11-26 shows another example looking at the bits of multicast IP 239.192.44.56. The IP address in hexadecimal is EF:C0:2C:38. The lower 23 bits get mapped into the lower 23 bits of the base multicast MAC to produce the multicast MAC address 01:00:5E:40:2C:38.

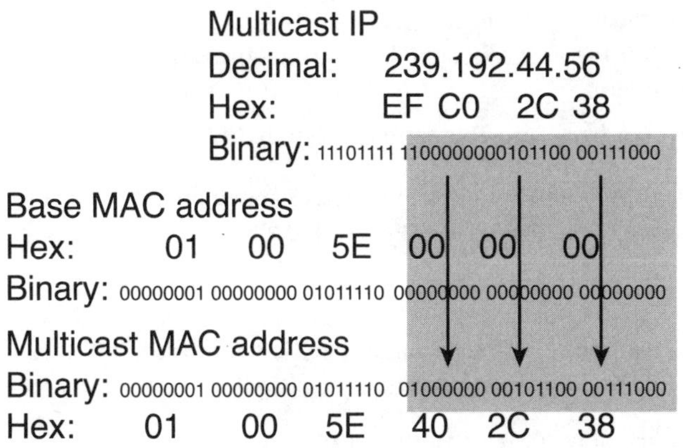

Multicast IP
Decimal: 239.192.44.56
Hex: EF C0   2C 38
Binary: 11101111 1100000000101100 00111000

Base MAC address
Hex: 01   00   5E   00   00   00
Binary: 00000001 00000000 01011110 00000000 00000000 00000000

Multicast MAC address
Binary: 00000001 00000000 01011110 01000000 00101100 00111000
Hex: 01   00   5E   40   2C   38

Figure 11-26 *Mapping of multicast IP addressing to MAC addresses*

IGMP

Internet Group Management Protocol is the protocol used in multicast implementations between the end hosts and the local router. RFC 2236 describes IGMP Version 2 (IGMPv2). RFC 3376 describes IGMP Version 3 (IGMPv3). RFC 1112 describes the first version of IGMP.

IP hosts use IGMP to report their multicast group memberships to routers. IGMP messages use IP protocol number 2. IGMP messages are limited to the local interface and are not routed.

IGMPv1

The first RFC describing IGMP (RFC 1112), written in 1989, describes the host extensions for IP multicasting. IGMPv1 provides simple message types for communication between hosts and routers. These messages are

- **Membership query:** Sent by the router to check whether a host wants to join a multicast group
- **Membership report:** Sent by the host to join a multicast group in the segment

The problem with IGMPv1 is the latency involved for a host to leave a group. With IGMPv1, the router sends membership queries periodically; a host must wait for the membership query message to leave a group. The query interval is 60 seconds, and it takes three query intervals (3 minutes) for a host to leave the group.

IGMPv2

IGMPv2 improves on IGMPv1 by allowing faster termination or leaving of multicast groups.

IGMPv2 has three message types, plus one for backward compatibility:

- **Membership query:** Sent by the router to check whether a host wants to join a group.
- **Version 2 membership report:** A message sent to the group address with the multicast group members (IP addresses). It is sent by hosts to join and remain in multicast groups on the segment.

11

- **Version 2 leave group:** Sent by the hosts to indicate that a host will leave a group; it is sent to destination 224.0.0.2. After the host sends the leave group message, the router responds with a group-specific query.
- **Version 1 membership report:** For backward compatibility with IGMPv1 hosts.

You enable IGMP on an interface when you configure a multicast routing protocol, such as PIM. You can configure the interface for IGMPv1, IGMPv2, or IGMPv3.

IGMPv3

IGMPv3 provides the extensions required to support source-specific multicast (SSM). It is designed to be backward compatible with both earlier versions of IGMP.

IGMPv3 has two message types, plus three for backward compatibility:

- **Membership query:** Sent by the router to check that a host wants to join a group.
- **Version 3 membership report:** A message sent to the group address with the multicast group members (IP addresses). It is sent by hosts to request and remain in multicast groups on the segment.
- **Version 2 membership report:** A message sent to the group address with the multicast group members (IP addresses). It is sent by hosts to request and remain in multicast groups on the segment. This message is used for backward compatibility with IGMPv2 hosts.
- **Version 2 leave group:** Sent by the hosts to indicate that a host will leave a group, to destination 224.0.0.2. The message is sent without having to wait for the IGMPv2 membership report message. This message is used for backward compatibility with IGMPv2 hosts.
- **Version 1 membership report:** A message used for backward compatibility with IGMPv1 hosts.

You enable IGMP on an interface when you enable a multicast routing protocol, such as PIM. You can configure the interface for IGMPv1, IGMPv2, or IGMPv3.

CGMP

CGMP is a Cisco proprietary protocol implemented to control multicast traffic at Layer 2. Because a Layer 2 switch is unaware of Layer 3 IGMP messages, it cannot keep multicast packets from being sent to all ports.

As shown in Figure 11-27, with CGMP the LAN switch can speak with the IGMP router to find out the MAC addresses of the hosts that want to receive the multicast packets. With CGMP, switches distribute multicast sessions only to the switch ports that have group members.

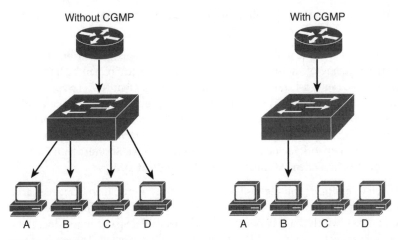

Figure 11-27 *CGMP*

When a router receives an IGMP report, it processes the report and then sends a CGMP message to the switch. The switch can then forward the multicast messages to the port with the host receiving multicast traffic. CGMP fast-leave processing allows the switch to detect IGMP Version 2 leave messages sent by hosts on any of the switch ports. When a host sends the IGMPv2 leave message, the switch can then disable multicasting for the port.

CGMP is no longer used and is not a CCDA topic. IGMP snooping is the standards-based protocol used in today's networks.

IGMP Snooping

IGMP snooping is a standards-based method for switches to control multicast traffic at Layer 2. It has replaced CGMP. It listens to IGMP messages between the hosts and routers. If a host sends an IGMP query message to the router, the switch adds the host to the multicast group and permits that port to receive multicast traffic. The port is removed from multicast traffic if the host sends an IGMP leave message to the router. The disadvantage of IGMP snooping is that it has to process every IGMP control message, which can impact the CPU utilization of the switch.

Sparse Versus Dense Multicast

IP multicast traffic for a particular (source, destination group) multicast pair is transmitted from the source to the receivers using a spanning tree from the source that connects all the hosts in the group. Multicast destinations are represented in the following form: (S,G) or (*,G). Any multicast transmission has a Class D multicast group address, G. A multicast group can have more than one source, and each such source will also have a "regular" (Class A, B or C, or CIDR) Internet address, S. The notation (*,G) means every possible source for the given group G, while (S,G) means a particular source, at the particular Internet address S, in the group G.

Each destination host registers itself as a member of interesting multicast groups through the use of IGMP. Routers keep track of these groups dynamically and build distribution trees that chart paths from each sender to all receivers. IP multicast routing protocols follow two approaches.

The first approach assumes that the multicast group members are densely distributed throughout the network (many of the subnets contain at least one group member), that all devices want to receive multicast traffic, and that bandwidth is plentiful. The approach with dense multicast routing protocols is to flood the traffic throughout the network and then, at the request of receiving routers, stop the flow of traffic on branches of the network that have no members of the multicast group. Multicast routing protocols that follow this technique of flooding the network include DVMRP, Multicast Open Shortest Path First (MOSPF), and Protocol-Independent Multicast-Dense Mode (PIM-DM).

The second approach to multicast routing assumes that multicast group members are sparsely distributed throughout the network, it assumes that not all devices want to receive multicast traffic, and that bandwidth is not necessarily widely available. Sparse mode does not imply that the group has few members, just that they are widely dispersed. The approach with sparse multicast routing protocols is to not send traffic until it is requested by the receiving routers or hosts. Multicast routing protocols of this type are Core-Based Trees (CBT) and Protocol-Independent Multicast-Sparse Mode (PIM-SM). CBT is not widely deployed and is not discussed in this book.

Multicast Source and Shared Trees

Multicast distribution trees control the path that multicast packets take to the destination hosts. The two types of distribution trees are source and shared. With *source* trees, the tree roots from the source of the multicast group and then expands throughout the network in spanning-tree fashion to the destination hosts. Source trees are also called shortest-path trees (SPTs) because they create paths without having to go through a rendezvous point (RP). The drawback is that all routers through the path must use memory resources to maintain a list of all multicast groups. PIM-DM uses a source-based tree.

Shared trees create the distribution tree's root somewhere between the network's source and receivers. The root is called the RP. The tree is created from the RP in spanning-tree fashion with no loops. The advantage of shared trees is that they reduce the memory requirements of routers in the multicast network. The drawback is that initially the multicast packets might not take the best paths to the receivers because they need to pass through the RP. After the data stream begins to flow from sender to RP to receiver, the routers in the path optimize the path automatically to remove any unnecessary hops. The RP function consumes significant memory on the assigned router. PIM-SM uses an RP.

PIM

PIM comes in two flavors: sparse mode (PIM-SM) and dense mode (PIM-DM). The first uses shared trees and RPs to reach widely dispersed group members with reasonable protocol bandwidth efficiency. The second uses source trees and reverse path forwarding (RPF) to reach relatively close group members with reasonable processor and memory efficiency in the network devices of the distribution trees.

With RPF, received multicast packets are forwarded out all other interfaces, allowing the data stream to reach all segments. If no hosts are members of a multicast group on any of the router's attached or downstream subnets, the router sends a prune message up the distribution tree (the reverse path) to tell the upstream router not to send packets for the multicast group. So, the analogy for PIM-DM is the push method for sending junk mail, and the intermediate router must tell upstream devices to stop sending it.

PIM-SM

PIM-SM is defined in RFC 2362. PIM-SM assumes that no hosts want to receive multicast traffic unless specifically requested. The RP gathers the information from senders and makes the information available to receivers. Routers with receivers have to register with the RP. The end-host systems request multicast group membership using IGMP with their local routers. The routers serving the end systems then register as traffic receivers with the RPs for the specified group in the multicast network.

Joining PIM-SM

With PIM-SM, DRs on end segments receive IGMP query messages from hosts wanting to join a multicast group. The router checks whether it is already receiving the group for another interface. If it is receiving the group, the router adds the new interface to the table and sends membership reports periodically on the new interface.

If the multicast group is not in the multicast table, the router adds the interface to the multicast table and sends a join message to the RP with multicast address 224.0.0.13 (all PIM routers) requesting the multicast group.

Pruning PIM-SM

When a PIM-SM does not have any more multicast receiving hosts or receiving routers out any of its interfaces, it sends a prune message to the RP. The prune message includes the group to be pruned or removed.

PIM DR

A designated router is selected in multiaccess segments running PIM. The PIM DR is responsible for sending join, prune, and register messages to the RP. The PIM router with the highest IP address is selected as the DR.

Auto-RP

Another way to configure the RP for the network is to have the RP announce its services to the PIM network. This process is called auto-RP. Candidate RPs send their announcements to RP mapping agents with multicast address 224.0.1.39 (**cisco-rp-announce**). RP mapping agents are also configured. In smaller networks, the RP can be the mapping agent. The 224.0.1.40 address used in AUTO-RP-DISCOVERY is the destination address for messages from the RP mapping agent to discover candidates. Configured RP mapping agents listen to the announcements. The RP mapping agent then selects the RP for a group based on the highest IP address of all the candidate RPs. The RP mapping agents then send RP-discovery messages to the rest of the PIM-SM routers in the internetwork with the selected RP-to-group mappings.

11

PIMv2 Bootstrap Router

Instead of using auto-RP, you can configure a PIMv2 bootstrap router (BSR) to automatically select an RP for the network. The RFC for PIM Version 2, RFC 2362, describes BSR. With BSR, you configure BSR candidates (C-BSR) with priorities from 0 to 255 and a BSR address. C-BSRs exchange bootstrap messages. Bootstrap messages are sent to multicast IP 224.0.0.13 (all PIM routers). If a C-BSR receives a bootstrap message, it compares it with its own. The largest priority C-BSR is selected as the BSR.

After the BSR is selected for the network, it collects a list of candidate RPs. The BSR selects RP-to-group mappings, which is called the RP set, and distributes the selected RPs using bootstrap messages sent to 224.0.0.13 (all PIM routers).

DVMRP

RFC 1075 describes DVMRP. It is the primary multicast routing protocol used in the multicast backbone (MBONE). The MBONE is used in the research community.

DVMRP operates in dense mode using RPF by having routers send a copy of a multicast packet out all paths. Routers that receive the multicast packets then send prune messages back to their upstream neighbor router to stop a data stream if no downstream receivers of the multicast group exist (either receiving routers or hosts on connected segments). DVMRP implements its own unicast routing protocol, similar to RIP, based on hop counts. DVMRP has a 32 hop-count limit. DVMRP does not scale suboptimally. Cisco's support of DVMRP is partial; DVMRP networks are usually implemented on UNIX machines running the **mrouted** process. A DVMRP tunnel is typically used to connect to the MBONE DVMRP network.

IPv6 Multicast Addresses

IPv6 retains the use and function of multicast addresses as a major address class. IPv6 prefix FF00::/8 is allocated for all IPv6 multicast addresses. IPv6 multicast addresses are described in RFC 2373. EIGRP for IPv6, OSPFv3, and RIPng routing protocols use multicast addresses to communicate between router neighbors.

The format of the IPv6 multicast address is described in Chapter 9, "Internet Protocol Version 6 Design." The common multicast addresses are repeated in Table 11-11.

Table 11-11   Well-Known Multicast Addresses

Multicast Address	Multicast Group
FF01::1	All nodes (node-local)
FF02::1	All nodes (link-local)
FF01::2	All routers (node-local)
FF02::2	All routers (link-local)
FF02::5	OSPFv3 routers
FF02::6	OSPFv3 DRs

Multicast Address	Multicast Group
FF02::9	Routing Information Protocol (RIPng)
FF02::A	EIGRP routers
FF02::B	Mobile agents
FF02::C	DHCP servers/relay agents
FF02::D	All PIM routers

References and Recommended Readings

Bruno, A. *CCIE Routing and Switching Exam Certification Guide*. Indianapolis: Cisco Press, 2002.

RFC 2740: OSPF for IPv6, available from www.ietf.org/rfc.

RFC 1587: The OSPF NSSA Option, www.ietf.org/rfc.

Martey, A. *IS-IS Network Design Solutions. Indianapolis*: Cisco Press, 2002.

RFC 1584: Multicast Extensions to OSPF, www.ietf.org/rfc.

RFC 2328: OSPF Version 2, www.ietf.org/rfc.

RFC 1142: OSI IS-IS Intra-domain Routing Protocol, www.ietf.org/rfc.

Border Gateway Protocol, www.cisco.com/univercd/cc/td/doc/cisintwk/ito_doc/bgp.htm.

RFC 1997: BGP Communities Attribute, www.ietf.org/rfc.

RFC 1112: Host Extensions for IP Multicasting, www.ietf.org/rfc.

Doyle, J. and J. Carroll. *Routing TCP/IP, Volume I, Second Edition*. Indianapolis: Cisco Press, 2005.

Doyle, J. and J. Carroll. *Routing TCP/IP, Volume II*. Indianapolis: Cisco Press, 2001.

RFC 2362: Protocol Independent Multicast-Sparse Mode (PIM-SM): Protocol Specification (experimental), www.ietf.org/rfc.

RFC 2236: Internet Group Management Protocol, Version 2, www.ietf.org/rfc.

RFC 1519: Classless Inter-Domain Routing (CIDR): An Address Assignment and Aggregation Strategy, www.ietf.org/rfc.

Halabi, S. *Internet Routing Architectures*. Indianapolis: Cisco Press, 2000.

"IP Multicast Technology Overview" (white paper), http://www.cisco.com/c/en/us/td/docs/ios/solutions_docs/ip_multicast/White_papers/mcst_ovr.html.

RFC 2365: Administratively Scoped IP Multicast, www.ietf.org/rfc.

A Border Gateway Protocol 4 (BGP-4), www.ietf.org/rfc.

RFC 1075: Distance Vector Multicast Routing Protocol, www.ietf.org/rfc.

11

Williamson, B. *Developing IP Multicast Networks*. Indianapolis: Cisco Press, 1999.

RFC 2858: Multiprotocol Extensions for BGP-4, www.ietf.org/rfc.

RFC 4271: A Border Gateway Protocol 4 (BGP-4), www.ietf.org/rfc.

RFC 5340: OSPF for IPv6, www.ietf.org/rfc.

RFC 5838: Support of Address Families in OSPFv3, www.ietf.org/rfc.

RFC 6969: OSPFv3 Instance ID Registry Update, www.ietf.org/rfc.

BGP Attributes: Atomic Aggregate Attribute, www.networkers-online.com/blog/2010/12/bgp-attributes-atomic-aggergate-atribute/.

Exam Preparation Tasks

Review All Key Topics

Review the most important topics in the chapter, noted with the Key Topic icon in the outer margin of the page. Table 11-12 lists a reference of these key topics and the page numbers on which each is found.

Table 11-12   Key Topics

Key Topic Element	Description	Page
Summary	OSPFv2 areas	432
Summary	OSPF router types	434
Summary	OSPF LSA types	436
Table 11-4	Major LSA Types	436
List	Major changes to OSPFv3	440
Summary	OSPFv3 LSAs	441
Table 11-6	OSPFv3 LSA Types	442
Summary	eBGP	445
Summary	iBGP	445
List	BGP administrative distances	449
Summary	BGP Path Attributes	449
Summary	Route summarization	455
Summary	Route redistribution	458
Summary	Route filtering	461
Summary	Multicast	463
Table 11-10	Multicast Addresses	464
Table 11-11	Well-Known Multicast Addresses	470

Complete Tables and Lists from Memory

Print a copy of Appendix D, "Memory Tables" (found on the book website), or at least the section for this chapter, and complete the tables and lists from memory. Appendix E, "Memory Tables Answer Key," also on the website, includes completed tables and lists to check your work.

11

Define Key Terms

Define the following key terms from this chapter, and check your answers in the glossary:

OSPFv2, OSPFv3, ABR, ASBR, DR, LSA, stub, BGP, iBGP, QPPB, MP-BGP, PBR, IGMP, PIM

Q&A

The answers to these questions appear in Appendix A, "Answers to the 'Do I Know This Already?' Quizzes and Q&A Questions." For more practice with exam format questions, use the exam engine on the CD.

1. True or false: A router needs to have all its interfaces in Area 0 to be considered an OSPF backbone router.

2. True or false: OSPF and IS-IS use a designated router in multiaccess networks.

3. Which multicast addresses do OSPFv2 routers use?

4. Which multicast addresses are used by OSPFv3 routers?

5. What is the Cisco administrative distance of OSPF?

6. Which OSPFv2 router type generates the OSPF Type 3 LSA?

7. Which OSPFv2 router type generates the OSPF Type 2 LSA?

8. What is included in an OSPFv2 router LSA?

9. True or false: The router with the lowest priority is selected as the OSPF DR.

10. True or false: You use iBGP to exchange routes between different autonomous systems.

11. True or false: BGP Version 4 does not include support for CIDR, only OSPF and EIGRP do.

12. True or false: eBGP and iBGP redistribute automatically on a router if the BGP peers are configured with the same autonomous system number.

13. eBGP routes have an administrative distance of ___, and iBGP routes have an administrative distance of ___.

14. True or false: IGMP snooping and CGMP are methods to reduce the multicast traffic at Layer 2.

15. True or false: PIM has a hop-count limit of 32.

16. True or false: PIM-SM routers use the multicast 224.0.0.13 address to request a multicast group to the RP.

17. True or false: Autonomous system path is the only attribute BGP uses to determine the best path to the destination.

18. List three IP routing protocols that use multicast addresses to communicate with their neighbors.

19. What IPv6 multicast address does EIGRP use for IPv6?

20. Match the routing protocol with the description:

    i.   EIGRP

    ii. OSPFv2

    iii. RIPv2

    iv. BGP

  a. Distance-vector protocol used in the edge of the network

  b. IETF link-state protocol used in the network core

  c. Hybrid protocol used in the network core

  d. Path-vector protocol

21. What is the default OSPF cost for a Fast Ethernet interface?

22. Which routing protocol do you use in the core of a large enterprise network that supports VLSMs for a network with a mix of Cisco and non-Cisco routers?

23. What is the benefit of designing for stub areas?

24. What constraint does the OSPF network design have for traffic traveling between areas?

25. How is OSPFv3 identified as the upper-layer protocol in IPv6?

26. Which routing protocols are recommended for large enterprise networks?

  a. RIPv2

  b. OSPFv2

  c. EIGRP

  d. IS-IS

  e. A and B

  f. B and C

  g. B and D

  h. A, B, C, and D

27. What OSPFv3 LSA has an LS type of 0x0008?

  a. Router LSA

  b. Inter-area-router LSA

  c. Link LSA

  d. Intra-area-prefix LSA

11

28. Which routing protocol does not support VLSMs?

    a. RIPv1

    b. OSPFv2

    c. EIGRP

    d. RIPv2

    e. B and C

    f. B, C, and D

29. Which routing protocols have fast convergence for IPv4 networks?

    a. BGP

    b. OSPFv2

    c. EIGRP

    d. RIPv2

    e. B and C

    f. B, C, and D

    g. A, B, and C

30. Which routing protocols have fast convergence for IPv6 networks?

    a. RIPng

    b. OSPFv3

    c. EIGRP for IPv6

    d. RIPv2

    e. MP-BGP

    f. B and C

    g. B, C, and D

    h. B, C, and E

31. A retail chain has about 800 stores that connect to the headquarters and a backup location. The company wants to limit the amount of routing traffic used on the WAN links. What routing protocol(s) is/are recommended?

    a. RIPv1

    b. RIPv2

    c. OSPFv2

    d. EIGRP

    e. IS-IS

    f. BGP

    g. B, C, and D

    h. C and D

    i. C, D, and E

32. Which of the following statements is correct?

    a. OSPFv3 provides changes to OSPFv2 for use in IPv4 networks.

    b. OSPFv3 provides changes to OSPFv2 for use in IPv6 networks.

    c. OSPFv3 provides changes to OSPFv2 for use in IPv6 and IPv4 networks.

    d. OSPFng provides changes to OSPFv2 for use in IPv6 networks.

Use Figure 11-28 to answer the following question.

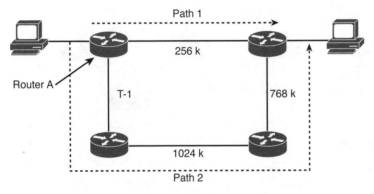

Figure 11-28   *Path selection*

33. If OSPF is enabled on all routers with the default metrics unchanged, what path is taken?

    a. Path 1

    b. Path 2

    c. Unequal load balance with Path 1 and Path 2

    d. Equal load balance with Path 1 and Path 2

11

Use Figure 11-29 to answer the following question.

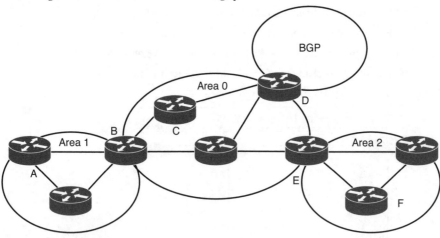

Figure 11-29   *OSPF router types*

34. Identify the OSPF router types shown in Figure 11-29.

Router A = _____

Router B = _____

Router C = _____

Router D = _____

Router E = _____

Router F = _____

35. Match the IP multicast address with its description.

i.   224.0.0.1

ii.   224.0.0.2

iii. 224.0.0.5

iv.   224.0.0.10

a. All OSPF routers

b. All routers

c. EIGRP routers

d. All hosts

36. Match the BGP attribute with its description.

i.   Local preference

ii.   MED

iii. Autonomous system path

iv.   Next hop

    a. IP address

    b. Indicates the path used to exit the autonomous system

    c. Tells external BGP peers the preferred path into the autonomous system

    d. List of ASNs

37. Which Cisco feature can you use instead of local preference to influence the selected path to external BGP routers?

38. What is the purpose of route reflectors?

39. When BGP confederations are used, which number do external peers see?

40. With _____ , all routers peer with each other within the private autonomous system. With _____ , client routers peer only with the reflector.

41. Which of the following shows the correct order that BGP uses to select a best path?

    a. Origin, lowest IP, autonomous system path, weight, local preference, MED

    b. Weight, local preference, autonomous system path, origin, MED, lowest IP

    c. Lowest IP, autonomous system path, origin, weight, MED, local preference

    d. Weight, origin, local preference, autonomous system path, MED, lowest IP

42. What feature did BGPv4 implement to provide forwarding of packets based on IP prefixes?

43. What route should be used to summarize the following networks?

10.150.80.0/23, 10.150.82.0/24, 10.150.83.0/24, 10.150.84.0/22

    a. 10.150.80.0/23, 10.150.82.0/23, and 10.150.84.0/22

    b. 10.150.80.0/22 and 10.150.84/22

    c. 10.150.80.0/21

    d. 10.150.80.0/20

44. Match the IPv6 multicast address with its description.

    i.   FF02::1

    ii.   FF02::2

    iii.   FF02::5

    iv.   FF02::9

    v.   FF02::A

    a. OSPFv3 routers

    b. RIPng routers

    c. All routers

    d. EIGRP routers

    e. All nodes

11

45. Route summarization and redistribution occur in which layer of the hierarchical model?

    a. Building access

    b. Distribution

    c. Core

    d. Server access

46. Which of the following best describes route summarization?

    a. Grouping contiguous addresses to advertise a large Class A network

    b. Grouping noncontiguous addresses to advertise a larger network

    c. Grouping contiguous addresses to advertise a larger network

    d. Grouping Internet addresses

47. Which standards-based routing protocol converges most quickly?

    a. RIPv2

    b. OSPF

    c. EIGRP

    d. BGP

48. Which routing protocol(s) do not require subinterfaces when operating over non-broadcast multiaccess point-to-multipoint networks?

    a. RIP

    b. OSPF

    c. EIGRP

    d. BGP

    e. IS-IS

49. Which link-state routing protocols support IPv6 routing?

    a. RIP

    b. OSPF

    c. EIGRP

    d. BGP

    e. IS-IS

50. Which OSPF area allows redistribution of external routers while preventing propagation of Type 5 LSAs?

    a. Area 0

    b. Stub area

    c. Not so stubby area

    d. ABR

    e. Area 1 over a Virtual Link

51. Which protocol is commonly used to connect to an ISP?

   a. RIPv2

   b. OSPF

   c. EIGRP

   d. BGP

52. Which of the following statements are true regarding OSPF? (Choose two.)

   a. ABRs require manual configuration for summarization.

   b. ABRs automatically summarize.

   c. External routes are injected into the autonomous system via the ABR.

   d. External routes are injected into the autonomous system via the ASBR.

53. Which routing protocol provides multivendor support with high scalability and fast convergence?

   a. RIPv2

   b. OSPF

   c. EIGRP

   d. BGP

54. Which routing protocol is recommended for large IPv6 multivendor networks?

   a. RIPng

   b. OSPFv3

   c. EIGRP for IPv6

   d. BGP

55. As a network designer, you need to influence the outbound routing with your ISP. Which are BGP options to do this?

   a. AS Path, Local Preference, Weight

   b. MED, Local Preference, Weight

   c. AS Path, BGP Communities, MED

   d. BGP Communities, Local Preference, MED

56. As a network designer, you need to influence the inbound routing with your ISP. Which are BGP options to do this?

   a. AS Path, Local Preference, Weight

   b. MED, Local Preference, Weight

   c. AS Path, BGP Communities, MED

   d. BGP Communities, Local Preference, MED

11

57. Which statements are correct? (Choose two.)

    a. The Dijkstra algorithm is used by both OSPF and IS-IS to calculate the shortest best path.

    b. IS-IS is a proprietary protocol. OSPF is a standards-based protocol.

    c. OSPF is only used on enterprise networks and IS-IS by service providers.

    d. ISIS boundaries are links; OSPF area boundaries are within the routers.

58. PIM-SM is configured on the network. Which protocol prevents media streams from being broadcast on the access switch?

    a. PIM-SM RD

    b. IGMPv3

    c. Auto-RP

    d. IGMP snooping

59. Which protocol is commonly used to connect to an ISP?

    a. RIPv2

    b. OSPF

    c. EIGRP

    d. BGP

60. Refer to Figure 11-30. Where should route redistribution occur?

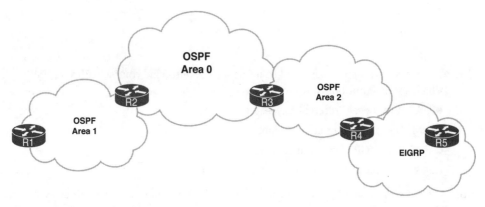

Figure 11-30 *Redistribution question*

    a. R1

    b. R2

    c. R3

    d. R4

    e. R5

Refer to Figure 11-31 to answer the following questions.

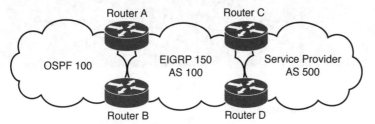

Figure 11-31   *Network scenario*

61. Where should you configure BGP?

   a. Routers A and B

   b. Routers C and D

   c. Answers A and B

   d. Routers A and C

62. On which router should you configure redistribution for OSPF and EIGRP?

   a. Router A only.

   b. Router B only.

   c. Routers A and B.

   d. Redistribution occurs automatically.

63. To announce the networks from autonomous system 100 to autonomous system 500, which routing protocols should you redistribute into BGP?

   a. OSPF only

   b. EIGRP only

   c. OSPF and EIGRP

   d. iBGP

64. Where should you use filters?

   a. Routers A and B

   b. Routers C and D

   c. Routers A and C

   d. Answers A and B

11

This chapter covers the following subjects:

Network Security Overview

Security Policy and Process

Trust and Identity Management

Secure Services

Threat Defense

Security Management Solutions

This chapter discusses network security in terms of security management and policy. Network security topics examined include security threats, risks, policy compliance, and securing network connectivity. The chapter then goes on to explain how network security management and policy provide a framework for secure networks. The chapter also explores trust and identity management, which defines how network access can occur, and threat defense, which adds increased levels of security into network endpoints.

CHAPTER 12

Managing Security

"Do I Know This Already?" Quiz

The "Do I Know This Already?" quiz helps you identify your strengths and deficiencies in this chapter's topics.

The ten-question quiz, derived from the major sections in the "Foundation Topics" portion of the chapter, helps you determine how to spend your limited study time.

Table 12-1 outlines the major topics discussed in this chapter and the "Do I Know This Already?" quiz questions that correspond to those topics.

Table 12-1 Do I Know This Already?" Foundation Topics Section-to-Question Mapping

Foundation Topics Section	Questions Covered in This Section
Network Security Overview	1–4
Security Policy and Process	5, 6
Trust and Identity Management	7
Secure Services	8
Threat Defense	9
Security Management Solutions	10

1. Which of the following security legislation applies protection for credit card holder data?

    a. SOX

    b. GLBA

    c. HIPAA

    d. PCI DSS

2. What classification of security threat gathers information about the target host?

    a. Unauthorized access

    b. Reconnaissance

    c. Denial of service

    d. None of the above

3. What type of security threat works to overwhelm network resources such as memory, CPU, and bandwidth?

  a. Denial of service

  b. Reconnaissance

  c. Unauthorized access

  d. NMAP scans

4. What is it called when attackers change sensitive data without proper authorization?

  a. VLAN filtering

  b. ACLs

  c. Integrity violation

  d. Loss of availability

5. What security document focuses on the processes and procedures for managing network events in addition to emergency-type scenarios?

  a. Acceptable-use policy

  b. Incident-handling policy

  c. Network access control policy

  d. Security management policy

6. Which of the following should be included in a security policy? (Select all that apply.)

  a. Identification of assets

  b. Definition of roles and responsibilities

  c. Description of permitted behaviors

  d. All of the above

7. Authentication of the identity is based on what attributes? (Select all that apply.)

  a. Something the subject knows

  b. Something the subject has

  c. Something the subject is

  d. All of the above

8. What VPN protocol uses encrypted point-to-point GRE tunnels?

  a. GRE-based VPN

  b. Cisco IPsec VPN

  c. Cisco GET VPN

  d. Cisco DMVPN

9. What are some physical security guidelines to consider for a secure infrastructure? (Select all that apply.)

    a. Evaluate potential security breaches.

    b. Use physical access controls such as locks or alarms.

    c. Assess the impact of stolen network resources and equipment.

    d. Use Syslog and SNMP analysis.

10. Which of the following benefits does a security management solution provide?

    a. SAINT scans

    b. Provisions network security policies for deployment

    c. Prevents unauthorized access

    d. NMAP scans

12

Foundation Topics

This chapter examines security management topics that you need to master for the CCDA exam. It begins by explaining reasons for network security and some techniques that can be used to prevent attacks. Next, the chapter describes the types of attacks that can compromise network security and classifies security threats. It goes on to cover the risks inherent in network security, along with a series of risk examples that illustrate how attacks can occur. The chapter then looks at what a "security policy" is and how it is used as a framework for network security.

In addition, this chapter explores ways to control and permit network access at any point within the network and discusses enabling security in network equipment by using traffic-isolation techniques. The chapter wraps up with examining some security management solutions.

Network Security Overview

For many years, networks were designed to be fairly open in nature and did not require much security. The greatest area of concern was physical access. Over time, networks grew in size, and complexity of attacks increased the need for network security. For today's businesses and organizations, security is now a mandatory part of designing IT systems, because the risks are too high if critical data is tampered with or lost. Security teams within organizations must provide adequate levels of protection for the business to conduct its operations.

Network security is used to prevent unauthorized access and defend against network attacks from intruders. In addition, network security protects data from manipulation and theft. Businesses today also need to comply with company policy and security legislation that is in place to help protect data and keep it private.

Here are some key security goals to think about when integrating security into the network:

- High availability and resiliency of the infrastructure
- Preventing unauthorized access, intrusions, network abuse, data leaks, theft, and fraud
- Protecting the end users and infrastructure
- Ensuring data confidentiality and integrity

Network security also needs to be transparent to the end users and should also be designed to prevent attacks by

- Blocking external attackers from accessing the network
- Permitting access to only authorized users
- Preventing attacks from sourcing internally
- Supporting different levels of user access
- Safeguarding data from tampering or misuse

Security Legislation

A number of legislative bodies along with the public have insisted that security controls be in place to protect private information and make certain that it is handled properly. These legislative bodies influence network security by imposing mandates with which organizations are required to comply. These requirements might include protecting customer information with regards to privacy and, in some cases, requiring encryption of the data.

The United States has a growing body of security legislation that you need to be aware of:

- **U.S. Public Company Accounting Reform and Investor Protection Act of 2002 (Sarbanes-Oxley or SOX):** Focuses on the accuracy and controls imposed on a company's financial records. This U.S. federal law was passed because of a number of corporate and accounting scandals that took place.

- **Payment Card Industry (PCI) Data Security Standard (DSS):** PCI is a data security standard that defines how to protect credit card holder data, including the storage and transfer of credit card holder information. Many retailers that accept credit cards have to meet PCI DSS standards or pay stiff penalties and are subject to regular and rigorous audits for PCI DSS compliance.

- **Gramm-Leach-Bliley Financial Services Modernization Act of 1999 (GLBA):** Provides protection against the sale of bank and account information that is regularly bought and sold by financial institutions. GLBA also guards against the practice of obtaining private information through false pretenses.

- **U.S. Health Insurance Portability and Accountability Act (HIPAA):** Applies to the protection of private health information that is used electronically. The purpose is to enable better access to health information, reduce fraud, and lower the cost of health care in the United States.

- **EU Data Protection Directive 95/46/EC:** Calls for the protection of people's right to privacy with respect to the processing of personal data.

Table 12-2 describes the security legislation and identifies its abbreviation.

Table 12-2 Security Legislation

Legislation Description	Legislation Abbreviation
Focuses on the accuracy and the controls imposed on a company's financial records	SOX
Data security standard that defines how to protect credit card holder data	PCI DSS
Protection against the sale of bank and account information that is regularly bought and sold by financial institutions	GLBA
Protection of private health information that is used electronically	HIPPA
Protection of people's privacy with respect to the processing of personal data	Directive 95/46/EC

12

Security Threats

It is important to be aware of the different types of attacks that can impact the security of IT systems. Security threats can be classified into the following categories:

- **Reconnaissance:** The goal of reconnaissance is to gather as much information as possible about the target host/network. Generally, this type of information gathering is done before an attack is carried out.

- **Unauthorized access:** Refers to the act of attacking or exploiting the target system or host. Operating systems, services, and physical access to the target host have known system vulnerabilities that the attacker can take advantage of and use to increase his or her privileges. Social engineering is another technique for obtaining confidential information from employees by manipulation. As a result of the attacker exploiting the host, can read, change, or delete information from the system causing interruption of service and/ or data loss in some cases.

- **Service disruption:** Attacks aimed at disrupting normal infrastructure services. The disruption can be caused by the following:

  - **Denial of service (DoS) attacks:** DoS attacks aim to overwhelm resources such as memory, CPU, and bandwidth that impact the target system and deny legitimate user's access. Distributed DoS (DDoS) attacks involve multiple sources working together to deliver the coordinated attack.

  - **Adware:** Automatic ads used to generate revenue for the hackers that are seeking monetary gains.

  - **Malware:** Hostile software used to gain access, gather information, or disrupt normal operations.

  - **Spyware:** Software that is used to obtain covert information secretly.

- **Disclosure and modification of data:** As data is in transit, an attacker can use packet-sniffing tools to read data on the wire while it is in flight. Man-in-the-middle attacks can also be used to inject new information into the data packets.

- **Network abuse:** The network can be abused from peer-to-peer file sharing, out-of-policy network browsing, and access to forbidden content on the network. Instant messaging systems can be a potential target for spammers to send unsolicited messages.

- **Data leaks:** The loss of data from servers or users' workstations while in transit or at rest. To prevent loss of data, data loss prevention (DLP) software can help to control what data users can transfer.

- **Identity theft and fraud:** Would-be attackers use phishing techniques such as email spam to gather personal information such as usernames, passwords, and credit card accounts by posing as a person who can be trusted.

Table 12-3 outlines the categorized security threats.

Table 12-3   Security Threats

Threat Description	Threat Category
Gathering information about a host/network segment	Reconnaissance
Attacks aimed at overwhelming resources such as memory, CPU, and bandwidth of an attacked system and the use of adware/malware/spyware	Service Disruption
Act of attacking or exploiting the target host system	Unauthorized access
Attackers using packet sniffing tools and conducting man-in-the-middle attacks	Disclosure and modification of data
Peer-to-peer file sharing, out-of-policy network browsing, and the spamming of instant messaging systems	Network Abuse
Loss of data from servers or user workstations	Data Leaks
Phishing with SPAM to gather personal information	Identity Theft and Fraud

Reconnaissance and Port Scanning

Reconnaissance network tools are used to gather information from the hosts attached to the network. They have many capabilities, including identifying the active hosts and which services the hosts are running. In addition, these tools can find trust relationships, determine OS platforms, and identify user and file permissions.

Some of the techniques that these scanning tools use include TCP connects (open), TCP SYNs (half open), ACK sweeps, Internet Control Message Protocol (ICMP) sweeps, SYN sweeps, and Null scans. Listed here are some of the more popular port-scanning tools and their uses:

- NMAP (Network Mapper) is designed to scan large networks or even a single host. It is an open source utility used for network exploration and security audits.

- NetscanTools is a collection over 40 network utilities designed for Windows machines. It includes tools for DNS, ping, traceroute, and port scanning.

- NetStumbler identifies wireless networks using 802.11a/b/g wireless LAN (WLAN) standards with or without the service set identifier (SSID) being broadcast. NetStumbler runs on Microsoft Windows–based platforms, including Windows Mobile.

- Kismet is an 802.11 wireless sniffer and intrusion detection system (IDS) application that can collect traffic from 802.11a/b/g/n networks. Kismet collects packets and detects wireless networks even when they are hidden.

Figure 12-1 shows NMAP scanning several hosts that have different operating systems. This particular scan displays the IP address, open ports, services, device type, uptime, OS details, and traceroute information.

12

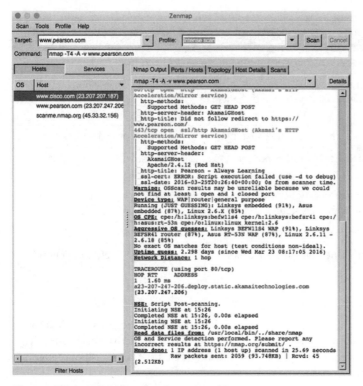

Figure 12-1   *NMAP: scanning several hosts*

Vulnerability Scanners

Vulnerability scanners determine what potential exposures are present in the network. Passive scanning tools are used to analyze the traffic flowing on the network. Active testing injects sample traffic onto the network. Here are some online resources for published vulnerability information:

- **CERT CC:** cert.org
- **MITRE:** cve.mitre.org
- **Microsoft:** technet.microsoft.com/en-us/security
- **Cisco Security Notices:** tools.cisco.com/security/center/

Here are some tools used for vulnerability scanning:

- **Nessus** is designed to automate the testing and discovery of known vulnerabilities. Nessus is an open source tool that runs natively on various operating systems, including Linux, Apple Mac OS, and Microsoft Windows-based operating systems.
- **SAINT** (Security Administrator's Integrated Network Tool) is a vulnerability-assessment application that runs on Linux and Apple Mac OS hosts.
- **MBSA** (Microsoft Baseline Security Analyzer) is used to scan systems and identify whether patches are missing for Windows products such as operating systems, Internet

Information Services (IIS), Structured Query Language (SQL), Exchange Server, Internet Explorer, Systems Management Server (SMS), and Microsoft Office applications. MBSA also alerts you if it finds any known security vulnerabilities such as weak or missing passwords and other common security issues.

The MBSA security report in Figure 12-2 displays several security issues on this host. Issues found include: Automatic updates is not configured to start automatically, some user account passwords have blank or missing passwords, and the Windows Firewall has some exceptions.

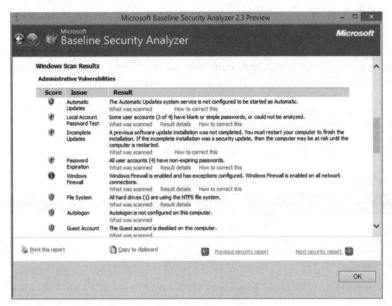

Figure 12-2 *MBSA: Security Report*

Unauthorized Access

Attackers use several techniques to gain unauthorized system access. One approach is when unauthorized people use usernames and passwords to escalate the account's privilege levels. Furthermore, some system user accounts have default administrative username and password pairings that are common knowledge, which makes them very unsecure. The trust relationships inherit between systems, and applications are yet another way unauthorized access takes place.

Social engineering is yet another method used to gain unauthorized access. Social engineering is the practice of acquiring confidential information by manipulating legitimate users. Actually, the most confidential information such as badges, usernames, and passwords can be uncovered just by walking around an organization. Many security items can be found unsecured in offices and cubicles. For example, it is not uncommon to find passwords written on notes or badges and keys left on tops of desks or in unlocked drawers. Another way of gaining confidential information is the pyschological method of social engineering. For example, someone pretending to be from the IT department calls a user and asks for his or her account information to maintain or correct an account discrepancy.

In addition to these approaches, hackers can obtain account information by using password-cracking utilities or by capturing network traffic.

Security Risks

To protect network resources, processes, and procedures, technology needs to address several security risks. Important network characteristics that can be at risk from security threats include system availability, data integrity, and data confidentiality:

- **System availability** should ensure uninterrupted access to critical network and computing resources to prevent service disruption and loss of productivity.

- **Data integrity** should ensure that only authorized users can change critical information and guarantee the authenticity of data.

- **Data confidentiality** should ensure that only legitimate users can view sensitive information to prevent theft, legal liabilities, and damage to the organization.

In addition, the use of redundant hardware and encryption can significantly reduce the risks associated with system availability, data integrity, and data confidentiality.

Table 12-4 summarizes security risks types with descriptions.

Table 12-4 Security Risks

Risk Description	Risk Type
Ensure only legitimate users can view sensitive information to prevent theft, legal liabilities, and damage to the organization.	Confidentiality of data
Ensure only authorized users can change critical information and guarantee the authenticity of data.	Integrity of data
Allow uninterrupted access to critical network and computing resources to prevent business disruption and loss of productivity.	System and data availability

Targets

Given the wide range of potential threats, just about everything in the network has become vulnerable and is a potential target. Ordinary hosts top the list as the favorite target, especially for worms and viruses. After a host has been compromised, it is frequently used as a new attack point. (A collection of such hosts is referred to as a botnet.)

Other high-value targets include devices that support the network. Here is a list of some network devices, servers, and security devices that stand out as potential targets:

- Infrastructure devices: Routers, switches

- Security devices: Firewalls, intrusion prevention systems (IPS)

- Network services: Dynamic Host Configuration Protocol (DHCP) and Domain Name System (DNS) servers

- Endpoints: Management stations and IP phones

- Infrastructure: Network throughput and capacity

Loss of Availability

Denial of service (DoS) attacks try to block or deny access to impact the availability of network services. These types of attacks can interrupt business transactions, cause considerable loss, and damage the company's reputation. DoS attacks are fairly straightforward to carry out, even by an unskilled attacker. Distributed DoS (DDoS) attacks are initiated by multiple source locations within the network to increase the attack's size and impact.

DDoS attacks occur when the attacker takes advantage of vulnerabilities in the network/host. Here are some common failure points:

- A network, host, or application fails to process large amounts of data sent to it, which crashes or breaks communication ability.
- A host or application is unable to handle an unexpected condition, such as improperly formatted data and memory or resource depletion.
- Nearly all DoS attacks are carried out with spoofing and flooding methods.

Table 12-5 lists some DoS-mitigating IOS software features.

Table 12-5   Software Features to Manage DoS Attacks

Feature Description	Feature
Verifies DHCP transactions and prevents rogue DHCP servers from interfering with production traffic	DHCP snooping
Intercepts Address Resolution Protocol (ARP) packets and verifies that the packets have valid IP-to-MAC bindings	Dynamic ARP Inspection (DAI)
Prevents unknown source addresses from using the network as a transport mechanism to carry out attacks	Unicast Reverse Path Forwarding (uRFP)
Controls what traffic is allowed or blocked on the network	Access control lists (ACL)
Controls the rate of bandwidth for incoming traffic, such as ARP packets and DHCP requests	QoS Policing
Set of rules that an IPS uses to detect unusual activity	IPS Signatures

Figure 12-3 shows a DoS threat on availability. The attacker is performing a DoS attack on the network and servers using a flood of packets. Keep in mind that this is an external attack; however, an internal attack is also certainly possible.

12

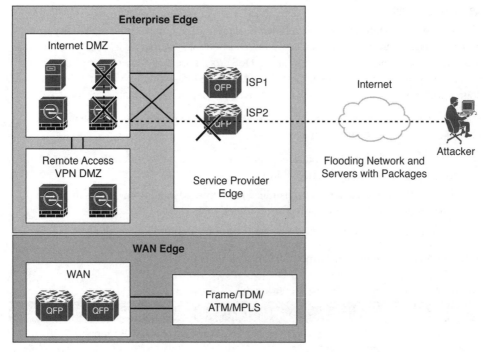

Figure 12-3 *DoS threat*

Integrity Violations and Confidentiality Breaches

When attackers change sensitive data without the proper authorization, this is called an integrity violation. For example, an attacker might access financial data and delete critical information. The effect of this change might not be felt for some time or until a significant loss has occurred. Integrity attacks like this are considered by many companies to be one of the most serious threats to their business. Furthermore, identifying these attacks can be difficult, and the effects can be devastating.

Confidentiality breaches occur when the attacker attempts to read sensitive information. It is difficult to detect these types of attacks, and loss of data can happen without the owner's knowledge.

It is important to use restrictive access controls to prevent integrity violations and confidentiality attacks. Here are some ways to enforce access control to reduce the risks:

- Restrict access by separating networks (VLANs) and by using stateful packet inspection firewalls.
- Restrict access with OS-based controls in both Windows and Linux.
- Limit user access by using user profiles for different departmental roles.
- Use encryption techniques to secure data or digitally sign data.

Figure 12-4 shows an attacker viewing, altering, and stealing competitive information. Pay particular attention to the obstacles the attacker must go through to get to the data.

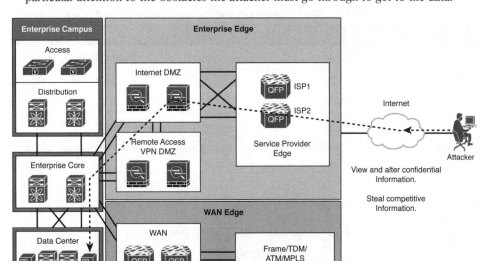

Figure 12-4 *Confidentiality and integrity threat*

Security Policy and Process

To provide the proper levels of security and increase network availability, a security policy is a crucial element in providing secure network services. This is an important concept to understand, and such business requirements should be considered throughout the system lifecycle. Business requirements and risk analysis are used in the development of a security policy. It is often a balance between ease of access versus the security risk and cost of implementing the security technology.

In terms of network security in the system lifecycle, the business needs are a key area to consider. Business needs define what the business wants to do with the network.

Risk analysis is another part of the system lifecycle. It explains the security risks and their associated costs. The business needs and the risk assessment feed information into the security policy.

The security policy describes the organization's processes, procedures, guidelines, and standards. Furthermore, industry and security best practices are leveraged to provide well-known processes and procedures.

Finally, an organization's security operations team needs to have processes and procedures defined. This information helps explain what needs to happen for incident response, security monitoring, system maintenance, and managing compliance.

12

Table 12-6 outlines key network security considerations.

Table 12-6   Key Network Security Elements of the Network Security Lifecycle

Security Consideration	Name
What are the business requirements?	Business needs
What is associated risk and cost?	Risk analysis
What policy governs the business requirements and risk?	Security policy
What are the recommend industry security best practices?	Best practices
What will the process be for incident, compliance, and change management?	Security operations

Figure 12-5 shows the flow of the network security lifecycle.

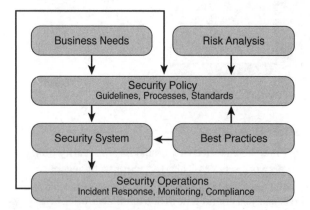

Figure 12-5   *Network security: system lifecycle*

Security Policy Defined

RFC 2196 says, "A security policy is a formal statement of the rules by which people who are given access to an organization's technology and information assets must abide." When you are developing security policies for an organization, RFC 2196 can serve as a guide for developing security processes and procedures. This RFC lists issues and factors that an organization must consider when setting its policies. Organizations need to make many decisions and come to agreement when creating their security policy.

Basic Approach of a Security Policy

To help create a security policy, here is a generally accepted approach from RFC 2196:

Step 1.   Identify what you are trying to protect.

Step 2.   Determine what you are trying to protect it from.

Step 3.   Determine how likely the threats are.

Step 4.   Implement measures that protect your assets in a cost-effective manner.

Step 5.   Review the process continuously, and make improvements each time a weakness is found.

Purpose of Security Policies

One of the main purposes of a security policy is to describe the roles and requirements for securing technology and information assets. The policy defines the ways in which these requirements will be met.

There are two main reasons for having a security policy:

- It provides the framework for the security implementation:
    - Identifies assets and how to use them
    - Defines and communicates roles and responsibilities
    - Describes tools and procedures
    - Clarifies incident handling of security events
- It creates a security baseline of the current security posture:
    - Describes permitted and unpermitted behaviors
    - Defines consequences of asset misuse
    - Provides cost and risk analysis

Here are some questions you might need to ask when developing a security policy:

- What data and assets will be included in the policy?
- What network communication is permitted between hosts?
- How will policies be implemented?
- What happens if the policies are violated?
- How will the latest attacks impact your network and security systems?

Security Policy Components

A security policy is divided into smaller parts that help describe the overall risk management policy, identification of assets, and where security should be applied. Other components of the security policy explain how responsibilities related to risk management are handled throughout the enterprise.

Further documents concentrate on specific areas of risk management:

- Acceptable-use policy is a general end-user document that is written in simple language. This document defines the roles and responsibilities within risk management and should have clear explanations to avoid confusion.
- Network access control policy defines general access control principles used in the network and how data is classified, such as confidential, top secret, or internal.
- Security management policy explains how to manage the security infrastructure.
- Incident-handling policy defines the processes and procedures for managing security incidents, including the handling of emergency scenarios.

12

Several other documents supplement these; they vary depending on the organization. The security policy requires the acceptance and support of all employees to make it successful. All the key stakeholders or business leaders, including members of senior management, should have input into the development of the security policy. In addition, key stakeholders should continue to participate in the ongoing maintenance and updates to the security policy in order to keep it up to date.

Table 12-7 summarizes additional security policy documents.

Table 12-7   Security Policy Documents

Policy Description	Document Name
Defines the roles and responsibilities within risk management	Acceptable-use policy
Defines general access control principles used and how data is classified, such as confidential, top secret, or internal	Network access control policy
Explains how to manage the security infrastructure	Security management policy
Defines the processes and procedures for managing incidents	Incident-handling policy

Risk Assessment

Within network security, proper risk management is a technique used to lower risks to within acceptable levels. A well thought-out plan for network security design implements the components that are part of the security policy. The security policies that an organization employs use risk assessments and cost-benefit analysis to reduce security risks.

Figure 12-6 shows the three major components of risk assessment. *Control* refers to how you use the security policy to minimize potential risks. *Severity* describes the level of the risk to the organization, and *probability* is the likeliness that an attack against the assets will occur.

Figure 12-6   *Risk assessment components*

Risk assessments should explain the following:

- What assets to secure
- The monetary value of the assets
- The actual loss that would result from an attack
- The severity and the probability that an attack against the assets will occur
- How to use security policy to control or minimize the risks

In many cases, security costs can be justified by describing the loss of productivity or revenue that could occur during security incidents.

Generally, network systems are built with just enough security to reduce potential losses to a reasonable level. However, some organizations have higher security requirements, such as complying with PCI DSS, SOX or HIPAA regulations, so they need to employ stronger security mechanisms.

Risk Index

A risk index is used to consider the risks of potential threats. The risk index is based on risk assessment components (factors):

- Severity of loss if the asset is compromised
- Probability of the risk actually occurring
- Ability to control and manage the risk

One approach to determining a risk index is to give each risk factor a value from 1 (lowest) to 3 (highest). For example, a high-severity risk would have a substantial impact on the user base and/or the entire organization. Medium-severity risks would have an effect on a single department or site. Low-severity risks would have limited impact and would be relatively straightforward to mitigate.

The risk index is calculated by multiplying the severity times the probability factor, and then dividing by the control factor:

Risk index = (severity factor * probability factor) / control factor

Table 12-8 shows a sample risk index calculation for a typical large corporation facing a couple of typical risks. If the risk index number calculated is high, there is more risk and therefore more impact to the organization. The lower the index number calculated means that there is less risk and less impact to the organization.

Table 12-8   Risk Index Calculation

Risk	Severity (S) Range 1 to 3	Probability (P) Range 1 to 3	Control Range 1 to 3	Risk Index (S * P)/C Range .3 to 9
DoS attack lasting for 1.5 hours on the email server	2	2	1	4
Breach of confidential customer lists	3	1	2	1.5

Continuous Security

As requirements change and new technology is developed, the network security policy should be updated to reflect the changes. Here are four steps used to facilitate continuing efforts in maintaining security policies:

12

Step 1.   **Secure:** Identification, authentication, ACLs, stateful packet inspection (SPI), encryption, and VPNs

Step 2.   **Monitor:** Intrusion and content-based detection and response

Step 3.   **Test:** Assessments, vulnerability scanning, and security auditing

Step 4.   **Improve:** Data analysis, reporting, and intelligent network security

Figure 12-7 shows the four-step process that updates and continues the development of security policies.

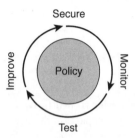

Figure 12-7   *Continuous security*

Table 12-9 lists the steps for continuous security.

Integrating Security Mechanisms into Network Design

Today's network designs demonstrate an increased use of security mechanisms and have become more tightly integrated with network design. Many security services such as IPS, firewalls, and IPsec virtual private network (VPN) appliances now reside within the internal network infrastructure. It is recommended that you incorporate network security during the network design planning process. This requires close coordination between the various engineering and operations teams.

Trust and Identity Management

Trust and identity management is crucial for the development of a secure network system. Trust and identity management defines who and what can access the network, and when, where, and how that access can occur. Access to the business applications and network equipment is based on the user-level rights that are granted and assigned by the administrators. Trust and identity management also attempts to isolate and keep infected machines off the network by enforcing access control. The three main components of trust and identity management are trust, identity, and access control, as shown in Figure 12-8. The following sections cover these components in detail.

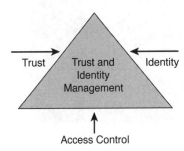

Figure 12-8   *Trust and identity management*

Trust

Trust is the relationship between two or more network entities that are permitted to communicate. Security policy decisions are largely based on this premise of trust. If you are trusted, you are allowed to communicate as needed. However, sometimes security controls need to apply restraint to trust relationships by limiting or preventing access to the designated privilege level. Trust relationships can be explicit or implied by the organization. Some trust relationships can be inherited or passed down from one system to another. However, keep in mind that these trust relationships can also be abused.

Domains of Trust

Domains of trust are a way to group network systems that share a common policy or function. Network segments have different trust levels, depending on the resources they are securing. When applying security controls within network segments, it is important to consider the trust relationships between the segments. Keep in mind that customers, partners, and employees each have their own unique sets of requirements from a security perspective that can be managed independently with "domains of trust" classifications. When domains of trust are managed in this way, consistent security controls within each segment can be applied.

Figure 12-9 shows two examples of trust domains with varying levels of trust segmented. The lighter shading indicates an internal environment with higher security, and the darker areas represent less-secure areas with lower security.

12

Example A

Example B

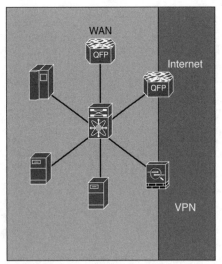
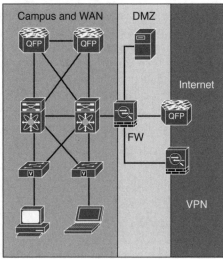

Figure 12-9   *Domains of trust*

Trust levels such as the internal network can be very open and flexible, whereas the outside needs to be considered unsafe and therefore needs strong security to protect the resources. Table 12-10 shows different levels of trust, from low to high.

Table 12-10   Domains of Trust: Risks from Low to High

Domain	Level	Safeguards Required
Production to lab	Low risk	ACLs and network monitoring
Headquarters to branch (IPsec VPN)	Medium risk	Authentication, confidentiality, integrity concerns, ACLs, route filtering
Inside (private) to outside (public)	High risk	Stateful packet inspection, intrusion protection (IPS), security monitoring

Identity

Identity is the "who" of a trust relationship. This can be users, devices, organizations, or all of the above. Network entities are validated by credentials. Authentication of the identity is based on the following attributes:

- **Something the subject knows:** Knowledge of a secret, password, PIN, or private key
- **Something the subject has:** Possession of an item such as a software token, token card, smartcard, or hardware key
- **Something the subject is:** Human characteristics, such as a fingerprint, retina scan, or voice recognition

Generally, identity credentials are checked and authorized by requiring passwords, pins, tokens, or certificates.

Passwords

Passwords are used to give users access and allow them to access network resources. Passwords are an example of the authentication attribute called "something you know." Typically, users do not want to use strong passwords; they usually prefer to use passwords that are easy to remember. Users present a weakness in password security that requires increased enforcement of the organization's password policy. Passwords should be valid for a limited amount of time and employ some password complexity such as upper/lowercase, numeric, and non-alphanumeric characters. Passwords should never be shared, use common dictionary words, or be posted on computer monitors.

Tokens

Tokens represent a way to increase security by requiring "two-factor authentication." This type of authentication is based on "something you know" and "something you have." For example, one factor may be a four-digit PIN, and another is the six-digit code on the physical token. The code on the tokens changes frequently, and it is not useful without the PIN. The code plus the PIN is transmitted to the authentication server for authorization. Then the server permits or denies access based on the user's predetermined access level. Some token-based systems even require a password instead of a pin and code from the token. This is known as two-factor authentication.

Figure 12-10 shows two-factor authentication using a username and password, along with a token access code.

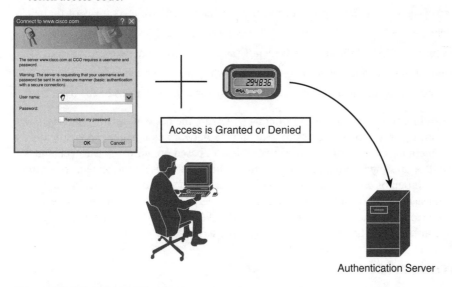

Figure 12-10 *Using tokens*

Certificates

Certificates are used to digitally prove your identity or right to access information or services. Certificates, also known as digital certificates, bind an identity to a pair of electronic keys that can be used to encrypt and sign digital information. A digital certificate is signed and issued by a certification authority (CA) with the CA's private key. A digital certificate contains the following:

- Owner's public key
- Owner's name
- Expiration date of the public key
- Name of the certificate authority
- Serial number
- Digital signature of the CA

Certificates can be read or written by an application conforming to the X.509 CCITT international standard and are typical when deploying server applications based on Secure Sockets Layer (SSL).

Network Access Control

Network access control is a security mechanism for controlling admission to networks and resources. These controls enforce the security policy and employ rules about which resources can be accessed. Network access control ensures the confidentiality and integrity of the network resources.

The core of network access control forms the AAA framework, which consists of the following:

- **Authentication** establishes the user's identity and access to the network resources.
- **Authorization** describes what can be done and what can be accessed.
- **Accounting** provides an audit trail of activities by logging the actions of the user.

Authentication, authorization, and accounting (AAA) are the network security services that help manage the network access control on your network equipment. AAA provides you with methods to secure access to network devices based on more granular techniques than just IP addressing information. For example, you might have a requirement to control access for a group of users regardless of their IP location. With AAA, you can integrate user directories such as LDAP and AD so that groups of users can have the same access levels decoupled from IP location. The implementation of AAA services requires authentication; however, authorization and accounting are optional services.

Secure Services

Secure Services is a component of the Cisco SAFE security reference architecture. This component of SAFE aims to protect the integrity and privacy of organizations' sensitive information. With increased security risks on the rise, it is critical that security be implemented within today's network environments. Consider, for example, the increased use of the Internet as a transport for extranet and teleworker connectivity via always-on broadband connectivity. Internal network segments have traditionally been considered trusted, but now require higher levels of network security. However, internal threats are now more than ten times more expensive and destructive than external threats. Data that flows across the network needs to be secured so that its privacy and integrity are preserved. These are important concepts to keep in mind when making business decisions about securing connectivity.

The Cisco Secure Services provides secure transport for data and applications using encryption and authentication techniques. Many security technologies exist for securing data, voice, and video traffic using wired, wireless, or remote access connectivity methods. Regardless of how the users connect to the network, they should have access to the applications and data that they are authorized to access.

Security technologies include

- IP Security (IPsec)
- Secure Shell (SSH)
- Secure Sockets Layer (SSL)
- MPLS VPNs with IPsec

Encryption Fundamentals

Cryptography uses encryption to keep data private, thus protecting its confidentiality. The encapsulated data is encrypted with a secret key that secures the data for transport. When the data reaches the other side of the connection, another secret key is used to decrypt the data and reveal the message transmitted. The encryption and decryption can be used only by authorized users. Most encryption algorithms require the user to have knowledge of the secret keys. IPsec is an example of a security protocol framework that uses encryption algorithms to hide the IP packet payload during transmission.

Encryption Keys

An encryption session between two endpoints needs a key to encrypt the traffic and a key to decrypt the traffic at the remote endpoint. There are two ways to send a key to the remote endpoint:

- Shared secrets
    - Both sides can use the same key or use a transform to create the decryption key.
    - The key is placed on the remote endpoint out of band.
    - This is a simple mechanism, but it has security issues because the key does not change frequently enough.
- PKI
    - It relies on asymmetric cryptography, which uses two different keys for encryption.
    - Public keys are used to encrypt and private keys to decrypt.
    - PKI requires a certificate to be issued by a certificate authority (CA) and is used by many e-commerce sites on the Internet.

12

Figure 12-11 shows what occurs during the encryption process using shared secret keys.

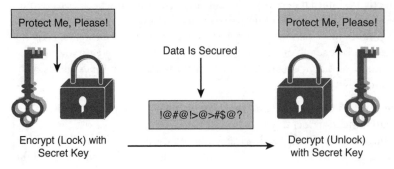

Figure 12-11   *Encryption keys*

VPN Protocols

There are several VPN protocols to choose from, each with varying benefits and uses:

- Standard IPsec

    - Uses Authentication Header (AH) and Encapsulating Security Payloads (ESP) to secure data.

    - Uses Internet Key Exchange (IKE) for dynamic key exchange.

    - Endpoints require IPsec software.

    - Choose when multivendor interoperability support is required.

- Cisco Dynamic Multipoint Virtual Private Network (DMVPN)

    - Secure encrypted point-to-point generic routing encapsulation (GRE) tunnels.

    - Provides on-demand spoke-to-spoke connectivity.

    - Routing, multicast, and quality of service (QoS) support.

    - Choose when simplified hub-and-spoke VPNs are needed.

- Cisco GRE-based VPN

    - Enables routing and multicast traffic across a VPN (IPsec is optional).

    - Non-IP protocol and QoS support.

    - Choose when more detailed configuration than DMVPN is required.

- Cisco GET VPN

    - Encryption integration on IP and MPLS WANs using private addressing.

    - Simplifies encryption management using group keying.

    - Any-to-any connectivity.

    - Support for routing, multicast, and QoS.

    - Choose when adding encryption to IP or MPLS WANs while allowing any-to-any connectivity.

Table 12-11 describes key features of VPN security protocols.

Key Topic

Table 12-11   VPN Protocols

VPN Description	VPN Name
Uses AH and ESP to secure data; requires endpoints have IPsec software.	Standard IPsec
Secure encrypted point-to-point GRE tunnels; on-demand spoke-to-spoke connectivity.	Cisco DMVPN
Enables routing and multicast traffic across an IPsec VPN; non-IP protocol and QoS support.	Cisco GRE-based VPN
Encryption integration on IP/MPLS WANs with private addressing; simplifies encryption using group keying; any-to-any connectivity.	Cisco GET VPN

IPsec comes in two forms: IP ESP and IP AH, which use protocol numbers 50 and 51, respectively. ESP is defined in RFC 2406, and AH is defined in RFC 2402. ESP provides confidentiality, data-origin authentication, integrity, and anti-replay service. AH allows for connectionless integrity, origin authentication, and anti-replay protection. These protocols can be used together or independently. Most IPsec-enabled clients or routers use IKE to exchange keys and ESP to encrypt the traffic.

Another type of VPN technology is SSL VPNs, which have become increasingly popular because of their clientless nature. The client only needs a standard web browser and a connection to the SSL VPN host, usually via the Internet.

Transmission Confidentiality

To ensure that data is kept private over unsecure networks such as the Internet, transmission confidentiality is used. Because the Internet is a public network, ordinary access control mechanisms are unavailable. Therefore, you need to encrypt the data before transporting over any untrusted network such as the Internet.

To provide transmission confidentiality, IPsec VPNs that support encryption can create a secure tunnel between the source and destination. As packets leave one site, they are encrypted; when they reach the remote site, they are decrypted. Eavesdropping on the Internet can occur, but with IPsec-encrypted packets, it is much more difficult.

IPsec VPNs commonly use well-known algorithms to perform the confidentiality treatment for packets. The well-known cryptographic algorithms include Triple Data Encryption Standard (3DES), Advanced Encryption Standard (AES), and Rivest Cipher 4 (RC4). These algorithms are thoroughly tested and checked and are considered trusted. However, keep in mind that cryptography can pose some performance problems, depending on the network's state. That is why it is important to carefully analyze the network before deploying VPNs with IPsec.

Data Integrity

Cryptographic protocols protect data from tampering by employing secure fingerprints and digital signatures that can detect changes in data integrity.

12

Secure fingerprints function by appending a checksum to data that is generated and verified with the secret key. Only those who are authorized also know the secret key. An example of secure fingerprints is Hash-based Message Authentication Code (HMAC), which maintains packet integrity and the authenticity of the data protected.

Digital signatures use a related cryptography method that digitally signs the packet data. A signer creates the signature using a key that is unique and known only to the original signer. Recipients of the message can check the signature by using the signature verification key. The cryptography inherent in digital signatures guarantees accuracy and authenticity because the originator signed it. Financial businesses rely on digital signatures to electronically sign documents and also to prove that the transactions did in fact occur.

Keep in mind the following data integrity guidelines:

- Analyze the need for transmission integrity.
- Factor in performance, but use the strongest cryptography.
- Always use well-known cryptographic algorithms.

Threat Defense

As part of the Cisco SAFE security reference architecture, threat defense enhances the security in the network by adding increased levels of security protection on network devices, appliances, and endpoints. Both internal and external threats have become much more destructive than in the past. DoS attacks, man-in-the-middle attacks, and Trojan horses have the potential to severely impact business operations. The Cisco Threat Defense System (Cisco TDS) provides a strong defense against these internal and external threats.

Threat defense has three main areas of focus:

- Enhancing the security of the existing network: Preventing loss of downtime, revenue, and reputation
- Adding full security services for network endpoints: Securing mobile devices and desktop endpoints with Cisco Identity Services Engine (ISE)
- Enabling integrated security in routers, switches, and appliances: Security techniques enabled throughout the network, not just in point products or locations

Physical Security

During your security implementations, it is essential to incorporate physical security to increase the strength of the overall security design. Physical security helps protect and restrict access to network resources and physical network equipment. Sound security policies must defend against potential attacks that can cause loss of uptime, reputation, or even revenue impacts.

Here are some considerations for potential physical threats:

- Attackers having unauthorized physical access can result in a full compromise of the IT asset.

- Vulnerabilities inherent in systems can be exploited by attackers when they access the hardware directly or through untrusted software.

- Physical access to the network, allowing attackers to capture, alter, or remove data flowing in the network.

- Attackers may use their own hardware, such as a laptop or router, to inject malicious traffic onto the network.

Keep in mind these physical security guidelines when designing physical security architectures:

- Use physical access controls such as card readers, retina scans, locks, or alarms.

- Ensure network devices have the proper environmental conditions that have controls for temperature, humidity, and fire suppression, and are free of magnetic interference.

- Incorporate UPS units to reduce the possibility of loss of power to devices.

- Evaluate potential security breach attack points.

- Assess the impact of stolen network resources and equipment.

- Use controls such as cryptography to secure traffic flowing on networks outside your control.

Figure 12-12 shows some physical security threat locations that an attacker could potentially exploit.

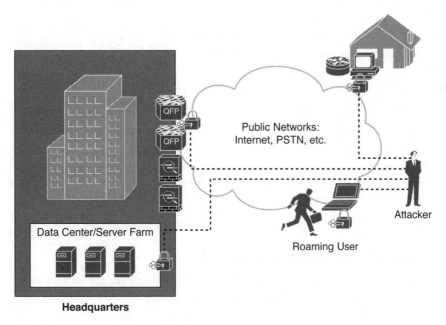

Figure 12-12 *Physical security threats*

12

Infrastructure Protection

The infrastructure needs to be protected using security features and services to meet the growing needs of business without disruption. Infrastructure protection is the process of taking steps to reduce the risks and threats to the network infrastructure and to maintain the integrity and high availability of network resources.

By using best practices and a security policy, you can secure and harden the infrastructure equipment to prevent potential attacks. To combat network threats, Cisco has enhanced Cisco IOS and IOS XE with security features to support the secure infrastructure and increase the network's availability.

Here are some recommended best practices for infrastructure protection:

- Use an out-of-band (OOB) management network to separate management-related traffic from production network traffic.

- Access network equipment remotely with SSH rather than with Telnet.

- In network switching infrastructure, use BPDU Guard, Root Guard, and VLAN Trunking Protocol (VTP) with mode Transparent.

- In network switching infrastructure, use ARP inspection and DHCP snooping.

- In network switching infrastructure, use Control Plane Policing (CoPP).

- Use AAA for authenticating administrative access, authorizing privileges, and logging all user sessions. Multiple AAA servers can also be used to increase fault tolerance of AAA services.

- Enable syslog collection; review the logs for further analysis.

- Use Simple Network Management Protocol Version 3 (SNMPv3) for its security and privacy features.

- Disable unused network services, such as tcp-small-servers and udp-small-servers.

- Use SFTP rather than TFTP to manage images.

- Use access classes to restrict access to management and the command-line interface (CLI).

- Enable routing protocol authentication when available, such as Enhanced Interior Gateway Routing Protocol (EIGRP), Open Shortest Path First (OSPF) protocol, Intermediate System-to-Intermediate System (IS-IS), and Border Gateway Protocol (BGP).

- Use unused VLANs for the native VLAN on trunk ports. Do not use VLAN1.

Security Management Solutions

Security management solutions are used to monitor, control, and support the network infrastructure. These same tools can be helpful during network audits and can save administrators a considerable amount of time.

Security management solutions provide the following:

- Collects, interprets, and presents information

- Provisions network security policies for deployment

- Maintains consistency by tracking policy changes
- Monitors account activity and provides role-based access control (RBAC)

A strong security implementation is only as good as the policies that are used. One of the biggest risks with a good security implementation is policy error. The network operations personnel need to fully understand the security policies, processes, and tools so that they can respond quickly when a security incident arises.

References and Recommended Readings

SecTools.org: Network Security Tools, sectools.org.

IANA protocol numbers, www.iana.org/assignments/protocol-numbers.

Module 4, "Enterprise Network Design," Designing for Cisco Internetwork Solution Course (DESGN) v3.0.

Safe Simplifies Security, http://www.cisco.com/c/dam/en/us/solutions/collateral/enterprise/design-zone-security/safe-poster-components.pdf

Cisco SAFE Solution Overview, www.cisco.com/en/US/docs/solutions/Enterprise/Security/SAFESolOver.html.

RFC 2196: Site Security Handbook, www.ietf.org/rfc/rfc2196.txt.

RFC 2402: IP Authentication Header, www.ietf.org/rfc/rfc2402.txt.

RFC 2406: IP Encapsulating Security Payload (ESP), www.ietf.org/rfc/rfc2406.txt.

Exam Preparation Tasks

Review All Key Topics

Review the most important topics in the chapter, noted with the Key Topic icon in the outer margin of the page. Table 12-12 lists a reference of these key topics and the page numbers on which each is found.

Table 12-12   Key Topics

Key Topic Element	Description	Page
Table 12-2	Security legislation	489
Table 12-3	Security threats	491
Table 12-4	Security risks	494
Table 12-5	Software features to manage DoS attacks	495
Table 12-6	Key network security elements of the network security lifecycle	498
Table 12-7	Security policy documents	500
List	Steps for continuous security	502
Table 12-10	Domains of Trust: Risks from Low to High	504
List	Encryption keys	507
List	VPN protocols	508
Table 12-11	VPN Protocols	509
List	Infrastructure protection	512
List	Security management solutions	512

Complete Tables and Lists from Memory

Print a copy of Appendix D, "Memory Tables" (found on the book website), or at least the section for this chapter, and complete the tables and lists from memory. Appendix E, "Memory Tables Answer Key," also on the website, includes completed tables and lists to check your work.

Define Key Terms

Define the following key terms from this chapter, and check your answers in the glossary:

U.S. Public Company Accounting Reform and Investor Protection Act of 2002, Gramm-Leach-Bliley Financial Services Modernization Act of 1999 (GLBA), U.S. Health Insurance Portability and Accountability Act (HIPAA), EU Data Protection Directive 95/46/EC, reconnaissance, unauthorized access, denial of service (DoS), NMAP, DHCP snooping, Dynamic ARP Inspection, Unicast RPF, access control lists (ACLs), QoS Policing, NetStumbler, Kismet, acceptable-use policy, network access control policy, security management policy, incident-handling policy, secure, monitor, test, improve, authentication, authorization, accounting, Adaptive Security Appliance (ASA), routers, Catalyst switches

Q&A

The answers to these questions appear in Appendix A, "Answers to the 'Do I Know This Already?' Quizzes and Q&A Questions." For more practice with exam format questions, use the exam engine on the CD.

1. What technique can be used to protect private information that is transported over the Internet between the headquarters and branch office? (Select the best answer.)

   a. Authentication

   b. Log all data

   c. Encryption

   d. Accounting

2. What would be recommended to protect database servers connected to or accessible from the Internet?

   a. Firewall

   b. Server load balancing (SLB)

   c. Syslog

   d. SPAN

3. What network security issue does 3DES encryption aim to solve?

   a. Data integrity

   b. User authentication

   c. Data authentication

   d. Data confidentiality

4. Users are reporting a DoS attack in the DMZ. All the servers have been patched, and all unnecessary services have been turned off. What else can you do to alleviate some of the attack's effects? (Select all that apply.)

   a. Police traffic on the firewall's ingress.

   b. Use ACLs to let only allowed traffic into the network.

   c. Block all TCP traffic from unknown sources.

   d. Perform DHCP snooping for the DMZ segment.

12

5. You are a network engineer for ABC Corp. You need to bring your coworkers up to date on network security threats. What would you discuss with them? (Select all that apply.)

   a. Reconnaissance and unauthorized access

   b. DHCP snooping

   c. DMZ security

   d. DoS

6. True or false: IPsec can ensure data integrity and confidentiality across the Internet.

7. What focuses on the accuracy and controls imposed on a company's financial records?

   a. HIPAA

   b. GLBA

   c. SOX

   d. EU Data Protection Directive

8. What are components of managing the security infrastructure? (Select all that apply.)

   a. Security management policy

   b. Incident-handling policy

   c. Network access control policy

   d. None of the above

9. Which security legislative body calls for the protection of people's privacy?

   a. HIPAA

   b. GLBA

   c. EU Data Protection Directive

   d. SOX

10. How can attackers obtain sensitive account information? (Select all that apply.)

    a. Password-cracking utilities

    b. Capturing network traffic

    c. Social engineering

    d. All of the above

11. What best describes how to protect data's integrity?

    a. System availability

    b. Data confidentiality

    c. Ensuring that only legitimate users can view sensitive data

    d. Allowing only authorized users to modify data

12. What provides an audit trail of network activities?

   a. Authentication

   b. Accounting

   c. Authorization

   d. SSHv1

13. What authenticates valid DHCP servers to ensure unauthorized host systems are not interfering with production systems?

   a. DHCP options

   b. ARP inspection

   c. DHCP snooping

   d. DHCP reservations

14. What contains the organization's procedures, guidelines, and standards?

   a. Security policy

   b. Acceptable use policy

   c. Procedure handling

   d. Process handling

15. How can you enforce access control? (Select all that apply.)

   a. Restrict access using VLANs

   b. Restrict access using OS-based controls

   c. Use encryption techniques

   d. All of the above

16. What is a general user document that is written in simple language to describe the roles and responsibilities within risk management?

   a. Security policy

   b. Acceptable-use policy

   c. Procedure handling

   d. Process handling

17. True or false: The network access control policy defines the general access control principles used and how data is classified, such as confidential, top secret, or internal.

18. What are the four steps used to facilitate continuing efforts in maintaining security policies?

   a. Secure, monitor, maintain, close out

   b. Monitor, test, evaluate, purchase

   c. Improve, test, purchase, evaluate

   d. Secure, monitor, test, improve

12

19. Match the encryption keys and VPN protocols with their definitions.

   i.   IPsec

   ii. SSL

   iii. Shared secret

   iv. PKI

   a. Both sides use the same key.

   b. Uses AH and ESP.

   c. Web browser TCP port 443.

   d. Asymmetric cryptography.

20. What does Cisco recommend as the foundation of any deployed security solution?

   a. Customer requirements

   b. Security audit

   c. SLA policy

   d. Security policy

21. Which of the following protocols are used for IP security?

   a. SSH and EIGRP

   b. BGP and TCP

   c. AH and ESP

   d. SSH and RIP

22. Which security solution best meets requirements for confidentiality, integrity, and authenticity when using the public network such as the Internet?

   a. Cisco IOS firewall

   b. Intrusion prevention

   c. Secure Services

   d. AAA

   e. Traffic Guard Protector

23. What uses security integrated into routers, switches, and appliances to defend against attacks?

   a. Trust and identity management

   b. Threat defense

   c. Secure Services

   d. Cisco SAFE

   e. Secure firewalling

24. Encryption and authentication are used to provide secure transport across untrusted networks by providing _____.

    a. Trust and identity management

    b. Threat defense

    c. Secure Services

    d. Cisco SAFE

    e. Secure firewalling

12

This chapter covers the following subjects:

Cisco SAFE Architecture

Trust and Identity Technologies

Detecting and Mitigating Threats

Security Management Applications

Integrating Security into Network Devices

Securing the Enterprise

This chapter covers Cisco Security Architecture for the Enterprise (SAFE), security technologies, and design options for securing the enterprise. The CCDA candidate can expect many questions related to integrating security technologies and mitigating security exposures. This chapter also focuses on how to integrate security into existing network devices and security platforms throughout your network. Furthermore, the CCDA must understand the different types of security features available and where to deploy them.

CHAPTER 13

Security Solutions

"Do I Know This Already?" Quiz

The "Do I Know This Already?" helps you identify your strengths and deficiencies in this chapter's topics.

The ten-question quiz, derived from the major sections in the "Foundation Topics" portion of the chapter, helps you determine how to spend your limited study time.

Table 13-1 outlines the major topics discussed in this chapter and the "Do I Know This Already?" quiz questions that correspond to those topics.

Table 13-1 "Do I Know This Already?" Foundation Topics Section-to-Question Mapping

Foundation Topics Section	Questions Covered in This Section
Cisco SAFE Architecture	1, 2
Trust and Identity Technologies	3, 4
Detecting and Mitigating Threats	5, 6
Security Management Applications	7
Integrating Security into Network Devices	8
Securing the Enterprise	9, 10

1. Which of the following are secure domains of the Cisco SAFE architecture? (Select all that apply.)

    a. Segmentation

    b. Compliance

    c. Management

    d. Data center

2. What network security platform combines a high-performance firewall with an IPS, antivirus, IPsec, and an SSL VPN in a single unified architecture?

    a. Integrated Services Routers

    b. Cisco Catalyst switches

    c. Adaptive Security Appliances

    d. Cisco ISE

3. Which media-level access control standard developed by IEEE permits and denies access to the network and applies traffic policy based on identity?

   a. AES

   b. 802.1X

   c. Cisco ISE

   d. ASA SM

4. What mechanism protects networks from threats by enforcing security compliance on all devices attempting to access the network?

   a. Cisco ISE

   b. SNMP

   c. ASDM

   d. 3DES

5. Which of the following can be used to perform firewall filtering with the use of ACLs? (Select all that apply.)

   a. ASA

   b. IPS

   c. ASA SM

   d. All of the above

6. What Cisco security appliance acts as an SMTP gateway for the enterprise?

   a. Cisco ISE

   b. Cisco ESA

   c. Cisco ASA

   d. Cisco WSA

7. Which security management solution integrates the configuration management of firewalls, VPNs, routers, switch modules, and IPS devices?

   a. CSM

   b. Cisco ISE

   c. ASDM

   d. ACS

8. When you're integrating security into the network devices, which of the following can be used? (Select all that apply.)

   a. RMON

   b. ASA

   c. Cisco IOS IPS

   d. Syslog

9. Which of the following technologies is used to detect and mitigate threats in network traffic?

    a. 802.1X

    b. NetFlow

    c. ASDM

    d. SSH

10. What Cisco security management platform is used to control the TACACS and RADIUS protocols?

    a. SSH

    b. IPS

    c. ACS

    d. IDM

13

Foundation Topics

This chapter covers security topics that you need to master for the CCDA exam. It begins with a discussion of the Cisco SAFE architecture and then covers the strategy for identifying and responding to security threats. Next, the "Trust and Identity Technologies" section discusses the technologies and services used on network security devices such as routers and firewalls. Then the "Detecting and Mitigating Threats" section covers the technologies that support threat defense, such as intrusion prevention systems (IPSs), Adaptive Security Appliances (ASAs), and Cisco Identity Services Engine (ISE).

Furthermore, the "Security Management Applications" section describes the Cisco security management products designed to support the Cisco SAFE architecture. Next, the "Integrating Security into Network Devices" section covers the security features integrated into Cisco network devices, such as routers, firewalls, IPS, endpoint security, and Catalyst service modules. To wrap up, the "Securing the Enterprise" section reviews the places in the network (PINs) used to deploy security devices and solutions in the enterprise, data center, and the enterprise edge.

Cisco SAFE Architecture

Cisco Security Architecture for the Enterprise (SAFE) is a secure architectural framework that simplifies the complexity of security and focuses on the areas in the network that a company needs to secure. Part of the SAFE architecture discusses organizing complexity into places in the network (PINs) along with secure domains. PINs consist of the places in the network such as branch, campus, cloud, data center, edge, Internet, and WAN. Secure domains are the functional areas used to protect the places in the network. Because enterprise networks are key enablers of business, networks must be designed with integrated security in mind to ensure confidentiality, integrity, and availability of network resources, especially those networks that support critical business activity.

One key principle of Cisco SAFE architecture relates to the need for deep security and protection from both the inside and outside of the organization. Cisco SAFE provides guidelines for handling today's threats and the capabilities needed to secure the network against those threats. The Cisco SAFE approach allows for the analysis of expected threats and supports the design of the network security strategy. In addition, the modular nature of Cisco SAFE allows for the security system to be expanded and scaled as the business grows.

The secure domains of Cisco SAFE are as follows:

- **Secure Services** provides access control, VPNs, and encryption. It protects insecure services such as applications and wireless networking.

- **Compliance** covers policies both internal and external, including PCI DSS, HIPAA, and SOX.

- **Threat Defense** provides visibility for cyber-threats and uses network traffic telemetry, reputation, and contextual information. It also includes the assessment of risks due to suspicious activities and provides next steps.

- **Security Intelligence** provides detection and aggregation of malware and threats. It enables the network to enforce policy dynamically as reputations are updated when new threats emerge.

- **Segmentation** creates boundaries for both users and data. Manual segmentation uses VLANs, network addressing, and firewalling for policy enforcement. Advanced segmentation uses identity-aware infrastructure to enforce policies automatically.

- **Management** provides services for devices and systems for consistent policy deployment, workflow-based change management, patch management, and alerting.

The benefits of Cisco SAFE include the following:

- SAFE is the basis for the design of highly available secure networks.

- SAFE provides for an open, modular, and expandable structure.

- SAFE facilitates the development, implementation, and management of secure networks.

Figure 13-1 shows Cisco SAFE PINs and the secure domains.

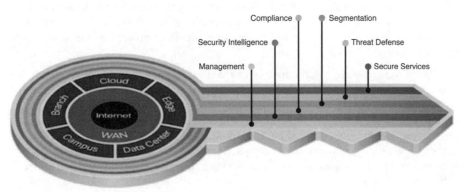

Figure 13-1 *Cisco SAFE PINs and the secure domains*

Network Security Platforms

Network security starts with having a secure underlying network. The underlying network provides an ideal place to implement core and advanced security solutions. The center of these secure network solutions consists of the Adaptive Security Appliances (ASAs), Integrated Services Routers (ISRs), and Cisco Catalyst switches that have integrated security features. These are intelligent network security devices with many built-in security features that provide a framework for incorporating security throughout the network. Here is a description of some important security device platforms:

- **ASA** is a high-performance firewall appliance with IPS, antivirus, IPsec, and Secure Shell (SSL) virtual private network (VPN) technologies integrated into a single unified architecture. ASA also has support for FirePOWER IPS module capabilities.

- **ISR G2** combines IOS firewall, VPN, and IPS services across the router portfolio, enabling new security features on existing routers. Supported VPNs include IPsec VPN, Dynamic Multipoint VPN (DMVPN), and SSL VPN.

13

■ **Cisco Catalyst switches** include denial of service (DoS) and man-in-the-middle attack mitigations and integration with service modules that provide firewall and VPN capabilities providing for secure connectivity. Unique security zones can be set up along with the virtualization of firewalls.

Cisco Security Control Framework

The Cisco Security Control Framework (SCF) is a security framework that provides a foundation for securing networks based on proven industry best practices and security architecture principles. Cisco SCF is designed to address current threats and threats that are still evolving by using common and comprehensive security solutions. The Cisco SAFE architecture uses SCF to develop secure network designs that ensure high availability of network services. Cisco SCF influences security product selection and helps guide network implementations to allow for better visibility and control.

SCF assumes the presence of security policies derived from threat and risk assessments that complement the goals of the business. Security policies and guidelines define the acceptable-use policy for the secure use of network services and devices in the organization. The security policies should also determine the process and procedures for handling security events, which help define the security operations. To achieve business goals, it is critical to businesses that security policy and procedures empower the business rather than prevent access.

Total visibility and complete control are two of the main components of SCF. Network security is a function of visibility and control. Without visibility, there is a lack of control, and without control, you are missing key elements of security. The success of a security policy depends on solid visibility and control. Within SCF, there are six security actions used to enforce security policy and allow for visibility and control. Visibility is improved with *identify*, *monitor*, and *correlate* security actions; and control is enhanced through the *harden*, *isolate*, and *enforce* security actions. Each of these security actions is further defined in the SCF model.

Figure 13-2 describes of components of the Cisco SCF model.

Cisco Security Control Framework Model					
Total Visibility			**Complete Control**		
Identify, Monitor, Collect, Detect and Classify Users, Traffic, Applications, and Protocols			Harden, Strengthen Resiliency, Limit Access, and Isolate Devices, Users, Traffic, Applications, and Protocols		
Identify	Monitor	Correlate	Harden	Isolate	Enforce
• Identify, Classify, and Assign Trust Levels to Subscribers, Services, and Traffic	• Monitor Performance, Behaviours, Events, and Compliance with Policies • Identify Anomalous Traffic	• Collect, Correlate, and Analyze System-Wide Events • Identify, Notify, and Report on Significant Related Events	• Harden Devices, Transport, Services and Applications • Strengthen Infrastructure Resiliency, Redundancy, and Fault Tolerance	• Isolate Subscribers, Systems, and Services • Contain and Protect	• Enforce Security Policies • Migrate Security Events • Dynamically Respond to Anomalous Event

Figure 13-2 *Cisco Security Control Framework*

Trust and Identity Technologies

Trust and identity technologies are security controls that enable network traffic security. The following are examples of technologies used to support trust and identity management:

- **Access control lists (ACL):** ACLs are used on routers, switches, and firewalls to control access. For example, ACLs are commonly used to restrict traffic on the ingress or egress of an interface by a wide variety of methods, such as using IP addresses and TCP or User Datagram Protocol (UDP) ports.

- **Firewall:** A security device designed to permit or deny network traffic based on source address, destination address, protocol, and port. The firewall enforces security by using the access and authorization policy to determine what is trusted and untrusted. The firewall also performs stateful packet inspection (SPI), which keeps track of the state of each TCP/UDP connection. SPI permits ingress traffic if the traffic originated from a higher security interface, such as the inside.

- **Port security:** Port security is a security technique used on switch ports to limit MAC addresses permitted on a switch port. It can be used to define specific MAC addresses or limit the number of MAC addresses allowed on the switch port.

- **802.1X:** An IEEE media-level access control standard that permits and denies admission to the network and applies traffic policy based on user or machine identity. 802.1X is used to control access to wired and wireless networks by allowing only authorized users and devices on the network.

- **Cisco Identity Services Engine (ISE):** Cisco ISE is a security policy management platform that automates access control by enforcing compliance, increasing network security, and improving operations. Cisco ISE provides accurate identification of users and devices on the network, including easy provisioning of all devices. ISE collects rich contextual data about the connected users and devices and can provide policy enforcement and security compliance before the device is even authorized to access the network.

The following sections cover some of these trust and identity technologies in more detail.

Firewall Fundamentals

A firewall is a security device that is responsible for enforcing the configured access control policy between network segments. Firewalls can be implemented with hardware appliances or with software-based solutions. The most important function for firewalls is preventing undesirable traffic on the outside of the firewall from accessing the internal network segments or DMZs on the inside. Because these network segment boundaries are so important, firewalls must adhere to some common functions. For example, if a software vulnerability were exploited in the firewall and became compromised, then the firewall would no longer be able to enforce the configured access control policy. Therefore, firewalls need to be resistant to attacks such as these.

For the firewall to create proper network segment boundaries, traffic needs to be pushed through the firewall so that the access control policy can be enforced. If there are alternate network paths, the traffic could flow around the firewall, thus bypassing the access control policy. Therefore, if there are redundant or additional paths in the network, firewalls should be used to enforce the firewall policy.

13

The access control policy defines the security rules about what traffic is allowed or blocked based on the company's business requirements and objectives. These security rules build the basis for the documented firewall security policy. These security rules should then be implemented on firewalls enforcing the company's access control policy.

Types of Firewalls

Today, there are many options when it comes to firewalls, each with its own capabilities and methods of implementing security services. Traditional firewall types include the following:

- **Packet filtering firewalls** use access control lists to permit or deny traffic and are sometimes referred to as *stateless firewalls*. The access control lists filter based on source and destination IP addresses, TCP/UDP port numbers, TCP flags, and ICMP types. As traffic flows through the ACL on the firewall, if traffic is matched by an ACL, then the action is taken without regard to any kind of state of the traffic flow. The packet filtering is actually occurring based on the information found in each packet that flows through the ACL. Packet filtering is typically used on routers and Layer 3 switches to restrict traffic flows and reduce the amount of traffic that needs to be further inspected.

- **Stateful firewalls** use stateful packet inspection (SPI) when evaluating traffic that passes through the firewall using a state table of existing traffic flows. As traffic enters the firewall, the traffic flow information is put into a state table to record the traffic flow. Then, as the return traffic comes back through the firewall, if a firewall record exists in the state table, the traffic is permitted back through. If the traffic flow does not exist in the state table, the traffic must be explicitly permitted by an ACL to be allowed through the firewall. A stateful firewall monitors the traffic from an initiating state, transferring state, or a terminating state. Most firewalls today are SPI firewalls.

  The two main advantages that SPI firewalls have over traditional packet filtering firewalls include the following:

  - The use of a state table where all of the firewall connections are tracked as they flow through the firewall

  - Capability to recognize the applications that use dynamic ports for additional connections during the communication between hosts

- **Application level gateways** work up to Layer 7 of the OSI model and are sometimes referred to as *proxy firewalls*. These proxy firewalls run software that acts as a proxy between the source clients and destination servers. As traffic flows through the proxy firewall, source client connections are terminated and new connections are originated to the destination servers. The application-level gateway sits in the middle and controls the connections between the client and the server, allowing very granular policy to be applied to the traffic flows.

- **Host-based firewalls** consist of firewall software running on clients and/or servers protecting traffic on ingress or egress network interfaces.

- **Transparent mode firewalls** can be the same SPI firewalls as mentioned previously but are implemented as a bump in the wire at Layer 2. Transparent mode firewalls use L2 bridged interfaces and enforce policy using ACLs consisting of IP and TCP/UDP port information.

- **Hybrid firewalls** are firewalls that include functions of multiple firewall types such as a stateful firewall with application-level gateway capabilities.

Next-Gen Firewalls

Next-generation firewalls (NGFWs) are the most recent generation of firewalls. They combine traditional firewall functionality with additional security technologies, including the following:

- **Application filtering** with deep packet inspection using application signatures.

- **Intrusion prevention system (IPS)** inspects content passing through a firewall and compares it against known malicious signatures. Matched signatures can drop the affected packets or the entire session. Zero-day attacks can also be detected by executing suspicious code using cloud services and mitigated using new IPS signatures based on the suspicious code.

- **User Identification** allows integration with LDAP or Microsoft Active Directory and can be used to apply security policy based on users or groups.

- **Decryption of encrypted traffic** provides visibility into SSL protected traffic. When decryption is enabled, the NGFW acts as a proxy by terminating the client SSL session on the firewall, and then it creates its own SSL session with the server. This allows for SSL traffic to be inspected.

- **Antivirus and antimalware inspection** provides protection against viruses and malware.

- **URL filtering** provides comprehensive alerting and control over suspicious web traffic.

NAT Placement

We need to use NAT because of the exhaustion of IPv4 public address space. Today, NAT is used extensively to enable Internet access on firewalls. In addition, port address translation (PAT) enables us to use many internal private addresses and translate them into a single public address. For servers that are public facing on the Internet, we need to use public IPv4 addressing. Either we can assign the server a public address without the need for NAT or we can assign the server a private address and have the firewall translate the address from public to private.

Using public IPv4 addressing simplifies the addressing and avoids NAT altogether; however, public IPv4 address blocks are very limited, and you might run out of space without being able to get more addresses assigned.

Another approach is to use NAT along with private addressing for your public-facing servers. This design allows you to use a firewall to handle the address translations between the public and private network segments. Firewall DMZs are typically used to place your public-facing servers into, and the firewall can use either static NAT or PAT to translate the addressing. With PAT, you can use a single public address on the firewall to translate traffic with different port numbers tied to different public-facing servers in the DMZ.

13

Firewall Guidelines

Here are some recommended guidelines to consider when implementing firewalls:

- Position firewalls at key network locations such as between the Internet and the inside network.

- Firewalls should be the primary security enforcement point, but not the only one. Consider other security devices such as IPS and email security appliances.

- Firewalls should be deployed with redundancy in mind, such as in an Active/Standby or Active/Active failover pair.

- A closed security model is more secure and preferred over an open security model. Closed security refers to denying everything by default and then adding **permit** statements as exceptions. An open security model is the opposite. It allows all traffic by default and then **deny** statements are added as exceptions, which is less secure.

- Firewall features should be used as needed, such as dynamic NAT/PAT for Internet traffic along with stateful packet inspection (SPI).

- Secure physical and management access points in locations with locks or badge readers. Enforce management access with authorized users using separate authentication servers.

- Analyze and monitor the firewall's events and logs. Look for anomalies and messages that might indicate further examination.

- Use change management to document the firewall change and the associated back-out plan should something go wrong during the change window.

Firewall ACLs

Firewalls control access to and from the Internet and provide interaction with customers, suppliers, and employees. But because the Internet is unsecure, firewalls need to use ACLs to permit and deny traffic flowing through it. Firewalls use security zones to define trust levels that are associated with the firewall's interfaces. For example, the trusted zone is associated with an interface connected to the internal network, and the untrusted zone is associated with an interface connected to outside of the firewall. Common security zones include the inside, outside, and demilitarized zone (DMZ), but others can be created as needed.

Figure 13-3 shows an ASA firewall with three zones and the permitted policy and flow of the traffic.

The policy for the firewall shown in Figure 13-3 includes the following:

- Allow HTTP and HTTPS to the Internet
- Allow HTTPS and FTP to the public web and FTP server
- Allow HTTPS to the public e-commerce server

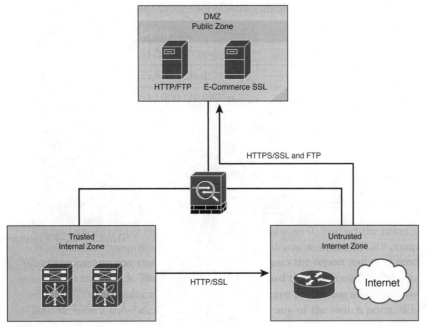

Figure 13-3 *Firewall ACLs and zones*

Cisco Identity-Based Network Services

The Cisco Identity-Based Network Services solution is a way to authenticate host access based on policy for admission to the network. IBNS supports identity authentication, dynamic provisioning of VLANs on a per-user basis, guest VLANs, and 802.1X with port security.

The 802.1X protocol is a standards-based protocol for authenticating network clients by permitting or denying access to the network. The 802.1X protocol operates between the end-user client seeking access and an Ethernet switch or wireless access point (AP) providing the connection to the network. In 802.1X terminology, clients are called *supplicants*, and switches and APs are called *authenticators*. A back-end Remote Authentication Dial-In User Service (RADIUS) server such as a Cisco Identity Services Engine (ISE) provides the user account database used to apply authentication and authorization.

With an IBNS solution, the host uses 802.1X and Extensible Authentication Protocol over LANs (EAPoL) to send the credentials and initiate a session to the network. After the host and switch establish LAN connectivity, username and password credentials are requested. The client host then sends the credentials to the switch, which forwards them to the RADIUS service running on Cisco ISE.

The RADIUS service performs a lookup on the username and password to determine the credentials' validity. If the username and password are correct, an accept message is sent to the switch or AP to allow access to the client host. If the username and password are incorrect, the server sends a message to the switch or AP to block the host port.

Figure 13-4 illustrates the communication flow of two hosts using 802.1X and EAPoL with the switch, AP, and back-end Cisco ISE server running RADIUS.

13

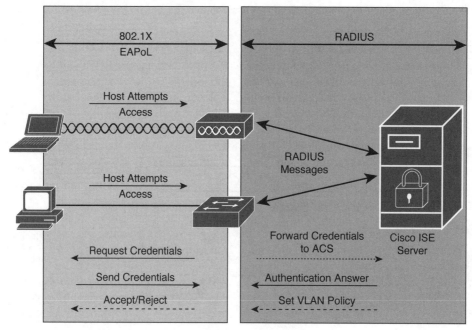

Figure 13-4 *802.1X and EAPoL with Cisco ISE*

Identity and Access Control Deployments

Validating user authentication should be implemented as close to the source as possible, with an emphasis on strong authentication for access from untrusted networks. Access rules should enforce policy deployed throughout the network with the following guidelines:

- Source-specific rules with any type destinations should be applied as close to the source as possible.

- Destination-specific rules with any type sources should be applied as close to the desti-nation as possible.

- Mixed rules integrating both source and destination should be used as close to the source as possible.

An integral part of identity and access control deployments is to allow only the necessary access. Highly distributed rules allow for greater granularity and scalability but, unfortunate-ly, increase the management complexity. On the other hand, centralized rule deployment eases management but lacks flexibility and scalability.

Figure 13-5 shows the importance of the authentication databases and how many network components in the enterprise rely on them for authentication services.

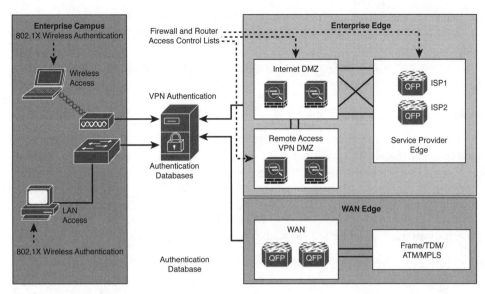

Figure 13-5 *Identity and access control*

Detecting and Mitigating Threats

The use of threat detection and mitigation techniques enables early detection of and notifications about unwanted malicious traffic. The goals are to detect, notify, and help stop unforeseen and unauthorized traffic. These techniques help increase the network's availability, particularly against unidentified and unexpected attacks. Threat detection and mitigation solutions include the following:

- **Endpoint protection:** Viruses and worms can create havoc by propagating infections from host to host throughout the network. Antivirus services can help hosts detect and remove infections based on known virus pattern markings.

- **Application security and content security defense:** Several new application layer network products have been released that help address new classes of threats, such as spam, phishing, spyware, packet abuse, and unauthorized point-to-point file sharing. Content security products such as Cisco WSA Appliances provide comprehensive antivirus, antispyware, file-blocking, antispam, URL blocking, and content-filtering services. These products supplement traditional firewalls and intrusion prevention system (IPS) solutions with more granular traffic inspection services, thereby quarantining traffic so that it does not propagate throughout the network.

- **Infection containment:** The Cisco ASA, ASA Services Module, and IOS firewalls protect the network by creating security zones that partition the network into separate segments. The firewall services provide perimeter network security but do not eliminate the need for continuous network monitoring. As part of the Cisco SAFE architecture, Cisco ISE can be used in the perimeter to perform policy-based admission control, thus reducing potential threats.

13

■ **Inline IPS:** Cisco has innovated in the area of IPS by being the first to incorporate IPS into the IOS on routing and switching platforms. In addition, IPS solutions have inline filtering features that can remove unwanted traffic with programmable features that classify traffic patterns. The Cisco IOS IPS can identify, analyze, and stop unwanted traffic from flowing on the network.

IPS/IDS Fundamentals

Intrusion prevention and intrusion detection systems are network security devices that proactively identify and block security threats. Today's security threats are far too complex to be secured by a single security device. Although security techniques such as access control, firewall services, and device hardening help secure the network from attacks, they cannot provide adequate protections from fast moving malware or zero-day attacks. Network security must adapt to these threats, and new network designs should include IDS and IPS that have features that can detect and block these new and evolving threats.

Both IPS and IDS look at packet payloads and compare these against security signatures that they know about.

Intrusion prevention systems are classified into two categories:

■ **Intrusion detection systems (IDSs)** are passive devices that monitor traffic and generate alerts or logs when suspicious traffic is detected from attacks such as reconnaissance or DoS attacks. Since IDS devices are only analyzing traffic flows, there is no impact at all to network performance.

■ **Intrusion prevention systems (IPSs)** are active devices that not only can detect but also block malicious traffic from coming into the network. For the IPS to actually block traffic, it has to be deployed in inline mode, where traffic is forced through the IPS. That way, the IPS can detect and prevent suspicious traffic in real time from accessing the internal network.

IPS/IDS technologies are commonly deployed as sensors, and they are available in many options. IPS sensors can be deployed on dedicated hardware appliances or using IPS software on routers, switches, or firewall modules. Both IPS and IDS technologies need to be able to detect malicious traffic, which has unique characteristics identified through the use of signatures. A *signature* is a set of rules that IPS/IDS sensors use to detect suspicious activity during network attacks. Signatures can detect viruses, malware, and protocol anomalies. Sensors are tuned to detect irregular traffic patterns or viruses by matching a signature.

Both IPS and IDS can be used together to increase security by providing extra visibility into the traffic flows. Because an IDS has zero impact on the network, it can be used to do deeper packet inspections in more areas within the network, and the IPS can be used for the most critical parts of the network.

Table 13-2 outlines the pros and cons of IDS and IPS devices.

Table 13-2   IDS/IPS Pros and Cons

	IDS	IPS
Pros	Zero impact to the network performance.	Can stop attacks.
	No network impact if sensor fails.	Use of stream normalization methods.
Cons	Attacks cannot be stopped.	Network performance impacts on latency and jitter.
	More vulnerable to intrusion techniques.	Network impact due to sensor failure.

IPS/IDS Guidelines

Here are some recommended guidelines to consider when deploying IPS/IDS services:

- Place IPS sensor appliances behind the firewall so that you only see traffic that has been filtered by the firewall policy

- Review the traffic load that it will need to handle as part of proper capacity planning for sizing the IPS sensors. Consider the performance impacts of enabling IPS features.

- Tune default signatures to reduce false positives. Monitor traffic for the first 30 days and tune the signatures afterwards to filter out noisy signatures.

- Develop an update schedule for downloading signatures near the release time of the new signatures. Tune the new signatures if needed.

- Monitor network events on a daily basis and look for malicious traffic patterns by correlating the events through a central monitoring system.

13

Figure 13-6 illustrates the recommended IPS placement behind the firewall.

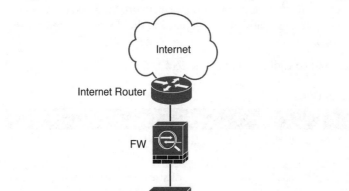

Figure 13-6 *IPS placement*

Threat Detection and Mitigation Technologies

Here are some examples of Cisco threat-detection and threat-mitigation technologies:

- ASA Service Module: Catalyst 6500 ASA Services Module
- ASA: Adaptive Security Appliance (robust firewall)
- IOS firewall: Cisco IOS software feature set
- FirePOWER IPS: Module for ASA appliance
- FirePOWER Next-Gen IPS appliances
- IPS: Intrusion prevention system (IOS feature)
- Cisco Web Security Appliance (Cisco WSA)
- Cisco Email Security Appliance (Cisco ESA)
- Network management protocols and solutions:
  - **NetFlow:** Stats on packets flowing through router (IOS feature)
  - **Syslog:** Logging data (IOS feature)
  - **SNMP:** Simple Network Management Protocol (IOS feature)

Threat-Detection and Threat-Mitigation Solutions

Threat-detection and threat-mitigation solutions are deployed throughout the network and can serve as an effective layered defense for secure network communications. For example, suppose your network is being attacked from the Internet (for example, via a worm or virus outbreak). The Internet WAN routers are your first line of protection and can be used to spot increasing network load or suspicious NetFlow data. After some information has been collected, you can use specific granular ACLs to further identify the attack.

Firewalls can perform stateful packet inspections and can ultimately block unwanted network traffic in the event of an attack. However, it is preferable to engage the ISP and have them block the attack from even entering your network.

To successfully detect threats and mitigate them, it is important to understand where to look for potential threats. The following are good sources of information for detecting and mitigating threats:

- NetFlow
- Syslog
- Remote Monitor (RMON) events
- Simple Network Management Protocol (SNMP) thresholds and traps
- CPU and interface statistics

Figure 13-7 depicts an attacker sourcing from the Internet and targeting the internal network and how to detect and mitigate the threat.

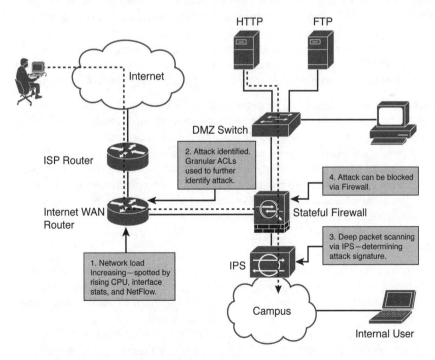

Figure 13-7 *Threat detection and mitigation*

FirePOWER IPS

The growth of data center resources along with increased security policy complexity are driving the need for next-generation security services. A comprehensive set of security capabilities is needed in order to combat advanced data security threats in addition to firewall security services. Cisco ASA clustering along with FirePOWER service modules provides increased security capabilities and simplicity to help mitigate these challenges.

FirePOWER module features and benefits for Cisco ASA appliances include the following:

- **Next-generation intrusion prevention system (NGIPS):** Provides threat protection and contextual awareness

- **URL filtering:** Provides over 80 categories and millions of URLs for filtering

- **Application Visibility and Control (AVC):** Provides over 3000 application layer and risk-based controls

- **Advanced Malware Protection (AMP):** Provides malware detection and blocking

Cisco ESA

Cisco Email Security Appliances (ESAs) are designed to protect networks from today's and tomorrow's email threats. Cisco ESA is a firewall and threat-monitoring appliance for SMTP-based traffic (on TCP port 25). Cisco ESAs are available as physical hardware appliances or as virtual Cisco ESA appliances. In the email delivery process, ESA acts as an SMTP gateway firewall for the enterprise. One of the advantages of using Cisco ESA for your MTA in the message transfer chain is that ESA can determine the source IP address and query that against the Cisco SensorBase to get the sender's reputation score. Cisco ESA uses the reputation score to stop spam, viruses, and malware from arriving in users' mailboxes.

Multiple deployment options are available depending on the number of interfaces used. It is generally recommended to place the ESA appliance close to the Internet firewall. The most common deployment option uses a single physical interface inserted in a dedicated or shared DMZ firewalled network segment. An alternative approach is to use two interfaces, one to send and receive email traffic located in the DMZ and another interface connected to an inside network to deliver mail to internal mail servers. With either approach, it is recommended to use a static Network Address Translation (NAT) on the Internet firewall to translate the public address into a private address located in the DMZ.

Cisco WSA

The Cisco Web Security Appliance (WSA) is designed to monitor and mitigate abnormal web traffic between users and the public Internet. WSA appliances provide web filtering, malware protection, identity-based polices, and SSL offload services. Cisco WSAs are available as physical hardware appliances or as virtual Cisco WSA appliances. The WSA acts as a web proxy for the corporate users residing on the internal network segments and is logically placed in the path between the users and the Internet. There are three ways to implement the WSA, two of which require Internet browser customizations.

Table 13-3 describes the Cisco WSA mode options.

Table 13-3   Cisco WSA Modes

Cisco WSA Mode	Description
Explicit mode with proxy auto-configuration (PAC) files	Proxy information stores in PAC
	Automatic download of PAC to browser using DHCP/DNS
	Supports redundancy; multiple WSAs listed in PAC
Explicit mode without PAC files	Requires changes to every browser
	Configuration of browser to point to the WSA as its proxy
	Does not support redundancy
Transparent mode with Web Cache Communication Protocol (WCCP)	Web traffic transparently directed to WSA using WCCP redirection
	No changes to browser necessary
	Requires configuration of WCCP-enabled FW/Router/L3 switch to point traffic to WSA
	Supports load sharing and redundancy

It is recommended to use explicit mode with PAC files for testing and then transition to WCCP for final implementation. The PAC file implementation is much easier to deploy during testing than WCCP because you just need to modify the test browser proxy settings; however, the WCCP mode is much more elegant in the long run because you do not need to modify all the users' browsers settings.

Security Management Applications

Security management applications consolidate network management and monitoring, which allows more secure control of the network. Security management provides several functions:

- Central repository for collecting network information for further analysis of security-related events. In addition, many applications have reporting capabilities to help network managers' present technical information to upper management. Some examples include authentication, authorization, and accounting (AAA) with TACACS and RADIUS servers, Cisco ISE, and syslog servers.

- Allows for easier deployment of security policies into the security devices via graphical user interface (GUI) tools. These tools help you maintain the consistency of the security policies across a broad spectrum of network device types.

- Role-based access control for all accounts to separate administrative tasks and user functions.

Security implementations need to be planned properly using the security policies governed by the organization to make good use of the security applications. From time to time, audits are necessary, which requires updates to the security policy and related security management applications. A major risk to security implementations is policy error. Management needs to be cognizant of the security policy and know how to manage incidents properly.

13

Security Platform Solutions

Cisco has a variety of security management products and technologies that allow scalable administration and enforcement of security policy for the Cisco SCF architecture. These solutions reduce the operational management and automate many of the common tasks, including configuration, analysis, incident response, and reporting. Security management platforms include the following:

- **Cisco Security Manager (CSM)** is an integrated solution for GUI configuration management of firewall, VPN, and IPS policies on Cisco security appliances, firewalls, routers, and switch modules. CSM has capabilities for security policies to be deployed by device, by group, or globally for all devices.

- **Cisco Secure Access Control Server (ACS)** provides centralized control for administrative access to Cisco devices and security applications. ACS provides for AAA security services and supports routers, switches, VPN services, and ASAs. In addition, Cisco ACS also supports back-end directory integration with Lightweight Directory Access Protocol (LDAP) and Microsoft Active Directory (AD) for authentication services.

- **Cisco Identity Services Engine (ISE):** Cisco ISE is a security policy management platform that automates access control by enforcing compliance, increasing network security, and improving operations. Cisco ISE provides accurate identification of users and devices on the network including easy provisioning of all devices. ISE collects rich contextual data about the connected users and devices and can provide policy enforcement and security compliance before the device is even authorized to access the network.

- **System Administration Jump Host** provides a centralized host used to stage configuration, software images, and implement network changes.

- **Network Time Protocol (NTP)** server provides time synchronization to NTP clients such as routers and switches. Time synchronization is crucial in the analysis of event correlations.

- **Configuration and Software Archive Host** serves as a repository to backup device configurations and software images.

Security Management Network

The SAFE architecture design incorporates a management network module dedicated to carrying network management and control plane traffic such as NTP, SSH, SNMP, TACACS, VPN, syslog, and NetFlow reporting. Two primary technologies are used in the management module: Cisco IOS routers acting as terminal servers and a management VLAN or separate network segment. Together, these technologies provide configuration management to nearly all network devices. The management VLAN provides the primary access method for devices using SSH and HTTPS. Hardened terminal servers provide console access and command-line interface (CLI) using reverse Telnet functions. It is a best practice to configure your network devices to send network management traffic such as NTP, SSH, SNMP, TACACS, syslog, and NetFlow traffic back to the dedicated network management VLAN.

Network management can be implemented in both in-band (IB) management and out-of-band (OOB) management configurations designed to provide secure management of network devices within the enterprise. OOB management is typically located at the headquarters and uses dedicated Ethernet ports on the devices connected to the OOB VLAN or network segment.

These Ethernet ports are intended to be used for management and monitoring functions of the network devices. The OOB management network can be a separate LAN or by using an isolated VLAN. The in-band management is used for remote devices such as branch site routers and the access is provided through a firewalled data path through the core network.

In some cases, console access to the network equipment is needed, and that functionality can be provided using an OOB console server.

Figure 13-8 illustrates the security management network using both IB and OOB networks for carrying control and management plane traffic. The firewall controls the security between the IB and OOB networks.

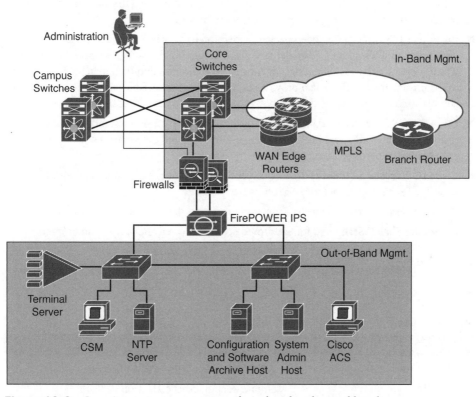

Figure 13-8 *Security management network: in-band and out-of-band*

Integrating Security into Network Devices

It is crucial to integrate security into all network devices throughout your network. Common device types include

- IOS routers and switches
- Adaptive Security Appliances (ASAs)
- Intrusion Prevention Systems (IPSs)
- Catalyst 6500 service modules
- Endpoint security

13

The following sections discuss device security integration in more detail.

IOS Security

Cisco has developed many security features that are integrated into the IOS base software or security-specific feature sets. Here are some of the major areas of security focus that have been included with IOS releases:

- **Cisco IOS firewall** is a security-specific option that provides stateful firewall functionality for perimeter IOS routers. Cisco IOS firewall provides effective control of application traffic flowing through the network. Key benefits of IOS firewall include protecting networks from network and application layer attacks, improving uptime, and offering policy enforcement for internal and external connections.

- **Cisco IOS IPS** offers inline deep packet inspection to successfully diminish a wide range of network attacks. IOS IPS can identify, classify, and block malicious traffic in real time. IOS IPS operates by loading attack signatures on the router and then matching the attacks based on signatures. Cisco also provides prebuilt signature definition files (SDF) that contain high-fidelity signatures that are based on the memory available on the router.

- **Cisco IOS IPsec** encrypts data at the IP packet level using a set of standards-based protocols. IPsec provides data authentication, anti-replay, and data confidentially, and is the preferred method of securing VPNs.

- **Cisco IOS Trust and Identity** is a set of core technologies that enables network traffic security. Technologies include the following:

    - **AAA:** Framework and mechanisms for controlling device access
    - **Secure Shell (SSH):** Used for encrypted access between applications and routers
    - **Secure Socket Layer (SSL):** Secure web application access
    - **PKI (Public Key Infrastructure):** Strong authentication for e-commerce applications

Table 13-4 describes the Cisco IOS integrated security features.

Table 13-4 Integrated Security for Cisco IOS

Cisco IOS Integrated Security	Description
Cisco IOS firewall	Stateful multiservice application-based filtering
Cisco IOS IPS	Inline deep packet inspection
Cisco IOS IPsec	Data encryption at the packet level
Cisco IOS Trust and Identity	AAA, PKI, SSH, SSL

ISR G2 Security Hardware Options

The Cisco G2 ISRs have additional hardware options that enhance the routers' security capabilities. Here are some of the available hardware options:

- **Built-In VPN Acceleration** is hardware-based encryption that offloads VPN processing from the router's internal CPU to improve VPN throughput.

- **High-Performance Advanced Integration Module (AIM)** is a VPN encryption advanced integration module used to terminate large numbers of VPN tunnels such as with Dynamic Multipoint VPN (DMVPN). The module supports Triple Digital Encryption Standard (3DES) and Advanced Encryption Standard (AES), which increases the router's encryption and compression performance.

- **IPS Enhanced Network Module (IPS NME)** provides technologies to prevent a large range of security threats using hardware-based intrusion prevention. Cisco IPS NME can identify, classify, and stop unwanted traffic, including spyware, malware, network viruses, and worms. The IPS NME can monitor up to 75 Mbps of traffic and supports T1/E1 and T3 WAN interfaces.

- **Universal serial bus (USB) port and removable credentials**: G2 ISRs were designed with onboard USB 1.1 ports, enabling security and storage capabilities. The USB ports allow for storing removable credentials for establishing IPsec VPN connections, configuration files, and software images.

- **Secure Voice**: Referred to as digital signal processor (DSP) slots on the ISR for use with packet voice/fax DSP modules (PVDMs). These offer capabilities such as conferencing and transcoding. In addition, Secure Real-time Transport Protocol (SRTP) protects the entire voice payload by encryption, except for the header, which remains in clear text to support QoS.

> **Note**   For a complete ISR G2 series comparison, go to www.cisco.com/en/US/products/ ps10536/prod_series_comparison.html.

Cisco Security Appliances

Cisco security appliances provide robust security services and protection for firewalling, VPN services, content defenses, intrusion prevention services, and network access control. The following is an overview of Cisco security appliances:

- **Adaptive Security Appliance (ASA):** The ASA is a high-performance, multifunction security appliance that offers a comprehensive set of services for securing network environments. The services are customized through product editions tailored for firewall, IPS, anti-virus, and VPN. The ASA is a critical component of the Cisco SAFE architecture that provides proactive threat mitigation, controls application data flows, and delivers flexible VPN and IPS services. In addition, the ASA is very cost-effective and easy to manage, and offers advanced integration modules that enhance the processing capabilities. ASA also has support for FirePOWER IPS module capabilities.

- **ASAs for VPNs:** The Cisco ASAs provide businesses with IPsec and SSL VPN connectivity. ASAs are flexible and offer many deployment scenarios. Although they are commonly used to terminate VPN sessions for remote-access connections, ASAs can also be used to terminate site-to-site tunnels with other ASAs, routers, or even non-Cisco firewalls. The centralized architecture and web-based management ease the administrative burden and consolidate the VPN connectivity for the enterprise.

13

- **Cisco Identity Services Engine (ISE):** Cisco ISE is a security policy management platform that automates access control by enforcing compliance, increasing network security, and improving operations. Cisco ISE provides accurate identification of users and devices on the network, including easy provisioning of all devices. ISE collects rich contextual data about the connected users and devices, and can provide policy enforcement and security compliance before a device is even authorized to access the network.

Catalyst 6500 Service Modules

The Catalyst 6500 switching platform supports additional security services and functionality through the use of service modules. Several service module options extend the capabilities of security-related services with the Cisco Catalyst 6500 platform. Many environments now combine many of these service modules together to form what is now referred to as *services switches*.

Catalyst 6500 security-related service modules include the following:

- **ASA Services Module** is a high-speed firewall module for use in the Cisco Catalyst 6500 and Cisco 7600 series routing platforms. Up to four ASA Service Modules can be installed in a single chassis, providing 20 Gbps of throughput performance per module. For service provider and large enterprise environments, the ASA Service Module supports advanced features such as multiple security contexts for both routed and transparent firewall modes. Running multiple contexts on the same firewall hardware is a technique used to virtualize the ASA into multiple firewalls, each with its own configuration and firewall policy.

- **IPsec VPN SPA** enables cost-effective and scalable VPN services using the Cisco Catalyst 6500 series switches and Cisco 7600 series routing platforms. The module does not have any interfaces, but instead uses the other LAN and WAN interfaces that are available on the chassis. Using the SPA Carrier-400, each slot of the Cisco Catalyst 6500 or Cisco 7600 router can support up to two Cisco IPsec VPN SPAs.

- **WebVPN Services Module** is a high-speed integrated SSL VPN Services Module for support of large-scale remote-access VPN deployments. The WebVPN Services Module supports up to 32,000 SSL VPN users, and up to 4 modules can be used in a single chassis.

- **Network Analysis Module 3** provides packet-capture capabilities and visibility into all the layers of the network data flows, including overlay technologies such as CAPWAP and VXLAN. You can analyze application traffic between hosts, networks, and servers. The NAM supports L4-7 visibility using Cisco Network-based Application Recognition 2 (NBAR2).

Endpoint Security

Endpoint security solutions protect server and desktop endpoints from the latest threats caused by malicious network attacks. Endpoint security solutions can identify and prevent network attacks that are considered unknown or "day-zero"-type threats. Cisco ISE enables the network to enforce security policies on both wired and wireless devices seeking access to the network infrastructure. Cisco ISE protects data and prevents unauthorized network access by initially confirming a user's identity before allowing access. Cisco ISE also provides posture assessment to reduce the risks associated with noncompliant devices by not allowing network access until the device is compliant with the configured policy.

Securing the Enterprise

The Cisco SAFE architecture provides the most comprehensive security systems for securing the enterprise network from the threats of today and tomorrow.

Each location in the enterprise network has unique security requirements because concerns are different and vary by location. In most cases, however, customizing network security solutions by functional area offers the best protection for the enterprise network.

The following sections examine some ways to use Cisco security solutions in the campus, data center, and enterprise edge.

Implementing Security in the Campus

Security for the campus begins with remembering that you need to implement security throughout your network. Several technologies, protocols, solutions, and devices work together to provide the secure campus. Network security should be implemented in the core, distribution, and access layers and can be grouped into four broad categories, as described in Table 13-5.

Table 13-5   Security in the Campus

Cisco Security Category	Security Solutions
Identity and access control	802.1X, ACLs, and firewalls
Threat detection and mitigation	NetFlow, syslog, SNMP, RMON, and IPS
Infrastructure protection	AAA, TACACS, RADIUS, SSH, SNMPv3, IGP/EGP MD5, and Layer 2 security features
Security management	CSM, Cisco ISE, and ACS

Figure 13-9 illustrates an enterprise campus security scenario and shows where security technologies, protocols, and mechanisms can be deployed in the enterprise campus.

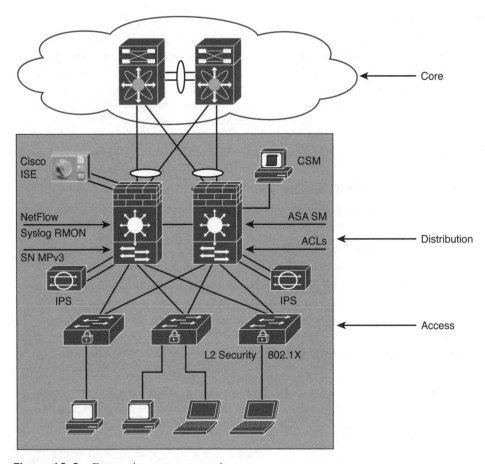

Figure 13-9   *Enterprise campus security*

Implementing Security in the Data Center

The enterprise data center hosts critical servers and applications for the main campus and the branch offices. Many of the servers require high availability because of the importance of the information and the high volume of users they serve. Several of the servers may contain sensitive information that is crucial to the business and therefore cannot become compromised. Therefore, it needs to be highly secured. Network performance is another area that is critically important, which can limit the choice of protection mechanisms and technologies. Here are some of the risks inherent with enterprise data centers:

■ Compromised applications and unauthorized access to critical information

■ Exploiting different servers in the business by launching an attack from the compromised servers

To provide adequate security protection, organizations can implement the network security solutions described in Table 13-6.

Table 13-6 Security in the Data Center

Cisco Security Category	Security Solutions
Identity and access control	802.1X, ACLs, and firewalls (ASA SM)
Threat detection and mitigation	NetFlow, syslog, SNMP, RMON, and IPS
Infrastructure protection	AAA, TACACS, RADIUS, SSH, SNMPv3, IGP/EGP MD5, and Layer 2 security features
Security management	CSM, Cisco ISE, and ACS

Figure 13-10 illustrates an enterprise data center security scenario and shows where security technologies, protocols, and mechanisms can be deployed in the enterprise data center.

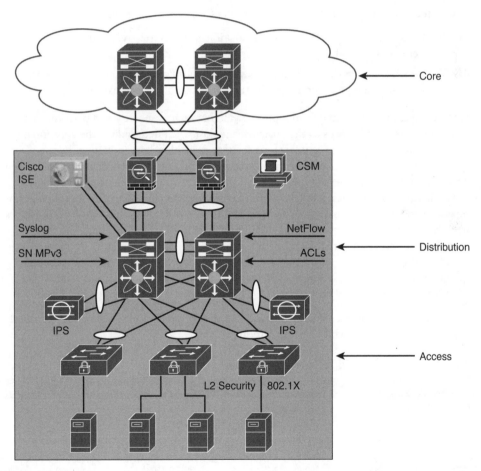

Figure 13-10 *Enterprise data center security*

13

Implementing Security in the Enterprise Edge

The enterprise edge provides connectivity to other parts of your network over insecure public networks. It is important to consider the available security options when transferring data between locations over Internet transports.

When you're selecting devices for the enterprise edge, design choices need to be factored in for levels of granularity of services per device. There are choices between all-in-one devices and dedicated device-per-service models. The all-in-one devices can simplify management and lower cost, but may lack some advanced features and increase the risk of exposure. The dedicated device per service, on the other hand, can enable increased levels of performance and security overall, but can add in more CAPEX and OPEX. Device types available include physical appliances, virtual appliance, or a cloud-based service for most of the security devices.

Integrated multiple services on Cisco routers and Cisco ASAs are as follows:

- **Cisco routers:** Provide VRFs to enable isolation at the router layer and can be stitched together over Layer 3 hops in the network.

- **Cisco ASAs:** Feature virtual contexts that allow multiple firewall instances to be run on the same hardware; however, not all features are available in context mode.

The design choices need to consider business factors such as security and performance characteristics, security risks to the business, and cost when determining the appropriate solution. There may be different levels of security available when evaluating the use of a public cloud service versus an on-premises private cloud option. Performance aspects need to be considered regarding the use of virtual workloads with dependencies on underlying server hardware or physical appliances with known performance characteristics. In addition, upgrades to virtual workloads are software- and license-based, whereas physical appliances require new purchases along with the install of new hardware and licensing. The virtualization layer can also add in redundancy for the virtual appliances without the typical cost of additional hardware. Security risks for cloud services are normally higher than with on-premises private cloud-based options. Then there is the cost evaluation for CAPEX and OPEX for the security solution.

Table 13-7 lists the device components with the device types of physical, virtual, or cloud service if the service provider has the offering available.

Table 13-7   Enterprise Edge Device Selection

Security Function	Cisco Device	Device Types
Network Firewall	Cisco ASA	Physical Virtual Cloud service (optional)
Remote Access VPN	Cisco ASA	Physical Virtual Cloud service (optional)

Security Function	Cisco Device	Device Types
Site-to-Site VPN	Cisco ASA	Physical
	Cisco CSR	Virtual Cloud service (optional)
Edge Routing	Cisco IOS routers	Physical
Intrusion Prevention System	Cisco ASA with FirePOWER	Physical
Email Security	Cisco ESA	Physical Virtual Cloud service (optional)
Web Security	Cisco WSA	Physical Virtual Cloud service (optional)
Security Policy Management	Cisco ISE	Physical Virtual
Access Policy System	Cisco ACS	Physical Virtual

Keep in mind the following potential risk areas when moving data between locations:

- Attackers obtain access to the network and compromise the confidentiality and integrity of sensitive information with eavesdropping or data manipulation.

- Misconfiguration of the enterprise edge devices could cause inappropriate device configurations and unwanted connectivity.

To provide adequate security protection between locations, organizations can implement the security solutions described in Table 13-8.

Table 13-8   Security in the Enterprise Edge

Cisco Security Category	Security Solutions
Identity and access control	Firewalls, IPS, IPsec, SSL VPN, and ACLs
Threat detection and mitigation	NetFlow, syslog, SNMP, RMON, and IPS
Infrastructure protection	AAA, CoPP, TACACS, RADIUS, SSH, SNMP v3, IGP/EGP MD5, RFC 2827 ingress filtering, and Layer 2 security features
Security management	CSM and ACS

13

Figure 13-11 illustrates the use of enterprise edge and where security technologies, protocols, and mechanisms can be deployed in the enterprise edge.

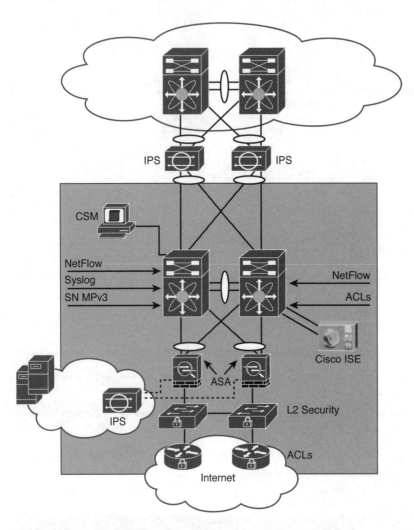

Figure 13-11 *Enterprise edge security*

References and Recommended Readings

The Cisco ASA 5500 as a Superior Firewall Solution, www.cisco.com/c/en/us/products/collateral/security/asa-5500-series-next-generation-firewalls/prod_white_paper0900a-ecd8058ec85.html.

Cisco SAFE Solution Overview, www.cisco.com/en/US/docs/solutions/Enterprise/Security/SAFESolOver.html.

SAFE Poster, www.cisco.com/c/dam/en/us/solutions/collateral/enterprise/design-zone-security/safe-poster-components.pdf.

Module 4 (Enterprise Network Design), Designing for Cisco Internetwork Solution Course (DESGN) 3.0.

Cisco Security Control Framework (SCF) Model, www.cisco.com/en/US/docs/solutions/Enterprise/Security/CiscoSCF.html.

RFC 2827: Network Ingress Filtering: Defeating Denial of Service Attacks Which Employ IP Source Address Spoofing, www.faqs.org/rfcs/rfc2827.html.

Cisco Identity Services Engine Data Sheet, www.cisco.com/c/en/us/products/collateral/security/identity-services-engine/data_sheet_c78-656174.html.

Exam Preparation Tasks

Review All Key Topics

Review the most important topics in the chapter, noted with the Key Topic icon in the outer margin of the page. Table 13-9 lists a reference of these key topics and the page numbers on which each is found.

Table 13-9 Key Topics

Key Topic Element	Description	Page
List	Secure Domains of SAFE	524
Summary	Cisco Security Control Framework	526
List	Trust and Identity technologies	527
List	Types of firewalls	528
List	Next-Gen Firewalls	529
List	Detecting and mitigating threats	533
List	IPS/IDS Fundamentals	534
Table 13-2	IDS/IPS Pros and Cons	535
List	FirePOWER module features	538
Table 13-3	Cisco WSA Modes	539
List	Security platform solutions	540
List	Integrating security into network devices	541
Table 13-4	Integrated security for Cisco IOS	542
List	Cisco security appliances	543
List	Catalyst 6500 service modules	544
Table 13-5	Security in the campus	545
Table 13-6	Security in the data center	547
Table 13-7	Enterprise Edge Device Selection	548
Table 13-8	Security in the enterprise edge	549

Complete Tables and Lists from Memory

Print a copy of Appendix D, "Memory Tables" (found on the book website), or at least the section for this chapter, and complete the tables and lists from memory. Appendix E, "Memory Tables Answer Key," also on the website, includes completed tables and lists to check your work.

Define Key Terms

Define the following key terms from this chapter, and check your answers in the glossary:

Adaptive Security Appliance (ASA), Integrated Services Router (ISR) G2, Cisco Catalyst switches, access control lists, firewall, FirePOWER IPS, Cisco ISE, 802.1X, Cisco

Identity-Based Network Services (IBNS), Cisco Security Manager (CSM), Cisco Secure Access Control Server (ACS), Cisco Adaptive Security Device Manager (ASDM)

Q&A

The answers to these questions appear in Appendix A, "Answers to the 'Do I Know This Already?' Quizzes and Q&A Questions." For more practice with exam format questions, use the exam engine on the CD.

1. What security device combines IOS firewall with VPN and IPS services?

   a. ASA

   b. ISR

   c. Cisco Catalyst switches

   d. IPS

2. Which of the following is a standards-based protocol for authenticating network clients?

   a. Cisco ISE

   b. PoE

   c. 802.1X

   d. CSM

3. The Cisco _____ is an integrated solution led by Cisco that incorporates the network infrastructure and third-party software to impose security policy on attached endpoints.

   a. ASA

   b. CSM

   c. ISR

   d. ISE

4. What software-based solution can network security administrators use to configure standalone ASA firewalls? (Select the best answer.)

   a. ISR

   b. Cisco ISE

   c. ASDM

   d. IDM

5. Cisco IOS Trust and Identity has a set of services that includes which of the following? (Select all that apply.)

   a. 802.1X

   b. SSL

   c. AAA

   d. ASDM

13

6. Cisco IOS _____ offers data encryption at the IP packet level using a set of standards-based protocols.

    a. IPS

    b. IPsec

    c. L2TP

    d. L2F

7. What provides hardware VPN encryption for terminating a large number of VPN tunnels for ISRs?

    a. ASA SM

    b. WebVPN Services Module

    c. Network Analysis Module 3

    d. High-Performance AIM

8. What are two ways to enhance VPN performance on Cisco ISR G2s?

    a. SSL Network Module

    b. IDS Network Module

    c. Built-In Hardware VPN Acceleration

    d. High-Performance AIM

9. Which Cisco security solution can prevent noncompliant devices from accessing the network until they are compliant?

    a. IPsec

    b. ASA Service module

    c. ACS

    d. Cisco ISE

10. Which of the following service modules do Cisco Catalyst 6500 switches support? (Select all that apply.)

    a. ASA SM

    b. Network Analysis Module 3

    c. High-Performance AIM

    d. FirePOWER IPS

11. What provides packet capture capabilities and visibility into all layers of network data flows?

    a. Network Analysis Module 3

    b. ASA Services Module

    c. WebVPN Services Module

    d. IPsec VPN SPA

12. Which of the following are identity and access control protocols and mechanisms? (Select all that apply.)

    a. 802.1X

    b. ACLs

    c. CSM

    d. NetFlow

13. Which two of the following are Cisco security management tools?

    a. CSM

    b. IDS module

    c. ACS

    d. Cisco ISE

14. True or false: NetFlow is used for threat detection and mitigation.

15. True or false: Cisco ASAs, ASA SM, and IOS firewall are part of infection containment.

16. What IOS feature offers inline deep packet inspection to successfully diminish a wide range of network attacks?

    a. IOS SSH

    b. IOS SSL VPN

    c. IOS IPsec

    d. IOS IPS

17. The Cisco _____ IPS Module for ASA can identify, analyze, and block unwanted traffic from flowing on the network.

18. What provides centralized control for administrative access to Cisco devices and security applications?

    a. CSM

    b. ACS

    c. NetFlow

    d. ASDM

19. Which of the following are PINs in the Cisco SAFE architecture?

    a. Core

    b. Data Center

    c. Telecommuter

    d. Distribution

20. Match each protocol, mechanism, or feature with its security grouping:

    i.   CSM

    ii. IGP/EGP MD5

    iii. NetFlow

    iv. Cisco ISE

    a. Identity and access control

    b. Threat detection and mitigation

    c. Infrastructure protection

    d. Security management

13

This chapter covers the following subjects:

Traditional Voice Architectures

Converged Multiservice Networks

IPT Design

The designs of enterprise voice networks are migrating from the traditional use of Private Branch Exchange (PBX) switches to the use of IP telephony architectures such as Cisco Unified Communications Manager (CUCM). Enterprise networks now have to be designed with IP telephony in mind. This chapter reviews public switched telephone network (PSTN) and PBX voice networks, converged multiservice networks, IP telephony (IPT) design, and quality of service (QoS) for IPT networks.

CHAPTER 14

Voice and Video Design

"Do I Know This Already?" Quiz

The "Do I Know This Already?" quiz helps you identify your strengths and deficiencies in this chapter's topics.

The ten-question quiz, derived from the major sections in the "Foundation Topics" portion of the chapter, helps you determine how to spend your limited study time.

Table 14-1 outlines the major topics discussed in this chapter and the "Do I Know This Already?" quiz questions that correspond to those topics.

Table 14-1 "Do I Know This Already?" Foundation Topics Section-to-Question Mapping

Foundation Topics Section	Questions Covered in This Section
Traditional Voice Architectures	5, 9
Converged Multiservice Networks	1, 2, 3, 4, 6, 7
IPT Design	8, 10

1. Which International Telecommunication Union (ITU) standard provides a framework for multimedia protocols for the transport of voice, video, and data over packet-switched networks?

    a. Session Initiation Protocol (SIP)

    b. Voice over IP (VoIP)

    c. H.323

    d. Weighted fair queuing (WFQ)

2. What is the default coder-decoder (codec) used with VoIP dial peers?

    a. G.711

    b. G.723

    c. G.728

    d. G.729

3. Real-time Transport Protocol (RTP) operates at what layer of the OSI model?

    a. Application

    b. Session

    c. Transport

    d. Network

4. Which H.323 protocol is responsible for call setup and signaling?

    a. H.245

    b. G.711

    c. H.225

    d. RTCP

5. What unit represents the average number of concurrent voice calls, commonly calculated for the period of 1 hour?

    a. Kbps

    b. Erlang

    c. DS0

    d. FXS

6. Which feature does not transmit packets when there is silence?

    a. Ear and mouth (E&M)

    b. Voice-activity detection (VAD)

    c. Dial peers

    d. Digital silence suppressor (DSS)

7. What does Compressed Real-time Transport Protocol (cRTP) compress?

    a. RTP headers

    b. RTP, TCP, and IP headers

    c. RTP, User Datagram Protocol (UDP), and IP headers

    d. Real-time Transport Control Protocol (RTCP) headers

8. Which QoS mechanism is recommended for VoIP networks?

    a. Custom queuing

    b. Low-latency queuing (LLQ)

    c. Priority queuing

    d. Switched-based queuing

9. Where is the local loop located?

    a. Between phones and the central office (CO) switch

    b. Between two PBXs

    c. Between the loopback interfaces of two VoIP routers

    d. Between two PSTN switches

10. What is jitter?

    a. The echo caused by mismatched impedance

    b. The loss of packets in the network

    c. The variable delay of received packets

    d. The fixed delay of received packets

Foundation Topics

This chapter covers traditional voice architectures, integrated voice design, and QoS in voice networks. The section "Traditional Voice Architectures" covers the architecture of time-division multiplexing (TDM) voice networks. It also discusses PSTN technologies and limitations.

The section "Converged Multiservice Networks" covers IP telephony design for Cisco Unified Communications. The "IPT Design" section covers QoS mechanisms used in IPT networks and provides IPT design recommendations.

Traditional Voice Architectures

This section reviews technologies and concepts to help you understand traditional voice networks. The content in this section is not in the CCDA exam blueprint. To focus on test material only, you can skip to the section "Converged Multiservice Networks."

The PSTN is the global public voice network that provides voice services. The PSTN is a variety of networks and services that are in place worldwide; it provides a circuit-switched service that uses Signaling System 7 (SS7) to control its calls. Central office (CO) switches exchange SS7 messages to place and route voice calls throughout the network. The PSTN uses TDM facilities to have multiple calls to be placed into a single signal. From the CO to the customer premises, the call can be analog, ISDN, or TDM digital. Each call consumes 64 Kbps of bandwidth, called digital service zero (DS0).

PBX and PSTN Switches

Traditional switches and PBXs route voice using TDM technology and analog technology. The CCDA must understand some of the differences between these devices. The PBX, as its name states, is used in a private network and uses proprietary protocols. The PBX is located in the enterprise's data center. Each PBX may scale up to thousands of phones. Companies deploy PBX networks to obtain enterprise feature such as extension dialing, dialing privilege control, voice mail, transfers, conferencing, and so on. Also companies that have multiple large locations with lots of intersite calling can implement tie lines to reduce long distance charges. On these types of circuits, there are no toll charges, but there are fixed costs associated with the circuits, which are provided by network carriers/phone companies.

PBXs are customer-owned voice switches. Enterprise companies install and configure their own PBXs to provide telephony service, abbreviated or extension dialing, remote-office extensions, voice mail, and private-line routing within other features. Organizations can reduce toll charges by using private tie lines between their switches. Calls that are placed between offices through the private voice network are called on-net. If a user needs to place a call outside the private network, the call is routed to the local PSTN. If the call is forwarded to the PSTN, it is called off-net.

Figure 14-1 shows a PBX network for an enterprise. Callers use the PBX network when they place calls from San Diego to Chicago, Atlanta, or Houston. The enterprise reduces toll charges by using its private voice network. A separate private network is in place for data traffic. If a user places a call from San Diego to Los Angeles, it is routed to the PSTN from the San Diego PBX. Then, toll charges are incurred for the call.

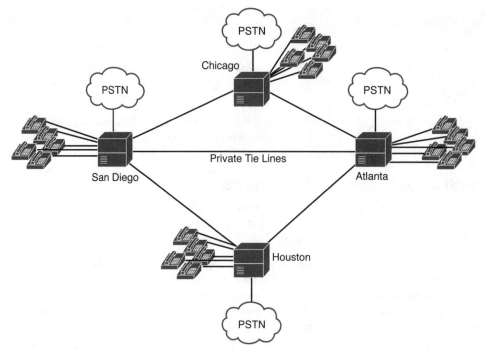

Figure 14-1   *PBX network*

Another issue in the design is the limitation on the number of calls per private line. If the private lines are T1s, they are each limited to carrying 24 concurrent calls at a time. This is because each call takes 64 Kbps of bandwidth with the G.711 codec, and 24 calls times 64 Kbps/call equals 1.536 Mbps, the bandwidth of a T1. All of this bandwidth is allocated for voice calls and cannot be used for data transport.

PSTN switches are not private. They can scale up to tens of thousands of phones and use open standards because they have to communicate with other switches, PBXs, fax machines, and home telephones. PSTN switches normally are located at the CO of the local or interexchange carrier.

Local Loop and Trunks

Depending on the dialed digits, a call routes through the local loop, one or more trunks, and the destination local loop to reach the destination phone. The local loop is the pair of wires that runs from the CO to the home or business office.

Trunks connect two switches. The type of trunk depends on the function of the switches the trunk is connecting. The term *tie line* is frequently used instead of *trunk* to describe a dedicated line connecting two telephone switches within a single organization. The following is a list of trunk types:

- **Interoffice trunk** connects two CO switches. Also called a PSTN switch trunk.
- **Tandem trunk** connects central offices within a geographic area.

- **Toll-connecting trunk** connects the CO to the long-distance office.

- **Intertoll trunk** connects two long-distance offices.

- **Tie trunk** connects two PBXs. Also called a private trunk.

- **PBX-to-CO trunk or CO-to-PBX business line** connects the CO switch to the enterprise PBX.

Figure 14-2 shows an example of the PSTN. All phones connect to their local CO via the local loop. Calls between Phones 1 and 2 and between Phones 4 and 5 go through interoffice trunks. Calls between Phones 2 and 3 go through tandem trunks within a region. When you place calls between Texas and Massachusetts, they are forwarded to the long-distance toll provider via a toll-connecting trunk and are routed through intertoll trunks.

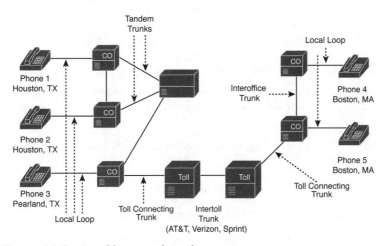

Figure 14-2 *Local loops and trunks*

Ports

You can use several ports to connect to voice end stations (phones) and private voice switches:

- **Foreign Exchange Station (FXS)** provides a connection from a switch to an analog end-point device such as traditional telephones or fax machines. It provides line power, dial tone, and ring voltage.

- **Foreign Exchange Office (FXO)** allows a switch such as a PBX to use a standard analog connection (FXS) from the PSTN or from another switch. In this case the PBX is emulating an endpoint device. Because this is a standard endpoint connection it uses two-wire connections just like a standard phone and often uses an RJ-11 connector interface.

- **Ear and Mouth (E&M)** connects private switches. It is an analog trunk used to connect to a voice switch; it supports tie-line facilities or signaling between phone switches. E&M can be connected with two-wire and four-wire. E&M is also called Earth and Magnet.

- **Channelized T1 (or E1)** circuits can be used to connect PBXs and the PSTN or two PBXs. These circuits can be provisioned in two different formats:
  - **Channel Associated Signaling (CAS) circuits** provide 24 (for T1) or 32 (for E1) channels (1 per DS0). CAS circuits get their name from the fact that switch-to-switch signaling (dialed digits, caller ID, and so on) occurs in-band on each individual channel with the voice traffic. Each DS0 channel is fixed at 64 Kbps, so this type of signaling takes a small number of bits away from the voice transmission to carry signaling data. Because of this CAS is also known as robbed-bit signaling.
  - **Common Channel Signaling (CCS) circuits** also use T1/E1 circuits. However, unlike CAS circuits, CCS circuits set aside one channel specifically for carrying signaling information for all of the other channels. This architecture allows for CCS circuits to provide a more robust feature set between switches. ISDN PRI uses CCS signaling and is the preferred connection type for PSTN-to-PBX or PBX-to-PBX connections. CCS support is not always available, and therefore CAS circuits are still widely used.

Major Analog and Digital Signaling Types

Signaling is needed to provide the state of telephones, digit dialing, and other information. For a call to be placed, managed, and closed, all of the following signaling categories have to occur:

- **Supervisory** provides call control and phone state (on-hook and off-hook).
- **Addressing** provides dialed digits.
- **Informational** provides information such as dial and busy tones and progress indicators.

These different signaling categories are provided by analog and digital circuit types.

The signaling type depends on the type of connection. The major areas are

- Loop start (CO to phone) is an analog signaling type commonly found in residential applications. The circuit is "started" when the loop is closed (connected) completing the circuit.
- Ground start (CO to phone) is an analog signaling that is an enhancement over loop start. Ground start allows for signaling between switches that allows one switch to signal to the other that it is fixing to go off-hook by "grounding" the line. This helps in preventing both sides from trying to seize access at the same time (called glare).
- E&M (PBX to PBX) is another analog switch-to-switch (PSTN-to-PBX or PBX-to-PBX) signaling type that provides additional signaling capability and can be a two-wire or four-wire implementation.
- CAS T1/E1 circuits get their name from the fact that switch-to-switch signaling (dialed digits, caller ID, and so on) occurs in-band on each individual channel with the voice traffic.

- CCS ISDN PRI circuits set aside one channel specifically for carrying signaling information for all the other channels.
- Q Signaling (Q.SIG).
- SS7 interswitch PSTN signaling.

Loop-Start Signaling

Loop-start signaling is an analog signaling technique used to indicate on-hook and off-hook conditions in the network. It is commonly used between the telephone set and the CO, PBX, or FXS module. As shown in Figure 14-3, with loop start, the local loop is open when the phone is on-hook. When the phone is taken off-hook, a −48 direct current (DC) voltage loops from the CO through the phone and back. Loop-start signaling is used for residential lines.

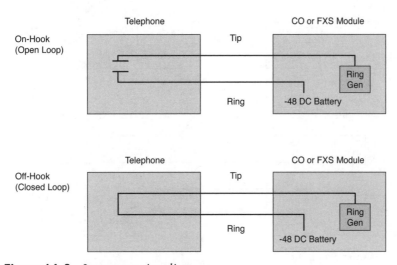

Figure 14-3 *Loop-start signaling*

Ground-Start Signaling

Ground-start signaling is an analog signaling technique used to indicate on-hook and off-hook conditions. Ground-start is commonly used in switch-to-switch connections. The difference between ground start and loop start is that ground start requires the closing of the loop at both locations. Ground start is commonly used by PBXs.

The standard way to transport voice between two telephone sets is to use tip and ring lines. Tip and ring lines are the twisted pair of wires that connect to your phone via an RJ-11 connector. As shown in Figure 14-4, the CO switch grounds the tip line. The PBX detects that the tip line is grounded and closes the loop by removing ground from the ring line.

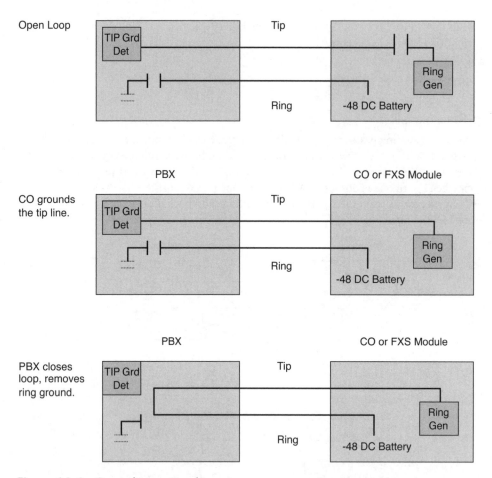

Figure 14-4 *Ground-start signaling*

E&M Signaling

E&M is an analog signaling technique often used in PBX-to-PBX tie lines. E&M is receive and transmit, or more commonly called Ear and Mouth. Cisco routers support four E&M signal types: Type I, Type II, Type III, and Type V. Types I and II are most popular on the American continents. Type V is common outside North America.

There are also three forms of E&M dial supervision signaling to seize the E&M trunk:

■ **Immediate start:** This is the most basic protocol. In this technique, the originating switch goes off-hook, waits for a finite period of time (for example, 200 ms), and then sends the dial digits without regard for the far end.

■ **Wink start:** Wink is the most commonly used protocol. In this technique, the originating switch goes off-hook, waits for a temporary off-hook pulse from the other end (which is interpreted as an indication to proceed), and then sends the dial digits.

■ **Delay dial:** In this technique, the originating side goes off-hook, waits for about 200 ms, and then checks whether the far end is on-hook. If the far end is on-hook, it outputs dial digits. If the far end is off-hook, it waits until it goes on-hook and then outputs dial digits.

CAS and CCS Signaling

Digital signaling has two major forms: Channel Associated Signaling (CAS) and Common Channel Signaling (CCS). The major difference is that with CAS the signaling is included in the same channel as the voice call. With CCS, the signaling is provided in a separate channel. Table 14-2 shows the common types of CAS and CCS. They are covered in the following sections.

Table 14-2 Common CAS and CCS Signaling Types

Signaling	Signaling/Circuit Type
CAS	T1 or E1 signaling
CCS	ISDN PRI or BRI
	QSIG
	SS7

T1/E1 CAS

Digital T1 CAS uses selected bits within each channel to transmit signaling information. CAS is also called *robbed-bit* signaling or *in-band* signaling in the T1 implementation. Robbed-bit CAS works with digital voice because losing an occasional voice sample does not affect the voice quality. The disadvantage of robbed-bit CAS is that it cannot be used on channels that might carry voice or data without reducing the data rate to 56 Kbps to ensure that signaling changes do not damage the data stream. Because of the implementation of signaling via a limited number of bits, CAS signaling is limited in signaling feature support.

E1 CAS uses a separate channel in the shared medium for CAS, so it does not have this disadvantage. The E1 signaling bits are channel associated, but they are not in-band.

CCS

CCS circuits set aside one channel specifically for carrying signaling information for all the other channels. This architecture allows for CCS circuits to provide a more robust feature set between switches. ISDN PRI uses CCS signaling and is the preferred connection type for PSTN-to-PBX or PBX-to-PBX connections.

ISDN PRI/BRI

ISDN T1 PRI provides twenty-three 64kbps B (bearer) channels for voice, with a separate 64kbps D (data signaling) channel for signaling. The ISDN E1 PRI provides 30 B channels. The use of messages in a separate channel, rather than preassigned bits, is also called

Common Channel Signaling. ISDN provides the advantage of not changing bits in the channels and thus is useful for data traffic in addition to voice traffic.

The ISDN BRI interface includes two 64kbps B channels for voice or data and a separate 16Kbps D channel that provides signaling for the interface.

Q.SIG

Q.SIG is the preferred signaling protocol used between PBX switches. It is a standards-based protocol, based on ISDN, that provides more robust features and services. It is feature transparent between PBXs. It is interoperable with public and private ISDN networks and imposes no restrictions on private dial plans. Q.SIG is also used between Cisco Unified Communications Manager (CUCM) and enterprise PBXs in hybrid implementations. It is also used on Cisco IOS voice gateways for PBX integration.

SS7

SS7 is a global ITU standard for telecommunications control that allows voice-network calls to be routed and controlled by call control centers. SS7 is used between PSTN switches. SS7 implements call setup, routing, and control, ensuring that intermediate and far-end switches are available when a call is placed. With SS7, telephone companies can implement modern consumer telephone services such as caller ID, toll-free numbers, call forwarding, and so on.

SS7 provides mechanisms for exchanging control, status, and routing messages on public telephone networks. SS7 messages pass over a separate channel than that used for voice communication. SS7 is a CCS technology. CCS7 controls call signaling, routing, and connections between CO, interexchange carrier, and competitive local-exchange carrier switches. Figure 14-5 shows the connectivity between SS7 components.

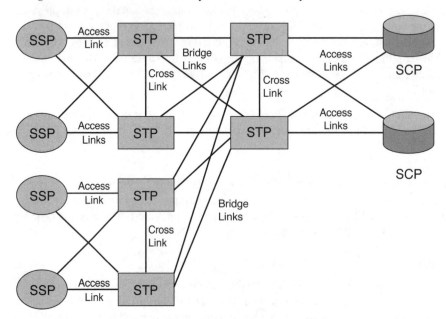

Figure 14-5 *SS7 signaling components*

As shown in Figure 14-5, SS7 has the following system components:

- **Signaling Control Point (SCP):** Databases that provide the necessary information for special call processing and routing, including 800 and 900 call services, credit card calls, local number portability, cellular roaming services, and advanced call center applications.

- **Signaling Transfer Point (STP):** Receives and routes incoming signaling messages toward their destinations. STPs are deployed in mated pairs and share the traffic between them.

- **Signaling Switching Point (SSP):** Telephone switches equipped with SS7 software and signaling links. Each SSP is connected to both STPs in a mated pair.

Addressing Digit Signaling

There are two methods for submitting analog address digits to place a call:

- Pulse or rotary dialing
- Dual-tone multifrequency (DTMF) dialing

Pulse dialing uses the opening and closing of a switch at the telephone set. A rotary register at the CO detects the opening and closing of the loop. When the number 5 is dialed on a rotary phone, the dial mechanism opens and closes five times, each one-tenth of a second apart.

DTMF uses two tones simultaneously to indicate the dialed number. Table 14-3 shows the phone keypad and the frequencies used. For example, when the number 5 is dialed, the frequencies 770 Hz and 1336 Hz are sent to the CO.

Table 14-3   DTMF Frequencies

Frequency	1209 Hz	1336 Hz	1477 Hz
697 Hz	1	ABC	DEF
		2	3
770 Hz	GHI	JKL	MNO
	4	5	6
852 Hz	PRS	TUV	WXY
	7	8	9
941 Hz	*	OPER	#
		0	

PSTN Numbering Plan

The PSTN uses the ITU E.164 standard for public network addressing. The E.164 standard uses a maximum of 15 digits and makes each phone unique in the PSTN. Examples of E.164 addresses are the residential, business, IP phones, and cell phones that you use every day. Each country is assigned a country code to identify it. The country codes can be one to three digits in length. Table 14-4 shows some examples of country codes.

Table 14-4   E.164 Country Codes

Country Code	Country
1	United States, Canada
1-787, 1-939	Puerto Rico
55	Brazil
39	Italy
86	China
20	Egypt
91	India
49	Germany
380	Ukraine
44	United Kingdom
81	Japan
52	Mexico
966	Saudi Arabia

The ITU website that lists country codes is located at www.itu.int/itudoc/itu-t/ob-lists/icc/e164_763.html.

Each country divides its network into area codes that identify a geographic region or city. The United States uses the North American Numbering Plan (NANP). NANP has the address format of *NXX-NXX-XXXX*, where *N* is any number from 2 to 9 and *X* is any number from 0 to 9. The first three digits are the area code. The address is further divided into the office code (also known as prefix) and line number. The prefix is three digits, and the line number is four digits. The line number identifies the phone.

An example of a PSTN address in the United States is 1-713-781-0300. The 1 identifies the United States; the 713 identifies an area code in the Houston, Texas, geographical region. The 781 identifies a CO in west Houston. The 0300 identifies the phone.

Another example of a PSTN address is 52-55-8452-1110. The country code 52 identifies the country of Mexico. The area code 55 identifies the geographic area of Mexico City. The office code 8452 and line number 1110 follow.

Other PSTN Services

The PSTN provides a suite of services in addition to call setup and routing:

- Centrex
- Voice mail
- Database services
- Interactive voice response (IVR)
- Automatic call distribution (ACD)

Centrex Services

Companies can use the local phone company to handle all their internal and external calls from the CO. In this voice model, the CO acts as the company's voice switch, with PBX features such as four-digit extension dialing, voice mail, and call holds and transfers. The Centrex service gives the company the appearance of having its own PBX network.

Voice Mail

PSTN service providers can enable voice messaging for customers who request the service. Voice mail provides automated call answering and message recording. Users can then retrieve the message and forward it to other extensions.

Database Services

The PSTN must keep call detail records (CDR) in the database systems. CDR information includes all types of call information, such as called party, caller, time, duration, locations, and user service plans. This information is used for billing and reporting.

IVR

IVR systems connect incoming calls to an audio playback system. IVR queues the calls, provides prerecorded announcements, prompts the caller for key options, provides the caller with information, and transfers the call to another switch extension or agent. IVR is used in customer call centers run by companies in all industries to gather and provide information to the customers before transferring them to agents.

ACD

ACD routes calls to a group of agents. ACD keeps statistics on each agent, such as the number of calls and their duration. Based on the statistics, the ACD system then can evenly distribute the calls to the agents or to the appropriate agent skill group. ACD is used by airline reservation systems, customer service departments, and other call centers.

Voice Engineering Terminology

You must consider voice traffic requirements when designing a network. The CCDA must be familiar with the following voice engineering terms.

Grade of Service

Grade of service (GoS) is the probability that a call will be blocked by a voice gateway when attempting to seize a circuit during the busiest hour. If it is determined that a network has a P.02 GoS, the probability is that 2 percent of all attempted calls will be blocked. A P.01 GoS indicates a 1 percent probability of callers being blocked.

Erlangs

An Erlang is a theoretical unit of measurement used to define the trunking (voice path) utilization in a voice application or environment. Erlangs values are used in Erlang formulas (Erlang B and Erlang C) to estimate capacity requirements. One Erlang represents the continuous use of one voice path for 3600 seconds (1 hour). Erlangs are used to describe aggregate trunk usage for a system and do not apply to any specific trunk or call. The hour used for the Erlang calculation should be the busiest hour (peak hour) in the day.

If a group of users makes/receives 20 calls in the average busiest hour and each call lasts an average of 10 minutes, the Erlangs are calculated as follows:

20 calls per hour * 10 minutes per call = 200 minutes per hour

Traffic volume = (200 minutes per hour) / (60 minutes per hour) = 3.33 Erlangs

The name Erlang came from the inventor, Agner Krarup Erlang, a Danish telecom engineer and mathematician who defined many formulas still used today in the design of voice systems. The most commonly used formulas are known as Erlang B, Extended Erlang B, and Erlang C.

There are three common Erlang models:

- **Erlang B** is a formula that estimates the amount of trunking capacity required given an Erlang value (busy-hour traffic) and a desired Grade of Service (also known as blocking percentage). It is the most common model used. Extending the previous example, 3.33 Erlangs (BHT) and a GoS of 1 percent results in an Erlang B value of nine trunks required. An Erlang B calculator can be found at www.erlang.com/calculator/erlb/.

- **Extended Erlang B** adds a "retry" percentage to the Erlang B model. It assumes that some blocked or failed calls will be reattempted, and therefore additional load is added.

- **Erlang C** queues excess calls instead of blocking them. This model is used to calculate the number of agents required in a call center environment. It is based on measurements of handling time, expected call volumes, and the amount of time a caller spends with an agent. This model is used in call centers where calls are queued for service.

Centum Call Second

A *call second* is equivalent to a single call lasting 1 second. A *Centum call second* (CCS) represents one call occupying a channel for 100 seconds. It is the equivalent of 1/36 of an Erlang. In other words, 36 CCS equals 1 Erlang (3600 seconds). The typical range is around 6 to 12 CCS per port.

Busy Hour

The *busy hour* is the specific hour within a 24-hour period in which the highest traffic load occurs. Most calls are placed and are of longer durations during this hour. It is also called *peak hour*.

Busy-Hour Traffic

Busy-hour traffic (BHT) is the amount of voice traffic that occurs in the busy hour, expressed in Erlangs. It is calculated by multiplying the average call duration by the number of calls in the hour and then dividing that by 3600.

For example, if 300 calls occurred during the busy hour, with an average duration of 150 seconds, the BHT is calculated as follows:

BHT = (150 seconds * 300 calls per hour) / (3600 seconds per hour)

BHT = 12.5 Erlangs

Blocking Probability

In voice environments, it is nearly impossible or at least cost-ineffective to provision capacity so that no calls are ever blocked. Therefore, planning for a target GoS is an important aspect in voice networks. The term *blocking* refers to those calls that cannot be completed due to capacity constraints, usually during peak periods or call spikes.

The blocking probability is the probability that a call will be blocked. Blocking probability is described as a percentage of calls. For example, a blocking probability of 0.02 means that 2 percent of the calls will be blocked, or 20 per every 1000 calls.

Call Detail Records

Call detail records include statistical and other information related to all calls placed. Information included in CDRs includes call time, call duration, source phone number, dialed (destination) phone number, and the amount billed. For VoIP networks, the CDR may also include source and destination IP addresses.

Converged Multiservice Networks

The introduction of packetized voice technology allows the convergence of data and voice networks. This lets companies save toll charges on voice telephone calls. It also reduces companies' total cost of ownership by not having to build and operate separate networks for voice, video, and data. Figure 14-6 shows an example of a Cisco Unified Communications network. The network provides a resilient and redundant foundation with QoS enabled to support the voice and video streams and Unified Communication applications. Call admission control is a mechanism for identifying capacity issues as part of the call routing process. *Call processing* is the term used to define the logical operations of a phone system.

The dial plan is used to define call routing (the physical/network paths that voice calls can take to connect two endpoints). It is responsible for defining what gateways, phone circuits, PSTN providers, or network paths should be taken to connect a call end to end based on goals such as cost, reliability, utilization, and redundancy.

Packetized voice systems allow for applications and services including voice mail and email combinations (unified messaging), multiparty calls (conferencing), integration of a user's availability status (presence), mobility, call centers, and collaboration applications such as integrated instant messaging, web meetings, and other rich communication applications.

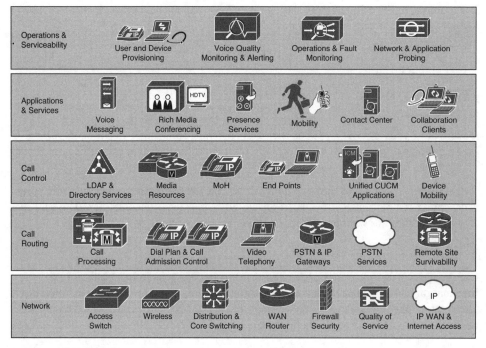

Figure 14-6   *Cisco Unified network*

In multiservice networks, digitized (coded) voice is packaged into packets, cells, or frames; sent as data throughout the networks; and converted back to analog voice. The underlying protocols used for these converged services are

- Voice over Frame Relay (VoFR)
- Voice over Asynchronous Transfer Mode (VoATM)
- Voice over Internet Protocol (VoIP)

Initially, VoFR and VoATM were used but lost ground to VoIP solutions. VoFR and VoATM are no longer exam topics for the CCDA and are not covered further. VoIP is also referred to as IP telephony (IPT) when it is integrated with IP-based signaling and call control. Most new phone system deployments are IPT systems.

VoIP

VoIP provides transport of voice over the IP protocol family. IP makes voice globally available regardless of the data-link protocol in use (Ethernet, ATM, Frame Relay). With VoIP, enterprises do not have to build separate voice and data networks. Integrating voice and data into a single converged network eliminates duplicate infrastructure, management, and costs.

Figure 14-7 shows a company that has separate voice and data networks. Phones connect to local PBXs, and the PBXs are connected using TDM trunks. Off-net calls are routed to the PSTN. The data network uses LAN switches connected to WAN routers. The WAN for data uses Frame Relay. Separate operations and management systems are required for these networks. Each system has its corresponding monthly WAN charges and personnel, resulting in additional costs. With separate voice and data networks,

- Data is primary traffic on many voice service provider networks.
- Companies want to reduce WAN costs.
- PSTN architecture is not flexible enough to accommodate data.
- PSTN cannot integrate voice, data, and video.

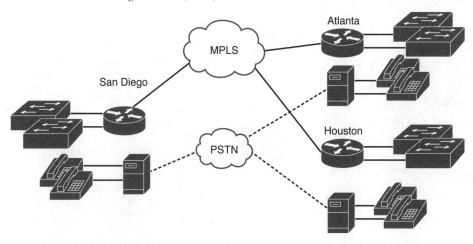

Figure 14-7 *Separate voice and data networks*

With IP telephony, you can reduce the number of systems, circuits, and support personnel. Figure 14-8 shows a converged IP telephony network that employs Ethernet-based phones with server-based call processing and integrated service gateway routers. Survivable Remote Site Telephony (SRST) is used for failover or backup call processing if WAN failure occurs. On-net calls travel through the Frame Relay network, and off-net calls are forwarded to the PSTN. The PSTN link is also used if voice overflow or congestion occurs on the WAN network. Calls are then routed to the PSTN.

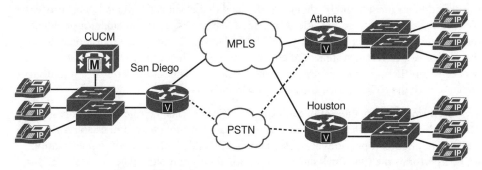

Figure 14-8 *Converged VoIP network*

IPT Components

The Cisco IPT architecture divides voice system architectures into four major VoIP components, as shown in Figure 14-9:

- Client endpoints
- Call processing
- Service applications
- Voice-enabled infrastructure

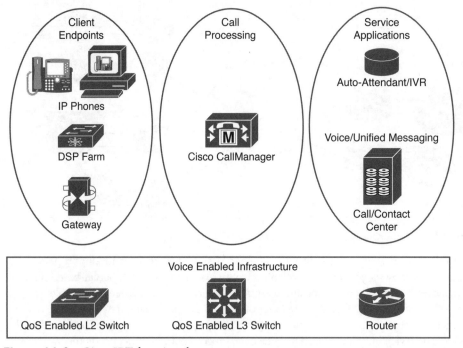

Figure 14-9 *Cisco IPT functional areas*

Client endpoints include the IP phones, analog and digital gateways, digital signal processor (DSP) farms, and software applications. Included here is Cisco's IP Communicator, which is the software-based IP phone that runs on a PC or laptop. Gateways are transitional devices that bridge two different systems and connection types. They can provide connections between VoIP/IPT systems and analog or digital circuits. This allows VoIP/IPT systems to integrate with the PSTN, PBXs, and analog endpoints.

The Cisco Unified Communications Manager (CUCM) fulfills the role of call processing. The CUCM servers are the "brains" of the voice dial plan and are used to establish IPT calls between IP phones. It provides a scalable and distributable VoIP call processing solution. CUCM performs the functions similar to traditional PBXs on older voice networks.

Service applications include IVR, Auto Attendant, and Unified Messaging (voice mail). Cisco IP Contact Center (IPCC) is used for enterprise call center applications. In addition, a standards-based Telephony Application Programming Interface (TAPI) allows third-party companies to develop applications for CUCM.

The voice-enabled infrastructure provides services to support IPT voice, including Power over Ethernet (PoE) and QoS. PoE allows a switch to detect a phone and provide it with power so that power does not have to be provided everywhere that phones are present. With this model, backup/redundant power can be provided from a centralized location. In addition, when a switch detects a phone, it can put that phone in a separate VLAN from other endpoints and allow QoS signaling from the phones. LAN switches and WAN routers work together to provide queuing of data and end-to-end prioritization of VoIP over other types of network traffic during times of congestion.

Table 14-5 summarizes the IPT functional areas.

Table 14-5   IPT Functional Areas

IPT Functional Area	Description
Service applications	Unity, IVR, TAPI interface
Call processing	Cisco CUCM
Client endpoints	IP phones, digital and analog gateways
Voice-enabled infrastructure	Layer 2 and Layer 3 switches and routers

Design Goals of IP Telephony

The overall goal of IP telephony is to replace the traditional, highly complex, expensive, and isolated TDM-based telephone systems and the required duplicate infrastructure with simpler, more cost-effective IPT components using existing data infrastructure and leveraging integration to provide flexibility and cost savings along with robust features and functionality. IPT also allows third-party software providers to develop new applications for IP phones.

The following summarizes the design goals for a VoIP network:

- To use end-to-end VoIP between sites
- To make VoIP widely usable
- To reduce access costs such as long distance toll charges and dedicated circuits costs
- To make VoIP cost-effective
- To provide the same reliability and high availability traditionally associated with older voice technologies
- To offer lower cost of ownership than traditional telephony
- To offer greater flexibility than traditional telephony (remote worker, mobility)
- To leverage integration to provide new applications (presence, IVR, contact centers)
- To improve remote worker, agent, and work-at-home staff productivity
- To facilitate data and telephony network consolidation
- To ensure backward compatibility with traditional systems and endpoints such as PBXs, faxes, and the PSTN

IPT Deployment Models

This section covers the Cisco IPT call-processing deployment models:

- Single-site deployment
- Multisite WAN with centralized call processing
- Multisite WAN with distributed call processing
- CallManager Express deployment

Single-Site Deployment

The single-site deployment model, shown in Figure 14-10, is a solution for enterprises located in a single large building or campus area with no voice on the WAN links. There are no remote sites.

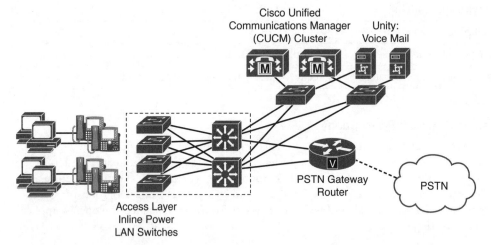

Figure 14-10 *Single-site deployment model*

A single cluster of CUCM servers is deployed for redundancy in the server farm. IP phones are deployed on PoE- and QoS-enabled LAN switches. The CUCM cluster supports up to 30,000 IP devices in a cluster. Gateway routers are configured with PRI cards to legacy PBXs and the PSTN. A single cluster of Unity or Unity Connection servers support voice-mail and unified messaging requirements. IP phones are deployed on PoE inline power LAN switches.

Multisite WAN with Centralized Call Processing Model

The centralized WAN call processing model is a solution for medium enterprises with one large location and many remote sites. Figure 14-11 shows the centralized call processing model. A CUCM cluster with multiple servers is deployed for redundancy at the large site. Call processing and voice-mail servers are located only at the main site. Remote-site IP phones register to the CUCM cluster located in the main site. PoE switches are used to power all IP phones. Remote sites use voice-enabled gateway routers with SRST for call processing redundancy in the event of a WAN failure.

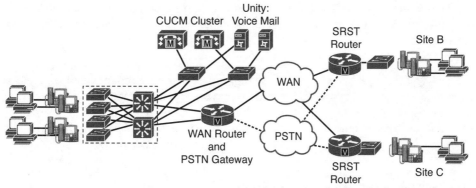

Figure 14-11 *Multisite WAN with centralized CM deployment model*

On the WAN, QoS features are configured to prioritize the VoIP packets over other packet types. In the event of WAN failure, SRST-configured routers forward calls through the PSTN. The PSTN circuit can be used for local inbound and outbound calls at the remote site. In this model, call admission control (CAC) is configured to impose a limit on the number of on-net calls permitted between sites.

Multisite WAN with Distributed Call Processing Model

The multisite WAN with distributed call processing is a solution for large enterprises with several large locations. Figure 14-12 shows the distributed WAN model. Up to 30,000 users are supported per CM cluster. Several CUCM clusters are deployed at the large sites for redundancy, and Unity servers are used for messaging. Intercluster trunks are created to establish communication between clusters. IP phones are deployed on PoE LAN switches.

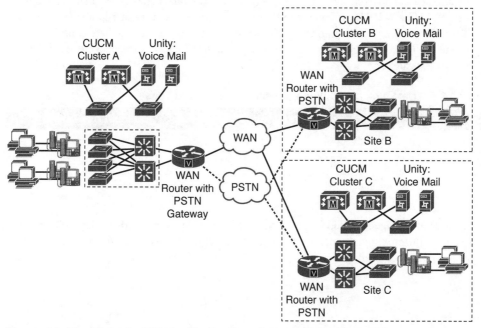

Figure 14-12 *Multisite WAN with distributed CM deployment model*

This model also supports remote sites to be distributed off the large sites. Cisco gatekeepers (special software feature on IOS routers) can be deployed to support a unified dial plan and enforce CAC.

> **Note**   CUCM currently has a maximum capacity of 20 servers per cluster, out of which eight can be with Cisco Communications Manager service started. That means we can have eight subscribers, which sum up to 30,000 endpoints per cluster. The CUCM Supercluster or Megacluster gives you the ability to have a maximum of 16 call processing servers in the cluster instead of eight, and can support up to 80,000 end points per cluster.

Unified CallManager Express Deployments

Cisco provides express versions of its CallManager and Unity solutions integrated in its Integrated Services Routers (ISRs). CallManager Express (CME) provides the call processing capabilities on a router. Unity Express provides voice-mail and auto-attendant functions on special modules that can be installed in a router. CME deployments support up to 450 Cisco IP phones (hardware dependent, based on 3945 ISR G2). It is a distributed, lower-cost solution for small branch offices.

Video Deployment Considerations

There has been an increase in the amount of video over IP traffic on data networks. In the workplace, the use of desktop video conferencing, video broadcasts, IP video surveillance is increasingly being seen on the network. Video surveillance requires high bandwidth and low loss and delay between the camera source and the storage device to produce the best video. We also see traffic from "unmanaged" sources from the Internet, such as video from news sites, YouTube, and TV programming shows. Video traffic is more susceptible to QoS issues than VoIP or data traffic, although end users are used to some intermediate chop in video as long as the audio going with it does not skip. Table 14-6 shows the packet-loss target for each traffic category.

Table 14-6   Data, Voice, and Video Sensitivities to Packet Loss

Traffic Type	Sensitivity to Multisecond Interruption	Packet-Loss Target
Data	Tolerant	1 % to 2 %
Voice	Less tolerant	< 1 %
Video	Intolerant	< 0.05 %

The network designer should be aware that different video applications behave differently and place different requirements on the network. Table 14-7 shows characteristics of video media application models.

Table 14-7   Video Media Application Models

Tool	Model	Flow Direction	Traffic Trends
TelePresence	Many to many	Client ←→ Client MCU ←→ Client	4 Mbps to 12 Mbps for high-def video.
Desktop video conferencing	Many to many	Client ←→ Client MCU ←→ Client	Collaboration across geographies.
Video surveillance	Many to few	Source → Storage Storage → Client Source → Client	Up to 3 Mbps to 4 Mbps per camera based on video quality and frame rates.
Desktop streaming media	Few to many	Storage → Client Source → Client	Increase in application driving more streams. Higher-quality video adds more bandwidth.

An architecture framework for media services supports different models of video models. As shown in Figure 14-13, the network provides service to video media in the Media Services Framework. Those services are access services, transport services, bridging services, storage servers, and session control services, which are provided to endpoints.

- **Access services** provide identity and access control of end devices, mobility, and location services.

- **Transport services** provide QoS for reliable packet delivery.

- **Bridging services** provide transcoding, conferencing, and recording services of media streams.

- **Storage services** provide capture and storage of media streams and content management and distribution.

- **Session control services** provide session signaling and control and gateway services.

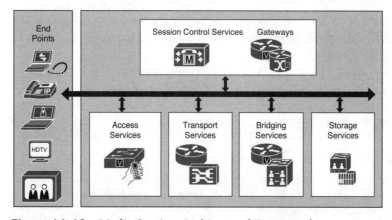

Figure 14-13   *Media Services Architectural Framework*

Codecs

Because speech is an analog signal, it must be converted into digital signals for transmission over digital systems. The first basic modulation and coding technique was pulse-code modulation (PCM). The international standard for PCM is G.711. With PCM, analog speech is sampled 8000 times a second. Each speech sample is mapped onto 8 bits. Thus, PCM produces (8000 samples per second) * (8 bits per sample) = 64,000 bits per second = 64kbps coded bit rate. Other coding schemes have been developed to further compress the data representation of speech. G.711 is used as the primary with IPT over LANs where high bandwidth is available.

Analog-to-Digital Signal Conversion

For clear voice communications, analog speech is converted in to digital format. Digitized voice can travel longer distances than analog voice. The steps involved to convert voice from analog into digital format are

Step 1.   Filtering

Step 2.   Sampling

Step 3.   Digitizing

Most of the spoken language range from 300 Hz to approximately 3400 Hz. In the first step, codecs are configured to filter signals over 4000 Hz out of the analog signal.

In the second step, the signal is sampled at 8000 times per second using pulse-amplitude modulation (PAM). It is sampled 8000 times a second because that is twice the highest frequency of the filtered voice stream at 4000 Hz. This produces a sample every 125 microseconds.

Third, the amplitude samples are converted to a binary code. This is a process where PCM occurs. The difference between PCM and PAM is that PCM does the additional step of encoding each analog sample into binary.

The digitizing process is divided further into two subprocesses:

- **Companding:** This term comes from "compressing and expanding." The analog samples are compressed into logarithmic segments. Then each segment is quantized and coded, which is the next subprocess.

- **Quantization and coding:** This process converts the analog value into a distinct value that is assigned a digital value. The standard word size is 8 bits, which allows for 256 distinct quantization intervals. The rate then becomes the sampling rate times the size of the codeword (2 * 4 KHz * 8 bits = 64 kbps).

Codec Standards

Codecs transform analog signals into a digital bit stream and digital signals back into analog signals. Figure 14-14 shows that an analog signal is digitized with a coder for digital transport. The decoder converts the digital signal into analog form.

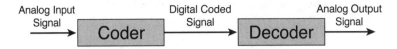

Figure 14-14 *Codec*

Each codec provides a certain quality of speech. Each codec provides a certain level of fidelity to the original audio, or quality of speech. The term *mean opinion score* (MOS) is used to rate the fidelity for a codec. An MOS score is not a scientific measure. Instead, it is a rating determined by sampling the output to a large group of listeners who judge the audio fidelity from 1 (bad) to 5 (best). The scores are then averaged to provide the MOS for each codec. For example, the established MOS score for G.711 is 4.1, and G.729 is 3.92. The default codec setting for VoIP dial peers in Cisco IOS software is G.729 (g729r8), but this can be configured with several other options, including G.711. Other codec standards are shown in Table 14-8. An explanation of the compression techniques is beyond the scope of the CCDA test.

Table 14-8   Codec Standards

Codec	Bit Rate	MOS	Description
G.711u	64 Kbps	4.1	PCM. Mu-law version used in North America and Japan. Samples speech 8000 times per second, represented in 8 bits.
G.711a	64 Kbps	4.1	PCM. A-law used in Europe and international systems.
G.726	16/24/32/40 Kbps	3.85	Adaptive differential pulse-code modulation (AD-PCM).
G.728	16 Kbps	3.61	Low-Delay CELP (LDCELP).
G.729	8 Kbps	3.92	Conjugate Structure Acelp (Cs-Acelp).
G.723.1	6.3 Kbps	3.9	Multipulse Excitation–Maximum Likelihood Quantization (MPE-MLQ).
G.723.1	5.3 Kbps	3.65	Algebraic Code–Excited Linear Prediction (ACELP).

VoIP Control and Transport Protocols

A number of different protocols are used in a VoIP environment for call control, device provisioning, and addressing.

Figure 14-15 shows those protocols focused on VoIP control and transport.

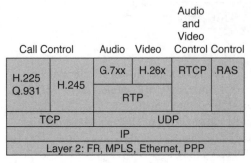

Figure 14-15 *VoIP control and transport protocols*

Some of the most significant protocols are

- **Dynamic Host Configuration Protocol (DHCP):** Used to provide device configuration parameters such as IP configuration (address, subnet mask, default gateway) and TFTP servers (via DHCP option 150).

- **TFTP:** To obtain ring tones, backgrounds, configuration files, and firmware files.

- **Skinny Client Control Protocol (SCCP):** Used for call control for Cisco IP phones (Cisco proprietary).

- **Real-time Transport Protocol (RTP):** For voice stream (VoIP) station-to-station traffic in an active call.

- **Real-time Transport Control Protocol (RTCP):** For RTP control and reporting (accompanying stream to RTP between endpoints).

- **Media Gateway Control Protocol (MGCP):** A client/server protocol for control of endpoints and gateways. In the MGCP model, intelligence resides on the call agent (server), and the device is controlled by the agent.

- **H.323:** An ITU standard for VoIP networks that is a peer-to-peer system (call processing logic is local to each device) used for gateways and endpoints.

- **Session Initiation Protocol (SIP):** A standard for VoIP networks defined by the IETF and used for gateways and endpoints. SIP is feature rich (native IM, presence, and video support), lightweight, and designed for easy troubleshooting (ASCII-based messages).

DHCP, DNS, and TFTP

IP phones use DHCP to obtain their IP addressing information: IP address, subnet mask, and default gateway. DHCP also provides the IP address of the DNS servers and the name or IP address of the TFTP server. You use TFTP to download the IP phone operating system and configuration. Both DHCP and TFTP run over UDP. These protocols are covered in detail in Chapter 8, "Internet Protocol Version 4 Design."

SCCP

SCCP is a Cisco proprietary client/server signaling protocol for call setup and control. SCCP runs over TCP. SCCP is called a "skinny" protocol because it uses less overhead than the

14

call-setup protocols used by H.323. IP phones typically use SCCP to register with CUCM and to establish calls. SCCP can also be used by the call agent to communicate with gateways and control analog endpoints such as FXS ports. It is also used to manage resources such as DSPs on voice gateways. SCCP is used for VoIP call signaling and for features such as message-waiting indicators. As shown in Figure 14-16, IP phones communicate with the CUCM server using SCCP, but RTP is the protocol used for voice media streams between IP phones.

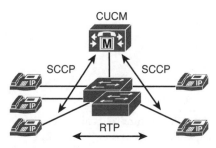

Figure 14-16   *SCCP*

RTP and RTCP

In VoIP, RTP transports audio streams. RTP is a transport layer protocol that carries digitized voice in its payload. RTP was initially defined in RFC 1889, and the current RFC is 3550. RTP runs over UDP, which has lower delay than TCP. Because of the time sensitivity of voice traffic and the delay incurred in retransmissions, UDP is used rather than TCP. Real-time traffic is carried over UDP ports ranging from 16,384 to 32767. The only requirement is that the RTP data be transported on an even port and that the RTCP data be carried on the next odd port. RTCP is also defined in RFC 3550. RTCP is a session layer protocol that monitors the delivery of data and provides control and identification functions. Figure 14-17 shows a VoIP packet with the IP, UDP, and RTP headers. Notice that the sum of the header lengths is 20 + 8 + 12 = 40 bytes.

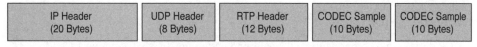

Figure 14-17   *IP, UDP, and RTP headers of a VoIP packet*

WAN links use RTP header compression to reduce the size of voice packets. This is also called Compressed RTP (cRTP), which is defined in RFC 2508. As shown in Figure 14-18, cRTP reduces the IP/UDP/RTP header from 40 bytes to 2 or 4 bytes (a significant decrease in overhead). cRTP happens on a hop-by-hop basis, with compression and decompression occurring on every link. It must be configured on both ends of the link. It is recommended for slow links up to 768 kbps. cRTP is not used much anyone because slow WAN link bandwidths are seen less. Higher speed links are not recommended because of the high CPU requirements and they reduce call quality.

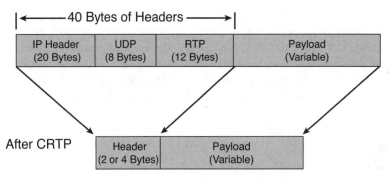

Figure 14-18 *cRTP*

MGCP

MGCP is a client/server signaling protocol that is used to allow centralized call processing agents (such as CUCM) to control gateways in VoIP networks. MGCP is defined in RFC 3661. MGCP's primary advantage is centralized device and dial plan configuration. Figure 14-19 shows a network where MGCP is used by the CUCM to control a voice gateway. MGCP gateways handle transition between TDM and IP voice network. MGCP is also used to provide enhanced functionality such as Q.SIG trunking, which is not supported in H.323 or SIP IOS gateways, and gateway failover and load balancing.

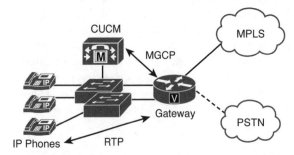

Figure 14-19 *MGCP*

MGCP defines two components: call agents and endpoints. In MGCP networks, endpoints cannot function without communication and control from the call agent. Call agents such as CUCM control the gateways. An endpoint is any gateway interface, such as a PRI trunk or analog interface.

H.323

H.323 is a standard published by the ITU that works as a framework document for multimedia protocols, including voice, video, and data conferencing, for use over packet-switched networks. H.323 standards describe terminal (endpoints), gateway, gatekeeper, and multipoint control unit (MCU) devices to be used in a multimedia network.

As shown in Figure 14-20, H.323 includes the following elements:

- **Terminals:** Telephones, video phones, and voice-mail systems (devices that provide real-time two-way voice).

- **MCUs:** An MCU is a device used for joining together multiple audio/video streams into a single bridge, or conference. The MCU is responsible for taking streams from the different conference participants, mixing the streams together, and then sending the combined stream back to the participants.

- **Gateways:** A device that provides transitional services from one network type to another such as connecting a VoIP network to a TDM network such as the PSTN (analog/T1 PRI). Gateways also provide translation services between H.323 endpoints and non-H.323 devices.

- **Gatekeepers:** Provide dial plan unification, CAC, device registration, and call routing services to the VoIP network and are often used to unify multiple different VoIP networks as a single call routing hub. Gatekeepers are recommended when interconnecting more than two CUCM networks, to reduce dial plan and call routing configuration and provide centralized CAC.

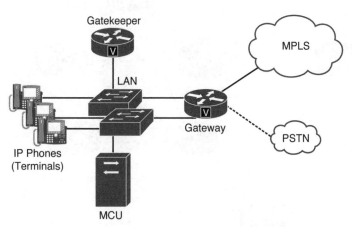

Figure 14-20 *H.323 components*

Gatekeeper Use for Scalability

By definition, H.323 networks are peer-to-peer, autonomous systems. This means that configuration is required on each device about all other devices in the network with which it needs to communicate (a mesh configuration), including network addressing, call routing, CAC, and other configuration parameters (a logical connection). As a network grows, the number of logical connections required grows exponentially. For example, if a gatekeeper is not used, logical connections need to be configured on each gateway to connect to every single other gateway on the network.

The number of logical connections is represented by the following formula:

$$L = (N * (N - 1)) / 2$$

where N is the number of devices in the network.

For example, in a network with seven devices, 21 logical connections must be configured to ensure that each device can communicate with every other device.

Alternatively, this configuration can be consolidated into a centralized system called a gate-keeper. In a gatekeeper-controlled system, each device needs to be configured with only a logical connection to the gatekeeper. In this fashion, the number of configurations required is exponentially reduced, and administration can be done from a central point.

Going back to the earlier configuration example, only seven logical connections need to be configured in a gatekeeper-controlled environment as opposed to the 21 that have to be configured without it. In a larger network of 100 devices, it is 100 versus 4950 connections!

As shown in Figure 14-21, for three gateways the number of logical connections is only three but grows to ten connections when there are only five gateways. With a gatekeeper, each gateway contains a simpler dial plan and connects only to the gatekeeper.

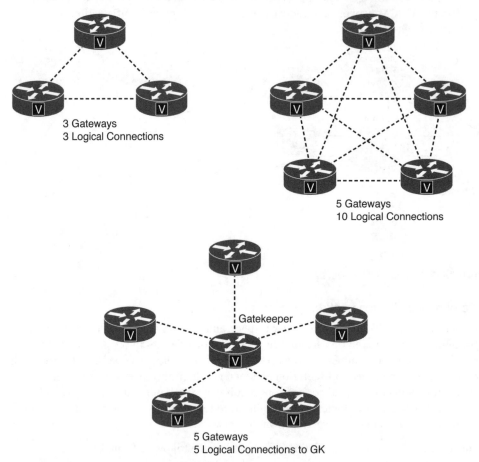

Figure 14-21   *A gatekeeper reduces the number of logical gateway connections*

H.323 terminals must support the following standards:

■ H.245 call capability control

■ Q.931 call setup signaling

- H.225 call signaling
- RTP/RTCP voice streams

H.245 specifies messages for opening and closing channels for media streams and other commands, requests, and indications. It is a control channel protocol.

Q.931 is a standard for call signaling used by H.323 within the context of H.225. It is also used by PRI links.

H.225 performs registration, admission, and status (RAS) signaling for H.323 sessions.

RTP is the transport layer protocol used to transport VoIP packets. RTCP is also a transport layer protocol.

H.323 includes a series of protocols for multimedia, as shown in Table 14-9.

Table 14-9   H.323 Protocols

	Video	Audio	Data	Transport
H.323 protocol	H.261	G.711	T.122	RTP
	H.263	G.722	T.124	H.225
	H.264	G.723.1	T.125	H.235
		G.728	T.126	H.245
		G.729	T.127	H.450.1
				H.450.2
				H.450.3
				X.224.0

H.264

H.264 is an ITU-T standard that defines video compression algorithm. It is identical to ISO/IEC MPEG-4 Part 10 and also called Advanced Video Coding (AVC). It is an upgrade from the H.263 standard that is found in Flash, YouTube, and Google video today. H.264 also handles encoding of pixel blocks more effectively, thus reducing the pixilation seen on video conferences when motion occurs. H.264 encodes and transmits two interlaced fields for each frame: 30 frames per second and 60 fields per second. H.263 only does 30 fields per second.

Table 14-10 provides typical bandwidth requirements of H.264 video sources.

Table 14-10   H.264 Video Bandwidth

Video Source	Resolution	Typical Load
TelePresence 3000	1080p	12.3 Mbps
TelePresence 3000	720p	6.75

Video Source	Resolution	Typical Load
TelePresence 1000	1080p	4.1 Mbps
TelePresence 1000	720p	2.25 Mbps
Cisco 4500 Video Surveillance	1080p	4–6 Mbps
Cisco DMS – Digital Sign SD	720×480	1.5–2.5 Mbps
Cisco DMS – Digital Sign HD	1080p	8–12 Mbps
Cisco Video Advantage	CIF	768 kbps
YouTube HD	720p	2 Mbps

SIP

SIP is a protocol defined by the IETF and specified in RFC 2543. It is an alternative multimedia framework to H.323, developed specifically for IP telephony. It is meant to be a simple lightweight replacement to H.323. Cisco now supports SIP on CUCM, IP phones, and gateways.

SIP is an application layer control (signaling) protocol for creating, modifying, and terminating IP multimedia conferences, Internet telephone calls, and multimedia distribution. Communication between members of a session can be via a multicast, a unicast mesh, or a combination.

SIP is designed as part of the overall IETF multimedia data and control architecture that incorporates protocols such as the following:

- Resource Reservation Protocol (RSVP) (RFC 2205) for reserving network bandwidth and priority (low-latency) queuing
- RTP and RTCP (RFC 3550) for transporting real-time data and providing QoS feedback
- Real-Time Streaming Protocol (RTSP) (RFC 2326) for controlling delivery of streaming media
- Session Announcement Protocol (SAP) (RFC 2974) for advertising multimedia sessions via multicast
- Session Description Protocol (SDP) (RFC 2327) for describing multimedia sessions

SIP supports user mobility by using proxy and redirect servers to redirect requests to the user's current location. Users can register their current locations, and SIP location services provide the location of user agents.

Figure 14-22 shows SIP components.

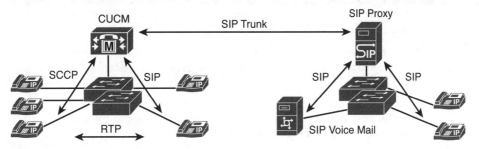

Figure 14-22 *SIP architecture*

SIP uses a modular architecture that includes the following components:

■ **SIP user agent (UA):** These endpoints create and terminate sessions, SIP phones, SIP PC clients, or gateways. A UA client (UAC) initiates a SIP request. A UA server (UAS) is a server application that contacts the user when it receives a SIP request. CUCM can act as both a server and a client.

■ **SIP proxy server:** Routes messages between SIP UAs. It acts as an intermediate that receives SIP requests from a client and forwards the requests on behalf of the client. SIP proxy servers perform authentication, authorization, routing, reliable request retransmission, and security.

■ **SIP redirect server:** Call control device used to provide routing information to user agents. It provides information about the next hop or hops that a message should take.

■ **SIP registrar server:** Stores the location of all user agents in the domain or subdomain. It processes requests from UACs for registration of their current locations. SIP proxy servers or redirect servers can contain registrar servers.

■ **SIP location services:** Provide logical location of UAs; used by the proxy, redirect, and registrar servers.

■ **Back-to-back user agent:** Call control device that divides a voice call into two call legs.

Table 14-11 summarizes protocols used in VoIP networks.

Table 14-11 Significant Protocols in VoIP Networks

Protocol	Description
DHCP	Dynamic Host Control Protocol. Provides IP address, mask, gateway, DNS address, and TFTP address.
TFTP	Trivial File Transfer Protocol. Provides the IP phone configuration and operating system.
SCCP	Skinny Client Control Protocol. Establishes calls between IP phones and CUCM.
RTP	Real-time Transport Protocol. Used for the transmission of real time traffic such as voice and video.

Protocol	Description
RTCP`	Real-time Transport Control Protocol. Provides out-of-band statistics and control information for RTP streams.
H.323	An ITU standard for VoIP networks. H.323 is older and more stable than SIP, but is also more process intensive and is limited to traditional voice and video functionality.
SIP	Session Initiation Protocol. An IETF standard for VoIP networks. Newer and less mature than H.323, but also less process intensive and has support for new features such as IM and presence.

IPT Design

This section covers network design issues and solutions that a designer needs to be aware of when designing a network for IPT. Topics such as bandwidth requirements, delay, and QoS schemes should be considered.

Bandwidth

VoIP calls need to meet bandwidth and delay parameters. The amount of bandwidth required depends on the codec used, the Layer 2 protocol, and whether voice-activity detection (VAD) is enabled. For the purpose of call control, you can use the following bandwidth requirements (minimum values) for VoIP design:

- G.729 calls use 26 kbps.
- G.711 calls use 80 kbps.

When you're designing for VoIP networks, the total bandwidth for voice, data, and video should not exceed 75 percent sustained of the provisioned link capacity during peak times. Best practice is to provision/plan for no more than one-third of any links for the priority queue/real time traffic. Use the following formula to provision interface speeds:

Bandwidth requirement (peak times) = [required bandwidth for voice] + [required bandwidth for video] + [required bandwidth for data]

Total Provisioned link bandwidth = Bandwidth Requirement / 0.75

The remaining bandwidth is used by routing, multicast, and management protocols.

VAD

As we listen and pause between sentences, typical voice conversations can contain up to 60 percent silence in each direction. In circuit-switched telephone networks, all voice calls use fixed-bandwidth 64Kbps links regardless of how much of the conversation is speech and how much is silence. In multiservice networks, all conversation and silence is packetized. Using VAD, you can suppress packets of silence. Silence suppression at the source IP telephone or VoIP gateway increases the number of calls or data volumes that can be carried over the links, more effectively utilizing network bandwidth. Bandwidth savings are at least

35 percent in conservative estimates. VAD is enabled by default for all VoIP calls. In real-world practice, is it suggested that VAD be avoided because it creates quality issues and breaks applications such as fax and modem transmissions.

Table 14-12 shows how much bandwidth is required based on different parameters. Notice that for G.729 bandwidth is reduced from 26.4 kbps to 17.2 kbps with VAD and to 7.3 kbps with VAD and cRTP enabled.

Table 14-12 VoIP Bandwidth Requirements with cRTP and VAD

Technique Codec Bit Rate (Kbps)	Payload Size (Bytes) (Default Uses 20ms Samples)	Bandwidth Multilink PPP (MLP) or FRF.12 (Kbps)	Bandwidth with cRTP for MLP or FRF.12	Bandwidth with VAD MLP or FRF.12 (Kbps)	Bandwidth with cRTP and VAD MLP or FRF.12 (Kbps)
G.711 (64)	240	76		50	43
G.711 (64)	160 (default)	83		54	44
G.726 (32)	120	44	34	29	22
G.726 (32)	80 (default)	50	35	33	23
G.726 (24)	80	38	27	25	17
G.726 (24)	60 (default)	42	27	27	18
G.728 (16)	80	25	18	17	12
G.728 (16)	40 (default)	35	19	23	13
G.729 (8)	40	17.2	9.6	11.2	6.3
G.729 (8)	20 (default)	26.4	11.2	17.2	7.3
G.723.1 (6.3)	48	12.3	7.4	8.0	4.8
G.723.1 (6.3)	24 (default)	18.4	8.4	12.0	5.5
G.723.1 (5.3)	40	11.4	6.4	7.4	4.1
G.723.1 (5.3)	20 (default)	17.5	7.4	11.4	4.8

Calculating Voice Bandwidth

The CCDA test expects the designer to be able to calculate some basic voice bandwidth estimates. Use the following assumptions when calculating voice bandwidth:

- IP/UDP/RTP header uses 40 bytes.
- cRTP reduces the IP/UDP/RTP header to 2 or 4 bytes.
- The WAN Layer 2 header adds 6 bytes on a point-to-point circuit.
- Voice packet size = (Layer 2 header) + (IP/UDP/RTP header) + (voice payload).
- Voice packets per second (pps) = codec bit rate / voice payload size.
- Voice bandwidth (bps) = (voice packet size) * (pps).

As an example, calculate the WAN bandwidth used at a site that will have ten concurrent G.729 calls with cRTP and a default voice payload of 20 bytes.

From this description, we obtain the following:

- G.729 codec is used: 8 kbps codec bit rate.
- cRTP = 2-byte IP/UDP/RTP header.
- Default voice payload= 20 bytes * (8 bits/bytes) = 160 bits.
- WAN header = 6 bytes.
- Voice packet size = 6 bytes + 2 bytes + 20 bytes = 28 bytes * (8 bits/byte) = 224 bits.
- PPS = 8 kbps / 160 bits = 8000/160 = 50 pps.
- BW per call = 224 (bits/packet) * 50 (pps) = 11200 bps = 11.2 kbps.
- BW for 10 calls = 11.2 kbps * 10 = 112 kbps.

Here is a second example: Calculate the WAN bandwidth used by a G.711 calls with no cRTP and a default voice payload.

From this description, we obtain the following:

- G.711 codec is used: 64kbps codec bit rate
- IP/UDP/RTP header = 40 bytes
- Default voice payload= 160 bytes * (8 bits/bytes) = 1280 bits
- WAN header = 6 bytes
- Voice packet size = 6 bytes + 40 bytes + 160 bytes = 206 bytes * (8 bits/byte) = 1648 bits
- PPS = 64 kbps / 1280 bits = 64,000/1280 = 50 pps
- BW per call = 1648 (bits/packet) * 50 (pps) = 82400 bps = 82.4 kbps

Cisco has developed a tool, available on its website, that you can use to obtain accurate estimates for IPT design. The tool is the Voice Codec Bandwidth Calculator, and it is available at http://tools.cisco.com/Support/VBC/do/CodecCalc1.do.

Delay Components in VoIP Networks

The ITU's G.114 recommendation specifies that the one-way delay between endpoints should not exceed 150 ms to be acceptable, commercial voice quality. In private networks, somewhat longer delays might be acceptable for economic reasons. The ITU G.114 recommendation specifies that 151-ms to 400-ms one-way delay might be acceptable provided that organizations are aware that the transmission time will affect the quality of user applications. One-way delays of above 400 ms are unacceptable for general network planning purposes.

Delay components are one of two major types: fixed delay and variable delay.

As shown in Figure 14-23, fixed delay includes the following types.

- Propagation delay
- Processing delay (and packetization)
- Serialization delay

Propagation delay is how long it takes a packet to travel between two points. It is based on the distance between the two endpoints. You cannot overcome this delay component. The speed of light is the theoretical limit. A reasonable planning figure is approximately 10 ms per 1000 miles, or 6 ms per 1000 m (6 ms per km). This figure allows for media degradation and devices internal to the transport network. Propagation delay is noticeable on satellite links.

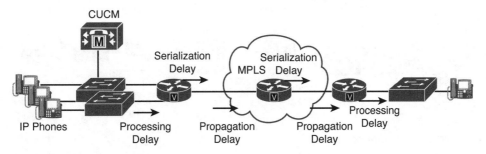

Figure 14-23 *Fixed delays*

Processing delay includes coding, compression, decoding, and decompression delays. G.729 has a delay of 15 ms, and G.711 PCM has a delay of 0.75 ms. The delay created by packetization is also a processing delay. Packetization delay occurs in the process of waiting for a number of digital voice samples before sending out a packet. Packetization delay is the time taken to fill a packet payload with encoded/compressed speech. This delay is a function of the sample block size required by the coder and the number of blocks placed in a single frame.

Serialization delay is how long it takes to place bits on the circuit. Faster circuits have less serialization delay. Serialization delay is calculated with the following formula:

Serialization delay = frame size in bits / link bandwidth in bps

A 1500-byte packet takes (1500 * 8) / 64,000 = 187 ms of serialization delay on a 64Kbps circuit. If the circuit is increased to 512 kbps, the serialization delay changes to (1500 * 8) / 512,000 = 23.4 ms. Data-link fragmentation using link fragmentation and interleaving (LFI) or FRF.12 mechanisms reduces the serialization delay by reducing the size of the larger data packets. This arrangement reduces the delay experienced by voice packets as data packet fragments are serialized and voice packets are interleaved between the fragments. A reasonable design goal is to keep the serialization delay experienced by the largest packets or fragments on the order of 10 ms at any interface.

Variable delays are

- Queuing delay
- Jitter delay

As packets cross a network, they pass through several devices. At every output port of these devices, it is possible that other voice and data traffic is sharing the link. Queuing delay is the delay experienced as a result of traffic having to compete to be queued for transmission on a link. It is the sum of the serialization delays of all the packets scheduled ahead of delayed packets. LFI is used as a solution for queuing delay issues. LFI is covered in the next section.

Figure 14-24 shows variable delays.

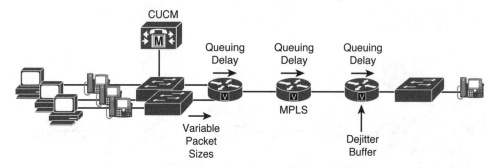

Figure 14-24 *Variable delays*

Packets might not arrive at a constant rate because they take different paths and have perhaps experienced congestion in the network. This variable delay is called *jitter*. The receiving end uses dejitter buffers to smooth out the variable delay of received VoIP packets. Dejitter buffers change the variable delay to fixed delay.

As the traffic load on a network increases, both the probability of delay and the length of the probable delay increase. The actual queuing delay depends on the number of queues, queue lengths, and queue algorithms. Queuing effects in VoIP networks are covered in the next section.

Table 14-13 summarizes the fixed and variable network delays, descriptions, and possible solutions.

Table 14-13   Network Delays

Fixed Delay	Description
Propagation delay	6 ms per km. No solution.
Serialization delay	Frame length/bit rate. A faster link and smaller packets help reduce.
Processing delay	Depends on codec used: coding, compression, and packetization. Add hardware DSPs.
Queuing delay	Variable packet sizes and number of packets. Use LLQ, CBWFQ, LFI.
Jitter	Caused by variable delay. Use dejitter buffers to make delay constant; design as much as possible for an uncongested network.

Packet Loss

Packet loss is another item that affects voice and video quality. It causes voice and video clipping and skips. It is caused by several factors: congested links, improper QoS configuration, bad packet buffer management, and routing issues. Packet loss is also caused by packets received outside of the dejitter buffer range, which are packets that are discarded.

14

Cisco VoIP uses 20-ms samples of voice payload per VoIP packet. Codec algorithms can then correct up to 30 ms of lost voice. For the codec correction to be effective, only one packet can be lost during any given time. When this occurs, the DSP interpolates the conversation with what it thinks the audio should be.

Echo Cancellation

In phone calls, sometimes speech is echoed back to the speaker. This is usually caused by an impedance mismatch. Echo cancellation involves first recognizing the originally transmitted signal that reappears, with some delay, in the transmitted or received signal. Once the echo is recognized, it can be removed by subtracting it from the transmitted or received signal. ITU-T defines that echo delays more than 15 ms should be suppressed with echo cancellers. Echo delays up to 15 ms do not need to be suppressed.

QoS and Bandwidth Mechanisms for VoIP and Video Networks

Cisco provides different QoS tools that you should use on edge and backbone routers to support VoIP networks. First, the CCDA should understand the different categories of QoS mechanisms:

- **Classification:** Process that identifies the class or group a packet belongs to. Matches are based on protocol, input port, IP precedence, DSCP, or 802.1P class of service (CoS). Classification is accomplished using class maps, access lists, and route maps.

- **Marking:** Process of marking packets with differentiated service codepoint (DSCP) values for QoS.

- **Congestion avoidance:** Mechanism that seeks to avoid congestion by preemptively dropping packets to signal traffic flows to slow sending rates. Examples are Weighted Random Early Discard (WRED) and Distributed WRED (DWRED).

- **Traffic conditioners:** These are of two types: traffic shaper and policer. The shaper delays excessive traffic by using a buffer or queuing mechanism and shape the flow of traffic. Traffic policing drops traffic or reclassifies excessive traffic to a lower priority. Frame Relay Traffic Shaping and Committed Access Rate (CAR) are examples. Figure 14-25 shows the differences.

- **Congestion management:** These queuing algorithms segregate traffic and use a determined method to prioritize traffic. Examples are weighted fair queuing (WFQ), priority queuing (PQ), custom queuing (CQ), class-based WFQ (CBWFQ), and low-latency queuing (LLQ).

- **Link efficiency:** Tools used to improve QoS characteristics on specific links within a network. Examples are Compressed RTP and LFI.

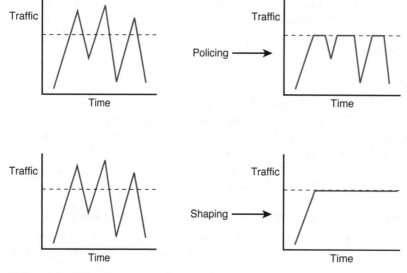

Figure 14-25   *Policing and shaping of traffic*

Several QoS and bandwidth management mechanisms are used on VoIP networks:

- cRTP
- IEEE 802.1Q/P
- RSVP
- LFI
- LLQ
- Auto QoS

cRTP

cRTP was covered in an earlier section. It compresses the IP/UDP/RTP headers from 40 bytes to 2 or 4 bytes. It is configured on a link-to-link basis. Cisco recommends using cRTP for links lower than 768 kbps. Do not configure cRTP if the router CPU is above 75 percent utilization.

IEEE 802.1P

The IEEE 802.1P signaling technique is an OSI Layer 2 standard for prioritizing network traffic at the data link/MAC sublayer. It can also be defined as best-effort QoS at Layer 2. IEEE 802.1P traffic is simply classified and sent to the destination; no bandwidth reservations are established.

IEEE 802.1P is a spin-off of the 802.1Q VLAN trunking standard. The 802.1Q standard specifies a tag that appends to a MAC frame. The VLAN tag carries VLAN information. The VLAN tag has two parts: the VLAN ID (12 bit) and Prioritization (3 bit). The Prioritization field was never defined in the VLAN standard. The 802.1P implementation defines this Prioritization field.

802.1P establishes eight levels (3 bits) of priority similar to IP precedence. Network adapters and switches route traffic based on the priority level. Using Layer 3 switches allows you to map 802.1P prioritization to IP precedence before forwarding to routers.

Resource Reservation Protocol

Resource Reservation Protocol (RSVP) is a signaling protocol that enables end stations or applications to obtain special QoS for their data flows. Basically, RSVP reserves bandwidth for the application. RSVP does not transport application data but is rather an Internet control protocol, like Internet Control Message Protocol (ICMP), Internet Group Management Protocol (IGMP), or routing protocols. RSVP is also known as Resource Reservation Setup Protocol. You can find the IETF charter at www.ietf.org/html.charters/rsvp-charter.html. The first "standards" version of the protocol can be found in RFC 2205.

RSVP is used by a host to request specific QoS from the network for particular application data streams or flows. RSVP requests generally result in resources being reserved in each node along the data path.

LFI

LFI is a QoS mechanism used to reduce the serialization delay. In a multiservice network, small VoIP packets have to compete with large data traffic packets for outbound interfaces. If the large data packet arrives at the interface first, the VoIP packet has to wait until the large data packet has been serialized. When the large packet is fragmented into smaller packets, the VoIP packets can be interleaved between the data packets. Figure 14-26 shows how LFI works. With no LFI, all VoIP packets and other small packets must wait for the FTP data to be transmitted. With LFI, the FTP data packet is fragmented. The queuing mechanism then can interleave the VoIP packets with the other packets and send them out the interface.

FRF.12 is a fragmentation and interleaving mechanism specific to Frame Relay networks. It is configured on Frame Relay permanent virtual circuits (PVC) to fragment large data packets into smaller packets and interleave them with VoIP packets. This process reduces the serialization delay caused by larger packets.

LLQ

As shown in Figure 14-27, LLQ provides a strict-priority queue for VoIP traffic. LLQ then is configured with multiple queues to guarantee bandwidth for different classes of traffic. Other traffic is WFQ'd based on its classification. With LLQ, all voice call traffic is assigned to the priority queue, VoIP signaling and video are assigned to a traffic class, FTP traffic is assigned to a low-priority traffic class, and all other traffic is assigned to a regular class. It also reduces jitter for voice and video streams because it gives priority to those traffic types. With LLQ for Frame Relay, queues are set up on a per-PVC basis. Each PVC has a PQ to support voice traffic. This congestion management method is considered the most optimal for voice.

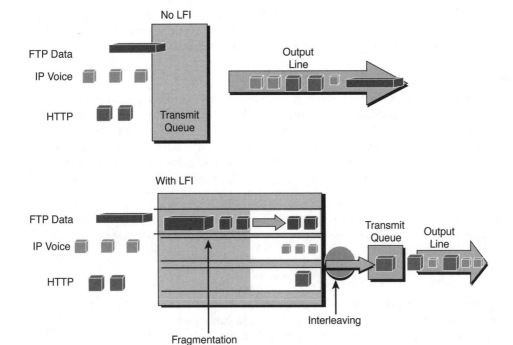

Figure 14-26 *LFI*

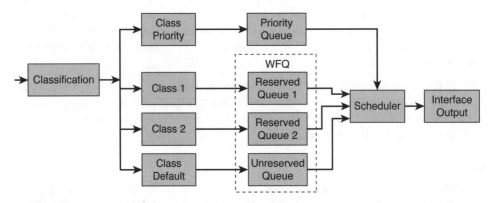

Figure 14-27 *LLQ*

If multiple classes are configured for LLQ, they share a single queue but are allocated bandwidth and policed individually. It is recommended that you place only voice in the priority queue, because voice traffic typically is well behaved, requiring fixed maximum amounts of bandwidth per call. The voice traffic is identified by IP precedence bits set to a value of 5 or a DSCP of Expedited Forwarding (EF) with values of 101*xxx*. When Class of Service (CoS) values are used, a CoS of 5 is used for voice traffic and a CoS of 3 is used for the signaling traffic.

Introducing video or other variable-rate, real-time or non-real-time traffic types could cause unacceptable jitter for the voice traffic. Video traffic normally is set to AF41 (100010). And signaling normally is set to an IP precedence of 3 or a DSCP of 011xxx.

Auto QoS

Auto QoS is a Cisco IOS feature that uses a simpler command-line interface (CLI) to enable QoS for VoIP in WAN and LAN environments. Auto QoS significantly reduces the number of configuration lines necessary to support VoIP in the network.

For the WAN, Auto QoS provides the following capabilities:

- Automatically classifies RTP and VoIP control packets
- Builds VoIP Modular QoS in the Cisco IOS software
- Provides LLQ for VoIP bearer traffic
- Provides minimum-bandwidth guarantees by using CBWFQ for VoIP control traffic

For the LAN, Auto QoS provides the following capabilities:

- Enforces a trust boundary at the Cisco IP phone
- Enforces a trust boundary on the Catalyst switch access and uplink and downlink ports
- Enables strict-priority queuing and weighted round robin for voice and data traffic
- Modifies queue admission criteria by performing CoS-to-queue mapping
- Modifies queue sizes and queue weights where required
- Modifies CoS-to-DSCP and IP precedence-to-DSCP mappings

AutoQoS is beneficial for small and medium-size businesses that need to deploy IPT quickly but lack the experience and staffing to plan and deploy IP QoS services.

AutoQoS also benefits large customer enterprises that need to deploy Cisco IPT on a large scale while reducing the costs, complexity, and timeframe for deployment and ensuring that the appropriate QoS for voice applications is being set consistently.

Table 14-14 summarizes QoS schemes used with IPT.

Table 14-14   QoS Scheme Summary

QoS Scheme	Description
cRTP	RTP header compression. Reduces header overhead from 40 bytes to 2 to 4 bytes.
LFI	Link fragmentation and interleaving. Fragments large data packets and interleaves VoIP packets between them.
LLQ	Uses a single strict queue for RTP traffic. Differentiated QoS available for all other traffic.
AutoQoS	AutoQoS is a Cisco IOS feature that enables QoS for VoIP in WAN and LAN environments. AutoQoS significantly reduces the number of configuration lines necessary to support VoIP in the network.

IPT Design Recommendations

The following are some best-practice recommendations when implementing IPT:

- Use separate VLANs and IP subnets for IP phones and data to provide ease of management and simplified QoS configuration.

- Use private IP addresses for IP phone subnets to allow for more security to voice devices.

- Place CallManager and Unity servers on filtered VLAN/IP subnets in the server access in the data center.

- Use IEEE 802.1Q trunking and 802.1P to allow for prioritization at Layer 2.

- Extend QoS trust boundaries to voice devices but not to PCs and other data devices.

- In the access layer, use multiple egress queues to provide priority queuing of RTP voice streams.

- Use DSCP for classification and marking.

- Use LLQ on WAN links.

- Use LFI on WAN links less than 768 kbps.

- Use CAC to avoid oversubscription of circuits.

IEEE 802.1Q should be configured on the PoE LAN switch ports to allow a voice VLAN for the IP phone and a data VLAN for the PC connected to the IP phone. These VLANs should be on separate IP subnets, and the IP phone should be an RFC 1918 private address subnet. Furthermore, the CallManager servers should be placed on a separate IP subnet in the data center. This lets you restrict access to the IPT environment.

IPT voice packets should be marked with a DSCP of EF (IP precedence 5), and signaling packets should be marked with CS3 (IP precedence 3). This allows QoS schemes to give precedence to the marked packets. LLQ takes the EF marked packets and places them in the strict-priority queue, guaranteeing bandwidth for voice. LFI should be configured on WAN links of a size less than 768 kbps to allow smaller IPT packets to get through larger packets. LFI and LLQ also reduce jitter in IPT conversations.

CAC should be used to keep excess voice traffic from the network by ensuring that there is enough bandwidth for new calls. Call admission control (CAC) is used to control the number of calls to reduce the WAN bandwidth for a site that has IPT. CAC is configured for the site on the CUCM servers. A maximum bandwidth or maximum number of calls is provisioned for the site. CAC enforces a maximum number of calls between two locations to ensure that call quality will not be degraded by allowing more calls than a network can support. CAC causes excessive calls between two locations to be refused. The IPT system must then either reroute the call to a different available path, such as the PSTN, or deny the call.

Service Class Recommendations

RFC 4594: Configuration Guidelines for DiffServ Services Classes (updated by RFC 5865) provides guidelines for specifying services. Six of these are specific for voice or video traffic. The 12 service classes are as follows:

- **Network Control:** For routing and network control functions
- **Operations, Administration, and Management (OAM):** For network configuration and management functions
- **Telephony:** Includes VoIP and circuit emulation
- **Signaling:** For peer-to-peer and client/server signaling, such as SIP, MGCP, H.323, and H.248
- **Multimedia Conferencing:** For applications that can change their encoding rate, such as H.323/V2
- **Real-Time Interactive:** For RTP/UDP streams for video conferencing applications that cannot change the encoding rate
- **Multimedia Streaming:** For variable-rate elastic streaming media applications and webcasts
- **Broadcast Video:** For inelastic streaming media with low jitter and low packet loss, such as broadcast TV, video surveillance, and security
- **Low-Latency Data:** For data processing applications, such as web-based ordering
- **High-Throughput Data:** For store-and-forward applications, such as FTP
- **Standard:** For traffic that has not been identified for any preferential treatment
- **Low-Priority Data:** For traffic types that do not required any bandwidth assurance

Cisco modified some of the DSCP per-hop behavior (PHB) recommendations (switched broadcast video and call signaling, for example) from the RFC and added queuing and dropping recommendations for MediaNetworks. Table 14-15 summarizes these.

Table 14-15   Cisco Service Class PHB Recommendations

Application Class	DSCP PHB	Queuing and Dropping	Applications
Network Control	CS6	BW queue	Network routing, EIGRP, OSPF, BGP, HSRP, IKE
Telephony	EF	PQ	IPT bearer traffic, VoIP, G.711, G.729
Broadcast Video	CS5	PQ (optional)	Cisco IP video surveillance
Multimedia Conferencing	AF4	BW queue + DSCP WRED	H.323/V2 video conferencing; Cisco Unified Personal Communicator
Real-Time Interactive	CS4	PQ (optional)	Video conferencing and interactive gaming; TelePresence
Multimedia Streaming	AF3	BW queue + DSCP WRED	Streaming video and audio on demand; Cisco Digital Media System (VoD)

Application Class	DSCP PHB	Queuing and Dropping	Applications
Call Signaling	CS3	BW queue	IPT signaling, H.323, SCCP, SIP
Low-Latency Transactional data	AF2	BW queue + DSCP WRED	Client/server, web-based ordering, Webex, MeetingPlace, ERP apps
Operations, Administration, Management (OAM)	CS2	BW queue	OAM&P, SNMP, SSH, syslog
High-Throughput Bulk Data	AF1	BW queue + DSCP WRED	Store-and-forward apps, email, FTP, backup
Low-Priority Scavenger Data	CS1	Minimum BW queue	Flows with no bandwidth assurance, YouTube, BitTorrent, Xbox
Standard Best Effort	CS0	Default queue + WRED	Default class

References and Recommended Readings

RFC 3435: Media Gateway Control Protocol (MGCP) Version 1.0, www.ietf.org/rfc.

RFC 2705: Media Gateway Control Protocol (MGCP) Version 1.0, www.ietf.org/rfc.

RFC 1890: RTP Profile for Audio and Video Conferences with Minimal Control, www.ietf.org/rfc.

RFC 1889: RTP: A Transport Protocol for Real-Time Applications, www.ietf.org/rfc.

RFC 2543: SIP: Session Initiation Protocol, www.ietf.org/rfc.

Keagy, S. *Integrating Voice and Data Networks*. Indianapolis: Cisco Press, 2000.

Kotha, S. "Deploying H.323 Applications in Cisco Networks" (white paper), www.cisco.com/c/en/us/td/docs/ios/voice/h323/configuration/guide/15_0/vh_15_0_book/vh_h323_overview.html.

Lovell, D. *Cisco IP Telephony*. Indianapolis: Cisco Press, 2002.

McQuerry, S., K. McGrew, S. Foy, *Cisco Voice over Frame Relay, ATM, and IP*. Indianapolis: Cisco Press, 2001.

Reference Guide, Packet Voice Networking, www.cisco.com/warp/public/cc/pd/rt/mc3810/prodlit/pvnet_in.htm.

Tech Notes: Voice Network Signaling and Control, www.cisco.com/warp/public/788/signalling/net_signal_control.html.

Voice over IP: Per Call Bandwidth Consumption, www.cisco.com/c/en/us/support/docs/voice/voice-quality/7934-bwidth-consume.html.

Cisco Recommendations for MediaNets, www.cisco.com/en/US/docs/solutions/Enterprise/Video/qosmrn.html.

www.erlang.com/.

RFC 3261: SIP: Session Initiation Protocol, www.ietf.org/rfc.

RFC 3262: Reliability of Provisional Responses in the Session Initiation Protocol (SIP), www.ietf.org/rfc.

RFC 3263: Session Initiation Protocol (SIP): Locating SIP Servers, www.ietf.org/rfc.

RFC 3264: An Offer/Answer Model with the Session Description Protocol (SDP), www.ietf.org/rfc.

RFC 3265: Session Initiation Protocol (SIP)-Specific Event Notification, www.ietf.org/rfc.

RFC 4594: Configuration Guidelines for DiffServ Service Classes, www.ietf.org/rfc.

RFC 2508: Compressing IP/UDP/RTP Headers for Low-Speed Serial Links, www.ietf.org/rfc.

Exam Preparation Tasks

Review All Key Topics

Review the most important topics in the chapter, noted with the Key Topic icon in the outer margin of the page. Table 14-16 lists a reference of these key topics and the page numbers on which each is found.

Table 14-16 Key Topics

Key Topic Element	Description	Page
List	Ports	561
Summary	CAS and CCS signaling	565
Table	Common CAS and CCS Signaling Types	565
Summary	Voice engineering terminology	569
List	IPT components	574
Table	IPT Functional Areas	575
Summary	Design goals for IPT	575
List	IPT deployment models	576
Table 14-6	Data, voice, and video sensitivities to packet loss	578
Table 14-8	Codec standards	581
Figure 14-15	VoIP control and transport protocols	582
Table 14-11	Significant Protocols in VoIP Networks	589
Summary	Delay components	592
List	QoS mechanisms	595
Table 14-14	QoS Scheme Summary	599
List	IPT design recommendations	600
Table 14-15	Cisco Service Class PHB Recommendations	601

Complete Tables and Lists from Memory

Print a copy of Appendix D, "Memory Tables" (found on the CD), or at least the section for this chapter, and complete the tables and lists from memory. Appendix E, "Memory Tables Answer Key," also on the CD, includes completed tables and lists to check your work.

Define Key Terms

Define the following key terms from this chapter, and check your answers in the glossary:

ACD, BHT, CAC, CCS, CDR, CO, Centrex, codec, companding, cRTP, CUCM, Erlang, E&M, FXS, FXO, gatekeeper, gateway, GoS, H.323, LLQ, MGCP, MOS, OAM, PSTN, PBX, RSVP, RTP, RTCP, SCCP, SIP, SS7, VAD

Q&A

The answers to these questions appear in Appendix A, "Answers to the 'Do I Know This Already?' Quizzes and Q&A Questions." For more practice with exam format questions, use the exam engine on the CD.

1. True or false: LLQ is recommended for VoIP networks.

2. True or false: H.323 is an IETF standard, and SIP is an ITU standard for multimedia protocols.

3. True or false: An Erlang is a unit that represents the continuous use of one voice path in 1 hour.

4. What do you implement to stop packets from being transmitted when there is silence in a voice conversation?

5. The variable delay of received VoIP packets is corrected with what kind of buffers?

6. True or false: Common Channel Signaling uses a separate channel for signaling.

7. True or false: FXO ports are used for phones, and FXS ports connect to the PSTN.

8. True or false: SS7 provides mechanisms for exchanging control and routing messages in the PSTN.

9. An organization uses what kind of system to gather and provide information for the customer before transferring her to an agent?

10. An organization uses what kind of system to route calls to agents based on the agent skill group or call statistics?

11. In addition to codec selection, both _____ and _____ can be used to reduce the bandwidth of VoIP calls.

12. Label each of the following delays as fixed or variable:
    a. Processing
    b. Dejitter buffer
    c. Serialization
    d. Queuing
    e. Propagation

13. How can you reduce serialization delay?

14. Which queuing technique uses a strict priority queue for RTP traffic?

15. True or false: The maximum one-way delay in the G.114 recommendation for acceptable voice is 200 ms.

16. True or false: FRF.12 is an LFI standard used in networks with VoFR and VoIP over Frame Relay.

17. An assessment of a network determines that the average round-trip time between two sites is 250 ms. Can an IPT solution be implemented between the sites?

18. Match each protocol with its description:

    i.   DHCP

    ii. SCCP

    iii. RTP

    iv. H.323

    v.   TFTP

  a. Transports coded voice streams

  b. Controls Cisco IOS gateways

  c. Provides call signaling between Cisco IP phones and CUCM

  d. Provides IP address

  e. Provides phone configuration

19. Match each CM deployment model with its description:

    i.   Single-site deployment

    ii. Multisite WAN with distributed call processing

    iii. Multisite WAN with centralized call processing

  a. Single CUCM cluster with SRST at remote sites

  b. Single CUCM cluster implemented in a large building

  c. Multiple CUCM clusters

20. Match each component with its Cisco IPT functional area:

    i.   CUCM

    ii. Layer 3 switch

    iii. Digital gateway

    iv. Unity

  a. Service applications

  b. Call processing

  c. Client endpoint

  d. Infrastructure

21. Which protocol is preferred for inter-PBX trunks?

   a. SS7

   b. RTP

   c. Q.SIG

   d. DTMF

22. cRTP compresses the IP/UDP/RTP header to what size?

   a. 2 or 4 bytes.

   b. 2 or 5 bytes.

   c. 40 bytes.

   d. It compresses the RTP header only.

23. The steps of converting an analog signal to digital format occur in which order?

   a. Sampling, filtering, digitizing

   b. Filtering, sampling, digitizing

   c. Digitizing, filtering, sampling

   d. Sampling, digitizing, filtering

24. Digitizing is divided into which two processes?

   a. Filtering and sampling

   b. Expanding and filtering

   c. Companding, quantizing, and coding

   d. Sampling, quantizing, and coding

25. Which of the following are goals of IP telephony?

   a. Use the existing IP infrastructure

   b. Provide lower cost of ownership

   c. Provide greater flexibility in voice communications

   d. All of the above

26. An analysis of a 384Kbps WAN link shows complaints of voice quality issues between two sites when large file transfers take place. The circuit is running at 45 percent utilization. What QoS schemes should be implemented to alleviate this?

   a. CQ and cRTP

   b. LFI and cRTP

   c. LLQ

   d. All of the above

27. Which codec is recommended for use in WAN links?

    a. G.711

    b. G.723

    c. G.726

    d. G.729

28. Which technology reduces the amount of bandwidth used? (Select all that apply.)

    a. QoS

    b. LFI

    c. cRTP

    d. VAD

29. Which of the following statements is true?

    a. CAC prevents voice calls from affecting other voice calls.

    b. CAC prevents voice calls from affecting data bandwidth.

    c. CAC prevents data from affecting voice calls.

    d. CAC prevents data from affecting other data traffic.

30. What IPT component contains the dial plan and is used to register IP phones?

    a. Gateway

    b. Unity server

    c. Gatekeeper

    d. Cisco Unified CallManager

31. Which are drivers for Unified Communications?

    a. Better quality

    b. Reduce WAN costs

    c. Flexibility to carry data, voice, and video

    d. Efficient integration with legacy PSTN infrastructure

    e. Improvement of QoS on the network

32. Match the H.323 component with its description.

    i.   IP phone

    ii.   Manages multipoint conferences

    iii.   Call control and signaling

    iv.   Provides translation services between H.323 endpoints

    a. Gateway

    b. Gatekeeper

    c. MCU

    d. Terminal

33. Which IPT component provides the call processing component?

    a. Cisco Call Processing Manager

    b. Cisco Gateway Manager

    c. Cisco Unified Communications Manager

    d. Cisco IP Contact Center

34. Which protocol is used for communications between two IP endpoints?

    a. SCCP

    b. SIP

    c. H.323

    d. MGCP

    e. RSVP

    f. CAC

    g. CUCM

    h. RTP

35. Which protocol is an IETF-defined application layer control protocol used to establish and terminate calls between two or more endpoints?

    a. SCCP

    b. SIP

    c. H.323

    d. MGCP

    e. RSVP

    f. CAC

    g. CUCM

    h. RTP

36. Which protocol is defined in RFC 3661 and used by CUCM to control gateways?

    a. SCCP

    b. SIP

    c. H.323

    d. MGCP

    e. RSVP

    f. CAC

    g. CUCM

    h. RTP

37. Which services from the Media Services Framework provide capture of media streams?

  a. Access services

  b. Transport services

  c. Bridging services

  d. Storage services

  e. Session control services

  f. Application services

  g. Endpoint services

  h. Reliable services

38. Which services from the Media Services Framework provide transcoding?

  a. Access services

  b. Transport services

  c. Bridging services

  d. Storage services

  e. Session control services

  f. Application services

  g. Endpoint services

  h. Reliable services

39. Which traffic type is recommended for AF4 PHB?

  a. Network control

  b. Telephony

  c. Broadcast video

  d. Multimedia conferencing

  e. Real time

  f. OAM

  g. FTP

  h. YouTube

40. Which traffic type is recommended for CS2 PHB?

  a. Network control

  b. Telephony

  c. Broadcast video

  d. Multimedia conferencing

  e. Real time

  f. OAM

  g. FTP

  h. YouTube

41. Which traffic type is recommended for CS4 PHB?

    a. Network control

    b. Telephony

    c. Broadcast video

    d. Multimedia conferencing

    e. Real time

    f. OAM

    g. FTP

    h. YouTube

42. Which CODEC generates an 8Kbps bit rate?

    a. G.711

    b. G.726

    c. G.728

    d. G.729

    e. G.723

43. Which CODEC is used to provide toll quality calls?

    a. G.711

    b. G.726

    c. G.728

    d. G.729

    e. G.723

44. Which is the recommended QoS mechanism for VoIP networks?

    a. WRED

    b. PQ

    c. WFQ

    d. LLQ

    e. DSCP

45. How much bandwidth is generated by Cisco TelePresence 3000 at 1080p?

    a. 12.3 Mbps

    b. 4.1 Mbps

    c. 6 Mbps

    d. 768 kbps

    e. 2 Mbps

46. How much bandwidth is generated by VT Advantage?

    a. 12.3 Mbps

    b. 4.1 Mbps

    c. 6 Mbps

    d. 768 kbps

    e. 2 Mbps

47. What protocol transports voice streams for IP telephony?

    a. SCCP

    b. SIP

    c. H.323

    d. MGCP

    e. RSVP

    f. CAC

    g. CUCM

    h. RTP

48. Which IPT deployment model is recommended for a single building with no voice on the WAN links but local PSTN is required?

    a. Single-site deployment

    b. Multisite WAN with centralized call processing

    c. Multisite WAN with distributed call processing

    d. CME

49. Which IPT deployment model is recommended for companies with several large locations?

    a. Single-site deployment

    b. Multisite WAN with centralized call processing

    c. Multisite WAN with distributed call processing

    d. CME

50. Which IPT deployment model is recommended for a companies with a large site and many remote sites?

    a. Single-site deployment

    b. Multisite WAN with centralized call processing

    c. Multisite WAN with distributed call processing

    d. CME

51. You perform some one-way delay tests between locations. What is the acceptable one-way delay for voice traffic?

    a. 50 ms

    b. 150 ms

    c. 400 ms

    d. 1 second

52. What is the size of the codeword created with each sample of voice?

    a. 8 bits

    b. 64k bits

    c. 8 bytes

    d. 8k Hz

53. What QoS mechanisms should be used ensure voice quality?

    a. Managing the buffers, compressing traffic

    b. Classifying the voice traffic, congesting management, and compression and fragmentation

    c. Provisioning enough bandwidth for voice, classifying traffic, and interface queuing and scheduling

    d. Classifying the voice traffic, buffering the voice traffic, and queuing the voice traffic

54. Which IPT functional area includes PoE, QoS, and VoIP traffic?

    a. Service applications

    b. Call processing

    c. Client endpoints

    d. Voice-enabled Infrastructure

55. Which information will help you decide which IP Telephony deployment model to use?

    a. Users will have to make off-net calls.

    b. LAN switches will require PoE+.

    c. Calls will be made between remote sites over the WAN.

    d. G.729 codec will be used for internal calls.

56. Which CoS values are used for voice media and signaling?

    a. CoS 1 and 5

    b. CoS 2 and 5

    c. CoS 3 and 5

    d. CoS 4 and 5

Use both the scenario described in the following paragraph and Figure 14-28 to answer the following questions.

The client has an existing Frame Relay network, as shown in Figure 14-28. The network has a large site and 50 small remote sites. The client wants a design for a VoIP network. The client wants to provide differentiated CoS for the voice, Systems Network Architecture (SNA), FTP, and other traffic.

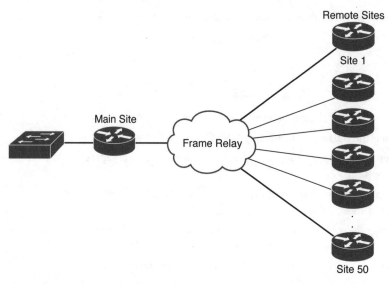

Figure 14-28 *Client's current frame relay network*

57. Based on the current network diagram, which Cisco IPT deployment model should you recommend?

58. What feature should you recommend to provide call processing in the event of a WAN failure?

59. Which queuing technique should you recommend?

60. For Site 1, the current data traffic is 512 kbps and video traffic is 0. What is the minimum bandwidth required to support four concurrent VoIP G.729 calls plus the data traffic to the site?

61. Should you implement a multisite WAN with a centralized call processing CUCM cluster?

62. What feature can you use to reduce bandwidth over the WAN links?

63. Which LFI technique should you use to reduce the serialization delay?

This chapter covers the following subjects:

Simple Network Management Protocol

Other Network Management Protocols

This chapter introduces the following network management protocols and components: Simple Network Management Protocol (SNMP), Management Information Base (MIB), Remote Monitoring (RMON) protocol, Cisco Discovery Protocol (CDP), and the use of NetFlow and system logging (syslog).

CHAPTER 15

Network Management Protocols

"Do I Know This Already?" Quiz

The "Do I Know This Already?" quiz helps you identify your strengths and deficiencies in this chapter's topics.

The ten-question quiz, derived from the major sections in the "Foundation Topics" portion of the chapter, helps you determine how to spend your limited study time.

Table 15-1 outlines the major topics discussed in this chapter and the "Do I Know This Already?" quiz questions that correspond to those topics.

Table 15-1 "Do I Know This Already?" Foundation Topics Section-to-Question Mapping

Foundation Topics Section	Questions Covered in This Section
Simple Network Management Protocol	1, 2, 3, 4, 6, 8
Other Network Management Technologies	5, 7, 9, 10

1. Which version of SNMP introduces security extensions for authentication and encryption?

   a. SNMPv1

   b. SNMPv2

   c. SNMPv3

   d. SNMPv4

2. SNMP runs over which protocol?

   a. TCP

   b. UDP

   c. IP

   d. MIB

3. Which SNMP component contains an agent?

   a. Managed device

   b. Agent

   c. NMS manager

   d. MIB

4. Which SNMP component is a collection of information that is stored on the local agent?

    a. Managed device

    b. Agent

    c. NMS manager

    d. MIB

5. CDP is an acronym for which Cisco function?

    a. Collection Device Protocol

    b. Cisco Device Protocol

    c. Campus Discovery Protocol

    d. Cisco Discovery Protocol

6. Which SNMP operation obtains full table information from an agent?

    a. Get

    b. GetNext

    c. GetBulk

    d. Inform

7. RMON1 provides information at what levels of the OSI model?

    a. Data link and physical

    b. Network, data link, physical

    c. Transport and network

    d. Application to network

8. Which of the following is not an SNMP operation?

    a. Get

    b. Community

    c. Set

    d. Trap

9. Which solution gathers information that can be used for accounting and billing applications?

    a. RMON

    b. NetFlow

    c. CDP

    d. Syslog

10. What is CDP?

    a. Client/server protocol

    b. Hello-based protocol

    c. Network management agent

    d. Request-response protocol

Foundation Topics

After a new network is designed, installed, and configured, it must be managed by the operations team. Network management tools are used to gather operating statistics and to manage devices. Statistics are gathered on WAN bandwidth utilization, router CPU and memory utilization, and interface counters. Configuration changes are also made through network management tools such as Cisco Prime. The ISO defines five types of network management processes that are commonly known as FCAPS. These processes are as follows:

- **Fault management:** Refers to detecting and correcting network fault problems
- **Configuration management:** Refers to baselining, modifying, and tracking configuration changes
- **Accounting management:** Refers to keeping track of circuits for billing of services
- **Performance management:** Measures the network's effectiveness at delivering packets
- **Security management:** Tracks the authentication and authorization information

Network management is supported by the elements listed in Table 15-2.

Table 15-2   Network Management Elements

Network Management Element	Description
NMS	Network management systems run the applications that manage and monitor managed devices.
Network management protocols and standards	These are used to exchange management information between the NMS and the managed devices. The key protocols and standards are SNMP, MIB, and RMON.
Managed devices	These are the devices managed by the NMS.
Management agents	Reside in the managed devices and include SNMP agents and RMON agents.

The protocols and tools described in this chapter perform some of these functions. SNMP is the underlying protocol used for network management. Agents are configured in managed devices (routers) that allow the NMS to manage the device. RMON is used for advanced monitoring of routers and switches. CDP is a Cisco proprietary protocol that allows the discovery of Cisco devices. NetFlow is a network monitoring solution that allows for greater scalability than RMON. Syslog allows system messages and error events to be gathered for review.

Simple Network Management Protocol

Simple Network Management Protocol (SNMP) is an IP application layer protocol that has become the standard for the exchange of management information between network devices. SNMP was initially described in RFC 1157. It is a simple solution that requires little code to implement, which allows vendors to build SNMP agents on their products.

SNMP runs over User Datagram Protocol (UDP) and therefore does not inherently provide for sequencing and acknowledgment of packets, but it still reduces the amount of overhead used for management information.

SNMP Components

SNMP has three network-managed components:

- The managed devices
- The agent that resides on the managed device
- The NMS

Figure 15-1 shows the relationship between these components.

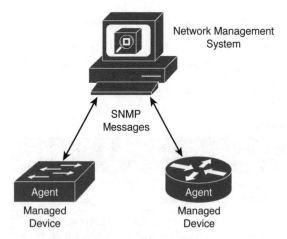

Figure 15-1   *SNMP components*

A managed device is a router or LAN switch or any other device that contains an SNMP agent. These devices collect and store management information and make this information available to the NMS. SNMP community strings (passwords) are configured on routers and switches to allow for SNMP management.

The agent is the network management software that resides in the managed device. The agent gathers the information and puts it in SNMP format. It responds to the manager's request for information and also generates traps.

The NMS has applications that are used to monitor and configure managed devices. It is also known as the manager. The NMS provides the bulk of the processing resources used for network management. It polls agents on the network and correlates and displays the management information.

MIB

A Management Information Base (MIB) is a collection of information that is stored on the local agent of the managed device. MIBs are organized hierarchically and are accessed by the NMS. MIBs are databases of objects organized in a tree-like structure, with each branch containing similar objects. Each object has an object identifier (number) that uniquely identifies the managed object of the MIB hierarchy. Read and write community strings are used to control access to MIB information.

The top-level MIB object IDs belong to different standards organizations, and lower-level object IDs are allocated to associated organizations. Standard MIBs are defined by RFCs. Vendors define private branches that include managed objects for their products. Figure 15-2 shows a portion of the MIB tree structure. RFC 1213 describes the MIBs for TCP/IP. Cisco defines the MIBs under the Cisco head object. For example, a Cisco MIB can be uniquely identified by either the object name, iso.org.dod.private.enterprise.cisco, or the equivalent object descriptor, 1.3.6.1.4.1.9.

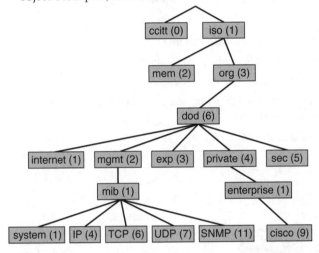

Figure 15-2 *MIB tree structure*

Each individual manageable feature in the MIB is called an MIB variable. The MIB module is a document that describes each manageable feature that is contained in an agent. The MIB module is written in Abstract Syntax Notation 1 (ASN.1). Three ASN.1 data types are required: name, syntax, and encoding. The name serves as the object identifier. The syntax defines the object's data type (integer or string). The encoding data describes how information associated with a managed object is formatted as a series of data items for transmission on the network. Some examples of standard managed objects that can be obtained from the MIB tree follow:

- Interfaces
- Buffers
- Memory
- Standard protocols

From the Cisco private tree, you can obtain the following additional information:

- Small, medium, large buffers
- Primary and secondary memory
- Proprietary protocols (Enhanced Interior Gateway Routing Protocol [EIGRP]), for example)

You can find more specific information about Cisco MIBs at www.cisco.com/public/sw-center/netmgmt/cmtk/mibs.shtml.

SNMP Message Versions

SNMPv1 was initially defined by RFC 1157. Since then, SNMP has evolved with a second and third version, each adding new message types. The CCDA should understand each message type and the version associated with each.

SNMPv1

SNMPv1 is defined by RFC 1157. It is a simple request-and-response protocol. The NMS manager issues a request, and managed devices return responses. The data types are limited to 32-bit values. SNMPv1 uses four protocol operations, with five message types to carry out the communication:

- **Get request:** Retrieves the value of a specific MIB variable.
- **GetNext request:** Retrieves the next instance of the MIB variable.
- **Get response:** Contains the values of the requested variable.
- **Set request:** This is a request from the manager to the agent to set a MIB variable. It can be used to modify the agent's configuration.
- **Trap:** Transmits an unsolicited alarm condition.

Figure 15-3 shows the SNMPv1 message types.

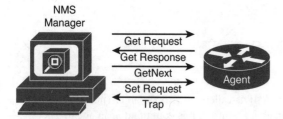

Figure 15-3 *SNMPv1 message types*

The NMS manager uses the Get operation to retrieve the value-specific MIB variable from an agent. The GetNext operation is used to retrieve the next object instance in a table or list within an agent. The Get Response contains the value of the requested variable.

The NMS manager uses the Set operation to set values of the object instance within an agent. For example, the Set operation can be used to set an IP address on an interface or to bring an interface up or down. Agents use the Trap operation to inform the NMS manager of a significant alarm event. For example, a trap is generated when a WAN circuit goes down.

SNMPv2

SNMPv2 is an evolution of the initial SNMPv1 and is defined in RFCs 1901 and 1902. SNMPv2 offers improvements to SNMPv1, including additional protocol operations. The Get, GetNext, and Set operations used in SNMPv1 are exactly the same as those used in SNMPv2. The SNMP Trap operation serves the same function as in SNMPv1, but it uses a different message format.

SNMPv2 defines two new protocol operations:

- **GetBulk:** Reduces repetitive requests for MIB variables
- **Inform request:** Alerts an SNMP manager of specific conditions with confirmation

The NMS manager uses the GetBulk operation to retrieve large blocks of data, such as multiple rows in a table. This is more efficient than repeating GetNext commands. If the agent responding to the GetBulk operation cannot provide values for all the variables in a list, it provides partial results. The Inform operation allows one NMS manager to send trap information to other NMS managers and to receive information. Another improvement is that data type values can be 64 bits.

Table 15-3 summarizes SNMP message types.

Table 15-3   SNMP Message Types

SNMP Message	Description
Get request	Retrieves the value of a specific MIB variable
GetNext request	Retrieves the next issuance of the MIB variable
Get response	Contains the values of the requested variable
Set request	Modifies the value of a MIB variable
Trap	Transmits an unsolicited alarm condition
GetBulk	Reduces repetitive requests for MIB variables
Inform request	Alerts an SNMP manager of specific conditions with confirmation

SNMPv3

SNMPv3 was developed to correct several deficiencies in the earlier versions of SNMP, security being a primary reason. SNMPv3 is defined in RFCs 3410 through 3415. SNMPv3 provides authentication and privacy via usernames and access control by using key management. Security levels are implemented to determine which devices a user can read, write, or create. SNMPv3 also verifies each message to ensure that it has not been modified during transmission. SNMPv3 removes the use of community-based authentication strings, which were sent in cleartext over the network. It is recommended that SNMPv1 and SNMPv2 be used only for read-only access, whereas SNMPv3 be used with read-write access.

SNMPv3 introduces three levels of security:

- **noAuthNoPriv:** No authentication and no encryption
- **authNoPriv:** Authentication and no encryption
- **authPriv:** Authentication and encryption

The noAuthNoPriv level provides no authentication and no privacy (encryption). At the authNoPriv level, authentication is provided but not encryption. The authPriv level provides authentication and encryption.

Authentication for SNMPv3 is based on Hash-based Message Authentication Code–Message Digest 5 (HMAC-MD5) or HMAC – Secure Hash (HMAC-SHA) algorithms. The Cipher Block Chaining–Data Encryption Standard (CBC-DES) standard is used for encryption.

Table 15-4 summarizes SNMP security levels.

Table 15-4 SNMP Security Levels

Version	Level	Authentication	Encryption
SNMPv1	NoAuthNoPriv	Community String	None
SNMPv2	NoAuthNoPriv	Community String	None
SNMPv3	NoAuthNoPriv	Username	None
SNMPv3	AuthNoPriv	MD5 or SHA	None
SNMPv3	AuthPriv	MD5 or SHA	DES, 3DES, AES

Other Network Management Technologies

This section covers RMON, NetFlow, CDP, LLDP, and syslog technologies used to gather network information.

RMON

RMON is a standard monitoring specification that enables network monitoring devices and console systems to exchange network monitoring data. RMON provides more information than SNMP, but more sophisticated data collection devices (network probes) are needed. RMON looks at MAC-layer data and provides aggregate information on the statistics and LAN traffic.

Enterprise networks deploy network probes on several network segments; these probes report back to the RMON console. RMON allows network statistics to be collected even if a failure occurs between the probe and the RMON console. RMON1 is defined by RFCs 1757 and 2819, and additions for RMON2 are defined by RFC 2021.

The RMON MIB is located at iso.org.dod.internet.mgt.mib.rmon or by the equivalent object descriptor, 1.3.6.1.2.1.16. RMON1 defines nine monitoring groups; each group provides specific sets of data. One more group is defined for Token Ring. Each group is optional, so vendors do not need to support all the groups in the MIB. Table 15-5 shows the RMON1 groups.

Table 15-5 RMON1 Groups

ID	Name	Description
1	Statistics	Contains real-time statistics for interfaces: packets sent, bytes, cyclic redundancy check (CRC) errors, fragments.
2	History	Stores periodic statistic samples for later retrieval.
3	Alarm	An alarm event is generated if a statistic sample crosses a threshold.

ID	Name	Description
4	Host	Host-specific statistics.
5	HostTopN	Most active hosts.
6	Matrix	Stores statistics for conversations between two hosts.
7	Filters	Allows packets to be filtered.
8	Packet Capture	Allows packets to be captured for subsequent analysis.
9	Events	Generates notification of events.

RMON2

RMON1 is focused on the data link and physical layers of the OSI model. As shown in Figure 15-4, RMON2 provides an extension for monitoring upper-layer protocols.

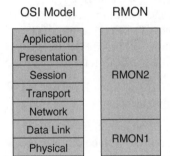

Figure 15-4   *RMON1 and RMON2 compared to the OSI model*

Defined by RFC 2021, RMON2 extends the RMON group with the MIB groups listed in Table 15-6.

Table 15-6   RMON2 Groups

ID	Name	Description
11	Protocol Directory	Lists the protocols the device supports
12	Protocol Distribution	Traffic statistics for each protocol
13	Address Mapping	Contains network-to-MAC-layer address mapping (IP to MAC)
14	Network Layer Host	Contains statistics for traffic sent to or from network layer hosts
15	Network Layer Matrix	Contains statistics for conversations between two network layer hosts
16	Application Layer Host	Contains application layer statistics for traffic sent to or from each host

ID	Name	Description
17	Application Layer Matrix	Contains application layer statistics for conversations between pairs of hosts
18	User History	Contains periodic samples of specified variables
19	Probe Configuration	Probes parameter configuration

NetFlow

Cisco NetFlow allows the tracking of IP flows as they are passed through routers and multilayer switches. An IP flow is a set of IP packets within a specific timeslot that share a number of properties, such as the same source address, destination address, type of service, and protocol number. NetFlow information is forwarded to a network data analyzer, network planning tools, RMON applications, or accounting and billing applications. NetFlow allows for network planning, traffic engineering, usage-based network billing, accounting, Denial of Service monitoring capabilities, and application monitoring. One big benefit is that NetFlow provides the necessary data for billing of network usage. The most recent version of NetFlow is NetFlow Version 9, which is defined in RFC 3954. The NetFlow protocol itself has been superseded by Internet Protocol Flow Information eXport (IPFIX). Based on the NetFlow Version 9 implementation, IPFIX is on the IETF standards track with RFCs 7011 and 7015.

As shown in Figure 15-5, NetFlow consists of three major components:

- **NetFlow accounting:** Collects IP data flows entering router or switch interfaces and prepares data for export. It enables the accumulation of data on flows with unique characteristics, such as IP addresses, application, and class of service (CoS).

- **Flow collector engines:** Captures exported data from multiple routers and filters and aggregates the data according to customer policies, and then stores this summarized or aggregated data. Examples of collectors are Cisco NetFlow Collector, SolarWinds, and CA NetQoS.

- **Network data analyzers:** Displays a graphical user interface (GUI) and analyzes NetFlow data collected from flow collector files. This allows users to complete near-real-time visualization or trending analysis of recorded and aggregated flow data. Users can specify the router and aggregation scheme and the desired time interval.

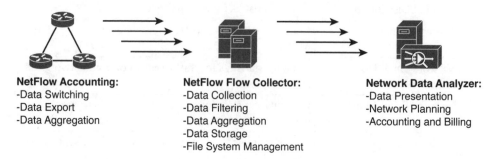

NetFlow Accounting:
-Data Switching
-Data Export
-Data Aggregation

NetFlow Flow Collector:
-Data Collection
-Data Filtering
-Data Aggregation
-Data Storage
-File System Management

Network Data Analyzer:
-Data Presentation
-Network Planning
-Accounting and Billing

Figure 15-5 *NetFlow components*

The benefits of using NetFlow include the following:

- Ability to obtain detailed information with minimal impact to the network devices
- Ability to customize the data captures for each interface
- Ability to include data timestamping across a large number of devices
- Ability to meter network traffic providing data for billing based on network usage
- Used to detect and mitigate threats

Routers and switches are the network accounting devices that gather the statistics. These devices aggregate data and export the information. Each unidirectional network flow is identified by both source and destination IP addresses and transport layer port numbers. NetFlow can also identify flows based on IP protocol number, type of service, and input interface. NetFlow data records contain the following information:

- Source and destination IP address
- Source and destination TCP/UDP ports
- Type of service (ToS)
- Packet and byte counts
- Start and end timestamps
- Input and output interface numbers
- TCP flags and encapsulated protocol (TCP/UDP)
- Routing information (next-hop address, source and destination autonomous system number, destination prefix mask)
- Data analyzers

The NetFlow export or transport mechanism sends the NetFlow data to a collection engine or network management collector. Flow collector engines perform data collection and filtering. They aggregate data from several devices and store the information. Different NetFlow data analyzers can be used based on the intended purpose. NetFlow data can be analyzed for the following key applications:

- **Accounting and billing:** Used by service providers for charging based on bandwidth and application usage and quality of service (QoS).
- **Network planning and analysis:** Link and router capacity.
- **Network and security monitoring:** Visualize real-time traffic patterns.
- **Application monitoring and profiling:** Time-based view of application usage.
- **User monitoring and profiling:** Identifies customer and user network utilization and resource application.
- **NetFlow data warehousing and mining:** NetFlow data can be warehoused for later retrieval and analysis.

Looking ahead, Cisco has introduced Flexible NetFlow as the next generation in flow technology. Flexible NetFlow has many benefits beyond the Cisco traditional NetFlow functionality available for years in Cisco hardware and software.

The key advantages to using Flexible NetFlow are as follows:

■ Flexibility, scalability of flow data beyond traditional NetFlow

■ The ability to monitor a wider range of packet information to produce new information about network behavior not available previously

■ Enhanced network anomaly and security detection

■ User configurable flow information to perform customized traffic identification and the ability to focus and monitor specific network behavior

■ Convergence of multiple accounting technologies into one accounting mechanism

Flexible NetFlow is an integral part of Cisco IOS Software that collects and measures data, allowing all routers or switches in the network to become a source of telemetry and a monitoring device. Flexible NetFlow allows extremely granular and accurate traffic measurements and high-level aggregated traffic collection. Because it is part of Cisco IOS Software, Flexible NetFlow enables Cisco product-based networks to perform traffic flow analysis without external probes being purchased, thus making traffic analysis economical for large IP networks.

Flexible NetFlow can track the following packet information for Layer 2, IPv4, and IPv6 flows:

■ Source and destination MAC addresses

■ Source and destination IPv4 or IPv6 addresses

■ Source and destination TCP/User Datagram Protocol (UDP) ports

■ Type of service (ToS)

■ DSCP

■ Packet and byte counts

■ Flow timestamps

■ Input and output interface numbers

■ TCP flags and encapsulated protocol (TCP/UDP) and individual TCP flags

■ Sections of packets for deep packet inspection

■ All fields in the IPv4 header, including IP-ID, TTL, and others

■ All fields in the IPv6 header, including Flow Label, Option Header, and others

■ Routing information such as next-hop address, source autonomous system (AS) number, destination AS number, source prefix mask, destination prefix mask, BGP Next Hop, and BGP Policy Accounting traffic index

NetFlow Compared to RMON and SNMP

NetFlow enables you to gather more statistical information than RMON with fewer resources. It provides greater detail of the collected data, with date- and timestamping. NetFlow has greater scalability and does not require network probes. As compared with SNMP, NetFlow reports on traffic statistics and is push based, whereas SNMP reports primarily on device statistics and is poll based.

NetFlow can be configured on individual Layer 3 interfaces on routers and Layer 3 switches. NetFlow provides detailed information on the following:

- Source and destination IP addresses
- Source and destination interface identifiers
- TCP/UDP source and destination port numbers
- Number of bytes and packets per flow
- Source and destination autonomous system numbers
- IP type of service (ToS)

CDP

Cisco Discovery Protocol (CDP) is a Cisco-proprietary protocol that can be used to discover only Cisco network devices. CDP is media and protocol independent, so it works over Ethernet, Frame Relay, ATM, and other media. The requirement is that the media support Subnetwork Access Protocol (SNAP) encapsulation. CDP runs at the data link layer of the OSI model. CDP uses hello messages; packets are exchanged between neighbors, but CDP information is not forwarded. In addition to routers and switches, IP phones and Cisco Unified Communication Manager (CUCM) servers also advertise CDP information.

Being protocol and media independent is CDP's biggest advantage over other network management technologies. CDP provides key information about neighbors, including platforms, capabilities, and IP addresses, which is significant for network discovery. It is useful when SNMP community strings are unknown when performing a network discovery.

When displaying CDP neighbors, you can obtain the following information:

- **Local interface:** Local interface that is connected to the discovered neighbor
- **Device ID:** Name of the neighbor device and MAC address or serial number
- **Device IP address:** IP address of the neighbor
- **Hold time:** How long (seconds) to hold the neighbor information
- **Device capabilities:** Type of device discovered: router, switch, transparent bridge, host, IGMP, or repeater
- **Version:** IOS or switch OS version
- **Platform:** Router or switch model number
- **Port ID:** Interface of the neighboring device

Network management devices can obtain CDP information for data gathering. CDP should be disabled on untrusted interfaces, such as those that face the Internet, third-party networks, or other secure networks. CDP works only on Cisco devices.

> **Note**   Disable CDP on interfaces for which you do not want devices to be discovered, such as Internet connections.

LLDP

The Link Layer Discovery Protocol (LLDP), defined in the IEEE 802.1AB (LLDP) specification, is an option of discovering network devices in multivendor networks. LLDP performs functions similar to CDP. With LLDP, devices send information at a fixed interval from each of their interfaces in the form of an Ethernet frame with an Ethertype of 0x88CC. The information shared includes the following:

- System name and description
- Port name and description
- VLAN name
- IP management address
- System capabilities
- MAC/PHY layer information
- Link aggregation

Syslog

The syslog protocol is defined in RFC 3164. Syslog transmits event notification messages over the network. Network devices send the event messages to an event server for aggregation. Network devices include routers, servers, switches, firewalls, and network appliances. Syslog operates over UDP, so messages are not sequenced or acknowledged. The syslog messages are also stored on the device that generates the message and can be viewed locally.

Syslog messages are generated in many broad areas. These areas are called facilities. Cisco IOS has more than 500 facilities. Common facilities include

- IP
- CDP
- OSPF
- TCP
- Interface
- IPsec
- SYS operating system
- Security/authorization
- Spanning Tree Protocol (STP)

Each syslog message has a level. The syslog level determines the event's criticality. Lower syslog levels are more important. Table 15-7 lists the syslog levels.

Table 15-7 Syslog Message Levels

Syslog Level	Severity	Level
0	Emergency	System is unusable.
1	Alert	Take action immediately.

Syslog Level	Severity	Level
2	Critical	Critical conditions.
3	Error	Error messages.
4	Warning	Warning conditions.
5	Notice	Normal but significant events.
6	Informational	Informational messages.
7	Debug	Debug level messages.

15

Common syslog messages are interface up and down events. Access lists can also be configured on routers and switches to generate syslog messages when a match occurs. Each syslog message includes a timestamp, level, and facility. Syslog messages have the following format:

mm/dd/yy:hh/mm/ss:FACILITY-LEVEL-mnemonic:description

Syslog messages can create large amounts of network bandwidth. It is important to enable only syslog facilities and levels that are of particular importance.

Table 15-8 summarizes some of the protocols just covered in this section.

Table 15-8 NetFlow, CDP, and Syslog

Technology	Description
NetFlow	Collects network flow data for network planning, performance, accounting, and billing applications.
CDP	Proprietary protocol for network discovery that provides information on neighboring devices.
Syslog	Reports state information based on facility and severity levels.
RMON	Remote Monitoring. Provides aggregate information of network statistics and LAN traffic.

References and Recommended Reading

NetFlow Performance Analysis, www.cisco.com/en/US/tech/tk812/technologies_white_paper0900aecd802a0eb9.shtml.

NetFlow Version 9, www.cisco.com/en/US/products/ps6645/products_ios_protocol_option_home.html.

Cisco IOS Netflow Data Sheet, http://www.cisco.com/c/en/us/products/collateral/ios-nx-os-software/ios-netflow/product_data_sheet0900aecd80173f71.html.

Tutorial on Link Layer Discovery Protocol, http://www.eetimes.com/document.asp?doc_id=1272069.

MIBs Supported by Product, http://tools.cisco.com/ITDIT/MIBS/servlet/index.

RFC 1157: A Simple Network Management Protocol (SNMP).

RFC 1441: Introduction to Version 2 of the Internet-Standard Network Management Framework.

RFC 1757: Remote Network Monitoring Management Information Base.

RFC 1901: Introduction to Community-Based SNMPv2.

RFC 1902: Structure of Management Information for Version 2 of the Simple Network Management Protocol (SNMPv2).

RFC 2021: Remote Network Monitoring Management Information Base Version 2 Using SMIv2.

RFC 2576: Coexistence Between Version 1, Version 2, and Version 3 of the Internet Standard Network Management Framework.

RFC 3164: The BSD Syslog Protocol.

RFC 3410: Introduction and Applicability Statements for Internet Standard Management Framework.

RFC 3411: An Architecture for Describing Simple Network Management Protocol (SNMP) Management Frameworks.

RFC 3412: Message Processing and Dispatching for the Simple Network Management Protocol (SNMP).

RFC 3414: User-Based Security Model (USM) for Version 3 of the Simple Network Management Protocol (SNMPv3).

RFC 3415: View-Based Access Control Model (VACM) for the Simple Network Management Protocol (SNMP).

RFC 3416: Protocol Operations for SNMPv2.

RFC 3418: Management Information Base for SNMPv2.

RFC 3954: Cisco Systems NetFlow Services Export Version 9.

RFC 5103: Bidirectional Flow Export Using IP Flow Information Export (IPFIX).

RFC 7011: Specification of the IP Flow Information Export (IPFIX) Protocol for the Exchange of Flow Information.

RFC 7015: Flow Aggregation for the IP Flow Information Export (IPFIX) Protocol.

Cisco IOS Flexible http://www.cisco.com/c/en/us/products/collateral/ios-nx-os-software/flexible-netflow/product_data_sheet0900aecd804b590b.html.

Exam Preparation Tasks

Review All Key Topics

Review the most important topics in the chapter, noted with the Key Topics icon in the outer margin of the page. Table 15-9 lists a reference of these key topics and the page numbers on which each is found.

Table 15-9 Key Topics

Key Topic Element	Description	Page
Table 15-2	Network Management Elements	619
Summary	Simple Network Management Protocol. Standard for the exchange of management information between network devices.	619
Table 15-3	SNMP Message Types	623
Table 15-4	SNMP Security Levels	624
Summary	Remote Monitoring. Provides aggregate information of network statistics and LAN traffic.	624
Summary	Tracks IP flows as they are passed through routers and multilayer switches.	626
Summary	Media- and protocol-independent Cisco protocol used to discover Cisco network devices.	629
Section	Use of Link Layer Discovery Protocol (LLDP) for network management purposes.	630
Table 15-7	Syslog Message Levels	630
Table 15-8	NetFlow, CDP, and Syslog	631

Complete Tables and Lists from Memory

Print a copy of Appendix D, "Memory Tables" (found on the CD), or at least the section for this chapter, and complete the tables and lists from memory. Appendix E, "Memory Tables Answer Key," also on the CD, includes completed tables and lists to check your work.

Define Key Terms

Define the following key terms from this chapter, and check your answers in the glossary:

Accounting management, CDP, LLDP, configuration management, fault management, FCAPS, MIB, NetFlow, performance management, RMON, SNMP, syslog

Q&A

The answers to these questions appear in Appendix A, "Answers to the 'Do I Know This Already?' Quizzes and Q&A Questions." For more practice with exam format questions, use the exam engine on the CD.

1. What does the acronym *FCAPS* stand for?

2. CDP runs at what layer of the OSI model?

3. Syslog level 5 is what level of severity?

4. True or false: RMON provides more scalability than NetFlow.

5. True or false: NetFlow provides detailed information on the number of bytes and packets per conversation.

6. What information can be obtained from a neighbor using CDP?

7. What SNMP message is sent by an agent when an event occurs?

   a. Get

   b. Set

   c. GetResponse

   d. Trap

8. What SNMP message is sent to an agent to obtain an instance of an object?

   a. Get

   b. Set

   c. GetResponse

   d. Trap

9. What SNMP message is used to configure a managed device?

   a. Get

   b. Set

   c. GetResponse

   d. Trap

10. About how many facilities are available for syslog in Cisco routers?

    a. 25

    b. 100

    c. 500

    d. 1000

11. Which SNMPv3 level provides authentication with no encryption?

    a. authPriv

    b. authNoPriv

    c. noAuthNoPriv

    d. noauthPriv

12. What encryption standard does SNMPv3 use?

    a. 3DES

    b. CBC-DES

    c. HMAC-MD5

    d. MD5

13. Which technologies can you use to assess a network and create documentation? (Select two.)

    a. RMON

    b. MIB

    c. CDP

    d. NetFlow

14. Which of the following are true about CDP? (Select three.)

    a. It uses UDP.

    b. It is a data-link protocol.

    c. It provides information on neighboring routers and switches.

    d. It is media and protocol independent.

    e. It uses syslog and RMON.

15. RMON2 provides information at what levels of the OSI model?

    a. Data link and physical

    b. Network, data link, and physical

    c. Transport and network only

    d. Network to application

16. Which network management technology operates over TCP?

    a. SNMP

    b. RMON

    c. NetFlow

    d. None of the above

17. Which statement is correct?

    a. SNMPv1 uses GetBulk operations and 32-bit values.

    b. SNMPv2 uses 32-bit values, and SNMPv3 uses 64-bit values.

    c. SNMPv1 uses 32-bit values, and SNMPv2 uses 64-bit values.

    d. SNMPv1 uses GetBulk operations, and SNMPv2 uses Inform operations.

18. Which SNMPv3 level provides authentication and privacy?

   a. authPriv

   b. authNoPriv

   c. noAuthNoPriv

   d. noauthPriv

19. Match the RMON group with its description.

   i.   Statistics

   ii.   Matrix

   iii.   alHost

   iv.   protocoldir

   a. Stores statistics for conversations between two hosts

   b. Lists the protocols that the device supports

   c. Contains real-time statistics for interfaces: packets sent, bytes, CRC errors, fragments

   d. Contains application layer statistics for traffic sent to or from each host

20. What is the most critical syslog priority level?

   a. 0

   b. 1

   c. 6

   d. 7

21. Which management protocol will help a company concentrate on Layer 4 monitoring and gain information to assist in long-term trending analysis?

   a. SNMPv3

   b. RMON2

   c. NetFlow

   d. CDP

   e. MIB

22. Which management protocol performs network traffic analysis?

   a. SNMPv3

   b. RMON2

   c. NetFlow

   d. CDP

   e. MIB

23. What virtual information store is used by SNMP?

   a. SNMPv3

   b. RMON2

   c. ASN.1

   d. CDP

   e. MIB

24. What standard language is used by SNMP?

   a. SNMPv3

   b. RMON2

   c. ASN.1

   d. CDP

   e. MIB

25. Which SNMPv3 method provides authentication but no encryption?

   a. noAuthNoPriv

   b. authPriv

   c. authNoPriv

   d. noauthPriv

26. Which is not an SNMP operation?

   a. GetNext

   b. Trap

   c. Inform Request

   d. Community

   e. GetBulk

27. Which protocol allows for vendor-specific information?

   a. SNMPv3

   b. RMON2

   c. ASN.1

   d. CDP

   e. MIB

28. Which protocol allows for ISPs to bill its customers for network usage?

   a. SNMPv3

   b. RMON2

   c. NetFlow

   d. CDP

   e. MIB

29. Which solution can be customized in each interface to include data timestamping across a large number of interfaces?

   a. SNMPv3

   b. RMON2

   c. NetFlow

   d. CDP

   e. MIB

30. Cisco NetFlow consists of which components? (Select three.)

   a. NetFlow Accounting

   b. FlowCollector

   c. NetFlow Billing Server

   d. Network Data Analyzer

   e. NetFlow Traffic Generator Tool

31. You are performing a manual network discovery using CDP when you encounter non-Cisco network devices. What options do you have to continue the manual discovery?

   a. Continue to use CDP; it discovers non-Cisco devices.

   b. Use CDP non-Cisco command options.

   c. Use LLDP.

   d. Give up; only CDP can be used.

This chapter covers four comprehensive scenarios that draw on several design topics covered in this book:

Scenario one: Friendswood Hospital

Scenario two: Big Oil and Gas

Scenario three: Video Games Spot

Scenario four: Diamond Communications

The case studies and questions in this chapter draw on your knowledge of the CCDA exam topics. Use these exercises to help you master the topics as well as to identify areas you still need to review for the exam.

Understand that each scenario presented encompasses several exam topics. Each scenario, however, does not necessarily encompass all the topics. Therefore, work through all the scenarios in this chapter to cover all the topics. Your CCDA exam will probably contain questions that require you to analyze a scenario. This chapter contains four case studies that are similar in style to the ones you might encounter on the CCDA exam. Read through each case study and answer the corresponding questions. You will find the answers to the case study questions at the end of the chapter. Sometimes more than one solution can satisfy the customer's requirements. In these cases, the answers presented represent recommended solutions developed using good design practices. An explanation accompanies the answer where necessary.

CHAPTER 16

Comprehensive Scenarios

Scenario One: Friendswood Hospital

Mr. Robertson, the IT director at Friendswood Hospital, is responsible for managing the network. Mr. Robertson has requested your help in proposing a network solution that will meet the hospital's requirements. The hospital is growing, and the management has approved funds for network improvements.

The medical staff would like to be able to access medical systems using laptops from any of the patient rooms. Doctors and nurses should be able to access patient medical records, x-rays, prescriptions, and recent patient information. Mr. Robertson purchased new servers and placed them in the data center. The wireless LAN (WLAN) has approximately 50 clients, with about 50 more due in six months. The servers must have high availability. Furthermore, an IP Telephony solution will be deployed and IP addresses should be allocated for the IP phones: 50 IP phones per floor.

Patient rooms are on floors 6 through 10 of the hospital building. Doctors should be able to roam and access the network from any of the floors. A wireless radio-frequency (RF) survey report mentions that three access points placed in the main hallways on each floor can provide full wireless coverage on each floor.

The current network has ten segments, with LAN switches with Fast Ethernet ports that reach a single router that also serves the WAN. Only a single link is used from the floors to the core router. The router is running EIGRP routing protocol, and they want to move to a standards-based routing protocol. The back-end new servers are located in the same segment as those used on floor 1. Mr. Robertson mentions that users have complained of slow access to the servers. He also hands you a table with the current IP addresses (see Table 16-1).

Table 16-1 Current IP Addresses

Floor	Servers	Clients	IP Network
1	15	40	200.100.1.0/24
2	0	43	200.100.2.0/24
3	0	39	200.100.3.0/24
4	0	42	200.100.4.0/24
5	0	17	200.100.5.0/24
6	0	15	200.100.6.0/24

Floor	Servers	Clients	IP Network
7	0	14	200.100.7.0/24
8	0	20	200.100.8.0/24
9	0	18	200.100.9.0/24
10	0	15	200.100.10.0/24

Mr. Robertson would like a proposal to upgrade the network with updated switches that support Gigabit Ethernet to the desktop, redundant 10 Gigabit Ethernet (10GE) fiber uplinks, and Power over Ethernet (PoE), and to provide 10 Gigabit Ethernet access to the servers. The proposal should also cover secure WLAN access on floors 6 through 10 with centralized management. Include an IP addressing scheme that reduces the number of Class C networks the hospital uses. Mr. Robertson wants to reduce the number of networks leased from the Internet service provider (ISP).

Scenario One Questions

The following questions/directives refer to scenario one:

1. What are Friendswood Hospital's business requirements?
2. Are there any business-cost constraints?
3. What are the network's technical requirements?
4. What are the network's technical constraints?
5. Prepare a logical diagram of the current network.
6. Does the hospital use IP addresses effectively?
7. What do you recommend to improve the switching speed between floors?
8. Based on the number of servers and clients provided, what IP addressing scheme would you propose?
9. What routing protocols do you recommend?
10. What solution do you recommend for WLAN access and the network upgrade?
11. Draw the proposed network solution.

Scenario Two: Big Oil and Gas

Mr. Drew is an IT director at Big Oil and Gas, a medium-sized petrochemical company based in Houston, Texas. It also has operations in the Gulf of Mexico and in South America. Mr. Drew is in charge of the network infrastructure. His group includes personnel who can install and configure Cisco routers and switches. Big Oil and Gas uses a legacy Time-Division Multiplex (TDM) voice network and old small PBXs for telephone services. Each site has separately managed PBXs with expired support contracts.

The Big Oil and Gas CIO wants to migrate from the legacy TDM voice network to a Unified Communications (UC) solution to reduce circuit and management costs. Existing data WAN circuits have 50 percent utilization or less but spike up to 80 percent when sporadic FTP transfers occur.

Mr. Drew hands you the diagram shown in Figure 16-1. The existing data network includes 35 sites with approximately 30 people at each site. The network is a Multiprotocol Label Switching (MPLS) WAN, with approximately 200 people at the headquarters. The WAN links range from 384Kbps circuits to 4xE1 speeds. Remote-site applications include statistical files and graphical-site diagrams that are transferred using FTP from remote sites to the headquarters.

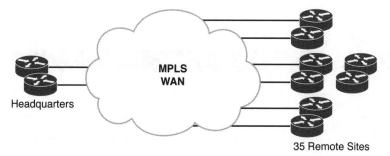

Figure 16-1 *The Big Oil and Gas current network*

Mr. Drew wants a UC solution that manages the servers at headquarters but still provides redundancy or failover at the remote site. He mentions that he is concerned that the FTP traffic might impact the VoIP traffic. He wants to choose a site to implement a test before implementing UC at all sites.

Scenario Two Questions

The following questions/directives refer to scenario two:

1. What are the business requirements for Big Oil and Gas?
2. Are there any business-cost constraints?
3. What are the network's technical requirements?
4. What are the network's technical constraints?
5. Approximately how many IP phones should the network support?
6. What type of UC architecture should you propose?
7. What quality of service (QoS) features would you propose for the WAN?
8. What PoE recommendations would you make?
9. Would you propose a prototype or a pilot?
10. What solution do you suggest for voice redundancy at the remote sites?
11. Diagram the proposed solution.

Scenario Three: Video Games Spot

Video Games Spot is a chain of stores that sells video games. Its headquarters is in Houston, Texas, and more than 60 stores are located throughout the United States. The CIO tells you that they are in the middle of a WAN migration from Frame Relay to MPLS L3 VPN. It will be completed in two months. Most WAN links at the stores are less than 1 Mbps.

After the WAN migration is complete, the CIO wants to use VoIP for voice calls between stores. Most of the traffic is from remote stores to the HQ locations. He wants to complete the VoIP project within the next six months and within the established budget. Each store will have five concurrent calls back to headquarters.

The WAN provider has one priority queue and three other queues for different traffic classifications: Platinum, Gold, Silver, and Bronze. Each is assigned the differentiated services code point (DSCP) listed in Table 16-2.

Table 16-2   DSCPs for Video Games Spot

Priority Queue	DSCP
Platinum	EF
Gold	AF31
Silver	AF21
Bronze	Default

Scenario Three Questions

The following questions refer to scenario three:

1. What are the business constraints for this project?

2. Is MPLS technology appropriate for VoIP?

3. Assuming a g.729 codec, how much bandwidth must be allocated for VoIP packets per store?

4. Assuming a g.729 codec, how much bandwidth must be reserved for VoIP traffic on the WAN link of the headquarters router?

5. Which MPLS priority queue is assigned for VoIP traffic?

   a. Gold

   b. Platinum

   c. Silver

   d. Bronze

6. Which MPLS QoS queue is assigned for FTP traffic?

   a. Platinum

   b. Gold

   c. Silver

   d. Bronze

7. What WAN interface solution must be used to prevent large file transfers from interfering and causing delays of VoIP packets?

   a. Priority queuing

   b. Policy routing

   c. Link fragmentation and interleaving

   d. Serialization delay

8. What is the recommended queuing technique for the WAN interfaces?

   a. PQ

   b. Policy queuing

   c. LLQ

   d. Custom queuing

Scenario Four: Diamond Communications

Diamond Communications has requested an assessment of its current network infrastructure. You are given the diagram shown in Figure 16-2. The current infrastructure contains three 6500 Catalyst switches connected using Layer 2 links. Building access switches, WAN routers, Internet firewalls, bare-metal servers, and VMware ESXi servers all connect to the 6500 switches. There are more than 2000 users attached to the campus access switches, and some Fast Ethernet hubs are still used on the network.

The IT manager mentions that they experience sporadic network outages several times during the day, and users are complaining that the network is slow. The CIO states that they want to consolidate and virtualize the network as much as possible, because the company expects to double in size in three years. They also want to prepare the network for Unified Communications (UC).

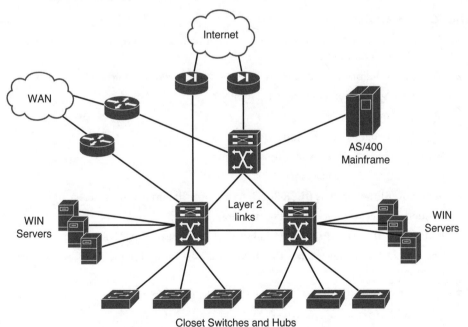

Figure 16-2 *The Diamond Communications current network*

Scenario Four Questions

The following questions/directives refer to scenario four:

1. Is this network scalable?

2. What do you recommend for the core and distribution switches?

3. How would you incorporate network and device virtualization?

4. What changes are required in the closet switches and hubs?

5. What do you recommend for the WAN routers and Internet firewalls?

6. What do you recommend for the bare-metal and virtualized servers?

7. What is the role of the distribution layer in the architecture?

8. What do you recommend for IP addressing?

9. Diamond Communications has a VLAN with a /22 IP subnet that is experiencing network delays. What do you recommend?

10. Diagram your proposed solution.

Scenario Answers

The sections that follow provide the answers/solutions to scenarios one through four.

Scenario One Answers

1. The hospital needs to provide access to patient records, prescriptions, and information from patient rooms.

2. No cost restrictions were discussed. The board approved the funds.

3. The technical requirements are as follows:

   IP Telephony

   Gigabit Ethernet to the desktop

   WLAN access from rooms on floors 6 through 10

   Centralized WLAN management

   Power over Ethernet plus (IEEE 802.3at) to power IP phones and wireless APs

   Redundant access to servers in the data center

   Redundant 10 Gigabit Ethernet uplinks switching between LAN segments

4. The only technical constraint is that servers must be located in the first floor data center rooms.

5. Figure 16-3 shows the logical diagram of the current network.

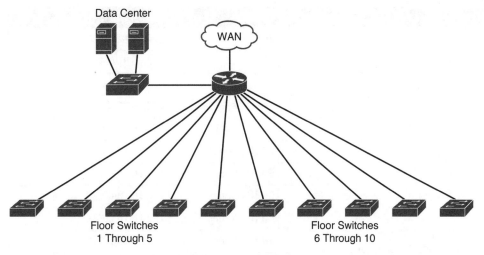

Figure 16-3 *Friendswood Hospital current network*

6. The hospital does not use IP addresses effectively. It uses public Class C networks on each floor. Each floor wastes more than 200 IP addresses, because each Class C network provides up to 254 IP addresses.

7. Recommend using high-speed 10 Gigabit Ethernet Layer 3 switches for the building collapsed core/distribution layer. They can use the existing router for WAN access.

8. The primary recommendation is to use private addresses for the network. Using private addresses has been a best-practice policy for private internal networks since 1996. With private addresses, the hospital could release eight of the Class C networks to the ISP, retaining two for ISP connectivity. In addition, this allows for the parallel infrastructure to be built prior to migrating users to the new network.

   With private addresses, the hospital can choose to use 172.16.0.0/16 for private addressing. The addressing scheme shown in Table 16-3 provides sufficient address space for each network.

Table 16-3   IP Addressing Scheme Using Private Addresses

Floor	Servers	Clients	IP Network
1	15	0	172.16.0.0/24
1	0	40	172.16.1.0/24
2	0	43	172.16.2.0/24
3	0	39	172.16.3.0/24
4	0	42	172.16.4.0/24
5	0	17	172.16.5.0/24
6	0	15	172.16.6.0/24
7	0	14	172.16.7.0/24

Floor	Servers	Clients	IP Network
8	0	20	172.16.8.0/24
9	0	18	172.16.9.0/24
10	0	15	172.16.10.0/24
WLAN: 6, 7, 8, 9, 10	0	100	172.16.20.0/24
1		50 IP phones	172.16.101.0/24
2		50 IP phones	172.16.102.0/24
3		50 IP phones	172.16.103.0/24
4		50 IP phones	172.16.104.0/24
5		50 IP phones	172.16.105.0/24
6		50 IP phones	172.16.106.0/24
7		50 IP phones	172.16.107.0/24
8		50 IP phones	172.16.108.0/24
9		50 IP phones	172.16.109.0/24
10		50 IP phones	172.16.110.0/24

Another solution is to retain the public addresses and use them in the internal network. This solution is less preferred than private addressing. Table 16-4 shows the recommended address scheme that would reduce the number of Class C networks.

Table 16-4   IP Addressing Scheme Using Public Address Space

Floor	Servers	Clients	IP Network
1	0	40	200.100.1.0/26
1	15	N/A	200.100.1.64/26
2	0	43	200.100.1.128/26
3	0	39	200.100.1.192/26
4	0	42	200.100.2.0/26
5	0	17	200.100.2.64/26
6	0	15	200.100.2.128/26
7	0	14	200.100.2.192/26
8	0	20	200.100.3.0/26
9	0	18	200.100.3.64/26
10	0	15	200.100.3.128/26
WLAN: 6, 7, 8, 9, 10	0	40	200.100.3.192/26

Floor	Servers	Clients	IP Network
1		50 IP phones	200.100.4.0/26
2		50 IP phones	200.100.4.64/26
3		50 IP phones	200.100.4.128/26
4		50 IP phones	200.100.4.192/26
5		50 IP phones	200.100.5.0/26
6		50 IP phones	200.100.5.64/26
7		50 IP phones	200.100.5.128/26
8		50 IP phones	200.100.5.192/26
9		50 IP phones	200.100.6.0/26
10		50 IP phones	200.100.6.64/26

Each subnet has 62 IP addresses for host addressing. Based on the preceding IP addressing scheme, Friendswood Hospital does not need networks 200.100.7.0/24 through 200.100.10.0/24.

9. Recommend routing protocols that support variable-length subnet masks (VLSMs). The network is small. Recommend the use of OSFP to satisfy the requirement to use a standards-based routing protocol.

10. Recommend using a primary and backup wireless LAN controller (WLC) and three 802.11ac wireless access points (AP) on each floor for redundancy. Use a VLAN that spans floors 6 through 10. Change the router to a Layer 3 switch. Use the router for WAN access.

11. Figure 16-4 shows the diagram. The router is replaced by the Layer 3 switch with 10 Gigabit Ethernet ports to provide high-speed switching between LANs. Dual 10GE links are used to provide redundancy between the access layer and the core/distribution layer. Each floor has a data IP subnet plus a subnet for the WLAN and another for the data center. Each floor has three access points for coverage and access switches with GE ports and 10GE Uplinks. Servers can connect using 10 Gigabit Ethernet.

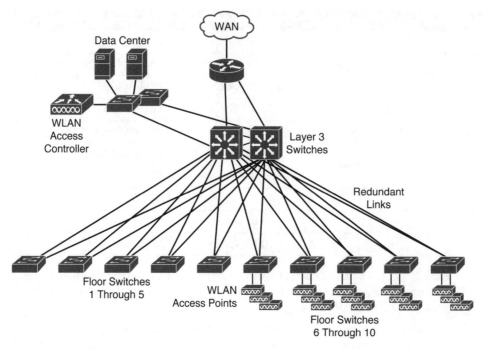

Figure 16-4   *The Friendswood Hospital proposed network solution*

Scenario Two Answers

1. The company wants to provide voice services in a converged network.

2. The solution should provide reduced costs over the existing separate voice and data networks.

3. The technical requirements are as follows:

   Provide UC over the data network.

   Provide voice redundancy or failover for the remote sites.

   Prevent FTP traffic from impacting the voice traffic.

4. The only technical constraint is that call-processing servers need to be located at headquarters, and IP phones need to continue to work even if the WAN goes down or has limited bandwidth.

5. There are 200 IP phones at headquarters, and 35 × 30 = 1050 remote IP phones, for a total of 1250 IP phones.

6. Propose the WAN centralized call-processing architecture with a Cisco Unified Communications Manager (CUCM) cluster at headquarters.

7. Use low-latency queuing (LLQ) on the WAN links to give the highest priority to voice traffic. Then define traffic classes for regular traffic and FTP traffic. Make bandwidth reservations for the voice traffic and maximum bandwidth restrictions for the FTP traffic. Call Admission Control (CAC) is recommended to limit the number of calls to and from a remote site. CAC should be used to reroute calls to the public switched

telephone network (PSTN) if there is no available bandwidth to support a new call. For example, you can limit calls at sites with 384K links to only three calls via the WAN. Any additional call gets routed to the PSTN.

8. Recommend standards-based Power over Ethernet (PoE), also known as IEEE (802.3af), for the switches to provide power to the IP phones.

9. To prove that calls can run over the WAN links, implement a pilot site. The pilot would test the design's functionality over the WAN with or without FTP traffic.

10. Recommend the use of Survivable Remote Site Telephony (SRST) to provide voice services in the event of WAN failure, and reroute calls to the (PSTN).

11. Figure 16-5 shows the diagram of the proposed solution, which shows headquarters and two remote sites for clarity. This architecture is duplicated for all remote sites. Each site uses a voice router that is connected to both the IP WAN and the PSTN. SRST provides voice survivability in the case of WAN failure. A CUCM cluster is implemented at the headquarters. The Cisco Unified Communications Manager (CUCM) servers are placed in the data center in a redundant network.

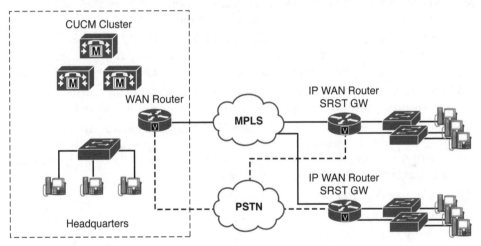

Figure 16-5 *Headquarters and two remote sites*

Scenario Three Answers

1. The WAN project is to be completed in two months. The VoIP project is to be completed in six months and within budget.

2. Yes, MPLS L3 VPN technology is the preferred WAN technology to support VoIP packets. MPLS provides QoS prioritization and guarantees.

3. 130 Kbps. This is calculated by taking five concurrent calls times 26 Kbps per call.

4. 7.8 Mbps. This is the sum of VoIP traffic per store multiplied by 60 remote stores.

5. B. VoIP traffic is marked with DSCP expedited forwarding, which corresponds to the Platinum queue.

6. D. FTP traffic does not require prioritization and therefore is assigned to the default Bronze queue.

7. C. LFI should be used on WAN links that are less than 768 Kbps. It is used to reduce the serialization delay associated with the transmission of large packets on low-speed links.

8. C. LLQ is the recommended queuing technique when VoIP packets are present on WAN links.

Scenario Four Answers

1. No. The current Diamond network is not scalable. It is a flat network architecture using Layer 2 links in the core with no hierarchy. It does not have core, distribution, and access layers.

2. Recommend creating a hierarchy with core, distribution, and access layers. Create a Nexus 7000 VDC for the core layer. Use Layer 3 links rather than Layer 2 links to prevent spanning-tree loop broadcast storms.

3. Network virtualization would be implemented using the Virtual Device Context (VDC) and Virtual Port Channel (VPC) features with the Nexus 7700 series pair of switches. Device virtualization is achieved using Nexus 7000 Virtual Device Contexts (VDC) for the core, edge, campus, and server distribution layers.

4. All hubs need to be replaced with switches. All switches should be replaced with 10GE LAN switches with PoE plus to provide power to future IP phones and wireless access points. All new switch purchases should be 10GE LAN switches with PoE plus.

5. Create a Nexus 7700 VDC enterprise edge layer that separates the campus LAN and the enterprise edge. Create another VPC for the campus distribution layer.

6. Create a Nexus 7700 VDC DC and Nexus 5500/Nexus 2000 access layer on which to place all the virtualized and bare-metal servers with support for 1GE/10GE copper and fiber connectivity. The Nexus 5500 also supports Unified Fabric for future Fibre Channel over Ethernet (FCoE) requirements.

7. The distribution layer has several functions:

Address summarization

Security ACLs

FHRP definition

VLAN routing

Link aggregation

8. Recommend allocating /30 subnets for the links between the core and distribution switches. Allocate separate IP subnets for the future IP phones and servers. This lets you apply security policies. Also, allocate separate IP subnets for wireless LAN networks.

9. Recommend splitting the IP subnet into separate /24 IP subnets, as needed, with 30 percent for future growth.

10. The solution shown in Figure 16-6 is a highly redundant and hierarchical network with core, edge, campus, and DC distribution layers. Campus access and separate server access for the server farm are used. Distribution switches are used to allocate security policies and route summarization. The solution is scalable and will support the growth plans of Diamond Communications. PoE plus switches are deployed to support the future UC deployment.

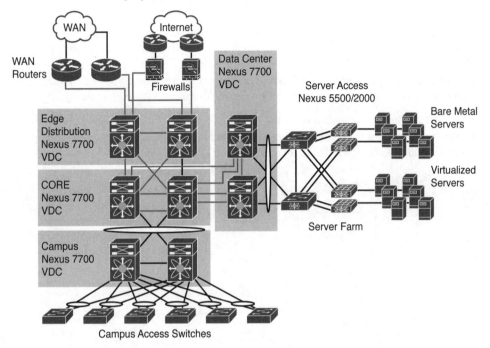

Figure 16-6 *The Diamond Communications proposed network solution*

The first 16 chapters of this book cover the technologies, protocols, design concepts, and considerations required to be prepared to pass the 200-310 CCDA exam. Although these chapters supply the detailed information, most people need more preparation than just reading the first 16 chapters of this book. This chapter details a set of tools and a study plan to help you complete your preparation for the exams.

This short chapter has two main sections. The first section lists the exam preparation tools useful at this point in the study process. The second section details a suggested study plan now that you have completed all the earlier chapters in this book.

Note Note that Appendix D, "Memory Tables," and Appendix E, "Memory Tables Answer Key," exist as soft-copy appendixes on the companion website.

CHAPTER 17

Final Preparation

Tools for Final Preparation

This section lists some information about the available tools and how to access them.

Review Tools on the Companion Website

The companion website for this book includes all the electronic files and review tools. To access this site, follow these steps:

Step 1. Go to http://www.pearsonitcertification.com/register.

Step 2. Either log in to your account (if you have an existing account already) or create a new account.

Step 3. Enter the ISBN of your book (9781587144547) and click **Submit**.

Step 4. Answer the challenge questions to validate your purchase.

Step 5. In your account page, click the **Registered Products** tab and then click the **Access Bonus Content** link.

After you have registered your book, to access the companion website, all you need to do is go to www.pearsonitcertification.com and sign in to your account. From there, select the Registered Products tab and click the Access Bonus Content link.

Pearson Cert Practice Test Engine and Questions

The companion website includes the Pearson Cert Practice Test engine (software that displays and grades a set of exam-realistic, multiple-choice questions). Using the Pearson Cert Practice Test, you can either study by going through the questions in Study mode or take a simulated (timed) CCDA exam.

The installation process requires two major steps. The companion website has a recent copy of the Pearson Cert Practice Test engine. The practice exam—the database of CCDA exam questions—can be downloaded after you redeem your access code found in the sleeve in the back of the book.

Download and Install the Software

The software installation process is routine compared with other software installation processes. To be complete, the following steps outline the download and installation process:

Note If you have purchased another Pearson study guide, you may have already installed the PCPT software. If you already have the software installed, there is no need to install the software again. Skip ahead to the next section to activate your new practice exams.

Step 1.   Go to the book's companion website (instructions for access are included in the previous section).

Step 2.   Locate the download link for the Pearson IT Certification Practice Test (PCPT) software and download the latest version of the engine to your computer.

Step 3.   When the download is complete, unzip the software and run the installer.

Step 4.   Respond to window prompts as with any typical software installation process.

The installation process will give you the option to activate your exam with the activation code supplied on the paper in the sleeve in the back of the book. This process requires that you establish a Pearson website logon. You will need this logon to activate the exam, so please do register when prompted. If you already have a Pearson website logon, there is no need to register again. Just use your existing logon.

Activate and Download the Practice Exam

Once the exam engine is installed, you should then activate the exam associated with this book (if you did not do so during the installation process), as follows:

Step 1.   Start the Pearson Cert Practice Test (PCPT) software from the Windows Start menu or from your desktop shortcut icon.

Step 2.   To activate and download the exam associated with this book, from the My Products or Tools tab, click the **Activate** button.

Step 3.   At the next screen, enter the activation key from the paper inside the cardboard sleeve at the back of the book. Then click the **Activate** button.

Step 4.   The activation process downloads the practice exam. Click Next, and then click **Finish**.

When the activation process has completed, the My Products tab should list your new exam. If you do not see the exam, make sure you have selected the My Products tab on the menu. At this point, the software and practice exam are ready to use. Just select the exam and click the **Use** button.

To update a particular exam you have already activated and downloaded, simply select the **Tools** tab and click the **Update Products** button. Updating your exams ensures you have the latest changes and updates to the exam data.

If you want to check for updates to the Pearson Cert Practice Test engine software, select the **Tools** tab and click the **Update Application** button. Doing so ensures that you are running the latest version of the software engine.

Activating Other Exams

The exam software installation process, and the registration process, only has to happen once. Then, for each new exam, only a few steps are required. For instance, if you buy another new Cisco Press Official Cert Guide or Pearson IT Certification Cert Guide, extract the activation code from the sleeve at the back of that book. From there, all you have to do is start the exam engine (if not still up and running), and perform steps 2 through 4 from the previous list.

Premium Edition

In addition to the free practice exam provided with this book, you can purchase additional exams with expanded functionality directly from Pearson IT Certification. The Premium Edition of this title contains an additional two full practice exams and an eBook (in PDF, EPUB, and Kindle formats). In addition, the Premium Edition title also has remediation for each question to the specific part of the eBook that relates to that question.

Because you have purchased the print version of this title, you can purchase the Premium Edition at a deep discount. There is a coupon code in the sleeve in the back of the book that contains a one-time-use code and instructions for where you can purchase the Premium Edition.

To view the Premium Edition product page, go to www.informit.com/title/9781587144547.

The Cisco Learning Network

Cisco provides a wide variety of CCDA preparation tools at a Cisco Systems website called the Cisco Learning Network. This site includes a large variety of exam preparation tools, including sample questions, forums on each Cisco exam, learning video games, and information about each exam.

To reach the Cisco Learning Network, go to www.cisco.com/go/learnnetspace, or just search for "Cisco Learning Network." You must use the logon you created at Cisco.com. If you do not have such a logon, you can register for free. To register, simply go to Cisco.com, click Register at the top of the page, and supply some information.

Memory Tables

Like most *Official Cert Guides* from Cisco Press, this book purposely organizes information into tables and lists for easier study and review. Rereading these tables can be very useful before the exam. However, it is easy to skim over the tables without paying attention to every detail, especially when you remember having seen the table's contents when reading the chapter.

Instead of just reading the tables in the various chapters, this book's Appendixes D and E give you another review tool. Appendix D lists partially completed versions of many of the tables from the book. You can open Appendix D (a PDF on the companion website) and print the appendix. For review, you can attempt to complete the tables. This exercise can help you focus on the review. It also exercises the memory connectors in your brain; plus it makes you think about the information without as much information, which forces a little more contemplation about the facts.

Appendix E, also a PDF located on the companion website, lists the completed tables to check yourself. You can also just refer to the tables as printed in the book.

Chapter-Ending Review Tools

Chapters 1 through 15 each have several features in the "Exam Preparation Tasks" and "Q&A" sections at the end of the chapter. You might have already worked through these in each chapter. It can also be useful to use these tools again as you make your final preparations for the exam.

Suggested Plan for Final Review/Study

This section lists a suggested study plan from the point at which you finish reading through Chapter 16, until you take the 200-310 CCDA exam. Certainly, you can ignore this plan, use it as is, or just take suggestions from it.

The plan uses five steps:

Step 1.   **Review key topics and DIKTA questions:** You can use the table that lists the key topics in each chapter, or just flip through the pages looking for key topics. Also, reviewing the DIKTA questions from the beginning of the chapter can be helpful for review.

Step 2.   **Complete memory tables:** Open Appendix D from the companion website and print the entire thing, or print the tables by major part. Then complete the tables.

Step 3.   **Review "Q&A" sections:** Go through the Q&A section at the end of each chapter to identify areas you need more study.

Step 4.   **Subnetting practice:** If you can no longer do subnetting well and quickly, without a subnetting calculator, take some time to get better and faster before going to take the 200-310 CCDA exam.

Step 5.   **Use the Pearson Cert Practice Test engine to practice:** The Pearson Cert Practice Test engine can be used to study using a bank of unique exam-realistic questions available only with this book.

Subnetting Practice

This book assumes that you have mastered subnetting and the related math. However, many people who progress through CCNA and move on to CCDA follow a path like this:

Step 1.   Learn subnetting conceptually.

Step 2.   Get really good at doing the math quickly.

Step 3.   Pass the CCNA.

Step 4.   Get a lot faster at doing the subnetting math.

Step 5.   Study for the 200-310 CCDA exam.

Although subnetting should not be assessed as an end to itself on the 200-310 CCDA exam, many questions require that you understand subnetting math and be able to do that math just as quickly as you did when you passed the CCNA exam. If you are a little slow on doing subnetting math, before you go to the 200-310 CCDA exam, try some of the following exercises:

- Practice finding the subnet number, broadcast address, and range of addresses in a subnet. To do so, pick a number and mask, calculate the values, and use your favorite subnet calculator to check your work. Look at the Cisco Learning Network for a calculator if you do not have one already.

- Use the Cisco Subnet Game, also at the Cisco Learning Network.

- Practice choosing the best summary for a range of subnets. Pick three or four addresses/masks. Calculate the subnet number and range. Then, try to choose the summary (subnet number/mask) that includes those three or four subnets, without including any more subnets than what is required. You can also check your math with a subnet calculator.

- If you like using binary/decimal conversions when you work through these problems, but just need to go faster, check out the Cisco Binary Game, also at the Cisco Learning Network.

Using the Exam Engine

The Pearson Cert Practice Test engine includes a database of questions created specifically for this book. The Pearson Cert Practice Test engine can be used either in Study mode or Practice Exam mode, as follows:

- **Study mode:** This mode is most useful when you want to use the questions for learning and practicing. In Study mode, you can select options such as randomizing the order of the questions and answers, automatically viewing answers to the questions as you go, testing on specific topics, and many other options.

- **Practice Exam mode:** This mode presents questions in a timed environment, providing you with a more exam-realistic experience. It also restricts your ability to see your score as you progress through the exam and view answers to questions as you are taking the exam. These timed exams not only allow you to study for the actual 200-310 CCDA exam, they help you simulate the time pressure that can occur on the actual exam.

When doing your final preparation, you can use Study mode, Practice Exam mode, or both. However, after you have seen each question a couple of times, you will likely start to remember the questions, and the usefulness of the exam database might diminish. So, consider the following options when using the exam engine:

- Use this question database for review. Use Study mode to study the questions by chapter, just as with the other final review steps listed in this chapter. Plan on getting another exam (possibly from the Premium Edition) if you want to take additional simulated exams.

- Save the question database, not using it for review during your review of each book part. Save it until the end, so you will not have seen the questions before. Then, use Practice Exam mode to simulate the exam.

Picking the correct mode from the exam engine's user interface is pretty obvious. The following steps show how to move to the screen from which to select Study or Practice Exam mode:

Step 1. Click the **My Products** tab if you are not already at that screen.

Step 2. Select the exam you want to use from the list of available exams.

Step 3. Click the **Use** button.

The engine should then display a window from which you can choose Study mode or Practice Exam mode. When in Study mode, you can further choose the book chapters, limiting the questions to those explained in the specified chapters of the book.

Summary

The tools and suggestions listed in this chapter have been designed with one goal in mind: to help you develop the skills required to pass the 200-310 CCDA exam. This book has been developed from the beginning to not just tell you the facts but to also help you learn how to apply the facts. No matter what your experience level leading up to when you take the exams, it is our hope that the broad range of preparation tools, and even the structure of the book, helps you pass the exam with ease. I hope you do well on the exam.

Answers to the Do I Know This Already?" Quizzes and Q&A Questions

Answers to the Do I Know This Already?" Quizzes

Chapter 1

1. B, D, and F. Borderless network, data center/virtualization, and collaboration are the three architectures for the enterprise.

2. A, B, C. Removal of borders, virtualization, and growth of applications are technology forces.

3. B. Network resiliency and control occur in the Borderless Network Services layer.

4. B. Presence occurs under Collaboration Services.

5. B. Solution Support provides dedicated resources to troubleshoot issues within the network.

6. A. The plan phase is when the network is designed.

7. D. The primary sources of network audits are existing documentation, existing management software, and new management tools.

8. D. The top-down design approach starts the design from the application layer.

9. B. These are examples of organization constraints.

10. C. These are examples of technical goals.

Chapter 2

1. B. The core layer of the hierarchical model is responsible for fast transport.

2. C. The enterprise edge consists of e-commerce, Internet connectivity, VPN/remote access, and WAN modules. The enterprise edge modules connect to SPs.

3. C. The distribution layer of the hierarchical model is responsible for security filtering, address and area aggregation, and media translation.

4. D. HSRP and VRRP provide default gateway redundancy.

5. F. The network management module monitors all components and functions except for the SP edge.

6. A. The SP edge includes Internet, PSTN, and WAN modules.

7. C. The server farm hosts campus servers, including Cisco CallManager servers.

8. D. The access layer functions are high availability, port security, rate limiting, ARP inspection, virtual access lists, and trust classification.

Chapter 3

1. F. Routers and Layer 3 switches are Layer 3 devices that control and filter network broadcasts.

2. C. The maximum distance of 100BASE-T is 100 meters.

3. G. Every port of a Layer 2 switch, Layer 3 switch, or LAN port on a router is a collision domain.

4. B. Routes are summarized at the distribution layer.

5. B. Layer 3 switches are recommended for the backbone of campus networks.

6. C. This is a peer-peer application.

7. C. Multimode fiber provides a cost-effective solution for that distance. Single-mode fiber is more expensive. UTP cannot go more than 100 meters.

8. C. PortFast bypasses the listening-learning phase for access ports and goes directly to the port-forwarding state.

Chapter 4

1. B and C. Fibre Channel over Ethernet (FCoE) and Internet Small Computer Systems Interface (iSCSI) are two methods for implementing unified fabric in the data center over 10 Gigabit Ethernet.

2. B. The data center foundation transparently provides end users application access through the intelligent use of the network, compute, and storage resources.

3. A. Data center facility aspects such as space, load, power capacity, and cabling are architectural and mechanical specifications.

4. D. Data center cooling requires the most power out of the overall power budget, next to servers and storage.

5. C. The data center access layer provides Layer 2/Layer 3 physical port density for servers in the data center.

6. D. The Layer 4 security and application services in the data center aggregation layer include server load balancing, SSL offloading, firewalling, and IPS services.

7. D. Virtualization technologies allow a physical device to share its resources by acting as multiple versions of itself.

8. A, B, and C. VRFs, VLANs, and VSANs are examples of network virtualization techniques where logical isolation is used.

9. C. Dark Fiber can be privately owned. VPLS, MPLS, and VPWS require a service provider to implement.

10. C. Dedicated L4-7 load balancers maintain TCP state information locally in their state tables.

Chapter 5

1. D. IEEE 802.11ac provides 1.3 Gbps of bandwidth.

2. B. The Industrial, Scientific, and Medical (ISM) band of frequencies provides 11 channels for WLANs.

3. D. CAPWAP is an Internet Engineering Task Force (IETF) standard for control messaging for setup, authentication, and operations between access points (APs) and WLAN controllers (WLCs).

4. B. The service-port interface is an optional interface that is statically configured for out-of-band management.

5. D. 1000. The WiSM WLC module supports up to 1000 access points.

6. C. With N+N+1 redundancy, an equal number of controllers back up each other, as with N+N. Plus, a backup WLC is configured as the tertiary WLC for the access points.

7. B. The recommended best practice is up to 20 WLAN clients.

8. D. Mesh access points (MAP) connect to the RAP to connect to the wired network.

Chapter 6

1. C. DMZ/e-commerce, Internet, remote-access VPN, and WAN/MAN are all network modules found in the enterprise edge.

2. B Metro Ethernet bandwidths can range from 10 Mbps to 1 Gbps, and even higher in some cases.

3. D. A TDM T1 circuit provides 1.5.44 Mbps of bandwidth.

4. C. The Cisco PBM methodology is used when designing the enterprise edge.

6. D. MPLS is a technology for the delivery of IP services using labels (numbers) to forward packets.

6. A. Low-latency queuing (LLQ) adds a strict-priority queue to CBWFQ.

7. D. Site-to-site VPNs over the Internet offer an alternative WAN transport for interconnecting sites instead of MPLS.

8. D. Dual-router dual-homed provides the highest level of resiliency for Internet connectivity with full redundancy in hardware, links, and Internet service providers.

9. A. A remote access VPN gives mobile users, home users, and partners connectivity to corporate intranets over the Internet.

10. A. Cisco ISR and Cisco ASR series routers are commonly used for site-to-site VPNs with IPsec over GRE to support the deployment of IGPs.

Chapter 7

1. A. Frame Relay and ATM are commonly used to connect to WAN services in the enterprise edge.

2. D. Leased lines have a higher cost disadvantage vs. VPNs or IPsec over the Internet.

3. B. Dynamic routing protocols and IP multicast are not supported with IPsec VPN.

4. D. DMVPN. In enterprise environments, DMVPN is used on routers with NHRP and mGRE.

5. B. Secondary WAN links offer both backup and load-sharing capabilities.

6. C. The goal of high availability is to remove the single points of failure in the design, either by software, hardware, or power. Redundancy is critical in providing high levels of availability.

7. C. SP MPLS/IP VPN has excellent growth support and high availability.

8. B. Cisco IOS S Releases 12.2SE and IOS XE 3.7 provide low-end to mid-range switching for enterprise access and distribution deployments.

9. A, B, and D. Common components used for designing enterprise branch architectures include routers, switches, and IP phones.

10. B. The medium branch design is recommended for branch offices of 50 to 100 users, with an additional access router in the WAN edge allowing for redundancy services.

Chapter 8

1. B.

2. B. There are 5 host bits: $2^5 - 2 = 30$ hosts.

3. D. Loopback addresses should have a /32 mask so that address space is not wasted.

4. C. The precedence bits are located in the Type of Service field of the IPv4 header.

5. B. Multicast addresses range from 224.0.0.1 to 239.255.255.255.

6. D. The summary route summarizes subnetworks from 150.10.192.0/24 to 150.10.199.0/24. Answer D is the only one that includes them.

7. D. Point-to-point links need only two host addresses. They use a /30 mask, which provides $2^2 - 2 = 2$ host addresses.

8. C. DHCP assigns IP addresses dynamically.

9. C. Static NAT is used to statically translate public IP addresses to private IP addresses.

10. C. The DS field allocates 6 bits in the ToS field, thus making it capable of 64 distinct codepoints.

Chapter 9

1. C. IPv6 uses 128 bits for addresses, and IPv4 uses 32 bits. The difference is 96.

2. C. The IPv6 header is 40 bytes in length.

3. C. The defining first hexadecimal digits for link-local addresses are FE8.

4. D. IPv6 addresses can be unicast, anycast, or multicast.

5. B. Answers A and C are incorrect because you cannot use the double colons (::) twice. Answers C and D are also incorrect because you cannot reduce b100 to b1.

6. C. NAT-PT translates between IPv4 and IPv6 addresses.

7. B. The IPv6 multicast address type handles broadcasts.

8. B. The IPv6 loopback address is ::1.

9. A. IPv4-compatible IPv6 addresses have the format ::d.d.d.d.

10. C. The DNS maps fully qualified domain names to IPv6 addresses using (AAAA) records.

11. B. IPv6 increases the address space, which allows globally unique IP addresses. Broadcasts are no longer used.

12. C.

13. D.

Chapter 10

1. B. The default metric for interfaces for IS-IS is 10.

2. C. You use an exterior gateway protocol (EGP) to receive Internet routes from a service provider.

3. A. RIPv2 is a classless distance-vector routing protocol.

4. B. Distance-vector routing protocols send periodic updates.

5. B. RIPng is a distance-vector routing protocol that is used in IPv6 networks.

6. B. If bandwidth is used, the path with the highest bandwidth is selected. If cost is used, the path with the lowest cost is selected.

7. B. OSPF has an administrative distance of 110. EIGRP has an administrative distance of 90. The route with the lower administrative distance is selected: EIGRP.

8. D. EIGRP, RIPv2, IS-IS, and OSPF are all classless routing protocols.

9. B. The default metrics for EIGRP are bandwidth and delay.

10. C. EIGRP implements DUAL.

Chapter 11

1. B. OSPF defines ABRs that connect areas to the OSPF backbone.

2. G. EIGRP, OSPF, and IS-IS support VLSMs.

3. B. OSPF defines the ASBR as the router that injects external routes into the OSPF autonomous system.

4. E. OSPFv2 Type 5 LSAs are autonomous system external LSAs.

5. C. OSPFv2 routers use 224.0.0.6 to communicate with DRs.

6. A. Type 1 LSAs (router LSAs) are forwarded to all routers within an OSPF area.

7. D. Intra-area-prefix LSAs carry IPv6 prefixes associated with a router, a stub network, or an associated transit network segment.

8. B. You use External Border Gateway Protocol (eBGP) to exchange routes between autonomous systems.

9. B. It is a best practice to summarize routes on the distribution routers toward the core.

10. B. You use IGMP between hosts and local routers to register with multicast groups.

11. B. The lower 23 bits of the IP multicast address are mapped to the last 23 bits of the Layer 2 MAC address.

12. A. The administrative distance of eBGP routes is 20. The administrative distance of Internal BGP (iBGP) routes is 200.

Chapter 12

1. D. Payment Card Industry Data Security Standards (PCI DSS) is a security standard that defines how to protect credit card holder data.

2. B. Reconnaissance is used to gather information from the hosts attached to the network.

3. A. DoS attacks aim to overwhelm resources such as memory, CPU, and bandwidth, thus impacting the target system and denying legitimate users access.

4. C. When attackers change sensitive data without the proper authorization, this is called an integrity violation.

5. B. Incident-handling policies define the processes and procedures for managing security incidents, including the handling of emergency-type scenarios.

6. D. All of these fall into the two main reasons for having a security policy by providing a framework for the security implementation and creating a security baseline of the current security posture.

7. D. Authentication of the identity can be based on any of the attributes or a combination thereof.

8. D. Cisco DMVPN provides encrypted point-to-point GRE tunnels. GRE-based VPNs do not use encryption.

9. A, B, and C. Evaluating security breaches, using locks or alarms, and assessing the impact of stolen resources are all physical security guidelines to consider for a secure infrastructure.

10. B. Security management solutions provide ways to provision network security policies for ease of deployment.

Chapter 13

1. A, B, and C. Segmentation, compliance, and management are secure domains of the Cisco SAFE architecture.

2. C. The Cisco ASAs provide high-performance firewall, IPS, antivirus, IPsec, and VPN services.

3. B. 802.1X is an IEEE media-level access control standard that permits and denies admission to the network and applies traffic policy based on identity.

4. A. Cisco ISE protects the network from security threats by enforcing security compliance on all devices attempting to access the network.

5. A and C. The Cisco FWSM and ASA SM security appliances all support firewall filtering with ACLs.

6. B. Cisco ESA is a firewall and threat-monitoring appliance for SMTP-based traffic (on TCP port 25).

7. A. Cisco Security Manager (CSM) is an integrated solution for configuration management of firewall, VPN, router, switch module, and IPS devices.

8. B and C. Cisco IOS IPS and ASA can be used to integrate security into the network.

9. B. NetFlow provides information for detecting and mitigating threats.

10. C. Cisco ACS is a security management platform for controlling administrative access for Cisco devices and security applications.

Chapter 14

1. C. H.323 is the ITU standard that provides a framework for the transport of voice, video, and data over packet-switched networks.

2. D. The default codec in Cisco VoIP dial peers is G.729, which has an 8Kbps bit rate.

3. C. RTP operates at the transport layer of the OSI model.

4. C. The H.225 standard defines the procedures for call setup and signaling.

5. B. An Erlang is a unit that describes the number of calls in an hour.

6. B. VAD reduces traffic by not transmitting packets when there is silence in voice conversations.

7. C. cRTP compresses the RTP, UDP, and IP headers.

8. B. LLQ is recommended for VoIP networks.

9. A. The local loop is located between the traditional phone and the CO switch.

10. C. Jitter is the variance in the amount of per-packet delay incurred during the transport of packets across the network, such as packets in an IP telephony voice call.

Chapter 15

1. C. SNMPv3 introduces authentication and encryption for SNMP.

2. B. SNMP runs over UDP.

3. A. Managed devices contain SNMP agents.

4. D. A MIB is a collection of information that is stored on the local agent of the managed device.

5. D. CDP is the Cisco Discovery Protocol.

6. C. The NMS manager uses the GetBulk operation to retrieve large blocks of data, such as multiple rows in a table.

7. A. RMON1 is focused on the data link and physical layers of the OSI model.

8. B. Community is not an SNMP operation.

9. B. NetFlow allows for network planning, traffic engineering, billing, accounting, and application monitoring.

10. B. CDP is a hello-based protocol.

Answers to the Q&A Questions

Chapter 1

1. Prepare, Plan, Design, Implement, Operate, Optimize.

2. E, F, G. Regulation, ROI, and competitiveness are business forces.

3. A. Identify customer requirements.

4. B, C, and E.

5. i = D, ii = F, iii = C, iv = B, v = E, vi = A.

6. C. The user services architecture provides mobility, performance, and security.

7. B, C, and D.

8. i = D, ii = A, iii = E, iv = B, v = F, vi = C.

9. B. A pilot site is an actual live location for testing.

10. A. A prototype network is a subset of the design in an isolated environment.

11. B.

12. A. Monitoring commands are not SNMP tools.

13. A and B.

14. C and D. The other answers are technical constraints.

15. A, C, and E.

16. B, D, and F. The other answers are organizational goals.

17. A, B, D, E. Answers C and F are not usually included in the design document.

18. i = D, ii = C, iii = B, iv = F, v = E, vi = A, vii = G.

19. C. The network health analysis is based on statistics obtained from the existing network.

20. C. WAN circuits with sustained utilization of more than 70 percent should have their provisioned bandwidth increased.

21. A, B, C, D, E. All these items are included in a network audit report.

22. B, C, and D.

23. B.

24. C, D, and E.

25. B, C, and D.

26. B.

27. The sequence for the stages of top-down design is as follows:

1. Identify customer requirements.
2. Define upper OSI layers.
3. Gather additional information.
4. Choose underlying technology.

28. B, D, and E.

29. C-1, A-2, B-3, C-4. Taking a top-down approach, the order of importance is security design, IP addressing (network layer) design, physical topology design, and then network modular design.

30. C and D.

31. A, B, C, and D.

32. C.

33. A, B, and E

34. B.

35. C.

36. C.

37. A.

38. D.

39. E. Operate.

40. F. Optimize.

41. C. Design.

42. B. Plan.

43. A. Prepare.

44. C. Build.

45. D. Manage.

Chapter 2

1. False.

2. True.

3. The server farm.

4. True.

5. The Internet submodule.

6. Enterprise campus, enterprise edge, enterprise WAN, enterprise branch, enterprise data center, and enterprise teleworker.

7. True.

8. False. A full-mesh network increases costs.

9. Use $n(n-1)/2$, where $n = 6$. $6(6-1)/2 = (6 * 5)/2 = 30/2 = 15$.

10. Option 1: Single router, dual links to one ISP.

Option 2: Single router, dual links to two ISPs.

Option 3: Dual routers, dual links to one ISP.

Option 4: Dual routers, dual links to two ISPs.

Option 4 provides the most redundancy, with dual local routers, dual links, and dual ISPs.

11. The SP edge Internet submodule connects to the enterprise edge Internet submodule.

12. Cost savings, ease of understanding, easy network growth (scalability), and improved fault isolation.

13. IP phones reside in the building access layer of the campus infrastructure. The CallManagers are placed in the server farm of the enterprise campus.

14. i = C, ii = D, iii = B, iv = A.

15. False. Small campus networks can have collapsed core and distribution layers and implement a two-layer design. Medium campus networks can have two-tier or three-tier designs.

16. Use the formula $n(n-1)/2$, where n = 10. $10(10-1)/2 = 90/2 = 45$ links.

17. B. The distribution layer provides routing between VLANs and security filtering.

18. E-commerce, Internet, VPN/remote access, and WAN.

19. Internet services, WAN services, and PSTN services.

20. Firewalls, Internet routers, FTP/HTTP servers, SMTP mail servers, and DNS servers.

21. B. The VPN/remote access submodule contains firewalls, VPN concentrators, and ASAs.

22. D and E. The access layer concentrates user access and provides PoE to IP phones.

23. B and C. The distribution layer concentrates the network access switches and routers and applies network policies with access lists.

24. A and F. The core layer provides high-speed data transport without manipulating the data.

25. D. The campus core connects to the server farm, the enterprise edge, and the building distribution.

26. E. The infrastructure at the remote site usually consists of a WAN router and a small LAN switch.

27. A, B, and C. Web, application, and database servers are placed in the e-commerce submodule.

28. D. Block 4.

29. A. Block 1.

30. F. Block 6.

31. B. Block 2.

32. E. Block 5.

33. C. Block 3.

34. C. The Cisco Virtual Office supports the teleworker with router, VPN, and IP telephony.

35. A and C.

36. A, C, and E. The teleworker, branch, and data center modules are part of the enterprise remote modules.

37. B, C, and E. Security, QoS, and high availability are borderless network infrastructure services.

38. C. Servers are located in the server farm module of the enterprise campus area.

39. B. Partial-mesh connectivity is best suited for the distribution layer.

40. A and B. Wireless APs function as a hub to connect wireless end devices to the network.

41. A and B.

42. A, B, and C.

43. B. VSS allows a Catalyst 6500 or 6800 switch pair to act as a single logical switch.

44. C.

45. C.

46. E, F, and G.

47. C and D.

48. C, E, and F.

49. B.

50. C.

51. A.

52. C.

53. C.

54. B.

55. D.

56. C.

57. D.

58. A and B.

59. B.

60. Access layer: A, D, E, F

Distribution layer: A, C, E, F

Core: B

61. Only section B.

62. Only section C.

63. Sections A, D, and E belong to the access layer.

Chapter 3

1. False. Layer 2 switches limit only the collision domain.

2. CGMP.

3. True.

4. True.

5. Inter-Switch Link (ISL) and IEEE 802.1p/802.1Q.

6. A. IP phone–to–IP phone communication is an example of peer-to-peer communication.

7. A, C, and E. Network applications, infrastructure devices, and environmental characteristics affect network design.

8. C. Multimode fiber provides the necessary connectivity at the required distance. UTP can reach only 100 m. Single-mode fiber is more expensive.

9. B. The DC aggregation layer is similar to the campus distribution layer.

10. C. Disabling trunking on host ports and using RPVST+ are best practices at the access layer.

11. B. The use of HSRP and summarization of routes are best practices in the distribution layer.

12. A. Best practices for the core include the use of triangle connections to reduce switch peering and using routing to prevent network loops.

13. D. Load balancers, SSL offloading, firewalls, and intrusion detection devices are deployed in the DC aggregation layer.

14. D. All are threats to the enterprise edge distribution.

15. C. Create a server farm that allows the enforcement of security policies.

16. B. These are design considerations for the distribution layer.

17. D. All are server connectivity options.

18. A. The core and the distribution should be connected using redundant Layer 3 triangular links.

19. B. The building subnets are too large and should be further segmented to reduce the broadcast domain.

20. B. Broadcasts are not forwarded by routers and are controlled by VLANs.

21. i = C, ii = A, iii = B, iv = E, v = D.

22. True. Layer 3 switches and routers control both the collision and broadcast domains.

23. i = A, ii = C, iii = B.

24. i = E, ii = A, iii = C, iv = D, v = B

25. i = B, ii = A, iii = D, iv = C

26. i = B, ii = D, iii = C, iv = A

27. True. IP phones reclassify incoming frames from the PC. Switches can accept or reclassify incoming frames.

28. CGMP and IGMP snooping control multicast traffic at Layer 2. The switch and local router exchange CGMP messages. With IGMP snooping, the switch listens to IGMP messages between the host and the router.

A

29. ISL and IEEE 802.1p/Q are two methods for CoS. ISL was created by Cisco and uses an external tag that contains 3 bits for marking. IEEE 802.1p specifies 3 bits for marking that is carried in the internal tag of IEEE 802.1Q. The IEEE 802.1p specification is not included in the IEEE 802.1D-1998 standard.

30. False. You can configure the CGMP only if both the router and switch are Cisco devices. IGMP snooping can be configured in mixed environments.

31. The campus backbone should have high-speed links. Recommend 10 Gigabit Ethernet links.

32. The IP phones should remap the workstation traffic to a value less than the value assigned to voice. Typically, it is recommended that you configure the IP phone to set the DSCP to EF for VoIP bearer traffic.

33. Inspect them at the Layer 3 switches in Building A. Packets should be marked and accepted as close as possible to the source.

34. No. There is no redundancy to the WAN module. A separate link to another building would provide that redundancy.

35. No. There is no redundancy to the Internet module. A separate link from another building would provide that redundancy.

36. Yes. The network uses Layer 2 switches at the building-access layer and Layer 3 switches at the building distribution and campus backbone layers.

37. A, C, and E.

38. C.

39. B and C.

40. C.

41. D.

42. C.

43. A. Use redundant triangle topology between the distribution and core layers.

44. B.

45. A.

46. A, B, G, and H.

47. A, C, and E.

48. C, D, F, and G.

49. A, E, and G.

50. B.

51. C.

52. A.

53. D.

54. A, E.

55. C.

56. B.

57. A.

Chapter 4

1. B. The data center services layer resides above the data center foundation and provides the necessary security firewall and IPS services that protect the applications and critical data in the data center.

2. D. Cisco Nexus 1000V virtual switch for VMware ESX and ESXi helps deliver visibility and policy control for VMs.

3. A. Converged network adapters (CNAs) run at 10GE and support FCoE and are available from Emulex and QLogic.

4. D. Cisco Unified Computing System (UCS) is an innovative next-generation data center platform that converges computing, network, storage, and virtualization all together into one system.

5. A. Cisco Nexus 7000 series switches are the only switches that support VDCs.

6. B. An effective way to address policy enforcement is to use an ASA SM in a Cisco Catalyst 6500 series switch to provide firewall services for the data center.

7. D. As a result of server virtualization, many data center applications are no longer bound to bare-metal hardware resources.

8. C. Virtual Switching System (VSS) is a network virtualization technology that allows two physical Cisco Catalyst 6500 series switches to act as a single logical virtual switch.

9. A. Virtual Port Channel (vPC) enables the spanning-tree topology to appear loop-free although multiple redundant paths are present in the physical topology.

10. A and C. Low-latency switching, distributed forwarding architecture, 10 and 40GE, and scalable IP multicast support.

11. B. The data center aggregation layer supports advanced application and security services and has a large STP processing load.

12. A, B, and D. 10 and 40 Gigabit Ethernet density, administrative domains and polices, and future growth are all drivers for the data center core layer.

13. C. The data center access layer provides benefits such as port density for server farms, high-performance low-latency Layer 2 switching, and a mix of oversubscription requirements.

A

14. B and C. Cable management is affected by the number of connections and media selection.

15. B. The cabinets and racks should be arranged in the data center with an alternating pattern of "cold" and "hot" aisles.

16. C. Within the unified computing resources, the service profile defines the identity of the server. The identity contains many items, such as memory, CPU, network cards, and boot image.

17. C. Overlay Transport Virtualization (OTV) is a Nexus/ASR software feature that provides for L2 extension functionality between data centers over any IP network.

18. B. Anycast based only works reliably for UDP traffic because TCP uses sessions that cannot be maintained while the servers change.

19. C. Path isolation involves the creation of independent logical network paths over a shared network infrastructure.

20. D. A Fabric Extender (FEX) is a physical grouping of copper or fiber switch ports that uplinks to a parent switch such as Nexus 5K or 7K.

Chapter 5

1. 1.3 Gbps

2. 200 Mbps

3. Having to configure SSIDs, frequency channels, and power settings on each individual AP.

4. Advanced Encryption Standard (AES).

5. Advanced Encryption Standard (AES)

   Reduced TCO

   Enhanced visibility and control

   Dynamic RF management

   WLAN security

   Unified wired and wireless network

   Enterprise mobility

   Enhanced productivity and collaboration

6. False. With split-MAC, control and data traffic frames are split. LAPs communicate with the WLCs with control messages over the wired network. LWAPP data messages are encapsulated and forwarded to and from wireless clients.

7. True. Controller MAC functions are association requests, resource reservation, and authentication and key management.

8. C. Layer 3 CAPWAP tunnels are the preferred solution.

9. B. Layer 2 intercontroller roaming is the preferred intercontroller roaming option.

10. B. The WLC places the user data on the appropriate VLAN and forwards the frame to the wired network.

11. C. Each 4400 series WLC supports 100 APs. 100 APs times 24 controllers in a mobility group equals 2400.

12. D. The recommended number of data devices per AP is 20.

13. B. The recommended number of voice over wireless devices per AP is seven for G.711 and eight for G.729.

14. C. Cisco Radio Resource Management controls AP radio frequency and power settings.

15. A. Typically, there is a latency per hop of 1 to 3 ms.

16. D. The RTT between the AP and WLC should not exceed 300 ms.

17. D. Cisco recommends deterministic controller redundancy.

18. D. EoIP is the recommended method for guest services.

19. A. H-REAP with centralized controllers is recommended for branch WLAN design.

20. B and D. Recommended practices are minimizing intercontroller roaming and centralizing controller placement.

21. D. The Cisco 6500 WLC module supports 300 access points.

22. i = D, ii = E, iii = A, iv = F, v = B, vi = C.

23. i = E, ii = D, iii = C, iv = B, v = A.

24. i = B, ii = A, iii = C.

25. i = B, ii = A, iii = G, iv = E, v = F, vi = C, vii = D.

26. i = C, ii = D, iii = A, iv = B.

27. B. For best performance, 20 MAP nodes or fewer is recommended per RAP.

28. D. Only answer D has the correct order.

29. B. Radio Resource Management (RRM) functions include radio resource monitoring, dynamic channel assignment, interference detection and avoidance, dynamic transmit power control, coverage hole detection and correction, and client and network load balancing.

30. B. Channels 1, 6, and 11 of the ISM frequencies do not overlap.

31. A. Only answer A is correct.

32. C. H-LEAP uses mutual authentication between the client and the network server and uses IEEE 802.1X for 802.11 authentication messaging. H-LEAP uses a RADIUS server to manage user information.

33. C.

34. A and E. DHCP and DNS can be used to find the WLAN controller.

35. B. The WLC copies the DSCP value of a received packet from the wired network to the DSCP value of the CAPWAP header.

36. D and E.

37. A and B.

38. A, C, and E.

39. B and E.

40. C. The service set identifier identifies the WLAN network.

41. C.

42. A and B.

43. A, B, C, and D.

44. B, C, and E.

45. C and D.

46. C. With N+N redundancy, an equal number of controllers back up each other.

47. B. Monitor mode is a feature designed to allow specified CAPWAP-enabled APs to exclude themselves from handling data traffic between clients and the infrastructure. They instead act as dedicated sensors for location-based services (LBS), rogue AP detection, and intrusion detection (IDS).

48. C. LAPs operate in Rogue Detector mode to monitor for rogue APs. The rogue detector (RD) should be able to see all the VLANs in the network, because rogue APs can be connected to any of the VLANs in the network. The LAN switch sends all the rogue AP/client MAC address lists to the RD. The RD then forwards these to the WLC to compare with the MAC addresses of clients that the WLC APs have heard over the air. If the MAC addresses match, the WLC knows that the rogue AP to which those clients are connected is on the wired network.

49. A. The Local mode is the default mode of operation. In this mode, every 180 seconds the AP measures noise floor and interference, and scans for IDS events.

50. C. 15.4 watts × 48 = 740 watts

Chapter 6

1. D. After analyzing the customer requirements, the next step is to characterize the existing network.

2. D. The remote access VPN module is within the enterprise edge module.

3. D. The high speeds and relatively low cost of DSL make this a popular Internet access technology for the enterprise telecommuter.

4.   C and D. DMZ/e-commerce, Internet, remote access VPN, and WAN/MAN are modules that are found in the enterprise edge.

5.   A. The window size defines the upper limit of frames that can be transmitted without getting a return acknowledgement. A larger window size uses a smaller number of acknowledgements than smaller window sizes.

6.   B. WFQ is the default QoS mechanism on interfaces below 2.0 Mbps.

7.   A, B, and D. The PBM design methodology includes the process of analyzing network requirements, characterizing the existing network, and designing the topology.

8.   D. DMZ/e-commerce, Internet, remote access VPN, and WAN/MAN are modules that are found in the enterprise edge.

9.   D. The service provider edge connects to ISPs and is found in the enterprise edge.

10.   D. The WAN edge connects using MPLS connectivity.

11.   B. WAN edge modules are used to connect to Frame Relay and ATM networks.

12.   B. After you analyze the network requirements and characterize the existing network, the design of the topology occurs, which includes the implementation planning.

13.   D. The WAN/MAN functional area or module provides connectivity to the remote sites via Frame Relay, TDM, ATM, or MPLS services.

14.   D. The framing for dark fiber is determined by the enterprise, not the provider.

15.   D. Low-latency queuing (LLQ) adds a strict priority queue to CBWFQ.

16.   Twenty-four timeslots are used in a T1.

17.   C. Wireless bridges are used to connect two separate wireless networks together, typically located in two separate buildings.

18.   DWDM maximizes the use of the installed base of fiber used by service providers and is a critical component of optical networks.

19.   CMTS. The equipment used on the remote access side is the cable modem, which connects to the Cable Modem Termination System (CMTS) on the Internet service provider side.

20.   A. The WAN/MAN module provides connectivity to the remote sites via Frame Relay, TDM, ATM, or SONET network services.

21.   DOCSIS. The Data Over Cable Service Interface Specifications (DOCSIS) protocol defines the cable procedures that the equipment needs to support.

22.   C. ISDN falls into the circuit-switched WAN category.

23.   D. The SLA defines the level of service offered by the provider, such as bandwidth, allowed latency, and loss.

24.   B. A WAN that occasionally becomes congested is a good candidate for queuing solutions.

A

Chapter 7

1. B. Leased lines are dedicated network connections provided by the service provider.

2. A. A major disadvantage of the hub-and-spoke topology is that the hub router represents a single point of failure.

3. B. Full-mesh topologies require that each site has a connection to all other sites in the WAN cloud.

4. B and D. WAN backup over the Internet is best effort and provides redundancy for the primary WAN connection.

5. B. The operation of VPLS allows for connecting L2 domains over an IP/MPLS network.

6. B, C, and D. Full mesh, partial mesh, and hub and spoke are all WAN topologies used with Cisco enterprise architectures in the WAN.

7. B. With MPLS L3 VPNs, enterprise routing information is exchanged with the service provider for connecting multiple sites together via L3.

8. A. A secondary WAN link provides a backup to the primary link and can also support load sharing of traffic with the primary link.

9. D. Medium branches use dual routers and dual external L2 switches.

10. C. Large branches support between 100 and 1000 users.

11. A and C. Both IPsec and DMVPN are methods that exist for tunneling private networks over a public IP network.

12. C. Factors for WAN architecture selection include ongoing expenses, ease of management, and high availability.

13. A. GRE provides simple Layer 3 tunneling for basic IP VPNs without using encryption.

14. D. Implementing the WAN is not part of the design process.

15. B. ISP service uses Internet-based site-to-site VPNs.

16. D. GETVPN is not typically used on the Internet because NAT does not work due to the original IP addressing preservation.

17. C. The large branch uses dual router and dual ASA firewalls.

18. B. A private WAN with self-deployed MPLS is usually reserved for large enterprises that are willing to make substantial investments in equipment and training to build out the MPLS network.

19. i = A, ii = D, iii = B, iv = C.

Chapter 8

1. 10/8, 172.16/12 (172.16.0.0 to 172.31.255.255), and 192.168/16.

2. True. You can use DHCP to specify several host IP configuration parameters, including IP address, mask, default gateway, DNS servers, and TFTP server.

3. False. The bit-number representation of 255.255.255.248 is /29. /28 is the same mask as 255.255.255.240.

4. True.

5. 20 (bytes).

6. DSCP uses 6 bits, which provides 64 levels of classification.

7. True.

8. False. The header checksum field only includes a checksum of the IP header; it does not check the data portion.

9. The subnet is 172.56.4.0/22, the address range is from 172.56.4.1 to 172.56.7.254, and the subnet broadcast is 172.56.7.255.

10. The IP layer in the destination host.

11. B. DHCP configures the IP address, subnet mask, default gateway, and other optional parameters.

12. C. Class B networks have 16 bits for host addresses with the default mask: $2^{16} - 2 = 65,534$.

13. B. A /26 mask has 26 network bits and 6 host bits.

14. C. Network 192.170.20.16 with a prefix of /29 summarizes addresses from 192.170.20.16 to 192.170.20.23.

15. B. AF3 is backward compatible with IP precedence priority traffic with a binary of 011.

16. A. IPv4 packets can be fragmented by the sending host and routers.

17. B. Multicast addresses are received by a set of hosts subscribed to the multicast group.

18. B, D, and E. The three types of IPv4 address are unicast, broadcast, and multicast.

19. A, C, and D. End-user workstations, Cisco IP phones, and mobile devices should have their IP addresses assigned dynamically.

20. B. Dynamic name resolution reduces administrative overhead. Name-to-IP-address tables do not need to be configured.

21. B. There are 4 bits to determine the number of host addresses: $2^4 - 2 = 16 - 2 = 14$.

22. B. Answer B allows up to six hosts. Answer A allows only two hosts, which is too small. Answer C allows 14 hosts, which is larger than Answer B.

A

23. D, G, and I.

24. C. PAT.

25. C. RIPE.

26. B. VLSM.

27. C. The American Registry for Internet Numbers allocates IP address blocks in for the United States, Canada, several parts of the Caribbean region, and Antarctica.

28. D. The Asia-Pacific Network Information Centre allocates IP address blocks for Asia, Australia, New Zealand, and neighboring counties.

29. B. The networks in answer B provide 126 addresses for hosts in each LAN at Site B.

30. A. Network 192.168.15.0/25 provides 126 addresses for LAN 1, network 192.168.15.128/26 provides 62 addresses for LAN 2, and network 192.168.15.192/27 provides 30 addresses for LAN 3.

31. D. You need only two addresses for the WAN link, and the /30 mask provides only two.

32. A. Private addresses are not announced to Internet service providers.

33. B. NAT translates internal private addresses to public addresses.

34. D. VLSM provides the ability to use different masks throughout the network.

Chapter 9

1. False. OSPFv3 supports IPv6. OSPFv2 is used in IPv4 networks.

2. True.

3. ARP.

4. 16.

5. 0110. The first field of the IPv6 header is the version field. It is set to binary 0110 (6).

6. False.

7. 0xFF (1111 1111 binary).

8. FE8/10.

9. True.

10. Version, Traffic Class, Flow Label, Payload Length, Next Header, Hop Limit, IPv6 Source Address, and IPv6 Destination Address.

11. B. IPv6 address types are unicast, anycast, and multicast.

12. True. Both compressed representations are valid.

13. 2001:1:0:ab0::/64.

14. 32.

15. It is a multicast address. All IPv6 multicast addresses begin with hexadecimal FF.

16. C. Answers A, B, and D are incorrect because 0100 does not compact to 01. Answer B is also incorrect because 0010 does not compact to 001.

17. A. The dual-stack backbone routers handle packets between IPv4 hosts and IPv6 hosts.

18. B. DNS indicates which stack to use. DNS A records return IPv4 addresses. DNS AAAA records return IPv6 addresses.

19. B.

20. A and D.

21. D. IPv4 packets can be fragmented by the sending host and routers. IPv6 packets are fragmented by the sending host only.

22. A. Anycast addresses reach the nearest destination in a group of hosts.

23. D.

24. D.

25. C and D.

26. A.

27. D.

28. C. Running dual-stack IPv4 and IPv6 on hosts and routers allows for full flexibility for communications for the corporation internally, with partners, and with the Internet.

29. B.

30. B.

31. A and C.

32. A.

33. C.

34. A.

35. D.

36. A. All the networks can be summarized with a 52-bit mask.

37. C. SLAAC is used first to assign the IPv6 address and then DHCPv6 is used to assign additional options.

38. C. Link-local and site-local are unicast addresses, and multicast addresses are sent to a group of hosts. Anycast addresses are routed to the nearest receiver from a group of hosts.

39. B. Link-local source addresses remain with the local link.

40. B and D. Only OSPF and IS-IS are link-state routing protocols.

A

41. A, C, E. Dual-stack, tunneled, and translation are transition models to IPv6.

42. A, D, G. Dual-stack, service block, and hybrid are deployment models to IPv6.

43. A. IPv6 anycast type addresses replace IPv4 broadcasts.

44. D. Unique local unicast IPv6 addresses use the FC00::/7 prefix.

45. B. The Réseaux IP Européens Network Coordination Centre allocates address blocks for Europe, Russia, the Middle East, and Central Asia.

46. Implement a dual-stack backbone, or implement IPv4 tunnels between the sites.

47. NAT-PT is required to provide network address translation and protocol translation between IPv6 and IPv4 hosts.

48. If a dual-stack backbone is implemented, only the WAN routers require an IPv6-IPv4 dual stack. End hosts do not need a dual stack.

49. No. All WAN routers still run the IPv4 stack, with two exceptions: the WAN routers at Sites A and B. These routers speak IPv6 within their sites and speak IPv4 to the WAN.

Chapter 10

1. False. Distance-vector routing protocols send periodic routing updates.

2. False. RIPng is used with IPv6 networks.

3. True.

4. True. The higher value for reliability is preferred.

5. False. The link with the lower load is preferred.

6. The EIGRP route. EIGRP routes have an administrative distance of 90, and OSPF routes have an administrative distance of 100. The lower administrative distance is preferred.

7. The IS-IS route. IS-IS routes have an administrative distance of 115, and RIP routes have an administrative distance of 120. The lower administrative distance is preferred.

8. The OSPF route, because it has a more specific route.

9. A. The best reliability is 255/255 (100 percent), and the best load is 1/255 (~0 percent).

10. G. IS-IS and OSPF permit an explicit hierarchical topology.

11. Delay measures the amount of time a packet takes to travel from one end to another in the internetwork.

12. The metric is 10^8/BW. If BW = 100 Mbps = 10^8, the metric = 10^8/10^8 = 1.

13. i = C, ii = A, iii = D, iv = B.

14. True.

15. B, D, E, and F.

16. B. OSPFv3 is the only standards-based routing protocol in the list that supports large networks. RIPng has limited scalability.

17. C, D, and E. Link-state routing protocols plus EIGRP's hybrid characteristics converge faster.

18. C. EIGRP supports large networks and does not require a hierarchical network.

19. B, C, D, and E. RIPv1 does not support VLSMs.

20. F. BGP is used to connect to ISPs.

21. C. EIGRP is supported only on Cisco routers.

22. D. OSPFv3 is the only correct answer. RIPv2 is for IPv4 networks. EIGRP is not a standards-based protocol. BGPv6 and RIPv3 do not exist.

23. B, C, and E.

24. B and C. IGPs converge faster than EGPs.

25. C. Faster routing convergence means more accurate information.

26. A. Classless networks have less routing overhead.

27. B and C. EIGRP uses DUAL for fast convergence and supports VLSMs.

28. i = D, ii = B, iii = A, iv = C.

29. C. To reduce broadcast traffic, use EIGRP for IPv4 as the routing protocol for the network. RIPng and EIGRPv6 are for IPv6 networks.

30. i = B, ii = D, iii = A, iv = C.

31. i = C, ii = A, iii = D, iv = B.

32. B. EIGRP route has a lower administrative distance.

33. C. EIGRP provides fast convergence and unequal load balancing.

34. D. IS-IS.

35. B. The default IS-IS cost metric for any interface type is 10.

36. D. IS-IS does not define BDRs.

37. C. EIGRP.

38. C. EIGRP.

39. C and E.

40. A, B, D, F.

41. B and C.

42. A and C.

43. B and C.

A

44. C. EIGRP for IPv6.

45. C. 1900.6500.0001 is the system ID, 49 is the AFI, and 0001 is the area ID.

46. A, B and C.

47. B. 2. The variance command configures EIGRP to accept unequal-cost routes with a metric of less than $2 \times 20 = 40$. The route with a metric of 35 is added.

48. A. Administrative distances are BGP=20, EIGRP=90, OSPF=110, IS-IS=115, and RIP=120.

49. B. Administrative distances are EIGRP=90, OSPF=110, IS-IS=115, RIP=120, iBGP=200.

50. A is EIGRP for IPv6, B is OSPFv2, C is RIPv2, D is EIGRP for IPv4, and E is OSPFv3.

51. A. The minimum bandwidth via Route 1 is 384 Kbps. The minimum bandwidth via Route 2 is 128 Kbps. The route with the higher minimum bandwidth is preferred, so the router chooses Route 1.

52. B. Route 2 has fewer router hops than Route 1.

53. A. Route 2 has a higher cost than Route 1. The Route 2 cost is 108/128 Kbps = 781.25. The Route 1 cost is 108/512 Kbps + 108/384 Kbps + 108/512 Kbps = 195.31 + 260.41 + 195.31 = 651.03. Therefore, Route 1 is preferred.

54. A. Path 1 has a lower hop count metric.

55. A. Path 1 has a lower hop count metric.

56. B. Path 2 has greater bandwidth.

57. C. Load sharing is enabled with the **variance** command.

58. B. By default, Path 2 has higher bandwidth and thus has the better metric.

58. A. IS-IS chooses Path 1 with a metric of 10 versus Path 2 with a metric of 30.

Chapter 11

1. False. A router with one or more interfaces in Area 0 is considered an OSPF backbone router.

2. True.

3. 224.0.0.5 for ALLSPFRouters and 224.0.0.6 for ALLDRouters.

4. FF02::5 for ALLSPFRouters and FF02::6 for ALLDRouters.

5. The administrative distance of OSPF is 110.

6. OSPF ABRs generate the Type 3 summary LSA for ABRs.

7. OSPF DRs generate Type 2 network LSAs.

8. Included are the router's links, interfaces, state of links, and cost.

9. False. The router with the highest priority is selected as the OSPF designated router.

10. False. You use eBGP to exchange routes between different autonomous systems.

11. False. BGPv4 added support for classless interdomain routing (CIDR), which provides the capability of forwarding packets based on IP prefixes only, with no concern for the address class.

12. True.

13. 20, 200.

14. True.

15. False. PIM does not have a hop-count limit. DVMRP has a hop-count limit of 32.

16. True.

17. False. BGP uses several attributes in the BGP decision process.

18. RIPv2, OSPF, and EIGRP.

19. FF02::A.

20. i = C, ii = B, iii = A, iv = D

21. Cost is calculated as 10^8 / BW, and BW = 100 Mbps = 10^8 bps for Fast Ethernet. Cost = 10^8 / 10^8 = 1.

22. OSPF. Although RIPv2 and EIGRP support VLSMs, RIPv2 is no longer recommended. EIGRP is not supported on non-Cisco routers.

23. You do not need to flood external LSAs into the stub area, which reduces LSA traffic.

24. All traffic from one area must travel through Area 0 (the backbone) to get to another area.

25. OSPFv3 is identified as IPv6 Next Header 89.

26. F. EIGRP and OSPFv2 are recommended for large enterprise networks.

27. C. Link LSAs are flooded to the local link.

28. A. RIPv1.

29. E. EIGRP and OSPFv2 have fast convergence.

30. F. EIGRP for IPv6 and OSPFv3 have fast convergence for IPv6 networks.

31. H. RIPv1 and RIPv2 generate periodic routing traffic. IS-IS is used in SP networks. BGP is used for external networks.

32. C. OSPFv3 is used in IPv6 and IPv4 networks.

33. B. From Router A, the OSPF cost for Path 1 is 10^8 / 256 Kbps = 390. The OSPF cost for Path 2 is (10^8 / 1536 Kbps) + (10^8 / 1024 Kbps) + (10^8 / 768 Kbps) = 65 + 97 + 130 = 292. OSPF selects Path 2 because it has a lower cost.

34. Router A = Internal; Router B = ABR; Router C = Backbone; Router D = ASBR; Router E = ABR; Router F = Internal.

35. i = D, ii = B, iii = A, iv = C.

36. i = B, ii = C, iii = D, iv = A.

37. Weight. Weight is configured locally and not exchanged in BGP updates. On the other hand, the local preference attribute is exchanged between iBGP peers and is configured at the gateway router.

38. Route reflectors reduce the number of iBGP logical mesh connections.

39. External peers see the confederation ID. The internal private autonomous system numbers are used within the confederation.

40. BGP confederations, route reflectors.

41. B. Only answer B has the correct order of BGP path selection, which is weight, local preference, autonomous system path, origin, MED, and lowest IP.

42. CIDR was first implemented in BGPv4.

43. C.

44. i = E, ii = C, iii = A, iv = B, v = D

45. B.

46. C.

47. B. OSPF.

48. C and D.

49. B and E.

50. C.

51. D. BGP.

52. A and D.

53. B.

54. B.

55. A.

56. C.

57. A and D.

58. D.

59. D. BGP.

60. D. R4.

61. B. BGP should be configured between autonomous system 100 and autonomous system 500.

62. C. Both Routers A and B perform the redistribution with route filters to prevent route feedback.

63. B. The OSPF routes are redistributed into EIGRP. Then you can redistribute EIGRP routes into BGP.

64. D. You should use filters on all routers performing redistribution.

Chapter 12

1. C. Encryption can protect data transported between sites over the Internet.

2. A. Firewalls have the capabilities to protect database servers in DMZ segments.

3. D. Encryption is a security technique for protecting the data confidentiality of information.

4. A and B. The use of ACLs and policing traffic can alleviate the effects of a DoS attack being performed.

5. A and D. DoS, reconnaissance, and gaining unauthorized access are security threats.

6. True. IPsec can ensure data integrity and confidentiality across the Internet.

7. C. SOX focuses on the accuracy and controls imposed on a company's financial records.

8. A, B, and C. Managing the security infrastructure has components that include the overall security management policy, incident-handling policy, and network access control policy.

9. C. EU Data Protection Directive calls for the protection of the people's right to privacy with respect to the processing of personal data.

10. D. Attackers can use password-cracking utilities, capture network traffic, and use social engineering to obtain sensitive information.

11. D. Data integrity allows only authorized users to modify data, ensuring that the data is authentic.

12. B. Accounting provides an audit trail of activities by logging the actions of the user.

13. C. DHCP snooping verifies DHCP transactions and prevents rogue DHCP servers from interfering with production traffic.

14. A. The security policy describes the organization's processes, procedures, guidelines, and standards.

15. D. Access control can be enforced by restricting access using VLANs, OS-based controls, and encryption techniques.

16. B. The acceptable-use policy is a general end-user document that is written in simple language that defines the roles and responsibilities within risk management.

17. True. The network access control policy defines the general access control principles used and how data is classified, such as confidential, top secret, or internal.

A

18. D.

19. i = B, ii = C, iii = A, iv = D.

20. D. The foundation of security solutions is a security policy.

21. C. AH and ESP are part of IP security.

22. C. The secure Services solution has requirements of confidentiality, integrity, and authenticity when using the Internet as a transport.

23. B. Threat defense integrates security into routers, switches, and appliances to ward off attacks.

24. C. The Secure Services component has requirements of encryption and authentication to provide secure transport access public networks.

Chapter 13

1. B. Integrated Services Router (ISR) combines IOS firewall, VPN, and IPS services.

2. C. The 802.1X protocol is a standards-based protocol for authenticating network clients by permitting or denying access to the network.

3. D. The Cisco Identity Services Engine is an integrated solution led by Cisco that incorporates the network infrastructure and third-party software to impose security policies on the attached endpoints.

4. C. Cisco Adaptive Security Device Manager (ASDM) is a web-based tool for managing Cisco ASA firewalls.

5. A, B, and C. Cisco IOS Trust and Identity is a set of services that includes AAA, SSH, SSL, 802.1X, and PKI.

6. B. Cisco IOS IPsec offers data encryption at the IP packet level using a set of standards-based protocols.

7. D. High-Performance Advanced Integration Module (AIM) is a hardware module for terminating large numbers of VPN tunnels.

8. C and D. Built-In Hardware VPN Acceleration is hardware-based encryption that offloads VPN processing from the router's internal CPU to improve VPN throughput. High-Performance Advanced Integration Module (AIM) is a hardware module for terminating large numbers of VPN tunnels.

9. D. Cisco ISE can restrict access to noncompliant devices but permit access to trusted wired or wireless endpoints such as desktops, laptops, PDAs, and servers.

10. A and B. Cisco Catalyst 6500 switches support ASA and NAM3 service modules.

11. A. Network Analysis Module 3 provides packet-capture capabilities and visibility into all the layers of the network data flows, including overlay technologies such as CAPWAP and VXLAN.

12. A and B. Some identity and access control protocols include 802.1X and ACLs.

13. A, C, and D. Cisco Security Manager (CSM), ACS, and Cisco ISE are security management tools.

14. True. NetFlow is used for threat detection and mitigation.

15. True. Cisco ASAs, ASA SM, and IOS firewall are part of infection containment.

16. D. The IOS Intrusion Prevention System (IPS) offers inline deep-packet inspection to successfully diminish a wide range of network attacks.

17. FirePOWER. The Cisco FirePOWER IPS Module for ASA can identify, analyze, and block unwanted traffic from flowing on the network.

18. B. Cisco Secure Access Control Server (ACS) provides centralized control for administrative access to Cisco devices and security applications.

19. B. PINs consist of the places in the network, such as branch, campus, cloud, data center, edge, Internet, and WAN.

20. i = D, ii = C, iii = B, iv = A

Chapter 14

1. True. Cisco recommends low-latency queuing for VoIP networks.

2. False. H.323 is an ITU standard, and SIP is an IETF standard for multimedia.

3. True. An Erlang is a telecommunications traffic unit of measurement representing the continuous use of one voice path for 1 hour.

4. VAD. Voice-activity detection suppresses packets when there is silence.

5. Dejitter buffers are used at the receiving end to smooth out the variable delay of received packets.

6. True. With CCS, a separate channel (from the bearer channels) is used for signaling.

7. False. You use FXS ports to connect to phones and FXO ports to connect to the PSTN.

8. True. SS7 implements call setup, routing, and control, ensuring that intermediate and far-end switches are available when a call is placed.

9. Interactive voice response (IVR) system. IVR systems connect incoming calls to an audio playback system that queues the calls, provides prerecorded announcements, prompts the caller for key options, provides the caller with information, and transfers the call to another switch extension or agent.

10. Automatic call distribution (ACD) system. ACD is used by airline reservation systems, customer service departments, and other call centers.

11. cRTP and VAD. Both cRTP and VAD reduce the amount of bandwidth used by VoIP calls. G.729 calls can be reduced from 26.4 kbps to 11.2 with cRTP and to 7.3 with cRTP and VAD.

12. A, B, C, and E are fixed; D is variable. Fixed-delay components include processing, serialization, dejitter, and propagation delays. Variable-delay components include only queuing delays.

13. You reduce the frame size with fragmentation or increase the link bandwidth. The formula is serialization delay = frame size/link bandwidth.

14. PQ-WFQ and LLQ. Both of these queuing techniques use a strict-priority queue. LLQ also provides class-based differentiated services.

15. False. The G.114 recommendation specifies a 150-ms one-way maximum delay.

16. True. FRF.12 specifies LFI for Frame Relay networks.

17. Yes. An RTT of 250 ms means that the average one-way delay is 125 ms, which is less than the recommended maximum of 150 ms.

18. i = D, ii = C, iii = A, iv = B, v = E

19. i = B, ii = C, iii = A

20. i = B, ii = D, iii = C, iv = A.

21. C. Q.SIG is the preferred protocol for inter-PBX trunks.

22. A. cRTP compresses the IP/UDP/RTP headers from 40 bytes to 2 or 4 bytes.

23. B. The analog signal is filtered and then sampled, and then samples are digitized.

24. C. The digitizing process is divided into companding, quantization, and coding.

25. D. All answers are correct.

26. B. LFI and cRTP should be implemented to help with the serialization delay on slow-speed WAN circuits. LLQ will not help because the circuit has no congestion.

27. D. The G.729 codec is recommended on WAN links because of its lower bandwidth requirements and relatively high MOS.

28. C and D. cRTP and VAD reduce the amount of IP bandwidth used in IPT calls.

29. A. CAC prevents new voice calls from affecting existing voice calls.

30. D. The Cisco Unified CallManager performs the call processing functions of the Cisco IPT solution.

31. B and C.

32. A = iv, B = iii, C = ii, D = i.

33. C.

34. H. RTP is used to transport voice streams between two endpoints.

35. B. SIP is defined in RFC 2453 and is used to establish, maintain, and terminate calls.

36. D. MGCP is used to control gateways.

37. D. Storage services provide capture and storage of media streams.

38. C. Bridging services provide transcoding and recording services of media streams.

39. D. Multimedia conferencing should be provisioned on DSCP AF4 PHB.

40. F. OAM should be provisioned on DSCP CS2 PHB.

41. D. Real-time interactive media should be provisioned on DSCP CS4 PHB.

42. D. G.729 generates an 8Kbps bit rate.

43. A. G.711 generates a 64kbps bit rate.

44. D. LLQ is recommended for most VoIP networks.

45. A. Cisco TelePresence 3000 generates 12.3Mbps worth of traffic at 1080p.

46. D. Cisco Video Advantage generates 768 kbps worth of CIF traffic.

47. H. RTP transports audio streams. RTP is the transport layer protocol that carries digitized voice in its payload.

48. A. The single-site deployment model is a solution for enterprises located in a single large building or campus area with no voice on the WAN links.

49. C. The multisite WAN with distributed call processing is a solution for large enterprises with several large locations. Several CUCM clusters are deployed at the large sites for redundancy, and Unity servers are used for messaging. Intercluster trunks are created to establish communication between clusters.

50. B. The centralized WAN call processing model is a solution for medium enterprises with one large location and many remote sites. Call processing and voice-mail servers are located only at the main site. Remote-site IP phones register to the CUCM cluster located in the main site.

51. B. The ITU's G.114 recommendation specifies that the one-way delay between endpoints should not exceed 150 ms to be acceptable, commercial voice quality.

52. A. With PCM, analog speech is sampled 8000 times a second. Each speech sample is mapped onto 8 bits.

53. C. The network design must provision enough bandwidth for voice (at peak times) and classify the voice traffic so that it can be prioritized.

54. D. Voice-enabled Infrastructure includes Layer 2 and Layer 3 switches and routers.

55. C.

56. C. CoS 5 is used for voice media and CoS 3 for signaling traffic.

57. Multisite WAN with centralized call processing with a CM cluster at the main site and SRST routers at the remote sites.

58. SRST enables the remote routers to provide call-handling support for IP phones when they lose connectivity to the CallManagers because of a WAN failure.

59. LLQ provides a strict queue for RTP (VoIP) traffic and differentiated class of service for all other traffic.

A

60. The minimum bandwidth is approximately 640 kbps. Each call is 30 kbps times 4, which equals 120 kbps. The existing 512 kbps of data traffic equals 640 kbps. The circuit should be provisioned at a higher speed to prevent the sustained peak utilization from being higher than 75 percent.

61. Yes, a multisite WAN with centralized call processing CUCM cluster should be implemented at the main site since all small remote sites connect back to the hub of the network.

62. cRTP compresses the RTP/UDP/IP headers from 40 bytes to 2 to 4 bytes.

63. FRF.12 is the link and fragmentation technique used in Frame Relay networks.

Chapter 15

1. Fault management, configuration management, accounting management, performance management, and security management.

2. Data link layer.

3. Notice level.

4. False.

5. True.

6. Device ID, IP address, capabilities, OS version, model number, and port ID.

7. D. A trap message is sent by the agent when a significant event occurs.

8. A. The NMS manager uses the Get operation to retrieve the value-specific MIB variable from an agent.

9. B. The NMS manager uses the Set operation to set values of the object instance within an agent.

10. C. More than 500 syslog facilities can be configured on Cisco IOS.

11. B. At the authNoPriv level, authentication is provided, but not encryption.

12. B. CBC-DES is the encryption algorithm used by SNMPv3.

13. C and D. Both CDP and NetFlow can be used to discover and document a network.

14. B, C, and D.

15. D. RMON2 provides monitoring information from the network to the application layers.

16. D. All work over UDP.

17. C.

18. A. The authPriv level provides authentication and encryption.

19. i = C, ii = A, iii = D, iv = B

20. A. Syslog level 0 indicates an emergency and that the system is unusable.

21. B. RMON2 allows for Layer 4 monitoring. NetFlow is not a long-term trending solution.

22. C. NetFlow does network traffic analysis.

23. E. MIB is the database that stores information.

24. C. ASN.1 is used to define information being stored.

25. C. authNoPriv provides authentication and no encryption.

26. D. Community is not an SNMP operation.

27. E. Private MIBs can be used for vendor specific information.

28. C. NetFlow allows for network planning, traffic engineering, usage-based network billing, accounting, Denial of Service monitoring capabilities, and application monitoring. One big benefit is that NetFlow provides the necessary data for billing of network usage.

29. C. NetFlow can be configured to provide timestamped data on multiple interfaces.

30. A, B, D. NetFlow consists of three major components: NetFlow Accounting, Flow Collector Engines, and Network Data Analyzers.

31. C. The Link Layer Discovery Protocol (LLDP), defined in the IEEE 802.1AB (LLDP) specification, is an option of discovering network devices in multivendor networks. LLDP performs functions similar to CDP.

A

CCDA 200-310 version 1.0. Exam Updates

Over time, reader feedback allows Pearson to gauge which topics give our readers the most problems when taking the exams. To assist readers with those topics, the authors create new materials clarifying and expanding on those troublesome exam topics. As mentioned in the Introduction, the additional content about the exam is contained in a PDF on this book's companion website, at http://www.ciscopress.com/title/9781587144547.

This appendix is intended to provide you with updated information if Cisco makes minor modifications to the exam upon which this book is based. When Cisco releases an entirely new exam, the changes are usually too extensive to provide in a simple update appendix. In those cases, you might need to consult the new edition of the book for the updated content. This appendix attempts to fill the void that occurs with any print book. In particular, this appendix does the following:

- Mentions technical items that might not have been mentioned elsewhere in the book
- Covers new topics if Cisco adds new content to the exam over time
- Provides a way to get up-to-the-minute current information about content for the exam

Always Get the Latest at the Book's Product Page

You are reading the version of this appendix that was available when your book was printed. However, given that the main purpose of this appendix is to be a living, changing document, it is important that you look for the latest version online at the book's companion website. To do so, follow these steps:

Step 1. Browse to http://www.ciscopress.com/title/9781587144547.

Step 2. Click the Updates tab.

Step 3. If there is a new Appendix B document on the page, download the latest Appendix B document.

Note The downloaded document has a version number. Comparing the version of the print Appendix B (Version 1.0) with the latest online version of this appendix, you should do the following:

- **Same version:** Ignore the PDF that you downloaded from the companion website.
- **Website has a later version:** Ignore the Appendix B in your book and read only the latest version that you downloaded from the companion website.

Technical Content

The current version of this appendix (version 1.0) does not contain additional technical coverage.

OSI Model, TCP/IP Architecture, and Numeric Conversion

The Open Systems Interconnection (OSI) model is a mandatory topic in any internetworking book. The CCDA candidate should understand the OSI model and identify which OSI layers host the different networking protocols. The OSI model provides a framework for understanding internetworking. This appendix provides an overview and general understanding of the OSI reference model.

The Transmission Control Protocol/Internet Protocol (TCP/IP) architecture provides the practical implementation of a layered model. This appendix provides an overview of the TCP/IP layers and how they map to the OSI model.

Also covered in this appendix is the numeric conversion of binary, decimal, and hexadecimal numbers. The ability to covert between binary, decimal, and hexadecimal numbers helps you manipulate IP addresses in binary and dotted-decimal format. Quickly converting these numbers will help you answer test questions.

OSI Model Overview

The International Organization for Standardization (ISO) developed the OSI model in 1984, and revisited it in 1994, to coordinate standards development for interconnected information-processing systems. The model describes seven layers that start with the physical connection and end with the application. As shown in Figure C-1, the seven layers are physical, data link, network, transport, session, presentation, and application.

The OSI model divides the tasks involved in moving data into seven smaller, more manageable layers. Each layer provides services to the layer above, performs at least the functions specified by the model, and expects the defined services from the layer below. The model does not define the precise nature of the interface between layers or the protocol used between peers at the same layer in different instantiations of a protocol stack. The model's design encourages each layer to be implemented independently. For example, you can run an application over IP (Layer 3), Fast Ethernet (Layer 2), Frame Relay (Layer 2), or Gigabit Ethernet (Layer 2). As the packets route through the Internet, the Layer 2 media change independently from the upper-layer protocols. The OSI model helps standardize discussion of the design and construction of networks for developers and hardware manufacturers. It also provides network engineers and analysts with a framework useful in understanding internetworking.

Layer Number	OSI Layer Name
7	Application
6	Presentation
5	Session
4	Transport
3	Network
2	Data Link
1	Physical

Figure C-1   *Seven-Layer OSI Model*

Layered implementations of internetworking technologies do not necessarily map directly to the OSI model. For example, the TCP/IP architecture model describes only four layers, with the upper layer mapping to the three upper layers of the OSI model (application, presentation, and session). The development of IP predates the OSI model. For a more thorough discussion of the TCP/IP model, see Chapter 8, "Internet Protocol Version 4 Design."

The following sections describe and provide sample protocols for each OSI layer.

Physical Layer (OSI Layer 1)

The physical layer describes the transportation of raw bits over physical media. It defines signaling specifications and media types and interfaces. It also describes voltage levels, physical data rates, and maximum transmission distances. In summary, it deals with the electrical, mechanical, functional, and procedural specifications for links between networked systems.

Examples of physical layer specifications are

- EIA/TIA-232 (Electronic Industries Association/ Telecommunications Industry Association)
- EIA/TIA-449
- V.35
- IEEE 802 LAN and metropolitan-area network (MAN) standards
- Physical layer (PHY) groups Synchronous Optical Network/Synchronous Digital Hierarchy (SONET/SDH)
- Maximum cable distances of the Ethernet standards

Data Link Layer (OSI Layer 2)

The data link layer is concerned with the reliable transport of data across a physical link. Data at this layer is formatted into frames. Data link specifications include frame sequencing, flow control, synchronization, error notification, physical network topology, and physical addressing. This layer converts frames into bits when sending information and converts bits into frames when receiving information from the physical media. Bridges and switches operate at the data link layer.

Because of the complexity of this OSI layer, the IEEE subdivides the data link layer into three sublayers for LANs. Figure C-2 shows how Layer 2 is subdivided. The upper layer is the logical link sublayer, which manages communications between devices. The bridging layer, defined by IEEE 802.1, is the middle layer. The lowest layer is the Media Access Control (MAC) sublayer, which manages the protocol access to the physical layer and ultimately the actual media. Systems attached to a common data link layer have a unique address on that data link layer. Be aware that you might find some references describing this layer as having two sublayers: the Logical Link Control (LLC) sublayer and the MAC sublayer.

OSI Model	IEEE 802 Specifications	
	802.2 Logical Link	
Data Link Layer	802.1 Bridging	
	Media Access Control	

Figure C-2 *IEEE Data Link Sublayers*

Examples of data link layer technologies are

- Frame Relay
- ATM
- Synchronous Data Link Control (SDLC)
- High-Level Data Link Control (HDLC)
- Point-to-Point Protocol (PPP)
- Ethernet implementations (IEEE 802.3)
- Wireless LAN (IEEE 802.11)

Network Layer (OSI Layer 3)

The network layer is concerned with routing information and methods to determine paths to a destination. Information at this layer is called packets. Specifications include routing protocols, logical network addressing, and packet fragmentation. Routers operate at this layer.

Examples of network layer specifications are

- Protocols
  - IPv4, IPv6
  - ICMP
  - ARP
  - Connectionless Network Protocol (CLNP)
- Routing protocols
  - Routing Information Protocol (RIP)
  - Open Shortest Path First (OSPF)
  - Enhanced Interior Gateway Routing Protocol (EIGRP)
  - Intermediate System-to-Intermediate System (IS-IS)

Transport Layer (OSI Layer 4)

The transport layer provides reliable, transparent transport of data segments from upper layers. It provides end-to-end error checking and recovery, multiplexing, virtual circuit management, and flow control. Messages are assigned a sequence number at the transmission end. At the receiving end, the packets are reassembled, checked for errors, and acknowledged. Flow control manages the data transmission to ensure that the transmitting device does not send more data than the receiving device can process.

Examples of transport layer specifications are

- Transmission Control Protocol (TCP)
- Real-Time Transport Protocol (RTP)
- User Datagram Protocol (UDP)

Note: Although UDP operates in the transport layer, it does not perform the reliable error-checking functions that other transport layer protocols do.

Session Layer (OSI Layer 5)

The session layer provides a control structure for communication between applications. It establishes, manages, and terminates communication connections called sessions. Communication sessions consist of service requests and responses that occur between applications on different devices.

Examples of specifications that operate at the session layer are

- DECnet's Session Control Protocol (SCP)
- H.245 and H.225

Presentation Layer (OSI Layer 6)

The presentation layer provides application layer entities with services to ensure that information is preserved during transfer. Knowledge of the syntax selected at the application layer allows selection of compatible transfer syntax if a change is required. This layer provides conversion of character-representation formats, as might be required for reliable transfer. Voice coding schemes are specified at this layer. Furthermore, compression and encryption can occur at this layer.

An example of a specification that operates at the presentation layer is Abstract Syntax Notation 1 (ASN.1).

Application Layer (OSI Layer 7)

The application layer gives the user or operating system access to the network services. It interacts with software applications by identifying communication resources, determining network availability, and distributing information services. It also provides synchronization between the peer applications residing on separate systems.

Examples of application layer specifications are

- Telnet
- File Transfer Protocol (FTP)
- Simple Mail Transfer Protocol (SMTP)
- Simple Network Management Protocol (SNMP)
- Network File System (NFS)
- Border Gateway Protocol (BGP)

TCP/IP Architecture

The suite of TCP/IP protocols was developed for use by the U.S. government and research universities. The suite is identified by its most widely known protocols: TCP and IP. As mentioned, the ISO published the OSI model in 1984. However, the TCP/IP protocols had been developed by the Department of Defense's Advanced Research Projects Agency (DARPA) since 1969. The TCP/IP uses only four layers (as described in RFC 791) versus the seven layers used by OSI. The TCP/IP layers are

- Application
- Host-to-host transport
- Internet
- Network interface

Figure C-3 shows how the TCP/IP layers map to the OSI model.

C

OSI Model	TCP/IP Architecture	TCP/IP Protocols
Application	Application	Telnet, SMTP, SNMP, FTP, TFTP, HTTPS, DNS
Presentation		
Session		
Transport	Host-to-Host Transport	TCP, UDP
Network	Internet	IP, ARP, OSPF, ICMP
Data Link	Network Interface	Use of lower layer protocols such as Ethernet and Frame Relay.
Physical		

Figure C-3   *The TCP/IP Architecture and the OSI Model*

Network Interface Layer

The TCP/IP network interface layer (also known as network access layer) maps to the OSI data link and physical layers. TCP/IP uses the lower-layer protocols for transport.

Internet Layer

The Internet layer is where IP resides. IP packets exist at this layer. It directly maps to the network layer of the OSI model. Other TCP/IP protocols at this layer are Internet Control Message Protocol (ICMP), Address Resolution Protocol (ARP), and Reverse ARP (RARP).

Host-to-Host Transport Layer

The host-to-host transport layer of TCP/IP provides two connection services: TCP and UDP. TCP provides reliable transport of IP packets, and UDP provides transport of IP packets without verification of delivery. This layer maps to the OSI transport layer, but the OSI model only defines reliable delivery at this layer.

Application Layer

The TCP/IP application layer maps to the top three layers of the OSI model: application, presentation, and session. This layer interfaces with the end user and provides for authentication, compression, and formatting. The application protocol determines the data's format and how the session is controlled. Examples of TCP/IP application protocols are Telnet, FTP, BGP, and Hypertext Transfer Protocol Secure (HTTPS).

Example of Layered Communication

Suppose that you use a Telnet application. Telnet maps to the top three layers of the OSI model. In Figure C-4, a user on Host 1 enables the Telnet application to access a remote host (Host 2). The Telnet application provides a user interface (application layer) to network services. As defined in RFC 854, ASCII is the default code format. No session layer is defined for Telnet (not an OSI protocol). Per the RFC, Telnet uses TCP for connectivity (transport layer). The TCP segment is placed in an IP packet (network layer) with a destination IP address of Host 2. The IP packet is placed in an Ethernet frame (data link layer), which is converted into bits and sent onto the wire (physical layer).

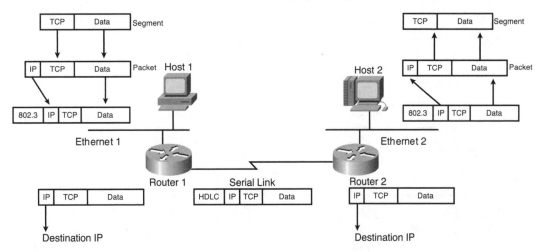

Figure C-4   *Telnet Example*

When the frame arrives at Router 1, it converts the bits into a frame; removes the frame headers (data link); checks the destination IP address (network); places a serial link header on the packet, making it a serial frame; and forwards the frame to the serial link (data link), which sends it as bits.

Router 2 receives the bits and converts them into a frame; removes the serial encapsulation headers; checks the destination IP address (network); adds an Ethernet header to the packet, making it a frame; and places the frame on Ethernet 2 (data link). Host 2 receives bits (physical) from the Ethernet cable and converts the bits into a frame (data link). Then, the IP protocol is examined and the packet data is forwarded to TCP, which checks the segment number for errors and then forwards the segment to TCP port 23 (Telnet), which is the application.

Numeric Conversion

This section focuses on the techniques for converting between decimal, binary, and hexadecimal numbers. Although the exam might not have a specific question about converting a binary number to decimal, you need to know how to convert these numbers to do problems on the test. An IPv4 address could be shown as binary or in traditional dotted-decimal format. MAC addresses and IPv6 addresses are represented in hexadecimal. Some show commands have output information in hexadecimal or binary formats.

Hexadecimal Numbers

The hexadecimal numeric system uses 16 digits instead of the 10 digits used by the decimal system. Table C-1 shows the hexadecimal digits and their decimal equivalent values.

Table C-1   Hexadecimal Digits

Hexadecimal Digit	Decimal Value
0	0
1	1
2	2
3	3
4	4
5	5
6	6
7	7
8	8
9	9
A	10
B	11
C	12
D	13
E	14
F	15
10	16
11	17
12	18
13	19
14	20

Hexadecimal Representation

It is common to represent a hexadecimal number with 0x before the number so that it is not confused with a decimal number. The hexadecimal number of decimal 16 is written as 0x10, not 10. Another method is to put a subscript h to the right of the number, such as 10_h. It is also common to use the term *hex* when speaking of hexadecimal. Much of the following text uses *hex*.

Converting Decimal to Hexadecimal

First things first: Memorize Table C-1. There are two ways to convert larger numbers. The first method is to convert decimal to binary and then convert binary to hex. The second method is to divide the decimal number by 16—the residual is the rightmost hexadecimal digit—and then keep dividing until the number is not divisible anymore. For the first method, use the schemes described in later sections. For the second method, follow the examples described here.

First, divide the decimal number by 16. The remainder of the division is the least-significant (first) hexadecimal digit. Continue to divide the quotients (answer) of the divisions by 16 until the quotient is 0. The remainder value of each later division is converted to a hexadecimal digit and prepended to the previous value. The final remainder is the most-significant digit of the hexadecimal equivalent. For large numbers, you might have to divide many times. The following examples make the process clearer.

Divide by 16:

$$
\begin{array}{r}
1 \\
16\overline{)\,26} \\
\underline{-16} \\
10 = A_h
\end{array}
$$

Answer: **1A_h**

Conversion Example C-1 *Convert 26 to Its Hex Equivalent*

Not divisible by 256; divide by 16:

$$
\begin{array}{r}
6 \\
16\overline{)\,96} \\
\underline{-96} \\
0 = 0_h
\end{array}
$$

Answer: **60_h**

Conversion Example C-2 *Convert 96 to Its Hex Equivalent*

Divide by 16 first:

$$
\begin{array}{r}
23 \\
16\overline{)\,375} \\
\underline{-32} \\
55 \\
\underline{-48} \\
7
\end{array}
$$

Now divide 23 by 16:

$$
\begin{array}{r}
1 \\
16\overline{)\,23} \\
\underline{-16} \\
7
\end{array}
$$

Now take the residual from the first division (7) and concatentate it with the residual from the second division (7), plus the result of the second division (1), and the answer is **177_h**.

Conversion Example C-3 *Convert 375 to Its Hex Equivalent*

Divide by 16:

```
         13 = Dh
16 | 218
    -16
     58
    -48
     10 = Ah
```

Answer: **DA_h**

Conversion Example C-4 *Convert 218 to Its Hex Equivalent*

Converting Hexadecimal to Decimal

To convert a hex number to decimal, take the rightmost digit and convert it to decimal (for example, 0xC = 12). Then add this number to the second rightmost digit multiplied by 16 and the third rightmost digit multiplied by 256. Do not expect to convert numbers larger than 255 on the CCDA exam, because the upper limit of IP addresses in dotted-decimal format is 255
(although Token Ring numbers reach 4096). Some examples follow.

```
1 x 256 = 256
7 x  16 = 112
7 x   1 =   7
          375d
```

Conversion Example C-5 *Convert 177_h to Decimal*

```
6 x 16 = 96
0 x  1 =  0
         96d
```

Conversion Example C-6 *Convert 60_h to Decimal*

```
1 x 256 = 256
0 x  16 =   0
0 x   1 =   0
          256d
```

Conversion Example C-7 *Convert 100_h to Decimal*

```
 1 x 256 = 256
13 x  16 = 208
10 x   1 =  10
           474d
```

Conversion Example C-8 *Convert $1DA_h$ to Decimal*

Alternative Method for Converting from Hexadecimal to Decimal

Another way is to convert from hex to binary and then from binary to decimal. The following sections discuss converting from binary to decimal.

Binary Numbers

The binary number system uses two digits: 1 and 0. Computer systems use binary numbers. IP addresses and MAC addresses are represented by binary numbers. The number of binary 1s or 0s is the number of bits, short for binary digits. For example, 01101010 is a binary number with 8 bits. An IP address has 32 bits, and a MAC address has 48 bits. As shown in Table C-2, IPv4 addresses are usually represented in dotted-decimal format; therefore, it is helpful to know how to convert between binary and decimal numbers.

MAC addresses are usually represented in hexadecimal numbers; therefore, it is helpful to know how to convert between binary and hexadecimal.

The CCDA candidate should memorize Table C-3, which shows numbers from 0 to 16 in decimal, binary, and hexadecimal formats.

Table C-2   Binary Representation of IP and MAC Addresses

IPv4 Address in Binary	IPv4 Address in Dotted Decimal
00101000 10001010 01010101 10101010	= 40.138.85.170
MAC Address in Binary	**MAC Address in Hexadecimal**
00001100 10100001 10010111 01010001 00000001 10010001	= 0C:A1:97:51:01:91

Table C-3   Decimal, Binary, and Hexadecimal Numbers

Decimal Value	Hexadecimal	Binary
0	0	0000
1	1	0001
2	2	0010
3	3	0011
4	4	0100
5	5	0101
6	6	0110
7	7	0111
8	8	1000
9	9	1001
10	A	1010

C

Decimal Value	Hexadecimal	Binary
11	B	1011
12	C	1100
13	D	1101
14	E	1110
15	F	1111
16	10	10000

Converting Binary to Hexadecimal

To convert binary numbers to hex, put the bits in groups of 4, starting with the right-justified bits. Groups of 4 bits are often called *nibbles*. Each nibble can be represented by a single hexadecimal digit. A group of two nibbles is an octet, 8 bits. Examples follow.

Group the bits:
    00 1001 1101
Answer: **09D**$_h$

Conversion Example C-9   *Convert 0010011101 to Hex*

Group the bits:
    0010 1010 0101 1001 0000 1011 0001
Answer: **2A590B1**$_h$

Conversion Example C-10   *Convert 0010101001011001000010110001 to Hex*

Converting Hexadecimal to Binary

This procedure is also easy. Just change the hex digits into their 4-bit equivalents. Examples follow.

Hex: 0   D   E   A   D   0
Binary: 0000 1101 1110 1010 1101 0000
Answer: **00001101111010101101 0000**

Conversion Example C-11   *Convert 0DEAD0 to Hex*

Hex: A   A   0   1   0   1
Binary: 1010 1010 0000 0001 0000 0001
Answer: **101010100000000100000001**

Conversion Example C-12   *Convert AA0101 to Hex*

Converting Binary to Decimal

To convert a binary number to decimal, multiply each instance of 0 or 1 by the power of 2 associated with the position of the bit in the binary number. The first bit, starting from the right, is associated with $2^0 = 1$. The value of the exponent increases by 1 as each bit is processed, working leftward. As shown in Table C-4, each bit in the binary number 10101010 has a decimal equivalent from 0 to 128 based on the value of the bit multiplied by a power of 2 associated with the bit position. This is similar to decimal numbers, in which the numbers are based on powers of 10: 1s, 10s, 100s, and so on. In decimal, the number 111 is $(1*100) + (1*10) + (1*1)$. In binary, the number 11111111 is the sum of $(1*2^7) + (1*2^6) + (1*2^5) + (1*2^4) + (1*2^3) + (1*2^2) + (1*2^1) + (1*2^0) = 128 + 64 + 32 + 16 + 8 + 4 + 2 + 1 = 255$. For 10101010, the result is $128 + 0 + 32 + 0 + 8 + 0 + 2 + 0 = 170$. Examples follow.

Table C-4   Decimal Values of Bits in a Binary Number

Power of 2	$2^7 = 128$	$2^6 = 64$	$2^5 = 32$	$2^3 = 8$	$2^2 = 4$	$2^0 = 1$
Binary	1	1	1	1	1	1

> **Note:**   Just memorize 1, 2, 4, 8, 16, 32, 64, and 128. Use it as you read a binary number from right to left. This technique should be helpful in fast conversions.

Sum: 128 + 0 + 32 + 16 + 0 + 4 + 2 + 1
Answer = **183**

Conversion Example C-13   *Convert 10110111 to Decimal*

Sum: 16 + 8 + 0 + 2 + 1
Answer = **27**

Conversion Example C-14   *Convert 00011011 to Decimal*

Sum: 128 + 64 + 32 + 16 + 8 + 4 + 2 + 1
Answer = **255**

Conversion Example C-15   *Convert 11111111 to Decimal*

Converting Decimal to Binary Numbers

This procedure is similar to converting from hex to decimal (by dividing), but now you divide the decimal number by 2. You use each residual to build the binary number by prepending each residual bit to the previous bit, starting on the right. Repeat the procedure until you cannot divide anymore. The only problem is that for large numbers, you might have to divide many times. You can reduce the number of divisions by first converting the decimal value to a hexadecimal value and then converting the intermediate result to the binary representation. After the following example, you will read about an alternate method suitable for use with decimal values between 0 and 255 that can be represented in a single octet.

```
      13                               6
 2 |  26                         2 |  13
     -26                              -12
       0                               1
```

The first bit is 0; now divide 13 by 2. [0]   The second bit is 1; now divide 6 by 2. [10]

```
       3                               1
 2 |   6                         2 |   3
      -6                              -2
       0                               1
```

The third bit is 0; now divide 3 by 2. [010]   The fourth bit is 1; the leftmost bit is the division
                                                result at the top, which is one. [11010]

                                                Answer: **11010**

Conversion Example C-16   *Convert 26 to Binary*

Alternative Method for Converting from Decimal to Binary

The dividing procedure just described works; it just takes a lot of time. Another way is to remember the bit position values within a byte—128, 64, 32, 16, 8, 4, 2, 1—and play with the bits until the sum adds up to the desired number. This method works when you convert integer values between 0 and 255, inclusive. Table C-5 shows these binary numbers and their decimal values.

Table C-5   Bit Values

Binary Number	Decimal Value
10000000	128
01000000	64
00100000	32
00010000	16
00001000	8
00000100	4
00000010	2
00000001	1

For example, to convert 26, you know that it is a number smaller than 128, 64, and 32, so those 3 bits are 0 (000?????). Now you need to find a combination of 16, 8, 4, 2, and 1 that adds up to 26. This method involves using subtraction to compute the remaining number. Start with the largest number, and make the bit at 16 a 1 (0001????). The difference between 26 and 16 is 10. What combination of 8, 4, 2, and 1 gives 10? 1010. Therefore, the answer is 00011010. You might think this method involves too much guesswork, but it becomes second nature after some practice.

The number is larger than 128; enable that bit. [1???????]

How far is 137 from 128: 9; enable the remaining bits for a value of 9 [1???1001].

The answer is 10001001.

Conversion Example C-17   *Convert 137 to Binary*

The number is larger than 128; enable that bit. [1???????]

Because 211–128 is greater than 64, enable that bit. [11??????] (Remember that

11000000 = 192.)

Because 211–192=19, enable bits 16, 2, and 1. [11?1??11]

The answer is 11010011.

Conversion Example C-18   *Convert 211 to Binary*

In addition to remembering the bit-position values (128, 64, 32, 16, 8, 4, 2, 1), it helps to remember network subnet mask values. Remembering them makes it easier to figure out whether you need to enable a bit. Table C-6 summarizes the binary subnet mask numbers and their decimal values.

Table C-6   Binary Masks and Their Decimal Values

Binary Mask	Decimal
10000000	128
11000000	192
11100000	224
11110000	240
11111000	248
11111100	252
11111110	254

References and Recommended Readings

ISO/IEC 7498-1: 1994. "Information Processing Systems - OSI Reference Model - The Basic Model."

RFC 791, Internet Protocol. www.ietf.org/rfc.

RFC 793, Transmission Control Protocol. www.ietf.org/rfc.

GLOSSARY

100BASE-TX IEEE specification for Fast Ethernet over UTP media.

802.1X An IEEE media-level access control standard that permits and denies access to the network and applies traffic policy based on identity.

ABR Area Border Router. Routers that connect to more than one OSPF area.

acceptable-use policy A document that defines the roles and responsibilities within risk management and should have clear explanations to avoid confusion.

access control Ensures that users and devices are identified and authorized for entry to their assigned network segment.

access control lists (ACL) Control what traffic is allowed on the network. ACLs are used on routers, switches, and firewalls to control access.

access layer Provides workgroup and user access to the network. Provides user access to local segments on the network. It is characterized by switched LAN segments in a campus environment.

access VPN These VPN connections give users connectivity over shared networks such as the Internet to the corporate intranet.

accounting Provides an audit trail of activities by logging the actions of the user.

accounting management Refers to keeping track of circuits for billing of services.

ACD Automatic call distribution systems route calls to a group of agents.

Adaptive Security Appliance (ASA) A high-performance firewall appliance with intrusion prevention system, antivirus, IPsec, and SSL VPN technologies integrated into a single unified architecture.

administrative distance Rating of the trustworthiness of a routing information source. An administrative distance value is assigned to each routing protocol, static, or connected route on Cisco routers.

ALG Application layer gateways.

AP Access point.

API Application programming interfaces.

ARP Address Resolution Protocol.

ASBR Autonomous System Boundary Router. Connects the OSPF backbone to external networks. Routers that inject external LSAs into the OSPF database (redistribution).

authentication Establishes the user's identity and access to the network resources.

authorization Describes what can be done and what can be accessed.

BGP   Border Gateway Protocol. Routing protocol used to exchange routing information between autonomous systems.

BHT   Busy-hour traffic. Expressed in Erlangs.

broadband cable   A technology used to transport data using a coaxial cable medium over cable distribution systems.

BW   Bandwidth. Metric used to determine the best path to a destination network. The highest bandwidth is preferred.

cabling in the data center   The cabling in the data center is known as the passive infrastructure.

CAC   Call admission control. Used to control the bandwidth or number of calls from a site.

CAPWAP   Control and Provisioning for Wireless Access Points.

Catalyst switch   Combines firewall, IPS, SSL VPN, IPsec VPN, DoS mitigation, and virtual services to build into security zones.

CCS   Centum Call Second. One call on a channel for 100 seconds.

CDP   Cisco Discovery Protocol. Cisco proprietary protocol that can be used to discover Cisco network devices. CDP is media and protocol independent, so it works over Ethernet, Frame Relay, ATM, and other media.

CDR   Call Detail Record.

Centrex   With Centrex services, the CO acts as the company's voice switch, giving the appearance that the company has its own PBX.

circuit switched   Data connections that can be brought up when needed and terminated when finished.

Cisco Adaptive Security Device Manager (ASDM)   A web-based tool for managing Cisco ASA 5500 series appliances, and Cisco Catalyst 6500 Firewall Services Modules (FWSM Version 3.1 or later).

Cisco Catalyst switches   Include DoS and man-in-the-middle attack mitigations.

Cisco Identity-Based Network Services (IBNS)   Based on several integrated Cisco solutions to enable authentication, access control, and user policies to secure network infrastructure and resources.

Cisco Intrusion Prevention System Device Manager (IDM)   A web-based application that configures and manages IPS sensors.

Cisco ISE   Cisco ISE is a security policy management platform that automates access control by enforcing compliance, increasing network security, and improving operations.

Cisco Nexus 1000V virtual switch for VMware ESX and ESXi   Helps deliver visibility and policy control for virtual machines (VM).

Cisco Router and Security Device Manager (SDM)   A web-based tool for routers that supports a wide range of IOS software.

Cisco Secure Access Control Server (ACS)   Provides centralized control for administrative access to Cisco devices and security applications.

Cisco Security Manager (CSM)   An integrated solution for configuration management of firewall, VPN, router, switch module, and IPS devices.

Cisco Security Monitoring, Analysis, and Response System (MARS)   An appliance-based solution for network security administrators to monitor, identify, isolate, and respond to security threats.

Cisco Unified Computing System (UCS)   An innovated next-generation data center platform that converges computing, network, storage, and virtualization together into one system.

CO   Central office.

Codec   Coder-decoder. Transforms analog signals into digital bit streams.

companding   Comes from "compressing and expanding." The analog samples are compressed into logarithmic segments decoder.

configuration management   Refers to baselining, modifying, and tracking configuration changes.

core layer   Provides fast transport between distribution switches within the enterprise campus. Provides high-speed switching backbone with high reliability and redundancy.

cRTP   Compressed RTP. Reduces header overhead from 40 bytes to 2 to 4 bytes.

CSMA/CA   Carrier sense multiple access with collision avoidance.

CSMA/CD   Carrier sense multiple access collision detection. Access protocol for Ethernet shared media.

CUCM   Cisco Unified Communications Manager. The call processing server.

data center access layer   The data center access layer's main purpose is to provide Layer 2 and Layer 3 physical port density for various servers in the data center.

data center aggregation (distribution) layer   Aggregates Layer 2/Layer 3 links from the access layer and connects with upstream links to the data center core.

data center core   Connects the campus core to the data center aggregation layer using high speed Layer 3 links.

Data Center Interconnect (DCI)   A Data Center Interconnect (DCI) is a network that connects two or more DCs together to transport traffic between them.

data center space element   Defines the number of racks for servers and telecommunications equipment that can be installed.

delay   Metric that refers to how long it takes a packet to reach the destination. Depends on many factors, such as link bandwidth, utilization, port queues, and physical distance traveled.

denial-of-service (DoS) attack   Tries to overwhelm resources such as memory, CPU, and bandwidth, thus impacting the attacked system and denying legitimate users access.

device virtualization   Allows for a single physical device to act like multiple copies of itself.

DHCP snooping   Verifies DHCP transactions and prevents rogue DHCP servers from interfering with production traffic.

DHCP   Dynamic Host Configuration Protocol. Used to dynamically configure IP parameters on hosts on the network.

DHCPv6   Dynamic Host Configuration Protocol Version 6.

dial backup   ISDN provides backup dialup services in the event of a failure of a primary WAN circuit.

digital subscriber line (DSL)   A technology that provides high-speed Internet data services over ordinary copper telephone lines.

distance vector   Routing protocols that advertise the entire routing table to its neighbors.

distribution layer   Provides policy-based connectivity and aggregation of access layer devices. Isolation point between access and core layers. At this layer, security filtering, aggregation of wiring closets, QoS, and routing between VLANs occur.

DMZ   Demilitarized zones are used to further divide network applications and are deployed with firewall policy protections. Common DMZs include Internet DMZ for e-commerce applications, remote access VPN for corporate users, and site-to-site VPN for connections to remote sites.

DNS   Domain Name Service. A distributed database system that returns the destination IP addresses given a domain name.

DR   Designated router. OSPF router on multiaccess networks (Ethernet) that is selected to collect all LSAs for the multiaccess network.

DSCP   Differentiated services code point. Uses 6 bits in the ToS field to support differentiated services.

DSSS   Direct sequence spread spectrum.

DUAL   Diffusing Update Algorithm. Used by EIGRP to select paths and guarantee freedom from routing loops.

DWDM   Dense wavelength-division multiplexing. Increases fiber-optics bandwidth capabilities by using different wavelengths of light called channels over the same fiber strand.

Dynamic ARP inspection   Intercepts ARP packets and verifies that the packets have valid IP- to-MAC bindings.

Dynamic Multipoint VPN (DMVPN)   A Cisco IOS solution for building IPsec + GRE VPNs in a dynamic and scalable manner.

E&M   Ear and Mouth; analog trunk.

EGP   Exterior gateway protocol. Used to communicate routing information with external networks.

EIGRP   Enhanced Interior Gateway Routing Protocol. Cisco proprietary routing protocol with hybrid characteristics that supports VLSMs and authentication and uses DUAL to select paths and guarantee freedom from routing loops.

enterprise campus module   Contains the campus core, building distribution, building access, and server farm/data center.

enterprise data center module   Consists of using the network to enhance the server, storage, and application servers.

enterprise edge   Contains the e-commerce, Internet connectivity and DMZ, VPN and remote-access, and enterprise WAN modules.

enterprise remote branch module   Consists of remote offices, small offices, or sales offices. Relies on WAN for services.

enterprise teleworker module   Supports mobile and home users providing access to corporate systems via VPN tunnels.

enterprise WAN module   Provides MPLS or other WAN technologies.

Erlang   Telecommunications traffic unit of measurement representing the continuous use of one voice path for one hour. Measure of total voice traffic volume in one hour. 1 Erlang = 36 CCS.

EtherChannel   Ethernet Channel ports bundle multiple Fast Ethernet, Gigabit Ethernet, or 10 Gigabit Ethernet links into a single Layer 2 or Layer 3 logical link.

EU Data Protection Directive 95/46/EC   Calls for the protection of people's privacy with respect to the processing of personal data.

extranet VPN   VPN infrastructure for business partner connectivity that also uses the Internet or a private infrastructure for access.

Fabric Extender (FEX)   A Fabric Extender (FEX) is a physical grouping of copper or fiber switch ports that uplinks to a parent switch such as a Nexus 5K or 7K.

fault management   Refers to detecting and correcting network problems.

FCAPS   Fault, configuration, accounting, performance, and security management.

FHSS   Frequency-hopping spread spectrum.

Fibre Channel over Ethernet (FCoE) and Internet Small Computer Systems Interface (iSCSI)   FCoE and iSCSI are two methods for implementing Unified Fabric in the data center over 10 Gigabit Ethernet.

FirePOWER IPS   A module for the ASA that provides NGIPS, URL filtering, application visibility, and advanced malware protection. In addition to a module it can also be a standalone appliance.

firewall   A security device designed to permit or deny network traffic based on source address, destination address, protocol, and port.

FQDN   Fully qualified domain name.

Frame Relay   A packet-switched connection-oriented Layer 2 WAN protocol.

full-mesh topology   Requires that each site be connected to every other site in the cloud.

FXO   Foreign Exchange Office.

FXS   Foreign Exchange Station.

gatekeeper   Provides call control and signaling services to H.323 endpoints.

gateway   Provides translation services between H.323 endpoints and non-H.323 devices.

GLBP   Global Load Balancing Protocol. Similar to HSRP, but provides load balancing between the redundant routers.

GoS   Grade of service. The probability that a call will be blocked when attempting to seize a circuit.

Gramm-Leach-Bliley Financial Services Modernization Act of 1999 (GLBA)   Provides protection against the sale of bank and account information that is regularly bought and sold by financial institutions.

Group Encrypted Transport VPN (GETVPN)   Similar to an IPsec VPN, but it differs by preserving the original IP addresses in the outer IP header of the packets.

H.323   ITU framework for multimedia protocols. Used to control Cisco IOS gateways.

hop count   Metric that counts the number of links between routers the packet must traverse to reach a destination.

H-REAP   Hybrid Remote Edge Access Point. Protocol that provides authentication for remote APs.

HSRP   Hot Standby Router Protocol. Provides a way for IP devices to keep communicating on the network even if the default gateway becomes unavailable by having an active and standby router on the network.

hub-and-spoke (or star) topology   Provides a hub router with connections to the spoke routers through the WAN cloud.

IANA   Internet Assigned Numbers Authority.

iBGP   Internal BGP: Used for peering between BGP neighbors in the same autonomous system. iBGP is used primarily in transit autonomous systems.

ICMPv6   Internet Control Message Protocol Version 6.

ID   Identifier.

IEEE 802.1x   IEEE standard for port-based authentication.

IEEE 802.3ab   IEEE standard that specifies the operation of Gigabit Ethernet over UTP.

IGMP   Internet Group Management Protocol. Protocol used in multicast implementations between the end hosts and the local router. IP hosts use IGMP to report their multicast group memberships to routers.

IGP   Interior Gateway Protocol. Meant for routing within an organization's administrative domain.

improve   Security data analysis, reporting, and intelligent network security.

incident-handling policy   Incident-handling policy defines the processes and procedures for managing incidents and even emergency-type scenarios.

Integrated Services Router (ISR) G2   Combines IOS firewall, VPN, and IPS services across the router portfolio, which enables new security features on existing routers.

intranet (site-to-site) VPN   Connect remote offices back to the headend office.

IPsec   A security architecture that operates in a host to protect IP traffic. The IETF defined IPsec in RFC 4301. IPsec uses open standards and provides secure communication between peers to ensure data confidentiality, integrity, and authentication through network layer encryption.

IPv4   Internet Protocol Version 4. The current version of the Internet protocol used today.

ISATAP   Intra-Site Automatic Tunnel Addressing Protocol.

Kismet   An 802.11 wireless sniffer and IDS that can collect traffic from 802.11a/b/g networks.

LAG   Link aggregation.

large branch design   Between 100 and 1000 users.

Layer 3 switches   Layer 3 switches perform the functions of both data link layer switches and network layer routers.

leased lines   Dedicated connections provided by the SP. These types of connections are "point to point" and generally more expensive.

Link Layer Discovery Protocol (LLDP)   An IEEE standard protocol (IEEE 802.1AB) that defines messages, encapsulated directly in Ethernet frames so they do not rely on a working IPv4 or IPv6 network, for the purpose of giving devices a means of announcing basic device information to other devices on the LAN. It is a standardized protocol similar to Cisco Discovery Protocol (CDP).

link-state protocols   Routing protocols that use the Dijkstra shortest path algorithm to calculate the best path.

LLQ   Low-latency queuing. Class-based weighted fair queuing plus priority queue (CBWFQ+PQ). LLQ provides a single priority queue; it can also configure guaranteed bandwidth for different classes of traffic.

load   Metric that measures the degree to which an interface link is busy.

LSA   Link-state advertisement. Flooded throughout an area or the entire OSPF autonomous system.

LWAPP   Lightweight Wireless Access Point Protocol.

MAP   Mesh access point. Remote APs that provide access to clients and communicate with the RAP.

medium branch design   Between 50 and 100 users.

Metro Ethernet   Metro Ethernet is based on Ethernet, IP, and optical technologies available in metro areas with Ethernet speeds and handoffs.

MGCP   Media Gateway Control Protocol. Used to control IOS gateways.

MIB   Management Information Base. Collection of information that is stored on the local agent of the managed device.

MIMO   Multiple input, multiple output.

monitor   Intrusion and content-based detection and response.

MOS   Mean Opinion Score. Measure used to describe the quality of speech.

MP-BGP   Multiprotocol BGP. Used to carry MPLS VPN information between all PE routers within a VPN community.

MPLS   Multiprotocol Label Switching. A technology for the delivery of IP services using an efficient encapsulation mechanism. MPLS uses labels appended to IP packets or Layer 2 frames for the transport of data.

MTU   Maximum transmission unit.

N+1 redundancy   A single WLC acts as the backup for multiple WLCs.

N+N redundancy   WLC redundancy scheme of overprovisioning of two controllers so that if either controller fails the wireless network is not impacted.

N+N+1 redundancy   WLC redundancy the same as N+N with one additional WLC acting as a backup for multiple WLC pairs.

NAT   Network Address Translation. NAT converts internal IP addresses into globally unique IP addresses.

NAT-PT   Network Address Translation - Protocol Translation.

NBAR   Network-Based Application Recognition. An intelligent classification engine.

ND   Neighbor discovery.

NetFlow   Gathers information on every flow in a network segment. Cisco's NetFlow allows the tracking of IP flows as they are passed through routers and multilayer switches.

NetStumbler   Identifies wireless networks using 802.11a/b/g WLAN standards.

network access control policy   A document that defines general access control principles used and how data is classified, such as confidential, top secret, or internal.

Network Admission Control (NAC)   Protects the network from threats by enforcing security compliance on all devices attempting to access the network.

Network load balancing   Can be hardware appliances, virtual appliances, or even software that provides L4-7 services.

network virtualization Encompasses logical isolated network segments that share the same physical infrastructure.

NMAP (Network Mapper) NMAP scans large networks or one host. It is an open source utility used for network exploration/security audits.

OAM Operations, administration, and management. For network operations and management.

OSPFv2 Open Short Path First Version 2. A link-state routing protocol that uses Dijkstra's shortest path first (SPF) algorithm to calculate paths to IPv4 destinations. Defined in RFC 2328.

OSPFv3 Open Short Path First Version 3. A link-state routing protocol that uses Dijkstra's shortest path first (SPF) algorithm to calculate paths to IPv6 destinations.

packet and cell switched Connections that use virtual circuits (PVC/SVC) established by the service provider.

partial-mesh topology Has fewer virtual circuit connections than a full-mesh topology.

PAT Port Address Translation. Maps multiple unregistered or private IP addresses to a single registered IP address by using different ports.

path isolation Provides independent logical traffic paths over a shared network.

PBM Plan, Build, and Manage network lifecycle. A top-down approach to network design that adapts the network infrastructure to the network applications' needs.

PBR Policy-based routing. Commonly used to modify the next-hop IP address based on the source address.

PBX Private Branch Exchange. Legacy voice switch.

performance management Measures the network's effectiveness at delivering packets.

PIM Protocol Independent Multicast. Routing protocol for multicast destinations.

PoE Power over Ethernet.

policy control Policies are applied to all users and devices across the architecture.

power in the data center facility Used to power cooling devices, servers, storage equipment, network, and some lighting.

PPDIOO Prepare, Plan, Design, Implement, Operate, and Optimize. Life cycle of the network.

PSTN Public switched telephone network.

QoS policing policy Controls the rate of bandwidth for incoming traffic, such as ARP packets and DHCP requests.

QPPB QoS Policy Propagation on BGP. Uses iBGP to spread common QoS parameters from one router to other routers in the network. It classifies packets using IP precedence bits based on BGP community lists, BGP autonomous system paths, and access lists.

RAP Rooftop AP. Connects the mesh to the wired network.

Rapid-PVST+   Rapid per VLAN Spanning Tree Plus, which is based on the Rapid STP (RSTP) IEEE 802.1W standard. RSTP (IEEE 802.1w) natively includes most of the Cisco proprietary enhancements to the 802.1D Spanning Tree, such as BackboneFast and UplinkFast. Rapid-PVST+ uses RSTP to provide faster convergence. When any RSTP port receives legacy 802.1D BPDU, it falls back to legacy STP, and the inherent fast convergence benefits of 802.1W are lost when it interacts with legacy bridges. Cisco recommends that Rapid-PVST+ be configured for best convergence.

rate limiting   Rate limiting controls the rate of bandwidth that incoming traffic is using, such as ARPs and DHCP requests.

reconnaissance   Reconnaissance gathers as much information as possible about the target host/network.

Remote access VPN   This type of VPN connection gives mobile users, home users, and partners connectivity to corporate intranets over the Internet. Users typically connect remotely using cable, wireless LAN, or 3G/4G WWAN. Remote access VPNs usually terminate on Cisco ASA appliances and can be grouped together to form a load-balancing cluster in a dedicated DMZ, or existing Cisco ASA firewalls can be used in smaller organizations

RF groups   Cluster of WLC devices that coordinate their RRM calculations.

RIPng   Routing Information Protocol next generation. RIPng is a distance-vector routing protocol for IPv6 networks.

RIPv2   Routing Information Protocol Version 2. RIPv2 is a distance-vector routing protocol for IPv4 networks that supports VLSMs, route authentication, and multicast of route updates.

RMON   Remote Monitoring. Standard monitoring specification that enables network monitoring devices and console systems to exchange network monitoring data. RMON1 looks at data link layer data. RMON2 looks at network to application layer data.

router   Routers consolidate IOS firewall, IPS, IPsec VPN, DMVPN, and SSL VPN into the routing platforms to secure the router if it is attacked.

RRM   Radio Resource Management. Method to manage AP radio frequency channels and power configuration.

RSVP   Signaling protocol that enables end stations or applications to obtain guaranteed bandwidth and low delays for their data flows.

RTCP   RTP Control Protocol. Session layer protocol that monitors the delivery of data and provides control and identification functions.

RTP   Real-time Transport Protocol. RTP is a transport layer protocol that carries digitized voice in its payload; RTP operates over UDP.

Scale out   To add additional servers with the application load distributed across the server farm pool.

Scale up   To buy larger servers with more memory and CPU cores.

SCCP   Skinny Client Control Protocol. Cisco proprietary client/server signaling protocol for call setup and control. Also known as "skinny."

secondary WAN link   The addition of a secondary WAN link makes the network more fault tolerant.

secure   Identification, authentication, ACLs, stateful packet inspection (SPI), encryption, and VPNs.

security management policy   Security management policy explains how to manage the security infrastructure.

service level agreement (SLA)-networked applications   SLA-networked applications rely on the underlying network between the client and server to provide its functions.

services edge   Services edge ensures the right services are accessible to the intended users, groups, or devices.

shadow PVC   Service providers can offer shadow PVCs that provide an additional PVC for use if needed.

SIP   Session Initiation Protocol. IETF framework for multimedia protocols.

Site-to-site VPN   Site-to-site VPNs over the Internet offer an alternative WAN transport for interconnecting sites. Generally, the remote sites use their Internet connection to establish the VPN connection back to the corporate head-end office. Site-to-site VPNs can also use an IP backbone provided by the service provider.

small branch design   Design for a site that has up to 50 users.

SNMP   Simple Network Management Protocol. IP application layer protocol that has become the standard for the exchange of management information between network devices.

SONET/SDH   SONET/SDH is circuit-based and delivers high-speed services over an optical network.

split-MAC   AP mode that splits MAC functions between the WLC and the remote AP.

SS7   Signaling 7. Allows voice calls to be routed and controlled by central call controllers. Permits modern consumer telephone services. Protocol used in the PSTN.

SSID   Service set identifier.

stub area   In a stub area, OSPF external LSAs (Type 5) are prevented from being flooded into that area. A default router is used instead.

Superscan   Superscan (made for Windows) provides high-speed scanning, host detection, and Windows host enumeration and banner grabbing.

syslog   Transmits event notification messages over the network. Network devices send the event messages to an event server for aggregation.

test   Assessments, vulnerability scanning, and security auditing.

time-division multiplexing (TDM)   A type of digital multiplexing in which multiple channels such as data, voice, and video are combined over one communication medium by interleaving pulses representing bits from different channels.

ToS   Type of Service field. This field of the IPv4 packet header specifies QoS parameters.

U.S. Health Insurance Portability and Accountability Act (HIPAA)   HIPAA applies to the protection of private health information that is used electronically.

U.S. Public Company Accounting Reform and Investor Protection Act of 2002 (Sarbanes-Oxley or SOX)   SOX focuses on the accuracy and the controls imposed on a company's financial records.

unauthorized access   Gaining unauthorized access is the act of attacking or exploiting the target host system.

Unicast RPF   Prevents unknown source addresses from using the network as a transport mechanism to carry out attacks.

VAD   Voice-activity detection. Used for detection and suppression of packets that do not contain actual speech content.

VDC   Virtual Device Context. Used for device virtualization on the Cisco Nexus 7000 series switches.

Virtual Port Channel (vPC)   Virtual Port Channel (vPC) technology works by combining two Cisco Nexus series switches with 10GE links, which are then represented to other switches as a single logical switch for port channeling purposes to the third downstream device.

Virtual Private LAN Services (VPLS)   Defines an architecture that enables Ethernet Multi-point Service (EMS) over an MPLS network.

Virtual Switching System (VSS)   Virtual Switching System (VSS) is a network virtualization technology used in the LAN that allows two physical Cisco Catalyst 4500, 6500, or 6800 series switches to act as a single logical virtual switch.

virtualization   Allows for the consolidation of servers and other network components and reduction of hardware infrastructure costs. It has gained popularity by industry leaders such as VMware.

virtualization technologies   Virtualization technologies share a common theme in their ability to abstract logical elements from hardware (applications or operating systems) or networks (LANs and SANs) and run them in a virtual state.

VLAN   Virtual LAN.

VLSM   Variable-link subnet mask. VLSMs allow the dividing of the IP address space into subnets of different sizes.

vPC   Virtual Port Channel (vPC) technology works by combining two Cisco Nexus 7000 series switches or two Cisco Nexus 5000 series switches with 10GE links, which are then represented to other switches as a single logical switch for port channeling purposes.

VRF   Virtual routing and forwarding. A routing virtualization technology that creates multiple logical Layer 3 routing and forwarding instances (route tables) that can function on the same physical router.

VRRP   Virtual Router Redundancy Protocol. Similar to HSRP. Provides a way for IP devices to keep communicating on the network even if the default gateway becomes unavailable by having a master and backup router on the network.

VSS   Virtual Switching System. Converts the distribution switching 6500 pair into a logical single switch.

wireless   Wireless as a technology uses electromagnetic waves to carry the signal between endpoints. Everyday examples of wireless technology include cell phones, wireless LANs, cordless computer equipment, and global positioning systems (GPS).

WLAN   Wireless local-area network.

WLC   Wireless LAN controller.

Index

C

G

J-K-L

M

W – X – Y – Z